Not For Tourists Guide™ to **NEW YORK CITY**

Get more on
notfortourists.com

Keep connected with:

Twitter:
twitter/notfortourists

Facebook:
facebook/notfortourists

iPhone App:
nftiphone.com

Not For Tourists, Inc

published and designed by:
Not For Tourists, Inc
NFT$_{TM}$—Not For Tourists$_{TM}$ Guide to New York City
www.notfortourists.com

Publisher
Jane Pirone

Information Design
Jane Pirone
Rob Tallia
Scot Covey

Director
Stuart Farr

Managing Editors
Craig Nelson
Rob Tallia

Production Manager
Aaron Schielke

Database Manager
Michael Dale

City Editor
Rob Tallia

Writing and Editing
Sara Bogush
Molly Fergus
Allix Geneslaw
Miles Klee
Nina Mandell
Tony Muller
Craig Nelson
Hannah Oberman
Lisa Prosser
Jessica Solt
Ethan Stanislawski
Rob Tallia
Josh Wellman

Research
Michael Dale
Susan Lee
Keely B. Hild
Zachary Wilson
John-Paul Anthony

Sales and Marketing
Deborah Blumenthal
Sarah Hocevar
Michael Salerno
Elina Salnikova
Cathy Vu

Graphic Design and Production
Annika Koski
Aaron Schielke
Sarah Wyman

Information Systems Manager
Juan Molinari

Proofreader
Scott Sendrow

Printed in China
ISBN# 978-0-9795339-5-2 $18.99

12th Edition

Every effort has been made to ensure that the information in this book is as up-to-date as possible at press time. However, many details are liable to change—as we have learned. The publishers cannot accept responsibility for any consequences arising from the use of this book.

Not For Tourists does not solicit individuals, organizations, or businesses for listings inclusion in our guides, nor do we accept payment for inclusion into the editorial portion of our book; the advertising sections, however, are exempt from this policy. We always welcome communications from anyone regarding ANYTHING having to do with our books; please visit us on our website at www.notfortourists.com for appropriate contact information.

Dear NFT User:

Once upon a time, there were unicorns and trolls, dog breeds were dog breeds, and guidebooks were widely agreed to be useful tools of navigation and exploration. But now that even your curmudgeonly old Uncle Max has an Android and Street View and a tiny Bluetooth delivering user ratings directly into his amygdala, why spend a hard-earned Andrew Jackson to take home this old-fashioned pack of paper?

You hold in your hands the anti-Yelp: a thoughtfully assembled, well-edited collection of maps, listings, and descriptions designed to help you find the best of New York City and not waste a nanosecond of your time on anything else. The notable. The bizarre. That indispensable boutique. That life-saving hospital. That cozy yet criminally overlooked bar. Bagels. Movie Theaters. Bookstores. Art Galleries. Supermarkets. Basically, the neighborhood staples…and neighborhood Staples!

That's right, friends, for less than the price of one cocktail at the Upper East Side's venerable Bemelman's Bar…or a little less than what you'd spend for 3 burgers at Corner Bistro…or for just about what you'd spend for a dozen or so bagels and cream cheese at David's—you'll have not one, not two, not three but four—yes, four—detailed maps for every Manhattan neighborhood that we cover—a fully updated catalog of local restaurants, bars, shops, and landmarks, plus extended coverage of parks, places, transit, sports arenas, museums, art galleries and everything else you need to know to survive and thrive in the greatest city on Earth. And if you're nonplussed by the super handy glossy foldout subway and bus map in the back, think about this: Do you really want to try puzzling out how to get from the Lower East Side to Washington Heights on a two-inch cell phone screen?

And new for this edition is a reconsidered, thoroughly revamped, and utterly revolutionary (for us, anyway) format that frees all those artful NFT blurbs from their former desolate perch in the forgotten back section of the guide. Now you will never, ever, ever have to frantically flip back and forth to know what NFT thinks about, say, Arturo's in Greenwich Village ("Classic NY pizza joint with live jazz. NFT Favorite.") Substantial neighborhood overviews now call out all the NFT Landmarks, and our incomparable team of crack writers and researchers have pounded the pavement and lent their invaluable, immeasurable body of knowledge to afford you, the reader, an expert's sense of the overall feel of the 35 neighborhoods in this guide. It's a big step forward for us, and we're so damn excited for you to reap the full benefits of our labor.

Face it: you need us. Wrap your furry paws around this superior guide of all things New York and get ready to scout the tastiest dim sum, the artiest art, the rowdiest pubs, the prettiest parks (including a whole new section on The High Line), the quirkiest bowling alleys, and all the rest of New York's hidden treasures. When you come across something we missed, send us a note at www.notfortourists.com. The only thing we like more than your incalculable admiration is snappy and pointed, yet pertinent, critique.

See you on the Subway!

Jane, Rob, Craig, et al.

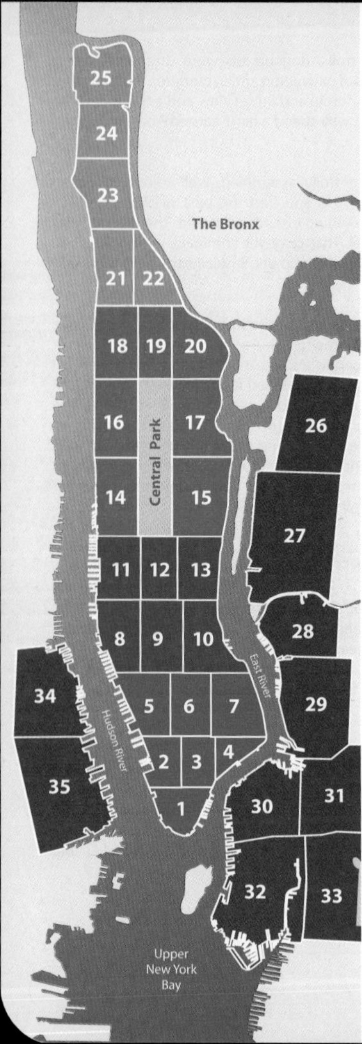

25
24
23
The Bronx
21
22
18
19
20
16
Central Park
17
26
14
15
27
11
12
13
8
9
10
28
East River
34
5
6
7
29
Hudson River
2
3
4
35
1
30
31
32
33
Upper
New York
Bay

Murray St
Greenwich St
W Broadway
City Hall Park
Park Pl
Park Row
Pace University
Spruce St
Frankfort St
Robert F Wagner
BROOKLYN BRIDGE
Barclay St
Park Place
Vesey St
St Paul's Chapel & Cemetery
Theatre Alley
Nassau St
Beekman St
Gold St
South Bridge Residential Tower
Pearl St
Bridge Café
Peck Slip
South St Seaport Historical District
World Trade Center
World Trade Center Site
World Trade Center
Ann St
Fulton Street-Broadway Nassau
Fulton St
Dey St
Church St
Cortlandt Street
Cortlandt Street
PAGE 270
Ryders Al
Cliff St
Beekman St
Water St
Front St
John St
Liberty Plaza
Liberty Plaza
Liberty St
Liberty Pl
Maiden Ln
Platt St
Fulton St
Burling Slip
American Stock Exchange
Cedar St
The Federal Reserve Bank
Chase Plaza
Battery Park City
Washington St
Greenwich St
Trinity Church
Thames St
Trinity Pl
Equitable Building
Canyon of Heroes
Legion Liberty Mem Sq
Fletcher St
John St
Albany St
Carlisle St
PAGE 234
Bankers Trust Company Building
The First JP Morgan Bank
Cedar St
American International Building
Maiden Ln
Pine St
Wall St Plaza
Rector Pl
West Side Hwy
Rector Street
Federal Hall
40 Wall St
Rector St
Rector Street
Wall Street
Broad Street
Wall Street
Wall St
Hanover Sq
Front St
South St
Wall St
Pier 13
Thames St
New York Stock Exchange
Exchange Pl
Exchange Alley
Vehicular Traffic Prohibited
Edgar St
20 Exchange Place
Broadway
William St
Gouverneur Ln
Delmonico's Building
India House
Mill Ln
Pier 11
Morris St
Cunard Building
Morris St
Little West St
Charging Bull
New St
Beaver St
Marketfield St
S William St
Stone St
Old Slip
Old Slip
FDR Dr
Pier 9
Standard Oil Building
Stone St
Bridge St
Water St
Vietnam Veterans Plaza
Alexander Hamilton U.S. Custom House
Bowling Green
Whitehall St
Battery Pl
Bowling Green
Battery Park Plaza
Moore St
Broad St
Heliport Auth
Robert F Wagner Jr Park
Battery Park
Pier A
Ferry to Ellis Island
Brooklyn Battery Tunnel
State St
New York Plaza
Peter Minuit Plaza
Whitehall Street
South Ferry
Battery Maritime Building
Battery Park Underpass
Battery Park
Staten Island Ferry Terminal
East River
Hudson River
1/4 mile
.25 km

Neighborhood Overview

Downtown is essentially New York's living museum—there are probably as many historical sites and markers in this neighborhood as there are in the entire rest of the city. This only makes sense, of course, since this is where New York started. To catch a little bit of that history, check out, in no particular order, **St. Paul's Chapel and Cemetery**, **Trinity Church**, and **Federal Hall**, where George Washington was inaugurated as first President of the United States. There is also a ferry which can take you to the Statue of Liberty, and, far more interestingly, to Ellis Island, where you can explore the history of immigration.

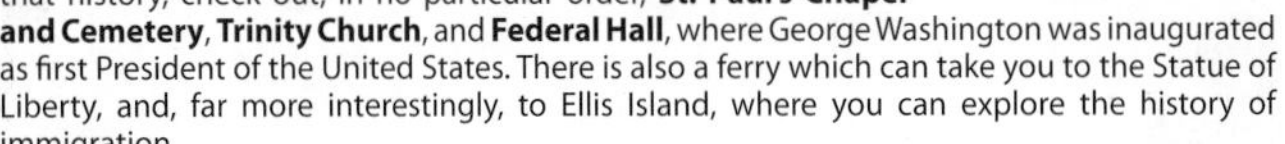

If you are interested in New York's mercantile and financial history, start off with the now well-guarded **New York Stock Exchange**, the **American Stock Exchange** (which was just recently acquired by the NYSE and is now referred to as the "NYSE Amex Equities"), the first **JP Morgan Bank** (still visibly scarred from a bombing in 1920), the **Federal Reserve Bank** (lots of cash, as well as being a main character in *Die Hard 3*), the gorgeous **Battery Maritime Building**, the stunning interior of the **Cunard Building**, the rich chocolate-colored federal-style **India House**, and the **Alexander Hamilton US Custom House**, now the National Museum of the American Indian. All of these buildings, along with John D. Rockefeller's **Standard Oil Building**, had or have major parts to play in New York's—and America's—mercantile and financial growth.

This financial growth led to the creation of the modern skyscraper, which New York had—and has—in abundance. Some of the most famous (remaining) downtown skyscrapers are **40 Wall Street** (now known as—what else—the "Trump Building"), art-deco gems **20 Exchange Place** and the **American International Building**, the massive **Equitable Building**, and **Bankers Trust Company Building**. But two of the most interesting skyscrapers are no longer around–Ernest Flagg's fabulous Singer Building, which was knocked down in 1968 to make way for the brutalist One Liberty Plaza, and, of course, Minoru Yamasaki's World Trade Center Towers, which were destroyed in a terrorist attack on September 11, 2001.

To take a break from all this soaring architecture, check out **Liberty Plaza**, with views of the new construction at the **Word Trade Center Site**, has great benches and sculpture. Near the East River, **Vietnam Veterans Plaza** is also a quiet spot to contemplate our forever-fading dreams of empire. Indoors, you can have a drink at New York's oldest bar, **The Bridge Cafe**. For the best of both worlds, get on the free **Staten Island Ferry**, have a tall boy, and contemplate all that you've seen while chilling out on the waves for a bit.

All this history brings hordes of tourists—for instance, tourist magnet **Bowling Green** has the famous **Charging Bull** on it, while the cobblestoned streets of **South Street Seaport** are awash with out-of-towners vainly searching for the Fulton Fish Market (it moved to The Bronx, folks) and shopping at the insidious Pier 17 Mall. At the same time, however, downtown, both before and after September 11, 2001, has become a magnet for New Yorkers seeking the perfect three-minute commute. You can see these locals hang out at one of two new strips of excellent dining and drinking—incredibly quaint Stone Street and up-and-coming Front Street. Both of these spots are a perfect end to a day of wandering around the madness of Downtown; we'll see you there!

Map 1 • Financial District

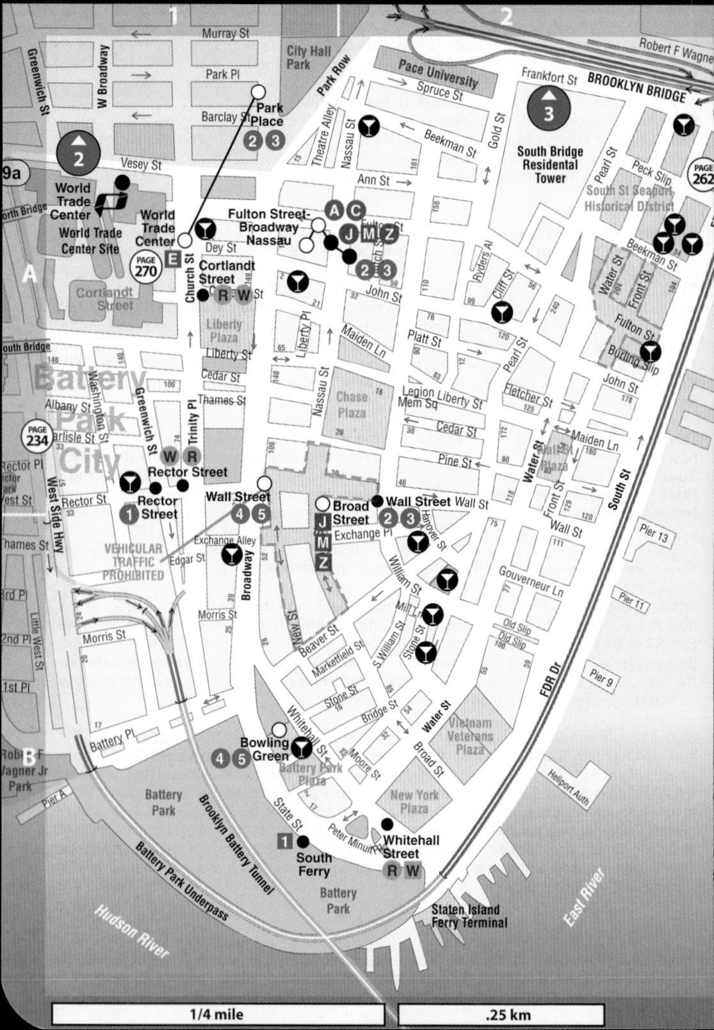

Well, it still ain't the Village by any stretch of the imagination, but at least newcomers such as wine bar **Bin 220** and **Fresh Salt** are viable options, along with old stalwarts **The Paris Cafe** and the **Bridge Cafe**. The secret bar at **India House**, however, is a new NFT favorite—you can thank us later.

Bars

- **The Beekman Pub** • 15 Beekman St [Nassau St] 212-732-7333 Guinness on tap and karaoke nights.
- **Bin 220** • 220 Front St [Beekman St] 212-374-9463 Escape the tourists at this excellent little wine bar.
- **Bridge Café** • 279 Water St [Dover St] 212-227-3344 Oldest bar in NYC; good whiskey selection.
- **Fresh Salt** • 146 Beekman St [Front St] 212-962-0053 Where architects go for happy hour.
- **Harry's Cafe & Steak** • 1 Hanover St [Wall St] 212-785-9200 The vintage French wine flows like a river. Or at least it used to.
- **Heartland Brewery** • 93 South St [Fulton St] 646-572-2337 Heartland HeartLAND HEARTLAND!
- **India House** • 1 Hanover Square [Stone St] 212-269-2323 Secret bar to the left up the stairs. You're welcome.
- **John Street Bar & Grill** • 17 John St [Nassau St] 212-349-3278 Nightmarish underground nonsense.
- **Killarney Rose** • 127 Pearl St [Hanover St] 212-422-1486 Irish pub where you can pregame for the Staten Island Ferry.
- **Liquid Assets** • 55 Church St [Fulton St] 212-693-2001 Plush seating and soft lighting.
- **Papoo's** • 55 Broadway [Exchange Aly] 212-809-3150 Popular Wall Street bar.
- **The Paris Café** • 119 South St [Peck Slip] 212-240-9797 Good, historic bar but used to be better. Best very late.
- **Pussycat Lounge** • 96 Greenwich St [Rector St] 212-349-4800 Wall Street strip club with live shows upstairs.
- **Ryan Maguire's Ale House** • 28 Cliff St [Fulton St] 212-566-6906 Decent Irish pub.
- **Ulysses'** • 95 Pearl St [Hanover Sq] 212-482-0400 Slightly hipper downtown bar.
- **Whitehorse Tavern** • 25 Bridge St [Whitehall St] 212-668-9046 Downtown dive. Not to be confused with the one in the West Village.

Murray St
Park Pl
Barclay St
Vesey St
City Hall Park
Park Row
Greenwich St
W Broadway
Park Place
2 3
World Trade Center
World Trade Center Site
World Trade Center
E
PAGE 270
Cortlandt Street
Cortlandt Street
R W
Church St
Dey St
Fulton Street-Broadway Nassau
A C
J M Z
2 3
Pace University
Spruce St
Beekman St
Theatre Alley
Nassau St
Ann St
Gold St
Frankfort St
BROOKLYN BRIDGE
Robert F Wagner
South Bridge Residental Tower
3
2
Pearl St
Peck Slip
South St Seaport Historical District
PAGE 262
Beekman St
Water St
Front St
Fulton St
Burling Slip
John St
John St
Liberty Plaza
Liberty St
Cedar St
Thames St
Trinity Pl
Liberty Pl
Maiden Ln
Platt St
Chase Plaza
Legion Mem Sq
Liberty St
Cedar St
Pine St
Fletcher St
Maiden Ln
Ryders Al
Cliff St
Battery Park City
Washington St
Albany St
Carlisle St
PAGE 234
West Side Hwy
Rector St
Rector Street
1
W R
Rector Street
Wall Street
4 5
Broad Street
J M Z
Wall Street
2 3
Wall St
Wall St
Exchange Pl
Exchange Alley
Edgar St
VEHICULAR TRAFFIC PROHIBITED
Broadway
New St
Hanover St
William St
Gouverneur Ln
Old Slip
Old Slip
Wall St Plaza
South St
Pier 13
Pier 11
Pier 9
FDR Dr
Morris St
Morris St
Little West St
Mill Ln
Stone St
S William St
Beaver St
Marketfield St
Stone St
Bridge St
Water St
Vietnam Veterans Plaza
Battery Pl
Bowling Green
4 5
Whitehall St
Battery Park Plaza
Moore St
Broad St
New York Plaza
Heliport Auth
Battery Park
Pier A
Brooklyn Battery Tunnel
State St
Peter Minuit Plaza
1
South Ferry
Whitehall Street
R W
Battery Park
Staten Island Ferry Terminal
Battery Park Underpass
Hudson River
East River
1/4 mile
.25 km

Our Stone Street favorite is pizzeria **Adrienne's**; on Front Street, it's the New Zealand goodness of **Nelson Blue**. You can eat cheaply at **Sophie's**, **Financier Patisserie**, **Zaitzeff**, **Barbarini Alimentari**, and greasy spoon **Pearl Street Diner** while you wait for financial success and a table at **SHO Shaun Hergatt** or **Mark Joseph**.

Restaurants

- **Adrienne's** • 54 Stone St [S William St]
  212-248-3838 • $$
  Modern, thin crust pizza.
- **Barbarini Alimentari** •
  225 Front St [Beekman]
  212-277-8890 • $$
  Take-out Italian goodness by the Seaport. Nice one.
- **Battery Gardens** • 17 Battery Park & State St [Across from 17 State St]
  212-809-5508 • $$$$$
  Panoramic views of NY harbor with a wood-burning fireplace.
- **Bayard's** • 1 Hanover Sq [Pearl St]
  212-514-9454 • $$$$
  Elegant Continental cuisine in the historic India House.
- **bread & olive** • 20 John St [Nassau]
  212-385-2144 • $$
  Middle Eastern goodness in the heart of downtown.
- **Bridge Café** • 279 Water St [Dover St]
  212-227-3344 • $$$$$
  Expensive but effective Seaport dining. Historic.
- **Financier Patisserie** • 62 Stone St [Mill Ln]
  212-344-5600 • $$
  Have your cake and a light meal too.
- **Grotto Pizzeria** • 69 New St [Beaver St]
  212-809-6990 • $$
  More quick, tasty Italian. Less nudity than that other grotto.
- **Harry's Cafe & Steak** • 1 Hanover St [Wall St]
  212-785-9200 • $$$$
  When the market is flush so is Harry.
- **Lemongrass Grill** • 84 William St [Maiden Ln]
  212-809-8038 • $$
  Serviceable Thai.
- **Les Halles** • 15 John St [Broadway]
  212-285-8585 • $$$
  Excellent French steakhouse. Thanks Mr. Bourdain.
- **Mark Joseph Steakhouse** •
  261 Water St [Peck Slip]
  212-277-0020 • $$$$
  Luger's wannabe: damn close, actually, and they take plastic.
- **Nelson Blue** • 233 Front St [Peck Slip]
  212-346-9090 • $$$
  New Zealand lollichop lollichop, whoah Lollichop…
- **Papoo's** • 55 Broadway [Exchange Aly]
  212-809-3150 • $$$$
  Good, if pricey, Italian cuisine.
- **The Paris Café** • 119 South St [Peck Slip]
  212-240-9797 • $$$
  Good burgers and seafood, a bit pricey though.
- **Pearl Street Diner** • 212 Pearl St [Platt St]
  212-344-6620 • $
  Greasy spoon hidden among the skyscrapers.
- **Red** • 19 Fulton St [South St]
  212-571-5900 • $$
  Acceptable Mexican.
- **SHO Shaun Hergatt** •
  40 Broad St [Exchange Pl]
  212-809-3993 • $$$$$
  Yup, it's great. If someone else is paying.
- **Smorgas Chef** • 53 Stone St [Mill Ln]
  212-422-3500 • $$
  Best 'balls on Wall Street…
- **Sophie's** • 73 New St [Beaver St]
  212-809-7755 • $
  Great cheap Cuban/Caribbean.
- **Spa 88** • 88 Fulton St [Gold St]
  212-766-8600 • $$
  Pre-and Post rub and tub grub.
- **Stella** • 213 Front St [Beekman St]
  212-233-2417 • $$$$
  Good for the power lunch; Pottery Barn decor.
- **Suteishi** • 24 Peck Slip [Front St]
  212-766-2344 • $$$
  Hip seaport sushi. Get the Orange/Red Dragon split.
- **Ulysses'** • 95 Pearl St [Hanover Sq]
  212-482-0400 • $$$
  Highlight: the buffet spread.
- **Zaitzeff** • 72 Nassau St [John St]
  212-571-7272 • $$
  Quick and organic burgers for lunch.
- **Zeytuna** • 59 Maiden Ln [William St]
  212-742-2436 • $$
  Gourmet take-out. NFT fave.

Murray St
Park Pl
Barclay St
Vesey St
City Hall Park
Park Row
Park Place
Pace University
Spruce St
Frankfort St
BROOKLYN BRIDGE
Robert F Wagr
South Bridge Residental Tower
Beekman St
Gold St
Theatre Alley
Nassau St
Ann St
Peck Slip
South St Seaport Historical District
World Trade Center
World Trade Center Site
Fulton Street-Broadway Nassau
Dey St
Cortlandt Street
Church St
PAGE 270
Cortlandt Street
Liberty Plaza
Liberty St
Cedar St
Thames St
John St
Maiden Ln
Platt St
Liberty Pl
Ryders Al
Cliff St
Pearl St
Water St
Front St
Fulton St
Burling Slip
Fletcher St
Legion Mem Sq
Liberty St
Chase Plaza
Battery Park City
Albany St
Washington St
Greenwich St
Trinity Pl
Carlisle St
PAGE 234
Rector Street
Rector St
Wall Street
Broad Street
Wall Street
Wall St
Pine St
Maiden Ln
Wall St Plaza
Hanover St
Exchange Pl
Exchange Alley
Edgar St
VEHICULAR TRAFFIC PROHIBITED
West Side Hwy
Broadway
New St
William St
Mill Ln
Gouverneur Ln
Old Slip
South St
Pier 13
Pier 11
Pier 9
Morris St
Little West St
Beaver St
Marketfield St
S William St
Stone St
FDR Dr
Bridge St
Water St
Vietnam Veterans Plaza
Battery Pl
Bowling Green
Whitehall St
Moore St
Battery Park Plaza
Broad St
New York Plaza
Heliport Auth
Battery Park
State St
Peter Minuit Plz
Whitehall Street
South Ferry
Brooklyn Battery Tunnel
Battery Park Underpass
Battery Park
Staten Island Ferry Terminal
Hudson River
East River
Pier A
Robert F Wagner Jr Park
1/4 mile
.25 km

Bagels, Coffee, & Shopping

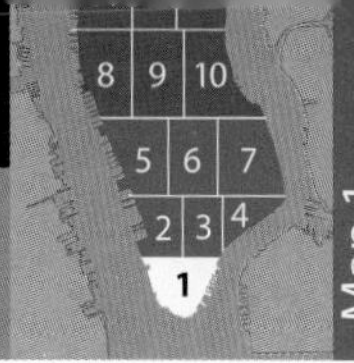

Gourmet markets **Jubilee** and **Zeytuna** are important destinations; then pick up some wine from **Greene Grape** or **Pasanella** to go with the food, add in some **Christopher Norman Chocolates**, buy something nice for her at the **ako store** or **Pylones**, then blow your own money at—where else? **J & R**.

Coffee

- **Dean & DeLuca Café** • 100 Broadway [Pine St]
  212-577-2153
  Expensive espresso for executives.
- **Financier Patisserie** • 35 Cedar St [William]
  212-952-3838
  Tres bien croissants.
- **Jack's Stir Brew Coffee** • 222 Front St [Peck Sl]
  212-929-0821
  Excellent little coffehouse, especially for these parts.
- **Zibetto** • 102 Fulton St [William St]
  A real Italian espresso bar. Un caffe, per favore!

Shopping

- **ako store** • 207 Front St [Fulton St]
  212-566-2727
  Jodie really digs this place.
- **Barbarini Mercato** • 227 Front St [Peck Slip]
  212-608-9622
  Italian imports, cheese, charcuterie, and groceries. Thank God.
- **Barclay Rex** • 75 Broad St [S William St]
  212-962-3355
  For all your smoking needs.
- **Browne & Co.** • 211 Water St [Beekman St]
  212-748-8651
  Old fashioned presses make prints, maps & cards.
- **Century 21** • 22 Cortlandt St [Broadway]
  212-227-9092
  Where most New Yorkers buy their underwear.
- **Christopher Norman Chocolates** •
  60 New St [Exchange Pl]
  212-402-1243
  Sweet chocolate shop. As if there were any other kind.
- **Compact Impact** • 71 Broadway [Rector St]
  212-677-0500
  Weird Japanese tech gadgets. By appointment only.
- **Dick's Hardware** • 9 Gold St [Platt St]
  212-425-1070
  Not a sex shop.
- **Firefly** • 224 Front St [Beekman]
  646-416-6560
  Cute children's boutique; not insanely priced.
- **Flowers of the World** • 110 Maiden Ln [Pearl]
  800-770-3125
  Fulfill any feeling, mood, budget, or setting.
- **Godiva Chocolatier** • 33 Maiden Ln [Nassau]
  212-809-8990
  Everyone needs a fix now and then.
- **The Greene Grape Downtown** •
  55 Liberty St [Nassau St]
  212-406-9463
  Fantastic everything—small label wines, champagnes, and spirits.
- **Hat Corner** • 139 Nassau St [Beekman]
  212-964-5693
  Look stylish with something from this old-school shop.
- **J&R Music & Computer World** •
  23 Park Row [Beekman St]
  212-238-9000
  Computers, electronics, and a good record store, to boot!
- **Jubilee Marketplace** • 99 John St [Cliff St]
  212-233-0808
  Godsend for Financial District dwellers.
- **Le Petite Cave** • 83 Maiden Ln [Liberty St]
  212-514-9817
  Friendly owner with well curated wine selection.
- **Little Airplane** • 207 Front St [Beekman]
  212-965-8999
  Cute little toy store run by "Wonder Pets" creators.
- **Pasanella** • 115 South St [Peck Slip]
  212-233-8383
  Great wine shop. Movies screenings in the back tasting room!
- **Pylones** • 183 Broadway [Maiden Ln]
  212-227-9273
  Impress your 15-year-old suburban niece with cool stuff.
- **Shoetrician Shoe Repair** •
  123 Fulton St [Dutch St]
  212-947-8496
  When your sole needs fixin'.
- **Silk Shop** • 132 Nassau St [Ann St]
  212-571-3130
  Wall Street secretaries shop here for trendy/sexy/sometimes slutty clothes.
- **The World of Golf** • 74 Broad St [Marketfield]
  212-385-1246
  Stop here on your way to Vanny.
- **Yankees Clubhouse Shop** • 8 Fulton St [South]
  212-514-7182
  27 and counting…
- **Zeytuna** • 59 Maiden Ln [William St]
  212-742-2436
  Excellent gourmet store--fish, meat, cheese counters. Yum.

Map 2 • TriBeCa

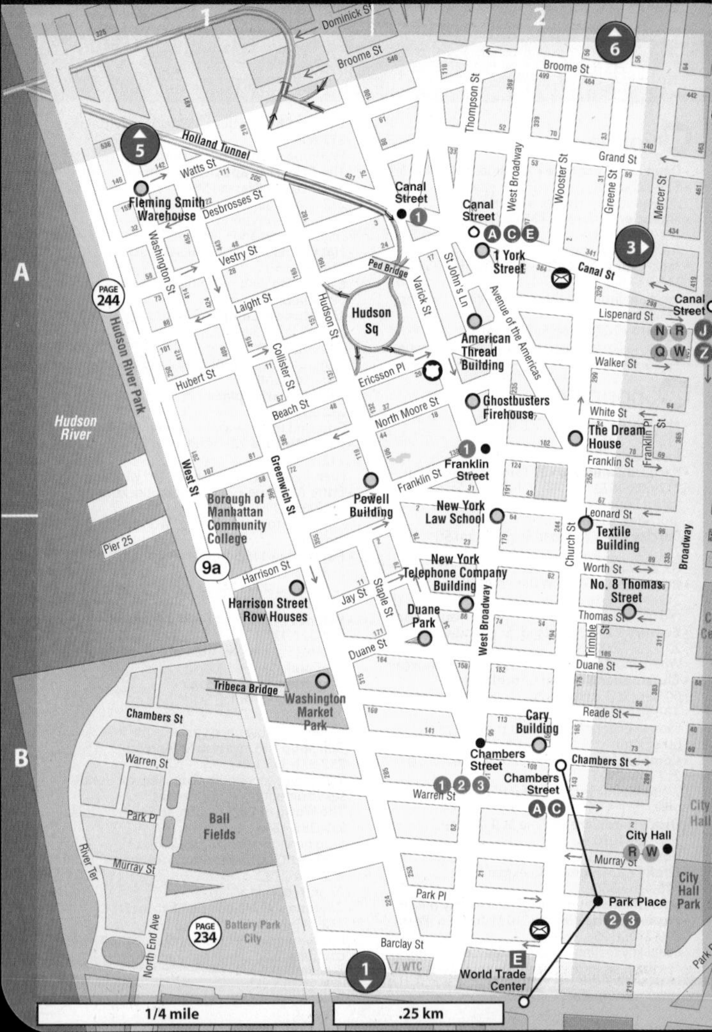

Canal Street 1
Canal Street A C E
1 York Street
American Thread Building
Ghostbusters Firehouse
The Dream House
Franklin Street 1
Fleming Smith Warehouse
Holland Tunnel
Hudson Sq
Powell Building
New York Law School
Textile Building
Borough of Manhattan Community College
New York Telephone Company Building
No. 8 Thomas Street
Harrison Street Row Houses
Duane Park
Washington Market Park
Tribeca Bridge
Cary Building
Chambers Street 1 2 3
Chambers Street A C
City Hall R W
Park Place 2 3
World Trade Center E
7 WTC
Canal Street N R J Q W Z
Hudson River
Hudson River Park
Pier 25
Ball Fields
Battery Park City
City Hall Park

PAGE 244
PAGE 234

1/4 mile
.25 km

Thinking of moving to TriBeCa? Well, then, congratulations—you've clearly made your first 10 million dollars! And, if you already live there...well, you're not reading a guidebook anyway...but maybe your assistant is. And for the rest of us, we'll just have to be content with walking around the neighborhood and choosing which fabulous converted loft building we'd live in when WE make our first $10 million.

Such is life in one of New York's prime neighborhoods—minutes away from downtown, the West Village, SoHo, and Chinatown, decent subway access, killer housing, a few minutes' walk to either the Battery Park City promenade or Hudson River Park, excellent restaurants, a few killer bars—life is pretty grand here, if you can afford it, of course.

But even if you can't, there's no question that walking around TriBeCa—as opposed to spending money in it—was and still is our favorite pastime in this 'nabe. There are simply tons of gorgeous old factory buildings that have now been lovingly converted to insanely expensive lofts, but that still shouldn't stop you from appreciating both the architecture and the preservation of these buildings, which can be found on almost every street in the Triangle Below Canal Street (Canal Street being the north side of the triangle, Broadway being the east side of the triangle, and the West Side Highway being the west side of the triangle).

On your walk, you'll pass one of the city's oldest parks (**Washington Market Park**), some ancient row houses (the **Harrison Street Row Houses**) and, perhaps our favorite TriBeCa landmark, the **Ghostbusters Firehouse** (you'll know it when you see it, trust us). A great starting (or ending point) for seeing TriBeCa is perhaps its nexus, lovely little **Duane Park**. It's a quaint little triangle surrounded on all sides by loft buildings you'd give an arm and a leg to live in.

As for the buildings themselves, there are a several you should definitely check out, including Henry J. Hardenbergh's **Textile Building**, Carrère & Hastings' **Powell Building**, which now houses **Nobu**, Ralph Walker's massive **New York Telephone Company Building**, the rounded front of the **American Thread Building**, the Venetian mash-up of **No. 8 Thomas Street**, cast-iron gem the **Cary Building**, and, the "pièce de résistance", Stephen Decatur Smith's **Fleming Smith Warehouse** on Washington Street, which houses TriBeCa classic **Capsouto Freres**.

Although most of the new construction (especially along Broadway) fits into the boring/puerile category, one new building to check out is Enrique Norten's postmodern **One York Street**; his insertion of a glass tower in the middle of two 19th-century buildings is pretty cool. **New York Law School's** new building at 185 West Broadway shines brightly at night as its law students burn the candle at both ends. Herzog & de Meuron's eagerly-awaited 56 Leonard Street project, however, is stalled (What? Recession? What?).

Unfortunately, we just don't get to TriBeCa as much at night any more, as two of its most interesting cultural hotspots—the Knitting Factory and Roulette—have both moved away (the **Knitting Factory** to Brooklyn and **Roulette** to SoHo). However, one of the coolest long-running sound and light installations in all the world is still here, at 275 Church Street, just steps from the posh **TriBeCa Grand Hotel**. La Monte Young and Marian Zazeela's **Dream House**, open October thru June on Thursday, Friday, and Saturday nights, is a special place to chill out, check your head, and get in touch with your inner being, before jumping it on the subway back to Bushwick.

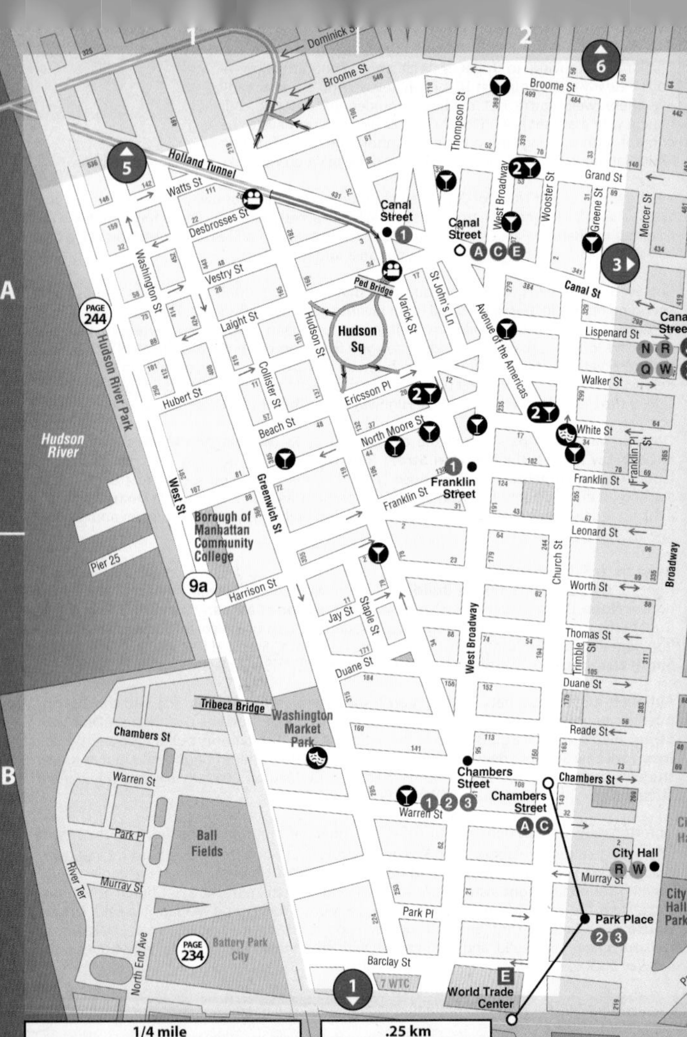

1
2
A
B
Dominick St
Broome St
Holland Tunnel
Watts St
Desbrosses St
Vestry St
Laight St
Hubert St
Beach St
Washington St
Hudson St
Collister St
Greenwich St
West St
Hudson River Park
Hudson River
Pier 25
9a
Canal Street
Canal Street
Ped Bridge
Hudson Sq
Varick St
St John's Ln
Ericsson Pl
North Moore St
Franklin St
Franklin Street
Thompson St
West Broadway
Wooster St
Greene St
Mercer St
Grand St
Canal St
Avenue of the Americas
Canal Street
Lispenard St
Walker St
White St
Franklin Pl
Franklin St
Leonard St
Worth St
Thomas St
Trimble Pl
Duane St
Reade St
Chambers St
Church St
Broadway
Borough of Manhattan Community College
Harrison St
Jay St
Staple St
Duane St
West Broadway
Tribeca Bridge
Washington Market Park
Chambers St
Chambers Street
Chambers Street
Warren St
Warren St
Park Pl
Ball Fields
River Ter
Murray St
North End Ave
Battery Park City
Park Pl
Barclay St
7 WTC
World Trade Center
City Hall
Murray St
Park Place
City Hall Park
PAGE 244
PAGE 234
1/4 mile
.25 km

While live music is no longer a nightly option with the **Knitting Factory's** move to Brooklyn, drinks both posh (**TriBeCa Grand, Bubble Lounge**) and dirty (**Nancy Whiskey, Puffy's**) can still be had. **Walker's** is a New York classic and should not be missed; otherwise, check out the **Flea Theatre's** calendar or wait for the **TriBeCa Film Festival**.

Bars

- **Anotheroom** • 249 W Broadway [Beach St]
  212-226-1418
  Cosy, cute, and narrow.
- **B Flat** • 277 Church St [White]
  212-219-2970
  Stylish Japanese basement cocktail den.
- **Brandy Library** •
  25 N Moore St [West Broadway]
  212-226-5545
  Refined but cozy with lots of free tasting events.
- **Broome Street Bar** •
  363 W Broadway [Broome]
  212-925-2086
  Real low-key for this part of town.
- **Bubble Lounge** • 228 W Broadway [White St]
  212-431-3433
  Champagne bar; the more $$$ you spend, the nicer they'll be.
- **Church Lounge** • 2 Sixth Ave
  212-519-6600
  Luxurious space with pricey drinks and occasional live music.
- **Lucky Strike** • 59 Grand St [West Broadway]
  212-941-0772
  Hipsters, locals, ex-smoky. Recommended.
- **Naked Lunch** • 17 Thompson St [Grand St]
  212-343-0828
  Average lounge.
- **Nancy Whisky Pub** •
  1 Lispenard St [West Broadway]
  212-226-9943
  Good dive. As if there were any other kind.
- **Puffy's Tavern** • 81 Hudson St [Harrison St]
  212-227-3912
  Suits, old timers, and hipsters. Top TriBeCa watering hole.
- **Roulette** • 20 Greene St [Canal]
  212-219-8242
  For the experimental at heart.
- **Smith & Mills** • 71 N Moore St [Greenwich St]
  Upscale cool cocktails. Limited seating.
- **Soho Grand Hotel** • 310 W Broadway [Canal]
  212-965-3000
  Swank sophistication.
- **Toad Hall** • 57 Grand St [West Broadway]
  212-431-8145
  Laid back vibe with SoHo locals.
- **Tribeca Grand Hotel** • 2 6th Ave [White St]
  212-519-6600
  Posh drinks in an uber-cool space; service is another matter.
- **Tribeca Tavern & Café** •
  247 W Broadway [Beach St]
  212-941-7671
  Good enough for us.
- **Walker's** • 16 N Moore St [West Broadway]
  212-941-0142
  Where old and new Tribeca neighbors mix.
- **Warren 77** • 77 Warren St [Greenwich St]
  212-227-8994
  Do you believe in miracles? A classy sports bar in NYC.

Movie Theaters

- **92Y Tribeca** • 200 Hudson St [Vestry St]
  212-601-1000
  Jewish-themed films mixed with popular indies.
- **Tribeca Cinemas** • 54 Varick St [Laight St]
  212-941-2001
  Home base of De Niro's Tribeca Film Festival.

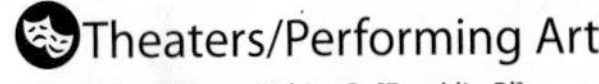

Theaters/Performing Arts

- **Flea Theatre** • 41 White St [Franklin Pl]
  212-226-0051
  Classic Off-Broadway combination of sex, politics and fun.
- **TriBeCa Performing Arts Center** •
  199 Chambers St [Greenwich St]
  212-220-1460
  Downtown performing arts center connected to BMCC. Cool.

Holland Tunnel
Dominick St
Broome St
Watts St
Desbrosses St
Vestry St
Laight St
Hubert St
Beach St
Washington St
Collister St
Hudson St
Hudson Sq
Ped Bridge
Varick St
St John's Ln
Canal Street
Thompson St
West Broadway
Wooster St
Greene St
Mercer St
Grand St
Canal St
Avenue of the Americas
Lispenard St
Walker St
White St
Franklin Pl
Franklin St
Leonard St
Worth St
Thomas St
Trimble Pl
Duane St
Reade St
Chambers St
Church St
Broadway
Ericsson Pl
North Moore St
Franklin Street
Greenwich St
West St
Borough of Manhattan Community College
Harrison St
Jay St
Staple St
Hudson River Park
Hudson River
Pier 25
PAGE 244
9a
Tribeca Bridge
Washington Market Park
Chambers Street
Warren St
Park Pl
Murray St
Barclay St
Ball Fields
River Ter
North End Ave
PAGE 234
Battery Park City
7 WTC
World Trade Center
City Hall
City Hall Park
Park Place
Park Row
1/4 mile
.25 km

If you've got the cash, this is the place—from **Nobu**'s top-shelf sushi to **Odeon**'s unquestioned hipness to **Landmarc**'s killer steaks to **Il Giglio**'s white-tablecloth-Italian to **Capsouto Freres**' upscale-but-warm French to **Bouley**'s top NYC dining experience. Otherwise, we go for the far-above-average pub grub at **Walker's** or cabbie favorite **Pakistan Tea House**.

Restaurants

- **Acapella** • 1 Hudson St [Chambers St]
212-240-0163 • $$$$
Sopranos-worthy Northern Italian cuisine.
- **Bouley** • 163 Duane St [Hudson St.]
212-964-2525 • $$$$$
Absolute top NYC dining. Love the apples in the foyer.
- **Bread Tribeca** • 301 Church St [Walker St]
212-334-0200 • $$$
Country-style Italian.
- **Bubby's** • 120 Hudson St [N Moore St]
212-219-0666 • $$
Great atmosphere—good home-style eats and homemade pies.
- **Capsouto Freres** • 451 Washington St [Watts]
212-966-4900 • $$$
Excellent brunch, great space, oldish (in a good way) vibe.
- **Centrico** • 211 W Broadway [Franklin St]
212-431-0700 • $$$$
Cha-cha upscale Mexican makes you forget the ka-ching.
- **City Hall** • 131 Duane St [Church St]
212-227-7777 • $$$$$
Bright, expensive, lots of suits, but still cool.
- **Corton** • 239 W Broadway [N Moore St]
212-219-2777 • $$$$
Bruni and Platt love this place. So should you.
- **Duane Park Café** • 157 Duane St [Hudson St]
212-732-5555 • $$$$$
Underrated New American.
- **Dylan Prime** • 62 Laight St [Greenwich St]
212-334-4783 • $$$$$
Excellent steakhouse, great location, TriBeCa prices.
- **Edward's** • 136 W Broadway [Duane St]
212-233-6436 • $$
Middle-of-the-road, kid's menu, mostly locals, sometimes great.
- **Estancia 460** • 460 Greenwich St [Watts St]
212-431-5093 • $$
Louche Argentines and brilliant french toast. Formerly Sosa Borella.
- **Flor de Sol** • 361 Greenwich St [Harrison St]
212-366-1640 • $$$$
Tapas with—of course—a scene.
- **The Harrison** • 355 Greenwich St [Harrison St]
212-274-9310 • $$$$$
Great New American—understandably popular.
- **Il Giglio** • 81 Warren St [Greenwich St]
212-571-5555 • $$$$$
Stellar Italian. Trust us.
- **Ivy's Bistro** • 385 Greenwich St [N Moore St]
212-343-1139 • $$
Down-to-earth neighborhood Italian.
- **Kitchenette** • 156 Chambers St [Hudson St]
212-267-6740 • $$
Great breakfast. Try the bacon.
- **Kori** • 253 Church St [Leonard St]
212-334-0908 • $$$
Korean. Hip space. It's TriBeCa.
- **Landmarc** • 179 W Broadway [Leonard St]
212-343-3883 • $$$$$
Modern, posh, great steaks and wines; and, of course, pricey.
- **Lupe's East LA Kitchen** • 110 6th Ave [Watts]
212-966-1326 • $
Tex-Mex. Quaint. Eat here.
- **Matsugen** • 241 Church St [Leonard St]
212-925-0202 • $$$$
Jean Georges's fantastic attempt at Japanese.
- **Nobu** • 105 Hudson St [Franklin St]
212-219-0500 • $$$$$
Designer Japanese. When we have 100 titles, we'll go here.
- **Nobu Next Door** • 105 Hudson St [Franklin St]
212-334-4445 • $$$$$
Nobu's cheaper neighbor.
- **Odeon** • 145 W Broadway [Thomas St]
212-233-0507 • $$$$
We can't agree about this one, so go and make your own decision.
- **Pakistan Tea House** • 176 Church St [Reade]
212-240-9800 • $
The real deal. Where cabbies eat. The Naan is perfect.
- **Tribeca Grill** • 375 Greenwich St [Franklin St]
212-941-3900 • $$$$$
Are you looking at me?
- **Walker's** • 16 N Moore St [West Broadway]
212-941-0142 • $$
Surprisingly good food for a pub!
- **Zutto** • 77 Hudson St [Harrison St]
212-233-3287 • $$$
Neighborhood Japanese.

Broome St
Dominick St
Holland Tunnel
Watts St
Desbrosses St
Vestry St
Laight St
Hubert St
Beach St
North Moore St
Ericsson Pl
Franklin St
Harrison St
Jay St
Staple St
Duane St
Chambers St
Warren St
Park Pl
Murray St
Barclay St
River Ter
North End Ave
Washington St
Collister St
Hudson St
Greenwich St
West St
Varick St
St John's Ln
Avenue of the Americas
West Broadway
Thompson St
Wooster St
Greene St
Mercer St
Grand St
Canal St
Lispenard St
Walker St
White St
Franklin Pl
Leonard St
Worth St
Thomas St
Trimble Pl
Reade St
Church St
Broadway
Canal Street
Franklin Street
Chambers Street
City Hall
Park Place
World Trade Center
7 WTC
Hudson Sq
Ped Bridge
Tribeca Bridge
Borough of Manhattan Community College
Washington Market Park
Ball Fields
Battery Park City
City Hall Park
Hudson River Park
Hudson River
Pier 25
9a
PAGE 244
PAGE 234
1/4 mile
.25 km

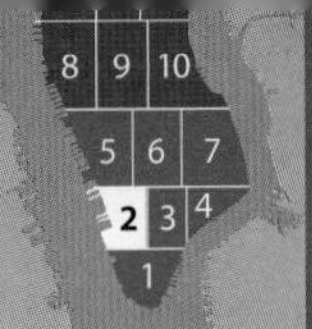

Two words here, folks: baked goods. TriBeCa's got 'em, with **Bouley Bakery**, **Grandaisy Bakery**, **Duane Park Patisserie**, and a **Le Pain Quotidien**. Then window shop at **Issey Miyake**, **Korin Japanese Trading**, **Jack Spade**, **Tent & Trails**, and **Steven Alan**. Top it off with a visit to **Bazzini**, **Vinovino**, or **MarieBelle's**.

Coffee

- **Kaffe 1668** • 275 Greenwich St [Murray St]
  212-693-3750
  Excellent coffee in a really cool space.
- **La Colombe Torrefaction** •
  319 Church St [Lipsenard St]
  212-343-1515
  Top-notch Philly coffee arrives in New York.
- **Le Pain Quotidien** • 81 W Broadway [Warren]
  646-652-8186
  Excellent coffee and pastries. Thanks Belgium.

Shopping

- **Amish Market** • 53 Park Pl [West Broadway]
  212-608-3863
  Lots of prepared foods. Do they deliver by horse and buggy?
- **Babesta Cribz** • 56 Warren St [West Broadway]
  646-290-5508
  Stuff for hipster babies and their parents.
- **Torly Kid** • 51 Hudson St [Thomas St]
  212-406-7440
  Children's store with clothing and educational toys.
- **Balloon Saloon** • 133 W Broadway [Duane St]
  212-227-3838
  We love the name.
- **Bazzini** • 339 Greenwich St [Jay St]
  212-334-1280
  Nuts to you!
- **Boffi SoHo** • 31 Greene St [Grand St]
  212-431-8282
  Hi-end kitchen and bath design.
- **Bouley Bakery & Market** •
  130 W Broadway [Reade]
  212-608-5829
  Fancy and fabulous pastries and breads.
- **Duane Park Patisserie** • 179 Duane St [Staple]
  212-274-8447
  Yummy!
- **Grandaisy Bakery** • 250 W Broadway [Beach]
  212-334-9435
  Breads and pizzas by the one and only.
- **Issey Miyake** • 119 Hudson St [N Moore St]
  212-226-0100
  Flagship store of this designer.
- **Jack Spade** • 56 Greene St [Broome St]
  212-625-1820
  Barbie's got Ken, Kate's got Jack. Men's bags.
- **Korin Japanese Trading** •
  57 Warren St [West Broadway]
  212-587-7021
  Supplier to Japanese chefs and restaurants.
- **Let There Be Neon** • 38 White St [Church St]
  212-226-4883
  Neon gallery and store.
- **Lucky Brand Dungarees** • 38 Greene St [Grand]
  212-625-0707
  Lucky you. If you can afford it.
- **MarieBelle's Fine Treats & Chocolates** •
  484 Broome St [Wooster St]
  212-925-6999
  Top NYC chocolatier. Killer hot chocolate.
- **New York Nautical** • 158 Duane St [Thomas]
  212-962-4522
  Armchair sailing.
- **Oliver Peoples** • 366 W Broadway [Watts St]
  212-925-5400
  Look as good as you see, and vice-versa.
- **Shoofly** • 42 Hudson St [Thomas St]
  212-406-3270
  Dressing your child for social success.
- **SoHo Art Materials** • 7 Wooster St [Crosby St]
  212-431-3938
  A painter's candy store.
- **Steven Alan** • 87 Franklin St [Church St]
  212-219-3305
  Trendy designer clothing and accessories. One-of-a-kind stuff.
- **Tent & Trails** • 21 Park Pl [Church St]
  212-227-1760
  Top outfitter for gearheads.
- **Tribeca Wine Merchants** • 40 Hudson St [Duane]
  212-393-1400
  High quality for a high rollers neighborhood.
- **Urban Archaeology** •
  143 Franklin St [West Broadway]
  212-431-4646
  Retro fixtures.
- **We Are Nuts About Nuts** •
  166 Church St [Chambers St]
  212-227-4695
  They're nuts. We're nuts. We're all nuts.
- **What Comes Around Goes Around** •
  351 W Broadway [Broome St]
  212-343-1225
  LARGE, excellent collection of men's, women's, and children's vintage.

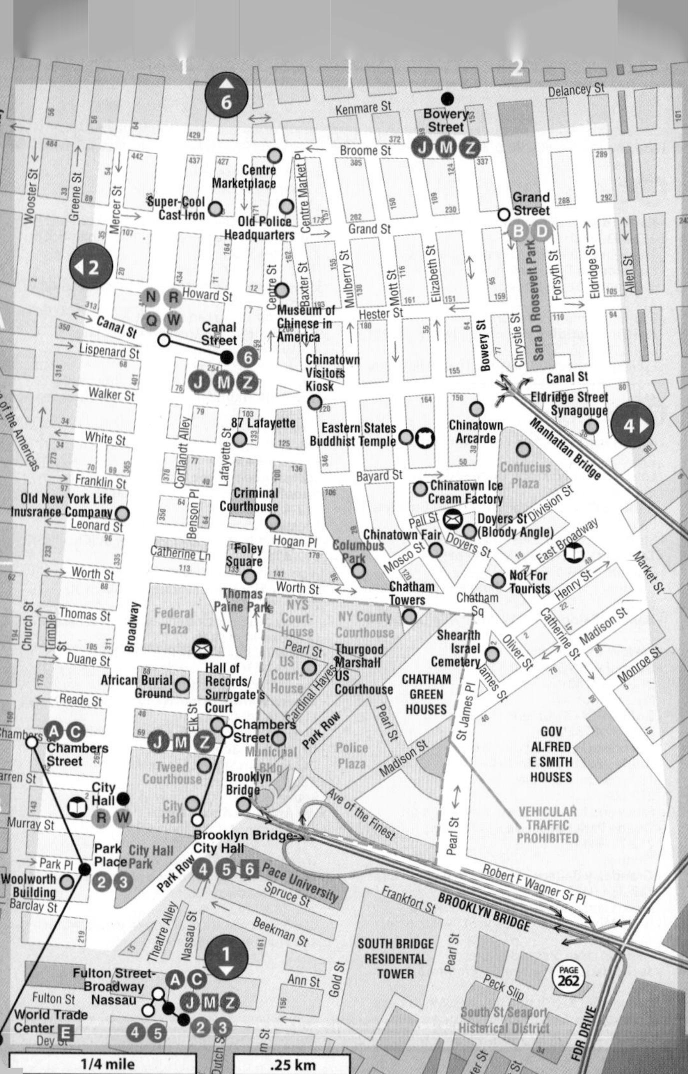

Kenmare St
Delancey St
Bowery Street
Broome St
Centre Marketplace
Super-Cool Cast Iron
Old Police Headquarters
Grand Street
Grand St
Howard St
Canal St
Canal Street
Museum of Chinese in America
Hester St
Lispenard St
Walker St
Chinatown Visitors Kiosk
Eldridge Street Synagouge
White St
87 Lafayette
Eastern States Buddhist Temple
Chinatown Arcarde
Manhattan Bridge
Confucius Plaza
Franklin St
Bayard St
Old New York Life Insurance Company
Criminal Courthouse
Chinatown Ice Cream Factory
Leonard St
Division St
Doyers St (Bloody Angle)
Chinatown Fair
Hogan Pl
Columbus Park
Catherine Ln
Foley Square
Worth St
Thomas Paine Park
Not For Tourists
Chatham Towers
Chatham Sq
Thomas St
Federal Plaza
NYS Court-House
NY County Courthouse
Duane St
Thurgood Marshall US Courthouse
Shearith Israel Cemetery
African Burial Ground
Hall of Records/ Surrogate's Court
CHATHAM GREEN HOUSES
Reade St
Chambers Street
Municipal Bldg
Police Plaza
GOV ALFRED E SMITH HOUSES
Tweed Courthouse
City Hall
Brooklyn Bridge
Ave of the Finest
VEHICULAR TRAFFIC PROHIBITED
Murray St
Brooklyn Bridge-City Hall
Park Place
City Hall Park
Park Pl
Woolworth Building
Barclay St
Pace University
Spruce St
Robert F Wagner Sr Pl
Frankfort St
BROOKLYN BRIDGE
Beekman St
SOUTH BRIDGE RESIDENTAL TOWER
Fulton Street-Broadway Nassau
Ann St
PAGE 262
Peck Slip
Fulton St
World Trade Center
South St Seaport Historical District
FDR DRIVE
1/4 mile
.25 km

Chinatown. Home of the NFT office since 1998, we truly have a love-hate relationship to this neighborhood. On one hand you have one of the highest concentrations of great (and cheap!) food in all of New York, one of the city's most interesting and diverse parks, lots of history, and a daytime hustle-and-bustle that is probably only matched by midtown Manhattan.

On the other hand…it's quite possibly New York's grimiest neighborhood, there is almost no nightlife, and peace and quiet is, of course, nonexistent during daylight hours. But hey—if you want peace and quiet, the Adirondacks are four hours away by car.

Otherwise, just get in and mix it up here with the locals, many of whom live in the huge **Confucius Towers** complex at the base of the Manhattan Bridge. And mixing it up is something that New Yorkers have been doing in this area for hundreds of years, starting with the incredibly dangerous "Five Points" area north of Collect Pond (the setting for Scorcese's seething Gangs of New York). Both the Five Points and Collect Pond are gone (the area itself is now **Columbus Park**), but even at the turn of the 20th century, little **Doyers Street** (aka "Bloody Angle") was the scene of Chinese gang wars for over 50 years.

Today, however, you can stroll around like the most clueless tourist and have absolutely no problems at all—gang wars have been replaced with street and shop commerce, from the tourist vendors of Mott Street to the produce market in the shadow of the Manhattan Bridge, with Canal Street's tourists and locals connecting the two. The mass of humanity is sometimes overwhelming.

Fortunately, there are some cool places to try and hide away for a few moments, including the **Eastern States Buddhist Temple** and Maya Lin's new **Museum of Chinese in America**. The best "living museum," however, is without a doubt **Columbus Park**, which has an incredible range of activities—from early-morning tai chi to afternoon mah-jongg—happening within its borders throughout the day. In summer, a stop at classic **Chinatown Ice Cream Factory** will also cool your jets momentarily.

Columbus Park also serves as the northeast border of the City Hall area. There are several standout examples of civic architecture, including **City Hall** itself, the **Tweed Courthouse**, the **US Courthouse**, the now-condo-ized **Woolworth Building**, the sublime **Hall of Records/Surrogate Court** building, and, one of our favorite buildings in all of New York, McKim, Mead, & White's masterful **Municipal Building**, complete with a wedding-cake top and the Brooklyn Bridge stop of the 4-5-6 trains underneath.

From the Municipal Building, a walk over the **Brooklyn Bridge** is almost a de rigueur activity; if you'd rather stay in Manhattan, though, check out the recently discovered **African Burial Ground** or watch Law & Order episodes being filmed from **Foley Square**. Or head back east a bit to discover another bit of New York City history, an ancient **Jewish Burial Ground** on St. James Place.

No matter what you see down here, however, don't forget to EAT. It's worth the traffic, the smells, the lines, and the general rudeness of people. Believe it.

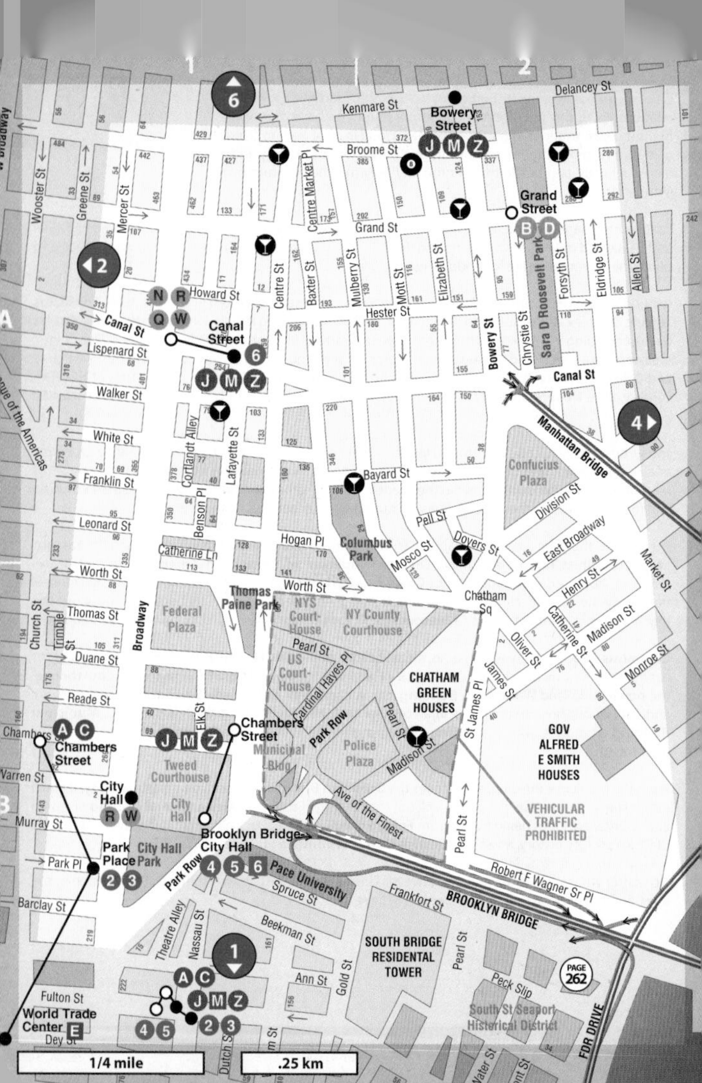

Delancey St
Kenmare St
Bowery Street
Broome St
Grand Street
Grand St
Howard St
Canal St
Canal Street
Lispenard St
Walker St
White St
Franklin St
Leonard St
Worth St
Thomas St
Duane St
Reade St
Chambers Street
Warren St
City Hall
Murray St
Park Place
Park Pl
Barclay St
Fulton St
World Trade Center
Dey St
Brooklyn Bridge-City Hall
Pace University
Spruce St
Beekman St
Ann St
Frankfort St
BROOKLYN BRIDGE
Robert F Wagner Sr Pl
SOUTH BRIDGE RESIDENTAL TOWER
Peck Slip
South St Seaport Historical District
FDR DRIVE
Manhattan Bridge
Confucius Plaza
Division St
East Broadway
Henry St
Madison St
Monroe St
Market St
Catherine St
Oliver St
James St
St James Pl
Chatham Sq
CHATHAM GREEN HOUSES
GOV ALFRED E SMITH HOUSES
VEHICULAR TRAFFIC PROHIBITED
Pearl St
Ave of the Finest
Police Plaza
Park Row
Municipal Bldg
Tweed Courthouse
City Hall Park
Federal Plaza
Thomas Paine Park
NYS Court-House
NY County Courthouse
US Court-House
Cardinal Hayes Pl
Columbus Park
Hogan Pl
Bayard St
Pell St
Doyers St
Mosco St
Hester St
Centre St
Baxter St
Mulberry St
Mott St
Elizabeth St
Bowery St
Chrystie St
Sara D Roosevelt Park
Forsyth St
Eldridge St
Allen St
Centre Market Pl
Lafayette St
Cortlandt Alley
Benson Pl
Catherine Ln
Elk St
Broadway
Church St
Trimble Pl
Wooster St
Greene St
Mercer St
Theatre Alley
Nassau St
Gold St
Dutch St
Water St
Ave of the Americas
1/4 mile
.25 km
PAGE 262

Nightlife

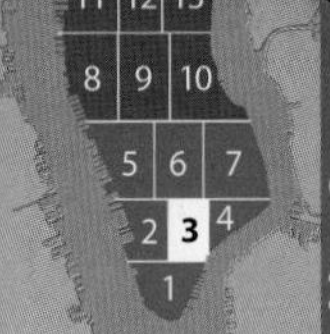

Think Kansas is boring at night? You haven't been to Chinatown at 10 pm on a Monday. Fortunately, one of the best dive/Chinese gangster Karaoke bars, the inimitable **Winnie's**, is here for your pleasure. Otherwise, hit sprawling **Fontana's** (the site of several NFT parties), or drink with the cops at **Metropolitan Improvement Company** or dance with hipsters at **Santos Party House**.

Bars

- **Apotheke** • 9 Doyers St [Bowery]
  212-406-0400
  Flaming expensive Euro-cocktails in a (supposedly) former opium den.
- **Capitale** • 130 Bowery [Grand St]
  212-334-5500
  Formerly the Bowery Savings Bank. Cool space.
- **Experimental Intermedia** •
  224 Centre St [Grand St]
  212-431-5127
  Experimental art/performance art shows involving a variety of artistic media.
- **Fontana's** • 105 Eldridge St [Grand St]
  212-334-6740
  A big, band-playing, art-hanging LES slice in borderline Chinatown.
- **Happy Ending** • 302 Broome St [Forsyth St]
  212-334-9676
  Still taking the edge off.
- **Metropolitan Improvement Company** •
  3 Madison St [Ave of the Finest]
  212-964-0422
  Where the cops drink.
- **Santos Party House** •
  96 Lafayette St [Walker St]
  212-584-5492
  Eclectic music is the rule at this terrific new venue.
- **Southside** • 1 Cleveland Pl [Broome St]
  212-680-5601
  Models, bankers, wealthy hipsters…you know the drill.
- **Winnie's** • 104 Bayard St [Mulberry St]
  212-732-2384
  Chinese gangster karaoke. We kid you not.

Billiards

- **Tropical 128** • 128 Elizabeth St [Broome St]
  212-925-8219
  Challenge the Chinatown champions.

Map 3 • City Hall / Chinatown

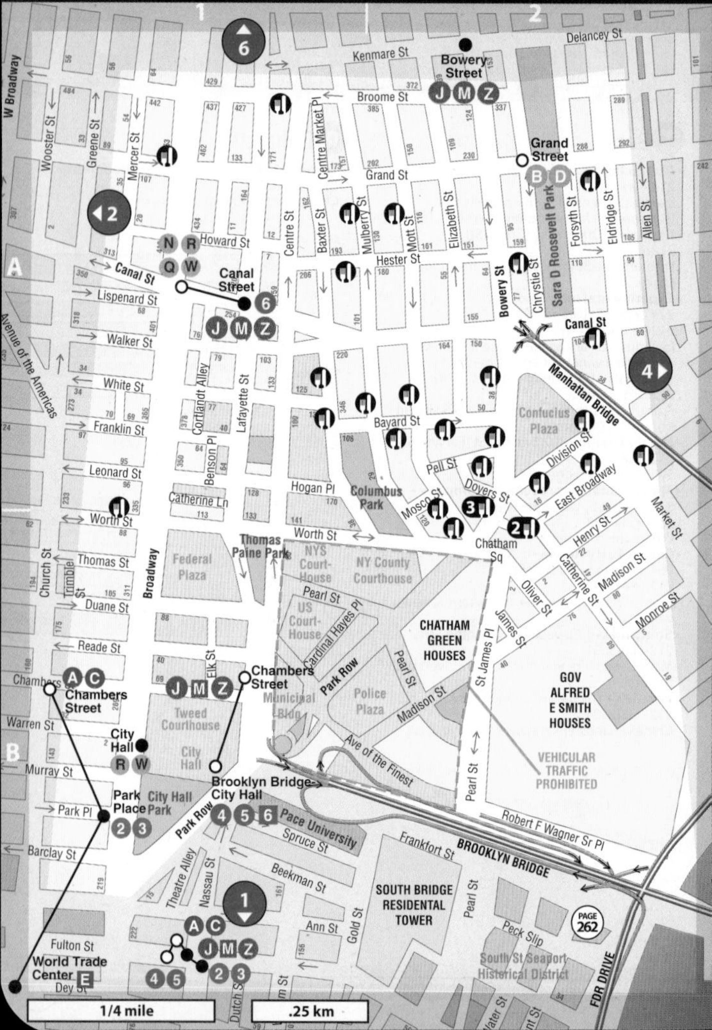

First stop: the crab soup dumplings at **Joe's Shanghai**. Second stop: the salt-and-pepper squid at **Pho Viet Huong**. On from there, classic Thai at **Pongsri Thai**, dim sum at **Mandarin Court**, **88 Palace**, or **Dim Sum Go Go**, or street cart **Xinjiang** for meat on a stick. Too much Asian? Head up to SoHo for Spanish sandwich gem **Despana**.

Restaurants

- **88 Palace** • 88 E Broadway [Forsyth St]
  212-941-8886 • $$
  Dim sum madness under the Manhattan Bridge.
- **Banh Mi Saigon** • 138 Mott St [Grand St]
  212-941-1541 • $
  The best Vietnamese sandwiches. Ever.
- **Bo Ky** • 80 Bayard St [Mott St]
  212-406-2292 • $
  Chinese/Vietnamese hybrid. Killer soups.
- **Buddha Bodai** • 5 Mott St [Worth St]
  212-566-8388 • $$
  Veg heads dig this place.
- **Cong Ly** • 124 Hester St [Chrystie St]
  212-343-1111 • $
  Most interesting Pho in the city. Plus grilled pork!
- **Cup & Saucer** • 89 Canal St [Eldridge St]
  212-925-3298 • $
  Where NFT eats when sick of Chinese food. Well, just Rob.
- **Despana** • 408 Broome St [Centre St]
  212-219-5050 • $
  Excellent Spanish take-out/gourmet grocery, complete w/ bull.
- **Dim Sum Go Go** • 5 E Broadway [Catherine St]
  212-732-0796 • $$
  New, hip, inventive dim sum; essentially, post-modern Chinese.
- **East Corner Wonton** • 70 E Broadway [Market]
  212-343-9896 • $
  Consistently good wonton noodle soups.
- **Excellent Pork Chop House** •
  3 Doyers St [Bowery]
  212-791-7007 • $
  Fried chicken leg & spicy wontons are excellent.
- **Farinella** • 90 Worth St [Broadway]
  212-608-3222 • $
  4-ft long pizzas and fresh panini. Napoli-style service.
- **Food Shing** • 2 E Broadway [Chatham Sq]
  212-219-8223 • $
  Outstanding beef soup with hand-pulled noodles.
- **Fuleen Seafood** • 11 Division St [Catherine St]
  212-941-6888 • $$$
  Chinatown gem; amazing lunch specials.
- **Great New York Noodle Town** •
  28 Bowery [Bayard St]
  212-349-0923 • $
  Cheap Chinese soups and BBQ and deep-fried squid. At 2 am.
- **Il Palazzo** • 151 Mulberry St [Grand St]
  212-343-7000 • $$$
  Good mid-range Italian.
- **Joe's Shanghai** • 9 Pell St [Bowery]
  212-233-8888 • $$
  Crab Soup Dumpling Mecca. Worth the wait.
- **L'Ecole** • 462 Broadway [Grand St]
  212-219-3300 • $$$$
  French Culinary Institute restaurant; new student menu every 6 weeks.
- **Mandarin Court** • 61 Mott St [Bayard St]
  212-608-3838 • $$
  Consistently good and frenetic dim sum.
- **May Wah Fast Food** • 190 Hester St [Baxter St]
  212-925-6428 • $
  Linoleum floors, fluorescent lights, and an amazing pork chop over rice.
- **New Malaysia** • 46 Bowery [Canal]
  212-964-0284 • $$
  A hidden gem that's literally hidden. Try the specials.
- **Nha Trang** • 87 Baxter St [White St]
  212-233-5948 • $$
  Excellent Vietnamese. Pho Beef Satee is good.
- **Nice Green Bo** • 66 Bayard St [Mott St]
  212-625-2359 • $
  Amazing Shanghainese. Nice alternative to Joe's.
- **Pho Viet Huong** • 73 Mulberry St [Bayard St]
  212-233-8988 • $$
  Very good Vietnamese—get the salt and pepper squid.
- **Ping's** • 22 Mott St [Mosco St]
  212-602-9988 • $$
  Eclectic Asian seafood. And we mean "eclectic."
- **Pongsri Thai** • 106 Bayard St [Baxter St]
  212-349-3132 • $$
  Ever wonder where district attorneys go for cheap, tasty Thai?
- **Sanur Restaurant** • 18 Doyers St [Bowery]
  212-267-0088 • $
  Amazing, super cheap Malaysian.
- **Tasty Hand-Pulled Noodle Inc** •
  1 Doyers St [Bowery]
  212-791-1817 • $
  Stop by for a bowl on your post office run.
- **Vanessa's Dumpling House** •
  118 Eldridge St [Broome St]
  212-625-8008 • $
  Famous Fat Dave recommends the sesame pancakes.
- **Xinjiang Kebab Cart** • Division St & Market St
  No phone • $
  Spicy, charcoal-grilled chicken hearts anyone?

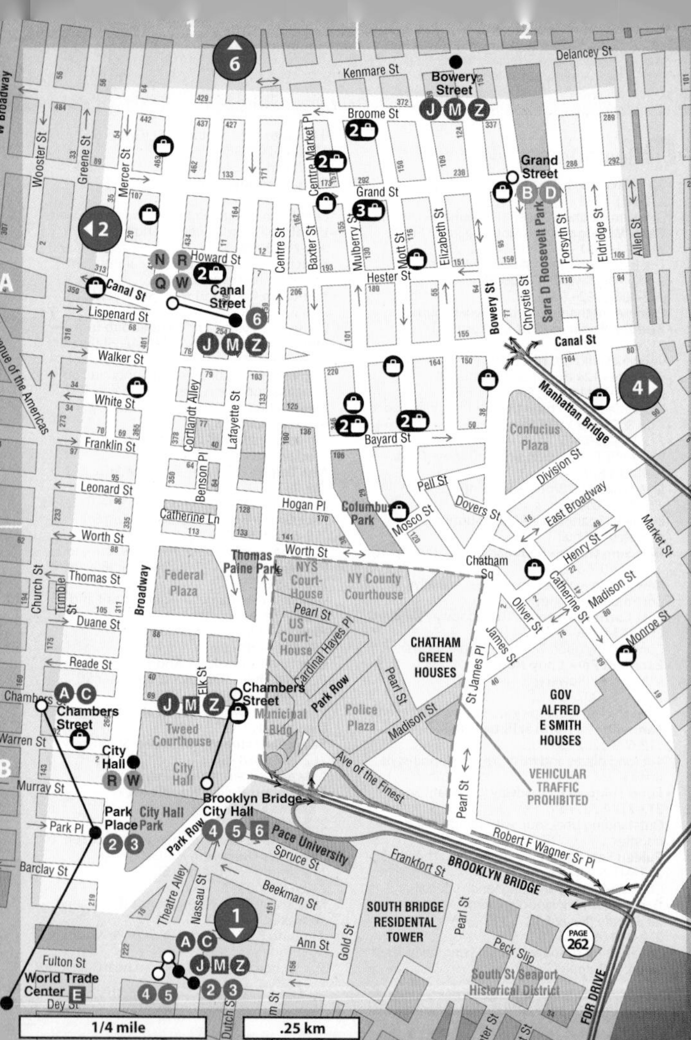

1
2
A
B
Delancey St
Kenmare St
Broome St
Grand St
Howard St
Hester St
Canal St
Lispenard St
Walker St
White St
Franklin St
Leonard St
Worth St
Thomas St
Duane St
Reade St
Chambers St
Warren St
Murray St
Park Pl
Barclay St
Fulton St
Dey St
W Broadway
Wooster St
Greene St
Mercer St
Centre Market Pl
Baxter St
Mulberry St
Mott St
Elizabeth St
Bowery St
Chrystie St
Forsyth St
Eldridge St
Allen St
Centre St
Lafayette St
Cortlandt Alley
Benson Pl
Catherine Ln
Hogan Pl
Bayard St
Pell St
Doyers St
Mosco St
Division St
East Broadway
Henry St
Madison St
Monroe St
Market St
Catherine St
Oliver St
James St
St James Pl
Pearl St
Cardinal Hayes Pl
Park Row
Ave of the Finest
Robert F Wagner Sr Pl
Frankfort St
Spruce St
Beekman St
Ann St
Gold St
Nassau St
Theatre Alley
Peck Slip
Water St
Dutch St
Church St
Trimble Pl
Broadway
Elk St
Avenue of the Americas
Sara D Roosevelt Park
Confucius Plaza
Columbus Park
Thomas Paine Park
Federal Plaza
NYS Court-House
NY County Courthouse
US Court-House
Police Plaza
Municipal Bldg
Tweed Courthouse
City Hall
City Hall Park
CHATHAM GREEN HOUSES
GOV ALFRED E SMITH HOUSES
VEHICULAR TRAFFIC PROHIBITED
Chatham Sq
Manhattan Bridge
BROOKLYN BRIDGE
Pace University
SOUTH BRIDGE RESIDENTAL TOWER
South St Seaport Historical District
FDR DRIVE
Bowery Street
Grand Street
Canal Street
Chambers Street
Brooklyn Bridge-City Hall
Park Place
World Trade Center
PAGE 262
1/4 mile
.25 km

So many places to shop, fortunately almost none of it on Canal Street (except for classic artists warehouse **Pearl Paint**, that is). Hit **New Beef King** for homemade jerky, **DiPalo Fine Foods** for Italian imports, **K & M Camera** for shutterbug stuff, and **Pearl River Mart** for a massive selection of imports. Or, simply walk the streets and window-shop.

Shopping

- **Aji Ichiban** • 167 Hester St [Mott St]
  212-925-1133
  Load up on free samples from the huge selection of Asian candies and snacks.
- **Alleva** • 188 Grand St [Mulberry St]
  212-226-7990
  Killer Italian import shop.
- **Bangkok Center Grocery** •
  104 Mosco St [Mulberry St]
  212-732-8916
  Curries, fish sauce, and other Thai products.
- **Built by Wendy** • 7 Centre Market Pl [Broome]
  212-925-6538
  Awesome NYC-based indie clothing label.
- **Catherine Street Meat Market** •
  21 Catherine St [Henry St]
  212-693-0494
  Fresh pig deliveries every Tuesday!
- **Chinatown Arcade** • 48 Bowery [Canal St]
  Bizarre indoor mall/passageway. Check it out.
- **Chinatown Ice Cream Factory** •
  65 Bayard St [Mott St]
  212-608-4170
  Take home a quart of mango. Oddest flavors in NYC.
- **Di Palo Fine Foods** • 200 Grand St [Mott St]
  212-226-1033
  Delicacies from across Italy. Excellent cheese.
- **Downtown Music Gallery** •
  13 Monroe St [Catherine]
  212-473-0043
  Independent labels and artists.
- **E. Vogel** • 19 Howard St [Crosby St]
  212-925-2460
  Beautiful custom-made boots that you probably can't afford.
- **Fay Da Bakery** • 83 Mott St [Canal St]
  212-791-3884
  Chinese pastry & boba like nobody's business.
- **Forsyth Outdoor Produce Market** •
  Forsyth St & Division St
  Cheapest veggies and fruit in Manhattan.
- **Fountain Pen Hospital** •
  10 Warren St [Broadway]
  212-964-0580
  They don't take Medicaid.
- **Hong Keung Seafood & Meat Market** •
  75 Mulberry St [Bayard St]
  212-571-1188
  Fresh seafood that you must eat today.
- **K & M Camera** • 385 Broadway [White]
  212-523-0954
  Good all-around camera store; open Saturdays!
- **Lendy Hardware** • 176 Grand St [Baxter St]
  212-941-1334
  Great bastion of the electrical supply world.
- **Lung Moon Bakery** • 83 Mulberry St [Canal St]
  212-349-4945
  Chinese bakery.
- **Muji Soho** • 455 Broadway [Grand St]
  212-334-2002
  Why is Japanese design so functional and cute?
- **New Beef King** • 89 Bayard St [Mulberry St]
  212-233-6612
  Serious jerky for serious jerks.
- **New York City Store** • 1 Centre St [Chambers]
  212-669-8246
  Specialty NYC books and municipal publications.
- **No 6** • 6 Centre Market Pl [Grand St]
  212-226-5759
  Notable selection of carefully selected original American and European vintage.
- **Ocean Star Market** • 250 Grand St [Chrystie]
  212-274-0990
  Cantonese market with fresh fish and veggies.
- **Opening Ceremony** • 35 Howard St [Crosby]
  212-219-2688
  Expensive hipster threads for tiny bodies.
- **Oro Bakery** • 375 Broome St [Mott St]
  212-941-6368
  Euro baked goods when you need a break from egg tarts.
- **Papabubble** • 380 Broome St [Mulberry St]
  212-966-2599
  Candy labratory. Willy Wonka would be proud.
- **Pearl Paint** • 308 Canal St [Mercer St]
  212-431-7932
  Mecca for artists, designers, and people who just like art supplies.
- **Pearl River Mart** • 477 Broadway [Broome St]
  212-431-4770
  Chinese housewares and more. Almost mind-numbing.
- **Piemonte Ravioli** • 190 Grand St [Mulberry St]
  212-226-0475
  Old-school and homemade.
- **Yunhong Chopsticks Shop** •
  50 Mott St [Bayard St]
  212-566-8828
  Super-cute chopstick shop in C-town.

Lilian Wald Houses
E 3rd St
E 2nd St
E 1st St
E Houston St
7
Hamilton Fish Park
Angel Orensanz Theatre
Stanton St
Rivington St
Masaryk Towers
Samuel Gompers Houses
Baruch Houses
Blue Condo
Delancey Street Essex Street
Williamsburg Bridge
Delancey St
Lower East Side Tenement Museum
Broome St
Bialystoker Synagogue
Hillman Houses
East River Houses
Grand St
Samuel Dickstein Plz
Seward Park Houses
Vladeck Houses
WH Seward Park
East Broadway
Corlears Hook Park
Hester St
Canal St
East Broadway
Gouverneur Hospital (old building)
La Guardia Houses
Rutgers Houses
FDR Dr
Pier 42
Pier 43
Marginal St
3
Knicker-bocker Village
East River
Gov Alfred E Smith Houses
Manhattan Bridge
30
Robert F Wagner Sr Pl
BROOKLYN
1/4 mile
.25 km
Empire Fulton-Ferry

Now characterized by a surfeit of bars and nightclubs and a perpetual congregation of gold lamé-wearing hipsters outside Houston Street's American Apparel, the Lower East Side was once a bustling cultural epicenter. Evidence of its predominantly Jewish roots is apparent in the dusting of tantalizing bagel, bialy, pastrami, and pickle joints as well as in the architecture—synagogues that either remained as such or were converted into avant-garde art spaces (Exhibit A: the **Angel Orensanz Foundation**). The center of entertainment is located at the northwestern tip, scattered throughout Orchard, Ludlow, Stanton, Clinton, Rivington, and Essex Streets and bordered by housing projects on the East and a sliver of Manhattan's sprawling Chinatown on the southern side. Though the majority of bar hopping twenty- and thirty-somethings revel in the Lower East Side's current hipness, the city's more decrepit folk still cringe at the neighborhood's crime-ridden days of yore. Grandma's apprehensive squawking about Lower Manhattan's violent 1970s and 1980s past enhances its already gritty appeal rather than deterring aforementioned scenesters and tourists from partaking in its lively nightlife and trendy dining options.

Not only a conspicuous hybrid of Jewish, Latino, and Chinese cultures, the Lower East Side is also a breathing representation of two intertwining generations: that of the 1920s working class and the present self-proclaimed artists and NYU party-seekers. The aged yet preserved "Louis Zuflacht Smart Clothes" sign, a testament to the neighborhood's now-defunct garment factories and retailers, presides over the recently opened **NY Studio Gallery**. Arched remnants of the First Roumanian-American Congregation ironically (and scandalously) face the dildo-vending **Babeland**, and Chinese markets stocked with overflowing barrels of pungent vegetables encounter pricey Broome Street boutiques. To learn more about the diverse ethnic groups who inhabited this busy area before, check out the **Lower East Side Tenement Museum**. You're supposed to feel content about your relatively spacious living quarters after viewing a day in the quotidian life of your ancestors, but chances are you'll grow envious of their decent digs.

Despite the bastion of Puerto Rican and Dominican immigrants who occupy the weathered but attractive red brick tenements, the influx of all-glass luxury condos built for those who believe coolness is quantified by monthly rent prices persists with a gentrifying vengeance (Exhibit B: **Blue Condo**). It may be located at Manhattan's southeastern tip, but the LES is undeniably one of the centers of the city's nightlife scene.

For a real taste of the neighborhood's Jewish roots, head down to the **Bialystoker Synagogue** (unfortunately, it claims no relation to the conniving protagonist of The Producers). Think it's tough to get into **Libation** now? Crowds that would easily engulf today's nightclub throngs used to swarm outside the synagogues in the 1920s, tamed only by an outpost of police officers. We don't know about you, but our idea of fun definitely involves Hebrew chanting and Manischewitz-drinking rather than table dancing in a skimpy miniskirt. If the excessive partying results in noxious effects on your health, **Gouverneur Hospital** is there to save the day. The building may be a century old, but the medical procedures are quite up-to-date. Or so we hope.

E 3rd St
E 2nd St
E 1st St
E Houston St
Lilian Wald Houses
Hamilton Fish Park
Stanton St
Rivington St
Delancey Street Essex Street
Delancey St
Williamsburg Bridge
Masaryk Towers
Samuel Gompers Houses
Baruch Houses
East River Houses
Hillman Houses
Broome St
Grand St
Seward Park Houses
Samuel Dickstein Plz
Vladeck Houses
Corlears Hook Park
WH Seward Park
Hester St
Canal St
East Broadway
La Guardia Houses
Rutgers Houses
Knickerbocker Village
Gov Alfred E Smith Houses
Manhattan Bridge
East River
FDR Dr
Pier 42
Pier 43
Robert F Wagner Sr Pl
BROOKLYN
1/4 mile
.25 km

Whether you're into chugging $1.75 PBRs at semi-grungy dive bars like **Welcome to the Johnsons** and **Motor City**, or licentious dance parties at **The Skinny**, or Punk Rock Karaoke at **Arlene's Grocery**, LES nightlife has something fun to offer spendthrifts, hipsters, and fist-pumpers alike. The later it gets, the heftier (and more boorish) the crowds become.

Bars

- **Arlene's Grocery** • 95 Stanton St [Ludlow St]
  212-995-1652
  Cheap live tunes.
- **Back Room** • 102 Norfolk St [Delancey St]
  212-228-5098
  The secret room is behind a bookcase.
- **Bar 169** • 169 E Broadway [Rutgers St]
  646-833-7199
  Sometimes good, sometimes not.
- **Barramundi** • 67 Clinton St [Rivington St]
  212-529-6999
  Great garden in summer.
- **Cake Shop** • 152 Ludlow St [Stanton St]
  212-253-0036
  Coffee, records, beer, rock shows, and a "Most Radical Jukebox."
- **Chloe 81** • 81 Ludlow St [Broome St]
  212-677-0067?
  Another secret bar you won't get into.
- **Clandestino** • 35 Canal St [Ludlow St]
  212-475-5505
  Inviting bar off the beaten track.
- **Dark Room** • 165 Ludlow St [Stanton St]
  212-353-0536
  For dark deeds. Ask Lindsay Lohan.
- **Donnybrook** • 35 Clinton St [Stanton St.]
  212-228-7733
  Upscale yet rustic pub for the professional crowd.
- **East Side Company** • 49 Essex St [Grand St]
  212-614-7408
  Fantastic cocktails. Intimate vibe. NFT approved.
- **Laugh Lounge NYC** • 151 Essex St [Stanton St]
  212-614-2500
  Where to get your HaHas on the LES.
- **Libation** • 137 Ludlow St [Rivington St]
  212-529-2153
  If you like this place, please leave New York.
- **Living Room** • 154 Ludlow St [Stanton St]
  212-533-7235
  Live music in your living room.
- **Local 138** • 138 Ludlow St [Rivington]
  212-477-0280
  Great happy hour. No douchebags most of the time.
- **Lolita** • 266 Broome St [Allen St]
  212-966-7223
  Hipster haven.
- **Los Feliz** • 109 Ludlow St [Delancey St]
  212-228-8383
  Taqueria/tequileria full of revolutionary splendor and a hidden subterranean labyrinth.
- **The Magician** • 118 Rivington St [Essex St]
  212-673-7851
  Hipster haven. The NFT cartographer loves it.
- **Max Fish** • 178 Ludlow St [Stanton St]
  212-529-3959
  Where the musicians go. Still.
- **Mehanata - The Bulgarian Bar** •
  113 Ludlow St [Delancey St]
  212-625-0981
  Keep an eye out for DJ Eugene Hutz.
- **Motor City** • 127 Ludlow St [Rivington St]
  212-358-1595
  Faux biker bar. Still good, though.
- **Rivington 151** • 151 Rivington [Suffolk St]
  212-228-4139
  2 for 1 until 10pm. Twice as sleazy all the time.
- **Roots & Vines** • 409 Grand St [Attorney St]
  212-260-2363
  Great wine bar, bizarre location.
- **The Skinny** • 174 Orchard St [Stanton St]
  212-228-3668
  Shimmy through sweating crowds in this appropriately named dive bar.
- **The Slipper Room** • 167 Orchard St [Stanton]
  212-253-7246
  Striptease for the arty crowd.
- **Spitzer's Corner** • 101 Rivington St [Ludlow]
  212-228-0027
  40 beers on tap best enjoyed Sunday through Wednesday.
- **Spur Tree** • 76 Orchard St [Broome St]
  212-477-9977
  Laid back Jamaican vibe. Great patio out back.
- **Ten Bells** • 247 Broome St [Ludlow St]
  212-228-4450
  Organic wine bar with candlelit Euro-vibe. Nice!
- **Verlaine** • 110 Rivington St [Essex St]
  212-614-2494
  Mellow, French-Vietnamese motif with deceptively sweet cocktails.
- **Welcome to the Johnsons** •
  123 Rivington St [Essex St]
  212-420-9911
  Great décor, but too crowded mostly.
- **White Star** • 21 Essex St [Canal St]
  212-995-5464
  Filled with absinthe and euro-hipsters.

1
2
A
B
E 3rd St
E 2nd St
E 1st St
E Houston St
Lilian Wald Houses
Hamilton Fish Park
Sheriff St
Columbia St
Baruch Pl
Mangin Pl
Stanton St
Attorney St
Rivington St
Masaryk Towers
Samuel Gompers Houses
Baruch Houses
Baruch Dr
Baruch Houses
Suffolk St
Clinton St
Ridge St
Delancey Street Essex Street
Williamsburg Bridge
Delancey St
Pitt St
Willett St
Abraham Kazan St
Cannon St
Lewis St
East River Houses
Hillman Houses
Hillman Houses
Broome St
Norfolk St
Essex St
Grand St
Samuel Dickstein Plz
Vladeck Houses
Cherry St
Seward Park Houses
Seward Park Houses
Forsyth St
Allen St
Orchard St
Ludlow St
Clinton St
East Broadway
Gouverneur St
Jackson St
Corlears Hook Park
Hester St
Eldridge St
Chrystie St
WH Seward Park
Montgomery St
Water St
Canal St
East Broadway
Division St
Henry St
Jefferson St
Madison St
La Guardia Houses
E Gouverneur Slip
W Gouverneur Slip
Marginal St
Pier 43
Forsyth St
Rutgers St
Cherry St
FDR Dr
Pier 42
Pike St
Rutgers Houses
East River
Monroe St
Market St
Catherine St
Knickerbocker Village
Water St
Manhattan Bridge
Gov Alfred E Smith Houses
Marshall
John St
Plymouth St
Bridge St
Water St
Jay St
Pearl St
BROOKLYN
Front St
Robert F Wagner Sr Pl
Anchorage Pl
Main St
York St
Empire
1/4 mile
.25 km
7
3
30

If the well-known **Clinton Street Baking Company** is bursting at the seams, head to the newer gastropub **Clerkenwell** for a starchy brunch. Be sure to take a group to **Stanton Social** for classy cocktails and unique sharing plates (but pad your wallet first). Check out **Kuma Inn** for one of our favorite dining spots in the city.

Restaurants

- **Barrio Chino** • 253 Broome St [Orchard St]
  212-228-6710 • $$
  Started as a tequila bar, but now more of a restaurant.
- **Bondi Road** • 153 Rivington St [Suffolk St]
  212-253-5311 • $$
  Aussie brunch. Unlimited drinks, mate.
- **Broadway East** • 171 E Broadway [Essex St]
  212-228-3100 • $$$
  Trendy veggie-focused menu.
- **Brown Cafe** • 61 Hester St [Ludlow St]
  212-477-2427 • $$
  Sleepy hipsters congregate here for breakfast.
- **Cafe Katja** • 79 Orchard St [Broome St]
  212-219-9545 • $$$
  The LES Euro zone welcomes Austria into the fold.
- **Clerkenwell** • 49 Clinton St [Rivington St]
  212-614-3234 • $$
  British pub food with great brunch menu.
- **Clinton St Baking Company** •
  4 Clinton St [E Houston St]
  646-602-6263 • $$
  Homemade buttermilk everything. LES laid back. Top 5 bacon.
- **Congee Village** • 100 Allen St [Delancey St]
  212-941-1818 • $$
  Porridge never tasted so good.
- **Creperie** • 135 Ludlow St [Rivington St]
  212-979-5543 • $
  A hole-in-the-wall that serves sweet and savory crepes.
- **Eat-pisode** • 123 Ludlow St [Rivington St]
  212-677-7624 • $
  Tasty Thai eatery near bustling nightlife and shops.
- **El Castillo de Jagua** • 113 Rivington St [Essex]
  212-982-6412 • $
  Great cheap Dominican.
- **El Sombrero** • 108 Stanton St [Ludlow St]
  212-254-4188 • $$
  Cheap margaritas. Dates back to earlier days of the LES.
- **Inoteca** • 98 Rivington St [Ludlow St]
  212-614-0473 • $$
  Late-night tapas, mafia-style.
- **Kuma Inn** • 113 Ludlow St [Delancey St]
  212-353-8866 • $$
  Spicy southeast Asian tapas.
- **Le Pere Pinard** • 175 Ludlow St [Stanton St]
  212-777-4917 • $$$$
  Cool, hip, swank French bistro with lovely back patio.
- **Les Enfants Terribles** • 37 Canal St [Ludlow St]
  212-777-7518 • $$$
  Cozy French-African. Recommended.
- **Little Giant** • 85 Orchard St [Broome St]
  212-226-5047 • $$$$$
  Quirky expensive LES newcomer.
- **Neighburrito** • 127 Rivington St [Norfolk St]
  212-260-2277 • $
  Made-to-order burritos that don't kill your stomach like Chipotle's!
- **Noah's Ark** • 399 Grand St [Suffolk St]
  212-674-2200 • $$
  Great Jewish deli.
- **San Marzano** • 71 Clinton St [Rivington St]
  212-228-5060 • $$
  Personal pies with gourmet toppings.
- **Schiller's Liquor Bar** •
  131 Rivington St [Norfolk St]
  212-260-4555 • $$$$
  Loud, good, loud, good.
- **Shopsin's** • 120 Essex St [Rivington St]
  No phone • $
  Kenny's back! Get your Blisters on My Sisters in the Essex St Market.
- **Sorella** • 95 Allen St [Delancey St]
  212-274-9595 • $$$$
  Top end Northern Italian.
- **Stanton Social** • 99 Stanton St [Ludlow St]
  212-995-0099 • $$$
  Cocktails and unique small plates for trendy thirty-somethings.
- **Sticky Rice** • 85 Orchard St [Broome St]
  212-274-8208 • $$
  Thai treats, Asian BBQ, BYOB, and Wi-Fi?!
- **T Poutine** • 168 Ludlow St [Stanton St]
  646-833-7444 • $
  Stick-to-your-ribs, French-Canadian street food.
- **Teany** • 90 Rivington St [Orchard St]
  212-475-9190 • $$
  Vegan tea room and Moby hang-out.
- **Two Boots** • 384 Grand St [Suffolk St]
  212-228-8685 • $
  Cajun pizza.
- **Zucco Le French Diner** •
  188 Orchard St [Houston St]
  212-677-5200 • $
  Cozy, inexpensive French brasserie where the owner serves your quiche.

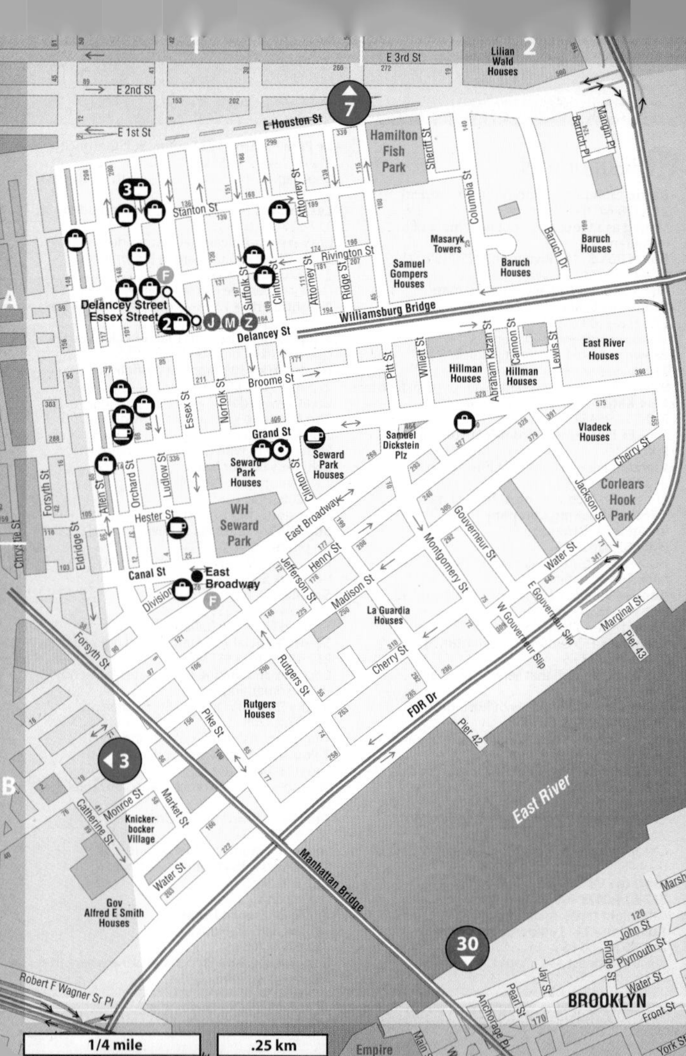

1
2
A
B
E 3rd St
E 2nd St
E 1st St
E Houston St
Lilian Wald Houses
Hamilton Fish Park
Sheriff St
Columbia St
Baruch Pl
Mangin Pl
Baruch Dr
Baruch Houses
Masaryk Towers
Samuel Gompers Houses
Stanton St
Rivington St
Attorney St
Ridge St
Suffolk St
Clinton St
Delancey Street Essex Street
Delancey St
Williamsburg Bridge
Broome St
Norfolk St
Essex St
Pitt St
Willett St
Abraham Kazan St
Cannon St
Lewis St
Hillman Houses
East River Houses
Grand St
Seward Park Houses
Samuel Dickstein Plz
Vladeck Houses
Cherry St
Corlears Hook Park
Jackson St
Forsyth St
Allen St
Orchard St
Ludlow St
Eldridge St
Chrystie St
Hester St
WH Seward Park
East Broadway
Henry St
Jefferson St
Gouverneur St
Montgomery St
Water St
Canal St
Division St
Madison St
La Guardia Houses
E Gouverneur Slip
W Gouverneur Slip
Marginal St
Pier 43
Rutgers St
Cherry St
FDR Dr
Rutgers Houses
Pike St
Pier 42
East River
Monroe St
Market St
Catherine St
Knickerbocker Village
Water St
Gov Alfred E Smith Houses
Manhattan Bridge
Robert F Wagner Sr Pl
Marshall
John St
Plymouth St
Bridge St
Jay St
Water St
Pearl St
Anchorage Pl
BROOKLYN
Front St
York St
Main St
Empire
1/4 mile
.25 km
7
3
30

Chari & Co, **Zarin Fabrics**, and **Foley & Corinna** are just some of the shops where you can score top-notch bike parts, designer fabric, or one-of-a-kind frocks. For tons of great food vendors, simply truck over to the **Essex Street Market**. Jewish culture lingers in the most delectable of forms at **Kossar's Bagels and Bialys**.

Bagels

- **Kossar's Bagels and Bialys** • 367 Grand St [Essex St]
  212-473-4810
  Where NFT gets its morning treats.

Coffee

- **Brown Cafe** • 61 Hester St [Ludlow St]
  212-477-2427
  Excellent hipster coffee is served starting at 8 am.
- **Roasting Plant** • 81 Orchard St [Broome St]
  212-775-7755
  Custom-ground coffee. Theatrical.
- **Roots & Vines** • 409 Grand St [Attorney St]
  212-260-2363
  Nice spot for a shot of espresso with a wine chaser.

Shopping

- **Babeland** • 94 Rivington St [Ludlow St]
  212-375-1701
  Sex toys without the creepy vibe.
- **Babycakes** • 248 Broome St [Ludlow St]
  212-677-5047
  A bakery dedicated solely to vegan, gluten-free goodies.
- **Bluestockings Bookstore Café and Activist Center** • 172 Allen St [Stanton St]
  212-777-6028
  Political/Left Wing.
- **Chari & Co.** • 175 Stanton St [Clinton St]
  212-475-0102
  Cozy Japanese bike shop with down-to-earth staff.
- **Dolce Vita** • 149 Ludlow St [Rivington St]
  212-529-2111
  Classic and funky shoes, expensive clothing, great afforable jewelry.
- **Doughnut Plant** • 379 Grand St [Norfolk St]
  212-505-3700
  Great, weird, recommended.
- **Earthmatters** • 177 Ludlow St [Stanton St]
  212-475-4180
  Organic groceries with a garden out back.
- **Economy Candy** • 108 Rivington St [Essex St]
  212-254-1531
  Candy brands from your childhood still being made and sold here!
- **Essex Street Market** • 120 Essex St [Rivington]
  212-388-0449
  Classic public market with a great combo of old-school and fresh-faced vendors.
- **Foley & Corinna** • 114 Stanton St [Essex St]
  212-529-2338
  Trendy handbags and dresses fit to parade around the LES.
- **Guss' Pickles** • 87 Orchard St [Broome St]
  212-334-3616
  Straight from a barrel on the street just like the olden days.
- **Il Laboratorio del Gelato** • 95 Orchard St [Broome St]
  212-343-9922
  Mind-bogglingly incredible artisanal gelato.
- **Ludlow Guitars** • 164 Ludlow St [Stanton St]
  212-353-1775
  New and used vintage guitars, accessories, and amps.
- **Moishe's Bakery** • 504 Grand St [E Broadway]
  212-673-5832
  Best babka, challah, hamantaschen, & rugalach.
- **Narnia** • 161 Rivington St [Clinton St]
  212-979-0661
  So many awesome articles. So few dollars to buy them with. Expensive, beautiful vintage.
- **Project 8** • 138 Division St [Ludlow St]
  212-925-5599
  Fashionable Euro-boutique.
- **Roni-Sue's Chocolates** • 120 Essex St [Rivington St]
  212-260-0421
  Chocolate-covered bacon and other sweets sold from inside Essex Market.
- **Saxelby Cheesemongers** • 120 Essex St [Rivington St]
  212-228-8204
  All-American and artisanal.
- **September Wines** • 100 Stanton St [Ludlow]
  212-388-0770
  Wines from a variety of family-operated vineyards. Free tastings!
- **TG170** • 170 Ludlow St [Stanton St]
  212-995-8660
  Fun funky fresh women's clothing.
- **Zarin Fabrics** • 314 Grand St [Allen St]
  212-925-6112
  Major destination in the fabric district.

Old Homestead
14th Street
8th Avenue
14th Street
14th Street
6th Avenue
PATH 14th St
The Highline
Little W 12th St
Gansevoort St
Horatio St
Jane St
W 12th St
Bethune St
Bank St
W 11th St
Perry St
Charles St
Charles Ln
W 10th St
Christopher St
Barrow St
Morton St
Leroy St
Clarkson St
W Houston St
King St
Charlton St
Vandam St
Spring St
Dominick St
Broome St
Watts St
Canal St
Grand St
Washington St
Greenwich St
Hudson St
Varick St
Renwick St
West Side Hwy
Weehawken St
Ninth Ave
Eighth Ave
Abingdon Sq
Greenwich Ave
Waverly Pl
W 4th St
Bleecker St
Seventh Ave S
Avenue of the Americas (Sixth Ave)
W 16th St
W 15th St
W 14th St
W 13th St
W 12th St
W 11th St
W 10th St
W 9th St
W 8th St
Patchin Place
PATH 9th St
Jefferson Market Courthouse
Stonewall Inn
Sheridan Sq
Gay St
Christopher Street Sheridan Square
White Horse Tavern
Westbeth Building
Washington Pl
Bob Dylan's One-Time Apt.
W 4th Street
W 4th St
The Cage
W 3rd St
Minetta Ln
Jones St
Cornelia St
Grove St
Commerce St
Bedford St
Carmine St
Downing St
St Luke's Pl
James J Walker Park
PATH Christopher St
Chumley's
Houston Street
W Houston
MacDougal St
Sullivan St
Prince St
Thompson St
Bleecker
Spring Street
Spring St
The Ear Inn
Holland Tunnel
Hudson River
Hudson River Park
9a
PAGE 272
PAGE 244
1/4 mile
.25 km
A
B
1
2

The eating, drinking, and shopping are all premium-grade, but the draw of the West Village runs deeper than finding the boots or the cheeseburger that will change your life.The fact that the writer and poet Dylan Thomas drank himself to death at the **White Horse Tavern**, or that **Chumley's** was once a speakeasy, enhances the appeal of hopping onto a bar stool in one of these joints. That's because a place that bears the exquisite distress of so many stories offers a richer experience than one where fewer interesting lives have come and gone (Bob Dylan lived at **161 West 4th Street** and wrote a song about it). Even though you're not thinking about that as you pick up after your dog on the next corner--which, by the way, a few more West Village residents could stand to do (you know who you are)--the feeling of the neighborhood descends from a tradition of creativity and free thought that was an institution when Jane (rather than Marc) Jacobs resided here. Even beyond the allure of the beautiful old brownstones and the most idyllic blocks, there's something magnetic about walking where Twain, Faulkner, and Baldwin (James, not Alec, or Stephen, you TMZ'ers) walked.

As long as there has been a grid, The West Village has been off of it. Literally speaking, many of the streets are named instead of numbered and turn at odd angles--a layout that even gives some New Yorkers fits (those who live above 14th Street, anyway). Culturally, the West Village as a bastion of Bohemianism emerged around the turn of the 20th century when an influx of immigrants and industry diversified the neighborhood and brought down real estate values to the point that upper-class citizens began to flee up fifth Avenue toward Central Park. Literary salons, private art galleries, shopping emporia, and experimental theatre soon proliferated. The writers' enclave at **Patchin Place** was established by the likes of e.e. cummings, Theodore Dreiser, and Djuna Barnes. By World War I, the neighborhood had become a tourist attraction known for its tolerance of radicalism and non-conformity, and its celebration of artistic innovation. In the decades that followed, the West Village saw the opening of Gertrude Vanderbilt Whitney's modern art museum on 8th Street, the Beat movement, performances by every jazz great you can name at the Village Vanguard, and the beginning of the gay and lesbian rights movement as marked by the rebellion at the **Stonewall Inn**.

While the population of the neighborhood currently reflects a very different socioeconomic stratum than it did during the true Bohemian Age--gelaterias now outnumber starving artists--much of the architecture and character of that era are still intact. This is thanks to the strong, and still persistent, preservation efforts that began in the 1940s. **The Ear Inn**, one of the oldest bars in Manhattan, was an early example of the New York City Landmarks Preservation Commission acting to protect a historic building. The **Jefferson Market Courthouse**, now part of the New York Public Library, was also saved by the outcry of the community when faced with demolition.

The atmosphere of creativity and tolerance still permeates the West Village; this neighborhood is still the gayest place straight men have ever clamored to live in. You can catch a poetry reading at the **Westbeth Building**, pick up some new trash talk at **The Cage**, tuck into a steak at **Old Homestead**, run it off at **Hudson River Park**, and see where Poe was treated at the **Northern Dispensary**. Simply put, the West Village is still perfect for eating, drinking, shopping, meandering, hanging out, going on dates, and generally having more fun than you can afford. And if you can't afford any of it, then simply walk the **High Line** and content yourself that you're (literally) above it all, anyway.

W 16th St
W 15th St
W 14th St
14th Street
8th Avenue
14th Street
14th Street
PATH 14th St
6th Avenue
W 13th St
Little W 12th St
Gansevoort St
The Highline
PAGE 272
Ninth Ave
Greenwich Ave
W 12th St
Abingdon Sq
Horatio St
Jane St
W 12th St
Washington St
Eighth Ave
Waverly Pl
W 11th St
Avenue of the Americas (Sixth Ave)
W 10th St
PATH 9th St
W 9th St
Bethune St
W 4th St
Seventh Ave S
Bank St
Bleecker St
W 11th St
W 8th St
Gay St
Sheridan Sq
Christopher Street Sheridan Square
Waverly Pl
Washington Pl
Perry St
Charles St
W 4th Street
W 4th St
Charles Ln
Grove St
Jones St
Cornelia St
W 10th St
PATH Christopher St
Christopher St
Weehawken St
West Side Hwy
W 3rd St
Commerce St
Minetta Ln
PAGE 244
Hudson River Park
Bedford St
Barrow St
Carmine St
Hudson River
Morton St
9a
St Luke's Pl
Bleecker
Leroy St
James J Walker Park
Downing St
Houston Street
W Houston
Clarkson St
W Houston St
MacDougal St
Sullivan St
King St
Varick St
Prince St
Hudson St
Charlton St
Washington St
Greenwich St
Spring Street
Spring St
Vandam St
Spring St
Dominick St
Renwick St
Broome St
Holland Tunnel
Canal St
Watts St
Broome
Grand
1/4 mile
.25 km
A
B

So many classics, so little time: check out **The Ear Inn** and **The White Horse Tavern** for history, the **Jazz Gallery** and the **Village Vanguard** for classic jazz, **SOB's** for world music, **Marie's Crisis** and the **Duplex** for show tunes and cabaret, and **Art Bar** and **Employees Only** to feel relatively (but not too) hip. Then catch a movie at either **IFC** or revival house **Film Forum**.

Bars

- **Art Bar** • 52 8th Ave [W 4th St]
  212-727-0244
  Great spaces, cool crowd.
- **Arthur's Tavern** • 57 Grove St [Bleecker St]
  212-675-6879
  Featuring great jazz and blues since 1937.
- **Barrow's Pub** • 463 Hudson St [Barrow St]
  212-741-9349
  Low-key, old man bar.
- **Blind Tiger Ale House** • 281 Bleecker St [Jones]
  212-462-4682
  Different location, same idea (beer).
- **Duplex** • 61 Christopher St [Seventh Ave S]
  212-255-5438
  Everything's still fun.
- **The Ear Inn** • 326 Spring St [Greenwich St]
  212-226-9060
  2nd oldest bar in NYC. A great place.
- **Employees Only** • 510 Hudson St [W 10th St]
  212-242-3021
  Classy cocktails for big bucks.
- **Gaslight Lounge** • 400 W 14th St [Ninth Ave]
  212-807-8444
  Laid back attitude.
- **Henrietta Hudson** • 438 Hudson St [Morton]
  212-924-3347
  Good lesbian vibe.
- **Jazz Gallery** • 290 Hudson St [Spring St]
  212-242-1063
  Not-for-profit jazz venue.
- **Johnny's Bar** • 90 Greenwich Ave [W 12th St]
  212-741-5279
  Occassional celeb sightings at this popular dive.
- **Kettle of Fish** • 59 Christopher St [7th Ave S]
  212-414-2278
  Cozy couches and darts.
- **Marie's Crisis** • 59 Grove St [7th Ave S]
  212-243-9323
  Showtunes only! And no, Billy Joel doesn't count.
- **The Otheroom** • 143 Perry St [Washington St]
  212-645-9758
  Surprisingly decent beer selection with great, low-key vibe.
- **Rusty Knot** • 425 West St [W 11th St]
  212-645-5668
  Who knew rich kids loved nautical themed bars?
- **SOB's** • 200 Varick St [W Houston St]
  212-243-4940
  World music venue with salsa lessons on Mondays.
- **Stonewall Inn** • 53 Christopher St [7th Ave S]
  212-488-2705
  From the L to the GB & T, this is where it all began.
- **Village Vanguard** • 178 7th Ave S [Perry St]
  212-255-4037
  Classic NYC jazz venue. Not to be missed.
- **Vol de Nuit** • 148 W 4th St [Sixth Ave]
  212-982-3388
  Belgian beers, cool vibe.
- **White Horse Tavern** • 567 Hudson St [11th St]
  212-243-9260
  Another NYC classic.
- **Wilfie and Nell** • 228 W 4th St [10th St]
  212-242-2990
  Cool space, good food; too bad someone told the i-bankers.

Billiards

- **Fat Cat Billiards** • 75 Christopher St [7th Ave S]
  212-675-6056
  Laid back vibe. Plus ping pong and jazz!

Movie Theaters

- **Film Forum** • 209 W Houston St [Varick St]
  212-727-8110
  Best place to pick up a film geek.
- **IFC Center** • 323 6th Ave [W 3rd St]
  212-924-7771
  Great midnights, special events, and Manhattan exclusives.

Theaters/Performing Arts

- **Actor's Playhouse** • 100 7th Ave S [Grove St]
  212-239-6200
  It definitely ain't the audience's playhouse.
- **Cherry Lane Theater** •
  38 Commerce St [Bedford St]
  212-989-2020
  Founded by Edna St. Vincent Millay & her boho buddies.
- **HERE** • 145 6th Ave [Dominick St]
  212-647-0202
  Cool avant-garde multiplex with a nice cafe.
- **Lucille Lortel Theatre** •
  121 Christopher St [Bedford St]
  212-279-4200
  Play Twister on the Off-Off Broadway Playwright's Walk of Fame.

W 16th St
W 15th St
W 14th St
14th Street
8th Avenue
14th Street
PATH
14th St
14th Street
6th Avenue
W 13th St
Little W 12th St
Gansevoort St
The Highline
Ninth Ave
Greenwich Ave
W 12th St
Horatio St
Jane St
W 12th St
Bethune St
Bank St
W 11th St
Perry St
Charles St
Charles Ln
W 10th St
Christopher St
Weehawken St
Washington St
Eighth Ave
Abingdon Sq
Waverly Pl
W 11th St
W 4th St
Bleecker St
Seventh Ave S
Avenue of the Americas (Sixth Ave)
W 10th St
PATH
9th St
W 9th St
W 8th St
Sheridan Sq
Christopher Street
Sheridan Square
Waverly Pl
Washington Pl
W 4th Street
W 4th St
W 3rd St
Minetta Ln
PATH
Christopher
St
Grove St
Commerce St
Jones St
Cornelia St
Bedford St
Carmine St
Barrow St
Morton St
St Luke's Pl
James J
Walker
Park
Leroy St
Clarkson St
Downing St
Houston
Street
W Houston St
W Houston
Bleecker
MacDougal St
Sullivan St
Prince St
King St
Charlton St
Vandam St
Spring
Street
Spring St
Spring St
Varick St
Hudson St
Greenwich St
Washington St
Dominick St
Broome St
Broome St
Watts St
Canal St
Renwick St
Thompson St
Grand St
Holland Tunnel
West Side Hwy
PAGE 272
PAGE 244
Hudson
River
Park
Hudson
River
9a
A
B
1
2
1/4 mile
.25 km

You'll never go hungry, and that's just at burger havens **Corner Bistro** and **BLT Burger**. Excellent French restaurants **Bar Six**, **French Roast**, and **Tartine** compete with Cornelia Street's trifecta of **Po**, **Home** and **Pearl Oyster Bar** for your hard-earned dollars. Cash-strapped? Hit **Waverly Restaurant** or **Joe's Pizza** while saving up for a night at **Spotted Pig**, **Aquagrill**, or **Spice Market**.

Restaurants

- **Aquagrill** • 210 Spring St [Sullivan St]
  212-274-0505 • $$$$$
  NFT's favorite straight-up seafood restaurant. Great feel.
- **Bar Six** • 502 6th Ave [W 13th St]
  212-691-1363 • $$$
  Pretty much a perfect French bistro.
- **BLT Burger** •
  470 6th Ave [W 11th St]
  212-243-8226 • $$
  Really, really freakin' good burgers.
- **Bobo** • 181 W 10th St [7th Ave]
  212-488-2626 • $$$$
  Hip eats, if you can find the unmarked basement entrance.
- **Café Asean** • 117 W 10th St [Patchin Pl]
  212-633-0348 • $$
  Pan-Asian, via Mr. Wong.
- **Corner Bistro** • 331 W 4th St [Jane St]
  212-242-9502 • $
  Top NYC burgers. Perfect at 3 am.
- **Ditch Plains** • 29 Bedford St [Downing St]
  212-633-0202 • $$$
  Great for seafood or breakfast.
- **Employees Only** • 510 Hudson St [W 10th St]
  212-242-3021 • $$$$
  Deco-decorated eatery with a damn good bar.
- **En Japanese Brasserie** •
  435 Hudson St [Leroy St]
  212-647-9196 • $$$$
  Amazing izakaya not to be missed.
- **Fatty Crab** • 643 Hudson St [Gansevoort St]
  212-352-3592 • $$$
  West Village favorite for Malaysian street food.
- **French Roast** • 78 W 11th St [Sixth Ave]
  212-533-2233 • $$
  Open 24 hours. French comfort food.
- **GoBo** • 401 Avenue of the Americas [W 8th St]
  212-255-3242 • $$$
  Even vegans deserve a decent place to eat.
- **Home** • 20 Cornelia St [W 4th St]
  212-243-9579 • $$$$
  There's no place like it.
- **Joe's Pizza** • 7 Carmine St [Bleecker St]
  212-366-1182 • $
  Excellent slices.
- **John's Pizzeria** • 278 Bleecker St [Jones St]
  212-243-1680 • $$
  Quintessential NY pizza.
- **Keste Pizzeria** • 271 Bleecker St [Jones St]
  212-243-1500 • $$$
  So authentic, it's the headquarters for the APN (look it up).
- **La Bonbonniere** • 28 8th Ave [Jane St]
  212-741-9266 • $
  Best cheap breakfast in the city.
- **Little Havana** • 30 Cornelia St [Sixth Ave]
  212-255-2212 • $$$
  Cuban food cooked by the Cuban grandma you never had.
- **Mary's Fish Camp** • 64 Charles St [W 4th St]
  646-486-2185 • $$$
  Amy Sedaris used to wait tables here for fun. Killer food!
- **Mercadito** • 100 7th Ave S [Grove St]
  212-647-0830 • $$$$
  Inventive Mexican with great fish taco choices.
- **Pearl Oyster Bar** • 18 Cornelia St [W 4th St]
  212-691-8211 • $$$
  For all your lobster roll cravings. NFT fave.
- **Po** • 31 Cornelia St [W 4th St]
  212-645-2189 • $$$$
  Creative Italian. Intimate feel.
- **Spice Market** • 403 W 13th St [Ninth Ave]
  212-675-2322 • $$$$$
  Another Jean-George joint. Thai-Malaysian street food and beautiful people.
- **Spotted Pig** • 314 W 11th St [Greenwich St]
  212-620-0393 • $$$$
  We finally got in. All great except for pig ears.
- **Taim** • 222 Waverly Pl [Perry St]
  212-691-6101 • $$
  Gourmet falafel with mind-blowing housemade sauces.
- **Tartine** • 253 W 11th St [W 4th St]
  212-229-2611 • $$$
  BYOB + Solid French = NFT pick.
- **Tea & Sympathy** • 108 Greenwich Ave [13th St]
  212-989-9735 • $$$
  Eccentric English. Cult favorite.
- **Wallse** • 344 W 11th St [Washington St]
  212-352-2300 • $$$$
  Top-notch Austrian cuisine keeps the West Villagers coming back.
- **The Waverly Inn** • 16 Bank St [Waverly Pl]
  212-243-7900 • $$$$
  Hip, revamped café-cum-speakeasy. Good luck getting in.
- **Waverly Restaurant** • 385 Avenue of the Americas [Waverly Pl]
  212-675-3181 • $$
  Great old-school diner with classy waiters.

1
2
A
B
8
9
9a
6
2
W 16th St
W 15th St
W 14th St
W 13th St
W 12th St
W 11th St
W 10th St
W 9th St
W 8th St
Waverly Pl
Washington Pl
W 4th St
W 3rd St
Minetta Ln
Bleecker St
W Houston St
Prince St
Spring St
Broome St
Grand St
Watts St
Canal St
Dominick St
Vandam St
Charlton St
King St
Clarkson St
Leroy St
Morton St
Barrow St
Christopher St
W 10th St
Charles St
Charles Ln
Perry St
W 11th St
Bank St
Bethune St
W 12th St
Jane St
Horatio St
Gansevoort St
Little W 12th St
Ninth Ave
Eighth Ave
Abingdon Sq
Greenwich Ave
Waverly Pl
W 4th St
Bleecker St
Seventh Ave S
Sheridan Sq
Gay St
Grove St
Commerce St
Bedford St
Jones St
Cornelia St
Carmine St
Downing St
St Luke's Pl
James J Walker Park
Hudson St
Varick St
Greenwich St
Washington St
Renwick St
MacDougal St
Sullivan St
Thompson St
Avenue of the Americas (Sixth Ave)
Washington St
Weehawken St
West Side Hwy
14th Street
8th Avenue
14th Street
14th Street
6th Avenue
PATH 14th St
PATH 9th St
Christopher Street Sheridan Square
PATH Christopher St
W 4th Street
Houston Street
Spring Street
PAGE 272
The Highline
PAGE 244
Hudson River Park
Hudson River
Holland Tunnel
1/4 mile
.25 km

Are you a foodie? Hit **Murray's Cheese, Myers of Keswick, Ottomanelli's, Citarella, Faicco's, Murray's Bagels,** and **Grandaisy Bakery**. Sip quality java at **Doma, Mojo,** or NFT hangout **Grey Dog**. Shop for tchotchkes at **Alphabets, Myxplyzyk** and **Flight 001**, or furniture at **Scott Jordan** and **Vitra**. Then blow your bonus in the Meatpacking Distict at **Jeffrey, Alexander McQueen**, or **Stella McCartney**. Done.

Bagels

- **Murray's Bagels** • 500 6th Ave [W 13th St]
  212-462-2830
  Classic. But they don't toast, so don't ask.

Coffee

- **Doma** • 17 Perry St [Waverly Pl]
  212-929-4339
  West Village intellectual hang out.
- **The Grey Dog's Coffee** •
  33 Carmine St [Bedford St]
  212-462-0041
  Good space for a meet up.
- **Mojo Coffee** • 128 Charles St [Greenwich St]
  212-691-6656
  Tiny, perfect cafe.
- **Roasting Plant** • 75 Greenwich Ave [7th Ave]
  212-775-7755
  Techno-coffee beans flying through the air!

Shopping

- **Alexander McQueen** • 417 W 14th St [9th Ave]
  212-645-1797
  Brit bad boy designs.
- **Alphabets** • 47 Greenwich Ave [Charles St]
  212-229-2966
  Fun miscellany store.
- **Bleecker Street Records** •
  239 Bleecker St [Leroy St]
  212-255-7899
  Classic Village record shop. Great selection.
- **Citarella** • 424 6th Ave [W 9th St]
  212-874-0383
  Wealthy foodies love this place.
- **CO Bigelow Chemists** • 414 6th Ave [W 9th St]
  212-533-2700
  Classic village pharmacy. Do try and patronize it.
- **The End of History** • 548 Hudson St [Perry St]
  212-647-7598
  Very cool shop specializing in antique glass.
- **Faicco's Pork Store** • 260 Bleecker St [Cornelia]
  212-243-1974
  Proscuitto bread, homemade sausage, huge heroes, pork heaven.
- **Flight 001** • 96 Greenwich Ave [Jane St]
  212-989-0001
  Cute hipster travel shop. And they sell NFT!
- **Grandaisy Bakery** • 73 Sullivan St [Spring St]
  212-334-9435
  The best bakery, period.
- **Health & Harmony** • 470 Hudson St [Barrow]
  212-691-3036
  Small health food store with good selection and decent prices.
- **House of Oldies** • 35 Carmine St [Bleecker St]
  212-243-0500
  Everything on vinyl.
- **Jacques Torres Chocolate Haven** •
  350 Hudson St [Charlton St]
  212-414-2462
  Tastebud bliss brought to you by the Master of Chocolate.
- **Jeffrey** • 449 W 14th St [Washington St]
  212-206-1272
  Avant-garde (and wildly expensive) mini-department store.
- **The Leather Man** • 111 Christopher St [Bedford]
  212-243-5339
  No, you won't look like James Dean. But it'll help.
- **Murray's Cheese Shop** • 254 Bleecker St [Leroy]
  212-243-3289
  We love cheese, and so does Murray's.
- **Mxyplyzyk** • 125 Greenwich Ave [W 13th St]
  800-243-9810
  Great, quirky, mid-range tchotchkes and home décor.
- **Myers of Keswick** • 634 Hudson St [Horatio St]
  212-691-4194
  Killer English sausages, pasties, etc. And "Bounty!"
- **O Ottomanelli's & Sons** • 285 Bleecker [Jones]
  212-675-4217
  High-quality meats and the friendliest butchers in town.
- **Rebel Rebel Records** •
  319 Bleecker St [Christopher St]
  212-989-0770
  Small CD and LP shop with knowledgeable staff.
- **Scott Jordan Furniture** • 137 Varick St [Spring]
  212-620-4682
  Solid hardwood furniture. Super-cool and mostly unaffordable.
- **Stella McCartney** • 429 W 14th St [Greene St]
  212-255-1556
  Hip, animal-friendly fashion.
- **Three Lives and Co** • 154 W 10th St [Waverly]
  212-741-2069
  General Interest books.
- **Vitra** • 29 9th Ave [W 13th St]
  212-463-5700
  Sleek and modern home furnishings. Super-cool.

W 16th St
E 16th St
Union Sq W
Union Sq E
Union Square
PAGE 266
Stuyvesant Square
Rutherford Pl
N D Perlman Pl
W 15th St
E 15th St
Con Edison Building
6th Ave
PATH 14th St
14th Street
W14th St
E 14th St
14th Street-Union Square
3rd Avenue
1st Ave
New School
PAGE 250
W 13th St
E 13th St
The Strand Bookstore
W 12th St
E 12th St
Salmagundi Club
Grace Church
W 11th St
E 11th St
Site of Weathermen Explosion
St Mark's-in-the-Bowery Church
W 10th St
E 10th St
Mark Twain House
PATH 9th St
W 9th St
E 9th St
Fifth Ave
University Pl
Fourth Ave
Third Ave
Stuyvesant St
Second Ave
First Ave
Wanamaker's
W 8th St
E 8th St
8th Street NYU
The Alamo (The Cube)
St Marks Pl
Gem Spa
MacDougal Aly
Washington Mews
Astor Pl
Astor Place
McSorley's
E 7th St
Washington Sq N
Waverly Pl
Colonnade Row
Cooper Union
T Shevchenko Pl
Ave of the Americas
Washington Square
PAGE 252
Brown Building of Science
Washington Pl
The Public Theater
Cooper Square
Cooper Union New Academic Building
E 6th St
E 5th St
W 4th Street
Washington Sq S
DeVinne Press Building
W 4th St
E 4th St
Old Merchant's House
Broadway
376 Lafayette Street
Great Jones Fire House
NYU
NOHO
W 3rd St
New York Marble Cemetery
Washington Square Village
Great Jones St
Joey Ramone Place
E 3rd St
James Aly
Bond Street Architecture
Bond St
E 2nd St
Minetta St
Bayard-Condict Building
Former location of CBGB & OMFUG
Bleecker St
Bleecker Street
Bowery
E 1st St
Lower East Side 2nd Avenue
MacDougal St
Sullivan St
Thompson St
LaGuardia Pl
Silver Towers
Mercer St
Lafayette St
W Houston St
E Houston St
E Houston St
Broadway-Lafayette Street
Milano's
Jersey St
Mott St
Stanton St
SOHO
Prada
New Museum of Contemporary Art
Chrystie St
Sara D Roosevelt Park
Forsyth St
Eldridge St
Allen St
Charlton St
Prince St
Little Singer Building
Prince Street
Rivington St
University Settlement House
Vandam St
West Broadway
Wooster St
Greene St
Crosby St
Mulberry St
Elizabeth St
Freeman Aly
Extra Pl
Spring St
Spring Street
Lombardi's
Spring Street
Cleveland Pl
Kenmare St
Delancey St
Bowery St
Dominick St
Broome St
Broome St
Centre St
Grand St
1/4 mile
.25 km

Simply put, this is still the center of the universe. Put your cursor (er, finger) down on the corner of Houston and Broadway. That's it, right there; not that anything is of interest in that intersection per se, but it all radiates out from there, including four of NY's top neighborhoods—Greenwich Village, SoHo, NoHo, and NoLiTa. It's hardly a bucolic lifestyle—green space is limited to a few patches of grass in **Washington Square Park**—but if it's greenery you want, what are you doing in the middle of New York City anyway? Consequently, this area has compensated for the lack of nature by providing, well, everything else one could possibly want in terms of culture. Architecture, art galleries, movie theaters, live music, shopping, restaurants, and nightlife—it's all here for the taking. Old New York, New New York, and every other kind of New York is represented here. Just walk the streets and you'll find it all.

One of this area's hidden secrets is the amount of stunning architecture from every period of New York City history. Check out the former stables in **Washington Mews**, now NYU offices, for a little bit of 18th century New York. Also ancient is the **St. Mark's-in-the Bowery Church** (1799), **Colonnade Row** (1830s), the **Old Merchant's House** (1832), **Grace Church** (1846) and the **Cooper Union Building** (1859).

In the latter half of the 1800s, two great architects, Louis Sullivan and Ernest Flagg, started building in this area. The results are Sullivan's only New York Building, the **Bayard-Condict Building** (1899), and Flagg's brilliant **Great Jones Fire House** (1899) and **Little Singer Building** (1904). In the early 20th century, Daniel Burnham (**Wanamaker's**, 1904/1907) and Henry J Hardenbergh (**376 Lafayette St**, 1888, and the **Con Edison Building**, 1914) also added their contributions to the area. Perhaps our ultimate favorite is the little-known **DeVinne Press Building** (1885) by Babb, Cook & Willard. Then, of course, there is the modern (or should we say postmodern?) era running rampant on the east side of this 'hood, especially on The Bowery (Cooper Union's new building, courtesy of Thom Mayne, and the brilliant **New Museum of Contemporary Art**) and on **Bond Street** (including Herzog & de Mauron's bizarre choices on 40 Bond).

There are several historical sites in this area, both famous and infamous. By far our favorite spot is the **New York City Marble Cemetery** on Second Street, tucked in between The Bowery and Second Avenue. Also in the area is the **Mark Twain House**, NYU's **Brown Building** (the site of the Triangle Shirtwaist Fire), and **18 West 11th St**, the Site of the Weatherman Explosion. Of more recent note, you can visit the former location of **CBGB & OMFUG** (now a John Varvatos store) right around the corner from **Joey Ramone Place** on East 2nd Street. Finally, for a lesson in NYC pizza history, **Lombardi's** is the place to learn about why eating pizza in New York is more than just a casual act.

The number of cultural institutions is dizzying and we'll talk about them a lot more in the "Nightlife" section, so we're going to mention only a few of our favorites for the area: Joseph Papp's **Public Theater** on Lafayette Street, and the **Salmagundi Club**, a center for artists since 1917, are two of the renowned institutions in the area. And to find more information about anything related to NYC, check out classic bookstore **The Strand**, where you'll find a great selection of New York City books amidst the dust and clutter.

As much as all the fabulous history and architecture of this area astounds us, so too do the grungier aspects of the area continue to divert us. You can always check out the skate punks at **The Alamo (The Cube)** at Astor Place, drink with professionals at dingy haven **Milano's**, and check out magazines and international newspapers at **Gem Spa**. St. Mark's Place between Bowery and Second Avenue was THE place in the '80s and '90s to see a wide range of Village denizens; unfortunately, that's not the case any more. It's a tourist trap now for the most part; head to Avenue C to get a sense of what this strip used to feel like.

W 16th St
E 16th St
W 15th St
E 15th St
W14th St
E 14th St
W 13th St
E 13th St
W 12th St
E 12th St
W 11th St
E 11th St
W 10th St
E 10th St
W 9th St
E 9th St
W 8th St
E 8th St
Union Sq W
Union Sq E
Union Square
Stuyvesant Square
Rutherford Pl
N D Perlman Pl
PAGE 266
PAGE 250
PAGE 252
6th Ave
PATH 14th St
14th Street
PATH 9th St
New School
14th Street-Union Square
3rd Avenue
1st Ave
Fifth Ave
University Pl
Fourth Ave
Third Ave
Second Ave
First Ave
Stuyvesant St
St Marks Pl
8th Street NYU
Broadway
Astor Pl
Astor Place
Cooper Square
MacDougal Aly
Washington Sq N
Washington Sq W
Washington Sq E
Washington Sq S
Washington Square
Waverly Pl
Washington Pl
Ave of the Americas
W 4th Street
W 4th St
E 4th St
E 7th St
E 6th St
E 5th St
T Shevchenko Pl
NYU
W 3rd St
NOHO
Great Jones St
E 3rd St
Lafayette St
Washington Square Village
James Aly
Bond St
E 2nd St
Minetta St
Bleecker St
Bleecker Street
Silver Towers
MacDougal St
Sullivan St
Thompson St
LaGuardia Pl
Mercer St
Bowery
E 1st St
Lower East Side 2nd Avenue
W Houston St
E Houston St
Broadway-Lafayette Street
SOHO
Jersey St
Mott St
Stanton St
Chrystie St
Sara D Roosevelt Park
Forsyth St
Eldridge St
Allen St
Rivington St
Charlton St
Vandam St
Spring St
Dominick St
Broome St
Prince St
West Broadway
Wooster St
Greene St
Prince Street
Crosby St
Mulberry St
Elizabeth St
Spring Street
Cleveland Pl
Kenmare St
Delancey St
Bowery St
Centre St
Grand St
1/4 mile
.25 km

You can spend a lot on a drink in this neighborhood if you so choose, but it's the many dive bars (**Blue & Gold**, **Grassroots**, **Holiday**, **Mars Bar**, **Milano's**) where you'll find us drinking. Hear writers at **Bowery Poetry Club** and **KGB**, watch European football at **Nevada Smith's**, and listen to music at **Joe's Pub** or **Le Poisson Rouge**.

Bars

- **Beauty Bar** • 231 E 14th St [3d Ave]
212-539-1389
Just a little off the top, dahling?
- **Blue & Gold** • 79 E 7th St [1st Ave]
212-777-1006
Another fine East Village dive.
- **Botanica** • 47 E Houston St [Mulberry St]
212-343-7251
Good bar, but we still miss the Knitting Factory.
- **Bowery Ballroom** • 6 Delancey St [Bowery]
212-533-2111
Great space that attracts great bands.
- **Bowery Poetry Club** • 308 Bowery [E 1st St]
212-614-0505
Slam poetry.
- **Decibel** • 240 E 9th St [2nd Ave]
212-979-2733
Hip, underground sake bar.
- **Fanelli's** • 94 Prince St [Mercer St]
212-226-9412
Old-time SoHo haunt. Nice tiles.
- **Grassroots Tavern** • 20 St Marks Pl [2nd Ave]
212-475-9443
That mass of fur in the corner is a cat.
- **Holiday Lounge** • 75 St Marks Pl [First Ave]
212-777-9637
Where to go to lose your soul.
- **Joe's Pub** • 425 Lafayette St [Astor Pl]
212-539-8776
Excellent range of acts in intimate space.
- **KGB** • 85 E 4th St [2nd Ave]
212-505-3360
Former CP HQ. Meet your comrades. Readings, too.
- **Le Poisson Rouge** • 158 Bleecker St [Sullivan]
212 505 3474
Seductive and strangely fun eclectic live music.
- **Lobby Bar** • 335 Bowery [E 2nd St]
212-505-9100
Great spot for a nightcap.
- **Mars Bar** • 25 E 1st St [2nd Ave]
212-473-9842
The king of grungy bars. Recommended.
- **Marshall Stack** • 66 Rivington St [Allen St]
212-228-4667
Winner for best bar that seemed like it would be awful.
- **Milady's** • 160 Prince St [Thompson St]
212-226-9340
Friendly spot keeping in real in this unreal 'hood.
- **Milano's** • 51 E Houston St [Mott St]
212-226-8844
Grungy, narrow, awesome, narrow, grungy.
- **Milk & Honey** • 134 Eldridge St [Broome St]
Good luck finding the phone number.
- **Nevada Smith's** • 74 3rd Ave [E 11th St]
212-982-2591
GooooaaaaaalllllLLL!
- **Peculier Pub** • 145 Bleecker St [LaGuardia Pl]
212-353-1327
Large beer selection. NYU hangout.
- **Sweet & Vicious** • 5 Spring St [Bowery]
212-334-7915
Great outdoor space.
- **Von** • 3 Bleecker St [Bowery]
212-473-3039
Great vibe. Great bar.

Bowling

- **Bowlmor Lanes** • 110 University Pl [12th St]
212-255-8188
Bright, loud, expensive, and sometimes really fun.

Movie Theaters

- **Angelika** • 18 W Houston St [Mercer St]
212-995-2000
Higher profile indies play here first.
- **Anthology Film Archives** • 32 2nd Ave [E 2nd]
212-505-5181
Quirky retrospectives, revivals, and other rarities.
- **Cinema Village** • 22 E 12th St [University Pl]
212-924-3363
Charming and tiny with exclusive documentaries and foreign films.
- **Landmark Theatres Sunshine Cinema** • 143 E Houston St [Eldridge St]
212-330-8182
High-luxury indie film multiplex.
- **Quad Cinema** • 34 W 13th St [Fifth Ave]
212-255-8800
Gay-themed world premieres and second-run Hollywood releases.

W 16th St
E 16th St
Union Sq W
Union Sq E
PAGE 266
Union Square
Stuyvesant Square
Rutherford Pl
N D Perlman Pl
W 15th St
E 15th St
6th Ave
PATH 14th St
14th Street
W14th St
E 14th St
14th Street-Union Square
3rd Avenue
1st Ave
New School
PAGE 250
W 13th St
E 13th St
W 12th St
E 12th St
W 11th St
E 11th St
W 10th St
E 10th St
Fifth Ave
University Pl
Fourth Ave
Third Ave
Stuyvesant St
Second Ave
First Ave
PATH 9th St
W 9th St
E 9th St
W 8th St
E 8th St
8th Street NYU
St Marks Pl
MacDougal Aly
Washington Sq W
Astor Pl
Astor Place
T Shevchenko Pl
E 7th St
Washington Sq N
Waverly Pl
Broadway
E 6th St
Ave of the Americas
Washington Square
PAGE 252
Washington Sq E
Washington Pl
Cooper Square
E 5th St
W 4th Street
Washington Sq S
W 4th St
E 4th St
NYU
W 3rd St
Lafayette St
Great Jones St
NOHO
E 3rd St
Minetta St
Washington Square Village
James Aly
Bond St
E 2nd St
Bleecker St
Bleecker Street
MacDougal St
Sullivan St
Thompson St
LaGuardia Pl
Silver Towers
Mercer St
Bowery
E 1st St
Lower East Side 2nd Avenue
W Houston St
E Houston St
Broadway-Lafayette Street
Jersey St
Mott St
SOHO
Stanton St
Sara D Roosevelt Park
Chrystie St
Forsyth St
Eldridge St
Allen St
Charlton St
Vandam St
Prince St
Prince Street
West Broadway
Wooster St
Greene St
Crosby St
Mulberry St
Elizabeth St
Rivington St
Spring St
Spring Street
Cleveland Pl
Delancey St
Dominick St
Kenmare St
Bowery St
Broome St
Centre St
Grand St

1/4 mile
.25 km

If we could only eat in one 'nabe, this would be it. There's everything from great pizza (**Arturo's**, **Basille's**) to hi-end madness at **Il Mulino** and **Babbo**. You can span the globe from **Sammy's Roumanian** to Australian at **Eight Mile Creek**. Then grab a lobster at 3 am at **Blue Ribbon** with the chefs. Cool.

Restaurants

- **Artichoke Basille's Pizza & Brewery** • 328 E 14th St [2nd Ave]
  212-228-2004 • $$
  Stand in line for amazing Sicilian slices.
- **Arturo's** • 106 W Houston St [Thompson St]
  212-677-3820 • $$
  Classic NYC pizza joint with live jazz. NFT favorite.
- **Babbo** • 110 Waverly Pl [MacDougal St]
  212-777-0303 • $$$$
  Super Mario—eclectic Italian. Go for the pasta tasting menu.
- **Balthazar** • 80 Spring St [Crosby St]
  212-965-1414 • $$$$$
  Simultaneously pretentious and amazing.
- **Blue Hill** • 75 Washington Pl [MacDougal St]
  212-539-1776 • $$$$$
  Wonderful food in an unexpected location.
- **Blue Ribbon** • 97 Sullivan St [Spring St]
  212-274-0404 • $$$$$
  Open 'til 4am. Everything's great.
- **Café Habana** • 17 Prince St [Elizabeth St]
  212-625-2001 • $$$
  Grilled corn + beautiful staff = amazing Cuban joint.
- **Café Spice** • 72 University Pl [E 11th St]
  212-253-6999 • $$$
  Designer Indian. Get the lababdar.
- **Eight Mile Creek** • 240 Mulberry St [Prince St]
  212-431-4635 • $$$$
  Awesome Australian. Get the kangaroo chops.
- **Five Points** • 31 Great Jones St [Lafayette St]
  212-253-5700 • $$$$
  Excellent NoHo destination. Cookshop's older sibling.
- **Frank** • 88 2nd Ave [E 5th St]
  212-420-0106 • $$
  Good food, great breakfast.
- **Freemans** • Freeman Alley [Rivington]
  212-420-0012 • $$$
  Taxidermy-filled hideaway with fab cocktails and delicious, rustic fare.
- **Hampton Chutney** • 68 Prince St [Crosby St]
  212-226-9996 • $
  Good take-out dosas.
- **Hummus Place** • 99 MacDougal St [Bleecker]
  212-533-3089 • $
  Authentic! Best hummus this side of Tel Aviv.
- **Il Buco** • 47 Bond St [Bowery]
  212-533-1932 • $$$$$
  Lovely Italian food. Great wines by the glass. Uber-hip scene.
- **Il Mulino** • 86 W 3rd St [Thompson St]
  212-673-3783 • $$$$
  Fine Italian dining at fine Italian dining prices.
- **Ippudo** • 65 4th Ave [10th St]
  212-388-0088 • $$$
  People waiting hours for a bowl of ramen? Yes, it's that good.
- **John's of 12th Street** • 302 E 12th St [2nd Ave]
  212-475-9531 • $$
  Classic Italian. Get the rollatini.
- **Jules** • 65 St Marks Pl [First Ave]
  212-477-5560 • $$$
  Small French bistro with live unimposing jazz.
- **La Esquina** • 114 Kenmare St [Cleveland Pl]
  646-613-7100 • $
  Taqueria trifecta: taco stand, corner cantina, and secret subterranean abode.
- **Lahore** • 132 Crosby St [E Houston St]
  212-965-1777 • $
  Indo-Pak deli popular with cabbies.
- **Mara's Homemade** • 342 E 6th St [2nd Ave]
  212-598-1110 • $$
  Ragin' Cajun. Recommended.
- **Momofuku Noodle Bar** • 171 1st Ave [E 10th]
  212-475-7899 • $$$$
  Because who can get into M. Ko?
- **Momofuku Ssam Bar** • 207 2nd Ave [13th St]
  212-254-3500 • $$
  Pork. Pork. Other stuff. Pork. Yum.
- **Olive's** • 120 Prince St [Wooster St]
  212-941-0111 • $
  Killer soups/sandwiches. A top take-out option.
- **Sammy's Roumanian** • 157 Chrystie St [Delancey St]
  212-673-0330 • $$$$
  An experience not to be missed. Chopped liver which will instantly kill you.
- **Strip House** • 13 E 12th St [Fifth Ave]
  212-328-0000 • $$$$$
  Super downtown steakhouse. NFT favorite.
- **Veselka** • 144 2nd Ave [E 9th St]
  212-228-9682 • $
  Pierogies absorb beer. At 4 am that's all you need to know.
- **Yonah Schimmel's Knish Bakery** • 137 E Houston St [Forsyth St]
  212-477-2858 • $
  Dishing delish knish since 1910-ish.

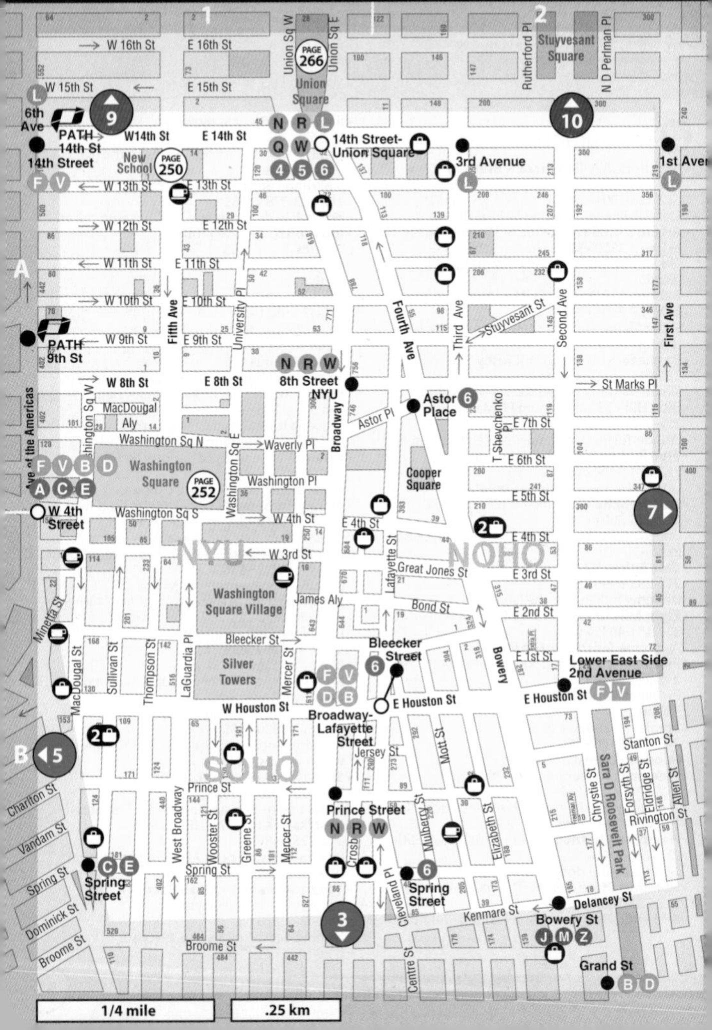
W 16th St
E 16th St
Union Sq W
Union Sq E
PAGE 266
Union Square
Stuyvesant Square
Rutherford Pl
N D Perlman Pl
W 15th St
E 15th St
6th Ave
PATH 14th St
W14th St
E 14th St
14th Street
14th Street-Union Square
3rd Avenue
1st Ave
New School
PAGE 250
W 13th St
E 13th St
W 12th St
E 12th St
W 11th St
E 11th St
W 10th St
E 10th St
W 9th St
E 9th St
PATH 9th St
Fifth Ave
University Pl
Fourth Ave
Third Ave
Stuyvesant St
Second Ave
First Ave
W 8th St
E 8th St
8th Street NYU
St Marks Pl
Astor Place
Astor Pl
Broadway
MacDougal Aly
Washington Sq N
Washington Sq W
Washington Sq E
Waverly Pl
Washington Square
PAGE 252
Washington Pl
Cooper Square
Ave of the Americas
T Shevchenko Pl
E 7th St
E 6th St
E 5th St
E 4th St
W 4th Street
Washington Sq S
W 4th St
E 4th St
NYU
NOHO
W 3rd St
Lafayette St
Great Jones St
E 3rd St
Washington Square Village
James Aly
Bond St
E 2nd St
Minetta St
Bleecker St
Bleecker Street
Bowery
E 1st St
Lower East Side 2nd Avenue
Silver Towers
MacDougal St
Sullivan St
Thompson St
LaGuardia Pl
Mercer St
W Houston St
E Houston St
Broadway-Lafayette Street
Jersey St
Mott St
Stanton St
Sara D Roosevelt Park
Chrystie St
Forsyth St
Eldridge St
Allen St
SOHO
Charlton St
Prince St
Prince Street
Vandam St
West Broadway
Wooster St
Greene St
Mercer St
Crosby St
Mulberry St
Elizabeth St
Rivington St
Spring St
Spring Street
Cleveland Pl
Spring Street
Dominick St
Kenmare St
Delancey St
Bowery St
Broome St
Broome St
Centre St
Grand St
1/4 mile
.25 km

Bagels, Coffee, & Shopping

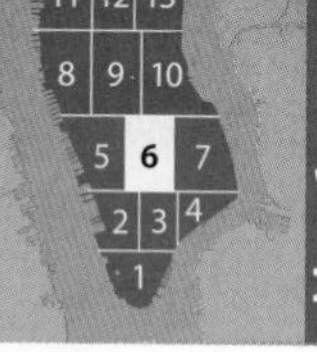

Lots of great stores, but very little of it is cheap (see: **Moss**, **Stereo Exchange**). At least you can eat some of it (**Black Hound**, **Bond Street Chocolate**, **East Village Cheese**, etc). **Kiehl's** is a must-stop for service and lotions; **Other Music** outlasted Tower Records and **Taschen** is one of our favorite publishers.

Coffee

- **Caffe Reggio** • 119 MacDougal St [W 3rd St] 212-475-9557 A New York classic. Check out the custom coffee cups.
- **Gimme Coffee** • 228 Mott St [Prince St] 212-226-4011 Amazing cappuccinos from the Ithaca experts.
- **Joe: The Art of Coffee** • 9 E 13th St [5th Ave] 212-924-7400 Joe really knows his joe.
- **Porto Rico Importing** • 201 Bleecker St [MacDougal St] 212-477-5421 Beans by the barrel full.
- **Think Coffee** • 248 Mercer St [W 3rd St] 212-228-6226 Collegiate coffee house. NYU hangout.

Shopping

- **Astor Wines & Spirits** • 399 Lafayette St [E 4th] 212-674-7500 NFT fav. The king of all NYC liquor stores.
- **Black Hound New York** • 170 2nd Ave [E 11th] 212-979-9505 Killer desserts. NFT Favorite.
- **Bond Street Chocolate** • 63 E 4th St [Bowery] 212-677-5103 The hippest chocolate this side of Belgium. Get the skulls.
- **Daily 235** • 235 Elizabeth St [Prince St] 212-334-9728 A little tchotchke store; has great journals.
- **Dual Specialty Store** • 91 1st Ave [6th St] 212-979-6045 Indian grocery store stocked with every spice imaginable.
- **East Village Cheese** • 40 3rd Ave [E 10th St] 212-477-2601 Super cheap cheeses, olives, and meats. No samples!
- **Global Table** • 107 Sullivan St [Spring St] 212-431-5839 Quietly elegant tableware.
- **Joe's Dairy** • 156 Sullivan St [W Houston St] 212-677-8780 Homemade mozzarella fresh daily.
- **Kiehl's** • 109 3rd Ave [E 13th St] 212-677-3171 Great creams, lotions, and unguents; laughably good service.
- **Lighting by Gregory** • 158 Bowery [Delancey] 212-226-1276 Bowery lighting mecca. Good ceiling fans.
- **MoMA Design Store** • 81 Spring St [Crosby St] 646-613-1367 Cutting-edge, minimalist, ergonomic, offbeat, and funky everything.
- **Moss Gallery** • 150 Greene St [Prince St] 212-204-7100 Awesome cool stuff you can't afford! Ever!
- **New York Central Art Supply** • 62 3rd Ave [E 11th St] 212-473-7705 Great selection of art, papers, and supplies.
- **Other Music** • 15 E 4th St [Lafayette St] 212-477-8150 Underground, experimental CDs, LPs, imports, and out-of-print obscurities.
- **Pageant Print Shop** • 69 E 4th St [2nd Ave] 212-674-5296 Just prints, really. But really great prints.
- **Pino's Prime Meats** • 149 Sullivan St [Prince] 212-475-8134 Old-world Italian butcher. Pino's tips are priceless.
- **Pylones** • 69 Spring St [Lafayette St] 212-431-3244 Colorful gifty things for your 15-year-old suburban niece.
- **Raffetto's** • 144 W Houston St [MacDougal St] 212-777-1261 Take-home Italian foods. Ravioli like mamma used to make.
- **Stereo Exchange** • 627 Broadway [Bleecker] 212-505-1111 Just-under-obscenely-priced audiophile equipment. Good for male depression.
- **The Strand** • 828 Broadway [E 12th St] 212-473-1452 Used mecca; world's messiest and best bookstore.
- **Taschen** • 107 Greene St [Prince St] 212-226-2212 God (and the Devil's) gift to publishing.
- **Trader Joe's** • 142 E 14th St [Irving Pl] 212-529-4612 Legendary bargain food chain with legendary long lines.

1
2
JOHN MURPHY PARK
Stuyvesant Town
E 16th St
E 15th St
East River
10
E 14th St
1st Avenue
A
E 13th St
E 12th St
E 11th St
Jacob Riis Houses
Szold Pl
Ped Bridge
Russian and Turkish Baths
Avenue A
Avenue B
E 10th St
First Ave
General Slocum Monument
Tompkins Square Park
Charlie Parker House
E 9th St
Avenue C
Avenue D
FDR Dr
PAGE 240
East River Park
St Marks Pl
E 8th St
6
St Brigid Roman Catholic Church
E 7th St
Pyramid Club
Joe Strummer Mural
E 6th St
Ped Bridge
Village View Houses
E 5th St
Lillian Wald Houses
E 4th St
E 3rd St
Nuyorican Poet's Café
E 2nd St
E Houston St
B
E 1st St
4
Second Ave
Katz's Deli
Hamilton Fish Park
Sheriff St
Columbia St
Baruch Pl
Mangin St
Baruch Houses
Attorney St
Masaryk Towers
Stanton St
Essex St
Norfolk St
Suffolk St
Clinton St
Ridge St
Pitt St
Samuel Gompers Houses
Forsyth St
Eldridge St
Allen St
Orchard St
Ludlow St
Rivington St
Williamsburg Bridge
Chrystie St
Delancey Street Essex Street
Delancey St
Willet St
Broome St
Lewis St
1/4 mile
.25 km

So many bars and restaurants, so little time. The East Village is no longer the city's Bohemian Center (we hear it's somewhere in Brooklyn), but there's no better neighborhood for food and drink. Inhabiting these rows of well-worn tenements are old timers, NYU kids, and everyone in between, which makes for fascinating people watching, day or night. A stroll through **Tompkins Square Park** sums it up. Cute pooches and their hip owners convene at the dog run, bongo drums echo over near Avenue B, and vestiges of a grittier past preside over the southwest entrance. Just a typical slice of life in the East Village, and a sweet life it is, if you can swing the rent.

In the early 19th and 20th centuries, when this area was considered part of the Lower East Side, it was home to waves of German, Irish, Italian, Jewish, Ukrainian, and Polish immigrants. A few historical sites have withstood the constant changes over the years. One of our favorites is **Saint Brigid's Church** (1848), which was built by Irish immigrants. It's currently undergoing restoration after nearly being demolished. If you like the idea of time travel, the next best thing might be a visit to the saunas at **Russian and Turkish Baths** (1892), where you can still get an old-world platza treatment. Another significant historical marker is the **General Slocum Monument**, which commemorates one of the worst disasters in the city's history—the sinking of the General Slocum steamship in 1904. Over 1,000 lives were lost, mainly German women and children from the neighborhood.

In the 1960s, Puerto Rican immigrants flooded into Alphabet City, another name for the blocks between Avenue A and Avenue D. Avenue C, also known as Loisaida Avenue, retains much of this character today. The loveliest aspects of this area are the many community gardens, planted on once-blighted lots and maintained by volunteers. We particularly like the always-tranquil **6BC Botanical Garden** on 6th Street between Avenue B and Avenue C. The best times to visit are Saturday and Sunday afternoons from May through October.

The term "The East Village" came into use in the 1960s, when artists, musicians, writers, performers, intellectuals, and political radicals flocked to the neighborhood. A hugely influential art scene sprang up from the 1960s through the '80s, but unfortunately, many of those galleries and performance spaces fell victim to skyrocketing rents. A few institutions have survived though—you can still catch a poetry slam at the **Nuyorican Poet's Café**, or dance the night away like it's 1984 at **The Pyramid Club**. One of our favorite summer events, The Charlie Parker Jazz Festival, takes place in **Tompkins Square Park**, right across the street from the **Charlie Parker House**. If you visit the park be sure to pass by the **Joe Strummer Mural**, a neighborhood landmark honoring one of the icons of punk rock. If it's rock n' roll you're looking for, **Mercury Lounge** on Houston is the last remaining venue from an earlier age.

1
2
A
B
JOHN MURPHY PARK
Stuyvesant Town
East River
E 16th St
E 15th St
10
1st Avenue
E 14th St
E 13th St
E 12th St
E 11th St
E 10th St
E 9th St
E 8th St
E 7th St
E 6th St
E 5th St
E 4th St
E 3rd St
E 2nd St
E 1st St
E Houston St
First Ave
Avenue A
Avenue B
Avenue C
Avenue D
Szold Pl
Jacob Riis Houses
Ped Bridge
FDR Dr
PAGE 240
East River Park
Tompkins Square Park
St Marks Pl
6
Village View Houses
Lillian Wald Houses
4
Second Ave
Hamilton Fish Park
Sheriff St
Columbia St
Baruch Pl
Mangin Pl
Baruch Houses
Masaryk Towers
Samuel Gompers Houses
Attorney St
Ridge St
Pitt St
Stanton St
Essex St
Norfolk St
Suffolk St
Clinton St
Ludlow St
Orchard St
Allen St
Eldridge St
Forsyth St
Chrystie St
Rivington St
Williamsburg Bridge
Delancey Street Essex Street
Delancey St
Willet St
Broome St
Lewis St
1/4 mile
.25 km

Doesn't matter if you're a punk, poet, or drag queen, there's a bar here with your name on it. We're partial to **Death and Company** for cocktails, **The Bourgeois Pig** for wine, **Zum Schneider** for beer, and **Drop Off Service** for happy hour. Looking for a bona fide dive? Try **Lucy's**. **7B** is a classic, upstairs at **2A** is cool, and **Mercury Lounge** still rocks.

Bars

- **11th Street Bar** • 510 E 11th St [Ave A]
212-982-3929
Darts, Irish, excellent.
- **2A** • 25 Avenue A [E 2nd St]
212-505-2466
Great upstairs space.
- **7B (Horseshoe Bar)** • 108 Avenue B [E 7th St]
212-473-8840
Godfather II shot here. What can be bad?
- **Ace Bar** • 531 E 5th St [Ave A]
212-979-8476
Darts, pinball, pool, and even skee-ball!
- **The Bourgeois Pig** • 111 E 7th St [Ave A]
212-475-2246
Dark, bordello-y den of vino for the romantically inclined.
- **Bua** • 122 St Marks Pl [First Ave]
212-979-6276
Neighborhood bar during the week, mobs of pretty people on the weekend.
- **Cherry Tavern** • 441 E 6th St [1st Ave]
212-777-1448
Get the Tijuana Special.
- **Death and Company** • 433 E 6th St [Ave A]
212-388-0882
Classy cocktails served Prohibition style. No password required.
- **Drop Off Service** • 211 Avenue A [13th St]
212-260-2914
$3 draft happy hour. Go early for best results.
- **Heathers** • 506 E 13th St [Ave A]
212-254-0979
Usually low-key for the East Village.
- **Hi-Fi** • 169 Avenue A [E 11th St]
212-420-8392
The BEST jukebox in town.
- **Joe's Bar** • 520 E 6th St [Ave A]
212-473-9093
Classic neighborhood hangout. A favorite.
- **Lakeside Lounge** • 162 Avenue B [E 10th St]
212-529-8463
Great jukebox, live music, décor, everything.
- **Mama's Bar** • 34 Avenue B [E 3rd St]
212-777-5729
Laid-back respite from the Avenue B craziness, with food from Mama's next door.
- **Manitoba's** • 99 Avenue B [E 6th St]
212-982-2511
Punk scene.
- **Mercury Lounge** • 217 E Houston St [Essex St]
212-260-4700
Rock venue with occasional top-notch acts.
- **Mona's** • 224 Avenue B [E 13th St]
212-353-3780
Depressing. Recommended.
- **Nublu** • 62 Avenue C [E 5th St]
212-375-1500
Sexy lounge with world music, nice ambience, and outdoor porch.
- **Nuyorican Poet's Café** • 236 E 3rd St [Ave C]
212-780-9386
Where mediocre poets die of humiliation.
- **Otto's Shrunken Head** • 538 E 14th St [Ave A]
212-228-2240
Not your grandma's tiki bar.
- **Parkside Lounge** • 317 E Houston St [Attorney]
212-673-6270
Good basic bar, live acts in the back.
- **PDT** • 113 St Marks Pl [Avenue A]
212-614-0386
Enter through a phone booth in a hot dog joint. No joke.
- **Pyramid Club** • 101 Avenue A [E 7th St]
212-228-4888
Classic '80s and '90s club.
- **The Stone** • 69 Ave C [E 2nd St]
212-473-0043
All proceeds go to the avant-garde jazz artists. Go now.
- **Ten Degrees** • 121 St Marks Pl [1st Ave]
212-358-8600
Cozy wine bar with live jazz on Wednesdays.
- **WCOU Radio (Tile Bar)** • 115 1st Ave [E 7th St]
212-255-9713
East Village survivor. Low key and great.
- **Zum Schneider** • 107 Avenue C [E 7th St]
212-598-1098
Get weisse, man. Prost.

Theaters/Performing Arts

- **Nuyorican Poet's Café** • 236 E 3rd St [Ave C]
212-780-9386
Where mediocre poets die of humiliation.
- **Performance Space 122** • 150 1st Ave [10th St]
212-477-5288
Where Penny Arcade turned vomiting into art.
- **Theater for the New City** • 155 1st Ave [E 10th]
212-254-1109
A hot box of crazy theatre.

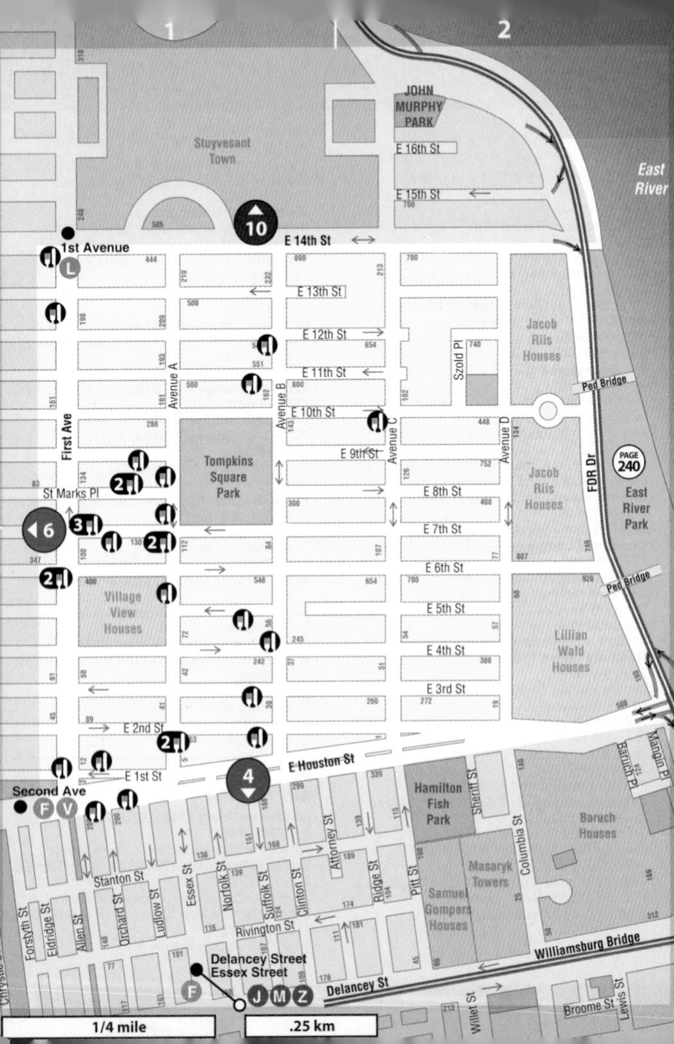
1
2
JOHN MURPHY PARK
Stuyvesant Town
E 16th St
E 15th St
East River
10
E 14th St
1st Avenue
E 13th St
E 12th St
E 11th St
E 10th St
E 9th St
E 8th St
E 7th St
E 6th St
E 5th St
E 4th St
E 3rd St
E 2nd St
E 1st St
St Marks Pl
First Ave
Avenue A
Avenue B
Avenue C
Avenue D
Szold Pl
Jacob Riis Houses
Ped Bridge
Tompkins Square Park
FDR Dr
PAGE 240
East River Park
Village View Houses
Lillian Wald Houses
6
4
E Houston St
Second Ave
Hamilton Fish Park
Sheriff St
Baruch Pl
Mangin Pl
Baruch Houses
Columbia St
Masaryk Towers
Samuel Gompers Houses
Attorney St
Stanton St
Essex St
Norfolk St
Suffolk St
Clinton St
Ridge St
Pitt St
Orchard St
Ludlow St
Allen St
Eldridge St
Forsyth St
Chrystie St
Rivington St
Williamsburg Bridge
Delancey Street Essex Street
Delancey St
Willet St
Broome St
Lewis St
1/4 mile
.25 km

The residents of this 'hood are spoiled rotten when it comes to restaurants. **7A's** always open, **Caracas Arepa Bar**'s always delicious (and packed), and brunch at **Supper** never lets us down. **Back Forty** is worth the wait, **Porchetta**'s sandwiches rock, **Banjara**'s lamb chops are to die for, and there's no place like **Hummus Place**.

Restaurants

- **7A** • 109 Avenue A [E 7th St]
  212-673-6583 • $$
  Open 24 hours. Great burgers.
- **Back Forty** • 190 Avenue B [12th St]
  212-388-1990 • $$
  Farm fresh, simple, and good.
- **Banjara** • 97 1st Ave [E 6th St]
  212-477-5956 • $$$
  Best Indian on 6th Street, hands-down. Awesome lamb chops.
- **Bereket Turkish Kebab House** •
  187 E Houston St [Orchard St]
  212-475-7700 • $
  Middle Eastern delights. Open late.
- **Big Arc Chicken** • 233 1st Ave [E 14th St]
  212-477-0091 • $
  Cheap Middle Eastern food complete with Arabic TV.
- **Black Iron Burger Shop** •
  540 E 5th St [Avenue B]
  212-677-6067 • $
  Burgers and shakes? Count us in.
- **Boca Chica** • 13 1st Ave [E 1st St]
  212-473-0108 • $$
  Excellent, fun South American. Great chimichurri sauce.
- **Caracas Arepa Bar** • 93 E 7th St [First Ave]
  212-228-5062 • $$
  Authentic Venezuelan.
- **Crif Dogs** • 113 St Marks Pl [Avenue A]
  212-614-2728 • $
  Kick-ass wieners.
- **Dirt Candy** • 430 E 9th St [Ave A]
  212-228-7732 • $$$
  Translation: gourmet vegetarian.
- **Dok Suni's** • 119 1st Ave [E 7th St]
  212-477-9506 • $$$
  Excellent Korean fusion. NFT fave.
- **Flea Market Café** • 131 Avenue A [St Marks Pl]
  212-358-9282 • $$
  French, good brunch.
- **Hummus Place** • 109 St Marks Pl [First Ave]
  212-529-9198 • $
  Authentic! Best hummus this side of Tel Aviv.
- **Il Posto Accanto** • 190 E 2nd St [Ave B]
  212-228-3562 • $$$
  Tiny, rustic Italian enoteca.
- **Kate's Joint** • 58 Avenue B [E 4th St]
  212-777-7059 • $$
  Inventive vegetarian and vegan.
- **Katz's Deli** • 205 E Houston St [Ludlow St]
  212-254-2246 • $$
  I'll have what she's having!
- **Luke's Lobster** • 93 E 7th St [1st Ave]
  212-387-8487 • $$
  Fresh-from-the sea lobster rolls, without sticker shock.
- **Luzzo's** • 211 1st Ave [E 13th St]
  212-473-7447 • $$
  Real coal oven. Top ten worthy.
- **Mama's Food Shop** • 200 E 3rd St [Ave B]
  212-777-4425 • $
  Great home-cooking and take-out. NFT Pick.
- **Mercadito Cantina** • 172 Avenue B [11th St]
  212-388-1750 • $$
  This gourmet taqueria is always packed.
- **Nicky's Vietnamese Sandwiches** •
  150 E 2nd St [Ave A]
  212-388-1088 • $
  Dirt-cheap Vietnamese treats.
- **Odessa** • 119 Avenue A [St Marks Pl]
  212-253-1470 • $
  Diner. Awesome deep-fried meat pierogies.
- **Porchetta** • 110 E 7th St [1st Ave]
  212-777-2151 • $$
  Best Italian pork sandwiches. Ever.
- **Punjabi Deli & Grocery** • 114 E 1st St [1st Ave]
  212-533-9048 • $
  Deli, grocery, and cabbie-worthy Indian eats.
- **Pylos** • 128 E 7th St [Ave A]
  212-473-0220 • $$
  Delicious Greek, cool hanging-pot ceiling.
- **Royale** • 157 Avenue C [10th St]
  212-254-6600 • $$
  Perfect burgers with stellar fixins, and a deal to boot.
- **Sigiri** • 91 1st Ave [E 6th St]
  212-614-9333 • $$
  Excellent BYOB Sri Lankan above a great beer shop.
- **Supper** • 156 E 2nd St [Ave A]
  212-477-7600 • $$$
  Spaghetti con limone is yummy. Great brunch. Otherworldly atmosphere.
- **Takahachi** • 85 Avenue A [E 6th St]
  212-505-6524 • $$$
  Super-good Japanese and sushi. A mainstay.

1
2
Stuyvesant Town
JOHN MURPHY PARK
E 16th St
E 15th St
East River
10
1st Avenue
E 14th St
E 13th St
E 12th St
E 11th St
E 10th St
E 9th St
E 8th St
E 7th St
E 6th St
E 5th St
E 4th St
E 3rd St
E 2nd St
E 1st St
First Ave
Avenue A
Avenue B
Avenue C
Avenue D
Szold Pl
Jacob Riis Houses
Ped Bridge
FDR Dr
PAGE 240
East River Park
St Marks Pl
6
3
2
Tompkins Square Park
Village View Houses
Lillian Wald Houses
E Houston St
4
Second Ave
Hamilton Fish Park
Sheriff St
Baruch Pl
Baruch Houses
Masaryk Towers
Samuel Gompers Houses
Columbia St
Stanton St
Essex St
Norfolk St
Suffolk St
Clinton St
Attorney St
Ridge St
Pitt St
Rivington St
Forsyth St
Eldridge St
Allen St
Orchard St
Ludlow St
Chrystie St
Delancey Street Essex Street
Delancey St
Williamsburg Bridge
Willet St
Broome St
Lewis St
1/4 mile
.25 km

Bagels, Coffee, & Shopping

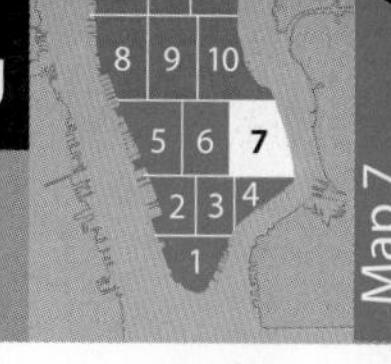

Not a chain retailer in sight, but there are boutiques a-plenty. We love browsing oddities at **Obscura Antiques**, jewelry at **The Shape of Lies**, kitschy gifts at **Alphabets**. Spanish Oenophiles, check out **Tinto Fino**. For spices in bulk try **Dual Specialty Store**. Jewish delicacies by the pound at **Russ & Daughters**. Or visit old school bodega **Ray's Candy Store**.

Coffee

- **Abraco** • 86 E 7th St [1st Ave]
  212-388-9731
  Sip an amazing espresso by the window.
- **The Bean Coffee & Tea** • 49 1st Ave [E 3rd St]
  212-353-1477
  Plenty of seating for the laptop armies.
- **Cafe Pick Me Up** • 145 Avenue A [E 9th St]
  212-673-7231
  Late-night caffeine hang out. Open 'til 12:30 am.
- **Ciao for Now** • 523 E 12th St [Ave A]
  212-677-2616
  Neighborhood fave for coffee and pastries.
- **Ninth Street Espresso** • 700 E 9th St [Ave C]
  212-358-9225
  Absolutely fantastic coffee drinks. Cool Portland vibe.
- **Ost Cafe** • 441 E 12th St [Ave A]
  212-477-5600
  Great space to hang out for a few hours.
- **Sympathy for the Kettle** •
  109 St Marks Pl [1st Ave]
  212-979-1650
  It's tea time Giles.

Shopping

- **11th Street Flea Market** • 1st Ave & E 11th St
  Stuff you didn't even know you needed!
- **Abed Bendahud Inkona Stationary** •
  66 Avenue A [5th St]
  212-228-7868
  If you're looking for a magazine, it's here. Somewhere.
- **Alphabets** • 115 Avenue A [E 7th St]
  212-475-7250
  Fun miscellany store.
- **Butter Lane** • 123 E 7th St [Ave A]
  212-677-2880
  Riding the cupcake trend…
- **East Village Books and Records** •
  99 St Marks Pl [1st Ave]
  212-477-8647
  Messy pile of used stuff.
- **East Village Wines** • 138 1st Ave [St Marks Pl]
  212-677-7070
  Classic EV liquor store. With booze!
- **Exit 9** • 64 Avenue A [E 5th St]
  212-228-0145
  Always fun and changeable hipster gifts. First place to sell NFT!
- **First Flight Music** • 174 1st Ave [E 11th St]
  212-539-1383
  Good guitars and amps, spotty service.
- **Gracefully** • 28 Avenue A [E 2nd St]
  212-677-8181
  Overpriced gourmet groceries. But better than the f***ing Key Food.
- **Gringer & Sons** • 29 1st Ave [E 2nd St]
  212-475-0600
  Kitchen appliances for every price range.
- **Lancelotti** • 66 Avenue A [E 5th St]
  212-475-6851
  Fun designer housewares, not too expensive.
- **Obscura Antiques & Oddities** •
  280 E 10th St [Ave A]
  212-505-9251
  Kitschy & Arbitrary Americana. Pricey, but sociologically fascinating.
- **Ray's Candy Store** • 113 Avenue A [7th St]
  212-505-7609
  Avenue A's Belgian fries-and-ice cream institution.
- **Russ & Daughters** • 179 E Houston St [Orchard St]
  212-475-4880
  Fab Jewish soul food—lox, herring, sable, etc.
- **Saifee Hardware** • 114 1st Ave [E 7th St]
  212-979-6396
  Classic East Village hardware store. It has everything.
- **The Shape of Lies** • 127 E 7th St [7th St]
  212-533-5920
  Vintage and locally made jewelry.
- **Sons + Daughters** • 35 Avenue A [E 3rd St]
  212-253-7797
  Great kid's toys/clothes destination, good prices.
- **Tinto Fino** • 85 1st Ave [5th St]
  212-254-0850
  Great selection of Spanish wines.
- **Two Boots Video** • 42 Avenue A [E 3rd St]
  212-254-1441
  We still might owe some overdue charges from 1996.
- **Zaragoza Mexican Deli and Grocery** •
  215 Avenue A [E 13th St]
  212-780-9204
  Bodega with burritos.

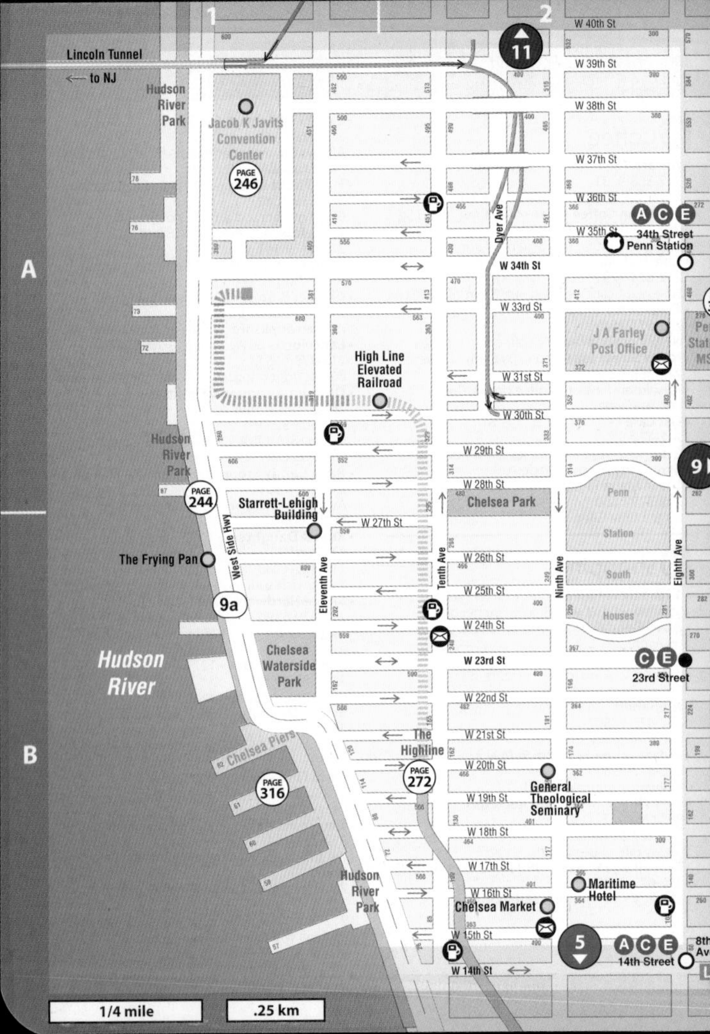
1
2
A
B
Lincoln Tunnel
to NJ
Hudson River Park
Jacob K Javits Convention Center
PAGE 246
11
W 40th St
W 39th St
W 38th St
W 37th St
W 36th St
W 35th St
W 34th St
W 33rd St
W 31st St
W 30th St
W 29th St
W 28th St
W 27th St
W 26th St
W 25th St
W 24th St
W 23rd St
W 22nd St
W 21st St
W 20th St
W 19th St
W 18th St
W 17th St
W 16th St
W 15th St
W 14th St
Dyer Ave
A C E
34th Street Penn Station
J A Farley Post Office
High Line Elevated Railroad
9
Hudson River Park
PAGE 244
Starrett-Lehigh Building
Chelsea Park
Penn Station South Houses
The Frying Pan
West Side Hwy
9a
Eleventh Ave
Tenth Ave
Ninth Ave
Eighth Ave
Hudson River
Chelsea Waterside Park
C E
23rd Street
Chelsea Piers
PAGE 316
The Highline
PAGE 272
General Theological Seminary
Hudson River Park
Maritime Hotel
Chelsea Market
5
A C E
14th Street
8th Av
1/4 mile
.25 km

8 9 10
5 6 7

Located due south of Midtown's gazillion office buildings and due north of the West Village and the Financial District, Chelsea is a magnet for the young, the beautiful, and the wealthy. A polished mix of quaint, restored townhouses and sparkling new condos in the sky combine to create a unique and appealing neighborhood that deftly bridges the transition from downtown to Midtown. With the opening of the long-awaited High Line Park in 2009, luxury marched west towards the river, with multiple shiny new buildings clustered around the new ribbon of green that cuts through the heart of the neighborhood.

While the neighborhood is diverse and welcoming to all, it would be dishonest to pretend that it isn't best known as the epicenter of all things gay. A substantial, muscle-bound gay population spawned the term "Chelsea boy," used either derisively or admiringly depending on one's taste. Several of the city's best gay bars, book stores, and social service organizations are located within the borders of this neighborhood. And while the gyms aren't exclusively gay, they know who their best and most loyal customers are.

But even if you're not a gay male, the charms of Chelsea are many and unmistakable: a thriving, inclusive nightlife with something for everyone, great dining for almost any budget, and great shopping for...middle budgets and upwards (though the odd deal can certainly be found tucked away on a side street or a more modest storefront on one of the avenues). On top of that, there are ample opportunities for recreation here—aside from the aforementioned High Line, there's the Hudson River Park (which, unsurprisingly, is alongside the body of water bearing the same name), and massive sports complex Chelsea Piers. Plus, there is the brilliant **Chelsea Market**, with its wonderfully diverse food vendors, and the safety-first, divided bike lanes on Eighth and Ninth Avenues.

The architecture of the neighborhood is some of New York's most noteworthy. Frank Gehry's translucent, iceberg/schooner hybrid **InterActiveCorp Building** is regrettably too short to be seen from vantage points that aren't near its location at the intersection of 18th Street and the West Side Highway. But it's a leading candidate for coolest building in Chelsea and one of the loveliest, most unique buildings erected in Manhattan in recent years. A few blocks away lies the gorgeous, Neo-Gothic campus of **The General Theological Seminary**, the oldest Episcopal theological school. Just north of there, the historic **London Terrace** luxury apartment complex fills an entire city block. Up a few blocks more, the **Starrett-Lehigh Building** is an art deco freight warehouse and factory that now houses several high-profile media and fashion companies including Martha Stewart.

Farther uptown, on Eighth Avenue between 31st and 33rd Streets, the **James A. Farley Post Office** stands in proud, marble magnificence across the street from the grotesquely ugly Madison Square Garden (the unworthy replacement for the demolished Penn Station). A couple blocks west of there is the **Javits Center**, the biggest exhibition hall in the city and another architectural lowlight. As a New Yorker, the best reason you'll ever have for going there is a jobs fair or an industry expo—the latter being preferable because there's likely to be free food or booze.

Instead of heading up into the 30s, take a walk through west Chelsea in the 20s and you'll find yourself in one of the great visual art districts of the world (see Art Galleries section for comprehensive listings). Over 300 galleries show the newest work of the best artists working today. Despite the occasional dud, you have a better-than-even chance of encountering exhilarating, high-quality work. Now and then, you might even find something you can afford to buy!

Add in some of the best people-watching in the city, and you'll know why so many other New Yorkers choose to pay a small fortune every month to live in a shoebox here.

Lincoln Tunnel
to NJ
Hudson River Park
Jacob K Javits Convention Center
PAGE 246
W 40th St
W 39th St
W 38th St
W 37th St
W 36th St
W 35th St
W 34th St
W 33rd St
W 31st St
W 30th St
W 29th St
W 28th St
W 27th St
W 26th St
W 25th St
W 24th St
W 23rd St
W 22nd St
W 21st St
W 20th St
W 19th St
W 18th St
W 17th St
W 15th St
W 14th St
Dyer Ave
34th Street Penn Station
J A Farley Post Office
Chelsea Park
Penn Station South Houses
23rd Street
14th Street
Eleventh Ave
Tenth Ave
Ninth Ave
Eighth Ave
West Side Hwy
9a
PAGE 244
Hudson River
Chelsea Waterside Park
Chelsea Piers
PAGE 316
The Highline
PAGE 272
Hudson River Park
1/4 mile
.25 km

The **Half King** is perfectly positioned for a drink après-gallery. **The Kitchen's** list of performances over the years is legendary, and rock shows still happen at the **Hammerstein** and **Highline Ballrooms**. Various gay crowds have their home bars here: **View Bar** (stylish on a budget), **Gym** (hunks!), and **The Eagle** (leather-daddies and cubs) are three of the best.

Bars

- **Billymark's West** • 332 9th Ave [W 29th St]
  212-629-0118
  Down and dirty dive.
- **Chelsea Brewing Company** •
  Pier 59 [W 18th St]
  212-336-6440
  When you're done playing basketball.
- **The Eagle** • 554 W 28th St [11th Ave]
  646-473-1866
  Get your leather on (or off).
- **Flight 151** • 151 8th Ave [W 17th St]
  212-229-1868
  Prepare for takeoff on Mondays with $4 Margaritas.
- **Gym Sports Bar** • 167 8th Ave [W 19th St]
  212-337-2439
  Where the boys go to watch the game…and each other.
- **Half King** • 505 W 23rd St [10th Ave]
  212-462-4300
  Always the perfect drinking choice in Chelsea. Amazing brunch.
- **Hammerstein Ballroom** •
  311 W 34th St [8th Ave]
  212-279-7740
  Lofty rock venue.
- **Highline Ballroom** • 431 W 16th St [16th St]
  212-414-5994
  New venue for rock, folk, dance, whatever.
- **Hiro Ballroom** • 88 9th Ave [9th Ave]
  212-727-0212
  DJs and events in a sleek, Japanese-themed setting.
- **Molly Wee Pub** • 402 8th Ave [W 30th St]
  212-967-2627
  You may just need a pint after a trip to Penn Station.
- **The Park** • 118 10th Ave [W 17th St]
  212-352-3313
  Good patio. We're split on this one.
- **Red Rock West** • 457 W 17th St [10th Ave]
  212-366-5359
  F***king loud!
- **View Bar** • 232 8th Ave [W 22nd St]
  212-929-2243
  View Drag Queen puppets playing Bingo on Friday nights.
- **Wakamba Cocktail Lounge** •
  543 8th Ave [W 37th St]
  212-564-2042
  Plastic palm trees & provocatively-clad barmaids.
- **West Side Tavern** • 360 W 23rd St [9th Ave]
  212-366-3738
  Local mixture.

Bowling

- **300** • W 23rd St & West Side Hwy
  212-835-2695
  VIP bowling on Chelsea Piers.

Movie Theaters

- **AMC Loews 34th Street 14** •
  312 W 34th St [8th Ave]
  212-244-4556
  The biggest and most comfortable of the midtown multiplexes.

Theaters/Performing Arts

- **American Place Theatre** •
  266 W 37th St [8th Ave]
  212-594-4482
  Theatre for the literary-minded.
- **Atlantic Theater Company** •
  336 W 20th St [8th Ave]
  212-691-5919
  David Mamet's theatre company. F*** you!
- **Hudson Guild** • 441 W 26th St [W 27th St]
  212-760-9800
  Nice, intimate space.
- **Joyce Theater** • 175 8th Ave [W 19th St]
  212-691-9740
  Built for dance, with excellent sightlines.
- **The Kitchen** • 512 W 19th St [10th Ave]
  212-255-5793
  The kind of place Jesse Helms would have hated.
- **Sanford Meisner Theatre** • 164 11th Ave [22nd]
  212-206-1764
  If you're swimming in the Hudson you've gone too far.
- **Upright Citizen's Brigade Theatre** •
  307 W 26th St [8th Ave]
  212-366-9176
  See hilarious improv comics before SNL makes them suck.

Lincoln Tunnel
to NJ
Hudson River Park
Jacob K Javits Convention Center
PAGE 246
W 40th St
W 39th St
W 38th St
W 37th St
W 36th St
W 35th St
W 34th St
W 33rd St
W 31st St
W 30th St
W 29th St
W 28th St
W 27th St
W 26th St
W 25th St
W 24th St
W 23rd St
W 22nd St
W 21st St
W 20th St
W 19th St
W 18th St
W 17th St
W 16th St
W 15th St
W 14th St
Dyer Ave
34th Street Penn Station
J A Farley Post Office
Chelsea Park
Penn Station South Houses
Eleventh Ave
Tenth Ave
Ninth Ave
Eighth Ave
West Side Hwy
9a
PAGE 244
23rd Street
Hudson River
Chelsea Waterside Park
Chelsea Piers
PAGE 316
The Highline
PAGE 272
Hudson River Park
14th Street
1/4 mile
.25 km

For some tasty Thai, try **Spice** or **Room Service**. For diner food, try the **Empire** (good) or the **Skylight** (cheap). **Grand Sichuan Int'l** is one of our favorite spots for Chinese in all of New York. Across the street, check out **Co.'s** stellar pizzas. Got a bailout bonus? Indulge at **Buddakan**, **Matsuri**, or **Morimoto**.

Restaurants

- **202** • 75 9th Ave [W 16th St]
  646-638-1173 • $$
  Simple European eats (and fancy dishware boutique).
- **Better Burger Chelsea** • 178 8th Ave [W 19th]
  212-989-6688 • $
  Ostrich burger? Check. Soy burger? Check. Antibiotic-free meat? Check.
- **Bottino** • 246 10th Ave [W 24th St]
  212-206-6766 • $$$
  Good, clean Italian. A good post-gallery spot.
- **Buddakan** • 75 9th Ave [W 16th St]
  212-989-6699 • $$$$$
  NYC branch of Stephen Starr's insanely popular Philadelphia behemoth.
- **Casa Havana** • 190 8th Ave [W 20th St]
  212-243-9421 • $$
  Great Cuban sandwiches.
- **Co.** • 230 9th Ave [24th St]
  212-243-1105 • $$
  Pizza of the gods.
- **Cola's** • 148 8th Ave [W 17th St]
  212-633-8020 • $
  Intimate and inexpensive.
- **Cookshop** • 156 10th Ave [W 20th St]
  212-924-4440 • $
  New, loft-like, local ingredient-focused eatery.
- **El Quinto Pino** • 401 W 24th St [9th Ave]
  212-206-6900 • $$
  Tiny, table-free tapas joint from owners of Tia Pol.
- **Empire Diner** • 210 10th Ave [W 22nd St]
  212-243-2736 • $$
  A Chelsea institution. 24 hours.
- **Grand Sichuan Int'l** • 229 9th Ave [W 24th St]
  212-620-5200 • $$
  Some of the best Chinese in NYC. Recommended.
- **La Luncheonette** • 130 10th Ave [W 18th St]
  212-675-0342 • $$$$
  A truly great French restaurant. Recommended.
- **La Taza de Oro** • 96 8th Ave [W 15th St]
  212-243-9946 • $$
  Sit at the counter with the locals for great Puerto Rican.
- **Manganaro Grosseria** • 488 9th Ave [W 37th]
  212-563-5331 • $$
  Locals-only Italian sandwich joint. Recommended.
- **Matsuri** • 369 W 16th St [9th Ave]
  212-243-6400 • $$$$$
  Gigantic, luxurious Japanese restaurant tucked beneath The Maritime Hotel.
- **Moonstruck Diner** • 400 W 23rd St [9th Ave]
  212-924-3709 • $$
  Not cheap as far as diners go, but generous portions.
- **Morimoto** • 88 10th Ave [W 16th St]
  212-989-8883 • $$$$$
  Stephen Starr's couture Japanese temple. Iron Chef-prepared cuisine.
- **Pepe Giallo** • 253 10th Ave [W 25th St]
  212-242-6055 • $$
  Takeout Italian.
- **Pomodoro** • 518 9th Ave [W 39th St]
  212-239-7019 • $$
  Takes "fast food" Italian to the next level; superb foccacia.
- **The Red Cat** • 227 10th Ave [W 23rd St]
  212-242-1122 • $$$$
  Hip and expensive.
- **Room Service** • 166 8th Ave [W 18th St]
  212-691-0299 • $$$
  This place is truly "Thai"rific—try the iced coffee.
- **Sandwich Planet** • 522 9th Ave [W 39th St]
  212-273-9768 • $
  Unlimited sandwich selection.
- **Skylight Diner** • 402 W 34th St [9th Ave]
  212-244-0395 • $
  24-hour diner. If you must.
- **Spice** • 199 8th Ave [W 20th St]
  212-989-1116 • $$
  Good, straightforward Thai.
- **Swich** • 104 8th Ave [W 15th St]
  212-488-4800 • $
  You'll be "pressed" to find a cooler sandwich on the go.
- **Tia Pol** • 205 10th Ave [W 22nd St]
  212-675-8805 • $$
  Very good, very popular (crowded) tapas joint.
- **Tick Tock Diner** • 481 8th Ave [W 34th St]
  212-268-8444 • $
  24-hour diner. Time's awastin'.
- **Trestle on Tenth** • 242 10th Ave [24th St]
  212-645-5659 • $$$
  Hip, local, small menu, recommended.
- **Txikito** • 240 9th Ave [W 24th St]
  212-242-4730 • $$$
  Unique gourmet Basque cooking.
- **Viceroy** • 160 8th Ave [W 18th St]
  212-633-8484 • $$$
  Stargazin' American.

Lincoln Tunnel
to NJ
Hudson River Park
Jacob K Javits Convention Center
PAGE 246
W 40th St
W 39th St
W 38th St
W 37th St
W 36th St
W 35th St
W 34th St
W 33rd St
W 31st St
W 30th St
W 29th St
W 28th St
W 27th St
W 26th St
W 25th St
W 24th St
W 23rd St
W 22nd St
W 21st St
W 20th St
W 19th St
W 18th St
W 17th St
W 16th St
W 15th St
W 14th St
Dyer Ave
34th Street
Penn Station
J A Farley Post Office
Chelsea Park
Penn Station South Houses
PAGE 244
West Side Hwy
9a
Eleventh Ave
Tenth Ave
Ninth Ave
Eighth Ave
23rd Street
Hudson River
Chelsea Waterside Park
Chelsea Piers
PAGE 316
The Highline
PAGE 272
Hudson River Park
14th Street
1/4 mile
.25 km

Bagels, Coffee, & Shopping

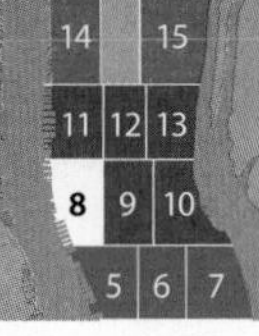

B&H Photo Video remains a go-to electronics store (closed Saturdays) and **Printed Matter**'s selection of artists' books is probably the best in the world. For food, simply hit brilliant **Chelsea Market** to get Italian imports (**Buon Italia**), wine (**Chelsea Wine Vault**), dairy (**Ronnybrook Farm**), fish (**The Lobster Place**), cheese (**Lucy's Whey**) and bread (**Amy's Bread**).

Bagels

- **Murray's Bagels** • 242 8th Ave [W 22nd St]
  646-638-1335
  Classic. But they don't toast, so don't ask.

Coffee

- **Billy's Bakery** • 184 9th Ave [W 21st St]
  212-647-9956
  Mindblowingly good cakes to go with your coffee.
- **Joe: The Art of Coffee** • 405 W 23rd St [9th Ave]
  212-206-0669
  Joe really knows his joe.
- **Ninth Street Espresso** • 75 9th Ave [W 15th]
  212-228-2930
  Gourmet coffee counter inside Chelsea Market.
- **Paradise Café & Muffins** • 139 8th Ave [17th St]
  212-647-0066
  Friendly spot. We'll let you decide if it's actually paradise.

Shopping

- **192 Books** • 192 10th Ave [W 21st St]
  212-255-4022
  Reads like a library—with a premium on art books and literature.
- **Amy's Bread** • 75 9th Ave [W 47th St]
  212-462-4338
  Perfect breads.
- **Aperture Book Center** •
  547 W 27th St [10th Ave]
  212-505-5555
  We love Aperture. Say hi for us.
- **B&H Photo** • 420 9th Ave [W 33rd St]
  212-444-6615
  Where everyone in North America buys their cameras and film. Closed Saturdays.
- **The Blue Store** • 206 8th Ave [W 21st St]
  212-924-8315
  Tobias Funke's dream store. Not kid-friendly.
- **Brooklyn Industries** • 161 8th Ave [18th St]
  212-206-0477
  A little bit of Brooklyn in the heart of Chelsea.
- **Buon Italia** • 75 9th Ave [W 16th St]
  212-633-9090
  Italian import mecca—get the 24-month prosciutto.
- **Chelsea Market Baskets** • 75 9th Ave [W 16th]
  212-727-1111
  Gift baskets for all occasions.
- **Chelsea Wholesale Flower Market** •
  75 9th Ave [W 16th St]
  212-620-7500
  Remember, you're in Manhattan, not Westchester.
- **Chelsea Wine Vault** • 75 9th Ave [W 16th St]
  212-462-4244
  Excellent shop inside the Chelsea Market.
- **Eleni's** • 75 9th Ave [W 16th St]
  888-4-ELENIS
  When a card won't do, iced cookies in every shape will.
- **Esposito's Pork Store** • 500 9th Ave [38th St]
  212-279-3298
  Authentic 1890 butcher shop.
- **Fat Witch Bakery** • 75 9th Ave [W 16th St]
  212-807-1335
  Excellent chocolate brownies.
- **Find Outlet** • 361 W 17th St [9th Ave]
  212-243-3177
  Find cheap(er) designer duds.!
- **Hell's Kitchen Flea Market** •
  9th Ave & W 39th St
  212-243-5343
  The famous flea market.
- **Knickerbocker Meat Market** •
  166 9th Ave [W 20th St]
  212-243-3151
  Fantastic butchers that serve only top-notch meat.
- **L'Arte del Gelato** • 75 9th Ave [W 15th St]
  212-366-0570
  Gelato to make you sing an aria. Or just pig out.
- **The Lobster Place** • 75 9th Ave [W 15th St]
  212-255-5672
  Fresh fish and Maine lobster, if you can afford it.
- **Lucy's Whey** • 75 9th Ave [W 15th St]
  212-463-9500
  American artisanal cheeses in Chelsea Market.
- **Printed Matter** • 195 10th Ave [W 22nd St]
  212-925-0325
  Astounding selection of artist's books; highly recommended.
- **Ronnybrook Farm Dairy** • 75 9th Ave [15th St]
  212-741-6455
  All things dairy, fresh from the Hudson Valley. Great shakes.

W 39th St
W 38th St
W 37th St
W 36th St
W 35th St
W 34th St
W 33rd St
W 32nd St
W 31st St
W 30th St
W 29th St
W 28th St
W 27th St
W 26th St
W 25th St
W 24th St
W 23rd St
W 22nd St
W 21st St
W 20th St
W 19th St
W 18th St
W 17th St
W 16th St
W 15th St
VEHICULAR TRAFFIC PROHIBITED
De Lamar Mansion
Morgan Library
Park Ave S
Herald Square
Macy's
34th Street Penn Station
34th Street Herald Square
Empire State Building
PAGE 242
33rd Street
PATH 33rd St
J A Farley Post Office
PAGE 326
Madison Square Garden
Penn Station
PAGE 303
Koreatown
Garment District
Flower District
Tin Pan Alley
28th Street
Eighth Ave
Seventh Ave (Fashion Ave)
Sixth Ave (Ave of the Americas)
Fifth Ave
Madison Ave
Broadway
New York Life Insurance Company
Croisic Building
Madison Sq Plz
New York State Appellate Court
Madison Square Park
Stern Brothers' Dry Goods Store
23rd Street
PATH 23rd St
Chelsea Hotel
Metropolitan Life Insurance Company
Flatiron Building
Hugh O'Neill's Dry Goods Store
Broadway Lord & Taylor
Theodore Roosevelt Birthplace
Arnold Constable's Dry Good Store
Siegel-Cooper Department Store
18th Street
Old Town Bar
Union Square
8th Avenue
14th Street
PATH 14th St
6th Avenue
14th Street-Union Square
PAGE 266
1/4 mile
.25 km

The amazing variety of people, places and things that typifies New York cannot be better experienced than in this area. Containing some of the most tourist-heavy areas—the **Empire State Building** and **Macy's** at Herald Square—you will also find the hip, expensive, and fabulously exclusive communities of Gramercy (to the east) and Chelsea (to the west). Flatiron is also the home to the lesser-known "Silicon Alley," coined as a reflection of the recent influx of start-up Internet companies in the area. In this incredibly diverse and unassuming neighborhood you will see moms pushing strollers, hipsters in low-slung pants, and wealthy elderly women walking their perfectly groomed poodles.

One of the most obvious draws of the area is the impressive architecture. You certainly can't miss the amazing sight of the towering **Empire State Building** or the aptly-named **Flatiron Building**. But also not to be missed is the less-obvious **Chelsea Hotel**, a favorite of many musicians and artists from Bob Dylan to Sid Vicious. Early 20th century additions to the area include the **MetLife Tower**, the **New York Life Building**, and the **New York State Appellate Court**, all of which are located on the east side of **Madison Square Park**. Equally impressive are the myriad number of current and former cast-iron department store buildings that make up the historic "Ladies' Mile" area, including the **Arnold Constable Dry Goods Store**, the **Broadway Lord & Taylor**, the **Croisic Building**, the **Hugh O'Neill Dry Goods Store**, the **Stern Brothers' Dry Goods Store**, and, our all-time favorite, the **Siegel-Cooper Department Store**. We can't help but mention that this area was also the scene of one of the greatest crimes against architecture—namely, the destruction of McKim, Mead & White's original Penn Station in 1963.

Venture to the **Garment District** and you will be surrounded by the shops and people that helped make New York City the fashion leader of the world in the late 1800's and early 1900's. The nearby **Flower District** was once several blocks filled with lush greenery of every variety. In 2010 however, high rent and massive competition have squeezed most retailers out, so it's less than a block in size now and can easily be missed. Luckily **Koreatown** is still going strong on 32nd Street (between Fifth and Broadway). Stroll through here on a Friday night to find the restaurants and bars packed to the brim.

Look down as you walk on 28th street between 5th avenue and Broadway and you will see a plaque in the sidewalk dedicated to **Tin Pan Alley**. If you're a music buff you'll want to take in the historical significance of this area, dating back to 1885 when a group of songwriters and music publishers got together to lobby for copyright laws.

For a piece of Presidential history, visit the **Birthplace of Theodore Roosevelt**. A recreated version of the brownstone President Roosevelt was born in on October 27 1858 now serves as a museum dedicated to the 26th President.

Finding a small patch of fresh green grass in Manhattan is almost as challenging as finding a parking spot, but in this area you have not one but two parks. **Madison Square Park** is a beautifully manicured park where you can be sure to catch hundreds of sunbathers on any summer Saturday. It is also home to the long lines of the **Shake Shack**. If you can afford to wait an hour or two, you will be treated to one of the best hamburgers of all-time. Farther south, **Union Square** is one of the more famous parks in Manhattan, having had several historic rallies and riots as well as being a main subway hub; it is busier than most parks. If you can squeeze yourself into a spot on one of the overflowing park benches, you'll be treated to some entertaining people watching. It's also worth noting for the dog lovers out there that both of these parks have sizable dog parks. And you can stop in at the nearby **Trixie and Peanut** and get your pup a matching Burberry jacket.

W 39th St
W 38th St
W 37th St
W 36th St
W 35th St
W 34th St
W 33rd St
W 32nd St
W 31st St
W 30th St
W 29th St
W 28th St
W 27th St
W 26th St
W 25th St
W 24th St
W 23rd St
W 22nd St
W 21st St
W 20th St
W 19th St
W 18th St
W 17th St
W 16th St
W 15th St
VEHICULAR TRAFFIC PROHIBITED
Herald Square
34th Street Herald Square
34th Street Penn Station
PATH 33rd St
Empire State Building
PAGE 242
PAGE 326
PAGE 303
PAGE 266
J A Farley Post Office
Madison Square Garden
Penn Station
33rd Street
28th Street
23rd Street
18th Street
8th Avenue
14th Street
PATH 23rd St
PATH 14th St
6th Avenue
14th Street-Union Square
Eighth Ave
Seventh Ave (Fashion Ave)
Sixth Ave (Ave of the Americas)
Broadway
Fifth Ave
Madison Ave
Park Ave S
Madison Sq Plz
Madison Square Park
Union Square
1/4 mile
.25 km

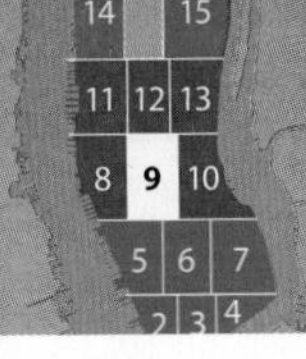

Whether you prefer celebrity sighting at **Raines Law Room**, dress code-mandatory joints like **230 5th**, classic NYC watering holes like **Old Town Bar** and **Peter McManus**, or gulping Guinness at low key Irish pubs like **Dewey's**, you have options. NFT cabaret experts state unequivocally that the **Metropolitan Room** is the best cabaret club in the city.

Bars

- **230 5th** • 230 5th Ave [26th St]
  212-725-4300
  Dress code and overpriced drinks. Best view of NYC makes it worthwhile.
- **Ace Hotel Lobby Bar** •
  20 W 29th St [Broadway]
  212-679-2222
  Amazing cocktails in an amazing space.
- **The Archive** • 12 E 36th St [Madison]
  212-213-0093
  Relaxed, subdued; solid cocktails.
- **Dewey's** • 210 5th Ave [25th St]
  212-696-2337
  Generic, inexpensive and comfortable.
- **Ginger Man** • 11 E 36th St [Madison Ave]
  212-532-3740
  Where button-down midtown types loosen up over bitter beers.
- **Honey** • 243 W 14th St [8th Ave]
  212-620-0222
  He who overcomes the cheese factor shall catch a groove.
- **Hotel Metro Rooftop Bar** •
  45 W 35th St [6th Ave]
  212-279-3535
  Fresh air + beer 14 floors above Manhattan.
- **Lillie's** • 13 E 17th St [5th Ave]
  212-337-1970
  Perfect for anyone with an Irish-Victorian fetish.
- **Limerick House** • 69 W 23rd St [6th Ave]
  212-243-8898
  Friendly bar. Plain and simple.
- **Live Bait** • 14 E 23rd St [Madison Ave]
  212-353-2400
  Still a great feel. A mainstay.
- **Mé Bar** • 17 W 32nd St [Broadway]
  212-290-2460
  Affordable rooftop bar with a kickass view of the ESB.
- **Merchants** • 112 7th Ave [W 17th St]
  212-366-7267
  Good mixed space.
- **Metropolitan Room** • 34 W 22nd St [6th Ave]
  212-206-0440
  Best cabaret club in the city.
- **No Idea Bar** • 30 E 20th St [Broadway]
  212-777-0100
  Very laid back for this part of town. Nice happy hour.
- **Old Town Bar** • 45 E 18th St [Broadway]
  212-529-6732
  Excellent old-NY pub.
- **Peter McManus** • 152 7th Ave [W 19th St]
  212-929-9691
  Refreshingly basic. Gorgeous old phone booths.
- **Raines Law Room** • 48 W 17th St [6th Ave]
  212-242-0600
  Cocktails worth your time. And money.
- **Splash Bar** • 50 W 17th St [6th Ave]
  212-691-0073
  Men dancing in waterfalls.

Movie Theaters

- **AMC Loews 19th St East 6** •
  890 Broadway [E 19th St]
  212-260-8173
  Standard multiplex.
- **Clearview Cinemas Chelsea** •
  260 W 23rd St [8th Ave]
  212-691-5519
  Manhattan's big, comfy, and gay multiplex.

Theaters/Performing Arts

- **29th Street Repertory Theatre** •
  212 W 29th St [7th Ave]
  212-465-0575
  "Where Brutal Theater Lives!"
- **Actor's Theater Workshop** •
  145 W 28th St [6th Ave]
  212-947-1386
  Classics and new plays from an exciting non-profit company.
- **Dance Theatre Workshop** •
  219 W 19th St [7th Ave]
  212-691-6500
  Great contemporary dance since 1965.
- **People's Improv Theater** •
  154 W 29th St [7th Ave]
  212-563-7488
  "The Pit" to all us insiders.
- **TADA! Theater** • 15 W 28th St [Broadway]
  212-252-1619
  Screw Disney; this is where you go for great affordable theatre for kids.

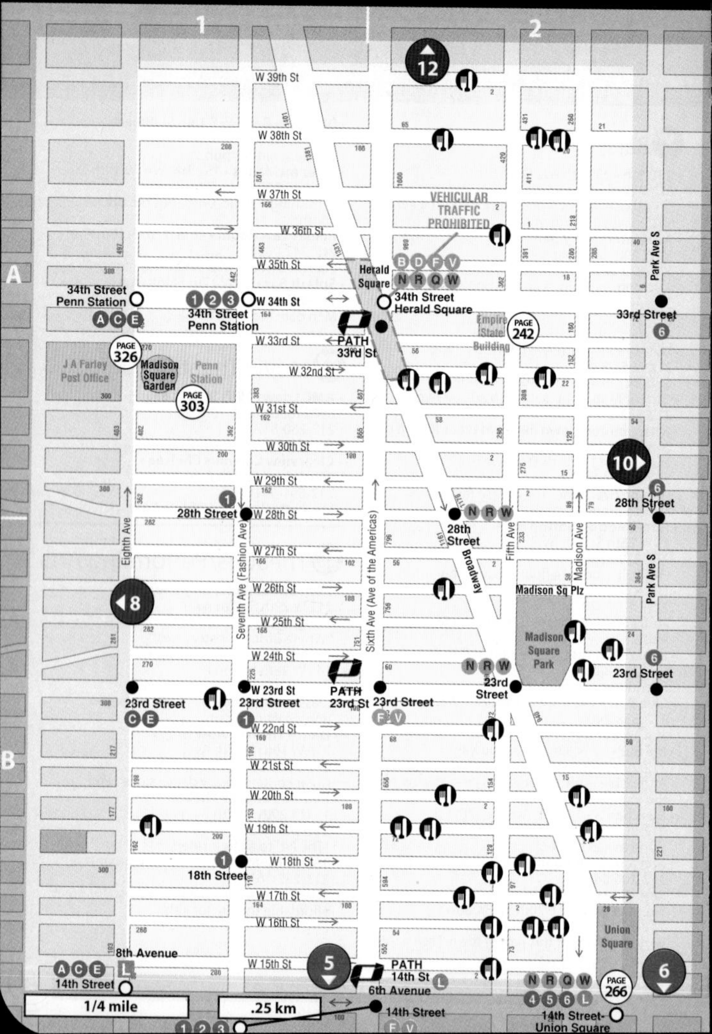

Map 9 • Flatiron / Lower Midtown

W 39th St
W 38th St
W 37th St
W 36th St
W 35th St
W 34th St
W 33rd St
W 32nd St
W 31st St
W 30th St
W 29th St
W 28th St
W 27th St
W 26th St
W 25th St
W 24th St
W 23rd St
W 22nd St
W 21st St
W 20th St
W 19th St
W 18th St
W 17th St
W 16th St
W 15th St

Eighth Ave
Seventh Ave (Fashion Ave)
Sixth Ave (Ave of the Americas)
Broadway
Fifth Ave
Madison Ave
Park Ave S
Madison Sq Plz

VEHICULAR TRAFFIC PROHIBITED
Herald Square
34th Street Herald Square
34th Street Penn Station
PATH 33rd St
Empire State Building
J A Farley Post Office
Madison Square Garden
Penn Station
33rd Street
28th Street
23rd Street
PATH 23rd St
Madison Square Park
18th Street
8th Avenue 14th Street
PATH 14th St
6th Avenue
14th Street
14th Street-Union Square
Union Square

PAGE 326
PAGE 303
PAGE 242
PAGE 266

1/4 mile
.25 km

Impress a date with the size of your wallet at **Gramercy Tavern**, **Tabla**, **Eleven Madison Park**, and NFT-fave **Craft**, or impress them with your wit and conversation over tapas at **Sala19**. Otherwise, hit **City Bakery** for their pretzel croissants, **Eisenberg's** for egg creams, **Dogmatic** for sausages, or **Kang Suh** for all-night Korean BBQ.

Restaurants

- **BLT Fish** • 21 W 17th St [Fifth Ave]
  212-691-8888 • $$$$$
  Downstairs: New England clam shack fare. Upstairs: Highbrow seafood.
- **Boqueria** • 53 W 19th St [Sixth Ave]
  212-255-4160 • $$$
  Cheese-stuffed dates wrapped in bacon? We're there.
- **Butterfield 8** • 5 E 38th St [Fifth Ave]
  212-679-0646 • $$$
  Walnut-paneled Murray Hill American with cool, Hitchcockian cityscape mural.
- **Chat 'n Chew** • 10 E 16th St [Fifth Ave]
  212-243-1616 • $$
  Home cookin'.
- **City Bakery** • 3 W 18th St [Fifth Ave]
  212-366-1414 • $$
  Stellar baked goods.
- **Coffee Shop** • 29 Union Sq W [E 16th St]
  212-243-7969 • $$
  Diner with a samba skew.
- **Craft** • 43 E 19th St [Broadway]
  212-780-0880 • $$$$$
  Outstanding. A top-end place worth the $$$$$.
- **Dogmatic** • 26 E 17th St [Broadway]
  212-414-0600 • $$
  Sausages magically stuffed into a fresh baked baguette.
- **Eisenberg's Sandwich Shop** •
  174 5th Ave [W 22nd St]
  212-675-5096 • $$
  Old-school corned beef and pastrami.
- **Eleven Madison Park** •
  11 Madison Ave [E 24th St]
  212-889-0905 • $$$$$
  Where the elite meet to greet.
- **Evergreen Shanghai Restaurant** •
  10 E 38th St [Fifth Ave]
  212-448-1199 • $
  Their scallion pancakes are worth the wait, and they know it.
- **Gramercy Tavern** • 42 E 20th St [Broadway]
  212-477-0777 • $$$$$
  Expensive, but good, New American.
- **HanGawi** • 12 E 32nd St [Fifth Ave]
  212-213-0077 • $$$$
  Serene, top-end vegetarian Korean.
- **Hill Country** • 30 W 26th St [Broadway]
  212-255-4544 • $$$
  Good ol' Texas 'cue; go for the wet brisket.
- **Kang Suh** • 1250 Broadway [W 32nd St]
  212-564-6845 • $$$
  Late-night Korean. Go for the private rooms.
- **Kunjip** • 9 W 32nd St [Broadway]
  212-216-9487 • $$
  The best Korean food in Manhattan; try the Bo Saam!
- **Olympic Pita** • 58 W 38th St [6th Ave]
  212-869-7482 • $
  Scrumptious shawarma.
- **Periyali** • 35 W 20th St [Fifth Ave]
  212-463-7890 • $$$$
  Upscale Greek. Pretty damned great.
- **RUB BBQ** • 208 W 23rd St [Seventh Ave]
  212-524-4300 • $$$
  Smokin' 'cue from Kansas pit master Paul Kirk.
- **Sala One Nine** • 35 W 19th St [6th ave]
  212-229-2300 • $$
  Garlic on everything, bring breathmints. Must try: Filet Mignon sandwich.
- **Seoul Garden** • 34 W 32nd St [Broadway]
  212-736-9002 • $$
  The soon tofu soup hits the spot.
- **Shake Shack** • 11 Madison Ave [E 23rd St]
  212-889-6600 • $
  Enjoy homemade shakes 'n burgers in the park. On a two-hour line.
- **Socarrat** • 259 W 19th St [8th Ave]
  212-462-1000 • $$$
  Authentic Paella feast, sit next to the Spaniards at the communal table.
- **Szechuan Gourmet** • 21 W 39th St [6th Ave]
  212-921-0233 • $$$
  Amazing Chinese in this part of the city? Believe it.
- **Tabla** • 11 Madison Ave [E 24th St]
  212-889-0667 • $$$$$
  Inventive Indian-inspired American. Recommended.
- **Tarallucci E Vino** • 15 E 18th St [5th Ave]
  212-228-5400 • $$
  Espresso in the morning, wine after work. Delicious and versatile.
- **Tocqueville** • 1 E 15th St [Fifth Ave]
  212-647-1515 • $$$$$
  Lovely everything—and you can actually hear each other speak!
- **Union Square Café** • 21 E 16th St [Union Sq W]
  212-243-4020 • $$$$$
  Someday we'll get in and like it.
- **Woo Chon** • 8 W 36th St [Fifth Ave]
  212-695-0676 • $$$
  All-night Korean. What could be better?

W 39th St
W 38th St
W 37th St
W 36th St
W 35th St
W 34th St
W 33rd St
W 32nd St
W 31st St
W 30th St
W 29th St
W 28th St
W 27th St
W 26th St
W 25th St
W 24th St
W 23rd St
W 22nd St
W 21st St
W 20th St
W 19th St
W 18th St
W 17th St
W 16th St
W 15th St
VEHICULAR TRAFFIC PROHIBITED
Herald Square
34th Street Herald Square
34th Street Penn Station
PATH 33rd St
Empire State Building
PAGE 242
PAGE 326
PAGE 303
PAGE 266
J A Farley Post Office
Madison Square Garden
Penn Station
33rd Street
28th Street
23rd Street
18th Street
Eighth Ave
Seventh Ave (Fashion Ave)
Sixth Ave (Ave of the Americas)
Broadway
Fifth Ave
Madison Ave
Park Ave S
Madison Sq Plz
Madison Square Park
PATH 23rd St
8th Avenue
14th Street
PATH 14th St
6th Avenue
Union Square
14th Street-Union Square
1/4 mile
.25 km

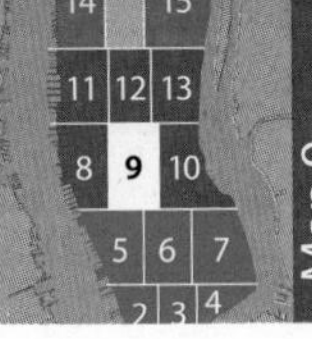

Need sporting goods? **Paragon** is the paragon of sporting goods stores (and a place to get tennis permits). **30th Street Guitars** and **Rogue Music** will rock your world. **Yamak** is a boutique alternative to the complete cluster-f*** of people that is **Macy's. Idlewild** is one of New York's finest bookshops, specializing in travel and literature.

Coffee

- **Café Grumpy** • 224 W 20th St [7th Ave]
  212-255-5511
  Best coffee on the island.
- **Culture Espresso** • 70 W 38th St [6th Ave]
  212-302-0200
  They serve Intelligentsia espresso? We're there.
- **Stumptown Coffee** • 18 W 29th St [Broadway]
  212-679-2222
  The real deal straight outta Portland.
- **Tbsp** • 17 W 20th St [5th Ave]
  646-230-7000
  Serving up Stumptown beans—coffee of the gods.

Shopping

- **30th Street Guitars** • 236 W 30th St [7th Ave]
  212-868-2660
  Axe heaven. Seriously.
- **ABC Carpet & Home** • 888 Broadway [19th St]
  212-473-3000
  A NYC institution for chic, even exotic, home décor and design.
- **Abracadabra** • 19 W 21st St [5th Ave]
  212-627-7523
  Magic, masks, costumes—presto!
- **Academy Records** • 12 W 18th St [5th Ave]
  212-242-3000
  Top Jazz/Classical mecca.
- **Adorama Camera** • 42 W 18th St [5th Ave]
  212-741-0052
  Good camera alternative to B&H. Still closed Saturdays, though.
- **Al Friedman** • 44 W 18th St [5th Ave]
  212-243-9000
  Art supplies, frames, office furniture, and more.
- **Ariston** • 110 W 17th St [6th Ave]
  212-929-4226
  Excellent florist with orchids as well.
- **Books of Wonder** • 18 W 18th St [5th Ave]
  212-989-3270
  Top NYC children's bookstore, always has signed copies around, too.
- **The Container Store** • 629 6th Ave [W 19th St]
  212-366-4200
  Organize your closet…and your life!
- **Fishs Eddy** • 889 Broadway [19th St]
  212-420-9020
  Bizarre dishes to complete your cool abode.
- **Idlewild Books** • 12 W 19th St [5th Ave]
  212-414-8888
  One of the best travel + literature bookstores on the planet.
- **Jazz Record Center** • 236 W 26th St [7th Ave]
  212-675-4480
  All that jazz!
- **Lush Cosmetics** • 1293 Broadway [W 33rd St]
  212-564-9120
  Fresh handmade cosmetics.
- **M&J Trimmings** • 1008 6th Ave [W 38th St]
  212-204-9595
  For your DIY sewing projects.
- **Macy's** • 151 W 34th St [7th Ave]
  212-695-4400
  Love the wooden escalators.
- **Mandler's** • 26 E 17th St [Broadway]
  212-255-8999
  Sausage emporium.
- **Muji Chelsea** • 16 W 19th St [5th Ave]
  212-414-9024
  Beautiful Japanese aesthetic applied to daily living.
- **NYC Racquet Sports** • 157 W 35th St [7th Ave]
  212-695-5353
  Serious tennis supplies.
- **Paragon Sporting Goods** •
  867 Broadway [E 18th St]
  212-255-8036
  Top NYC sporting goods store, plus tennis permits!
- **Rogue Music** • 220 W 30th St [7th Ave]
  212-629-5073
  Used equipment you probably still can't afford.
- **Sound by Singer** • 18 E 16th St [5th Ave]
  212-924-8600
  High end audio and video. And we mean "high-end."
- **Tekserve** • 119 W 23rd St [6th Ave]
  212-929-3645
  Apple computer sales and repairs.
- **Trixie and Peanut** • 23 E 20th St [Broadway]
  212-358-0881
  The "Nordstrom" of the dog world.
- **Whole Foods** • 250 7th Ave [W 24th St]
  212-924-5969
  Healthy shopping of the gayborhood.
- **Yamak** • 6 W 23rd St [5th Ave]
  212-255-7771
  Unique clothing/jewelry from Japan/Europe.

Map 10 • Murray Hill / Gramercy

1
2
13
E 39th St
E 38th St
Second Ave
Tunnel Approach St
Tunnel Exit St
E 37th St
Queens Midtown Tunnel
E 36th St
Sniffen Court
Sniffen Ct
St. Vartan Park
E 35th St
E 34th St
A
33rd Street
6
E 33rd St
E 32nd St
Kips Bay Plaza
NYU Medical Center
East River
E 31st St
Park Ave S
Lexington Ave
Third Ave
E 30th St
Second Ave
First Ave
E 29th St
Curry Hill
E 28th St
28th Street
6
Bellevue Hospital Center
E 27th St
Broadway Aly
9
E 26th St
69th Armory
Waterside Plaza
Baruch College
E 25th St
Vet Adm Medical Center
Asser Levy Pl
E 24th St
E 23rd St
Marina & Skyport
23rd Street
6
Protestant Welfare Agencies Building
201
E 22nd St
FDR Dr
Marginal St
Mayor James Harper Residence
B
E 21st St
Peter Cooper Village
Gramercy Park
National Arts Club
The Players
E 20th St
E 19th St
Pete's Tavern
Irving Pl
Tammany Hall/ Union Sq Theater
E 18th St
E 17th St
Stuyvesant Town
Union Square
Union Sq E
Friends Meeting House
E 16th St
Rutherford Pl
Stuyvesant Square
Nathan D Perlman Pl
E 16th St
Avenue C
E 16th St
PAGE 266
4 5 6 L
N R Q W
14th Street-Union Square
6
E 15th St
L
L
7
E 15th St
3rd Avenue
1st Avenue
E 14th St
1/4 mile
.25 km

The Murray Hill/Gramercy area of New York is one of New York's largest studies in contrast. On one hand, there are massive housing and hospital complexes that take up several city blocks; on the other hand, there are narrow alleys and small, gated parks of unparalleled beauty. Add it all together and we get (ho-hum) just another brilliant slice of New York.

Murray Hill's contrast, for instance, can be found by checking out lovely little **Sniffen Court**, one's of Manhattan's finest residential alleys, and then walking south to teeming **Kips Bay Plaza**, a set of two parallel housing towers designed by I.M. Pei. Or by watching kids play in **St. Vartan's Park**, then walking south on First Avenue to gaze at the humongous **NYU** and **Bellevue Medical Centers** (by which point, the "hill" portion of Murray Hill has evaporated). For the hill itself, head to Park Avenue and Lexington Avenue in the upper 30s--from there, you can get a sense of why this area is so-named (our unofficial guess is that Park Avenue and 38th Street is about the highest point in these parts). Then walk the side streets in the East 30s to see some really prime real estate, as well as consulates, hotels, and lots of other stuff you can't afford.

Moving south from Murray Hill, the neighborhood changes rather dramatically in the East 20s. You first encounter **"Curry Hill"** on Lexington Avenue in the upper 20s, a fantastic strip of Indian restaurants and groceries. Two large landmarks, one old and one new, punctuate the southern end of this strip—the looming brickwork of the **69th Armory**, now home to many special events throughout the year, and then **Baruch College's** postmodern new main building just south of there (architects like to call this type of building a "vertical campus;" what that means is a 15-minute wait for an elevator between classes). Baruch is joined in this area by two other schools of note, the **School of Visual Arts** and NYU's **Dental School**, both on East 23rd Street.

The area changes again south of 23rd Street, becoming one of New York's loveliest residential neighborhoods, Gramercy Park. The park itself is gated, controlled and only accessed by those who actually live around it. For the rest of us, we'll just need to be content with looking in at the park through its wrought-iron gates and staring at incredible period architecture facing the park. Our favorite three examples of this architecture are the **Mayor James Harper Residence** on the west side of the park, and the **Players** and **National Arts Clubs** on the southwestern side of the park. Then stroll down hidden Irving Place, a six-block long stretch of restaurants and nightlife options which dead-ends at 14th Street. Classic watering hole **Pete's Tavern**, where writer O. Henry drank, is a must-stop on this walk.

But the aforementioned contrast is still alive and kicking down here, because a few blocks to the east of warm, intimate Gramercy are the hulking **Stuyvesant Town** and Peter Cooper Village housing complexes, which together comprise over 11,000 residential units. Controversy has marked these two huge complexes for the past several years, as longtime owner Met Life spurned a (lower) offer from a tenant's group to buy the complex, instead selling to Tishman Speyer for $5.4 billion in 2006. It was the largest single sale of American property, which, now thanks to a deflated housing market, is now undoubtedly the largest property fiasco in American history (since Tishman had to turn over the property to its creditors to avoid bankruptcy). For us: no thanks, we'll stick with our Brooklyn walk-ups, and just visit.

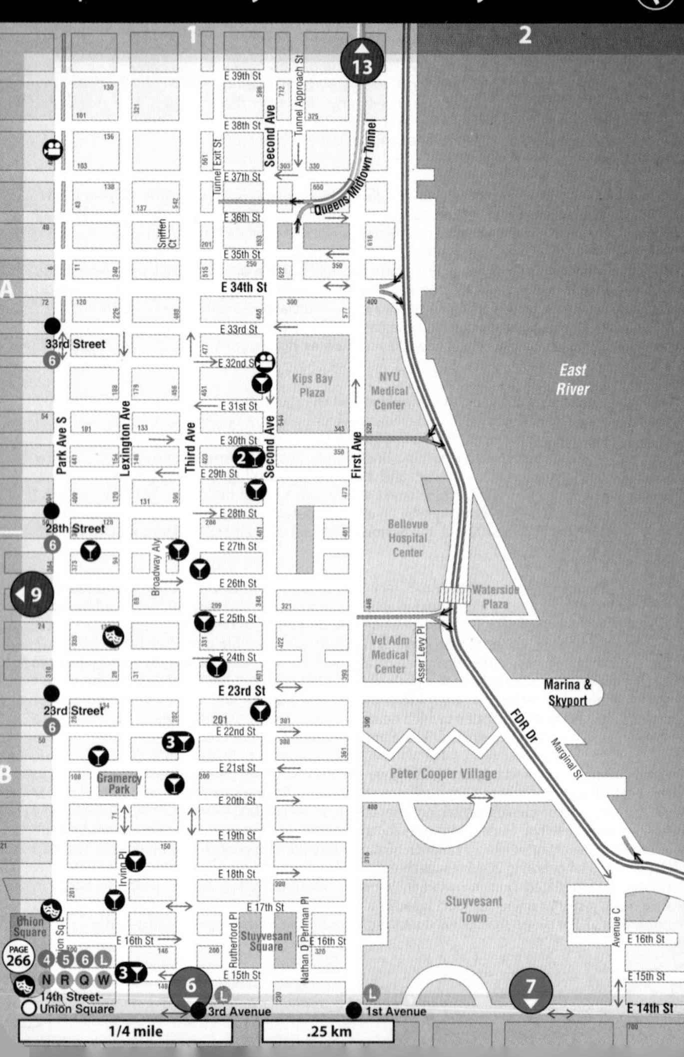
1
2
13
A
B
E 39th St
E 38th St
E 37th St
E 36th St
E 35th St
E 34th St
E 33rd St
E 32nd St
E 31st St
E 30th St
E 29th St
E 28th St
E 27th St
E 26th St
E 25th St
E 24th St
E 23rd St
E 22nd St
E 21st St
E 20th St
E 19th St
E 18th St
E 17th St
E 16th St
E 15th St
E 14th St
Tunnel Approach St
Tunnel Exit St
Queens Midtown Tunnel
Second Ave
Third Ave
Lexington Ave
Park Ave S
First Ave
Sniffen Ct
Broadway Aly
Irving Pl
Rutherford Pl
Nathan D Perlman Pl
Asser Levy Pl
Avenue C
FDR Dr
Marginal St
33rd Street
28th Street
23rd Street
Kips Bay Plaza
NYU Medical Center
Bellevue Hospital Center
Waterside Plaza
Vet Adm Medical Center
Marina & Skyport
Peter Cooper Village
Stuyvesant Town
Gramercy Park
Stuyvesant Square
Union Square
East River
9
6
7
PAGE 266
14th Street-Union Square
3rd Avenue
1st Avenue
1/4 mile
.25 km

Irish pubs abound in this neighborhood, and all of them (**Failte**, **Molly's**, **Paddy Reilly's**, **Rocky Sullivan's**) have their devotees. We prefer dive bars **McSwiggan's**, **119 Bar**, or **Whiskey River**, live music venues **The Fillmore at Irving Plaza**, **Rodeo Bar**, or the **Jazz Standard**, and (of course!) classic watering hole **Pete's Tavern**.

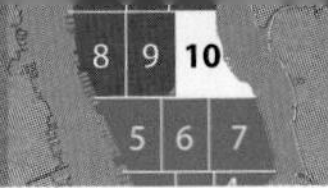

 Bars

- **119 Bar** • 119 E 15th St [Irving Pl]
  212-777-6158
  A dirty little dive right where you'd least expect it.
- **Bar Jamon** • 125 E 17th St [Irving Pl]
  212-253-2773
  Pig out at this wine bar.
- **Belmont Lounge** • 117 E 15th St [Irving Pl]
  212-533-0009
  Be seen.
- **Black Bear Lodge** • 274 3rd Ave [22nd St]
  212-253-2178
  Get a bucket of PBRs for $15.
- **Failte Irish Whiskey Bar** •
  531 2nd Ave [E 29th St]
  212-725-9440
  Sip Guiness by the fire. Shoot a round of pool. A favorite of Irish Ex-pats.
- **The Fillmore New York at Irving Plaza** •
  17 Irving Pl [E 15th St]
  212-777-6800
  Staple rock venue.
- **Hairy Monk** • 337 3rd Ave [E 25th St]
  212-532-2929
  Best place to harass a Red Sox fan.
- **The Jazz Standard** • 116 E 27th St [Lexington]
  212-576-2232
  Solid shows. BBQ upstairs!
- **McCormack's** • 365 3rd Ave [E 27th St]
  212-683-0911
  Good spot to watch World Cup action here. Food a bonus.
- **McSwiggan's** • 393 2nd Ave [E 23rd St]
  212-683-3180
  One of the best dive bars on the island.
- **Molly's** • 287 3rd Ave [E 22nd St]
  212-889-3361
  Great Irish pub with a fireplace.
- **New York Comedy Club** •
  241 E 24th St [3rd Ave]
  212-696-5233
  ...and the bartender asks, "where did you get that?"
- **Paddy Reilly's Music Bar** •
  519 2nd Ave [E 29th St]
  212-686-1210
  Sunday night means pints of Guinness and live Irish fiddlin'.
- **Pete's Tavern** • 129 E 18th St [Irving Pl]
  212-473-7676
  Where O Henry hung out. And so should you, at least once.
- **Plug Uglies** • 257 3rd Ave [E 20th St]
  212-780-1944
  Full length shuffle board table!
- **Rodeo** • 375 3rd Ave [E 27th St]
  212-683-6500
  As close to a honky-tonk as you'll get, partner.
- **Rolf's** • 281 3rd Ave [E 22nd St]
  212-477-4750
  December holiday visit is a must for some German bier.
- **Rose Bar** • 2 Lexington Ave [E 21st St]
  212-920-3300
  Another classy hotel bar NFT can't afford.
- **Waterfront Ale House** • 540 2nd Ave [30th St]
  212-696-4104
  Decent local vibe.
- **Whiskey River** • 575 2nd Ave [E 32nd St]
  212-679-6799
  Dive bar. Neighborhood joint. Great beer selection.

Movie Theaters

- **AMC Loews Kips Bay 15** • 570 2nd Ave [31st St]
  212-447-0638
  This multiplex is starting to show its age.
- **The Scandinavia House** • 58 Park Ave [38th St]
  212-879-9779
  Scandinavian movies. Bergman and beyond.

Theaters/Performing Arts

- **Baruch Performing Arts Center** •
  55 Lexington Ave [E 25th St]
  646-312-4085
  Leave a trail of bread crumbs to find your way out.
- **Daryl Roth Theatre** • 101 E 15th St [Park Ave S]
  212-239-6200
  Used to be a bank; now loses money with theatre.
- **Union Square Theater** •
  100 E 17th St [Park Ave S]
  212-307-4100
  The former site of Tammany Hall.

1
2
13
A
B
E 39th St
E 38th St
E 37th St
E 36th St
E 35th St
E 34th St
E 33rd St
E 32nd St
E 31st St
E 30th St
E 29th St
E 28th St
E 27th St
E 26th St
E 25th St
E 24th St
E 23rd St
E 22nd St
E 21st St
E 20th St
E 19th St
E 18th St
E 17th St
E 16th St
E 15th St
E 14th St
Second Ave
Tunnel Approach St
Tunnel Exit St
Queens Midtown Tunnel
Sniffen Ct
33rd Street
28th Street
23rd Street
Park Ave S
Lexington Ave
Third Ave
First Ave
Broadway Aly
Kips Bay Plaza
NYU Medical Center
Bellevue Hospital Center
Waterside Plaza
Vet Adm Medical Center
Asser Levy Pl
Marina & Skyport
FDR Dr
Marginal St
Peter Cooper Village
Stuyvesant Town
East River
Gramercy Park
Irving Pl
Union Square
Union Sq E
Rutherford Pl
Stuyvesant Square
Nathan D Perlman Pl
Avenue C
PAGE 266
14th Street-Union Square
3rd Avenue
1st Avenue
9
6
7
1/4 mile
.25 km

Everyone has their Curry Hill favorite; ours is vegetarian dosa house **Pongal**. If you're into meat, upscale burger joint **Rare** or steakhouses **Angelo & Maxie's** or **BLT Prime** will make you smile. Good Vietnamese (**L'annam**) and Thai (**Jaiya Thai**) can be found, but the sleeper pick here is **Turkish Kitchen**, our favorite Turkish in all of New York.

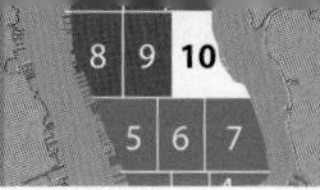

Restaurants

- **Angelo & Maxie's** • 233 Park Ave S [E 19th St]
  212-220-9200 • $$$
  Excellent steaks, burgers, etc.
- **Baoguette** • 61 Lexington Ave [E 25th St]
  212-532-1133 • $
  Gourmet sandwiches like catfish and sloppy bao.
- **BLT Prime** • 111 E 22nd St [Park Ave S]
  212-995-8500 • $$$$$
  Steakhouse with Craft-like, a-la-carte sides.
- **Butai** • 115 E 18th St [Irving Pl]
  212-387-8885 • $$$
  Impressive Japanese cuisine.
- **Carl's Steaks** • 507 3rd Ave [E 34th St]
  212-696-5336 • $
  Cheesesteaks, chickensteaks, and chili fries.
- **Chennai Garden** • 129 E 27th St [Lexington]
  212-689-1999 • $$
  Indian food that happens to be vegetarian, kosher, and very tasty.
- **Chinese Mirch** • 120 Lexington Ave [E 28th St]
  212-532-3663 • $$$
  Fiery Chinese food by way of Mumbai.
- **Curry Leaf** • 99 Lexington Ave [E 27th St]
  212-725-5558 • $$$
  Best basic Indian.
- **Defonte's of Brooklyn** •
  261 3rd Ave [E 21st St]
  212-614-1500 • $$
  Legendary Brooklyn sandwich takes Manhattan.
- **El Parador Café** • 325 E 34th St [2nd Ave]
  212-679-6812 • $$$
  NY's oldest and friendliest Mexican.
- **Gramercy Cafe** • 184 3rd Ave [E 17th St]
  212-982-2121 • $$
  Open 24 hours. Diner. You know the drill.
- **Haandi** • 113 Lexington Ave [E 28th St]
  212-685-5200 • $$
  Stellar Pakistani grilled meats.
- **I Trulli** • 122 E 27th St [Lexington Ave]
  212-481-7372 • $$$$$
  Italian. Great garden.
- **Jaiya Thai** • 396 3rd Ave [E 28th St]
  212-889-1330 • $$$
  Inventive, spicy Thai.
- **L'annam** • 393 3rd Ave [E 28th St]
  212-686-5168 • $$
  Cheap and quick Vietnamese, good—but not for serious enthusiasts.
- **L'Express** • 249 Park Ave S [E 20th St]
  212-254-5858 • $$
  Always-open French diner.
- **La Posada** • 364 3rd Ave [E 26th St]
  212-213-4379 • $
  Authentic Mexican burritos, tacos and enchiladas.
- **Les Halles** • 411 Park Ave S [E 29th St]
  212-679-4111 • $$$
  The original. Steak frites and French vibe.
- **Maoz** • 38 Union Square E [E 16th St]
  212-260-1988 • $
  Cheap and tasty falafel take-out chain from Amsterdam.
- **Mexico Lindo** • 459 2nd Ave [E 26th St]
  212-679-3665 • $$$
  Famous Mexican food.
- **Penelope** • 159 Lexington Ave [E 30th St]
  212-481-3800 • $$
  Gingham décor but oh, what a menu!
- **Pongal** • 110 Lexington Ave [E 28th St]
  212-696-9458 • $$
  Possibly NY's best vegetarian Indian. Sada dosa…mmmm.
- **Pongsri Thai** • 311 2nd Ave [E 18th St]
  212-477-4100 • $$
  Great, spicy Thai. Get the jungle curry.
- **Posto** • 310 2nd Ave [E 18th St]
  212-716-1200 • $$
  Savory thin-crust pizza, salads.
- **Rare Bar & Grill** •
  303 Lexington Ave [E 37th St]
  212-481-1999 • $$$
  Should be better, given the focus. We're divided on this one.
- **Resto** • 111 E 29th St [Park Ave S]
  212-685-5585 • $$
  Belgian gastropub that's pretty darn great.
- **Tiffin Wallah** • 127 E 28th St [Lexington Ave]
  212-685-7301 • $
  Veggie lunch buffet for a few bucks.
- **Turkish Kitchen** • 386 3rd Ave [E 28th St]
  212-679-6633 • $$$
  Excellent Turkish, great décor, brilliant bread. NFT pick!
- **The Water Club** • FDR Drive & E 30th St
  212-683-3333 • $$$$
  Romantic, good brunch on the East River.

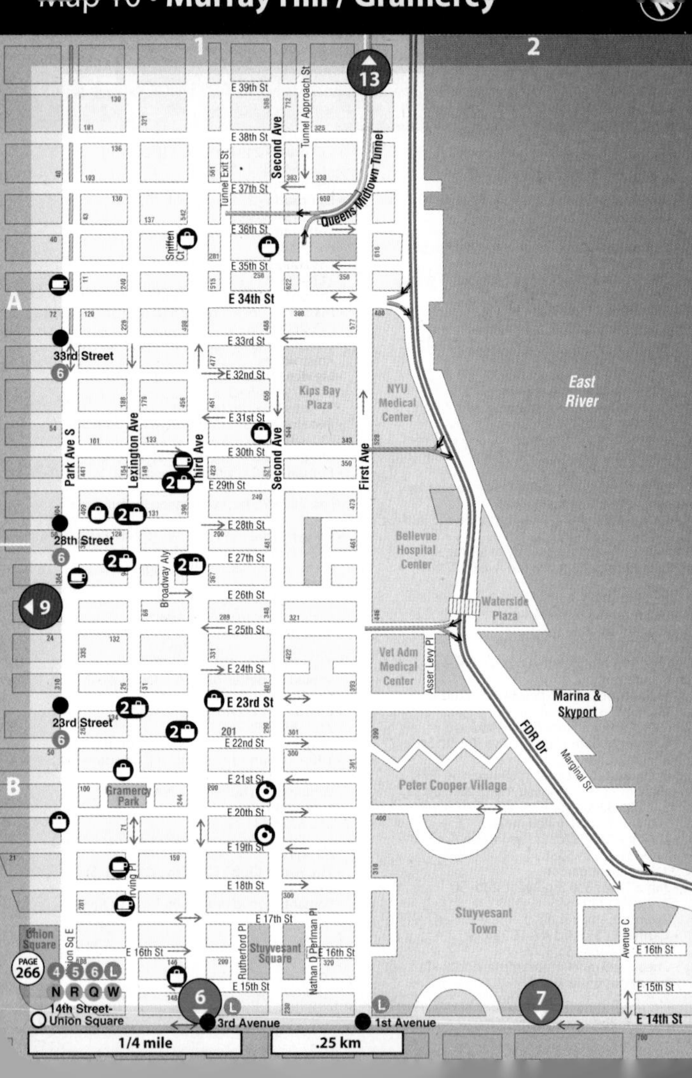

E 39th St
E 38th St
E 37th St
E 36th St
E 35th St
E 34th St
E 33rd St
E 32nd St
E 31st St
E 30th St
E 29th St
E 28th St
E 27th St
E 26th St
E 25th St
E 24th St
E 23rd St
E 22nd St
E 21st St
E 20th St
E 19th St
E 18th St
E 17th St
E 16th St
E 15th St
E 14th St
Second Ave
Tunnel Approach St
Tunnel Exit St
Queens Midtown Tunnel
Sniffen Ct
33rd Street
28th Street
23rd Street
Park Ave S
Lexington Ave
Third Ave
First Ave
Kips Bay Plaza
NYU Medical Center
Bellevue Hospital Center
Waterside Plaza
Vet Adm Medical Center
Asser Levy Pl
Marina & Skyport
FDR Dr
Marginal St
East River
Broadway Aly
Gramercy Park
Irving Pl
Peter Cooper Village
Stuyvesant Town
Union Square
Union Sq E
Rutherford Pl
Stuyvesant Square
Nathan D Perlman Pl
Avenue C
PAGE 266
14th Street-Union Square
3rd Avenue
1st Avenue
1/4 mile
.25 km

Bagels, Coffee, & Shopping

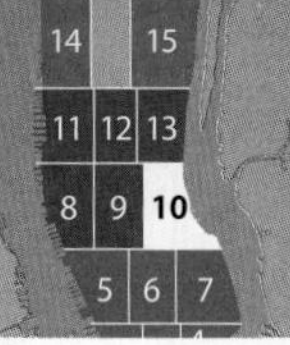

Hit either **Lamarca** or **Lamazou** cheese shops to go along with pastries from **La Delice**. Indian shops **Kenara**, **Kalustyan's**, **Foods of India**, and **Om Sari Palace** are always worth a look. **Jam** will have any envelope you could ever need and **Nuthouse Hardware** is New York's only 24-hour hardware store, with power tool rentals. Cool.

Bagels

- **David's Bagels** • 331 1st Ave [E 19th St]
  212-780-2308
  Hands-down best NYC bagel. Try to argue.
- **Ess-A-Bagel** • 359 1st Ave [E 21st St]
  212-260-2252
  Bagels (and service) with attitude.

Coffee

- **71 Irving** • 71 Irving Pl [E 19th St]
  212-995-5252
  Brilliant coffee.
- **Fika** • 407 Park Ave S [28th St]
  646-649-5133
  Swedish coffee is really great. Seriously!
- **Franchia Teahouse & Restaurant** •
  12 Park Ave [E 35th St]
  212-213-1001
  Modern Korean tea and treats.
- **Lady Mendl's Tea Salon** • 56 Irving Pl [17th St]
  212-533-4600
  It's tea time for the ladies of Manhattan.
- **Oren's Daily Roast** • 434 3rd Ave [E 30th St]
  212-779-1241
  Hip staff pours superior java at local mini-chain.

Shopping

- **City Opera Thrift Shop** • 222 E 23rd St [3rd Ave]
  212-684-5344
  They always have something or other.
- **DaVinci Artist Supply** •
  137 E 23rd St [Lexington Ave]
  212-982-8607
  Discounts to students, teachers, and art professionals.
- **Foods of India** • 121 Lexington Ave [E 28th St]
  212-683-4419
  Huge selection including harder-to-find spices.
- **Homefront Kids/Kids Cuts** •
  202 E 29th St [3rd Ave]
  212-381-1966
  Clothes, furniture, toys, gifts, haircuts, free gift wrap.
- **Housing Works Thrift Shop** •
  157 E 23rd St [Lexington Ave]
  212-529-5955
  Our favorite thrift store.
- **Jam Paper & Envelope** • 135 3rd Ave [15th St]
  212-473-6666
  And…the envelope, please.
- **Kalustyan's** • 123 Lexington Ave [E 28th St]
  212-685-3451
  Indian specialty foods.
- **Kenara Paan Shop** • 134 E 27th St [Lexington]
  212-481-1660
  Make like a cabbie and give paan a try.
- **La Delice Pastry Shop** • 372 3rd Ave [27th St]
  212-532-4409
  Delectable pastries, buttery croissants, layer cakes.
- **Lamarca Cheese Shop** •
  161 E 22nd St [3rd Ave]
  212-673-7920
  Italian culinary goodies.
- **Lamazou Cheese** • 370 3rd Ave [E 27th St]
  212-532-2009
  Great selection of cheese and gourmet products.
- **Ligne Roset** • 250 Park Ave S [E 20th St]
  212-375-1036
  Modern, sleek furniture. Only for people with very good jobs.
- **Max Nass Inc.** • 118 E 28th St [Lexington Ave]
  212-679-8154
  Vintage jewelry., repairs, restringing, and restoration.
- **Nemo Tile Company** • 48 E 21st St [Broadway]
  212-505-0009
  Good tile shop for small projects.
- **Nuthouse Hardware** • 202 E 29th St [3rd Ave]
  212-545-1447
  Open 24-hours; equipment rentals, too.
- **Om Sari Palace** • 134 E 27th St [Lexington]
  212-532-5620
  Saris, bangles, earrings, sandals and accessories.
- **Pookie & Sebastian** • 541 3rd Ave [E 36th St]
  212-951-7110
  Murray Hill outpost for fun, flirty, girly garb.
- **Shambhala** • 655 2nd Ave [E 36th St]
  212-213-2001
  Hand-crafted jewelry, coffee and empanadas.
- **Todaro Bros** • 555 2nd Ave [E 30th]
  212-532-0633
  Home made mozzeralla, pastas, high quality groceries.
- **Vintage Thrift Shop** • 286 3rd Ave [E 22nd St]
  212-871-0777
  Vintage clothes you can actually afford.

1
2
A
B

W 60th St
W 59th St
W 58th St
W 57th St
W 56th St
W 55th St
W 54th St
W 53rd St
W 52nd St
W 51st St
W 50th St
W 49th St
W 48th St
W 47th St
W 46th St
W 45th St
W 44th St
W 43rd St
W 42nd St
W 41st St
W 40th St
W 39th St
W 38th St
W 37th ST

Henry Hudson Pkwy
West Side Hwy
Hudson River Park
Eleventh Ave
Tenth Ave
Ninth Ave
Eighth Ave
Dyer Ave

Hudson River

Time Warner Center
Columbus Circle
59th Street Columbus Circle
Dewitt Clinton Park
Daily Show Studio
50th Street
Intrepid Sea, Air and Space Museum
Restaurant Row
Broadway Dance Center
42nd Street Port Authority Bus Terminal
Theatre Row
Port Authority Bus Terminal
The Annex/ Hell's Kitchen Flea Market
Lincoln Tunnel
Jacob K Javits Convention Center

PAGE 248
PAGE 244
PAGE 306
PAGE 246
14
12
8

1/4 mile
.25 km

Neighboorhood Overview

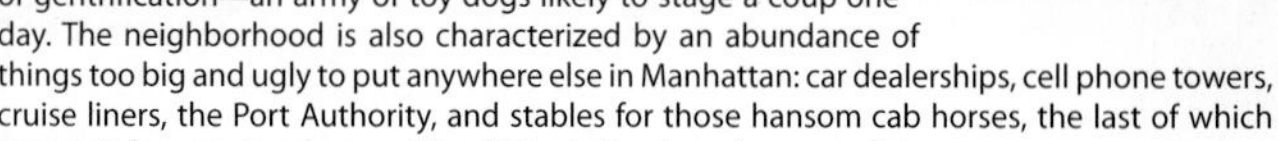

This scruffy patch of bodega-infused real estate between Broadway and that unlikely landing strip known as the Hudson is home to intimate theaters, niche restaurants and—along with a rising tide of gentrification—an army of toy dogs likely to stage a coup one day. The neighborhood is also characterized by an abundance of things too big and ugly to put anywhere else in Manhattan: car dealerships, cell phone towers, cruise liners, the Port Authority, and stables for those hansom cab horses, the last of which accounts for certain odors and the distinct clip-clop of every rush hour.

It's also farther west than the subways venture, harshly industrial looking and often beset by Lincoln Tunnel traffic or gale-force nautical winds. Yes, Hell's Kitchen may seem like the edge of the civilized world, and the panoramic view of New Jersey does little to dampen this grungy impression. Yet most locals come to cherish the mellow vibe and dearth of McDonald's locations that come with living just outside Manhattan's hyperkinetic and tourist-infested core. Here you'll have no trouble hailing a cab, or getting the bartender's attention. And as for the out-of-towners—well, they only get as far in as Ninth Avenue before their legs get tired.

Hell's Kitchen may be close to Central Park, but why fight the crowds? Instead explore Hudson River Park, an elegantly sculpted swath of greenery running along the coast of the island. Its linearity makes for ideal bikers and joggers, but the idle will find plenty of lovely spots to spread a picnic blanket and watch lunatics paddle by in kayaks. **Dewitt Clinton Park** always has an entertaining game going on its baseball/soccer/everything field; it also boasts two popular dog runs for the bonding of canines and their owners alike. Community gardens have sprung up there and close by, thanks to green-thumbed volunteers from the area.

Two entertainment elements to absorb: one you find on stage, and the other you find on the end of a fork—usually in that order. The former is available at one of the countless Off and Off-Off-Broadway theatres lying around—you know, the type that aren't showing something along the lines of "A Musical Loosely Cobbled Together From A String Of #1 Hit Singles"? **Theatre Row** is, as the name suggests, a lineup of such venues featuring, ahem, riskier fare—though perhaps not as scandalous as the peepshows that once littered that stretch of 42nd Street. Satirical mainstays **The Daily Show** and The Colbert Report also tape around here, if you're looking for entertainment that's as free as it is hilarious. Head up to **Restaurant Row** on 46th to sample one of the cozy eateries and candlelit nightlife nooks that cater to audiences after the curtain falls. Almost every type of food is accounted for, and authenticity is the rule—don't be surprised to find actual French people eating at a French bistro!

Hell's Kitchen is a great place to shop because mom-and-pop places have proved resilient—everything from artisanal bread to custom-made paints can be got at tiny stores run by devoted experts. You might even see an old-school coffee shop without so much as a name on a sign out front. But the best spot for browsing is: the **Hell's Kitchen Flea Market**, nestled between bus ramps on 39th Street, offers outdoor bargain-hunting on summer weekends. The usual gridlock is traded for a bazaar of vintage clothing, jewelry and collectibles, most priced a bit cheaper than they were before these particular vendors moved from a Chelsea location known as The Annex.

1
2
A
B
W 60th St
W 59th St
W 58th St
W 57th St
W 56th St
W 55th St
W 54th St
W 53rd St
W 52nd St
W 51st St
W 50th St
W 49th St
W 48th St
W 47th St
W 46th St
W 45th St
W 44th St
W 43rd St
W 42nd St
W 41st St
W 40th St
W 39th St
W 38th St
W 37th ST
HENRY HUDSON PKWY
West Side Hwy
Hudson River Park
Eleventh Ave
Tenth Ave
Ninth Ave
Eighth Ave
Dyer Ave
Hudson River
Dewitt Clinton Park
Time Warner Center
Columbus Circle
59th Street Columbus Circle
50th Street
42nd Street Port Authority Bus Terminal
Port Authority Bus Terminal
Lincoln Tunnel
Jacob K Javits Convention Center
PAGE 248
PAGE 244
PAGE 306
PAGE 246
14
12
8
1/4 mile
.25 km

Land of contrast: there's the swanky **Fusion**, with knockout girly drinks and an outdoor garden—and then there's an utter dive like **Rudy's Bar & Grill**, which serves each beer with a free hot dog. Elsewhere, you've got a decadent club-style concert venue and legendary smoker's roof in **Terminal 5**.

Bars

- **Bar Centrale** • 324 W 46th St [8th Ave]
  212-581-3130
  Make reservations to see Broadway stars relaxing after the show.
- **Birdland** • 315 W 44th St [Eighth Ave]
  212-581-3080
  Top-notch jazz.
- **Blue Ruin** • 538 9th Ave [W 40th St]
  917-945-3497
  Pressed tin ceiling and lots of booze.
- **Don't Tell Mama** • 343 W 46th St [8th Ave]
  212-757-0788
  Good cabaret space.
- **Fusion** • 818 10th Ave [54th Street]
  212-397-1133
  Slick lounge with potent girly drinks.
- **Holland Cocktail Lounge** •
  532 9th Ave [40th St]
  212-502-4609
  One of the last great dives of New York.
- **House of Brews** • 363 W 46th St [9th Ave]
  212-245-0551
  Fratty but friendly atmosphere, great beer selection.
- **Hudson Hotel Library** •
  356 W 58th St [9th Ave]
  212-554-6000
  Super-super-super pretentious.
- **The Pony Bar** • 637 10th Ave [W 45th St]
  212-586-2707
  Beer beer everywhere. Get a growler to go.
- **Port 41** • 355 W 41st St [9th Ave]
  212-947-1188
  Perfect stop before or after a grueling trip on Greyhound.
- **Rudy's Bar & Grill** • 627 9th Ave [W 44th St]
  212-974-9169
  Classic Hell's Kitchen. Recommended.
- **Smith's** • 701 8th Ave [44th St]
  212-246-3268
  Beautiful sign, but beware the testosterone.
- **Swing 46** • 349 W 46th St [9th Ave]
  212-262-9554
  Good place for a drink before a show.
- **The Tank** • 354 45th St [9th Ave]
  212-563-6269
  Major destination for experimental music.
- **Terminal 5** • 610 W 56th St [11th Ave]
  212-665-3832
  Ex-club space now used for mid-level indie bands.
- **Valhalla** • 815 9th Ave [54th St]
  212-757-2747
  Warm, wooden watering hole with staggering beer selection.
- **Vintage** • 753 9th Ave [W 51st St]
  212-581-4655
  Ginormous martini menu. Good beers.
- **Xth** • 642 10th Ave [W 45th St]
  212-245-9088
  Good local vibe.

Bowling

- **Lucky Strike Lanes** •
  624 W 42nd St [12th Ave]
  646-829-0170
  America's other, drunker pastime—with a lounge and dress code.

Theaters/Performing Arts

- **Mint Theatre** • 311 W 43rd St, 3rd Fl [8th Ave]
  212-315-0231
  Terrific company that does old plays even Michael Dale has never heard of.

W 60th St
W 59th St
W 58th St
W 57th St
W 56th St
W 55th St
W 54th St
W 53rd St
W 52nd St
W 51st St
W 50th St
W 49th St
W 48th St
W 47th St
W 46th St
W 45th St
W 44th St
W 43rd St
W 42nd St
W 41st St
W 40th St
W 39th St
W 38th St
W 37th ST
Henry Hudson Pkwy
West Side Hwy
Hudson River Park
Hudson River
Eleventh Ave
Tenth Ave
Ninth Ave
Eighth Ave
Dyer Ave
Dewitt Clinton Park
Time Warner Center
Columbus Circle
59th Street Columbus Circle
50th Street
42nd Street Port Authority Bus Terminal
Port Authority Bus Terminal
Lincoln Tunnel
Jacob K Javits Convention Center
PAGE 248
PAGE 244
PAGE 306
PAGE 246
1/4 mile
.25 km

The breadth and depth of deliciousness is staggering here. **Hallo Berlin** boasts German soul food, **Agua Dulce** a spicy Caribbean brunch, and **Island Burgers** about forty variations of their signature dish. Middle Eastern lovers get their fix at BYOB gem **Gazala Place** or **Hummus Kitchen**. Pre-theater pick is French stalwart **Tout Va Bien**.

Restaurants

- **Afghan Kebab House** • 764 9th Ave [51st St]
  212-307-1612 • $$
  Great kebabs, friendly.
- **Agua Dulce** • 802 9th Ave [W 53rd St]
  212-262-1299 • $$$
  Latin fusion that kicks, plus killer brunch deals.
- **Asiate** • 80 Columbus Cir [Broadway]
  212-805-8881 • $$$$$
  Highest-end Japanese/French. Bring lots of Yen/Euro.
- **Breeze** • 661 9th Ave [W 46th St]
  212-262-7777 • $$
  Always great Thai/French fusion.
- **Burrito Box** • 885 9th Ave [W 57th St]
  212-489-6889 • $
  Cheap and tasty Mexican with killer guac.
- **Casellula** • 401 W 52nd St [9th Ave]
  212-247-8137 • $$$
  Sophisticated wine and cheese pairings.
- **Chez Josephine** • 414 W 42nd St [Dyer Ave]
  212-594-1925 • $$$
  Yes, the owner really is Josephine Baker's son.
- **Chili Thai** • 712 9th Ave [W 49th St]
  212-265-5054 • $
  Tiny, friendly, and delicious.
- **Churrascaria Plataforma** •
  316 W 49th St [8th Ave]
  212-245-0505 • $$$$
  Brazilian Feast! Don't eat all day, then come here.
- **Daisy May's BBQ USA** • 623 11th Ave [46th St]
  212-977-1500 • $$
  Takeout BBQ and sides Mon-Fri. Plus, various Manhattan street carts!
- **Don Giovanni** • 358 W 44th St [Ninth Ave]
  212-581-4939 • $$
  One of the better cheap pies in the city.
- **Eatery** • 798 9th Ave [W 53rd St]
  212-765-7080 • $$
  A Hell's Kitchen comfort food favorite. All de-lish.
- **El Centro** • 824 9th Ave [54th St]
  646-763-6585 • $
  Open late for those sudden south-of-the-border cravings.
- **Empanada Mama** • 763 9th Ave [W 51st St]
  212-698-9008 • $
  No one fries them better.
- **etcetera etcetera** • 352 W 44 St [9th Ave]
  212-399-4141 • $$$$
  Beautiful bar, delicious Italian food.
- **Gazala Place** • 709 9th Ave [48th St]
  212-245-0709 • $$
  Brilliant Middle Eastern food. Share an appetizer platter.
- **Hallo Berlin** • 626 10th Ave [W 44th St]
  212-977-1944 • $$
  The best wurst in the city! Check out their street cart at 54th & Fifth.
- **Hudson Cafeteria** • 356 W 58th St [Ninth Ave]
  212-554-6000 • $$$$$
  Lovely and pricey and goody.
- **Hummus Kitchen** • 768 9th Ave [W 51st St]
  212-333-3009 • $$
  Hummus so good they named a kitchen after it.
- **Island Burgers & Shakes** • 766 9th Ave [51st St]
  212-307-7934 • $$
  Aptly named. A classic.
- **Joe Allen** • 326 W 46th St [8th Ave]
  212-581-6464 • $$$
  De rigueur stargazing, open late.
- **Marseille** • 630 9th Ave [W 44th St]
  212-333-3410 • $$$$
  True to the name, an expatriate's delight.
- **Meskerem** • 468 W 47th St [Tenth Ave]
  212-664-0520 • $$
  Friendly and consistently good Ethiopian.
- **Nizza** • 630 9th Ave [45th St]
  212-956-1800 • $$
  Share some fantastic antipasti: socca, tapenade, focaccette, and more.
- **The Nook** • 746 9th Ave [W 50th St]
  212-247-5500 • $$$
  Delicious New American (with after-hours parties).
- **Per Se** • 10 Columbus Cir [W 58th St]
  212-823-9335 • $$$$$
  Divine…but you practically have to sell a kidney to afford it.
- **Ralph's** • 862 9th Ave [W 56th St]
  212-581-2283 • $$
  Classic Italian cuisine.
- **Shorty's** • 576 9th Ave [W 42nd St]
  212-967-3055 • $
  Philly cheese steak without the snobbery. Extra Cheez Whiz, please.
- **Tout Va Bien** • 311 W 51st St [8th Ave]
  212-265-0190 • $$$$
  Warm, homey, pre-theater, French. NFT approved.
- **Turkish Cuisine** • 631 9th Ave [W 44th St]
  212-397-9650 • $$
  Turkish food, in case you were wondering. It's always good.

W 60th St
W 59th St
W 58th St
W 57th St
W 56th St
W 55th St
W 54th St
W 53rd St
W 52nd St
W 51st St
W 50th St
W 49th St
W 48th St
W 47th St
W 46th St
W 45th St
W 44th St
W 43rd St
W 42nd St
W 41st St
W 40th St
W 39th St
W 38th St
W 37th ST
HENRY HUDSON PKWY
Time Warner Center
59th Street Columbus Circle
Columbus Circle
Dewitt Clinton Park
Hudson River
Hudson River Park
West Side Hwy
Eleventh Ave
Tenth Ave
Ninth Ave
Eighth Ave
Dyer Ave
50th Street
42nd Street Port Authority Bus Terminal
Port Authority Bus Terminal
Lincoln Tunnel
Jacob K Javits Convention Center
PAGE 248
PAGE 244
PAGE 306
PAGE 246
1/4 mile
.25 km

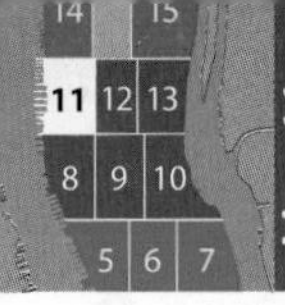

Amish Market is the top-end supermarket; **Ninth Avenue International** is amazing for Greek groceries. **Sullivan Street Bakery** makes bundles of heaven disguised as bread. **Delphinium** is the store where you can buy a non-Hallmark card, and the misnamed **Chelsea Garden Center** can provide the perfect flowers to go with it.

Bagels

- **H&H Bagels** • 639 W 46th St [Twelfth Ave]
  212-765-7200
  Hot & heavenly at their world headquarters.

Coffee

- **Bis.Co. Latte** • 667 10th Ave [W 47th St]
  212-581-3900
  Mmmm…homemade biscotti.
- **The Coffee Pot** • 350 W 49th St [Ninth Ave]
  212-265-3566
  The Wi-Fi is nice. Coffee not too bad.
- **Empire Coffee & Tea** • 568 9th Ave [W 41st St]
  212-268-1220
  Best coffee in these tourist-filled parts.

Shopping

- **10th Avenue Wines & Liquors** •
  812 10th Ave [54th St]
  212-245-6700
  Boozehound specials and tastings.
- **Amish Market** • 731 9th Ave [W 50th St]
  212-245-2360
  Lots of prepared foods. Do they deliver by horse and buggy?
- **Amy's Bread** • 672 9th Ave [W 47th St]
  212-977-2670
  Providing the heavenly smells that wake up Hell's Kitchen.
- **Annex/Hell's Kitchen Flea Market** •
  W 39th St & Dyer Ave
  212-243-5343
  Vintage treasures abound every Sat & Sun.
- **Bouchon Bakery** • 10 Columbus Cir [8th Ave]
  212-823-9366
  Heavenly pastries in a gigantic mall.
- **Chelsea Garden Center** • 580 11th Ave [38th St]
  212-727-7100
  Urban gardener's delight.
- **Coup de Coeur** • 609 9th Ave [W 43rd St]
  212-586-8636
  Trendy, eclectic shop with great vibes.
- **Cupcake Café** • 545 9th Ave [W 40th St]
  212-465-1530
  Three words: sweet potato doughnuts.
- **Delphinium Card & Gift** •
  358 W 47th St [9th Ave]
  212-333-7732
  For the "too lazy to make my own card" set.
- **Delphinium Home** • 653 9th Ave [W 46th St]
  212-333-3213
  Everything from rubber duckies to WASP cookbooks.
- **Epstein's Paint Center** • 822 10th Ave [55th St]
  212-265-3960
  Honest advice, top quality from century-old shop.
- **Janovic** • 771 9th Ave [W 52nd St]
  212-245-3241
  Top NYC paint store. Shades/blinds too.
- **Liberty Bicycles** • 846 9th Ave [W 55th St]
  212-757-2418
  This bike shop totally rocks.
- **Little Pie Company** • 424 W 43rd St [9th Ave]
  212-736-4780
  A homemade dessert equals happiness.
- **Luthier Music** • 341 W 44th St [9th Ave]
  212-397-6038
  One of the best for classical and flamenco guitars.
- **Ninth Avenue International** •
  543 9th Ave [W 40th St]
  212-279-1000
  Mediterranean/Greek specialty store.
- **Ninth Avenue Vintner** • 669 9th Ave [46th St]
  212-664-9463
  Good suggestions from the staff.
- **Pan Aqua Diving** • 460 W 43rd St [10th Ave]
  212-736-3483
  SCUBA equipment and courses.
- **Poseidon Greek Bakery** • 629 9th Ave [44th St]
  212-757-6173
  Old-school Greek delicacies like spanakopita.
- **Radio Shack** • 333 W 57th St [8th Ave]
  212-586-1909
  Kenneth, what is the frequency?
- **Sea Breeze** • 541 9th Ave [W 40th St]
  212-563-7537
  Bargains on fresh seafood.
- **Sullivan Street Bakery** •
  533 W 47th St [11th Ave]
  212-265-5580
  Artisan breads, foodie approved. NFT approved. God approved.
- **Tumi** • 10 Columbus Cir [Broadway]
  212-823-9390
  When your luggage gets lost and insurance is paying.

Central Park
Columbus Circle
59th Street Columbus Circle
Central Park S
5th Avenue/ 59th Street
Grand Army Plaza
E 59th St
Alwyn Court Apartments
W 58th St
Plaza Hotel
E 58th St
Eighth Ave
Broadway
57th Street
Carnegie Hall
57th Street
W 57th St
E 57th St
Hearst Tower
Seventh Ave
Avenue of the Americas (Sixth Ave)
W 56th St
E 56th St
Carnegie Deli
W 55th St
E 55th St
Fifth Ave
Madison Ave
Museum of Modern Art (MoMA)
W 54th St
E 54th St
W 53rd St
E 53rd St
7th Avenue
5th Avenue/ 53rd Street
W 52nd St
E 52nd St
W 51st St
E 51st St
Villard House
50th Street
W 50th St
E 50th St
St Patrick's Cathedral
50th Street
Rockefeller Center
Rockefeller Plz
W 49th St
E 49th St
49th Street
GE Building
Top of the Rock
VEHICULAR TRAFFIC PROHIBITED
W 48th St
E 48th St
47th-50th Streets Rockefeller Center
W 47th St
E 47th St
TKTS
Diamond District
W 46th St
E 46th St
Little Brazil
W 45th St
E 45th St
THEATER DISTRICT
Algonquin Hotel
The Debt Clock
W 44th St
E 44th St
Royalton Hotel
W 43rd St
E 43rd St
42nd Street Port Authority Bus Terminal
Times Square
Times Square 42nd Street
5th Avenue E 42nd St
W 42nd St
Port Authority Bus Terminal
W 41st St
E 41st St
Bryant Park
New York Public Library
42nd Street
New York Times Building
W 40th St
E 40th St
American Radiator Building
W 39th St
E 39th St
W 38th St
E 38th St
1/4 mile
.25 km

Hello, New York. Welcome to the heart of the city. To some this is total tourist hell. To others it's their home away from home where they slave away cooped up in a giant office tower. To the rest of us it's just a place we try to avoid, but sometimes find ourselves wandering around with our cousins from Ohio in tow. If you do stick around to explore these vast urban canyons, you'll be rewarded with some of the finest art, the biggest buildings, the brightest lights, world-famous hotels and cathedrals, and a pair of the most iconic animal statues ever. Maybe Midtown isn't so bad after all.

At the top of our Midtown list is **The Museum of Modern Art**. Sure it's pricey and can get packed on the weekend, but the art will blow your mind and the sculpture garden in summer is divine. Bargain tip: It's free on Friday evenings or splurge for a membership which includes admission to all of the excellent films. If you still enjoy the smell and feel of books, the main branch of the **New York Public Library** (guarded by the famous lion statues Patience and Fortitude) is spectacular. We love visiting The Map Room (no surprise there) and The Rose Main Reading Room, one of the most beautiful spaces in the world to sit down with a book. Then you can bask on the lawn of beautiful **Bryant Park**, stare up at the sky, and transcend the chaos of the city. At least until a pigeon poops on you or the crazy guy next to you starts yelling at himself.

For a trip down memory lane stop in at the **Algonquin Hotel** where famous writers, entertainers, and socialites used to cavort and carouse in the 1920s. To see how the ultra-rich used to (and still) live, take a stroll though the gorgeous **Plaza Hotel**. If you have an extra $1,095 lying around, we hear the Edwardian Suite is very nice. Walk by the beautiful **Alwyn Court Apartments** from 1908 and pretend you live in luxury as you gawk at the exquisite facade. Or experience a trip to the cinema before soulless multiplexes existed at the **Ziegfeld Theatre**. This movie palace is adorned with red carpeting, gold trim, and the biggest screen in the city.

Times Square is most definitely for tourists. The real gems of Times Square are on located on the periphery, like the striking **New York Times Building** and NFT's favorite bar **Jimmy's Corner**. If you really have to experience Times Square, take a quick, awe inspiring peek at the bright lights and check out the new car-free street design. Or if you're in the need of cheap Broadway tickets, wade through the crowds to **TKTS**. After you score some tickets for a show that night, take a quick break on the colorful TKTS bleachers. But don't linger too long or you'll end up in approximately 7,048 photos taken by clueless tourists who think they're documenting the real New York.

Midtown is home to a ridiculous amount of brilliant architecture. One of the world's most cutting-edge masterpieces is the **Hearst Tower**, a stunning blend of old and new, and the first green skyscraper in New York. On top of the original 1928 building is a structure made out of recycled steel that was added in 2006. Step into the lobby to check out the one-of-a-kind the water sculpture. Other classic architectural marvels include **Carnegie Hall**, **St Patrick's Cathedral**, **St Thomas Church**, **Villard House**, **Rockefeller Center**, and **American Radiator Building**. And finally, don't miss the trippy **Austrian Cultural Forum** which hosts a number of interesting events open to the public.

For something a little different check out **Little Brazil** for a small strip of restaurants, bars (some with live music), and businesses from the land of sun, sand, and soccer. Or go north a block to the famous **Diamond District** which started in the 1940s when Orthodox Jews fled Europe and set up shop here. Finally, stare up at **The Debt Clock** and watch in horror as the nation's money disappears by the nanosecond. Ok, now it's back to Jimmy's Corner for a drink. Better make it a double.

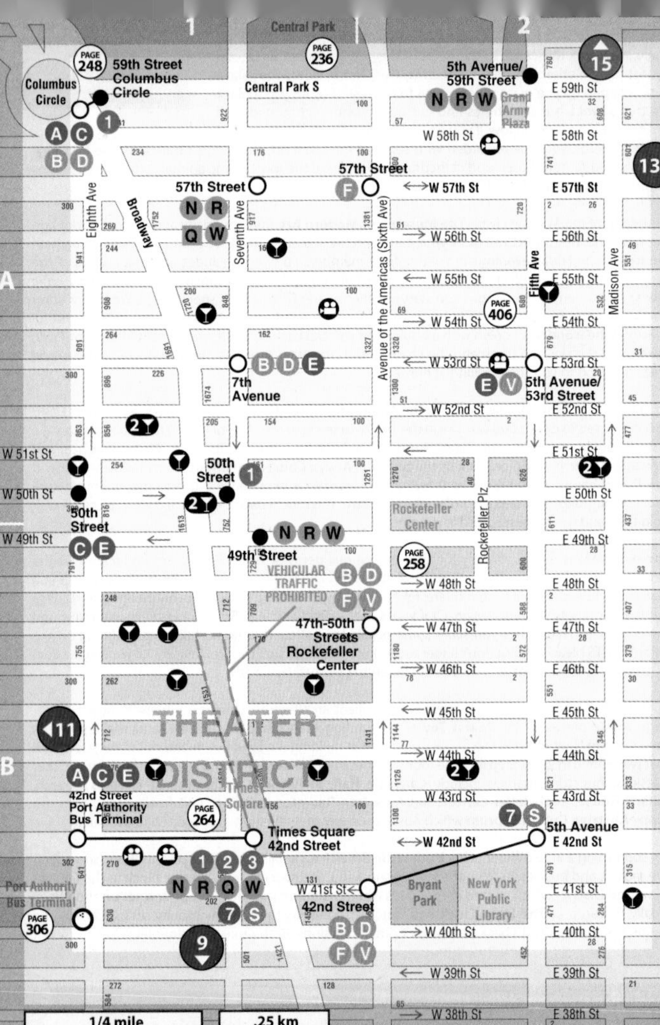
Central Park
Columbus Circle
59th Street Columbus Circle
Central Park S
5th Avenue/ 59th Street
Grand Army Plaza
E 59th St
W 58th St
E 58th St
57th Street
57th Street
W 57th St
E 57th St
Eighth Ave
Broadway
Seventh Ave
Avenue of the Americas (Sixth Ave)
Fifth Ave
Madison Ave
W 56th St
E 56th St
W 55th St
E 55th St
W 54th St
E 54th St
W 53rd St
E 53rd St
7th Avenue
5th Avenue/ 53rd Street
W 52nd St
E 52nd St
W 51st St
E 51st St
50th Street
W 50th St
E 50th St
50th Street
Rockefeller Center
Rockefeller Plz
W 49th St
E 49th St
49th Street
VEHICULAR TRAFFIC PROHIBITED
W 48th St
E 48th St
W 47th St
E 47th St
47th-50th Streets Rockefeller Center
W 46th St
E 46th St
W 45th St
E 45th St
THEATER DISTRICT
W 44th St
E 44th St
42nd Street Port Authority Bus Terminal
Times Square
W 43rd St
E 43rd St
5th Avenue
Times Square 42nd Street
W 42nd St
E 42nd St
Port Authority Bus Terminal
W 41st St
E 41st St
42nd Street
Bryant Park
New York Public Library
W 40th St
E 40th St
W 39th St
E 39th St
W 38th St
E 38th St
1/4 mile
.25 km

Bowl some frames at **Leisure Time** in Port Authority. Saddle up to the bar at **Jimmy's Corner** for a beer and a shot. Other options: **Oak Room** for cabaret, **Iridium** for jazz, **King Cole** for class, **Caroline's** for comedy, or escape it all on the patio of **Bookmarks**.

Bars

- **Blue Bar** • 59 W 44th St [Sixth Ave]
  212-840-6800
  If you're in the mood for a Harvey Wallbanger.
- **Bookmarks** • 299 Madison Ave [E 41st St]
  212-983-4500
  Escape the Midtown ruckus at this nifty rooftop bar.
- **Carnegie Club** • 156 W 56th St [7th Ave]
  212-957-9676
  Drink your 50-year-old cognac with your 22-year-old date.
- **Caroline's on Broadway** • 1626 Broadway [W 50th St]
  212-757-4100
  Laughs in Times Square. A classic.
- **China Club** • 268 W 47th St [Eighth Ave]
  212-398-3800
  Think *Night at the Roxbury*.
- **Flute** • 205 W 54th St [Seventh Ave]
  212-265-5169
  Munch on strawberries and cream with your bubbly.
- **Gilt** • 455 Madison Ave [E 51st St]
  212-891-8100
  When the economy recovers, you'll find us drinking here.
- **Harmony View Bar & Grill** • 210 W 50th St [Broadway]
  212-957-5100
  Above-average Irish pub popular with the after-work crowd.
- **House of Brews** • 302 W 51st St [Eighth Ave]
  212-541-7080
  Fratty but friendly atmosphere, great beer selection.
- **Iridium** • 1650 Broadway [W 51st St]
  212-582-2121
  Good mainstream jazz venue. Pricey.
- **Jimmy's Corner** • 140 W 44th St [Broadway]
  212-221-9510
  This cozy joint is the best bar around here, trust us.
- **King Cole Bar** • 2 E 55th St [5th Ave]
  212-753-4500
  Drink a red snapper and admire the gorgeous mural.
- **Oak Room** • 59 W 44th St [Sixth Ave]
  212-840-6800
  Classic and classy cabaret.
- **Paramount Bar** • 235 W 46th St [Broadway]
  212-764-5500
  Tiny, pretentious, unavoidable.
- **Roseland** • 239 W 52nd St [Broadway]
  212-247-0200
  Big-time rock venue.
- **Royalton Hotel** • 44 W 44th St [Fifth Ave]
  212-869-4400
  Phillippe Starck is the SH—!
- **The Rum House** • 228 W 47th St [Broadway]
  212-869-3005
  It ain't pretty, but it's usually open.
- **Russian Vodka Room** • 265 W 52nd St [8th Ave]
  212-307-5835
  Russian molls and cranberry vodka. Awesome.
- **Sardi's** • 234 W 44th St [7th Ave]
  212-221-8440
  Absorb the sacred DNA at the upstairs bar.
- **St Andrews** • 140 W 46th St [Sixth Ave]
  212-840-8413
  Over 200 Scotches at this bar and restaurant.

Bowling

- **Leisure Time** • 625 8th Ave [W 40th St]
  212-268-6909
  Bowl before you get on the bus at Port Authority.

Movie Theaters

- **AMC Empire 25** • 234 W 42nd St [7th Ave]
  212-398-2597
  Buy tickets ahead. It's Times Square.
- **MoMA** • 11 W 53rd St [Fifth Ave]
  212-708-9400
  Arty programming changes every day.
- **Paris Theatre** • 4 W 58th St [5th Ave]
  212-688-3800
  Art house equivalent of the Ziegfeld.
- **Regal E-Walk Stadium 13** • 247 W 42nd St [7th Ave]
  212-505-6397
  Across the street from the Empire, but not nearly as nice.
- **Ziegfeld Theatre** • 141 W 54th St [6th Ave]
  212-307-1862
  Beloved NY classic with a gigantic screen. Don't miss.

Central Park
Columbus Circle
59th Street Columbus Circle
Central Park S
5th Avenue/ 59th Street
Grand Army Plaza
W 58th St
E 58th St
57th Street
57th Street
W 57th St
E 57th St
Eighth Ave
Broadway
Seventh Ave
W 56th St
E 56th St
Avenue of the Americas (Sixth Ave)
W 55th St
E 55th St
Fifth Ave
Madison Ave
W 54th St
E 54th St
W 53rd St
E 53rd St
7th Avenue
5th Avenue/ 53rd Street
W 52nd St
E 52nd St
W 51st St
E 51st St
50th Street
W 50th St
E 50th St
50th Street
Rockefeller Center
Rockefeller Plz
W 49th St
E 49th St
49th Street
VEHICULAR TRAFFIC PROHIBITED
W 48th St
E 48th St
47th-50th Streets Rockefeller Center
W 47th St
E 47th St
W 46th St
E 46th St
W 45th St
E 45th St
THEATER DISTRICT
W 44th St
E 44th St
W 43rd St
E 43rd St
42nd Street Port Authority Bus Terminal
Times Square
Times Square 42nd Street
5th Avenue E 42nd St
W 42nd St
W 41st St
E 41st St
Bryant Park
New York Public Library
42nd Street
Port Authority Bus Terminal
W 40th St
E 40th St
W 39th St
E 39th St
W 38th St
E 38th St
1/4 mile
.25 km

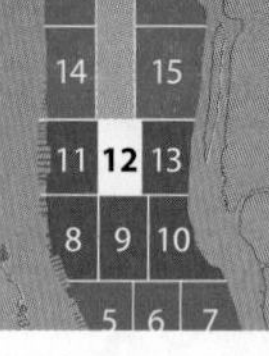

Greasy burgers hidden in a fancy hotel lobby? Dreams do come true at **Burger Joint**. For street food try **Jamaican Dutchy** or the halal cart at **53rd & 6th**. High-end arty diners get satisfaction at **The Modern**, Italian lovers at **Insieme**, and old-school chaps at **21 Club**. Jewish deli fans line up at **Stage** and **Carnegie** while **Edison Cafe** flies under the radar.

Restaurants

- **21 Club** • 21 W 52nd St [Fifth Ave]
  212-582-7200 • $$$$
  Old, clubby New York.
- **53rd & 6th Food Cart** •
  W 53rd St & 6th Ave
  No phone • $
  Serving halal food to cabbies and devoted fans (7:30 pm-4 am).
- **Akdeniz** • 19 W 46th St [5th Ave]
  212-575-2307 • $$
  Turkish oasis in Midtown.
- **Beacon Restaurant & Bar** •
  25 W 56th St [5th Ave]
  212-332-0500 • $$$$$
  Spend $100 on wood-fired goodness. If you can.
- **Bos & Lucky Sunday** • 858 8th Ave [W 51st St]
  212-459-3610 • $
  The only Chinese takeout you'll need.
- **Brasserie 8 1/2** • 9 W 57th St [Fifth Ave]
  212-829-0812 • $$$$$
  A must for brunch. Lovely for cocktails and dinner too.
- **Bread & Olive** • 24 W 45th St [5th Ave]
  212-764-1588 • $$
  Brick oven-baked Middle Eastern delights.
- **Burger Joint** • 119 W 56th St [Sixth Ave]
  212-708-7414 • $
  Fancy hotel lobby leads to unexpected burger dive. Awesome.
- **Cafe Zaiya** • 18 E 41st St [Madison Ave]
  212-779-0600 • $$
  Japanese food court that's cheap and fast.
- **Carnegie Deli** • 854 7th Ave [W 55th St]
  212-757-2245 • $$$
  Still good. Still really, really good.
- **Edison Café** • 228 W 47th St [Broadway]
  212-840-5000 • $
  Theater district mainstay for Jewish soul food.
- **Gallagher's Steak House** •
  228 W 52nd St [Broadway]
  212-245-5336 • $$$$
  Dine on fancy steak with grizzled old New Yorkers.
- **Haru** • 205 W 43rd St [7th Ave]
  212-398-9810 • $$$$
  Excellent mid-range Japanese. Loud, good.
- **Insieme** • 777 7th Ave [W 50th St]
  212-582-1310 • $$$$$
  Closest culinary escape to Times Square. Michelin-starred Italian.
- **Jamaican Dutchy Cart** • 7th Ave & W 51st St
  646-287-5004 • $
  This jerk is the worth the wait. Spicy!
- **Joe's Shanghai** • 24 W 56th St [Fifth Ave]
  212-333-3868 • $$
  Uptown version of killer dumpling factory.
- **La Bonne Soupe** • 48 W 55th St [Fifth Ave]
  212-586-7650 • $$
  Ooh la la, the best salad dressing accompanies my soupe a l'oignon.
- **Le Bernardin** • 155 W 51st St [Seventh Ave]
  212-554-1515 • $$$$$
  Top NYC seafood.
- **Margon** • 136 W 46th St [7th Ave]
  212-354-5013 • $
  If MidtownLunch.com likes it, so should you.
- **The Modern** • 9 W 53rd St [Fifth Ave]
  212-333-1220 • $$$$
  With gnocchi to die for, spend a lot and then STILL splurge on dessert.
- **Molyvos** • 871 7th Ave [W 56th St]
  212-582-7500 • $$$$
  Top Greek. Someday we'll check it out w/ your credit card.
- **Pongsri Thai** • 244 W 48th St [Broadway]
  212-582-3392 • $$
  Great, spicy Thai.
- **Primeburger** • 5 E 51st St [Madison Ave]
  212-759-4730 • $
  Truly retro diner with kitschy swiveling-tray seating.
- **Shelly's New York** • 41 W 57th St [Fifth Ave]
  212-245-2422 • $$$$
  Come starved, leave stuffed.
- **Stage Deli** • 834 7th Ave [W 54th St]
  212-245-7850 • $$
  Deliciously clogs your arteries just as well as Carnegie.
- **Sukhadia's** • 17 W 45th St [5th Ave]
  212 395-7300 • $$
  Indian buffet. Best food in Midtown at Midtown prices.
- **Toloache** • 251 W 50th St [8th Ave]
  212-581-1818 • $$$
  Designer Mexican in Midtown.
- **Virgil's Real BBQ** • 152 W 44th St [Sixth Ave]
  212-921-9494 • $$$
  It's real. Hush puppies and CFS to die for.

Map 12 • Midtown

Central Park

PAGE 248

59th Street Columbus Circle

Columbus Circle

PAGE 236

Central Park S

5th Avenue/ 59th Street

N R W

Grand Army Plaza

E 59th St

A C B D 1

W 58th St

E 58th St

57th Street

N R Q W

57th Street

F

W 57th St

E 57th St

Eighth Ave

Broadway

Seventh Ave

Avenue of the Americas (Sixth Ave)

W 56th St

E 56th St

Fifth Ave

Madison Ave

W 55th St

E 55th St

PAGE 406

W 54th St

E 54th St

B D E

7th Avenue

W 53rd St

E 53rd St

E V

5th Avenue/ 53rd Street

W 52nd St

E 52nd St

W 51st St

E 51st St

50th Street 1

W 50th St

E 50th St

50th Street

C E

W 49th St

Rockefeller Center

Rockefeller Plz

E 49th St

N R W

49th Street

VEHICULAR TRAFFIC PROHIBITED

B D F V

PAGE 258

W 48th St

E 48th St

47th-50th Streets Rockefeller Center

W 47th St

E 47th St

W 46th St

E 46th St

W 45th St

E 45th St

THEATER DISTRICT

W 44th St

E 44th St

A C E

42nd Street Port Authority Bus Terminal

PAGE 264

Times Square

W 43rd St

E 43rd St

7 S

Times Square 42nd Street

W 42nd St

5th Avenue E 42nd St

1 2 3 N R Q W 7 S

Port Authority Bus Terminal

PAGE 306

W 41st St

42nd Street

B D F V

Bryant Park

New York Public Library

E 41st St

W 40th St

E 40th St

W 39th St

E 39th St

W 38th St

E 38th St

15 13 11 9

1 2 A B

1/4 mile

.25 km

Bagels, Coffee, & Shopping

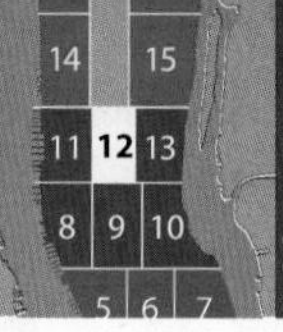

The ruling class lingers at places like **Bergdorf Goodman** and **Henri Bendel** for clothes and **Petrossian Boutique** for caviar, while you'll find us at the **MoMA Design Store**, **Muji**, or **Urban Center Books**. Single malt scotch lovers drool at **Park Avenue Liquor**.

Coffee

- **Fika** • 41 W 58th St [5th Ave]
  212-832-0022
  Swedish oasis in Midtown: strong coffee and homemade pastries.
- **Zibetto** • 1385 6th Ave [W 56th St]
  A real Italian espresso bar. Un caffe, per favore!

Shopping

- **Apple Store** • 767 5th Ave [E 59th St]
  212-336-1440
  Giant glass shrine houses all things Apple.
- **Bergdorf Goodman** • 754 5th Ave [W 57th St]
  212-753-7300
  Hands down—the best windows in the business.
- **Burberry** • 9 E 57th St [Fifth Ave]
  212-407-7100
  Signature "beige plaid" purveyor.
- **Chanel** • 15 E 57th St [Fifth Ave]
  212-355-5050
  Official outfitter of "ladies who lunch."
- **Colony Music** • 1619 Broadway [W 49th St]
  212-265-2050
  Sheet music galore.
- **Drummer's World** • 151 W 46th St [Sixth Ave]
  212-840-3057
  All-encompassing stop for drummers—from beginning to pro.
- **Ermenegildo Zegna** • 663 5th Ave [E 57th St]
  212-421-4488
  A truly stylish and classic Italian designer.
- **Felissimo** • 10 W 56th St [Fifth Ave]
  212-956-4438
  Cool design store, Great townhouse.
- **Henri Bendel** • 712 5th Ave [W 56th St]
  212-247-1100
  Offbeat department store specializing in the unusual and harder-to-find.
- **Kate's Paperie** • 140 W 57th St [Sixth Ave]
  212-459-0700
  Excellent stationery. NYC favorite.
- **Lee's Art Shop** • 220 W 57th St [Broadway]
  212-247-0110
  Excellent art store in surprising location.
- **Manny's Music** • 156 W 48th St [Seventh Ave]
  212-819-0576
  Uptown musical instruments mecca.
- **Mets Clubhouse Shop** •
  11 W 42nd St [5th Ave]
  212-764-4733
  For Amazin' stuff!
- **MoMA Design Store** • 11 W 53rd St [Fifth Ave]
  212-708-9400
  Cutting-edge, minimalist, ergonomic, offbeat, and funky everything.
- **Muji Times Square** • 620 8th Ave [W 40th]
  212-382-2300
  Like a Japanese IKEA, but cooler and without meatballs.
- **Museum of Arts and Design Shop** •
  2 Columbus Cir [Eighth Ave]
  212-299-7700
  Not your average museum store.
- **Park Avenue Liquor Shop** •
  292 Madison Ave [E 41st St]
  212-685-2442
  Amazing selection of scotch. Makes us wish we had more $$$.
- **Petrossian Boutique** • 911 7th Ave [58th St]
  212-245-2217
  Caviar and other delectables. Bring the Gold Card.
- **Roberto's Woodwind Repair Shop** •
  149 W 46th St [Sixth Ave]
  212-391-1315
  Saxophones, horns, clarinets, and flutes. If it blows, bring it here.
- **Saks Fifth Avenue** • 611 5th Ave [E 49th St]
  212-753-4000
  Fifth Avenue mainstay with lovely holiday windows and bathrooms.
- **Sam Ash** • 160 W 48th St [Seventh Ave]
  212-719-2299
  Musical instrument superstore.
- **Steinway and Sons** • 109 W 57th St [6th Ave]
  212-246-1100
  Cheap knockoff pianos. Just kidding.
- **Takashimaya** • 693 5th Ave [E 54th St]
  212-350-0100
  Elegant tea, furniture, accessory store. Highly recommended.
- **Tiffany & Co** • 727 5th Ave [E 56th St]
  212-755-8000
  Grande dame of the little blue box.
- **Urban Center Books** •
  457 Madison Ave [E 50th St]
  212-935-3595
  Sublime architecture & urban planning destination.

E 61st St
Lexington Avenue/ 59th Street
N R W
E 60th St
ROOSEVELT ISLAND TRAMWAY
Queensboro Bridge
to Queens
15
59th Street
4 5 6
Roosevelt Island Tram
E 59th St
E 58th St
E 57th St
E 56th St
FDR Dr
A
Central Synagogue
E 55th St
Sutton Place
Sutton Pl
E 54th St
Citicorp Center
E V
The Lever House
Lexington Ave/ 53rd Street
E 53rd St
to Queens
51st Street
The Seven Year Itch
E 52nd St
Seagram Building
6
12
E 51st St
Madison Ave
Park Ave
Lexington Ave
Third Ave
Second Ave
First Ave
Beekman Pl
E 50th St
Waldorf-Astoria
E 49th St
Mitchell Pl
General D MacArthur Plaza
E 48th St
East River
E 47th St
Dag Hammarskjold Plaza
Peace Garden
Vanderbilt Ave
E 46th St
E 45th St
PAGE 304
Grand Central Terminal
Depew Pl
E 44th St (Archbishop Fulton J Sheen Pl)
United Nations
United Nations Plaza
B
E 43rd St
to Queens
Citi Field
Tennis Center
PAGE 268
Grand Central 42nd Street
4 5 6
7 S
Chrysler Building
E 42nd St
Tudor City
Tudor City Pl
Robert Moses Playground
Queens Midtown Tunnel
To Queens
495
E 41St St
E 40th St
10
FDR Dr
E 39th St
Exit St
Entrance St
E 38th St
1/4 mile
.25 km

No matter how angry, late, or tired we are from dealing with the overwhelming crowds in this part of town, one glance up at Grand Central Terminal with the Chrysler Building looming in the background never fails to give us a burst of energy and a shot of civic pride. Welcome to East Midtown which has a major personality disorder—in a good way. It's got the tranquility of elegant Sutton Place and Tudor City, the rowdy nightlife along Second Avenue, the commuter bustle of Grand Central, the international crowd around the UN, and legendary architecture bursting from every corner of this neighborhood.

The hub of this neighborhood—and arguably the city—is **Grand Central Terminal**. One of the busiest train stations in the world, this gorgeous building also houses many hidden surprises under its vaunted ceiling. Start in the main concourse where you'll see a magnificent clock above the information booth. This spot is what New Yorkers mean when they say, "Meet me at the clock." Some of these meet ups turn into dates at the deluxe and hard-to-find cocktail lounge **Campbell Apartment**. Others wisely opt for a trip into the world of old-school New York dining at the highly recommended **Oyster Bar**. Ask to sit in the Saloon for a real treat. Shopping options abound here with lots of cool shops (books, MTA souvenirs, etc.) and the best food shopping in Midtown at **Grand Central Market**. For a real inside look, even locals enjoy the free tours on Wednesdays at 12:30 pm. Just meet at the clock.

You may have heard of a little organization called the **United Nations**. It's housed in an iconic glass building perched on the edge of the East River. We highly recommend the public tour where you get to see the General Assembly, an amazing art collection, and international diplomats scurrying about. Currently the UN headquarters is undergoing a massive $3 billion renovation. The project is estimated to be completed in 2013 or around the same time the UN finally ends world poverty. We can still dream, right?

Architecture nerds rave and worship at Mies van der Rohe's **Seagram Building**, argue over the value of Phillip Johnson's **Lipstick Building**, and contemplate the public art underneath **The Lever House**. One of the city's most unique places of worship is the **Central Synagogue** with vivid Moorish details. Stroll by at night for an otherworldly experience. **St. Bart's** on Park Avenue is gorgeous in a more traditional way, while the **Chrysler Building**, **Chanin Building**, and **GE Building** are worshipped for their Art Deco brilliance.

If you want a break from all the tall buildings, check out the **Seven Year Itch** subway grate where Marilyn Monroe's dress blows up for all the world to see. Head way east to walk down **Sutton Place** to see where lots of exclusive New Yorkers take up residence. Or stroll around Tudor City and marvel at the handsome Neo Gothic apartments that diplomats and divas call home. Make a reservation at Italian wonder **Convivio** in the heart of Tudor City. It's a nice way to unwind and enjoy this unique urban enclave without having to drop $2.7 million on a condo.

E 61st St
Lexington Avenue/ 59th Street
N R W
E 60th St
ROOSEVELT ISLAND TRAMWA
Queensboro Bridge
to Queens
15
59th Street
4 5 6
E 59th St
E 58th St
E 57th St
E 56th St
E 55th St
E 54th St
E 53rd St
E 52nd St
E 51st St
E 50th St
E 49th St
E 48th St
E 47th St
E 46th St
E 45th St
E 44th St (Archbishop Fulton J Sheen Pl)
E 43rd St
E 42nd St
E 41St St
E 40th St
E 39th St
E 38th St
FDR Dr
Sutton Place
Sutton Pl
to Queens
E V
Lexington Ave/ 53rd Street
51st Street
6
12
Madison Ave
Park Ave
Lexington Ave
Third Ave
Second Ave
First Ave
Beekman Pl
Mitchell Pl
General D MacArthur Plaza
East River
Dag Hammarskjold Plaza
Peace Garden
Vanderbilt Ave
PAGE 304
Grand Central Terminal
Depew Pl
United Nations Plaza
United Nations
PAGE 268
to Queens
Citi Field
Tennis Center
Grand Central 42nd Street
4 5 6
7 S
Tudor City
Tudor City Pl
Robert Moses Playground
Queens Midtown Tunnel
To Queens
495
10
Exit St
Entrance St
FDR Dr
1/4 mile
.25 km
A
B
1
2

Not many budget drinking options around here (except **Blarney Stone**), so go highbrow at **The Brasserie** inside The Seagram Building, **Campbell Apartment** inside Grand Central, **World Bar** inside the Trump Tower, or **Sir Harry's** inside the Waldorf. If you like to drink with the suits after work, **PJ Clarke's** is your spot.

Bars

- **Bill's Gay Nineties** • 57 E 54th St [Madison Ave] 212-355-0243 Party like it's 1899.
- **Blarney Stone** • 710 3rd Ave [E 45th St] 212-490-0457 The only bar in purgatory.
- **The Brasserie** • 100 E 53rd St [Park Ave] 212-751-4840 Posh drinks in hip Diller + Scofidio-designed space.
- **The Campbell Apartment** • 15 Vanderbilt Ave [E 42nd St] 212-953-0409 Awesome space, awesomely snooty!
- **Le Bateau Ivre** • 230 E 51st St [2nd Ave] 212-583-0579 Open 'til 4 am. French wine bar.
- **Manchester Pub** • 920 2nd Ave [E 49th St] 212-935-8901 You could do a lot worse in this part of town.
- **Metro 53** • 307 E 53rd St [Second Ave] 212-838-0007 Celebrities and suits.
- **P.J. Clarke's** • 915 3rd Ave [E 55th St] 212-317-1616 Old-timey midtown pub.
- **Sir Harry's** • 301 Park Ave [49th St] 212-872-4890 Nice little Art-Deco bar inside the Waldorf-Astoria. Bring $$$.
- **Sofia Wine Bar & Cafe** • 242 E 50th St [2nd Ave] 212-888-8660 Italian wine bar, plus food goodies...
- **Sutton Place** • 1015 2nd Ave [E 54th St] 212-207-3777 Fabulous roofdeck makes it worth the climb.
- **World Bar** • 845 United Nations Plaza [46th St] 212-935-9361 Expensive, classy hideaway for diplomats and Derek Jeter.

Movie Theaters

- **Instituto Cervantes New York** • 211 E 49th St [Third Ave] 212-308-7720 Spanish gems, but call to make sure there's subtitles.

Theaters/Performing Arts

- **59E59 Theaters** • 59 E 59th St [Madison Ave] 212-753-5959 Primary Stages always has something interesting playing here.
- **St Bart's Playhouse** • E 50th St & Park Ave 212-378-0248 Manhattan's most beloved community theatre.

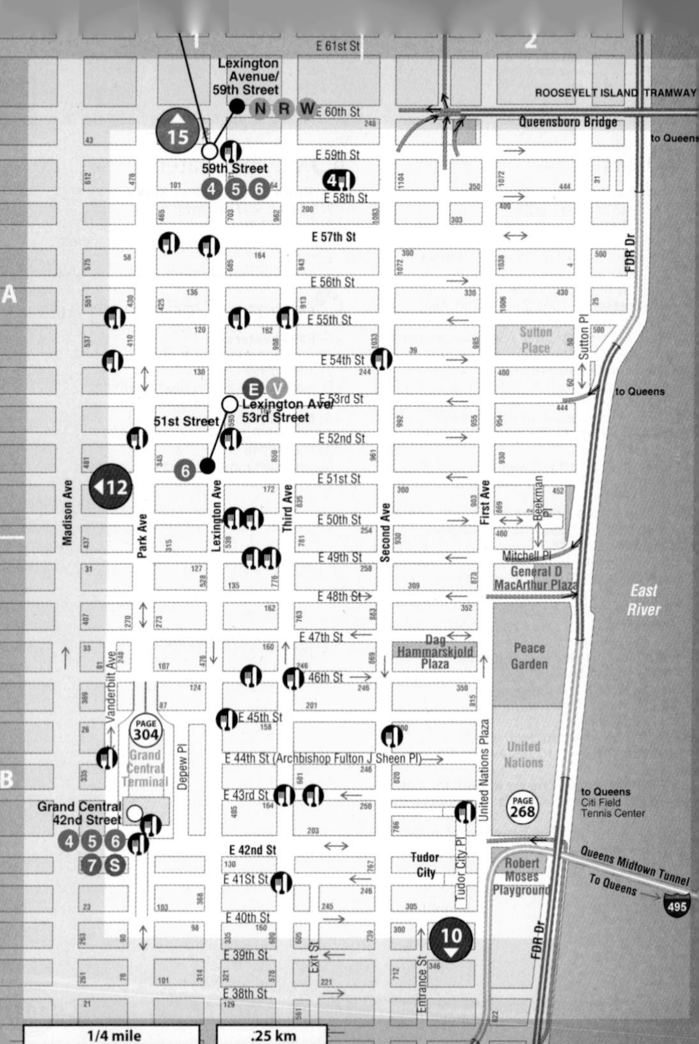

Lexington Avenue/ 59th Street
59th Street
E 61st St
E 60th St
E 59th St
E 58th St
E 57th St
E 56th St
E 55th St
E 54th St
E 53rd St
E 52nd St
E 51st St
E 50th St
E 49th St
E 48th St
E 47th St
46th St
E 45th St
E 44th St (Archbishop Fulton J Sheen Pl)
E 43rd St
E 42nd St
E 41St St
E 40th St
E 39th St
E 38th St
ROOSEVELT ISLAND TRAMWAY
Queensboro Bridge
to Queens
Lexington Ave/ 53rd Street
51st Street
Sutton Place
Sutton Pl
FDR Dr
Beekman Pl
Mitchell Pl
General D MacArthur Plaza
East River
Dag Hammarskjold Plaza
Peace Garden
United Nations
United Nations Plaza
to Queens Citi Field Tennis Center
Queens Midtown Tunnel
To Queens
Robert Moses Playground
Tudor City
Tudor City Pl
Entrance St
Exit St
Madison Ave
Park Ave
Lexington Ave
Third Ave
Second Ave
First Ave
Vanderbilt Ave
Depew Pl
Grand Central Terminal
Grand Central 42nd Street
PAGE 304
PAGE 268
1/4 mile
.25 km

The Oyster Bar should be on any New Yorker's list of must eats. **Aquavit's** Scandanavian Sunday buffet brunch is as amazing as it is expensive. **Sakagura** is a great option for Japanese and sake, while **Sushi Yasada** has the best raw fish in the city. For a classic NYC burger, **PJ Clarke's** is a good bet.

Restaurants

- **Aquavit** • 65 E 55th St [Park Ave]
  212-307-7311 • $$$$$
  Stellar dining experience: top-drawer Scandinavian.
- **BLT Steak** • 106 E 57th St [Park Ave]
  212-752-7470 • $$$$$
  Pricey and good, not great.
- **Burke in the Box at Bloomingdale's** •
  150 E 59th St [Lexington Ave]
  212-705-3800 • $$
  Chef David Burke's offbeat take-out eatery inside Bloomies.
- **Chola** • 232 E 58th St [Third Ave]
  212-688-4619 • $$$$
  Pricey south Indian cuisine.
- **Convivio** • 45 Tudor City Pl [E 42nd St]
  212-599-5045 • $$$
  Solid Italian on one of the coolest blocks in the city.
- **Dawat** • 210 E 58th St [Third Ave]
  212-355-7555 • $$$$
  Top-end Indian.
- **Docks Oyster Bar** • 633 3rd Ave [E 40th St]
  212-986-8080 • $$$$
  Great seafood, good atmosphere.
- **F&B** • 150 E 52nd St [Lexington Ave]
  212-421-8600 • $
  Belgian street food that makes our carts look nasty.
- **Felidia** • 243 E 58th St [Third Ave]
  212-758-1479 • $$$$
  Top Northern Italian.
- **Four Seasons** • 99 E 52nd St [Park Ave]
  212-754-9494 • $$$$$
  Designer everything. Even the cotton candy.
- **La Fonda Del Sol** • E 44th St & Vanderbilt Ave
  212-867-6767 • $$$$$
  Tapas in a semi-corporate setting.
- **Menchanko-tei** • 131 E 45th St [Lexington]
  212-986-6805 • $$
  Japanese noodle shop.
- **Monkey Bar** • 60 E 54th St [Madison Ave]
  212-308-2950 • $$$$
  Graydon Carter does Midtown with old-New York menu.
- **Nikki** • 151 E 50th St [Lexington Ave]
  212-753-1144 • $$$
  Eclectic Miami vice with pillows.
- **NY Luncheonette** •
  135 E 50th St [Lexington Ave]
  212-838-0165 • $$
  Diner where Obama lunched with Bloomy.
- **Opia** • 130 E 57th St [Lexington Ave]
  212-688-3939 • $$$$
  Midtown spot for moules frites and steak au poivre.
- **Oyster Bar** • Grand Central Terminal, Lower Level [Park Ave & E 42nd St]
  212-490-6650 • $$$
  Classic New York seafood joint. Go for the Saloon.
- **P.J. Clarke's** • 915 3rd Ave [E 55th St]
  212-317-1616 • $$$
  Pub grub. A fine burger.
- **Palm** • 837 2nd Ave [E 45th St]
  212-687-2953 • $$$$$
  Steaks and chops. Go to Luger's.
- **Patroon** • 160 E 46th St [3rd Ave]
  212-883-7373 • $$$$$
  An oasis of civility.
- **Pershing Square** • 90 E 42nd St [Park Ave]
  212-286-9600 • $$$$
  Excellent food and awesome space.
- **Sakagura** • 211 E 43rd St [3rd Ave]
  212-953-7253 • $$$
  Midtowners are very happy to have this excellent izakaya.
- **Shun Lee Palace** • 155 E 55th St [Lexington]
  212-371-8844 • $$$$$
  Top-end Chinese.
- **Smith & Wollensky** • 797 3rd Ave [E 49th St]
  212-753-1530 • $$$$$
  Don't order the fish.
- **Sparks Steak House** • 210 E 46th St [3rd Ave]
  212-687-4855 • $$$$$
  If you can't go to Luger's.
- **Sushi Yasuda** • 204 E 43rd St [3rd Ave]
  212-972-1001 • $$$$
  Best sushi in NYC. Let the debate begin...
- **Taksim** • 1030 2nd Ave [E 54th St]
  212-421-3004 • $$$
  All manner of Turkish delights.
- **Wollensky's Grill** • 201 E 49th St [3rd Ave]
  212-753-0444 • $$$$
  For those who want the same food as S&W with less wait time.
- **Yuva** • 230 E 58th St [3rd Ave]
  212-339-0090 • $$$$
  Inventive new addition to upscale Indian row.

E 61st St
Lexington Avenue/ 59th Street
N R W
E 60th St
ROOSEVELT ISLAND TRAMWAY
Queensboro Bridge
to Queens
15
59th Street
4 5 6
E 59th St
E 58th St
E 57th St
E 56th St
E 55th St
E 54th St
E 53rd St
E 52nd St
E 51st St
E 50th St
E 49th St
E 48th St
E 47th St
E 46th St
E 45th St
E 44th St (Archbishop Fulton J Sheen Pl)
E 43rd St
E 42nd St
E 41St St
E 40th St
E 39th St
E 38th St
FDR Dr
Sutton Place
Sutton Pl
to Queens
E V
Lexington Ave/ 53rd Street
51st Street
6
12
Madison Ave
Park Ave
Lexington Ave
Third Ave
Second Ave
First Ave
Beekman Pl
Mitchell Pl
General D MacArthur Plaza
East River
Dag Hammarskjold Plaza
Peace Garden
Vanderbilt Ave
PAGE 304
Grand Central Terminal
Depew Pl
United Nations Plaza
United Nations
to Queens
Citi Field
Tennis Center
PAGE 268
Grand Central 42nd Street
4 5 6
7 S
Tudor City
Tudor City Pl
Robert Moses Playground
Queens Midtown Tunnel
To Queens
495
Exit St
Entrance St
10
1/4 mile
.25 km
A
B
1
2

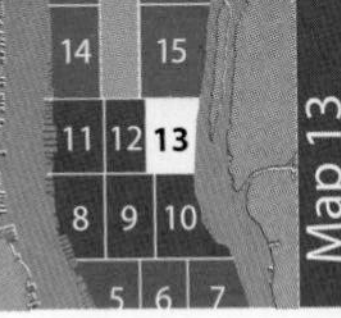

Sam Flax is where we stock up on art and office supplies. **The Food Emporium** under bridge is actually kind of cool. **Sherry Lehmann** has a ridiculous selection of fancy booze you can't afford. **Jeffrey Wine** has been serving the 'hood for over 30 years. And there's a **Home Depot** in a basement on 59th Street? That's just plain weird.

Bagels

- **Ess-A-Bagel** • 831 3rd Ave [E 51st St]
  212-980-1010
  Bagels with attitude.
- **Tal Bagels** • 977 1st Ave [E 54th St]
  212-753-9080
  Pretty good. Lots of cream cheese options.

Coffee

- **Aroma Espresso** • 205 E 42nd St [3rd Ave]
  212-557-1010
  The Israeli version of Starbucks comes stateside.
- **ING Direct Cafe** • 968 3rd Ave [E 58th St]
  212-752-8432
  Good coffee, inexpensive, clean & uncrowded.
- **Joe: The Art of Coffee** •
  44 Grand Central Terminal
  212-661-8580
  Joe really knows his joe.
- **Macchiato Espresso Bar** •
  141 E 44th St [Lexington Ave]
  212-867-6772
  Nice coffee shop for this part of town.

Shopping

- **A&D Building** • 150 E 58th St [Lexington Ave]
  212-644-2766
  Over 200,000 sq. ft. of commercial and residential furnishings. Wow.
- **Alkit Pro Camera** • 227 E 45th St [3rd Ave]
  212-674-1515
  Good camera shop; developing; rentals.
- **Amish Market** • 240 E 45th St [Third Ave]
  212-370-1761
  Lots of prepared foods. Do they deliver by horse and buggy?
- **Buttercup Bake Shop** • 973 2nd Ave [52nd St]
  212-350-4144
  Move over Magnolia. Buttercup's all grown up.
- **Crush Wine & Spirits** • 153 E 57th St [Lexington]
  212-980-9463
  Stock up on booze to survive the walk through Midtown.
- **Food Emporium** • 405 E 59th St [First Ave]
  212-752-5836
  Unique market design underneath the Queensboro Bridge.
- **Grand Central Market** • 105 E 42nd St [Park Ave]
  212-338-0014
  Pick up fixings for a gourmet dinner before jumping on the train.
- **Home Depot** • 980 3rd Ave [E 59th St]
  212-888-1512
  Mega home improvement chain comes to the city.
- **Ideal Cheese** • 942 1st Ave [E 52nd St]
  800-382-0109
  All cheese is ideal.
- **Innovative Audio** • 150 E 58th St [Lexington]
  212-634-4444
  Quality music systems and home theaters.
- **Jeffrey Wine & Liquors** • 939 1st Ave [52nd St]
  212-753-3725
  Jeffrey will treat you right. No Midtown attitude.
- **Nicola's Specialty Emporium** •
  997 1st Ave [55th St]
  212-753-9275
  Italian brothers with top Italian goods.
- **Posman Books** • 9 Grand Central Terminal
  212-983-1111
  Nice little bookshop. Lots of NFTs.
- **Radio Shack** • 940 3rd Ave [E 57th St]
  212-750-8409
  Kenneth, what's the frequency?
- **Richard B Arkway Books** •
  59 E 54th St [Madison Ave]
  212-751-8135
  Antique maps and rare travel books. Cool!
- **Sam Flax** • 900 3rd Ave [E 55th St]
  212-813-6666
  Portfolios, frames, furniture, and designer gifts.
- **Sherry-Lehmann** • 505 Park Ave [E 59th St]
  212-838-7500
  Wines and spirits for the connaisseur.
- **Sports Authority** • 845 3rd Ave [E 51st St]
  212-355-9725
  Sporting goods for the masses.
- **Terence Conran Shop** • 407 E 59th St [1st Ave]
  866-755-9079
  Awe-inspiring modern designs for the home. Can we live here?
- **The World of Golf** • 147 E 47th St [Lexington]
  212-775-9398
  Stop here on your way to Vanny.
- **Yankee Clubhouse Shop** • 110 E 59th St [Park]
  212-758-7844
  Any Yankee fan's paradise.

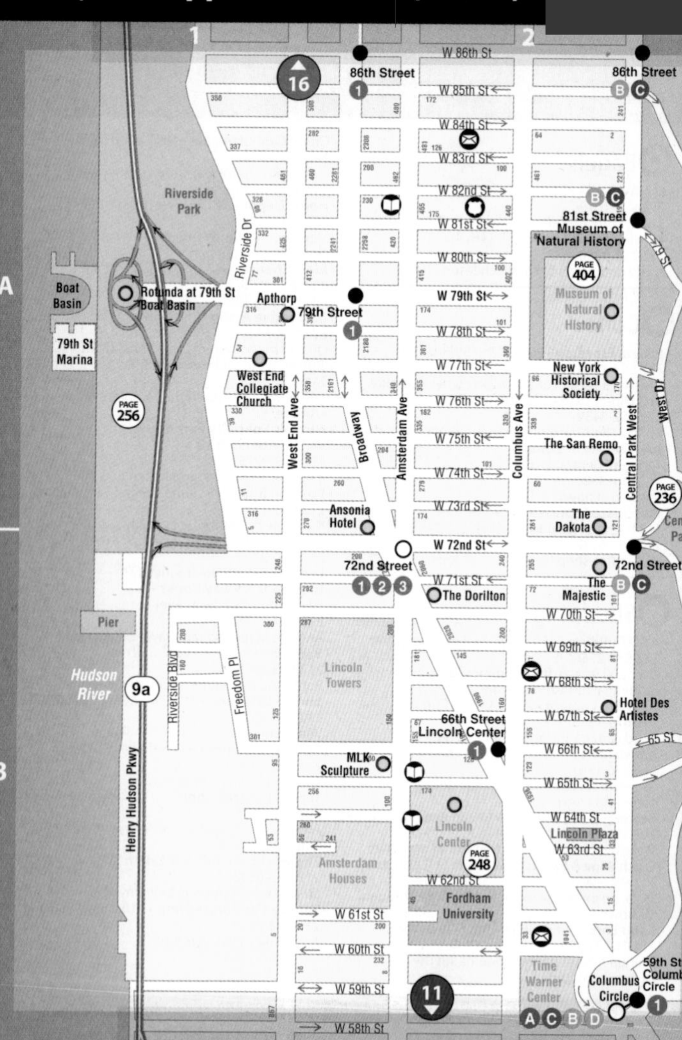

86th Street
W 86th St
W 85th St
W 84th St
W 83rd St
W 82nd St
W 81st St
W 80th St
W 79th St
W 78th St
W 77th St
W 76th St
W 75th St
W 74th St
W 73rd St
W 72nd St
W 71st St
W 70th St
W 69th St
W 68th St
W 67th St
W 66th St
W 65th St
W 64th St
W 63rd St
W 62nd St
W 61st St
W 60th St
W 59th St
W 58th St
Riverside Park
Riverside Dr
Boat Basin
Rotunda at 79th St Boat Basin
79th St Marina
Apthorp
79th Street
West End Collegiate Church
West End Ave
Broadway
Amsterdam Ave
Columbus Ave
Central Park West
West Dr
81st Street Museum of Natural History
Museum of Natural History
New York Historical Society
The San Remo
The Dakota
72nd Street
The Majestic
Ansonia Hotel
The Dorilton
Hotel Des Artistes
65 St
66th Street Lincoln Center
Lincoln Towers
Lincoln Plaza
Lincoln Center
MLK Sculpture
Amsterdam Houses
Fordham University
Time Warner Center
Columbus Circle
59th Str
Columb Circle
Pier
Hudson River
9a
Riverside Blvd
Freedom Pl
Henry Hudson Pkwy
PAGE 256
PAGE 404
PAGE 236
PAGE 248
16
11
A
B
Centr Park

Neighborhood Overview

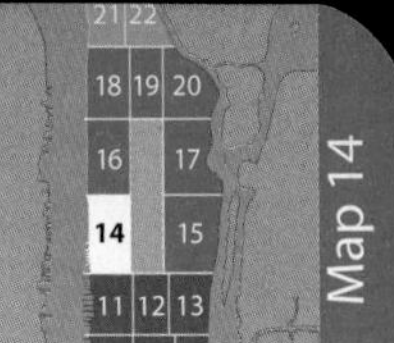

Away from the bustle of midtown and downtown Manhattan, the lower part of the Upper West Side offers a decidedly different, slower pace. But by no means does this neighborhood feel sleepy. Sandwiched between two parks, this neighborhood offers great food, museums, dive bars, and beautiful Art Deco architecture, not to mention the cultural meccas of Lincoln Center and the American Museum of Natural History, all of which remind you that New York is a livable city after all.

Many of the buildings that line the streets of the Upper West Side are landmarks. **The Ansonia** (built between 1899 and 1904) was originally a hotel and is now an exclusive apartment building. It has had many famous residents including Babe Ruth and Theodore Dreiser. **The Dakota** (built from 1880-1884) is best known for being the home of John Lennon and Yoko Ono, and the place where Lennon was killed at the entrance to the building. **The Dorilton** (built in 1902), the **Majestic** (built in 1894), and the **San Remo** (completed in 1931) all attest to bygone days of elaborate building construction.

Green space surrounds this neighborhood. To the east lies Central Park, but most locals head west to the gorgeous Riverside Park. It is filled with beautiful flower gardens, wonderful playgrounds, and some great spots to sit down and relax by the water. For those looking for something more active, a path runs along the Hudson River, perfect for jogging and biking. **The Boat Basin at 79th Street** is the only facility in the city that allows year-round residency in boats. It is also used as a launch site for kayaks, canoes, and sailboats, which you can rent in the summer. The rotunda overlooks the marina and is the site of the Boat Basin café (open April to October), a great place to unwind with a beer as the sun sets over the Hudson.

Like a city unto itself, **The American Museum of Natural History** is one of the largest museums in the world. Founded in 1869, the museum contains 25 interconnected buildings with lots of famous permanent exhibits (anthropological collections, rooms on human biology and evolution, a life-sized model blue whale, and the world's largest sapphire in the world, to name a few). Connected to the museum is the always popular **Hayden Planetarium**, part of the Rose Center for Earth and Space. It's a great spot to experience the wonders of the universe narrated by Robert Redford or Whoopi Goldberg.

Just south of AMNH is **The New-York Historical Society** which has a fabulous collection documenting the history of New York and the United States. Some highlights include many of James Audubon's watercolors, paintings from the Hudson River School, and materials from the Civil War and Reconstruction.

When Upper West Siders tire from museums, they join the rest of the city's cultural elite at **Lincoln Center**, probably the most famous arts and culture center in the world. Home of the Film Society of Lincoln Center, Jazz at Lincoln Center, the Lincoln Center Theater, the Metropolitan Opera, the City Opera, the City Ballet, and the New York Philharmonic, as well as Juilliard, the School of American Ballet, and the Library for the Performing Arts, this place is just bursting with artistic brilliance.

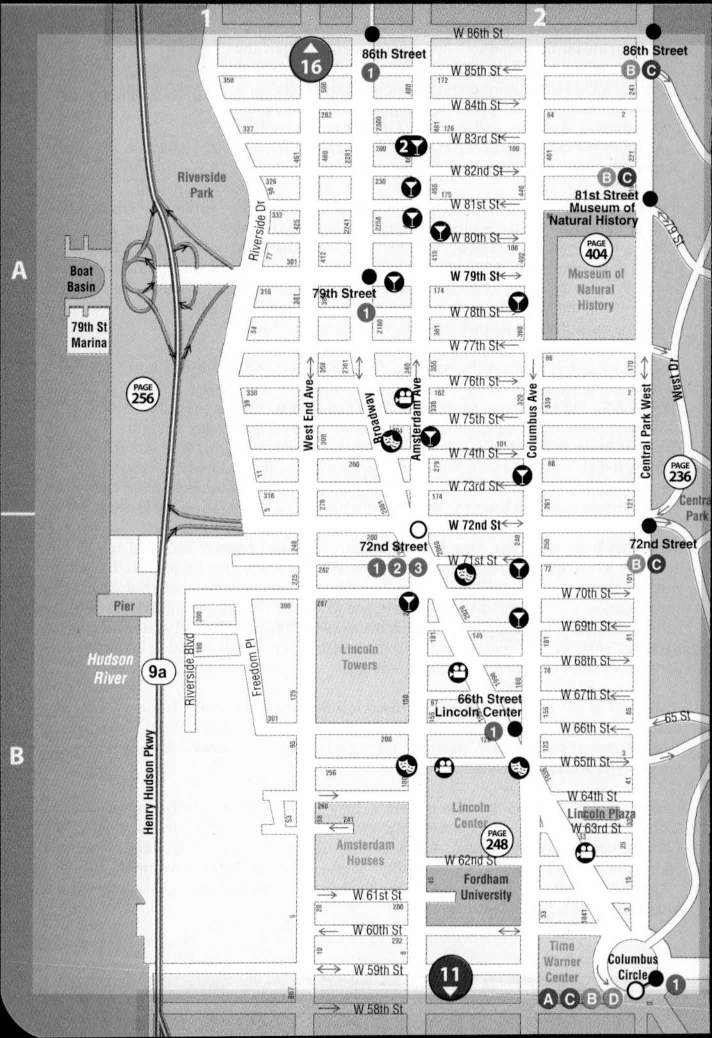

W 86th St
86th Street
W 85th St
W 84th St
W 83rd St
W 82nd St
W 81st St
81st Street
Museum of Natural History
W 80th St
W 79th St
79th Street
W 78th St
W 77th St
W 76th St
W 75th St
W 74th St
W 73rd St
W 72nd St
72nd Street
W 71st St
W 70th St
W 69th St
W 68th St
W 67th St
66th Street
Lincoln Center
W 66th St
W 65th St
W 64th St
Lincoln Plaza
W 63rd St
W 62nd St
W 61st St
W 60th St
W 59th St
W 58th St
65 St
79 St
Riverside Park
Riverside Dr
Boat Basin
79th St Marina
Museum of Natural History
West End Ave
Broadway
Amsterdam Ave
Columbus Ave
Central Park West
West Dr
Central Park
Pier
Hudson River
9a
Henry Hudson Pkwy
Riverside Blvd
Freedom Pl
Lincoln Towers
Lincoln Center
Fordham University
Amsterdam Houses
Time Warner Center
Columbus Circle

16
11
PAGE 256
PAGE 404
PAGE 236
PAGE 248

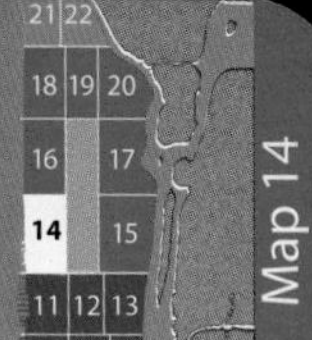

For a night of culture, go to Lincoln Center or see a concert at the **Beacon Theater.** For drunken revelries, seek out the **Dublin House**. Or class it up at **Cava**, a tiny wine bar. Go to **Café Luxembourg** to spot celebrities. And don't pass up a trip to the new location of **P&G Bar**, still going strong after all these years.

Bars

- **Bin 71** • 237 Columbus Ave [71st St]
  212-362-5446
  Sip wine with 30-something Upper West Siders.
- **Café Luxembourg** •
  200 W 70th St [Amsterdam Ave]
  212-873-7411
  Hey, is that Tom Hanks over there?
- **Candle Bar** • 309 Amsterdam Ave [74th St]
  212-874-9155
  Only gay bar in this part of the UWS. Strong drinks!
- **Cava** • 185 W 80th St [Amsterdam]
  212-724-2282
  Cozy. Can you say date night?
- **Dead Poet** • 450 Amsterdam Ave [W 82nd St]
  212-595-5670
  Good Irish feel. No secret society that we know of.
- **Dublin House** • 225 W 79th St [Broadway]
  212-874-9528
  Great dingy Irish pub. Recommended.
- **Emerald Inn** • 205 Columbus Ave [W 69th St]
  212-874-8840
  Another good Irish pub!
- **Fred's** • 476 Amsterdam Ave [W 83rd St]
  212-579-3076
  Sort of old-school. Sort of fun.
- **Hi Life Bar & Grill** •
  477 Amsterdam Ave [W 83rd St]
  212-787-7199
  Not a bad option for this part of town.
- **Jake's Dilemma** •
  430 Amsterdam Ave [W 81st St]
  212-580-0556
  Drink beer and pretend you're still in college.
- **P&G Bar** • 380 Columbus Ave [W 78th St]
  Reincarnated version not as divey but still a welcome return.
- **Wine and Roses** •
  286 Columbus Ave [W 73rd St]
  212-579-9463
  A wino's paradise. Not as sappy as it sounds.

Movie Theaters

- **AMC Loews Lincoln Square 13** •
  1998 Broadway [W 68th St]
  212-336-5020
  Classy Upper West Side multiplex with IMAX.
- **Jewish Community Center in Manhattan** •
  334 Amsterdam Ave [W 77th St]
  646-505-4444
  Jewish premieres, previews, and festivals.
- **Lincoln Plaza Cinemas** •
  1886 Broadway [W 63rd St]
  212-757-2280
  Uptown version of the Angelika.
- **Walter Reade Theater** •
  70 Lincoln Center Plaza [W 65th St]
  212-875-5600
  Amazing festivals and rare screenings.

Theaters/Performing Arts

- **Alice Tully Hall** • Broadway & W 65th St
  212-875-5050
  Lincoln Center's house for chamber music and small ensembles.
- **ArcLight Theatre** •
  152 W 71st St [Amsterdam Ave]
  212-595-0355
  A classic church basement theatre.
- **Beacon Theater** • 2124 Broadway [W 74th St]
  212-465-6500
  Former movie palace with beautiful neo-Grecian interior.
- **Mitzi E Newhouse Theater** •
  Amsterdam Ave & W 65th St
  212-239-6200
  Lincoln Center's Off-Broadway space

86th Street
W 86th St
W 85th St
W 84th St
W 83rd St
W 82nd St
W 81st St
W 80th St
W 79th St
W 78th St
W 77th St
W 76th St
W 75th St
W 74th St
W 73rd St
W 72nd St
W 71st St
W 70th St
W 69th St
W 68th St
W 67th St
W 66th St
W 65th St
W 64th St
W 63rd St
W 62nd St
W 61st St
W 60th St
W 59th St
W 58th St
65 St
79 St
81st Street
Museum of
Natural History
PAGE 404
Museum of Natural History
79th Street
72nd Street
66th Street
Lincoln Center
Riverside Park
Riverside Dr
Boat Basin
79th St Marina
PAGE 256
PAGE 236
PAGE 248
Central Park
West End Ave
Broadway
Amsterdam Ave
Columbus Ave
Central Park West
West Dr
Pier
Hudson River
9a
Henry Hudson Pkwy
Riverside Blvd
Freedom Pl
Lincoln Towers
Lincoln Center
Lincoln Plaza
Amsterdam Houses
Fordham University
Time Warner Center
Columbus Circle

Big Nick's has the largest, if not best, burgers in town and is open late. **Kefi** has awesome (and affordable) Greek food. The tiny **Celeste** is a neighborhood fave for Italian. **Ouest** is routinely touted as the finest restaurant on the Upper West Side. For all night eats, **French Roast** is the spot.

Restaurants

- **'cesca** • 164 W 75 St [Amsterdam Ave]
  212-787-6300 • $$$$
  Sunday Sauce worthy of a cameo in *Goodfellas*.
- **Artie's Deli** • 2290 Broadway [W 83rd St]
  212-579-5959 • $$
  Hot pastrami on rye never goes out of style.
- **Bar Boulud** • 1900 Broadway [W 63rd St]
  212-595-0303 • $$$
  Before the opera, stop in for the fabulous charcuterie plate.
- **Big Nick's** • 2175 Broadway [W 77th St]
  212-362-9238 • $$
  Death by burger. Recommended.
- **Café Luxembourg** •
  200 W 70th St [Amsterdam Ave]
  212-873-7411 • $$$$$
  Top-end bistro. Anyone know what Luxembourgian cuisine is?
- **Celeste** • 502 Amsterdam Ave [W 84th St]
  212-874-4559 • $$
  Cheap and tasty homemade pastas. A true gem.
- **Earthen Oven** • 53 W 72nd St [Columbus Ave]
  212-579-8888 • $$$
  Solid Indian cuisine. Nice weekend buffet.
- **Epices du Traiteur** • 103 W 70th St [Columbus]
  212-579-5904 • $$$
  Charming atmosphere, eclectic and flavorful food.
- **Fatty Crab** • 2170 Broadway [77th St]
  212-496-2722 • $$
  Malaysian when Upper West Siders need to spice it up a little.
- **The Firehouse** • 522 Columbus Ave [85th St]
  212-787-3473 • $$
  Where to go for after-softball wings.
- **Freddy & Peppers** •
  303 Amsterdam Ave [W 74th St]
  212-799-2378 • $
  Thin crust pizza. Has been around forever.
- **French Roast** • 2340 Broadway [W 85th St]
  212-799-1533 • $$
  Open 24 hours. Good croque-monsieur.
- **Gabriel's** • 11 W 60th St [Broadway]
  212-956-4600 • $$$
  Local-draw; good all-around.
- **Gari** • 370 Columbus Ave [W 78th St]
  212-362-4816 • $$$$$
  Why UWS sushi snobs no longer have to take the cross-town bus.
- **Good Enough to Eat** •
  483 Amsterdam Ave [W 83rd St]
  212-496-0163 • $$$
  Good brunch but Sunday line starts early.
- **Gray's Papaya** • 2090 Broadway [W 71st St]
  212-799-0243 • $
  Open 24 hours. An institution.
- **Josie's** • 300 Amsterdam Ave [W 74th St]
  212-769-1212 • $$$
  Good place to take the parents if they're vegetarian.
- **Kefi** • 505 Columbus Ave [W 84th St]
  212-873-0200 • $$
  Greek food gets an upgrade at this amazingly affordable gem.
- **La Caridad 78** • 2199 Broadway [W 78th St]
  212-874-2780 • $$
  Cheap Cuban paradise.
- **Le Pain Quotidien** • 50 W 72nd St [Central Pk W]
  212-712-9700 • $$
  Great breads. Communal Table. Euro vibe.
- **Monaco Restaurant** •
  421 Amsterdam Ave [80th St]
  212-873-3100 • $$
  Cute bistro. Outdoor tables in the summer.
- **Nanoosh** • 2012 Broadway [W 69th St]
  212-362-7922 • $
  Cheap, fast Middle-Eastern food. Good for before the movies.
- **Nougatine** • 1 Central Park West [Columbus Cir]
  212-299-3900 • $$$$$
  Brilliant $24.07 prix fixe lunch!
- **Ouest** • 2315 Broadway [W 84th St]
  212-580-8700 • $$$$
  Trendy and upscale. Just the way some Upper Westsiders like it.
- **Rosa Mexicano** • 61 Columbus Ave [62nd St]
  212-977-7700 • $$$$
  Inventive Mexican. Great guac.
- **Salumeria Rosi** • 283 Amsterdam Ave [73rd St]
  212-877-4800 • $$
  Eatery doubles as excellent salami shop. Beware of '80s glam interior.
- **Shake Shack** • 366 Columbus Ave [W 77th St]
  212-889-6600 • $$
  Now you can get your Shack Burger year round.
- **Vince and Eddie's** • 70 W 68th St [Columbus]
  212-721-0068 • $$$$
  Cozy comfort food. Fireplace in the winter.
- **West Branch** • 2178 Broadway [W 77th St]
  212-777-6764 • $$$$
  Favorite spot of the UWS dining elite. French-American fare.

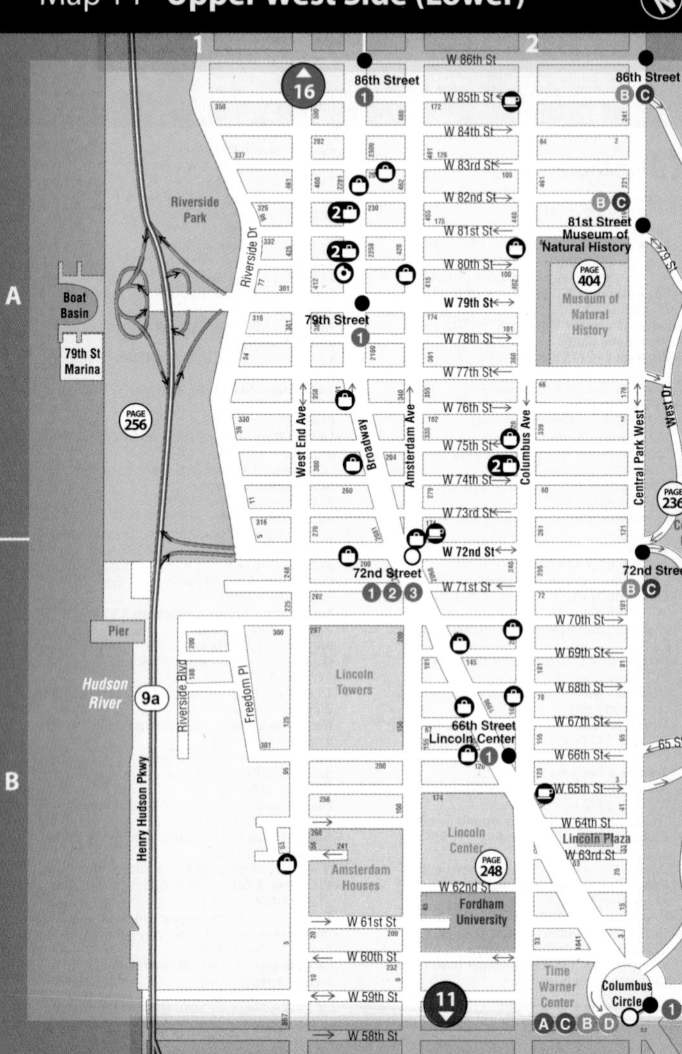

Map 14 · Upper West Side (Lower)
W 86th St
86th Street
W 85th St
W 84th St
W 83rd St
W 82nd St
W 81st St
81st Street
Museum of
Natural History
W 80th St
W 79th St
79th Street
W 78th St
W 77th St
W 76th St
W 75th St
W 74th St
W 73rd St
W 72nd St
72nd Street
W 71st St
72nd Street
W 70th St
W 69th St
W 68th St
W 67th St
66th Street
Lincoln Center
W 66th St
W 65th St
W 64th St
Lincoln Plaza
W 63rd St
W 62nd St
W 61st St
W 60th St
W 59th St
W 58th St
Riverside Park
Riverside Dr
Boat Basin
79th St Marina
PAGE 256
PAGE 404
PAGE 236
PAGE 248
Museum of Natural History
West End Ave
Broadway
Amsterdam Ave
Columbus Ave
Central Park West
West Dr
65 St
Pier
Hudson River
9a
Riverside Blvd
Freedom Pl
Lincoln Towers
Lincoln Center
Amsterdam Houses
Fordham University
Time Warner Center
Columbus Circle
Henry Hudson Pkwy

New York's prime food shopping can be found in this neighborhood. **Zabar's** (cheeses, fish, coffee, free samples), **H & H** (world famous bagels), and **Fairway** (fresh produce, breads, dry goods, total chaos) are within six blocks of one another. To pair some wine with that fine food, we like **67 Wine & Spirits**.

Bagels

- **H&H Bagels** • 2239 Broadway [W 80th St]
  212-595-8000
  Hot & heavenly.

Coffee

- **Aroma Espresso** • 161 W 72nd St [Amsterdam]
  212-595-7700
  The Israeli version of Starbucks comes stateside.
- **Joe: The Art of Coffee** •
  514 Columbus Ave [W 85th St]
  212-875-0100
  Joe really knows his joe.
- **Le Pain Quotidien** • 60 W 65th St [Columbus]
  212-721-4001
  Excellent coffee and pastries. Thanks Belgium.

Shopping

- **67 Wine & Spirits** • 179 Columbus Ave [68th St]
  212-724-6767
  Top-notch selection and helpful staff. Lots of tastings.
- **Allan & Suzi** • 416 Amsterdam Ave [W 80th St]
  212-724-7445
  UWS vintage clothing & designer resale mainstay.
- **Barnes & Noble** • 1972 Broadway [W 67th St]
  212-595-6859
  Nice performing arts section. Cafe on top floor.
- **Best Cellars** • 2246 Broadway [W 81st St]
  212-0362-8730
  Great combo of cheap wine and tons of tastings.
- **Bruce Frank** • 215 W 83rd St [Amsterdam Ave]
  877-232-3776
  Great bead shop. We're actually not joking.
- **Fairway Market** • 2127 Broadway [W 74th St]
  212-595-1888
  Top-notch supermarket, but always packed.
- **Gracious Home** • 1992 Broadway [W 68th St]
  212-231-7800
  A side of hardware with your fancy housewares.
- **Grandaisy Bakery** •
  176 W 72nd St [Amsterdam Ave]
  212-334-9435
  Uptown outpost of famous Sullivan Street location.
- **Grom** • 2165 Broadway [W 76th St]
  212-362-1837
  Really kick-ass gelato made by actual Italians.
- **Jonathan Adler** • 304 Columbus Ave [74th St]
  212-787-0017
  Funky, fun housewares.
- **Laytner's Linens** • 2270 Broadway [82nd St]
  212-724-0180
  Things that'll make you want to stay home more.
- **Nancy's Wine For Food** •
  313 Columbus Ave [W 75th St]
  212-877-4040
  Nancy will help you plan your next tasting party.
- **Patagonia** • 426 Columbus Ave [W 81st St]
  917-441-0011
  Eco-conscious store selling fleece for your adventurous subway ride.
- **Pookie & Sebastian** •
  322 Columbus Ave [W 75th St]
  212-580-5844
  Flirty tops, girly dresses, and fly jeans—for UWS chicks.
- **Soutine** • 104 W 70 St [Columbus Ave]
  212-496-1450
  Delicious French pastries.
- **Tani Shoes** • 2020 Broadway [69th St]
  212-873-4361
  Excellent selection of men's and women's shoes.
- **Townshop** • 2273 Broadway [W 82nd St]
  212-787-2762
  Where experts will fit you for the perfect bra.
- **Western Beef** • 75 West End Ave [W 63rd St]
  If you don't have time for Fairway and Zabar's.
- **Westsider Records** • 233 W 72nd St [Broadway]
  212-874-1588
  Cool record store. You'll find some interesting stuff.
- **Yarn Co** • 2274 Broadway [W 82nd St]
  212-787-7878
  The nitty gritty for knitters in the city.
- **Zabar's** • 2245 Broadway [W 80th St]
  212-787-2000
  Manhattan supermarket legend. NFT's favorite.

86th Street
The Jeffersons High-rise
Zion-St Marks Evangelical Lutheran Church
Carl Schurz Park
E 86th St
E 85th St
E 84th St
E 83rd St
E 82nd St
E 81st St
E 80th St
E 79th St
E 78th St
E 77th St
E 76th St
E 75th St
E 74th St
E 73rd St
E 72nd St
E 71st St
E 70th St
E 69th St
E 68th St
E 67th St
E 66th St
E 65th St
E 64th St
E 63rd St
E 62nd St
E 61st St
E 60th St
E 59th St
Metropolitan Museum of Art
PAGE 402
PAGE 236
Frank E. Campbell Funeral Chapel
Parisian-style Chimneys
New York Society Library
77th Street
John Jay Park
Bemelmans Bar
Whitney Museum of American Art
Fifth Ave
Madison Ave
Park Ave
Lexington Ave
Third Ave
Second Ave
First Ave
York Ave
East End Ave
Bobby Wagner Walk
Breakfast at Tiffany's Apartment Building
Frick Collection
Asia Society
The Explorers Club
Central Park
Weill Medical College (Cornell)
68th Street Hunter College
Memorial Sloane Kettering Cancer Center
Park East Synagouge
The Manhattan House
Rockefeller University
FDR Dr
The Lotos Club
Temple Emanu-El
Bernie Madoff Apartment
Foot Bridge
Lexington Avenue 63rd Street
East River
Mount Vernon Hotel Museum and Garden
The Metropolitan Club
5th Avenue/ 59th Street
Lexington Avenue/ 59th Street
Roosevelt Island Tram
59th Street
Roosevelt Island Tramwa
Queensboro Brid
To Queens
1/4 mile
.25 km

Neighborhood Overview

If you've ever watched the TV show Gossip Girl, you know the reputation of the Upper East Side: snooty, fancy and rich. While this historical neighborhood is also home to some of the oldest wealth in New York, it's home to a lot more than you see on the CW: on the weekends, especially in the warm days, check out everyone in their flip flops and sunglasses (designer please) heading to the most green space in Manhattan, Central Park. If you're not sunbathing or throwing a Frisbee, check out some of the most famous museums in the world, lively restaurants, shopping and brunch–oh you must be a lady/gentleman who brunches if you wander up here. Old or young, this neighborhood is changing–and especially in the summer, sans a trip to the Hamptons, there is no better place to be.

Long before **Bernie Madoff** made this neighborhood infamous, the fabulously wealthy started settling into the Upper East Side over a century ago. As a result, there are beautiful highrises up and down Park Avenue. Fifth Avenue is the home of what was dubbed "Millionaires Row" at the turn of the 19th century–the Carnegies, the Vanderbilts, the Astors, and their friends all walked the streets lined with glorious mansions, now known as Museum Mile. For a different sort of landmark head up to 85th for **The Jeffersons High Rise**...you know, that dee-luxe apartment in the sky from the classic TV show. Or walk by where Holly Golightly frolicked at the **Breakfast at Tiffany's Apartment**.

There are many historical sites to check out in one of the most historic districts in New York. Check out the **New York Society Library**, which moved to its current location on 79th Street from University Place in 1937. **Temple Emanu-El** on 72nd Street is one of the oldest temples in New York City—it was founded as a result of the second wave of immigration of Jews to America. Established in 1845, the reform congregation moved to its current location in 1927, where it welcomes Jews whose families have been going for generations and those who just moved to the city.

Want to stop and see a couple of exhibits? How about some of the most famous museums in the world. **The Frick Collection**, housed in the 1914 mansion of industrialist Henry Clark Frick, includes works by Rembrant, Degas, Goya, and many more of the art world's best-known names. (Visitor's tip: Free admission every Sunday between 11 am and 1 pm.) the **Whitney Museum** is a smaller and edgier house of contemporary American art. For a look into the art of worlds past, head over to **The Met** which houses over two million pieces and can take days to see it all. One last stop? **The Asia Society and Museum**, which houses an impressive art collection and performing arts program.

If you love classic New York entertainment (and have a large wad of cash), this your neighborhood. Step inside the Carlye Hotel to find **Bemelmans Bar**, named for the Austrian-born artist who created the Madeline children's books. It's a lovely place to stop for a drink and hear some piano during happy hour. Right next door is **Café Carlye** which attracts stars like Judy Collins, Elaine Strich, and Woody Allen on clarinet. Or head to **Feinstein's at the Regency** for legendary performers including Patti LuPone and Betty Buckley.

Map 15 • Upper East Side (Lower)

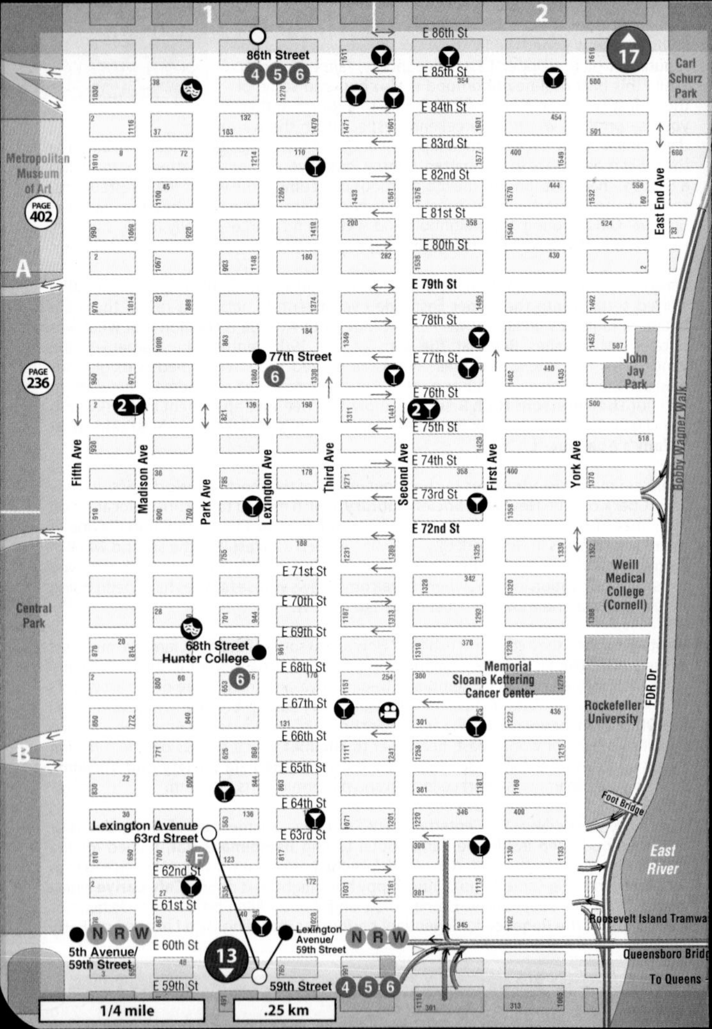

Metropolitan Museum of Art
PAGE 402
PAGE 236
Central Park
Carl Schurz Park
John Jay Park
Weill Medical College (Cornell)
Memorial Sloane Kettering Cancer Center
Rockefeller University
East River
Bobby Wagner Walk
FDR Dr
Foot Bridge
Roosevelt Island Tramway
Queensboro Bridge
To Queens

86th Street 4 5 6
77th Street 6
68th Street Hunter College 6
Lexington Avenue 63rd Street F
Lexington Avenue/ 59th Street N R W
5th Avenue/ 59th Street N R W
59th Street 4 5 6

Fifth Ave
Madison Ave
Park Ave
Lexington Ave
Third Ave
Second Ave
First Ave
York Ave
East End Ave

E 86th St
E 85th St
E 84th St
E 83rd St
E 82nd St
E 81st St
E 80th St
E 79th St
E 78th St
E 77th St
E 76th St
E 75th St
E 74th St
E 73rd St
E 72nd St
E 71st St
E 70th St
E 69th St
E 68th St
E 67th St
E 66th St
E 65th St
E 64th St
E 63rd St
E 62nd St
E 61st St
E 60th St
E 59th St

1/4 mile
.25 km

For a down-and-out dive (translation: our kind of bar) ride the **Subway Inn** or go old country Irish whiskey tasting at **Donohue's.** For a little more class grab the perfect glass of wine at **Accademia de Vino**. For even more class, no old money Upper East Side evening is complete without a visit to **Bemelmans Bar.**

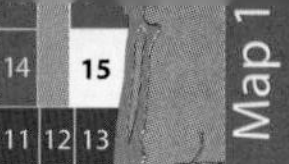

Bars

- **Accademia di Vino** • 1081 3rd Ave [E 63rd St]
  212-888-6333
  Wine bar. Laid back. Affordable. Uptown. Believe it.
- **American Trash** • 1471 1st Ave [77th St]
  212-988-9008
  Punk rockin' I-Bankers unite.
- **Bailey's Corner** • 1607 York Ave [E 85th St]
  212-650-1341
  Friendly Irish local. Watch the game or play darts.
- **Baker Street** • 1152 1st Ave [63rd St.]
  212-688-9663
  Flat screen TVs with above average bar food.
- **Bemelmans Bar** • 35 E 76th St [Madison Ave]
  212-744-1600
  When NFT actually has money, we drink here. Classic UES vibe.
- **Brandy's Piano Bar** • 235 E 84th St [Third Ave]
  212-744-4949
  Good ol' rollicking time.
- **Café Carlyle** • 35 E 76th St [Madison Ave]
  212-744-1600
  Classic cabaret venue where Woody plays. Hellishly expensive.
- **Donohue's Steak House** • 845 Lexington Ave [E 64th St]
  212-650-0748
  Old-school Irish. Sit at the bar & drink whiskey.
- **Feinstein's at the Regency** • 540 Park Ave [E 61st St]
  212-339-4095
  Life is a cabaret. At least if you work here.
- **Finnegan's Wake** • 1361 1st Ave [E 73rd St]
  212-737-3664
  Standard Irish pub. Therefore, pretty good.
- **Iggy's Karaoke Bar & Grill** • 1452 2nd Ave [66th St.]
  212-327-3043
  Super-friendly bartenders help cue up the cheesy karaoke action.
- **Lexington Bar & Books** • 1020 Lexington Ave [E 73rd St]
  212-717-3902
  Sip cognac and smoke a stogie. Stupid dress code policy.
- **Molly Pitchers** • 1641 2nd Ave [85th St]
  212-249-3067
  Where Ravens, Steelers fans find refuge on Sundays.
- **O'Flanagan's** • 1215 1st Ave [66th St]
  212-439-0660
  Unpretentious bar where recent grads and college kids mix peacefully.
- **Phoenix Park** • 206 E 67th St [3rd Ave.]
  212-717-8181
  Chill place to watch the Yankees or eat some burgers.
- **Pudding Stone's** • 1457 3rd Ave [E 82nd St]
  212-717-5797
  Long-countered locale to sip various vinos.
- **Ryan's Daughter** • 350 E 85th St [Second Ave]
  212-628-2613
  Free chips!
- **Stumble Inn** • 1454 2nd Ave [E 76th St]
  212-650-0561
  Thanks to the amazing specials, expect to stumble out.
- **Subway Inn** • 143 E 60th St [Lexington Ave]
  212-223-8929
  Sad, bad, glare, worn-out, ugh. Totally great.
- **Trinity Pub** • 299 E 84th St [Second Ave]
  212-327-4450
  Low on the UES meathead scale. Thank goodness!
- **Vero** • 1483 2nd Ave [77th St.]
  212-452-3354
  Escape a row of beer bars for a glass of wine.
- **Vudu** • 1487 1st Ave [E 78th St]
  212-249-9540
  They actually dance on the Upper East Side?

Movie Theaters

- **Beekman Theatre** • 1271 2nd Ave [E 67th St]
  212-585-4141
  Another good choice owned by the folks behind the Paris.

Theaters/Performing Arts

- **Sylvia and Danny Kaye Playhouse** • 695 Park Ave [E 69th St]
  212-772-5207
  Guess which one slept with Laurence Olivier.
- **Theater Ten Ten** • 1010 Park Ave [E 85th St]
  212-288-3246
  Good resident company puts on musicals and plays.

1
2
17
E 86th St
86th Street
4 5 6
E 85th St
E 84th St
E 83rd St
E 82nd St
E 81st St
E 80th St
E 79th St
E 78th St
E 77th St
77th Street
6
E 76th St
E 75th St
E 74th St
E 73rd St
E 72nd St
E 71st St
E 70th St
E 69th St
68th Street
Hunter College
6
E 68th St
E 67th St
E 66th St
E 65th St
E 64th St
E 63rd St
Lexington Avenue
63rd Street
F
E 62nd St
E 61st St
E 60th St
E 59th St
N R W
5th Avenue/
59th Street
Lexington
Avenue/
59th Street
N R W
59th Street
4 5 6
13
Carl
Schurz
Park
Metropolitan
Museum
of Art
PAGE
402
PAGE
236
A
B
Central
Park
Fifth Ave
Madison Ave
Park Ave
Lexington Ave
Third Ave
Second Ave
First Ave
York Ave
East End Ave
John
Jay
Park
Bobby Wagner Walk
Weill
Medical
College
(Cornell)
Memorial
Sloane Kettering
Cancer Center
Rockefeller
University
FDR Dr
Foot Bridge
East
River
Roosevelt Island Tramwa
Queensboro Brid
To Queens
1/4 mile
.25 km

The burger at **JG Melon** is one of the best reasons to go above 14th Street. Wallet friendly Mexican from the counter at **Cascabel** is pretty awesome. Get your diner fix at **Neil's** or **Lexington Candy Shop**, french fix at **La Chat Noir**, German fix at **Heidelberg** (with waiters in lederhosen!), and upscale vegetarian at **Candle 79**.

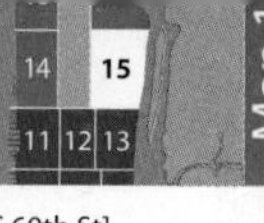

Restaurants

- **Alice's Tea Cup Chapter II** •
  156 E 64th St [Lexington Ave]
  212-486-9200 • $$
  Eat brunch or take tea in a fairy tale setting.
- **Andre's Cafe** • 1631 2nd Ave [E 85th St]
  212-327-1105 • $$
  Low-key Hungarian savories (goulash) and sweets (strudel).
- **Atlantic Grill** • 1341 3rd Ave [E 77th St]
  212-988-9200 • $$$$$
  Seafood galore. Old money loves this place.
- **Beyoglu** • 1431 3rd Ave [E 81st St]
  212-650-0850 • $$$
  Make a meal out of meze.
- **Café Boulud** • 20 E 76th St [Madison Ave]
  212-772-2600 • $$$$$
  Elegant, slightly more relaxed sibling of Daniel.
- **Café Mingala** • 1393 2nd Ave [E 73rd St]
  212-744-8008 • $
  Burmese. $5.50 lunch special!
- **Candle 79** • 154 E 79th St [Lexington Ave]
  212-537-7179 • $$$$
  Upscale vegetarian cuisine in luxurious surroundings.
- **Candle Café** • 1307 3rd Ave [E 75th St]
  212-472-0970 • $$$
  Delicious vegetarian café ironically next door to Le Steak.
- **Cascabel Taqueria** • 1542 2nd Ave [80th St]
  212-717-7800 • $
  Great Mexican food at Taco Bell prices.
- **Donguri** • 309 E 83rd St [Second Ave]
  212-737-5656 • $$$$$
  Transcendent, UES Japanese standout.
- **EAT** • 1064 Madison Ave [E 81st St]
  212-772-0022 • $$$
  Great brunch spot—part of the Eli Zabar empire.
- **Elio's** • 1621 2nd Ave [E 84th St]
  212-772-2242 • $$$$$
  UES Italian where schmoozing with the "who's-who" goes down.
- **Ethiopian Restaurant** • 1582 York Ave [83rd St]
  212-717-7311 • $$$
  Ethiopian in a sea of mediocre Italian.
- **Flex Mussels** • 174 E 82nd St [3rd Ave]
  212-717-7772 • $$$
  23 flavors--try the Abbey or Spaniard.
- **Gino** • 780 Lexington Ave [E 60th St]
  212-758-4466 • $$$$
  Pricey, OK food that's almost worth the old-school Italian atmosphere.
- **Heidelberg** • 1648 2nd Ave [E 86th St]
  212-628-2332 • $$$$
  Dirndls and lederhosen serving colossal beers and sausage platters.
- **Hummus Kitchen** • 1613 2nd Ave [E 84th St]
  212-988-0090 • $$
  Hummus so good they named a Kitchen after it.
- **Indian Tandoor Oven Restaurant** •
  175 E 83rd St [Third Ave]
  212-628-3000 • $$
  Delectable Indian specialties in cozy, color-draped surroundings.
- **Jacques Brasserie** • 204 E 85th St [Third Ave]
  212-327-2272 • $$$$
  UES spot for tasty moules frites and Stella on tap.
- **JG Melon** • 1291 3rd Ave [E 73rd St]
  212-744-0585 • $$
  Top NYC burgers. Always crowded. Open 'till 2:30 a.m.
- **JoJo** • 160 E 64th St [Lexington Ave]
  212-223-5656 • $$$$$
  Charming French bistro.
- **La Chat Noir** • 22 E 66th St [Madison Ave]
  212-794-2428 • $$$$
  Flavorful and quaint. Prices aren't too shabby for Madison Ave.
- **Le Veau d'Or** • 129 E 60th St [Lexington Ave]
  212-838-8133 • $$$
  Classic Parisian bistro with a $20 prix fixe.
- **Lexington Candy Shop/Luncheonette** •
  1226 Lexington Ave [E 83rd St]
  212-288-0057 • $
  Charming old-timey soda shop with twirly stools.
- **Malaga** • 406 E 73rd St [First Ave]
  212-737-7659 • $$$
  Sleeper Spanish joint dishing up terrific tapas and swell sangria.
- **Neil's Coffee Shop** • 961 Lexington Ave [70th St]
  212-628-7474 • $$
  Friendly diner for Hunter students & old timers.
- **Pastrami Queen** • 1125 Lexington Ave [78th St]
  212-734-1500 • $$
  Meats worthy of their royal names.
- **Poke** • 343 E 85th St [Second Ave]
  212-249-0569 • $$
  Good sushi. BYO Sake.
- **Uva** • 1486 2nd Ave [77th St.]
  212-472-4552 • $
  Come for the wine list, food optional.

86th Street
E 86th St
E 85th St
E 84th St
E 83rd St
E 82nd St
E 81st St
E 80th St
E 79th St
E 78th St
77th Street
E 77th St
E 76th St
E 75th St
E 74th St
E 73rd St
E 72nd St
E 71st St
E 70th St
E 69th St
68th Street
Hunter College
E 68th St
E 67th St
E 66th St
E 65th St
E 64th St
Lexington Avenue
63rd Street
E 63rd St
E 62nd St
E 61st St
E 60th St
E 59th St
5th Avenue/
59th Street
Lexington
Avenue/
59th Street
59th Street
Carl
Schurz
Park
Metropolitan
Museum
of Art
PAGE
402
PAGE
236
17
13
Fifth Ave
Madison Ave
Park Ave
Lexington Ave
Third Ave
Second Ave
First Ave
York Ave
East End Ave
John
Jay
Park
Bobby Wagner Walk
Weill
Medical
College
(Cornell)
Memorial
Sloane Kettering
Cancer Center
Rockefeller
University
FDR Dr
Foot Bridge
East
River
Central
Park
Roosevelt Island Tramwa
Queensboro Brid
To Queens
1/4 mile
.25 km

Can't afford $600 socks on Madison Avenue? Check out **Housing Works Thrift Shop** or **BIS Designer Resale** for affordable clothes handed down from Park Avenue. For drugs nothing beats the historic **Lascoff Apothecary**, and for unique wine breads try **Orwasher's**. If you can afford it, **Eli's** is one of the best places to buy food in the city.

Bagels

- **Bagelworks** • 1229 1st Ave [E 67th St]
  212-744-6444
  Truly excellent.
- **H&H Midtown Bagel East** •
  1551 2nd Ave [E 81st St]
  212-717-7312
  Hot & Heavenly.

Coffee

- **Beanocchio Café** • 1413 York Ave [E 75th St]
  212-861-8060
  Nice little spot, despite the lame name.
- **Le Pain Quotidien** • 1270 1st Ave [E 68th St]
  212-988-5001
  Excellent coffee and pastries. Thanks Belgium.
- **Oren's Daily Roast** • 985 Lexington Ave [71st St]
  212-717-3907
  Hip staff pours superior java at local mini-chain.
- **Via Quadronno** • 25 E 73rd St [Madison Ave]
  212-650-9880
  Straight up Italian espresso from Milan.

Shopping

- **Barneys New York** • 660 Madison Ave [61st St]
  212-826-8900
  Museum-quality fashion (with prices to match). Recommended.
- **Beneath** • 265 E 78th St [Second Ave]
  212-288-3800
  New, tiny shop with hipster brands and girly lingerie.
- **Bis Designer Resale** •
  1134 Madison Ave [E 84th St]
  212-396-2760
  Where you can actually afford Gucci and Prada.
- **Butterfield Market** •
  1114 Lexington Ave [E 78th St]
  212-288-7800
  UES gourmet grocer circa 1915.
- **Cheese on 62nd** • 134 E 62nd St [Lexington]
  212-980-5544
  For your next marvelous cocktail party.
- **Crawford Doyle Booksellers** •
  1082 Madison Ave [E 82nd St]
  212-288-6300
  Lovely place to browse and find a classic.
- **Eli's Manhattan** • 1411 3rd Ave [E 80th St]
  212-717-8100
  Blissful gourmet shopping experience. Just bring $$$.
- **Garnet Wines & Liquors** •
  929 Lexington Ave [E 69th St]
  212-772-3211
  Huge selection for people with money.
- **Housing Works Thrift Shop** •
  202 E 77th St [Third Ave]
  212-772-8461
  Our favorite thrift store.
- **In Vino Veritas** • 1375 1st Ave [E 73rd St]
  212-288-0100
  These bros know their wine.
- **Just Bulbs** • 220 E 60th St [Fifth Ave]
  212-888-5707
  Do you have any lamps? How about shades?
- **Kate's Paperie** • 1282 3rd Ave [E 74th St]
  212-396-3670
  Excellent stationery. NYC favorite.
- **Lascoff Apothecary** •
  1209 Lexington Ave [E 82nd St]
  212-288-9500
  Delightfully well-preserved apothecary, circa 1899.
- **Lyric Hi-Fi** • 1221 Lexington Ave [E 83rd St]
  212-439-1900
  Friendly, high-end stereo shop.
- **Oldies, Goldies & Moldies** •
  1609 2nd Ave [E 84th St]
  212-737-3935
  Deliciously Deco antiques and collectibles.
- **Orwasher's** • 308 E 78th St [Second Ave]
  212-288-6569
  Handmade wine breads. Best challah on the east side.
- **Ottomanelli Brothers** • 1549 York Ave [82nd St]
  212-772-7900
  Old-school butcher still going strong.
- **Two Little Red Hens** • 1652 2nd Ave [86th St]
  212-452-0476
  Lovely cases of cakes and pies flanked by kitschy hen memorabilia.
- **Venture Stationers** •
  1156 Madison Ave [E 85th St]
  212-288-7235
  Great neighborhood stationers. Do people still use paper?

W 111th St
St John
the Divine
1
2
W 110th St (Cathedral Pkwy)
18
Cathedral
Parkway
110 Street
W 109th St
W 108th St
Maurice
Schinasi
House
Straus Park
W 107th St
W 106th St
(Duke Ellington Blvd)
PAGE
256
Riverside
Park
Broadway
Riverside Dr
W 105th St
W 104th St
El Taller
Latino
Americano
Manhattan Ave
A
Frederick
Douglass
Houses
W 103rd St
103rd
Street
W 102nd St
Henry Hudson Pkwy
W 101st St
Fireman's
Memorial
W 100th St
W 99th St
Park West
Village
Central
Park
W 98th St
PAGE
236
Hudson
River
W 97th St
96th Street
W 96th St
Broadway
Mall
Community
Center
W 95th St
W 94th St
Pomander
Walk
Joan
of Arc
Memorial
West End Ave
Amsterdam Ave
W 93rd St
Columbus Ave
Central Park West
West Dr
9a
W 92nd St
B
W 91st St
W 90th St
(Henry J Browne Blvd)
Soldiers and
Sailors
Monument
W 89th St
W 88th St
W 87th St
W 86th St
86th Street
14
W 85th St
1/4 mile
.25 km

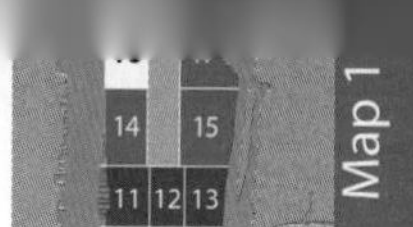

Close to Columbia University, this neighborhood is home to much of New York's liberal intelligentsia. It is not uncommon to overhear discussions about the fate of health care reform or the latest Phillip Roth novel at the dog run, or on line for coffee at a neighborhood bakery. But the neighborhood is far from snobby. Mixed in with the college professors, theater directors, doctors, and lawyers are many families with young children, and twenty-somethings, all of whom enjoy the slower pace of life and physical beauty of Manhattan's Upper West Side.

This neighborhood is one of the greenest spaces in New York. Situated between Riverside and Central Park, there are many places to run, bike, or sit in the shade of a tree. There are few tourist attractions in this part of Central Park, but the natural beauty of the park and its recreational spaces are abundant. You can enter the reservoir from this end of the park, and enjoy a scenic view while running 1.6 miles around a dirt path. Walking West from Central Park to Riverside Park, peak into **Pomander Walk**, a tiny, pedestrian-only street of tiny houses. In Riverside Park, take the time to explore the many famous monuments. After 9/11, neighborhood residents gathered at the **Fireman's Memorial** to commemorate those that were lost. The statue of **Joan of Arc** sits within an island on Riverside Drive that is maintained by neighborhood residents. **The Soldiers and Sailors Monument** commemorates those who served during the Civil War and was dedicated on Memorial Day in 1902, and is modeled after a Corinthian temple. If you're just looking for someplace to sit and read, **Straus Park**, a small green island between West End and Broadway offers a quiet place to rest amid the bustle of the street.

For a neighborhood so far from the bustling theater hub of Times Square and Museum Mile, the Upper West Side offers its fair share of cultural entertainment. **Symphony Space** is a multidisciplinary arts center. There is always a reading or concert on the main stage, and the **Leonard Nimoy Thalia** next door is always showing a classic movie. Symphony Space also occasionally hosts free marathon concerts, most recently Wall-to-Wall Broadway. Come early to get a seat and stay as long as you want. For jazz, check out **Smoke**; many well-known musicians perform. They also have excellent food. **Cleopatra's Needle** also has jazz, as well as inexpensive Middle Eastern food. **The Underground Lounge** hosts decent comedy nights and also occasionally has live music. The West Side Arts Coalition sponsors visual arts exhibitions at the **Broadway Mall Community Center** in the renovated Beaux-Arts Community Center. **El Taller Latino Americano** has live music, salsa dancing and an occasional film, as well as Spanish classes, all very affordable.

This neighborhood has some of the best food to eat on the move. Start at **Roti Roll** for a cheap Indian treat. At **Absolute Bagels**, you can eat fresh, warm bagels right out of the oven. If you're not too full, a few blocks down, sip delicious coffee or a eat pastry as good as any you would find in Paris at **Silver Moon Bakery**. At **Georgia's Bakery**, get a fresh lemonade.

W 111th St
Cathedral of St John the Divine
W 110th St (Cathedral Pkwy)
Cathedral Parkway 110 Street
Cathedral Parkway 110 Street
W 109th St
W 108th St
W 107th St
W 106th St
(Duke Ellington Blvd)
W 105th St
W 104th St
W 103rd St
103rd Street
103rd Street
W 102nd St
W 101st St
W 100th St
W 99th St
W 98th St
W 97th St
96th Street
W 96th St
96th Street
W 95th St
W 94th St
W 93rd St
W 92nd St
W 91st St
W 90th St
(Henry J Browne Blvd)
W 89th St
W 88th St
W 87th St
W 86th St
86th Street
86th Street
W 85th St
Riverside Park
Riverside Dr
Broadway
Henry Hudson Pkwy
Frederick Douglass Houses
Park West Village
Central Park
Hudson River
West End Ave
Amsterdam Ave
Columbus Ave
Manhattan Ave
Central Park West
West Dr
9a
1/4 mile
.25 km

For cheap drinks, check out **Abbey Pub**, **Broadway Dive**, or the **Ding Dong Lounge**. If you're LGBT, head to **Suite**. Go Euro with the Beligum brews at **B Cafe**. **Smoke** is smokin' with live jazz. **The Village Pourhouse** is where the football fans and softball teams go. **Amsterdam 106** is just fine, but we still miss the total dump of Night Cafe.

Bars

- **Abbey Pub** • 237 W 105th St [Broadway]
  212-222-8713
  Cozy Columbia hangout.
- **Amsterdam 106** •
  938 Amsterdam Ave [106th St]
  212-280-8070
  Great beer selection. Annoying TVs.
- **B Cafe** • 566 Amsterdam Ave [W 87th]
  212-873-1800
  Belgian beer tastes good. Really good.
- **Broadway Dive** • 2662 Broadway [W 101st St]
  212-865-2662
  Where everyone who reads this book goes.
- **Cleopatra's Needle** •
  2485 Broadway [92nd St]
  212-769-6969
  Solid Middle Eastern food and solid live jazz performances.
- **The Ding Dong Lounge** •
  929 Columbus Ave [W 105th St]
  212-663-2600
  Downtown punk brought Uptown.
- **Dive Bar** • 732 Amsterdam Ave [W 96th St]
  212-749-4358
  Columbia hangout. Not really a dive.
- **La Negrita** • 999 Columbus Ave [W 109th St]
  212-961-1676
  Latin-themed cocktails. Trivia night is popular.
- **Lion's Head Tavern** •
  995 Amsterdam Ave [109th St]
  212-866-1030
  Sports bar where locals and Columbia students drink cheaply.
- **The Parlour** • 250 W 86th St [Broadway]
  212-580-8923
  Irish pub, two spaces, good hangout.
- **Sip** • 998 Amsterdam Ave [W 109th St]
  212-316-2747
  Organic coffee by day, cool mojitos by night.
- **Smoke** • 2751 Broadway [W 106th St]
  212-864-6662
  Local jazz hangout. Sunday nights are fun.
- **Suite Bar** • 992 Amsterdam Ave [109th St]
  212-222-4600
  Karaoke on Thursdays. Only gay bar in the neighborhood.
- **Tap A Keg** • 2731 Broadway [104th St]
  212-749-1734
  Cheap beer and pool tables!
- **Underground Lounge** •
  955 West End Ave [W 107th]
  212-531-4759
  Stand up comedy and live music. Some really good!
- **Village Pourhouse** •
  982 Amsterdam Ave [W 109th St]
  212-979-2337
  Drink good beer and catch the big game here.

Movie Theaters

- **Leonard Nimoy Thalia at Symphony Space** •
  2537 Broadway [W 95th St]
  212-864-5400
  A different classic movie every week. Good variety.

Theaters/Performing Arts

- **Symphony Space** •
  2537 Broadway [W 95th St]
  212-864-5400
  Neighborhood concert hall with eclectic programs.
- **West End Theatre** • 263 W 86th St [Broadway]
  212-352-3101
  The Prospect Theater Company does some kickass musicals here.

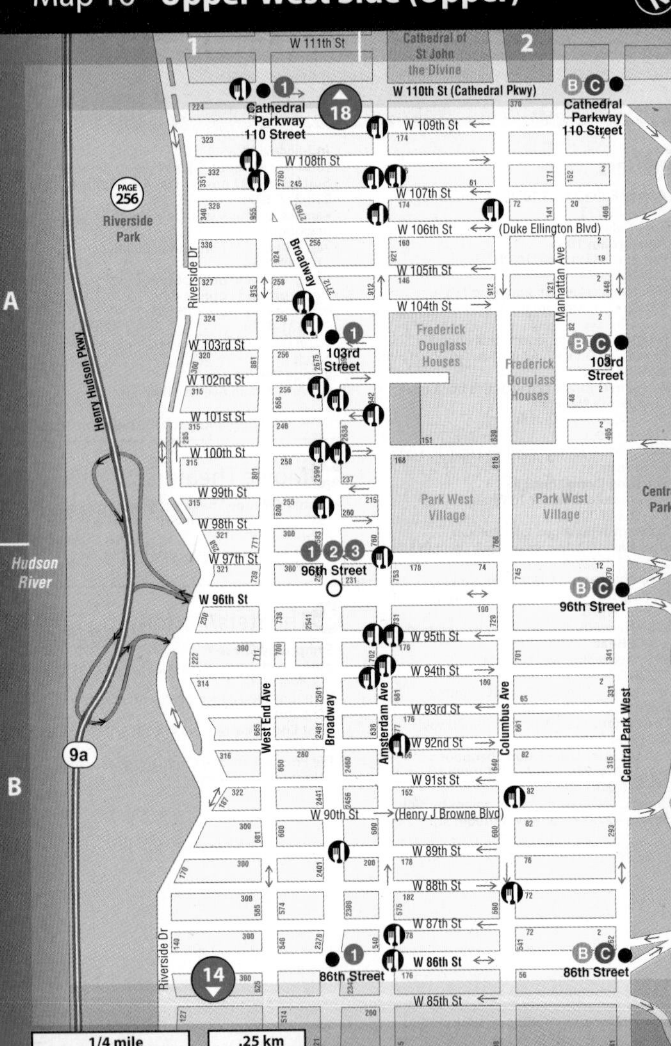

W 111th St
Cathedral of St John the Divine
W 110th St (Cathedral Pkwy)
Cathedral Parkway 110 Street
Cathedral Parkway 110 Street
18
W 109th St
W 108th St
W 107th St
W 106th St
(Duke Ellington Blvd)
W 105th St
W 104th St
W 103rd St
103rd Street
103rd Street
W 102nd St
W 101st St
W 100th St
W 99th St
W 98th St
W 97th St
96th Street
W 96th St
96th Street
W 95th St
W 94th St
W 93rd St
W 92nd St
W 91st St
W 90th St
(Henry J Browne Blvd)
W 89th St
W 88th St
W 87th St
W 86th St
86th Street
86th Street
W 85th St
14
PAGE 256
Riverside Park
Riverside Dr
Broadway
West End Ave
Amsterdam Ave
Columbus Ave
Manhattan Ave
Central Park West
West Dr
Frederick Douglass Houses
Frederick Douglass Houses
Park West Village
Park West Village
Central Park
Henry Hudson Pkwy
9a
Hudson River
A
B
1
2
1/4 mile
.25 km

Have the quintessential New York breakfast of bagels and lox at **Barney Greengrass**. Eat old-school at the diner **Broadway Restaurant**. For cheap rice and beans, try **Flor de Mayo** or **Malecon**. Dine on awesome Mexican at the tiny and cheap **Taqueri Y Fonda**, rich Indian food at **Indus Valley**, or glorious fried chicken at **Rack and Soul**.

Restaurants

- **Asiakan** • 710 Amsterdam Ave [W 94th St]
  212-280-8878 • $$$
  Super sushi & so hip!
- **Awash** • 947 Amsterdam Ave [W 106th St]
  212-961-1416 • $$
  Tasty Ethiopian.
- **Barney Greengrass** •
  541 Amsterdam Ave [W 86th St]
  212-724-4707 • $$$
  Sturgeon and eggs make the perfect NYC b-fast.
- **Bella Luna** • 584 Columbus Ave [W 88 St]
  212-877-2267 • $$$
  Old fashion Italian with live jazz Tuesdays.
- **Broadway Restaurant** •
  2664 Broadway [101st St]
  212-865-7074 • $
  Great breakfast and sandwiches, good place to start the day.
- **Café Con Leche** • 726 Amsterdam Ave [96th St]
  212-678-7000 • $$
  Cuban-Dominican haven.
- **Café du Soleil** • 2723 Broadway [W 104th St]
  212-316-5000 • $$$$
  French bistro that draws locals. Nice bar.
- **Charm Thai** • 722 Amsterdam Ave [95th St]
  212-866-9800 • $$
  Solid, cheap Thai. Comfortable seating. Good drinks too!
- **El Malecon** • 764 Amsterdam Ave [W 97th St]
  212-864-5648 • $
  Roast chicken and a con leche.
- **El Rey de la Caridad** •
  973 Amsterdam Ave [108th St]
  212-222-7383 • $$
  Enjoy a Dominican feast. Bring your Spanish dictionary.
- **Flor de Mayo** • 2651 Broadway [W 101st St]
  212-663-5520 • $$
  Cuban-Chinese-Chicken-Chow.
- **Gennaro** • 665 Amsterdam Ave [W 92nd St]
  212-665-5348 • $$$
  Crowded Italian.
- **Georgia's Bake Shop** •
  2418 Broadway [W 89th St]
  212-362-2000 • $
  Good pastries and space to linger.
- **Hummus Place** • 2608 Broadway [W 99th St]
  212-222-1554 • $
  It's like Sutton Place, except with Hummus.
- **Indian Cafe** • 2791 Broadway [108th St]
  212-749-9200 • $$
  Neighborhood Indian. Nice ambiance.
- **Indus Valley** • 2636 Broadway [W 100th St]
  212-222-9222 • $$$
  Locals rave about this Indian food but it costs.
- **Jerusalem Restaurant** •
  2715 Broadway [W 104th St]
  212-865-1511 • $
  Good Middle Eastern, friendly service, open late.
- **Krik Krak** • 844 Amsterdam Ave [W 101st St]
  212-222-3100 • $$
  Cozy Haitian for great island meal.
- **Lime Leaf** • 2799 Broadway [W 108th St]
  212-864-5000 • $$$
  Yummy pad thai.
- **Pio Pio Salon** • 702 Amsterdam Ave [94th St]
  212-665-3000 • $$
  Tasty rotisserie chicken with all the fixins. Thanks Peru!
- **Popover Cafe** • 551 Amsterdam Ave [87th St]
  212-595-8555 • $$
  Neighborhood favorite. Popovers with strawberry butter are a must-try.
- **Rack and Soul** • 258 W 109 St [Broadway]
  212-222-4800 • $$
  Instant neighborhood fave features NYC's best fried chicken.
- **Roti Roll Bombay Frankie** •
  994 Amsterdam Ave [W 109th St]
  212-666-1500 • $
  Hole-in-the-wall rotis to soak up alcohol.
- **Sal & Carmine's Pizza** •
  2671 Broadway [W 102nd St]
  212- 663-7651 • $
  The masters serve up perfect slices. Don't expect small talk.
- **Taqueria Y Fonda La Mexicana** •
  968 Amsterdam Ave [W 108th St]
  212-531-0383 • $$
  Amazing Mexican dive. Columbia kids love this place.
- **Trattoria Pesce & Pasta** •
  625 Columbus Ave [W 91st St]
  212-579-7970 • $$$
  Decent neighborhood Italian. Good antipasti.
- **Turkuaz** • 2637 Broadway [W 100th St]
  212-665-9541 • $$
  Craving gelenseksel yemekler (traditional dish)? It's all here.
- **Voza** • 949 Columbus Ave [107th St]
  212-666-8602 • $$$
  Cozy French-Italian. Can you say date night?

W 111th St
Cathedral of St John the Divine
W 110th St (Cathedral Pkwy)
Cathedral Parkway 110 Street
Cathedral Parkway 110 Street
W 109th St
W 108th St
W 107th St
W 106th St
(Duke Ellington Blvd)
W 105th St
W 104th St
Broadway
Riverside Dr
Riverside Park
PAGE 256
Manhattan Ave
Frederick Douglass Houses
Frederick Douglass Houses
103rd Street
103rd Street
W 103rd St
W 102nd St
W 101st St
W 100th St
W 99th St
W 98th St
W 97th St
Park West Village
Park West Village
Central Park
PAGE 236
96th Street
96th Street
W 96th St
W 95th St
W 94th St
W 93rd St
W 92nd St
W 91st St
W 90th St
(Henry J Browne Blvd)
W 89th St
W 88th St
W 87th St
W 86th St
86th Street
86th Street
W 85th St
West End Ave
Amsterdam Ave
Columbus Ave
Central Park West
West Dr
Henry Hudson Pkwy
Hudson River
9a
1/4 mile
.25 km

Barzini's has nice fresh produce as does **Garden of Eden** and the new **Whole Foods**. For smoked fish and prepared foods try the **Kosher Marketplace**. **Schatzie's** is the best butcher around. **Janovic** is great for home improvement projects. Supplies for any arts and crafts project can be found at **Michael's**.

Bagels

- **Absolute Bagels** • 2788 Broadway [108th St]
  212-932-2052
  Amazing. Home of the hard-to-find pumpernickel raisin.
- **Barney Greengrass** •
  541 Amsterdam Ave [W 86th St]
  212-724-4707
  Classic New York shop. Good bagels.

Coffee

- **Le Pain Quotidien** • 2463 Broadway [91st St]
  212-769-8879
  Excellent coffee and pastries. Thanks Belgium.
- **Silver Moon Bakery** • 2740 Broadway [105th St]
  212-866-4717
  Delicious morning coffee and croissant.
- **Three Star Coffee Shop** •
  541 Columbus Ave [W 86th St]
  212-874-6780
  Old-school diner.

Shopping

- **Ace Hardware** • 610 Columbus Ave [90th St]
  212-580-8080
  The place.
- **Barzini's** • 2455 Broadway [W 91st St]
  212-874-4992
  Huge selection of cheeses. Fresh bread and produce.
- **Garden of Eden Gourmet** •
  2780 Broadway [W 107th St]
  212-222-7300
  Produce is pretty good here.
- **Gotham Wines And Liquors** •
  2517 Broadway [W 94th St]
  212-932-0990
  Friendly neighborhood favorite.
- **Gothic Cabinet Craft** • 2652 Broadway [101st St]
  212-678-4368
  Real wood furniture. Made in Queens!
- **Health Nuts** • 2611 Broadway [W 99th St]
  212-678-0054
  Standard health food store.
- **Janovic** • 2680 Broadway [W 102nd St]
  212-531-2300
  Top NYC paint store.
- **Joon's Fine Seafood** •
  774 Amsterdam Ave [W 98th St]
  212-531-1344
  Fresh fish market that will fry 'em up right there.
- **Kosher Market Place** • 2442 Broadway [90th St]
  212-580-6378
  For all of your Kosher needs.
- **Mani Marketplace** •
  697 Columbus Ave [W 94th St]
  212-662-4392
  Fantastic little grocery with jazz on the sound system.
- **Mitchell's Wine & Liquor Store** •
  200 W 86th St [Amsterdam Ave]
  212-874-2255
  Worth a trip just for the gorgeous neon sign.
- **Mugi Pottery** • 993 Amsterdam Ave [109th St]
  212-866-6202
  Handcrafted pottery. Like in the movie Ghost.
- **Murray's Sturgeon** • 2429 Broadway [90th St]
  212-724-2650
  UWS comfort food: rugelah, knishes, and, lots of sturgeon.
- **New York Flowers & Plant Shed** •
  209 W 96th St [Amsterdam Ave]
  212-662-4400
  Makes you wish you had more (or any) garden space.
- **Schatzie's Prime Meats** •
  555 Amsterdam Ave [E 87th St]
  212-410-1555
  Butcher with good prime meat and poultry.
- **Sport Trax** • 2621 Broadway [W 99th St]
  212-866-0217
  Affordable sporting equipment and clothing.
- **Upper 90** • 697 Amsterdam Ave [94th St]
  646-863-3105
  Great selection of soccer apparel & accessories.
- **Variazioni Clothing** • 2389 Broadway [88th St]
  212-595-1760
  Funky tops, designer jeans, high prices.
- **Westlane Wines & Liquor** •
  689 Columbus Ave [W 93rd St]
  212-749-0990
  Behind the bullet proof glass is a pretty good selection.
- **Whole Foods** • 808 Columbus Ave [97th St]
  212-222-6160
  Finally. Good fresh food north of 96th Street.
- **Whole Foods Wine** •
  808 Columbus Ave [W 100th St]
  212-222-6160
  Featuring lots of NY State wines.

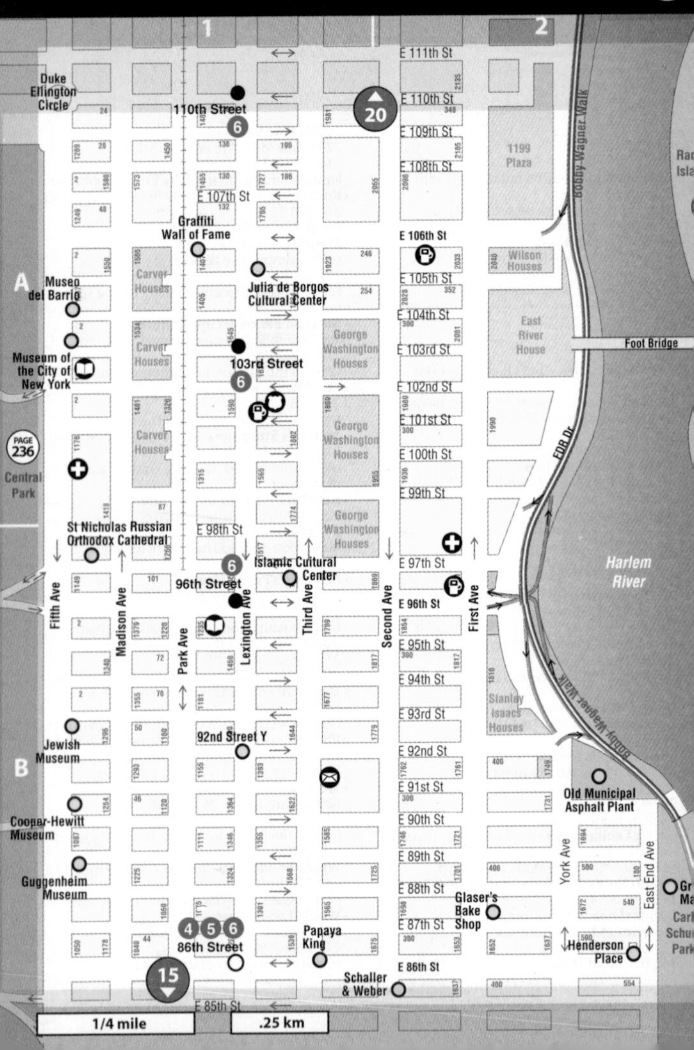

Duke Ellington Circle
110th Street
Graffiti Wall of Fame
Museo del Barrio
Julia de Borgos Cultural Center
Carver Houses
George Washington Houses
Museum of the City of New York
103rd Street
PAGE 236
Central Park
St Nicholas Russian Orthodox Cathedral
Islamic Cultural Center
96th Street
92nd Street Y
Jewish Museum
Cooper-Hewitt Museum
Guggenheim Museum
86th Street
Papaya King
Schaller & Weber
Glaser's Bake Shop
Henderson Place
Old Municipal Asphalt Plant
1199 Plaza
Wilson Houses
East River House
Stanley Isaacs Houses
Foot Bridge
Harlem River
Bobby Wagner Walk
FDR Dr
Fifth Ave
Madison Ave
Park Ave
Lexington Ave
Third Ave
Second Ave
First Ave
York Ave
East End Ave
E 111th St
E 110th St
E 109th St
E 108th St
E 107th St
E 106th St
E 105th St
E 104th St
E 103rd St
E 102nd St
E 101st St
E 100th St
E 99th St
E 98th St
E 97th St
E 96th St
E 95th St
E 94th St
E 93rd St
E 92nd St
E 91st St
E 90th St
E 89th St
E 88th St
E 87th St
E 86th St
E 85th St
1/4 mile
.25 km

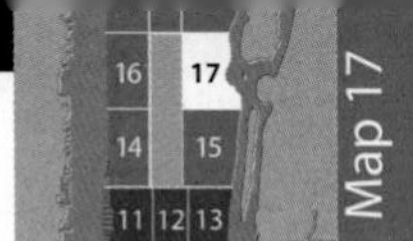

Whew, finally a break from the chaos. This part of the Upper East Side is a place for families—young, old, black, white, Latino, rich, poor—it just depends what block you stumble upon. Head above 96th Street for some of the best Mexican food on the planet, or head west to Central Park, where you'll find kids and adults playing soccer, softball, and football. Get some culture at the neighborhood's museums, get some knowledge at a lecture at the 92nd Street Y, but most importantly, get ready to be somewhere where people can actually live, work, and shop. Nothing hip or cool here, this is just a good old-fashioned New York neighborhood.

Much of this part of the Upper East Side is known as Carnegie Hill, named for the Carnegie Mansion on 91 stand Fifth Avenue (it's now the **Cooper-Hewitt Design Museum**). Though he doesn't actually live there, you may still catch a glimpse of Mayor Bloomberg at **Gracie Mansion**, which serves as the official residence of New York City mayors. **Henderson Place**, built in 1881 for families of 'moderate means', was designed by the architectural firm of Lamb and Rich and with 24 units still remaining, serves as an example of middle-class living in the Big Apple.

Ever think a Soviet battle could take place on American soil? The **Russian Orthodox Cathedral of St. Nicholas** was the site of a power struggle between czarist and Soviet Russians after its founding in 1902. Now it's undergoing renovations and finally conflict-free, but still an amazing sight to see. **The Old Municipal Asphalt Plant** now houses sports fields but was the source of much controversy: some called it the ugliest thing they'd ever seen, but the MOMA hailed it as a masterpiece of functional design. Head over to 91st Street and decide for yourself. **The Museum of the City of New York** can not only help visitors understand the history of the neighborhood but the whole city as well with 1.5 million objects and images connected to the city's past.

The Jewish Museum features works by Chagall, a video and film archive and traveling exhibits that are always worth a peek. Head up to 104th Street and down to the Caribbean in the newly renovated **Museo del Barrio**, where you can find an excellent collection of Latin American art. Another name you're sure to have heard of? **The Guggenheim**, which not only houses Picasso, Chagall, Mondrian, and Kandisky but is also a piece of art itself, with Frank Lloyd Wright's influence seen on the swirling staircase that guides visitors through. One of the best ways to see the Guggenheim is on the first Friday of every month during Art After Dark, where visitors can tour the museum and enjoy cocktails and music along the way. Before you leave, check the schedule at the **92nd Street Y**, which hosts speakers from Al Gore to Mos Def.

When you get tired of shelling out the benjamins for food, head over to **Papaya King** on 86th Street. A favorite of New Yorkers, it serves up hot dogs for cheap that it brags are "tastier than a filet mignon." Maybe not, but still worth a bite. While the Upper East Side isn't at a loss for bakeries, the best is **Glaser's Bake Shop** which has been serving up deliciousness since 1902. The **Graffiti Wall of Fame** at 106th and Park (yes, that 106 & Park for those BET fans out there), is an awesome collection of street art at its best.

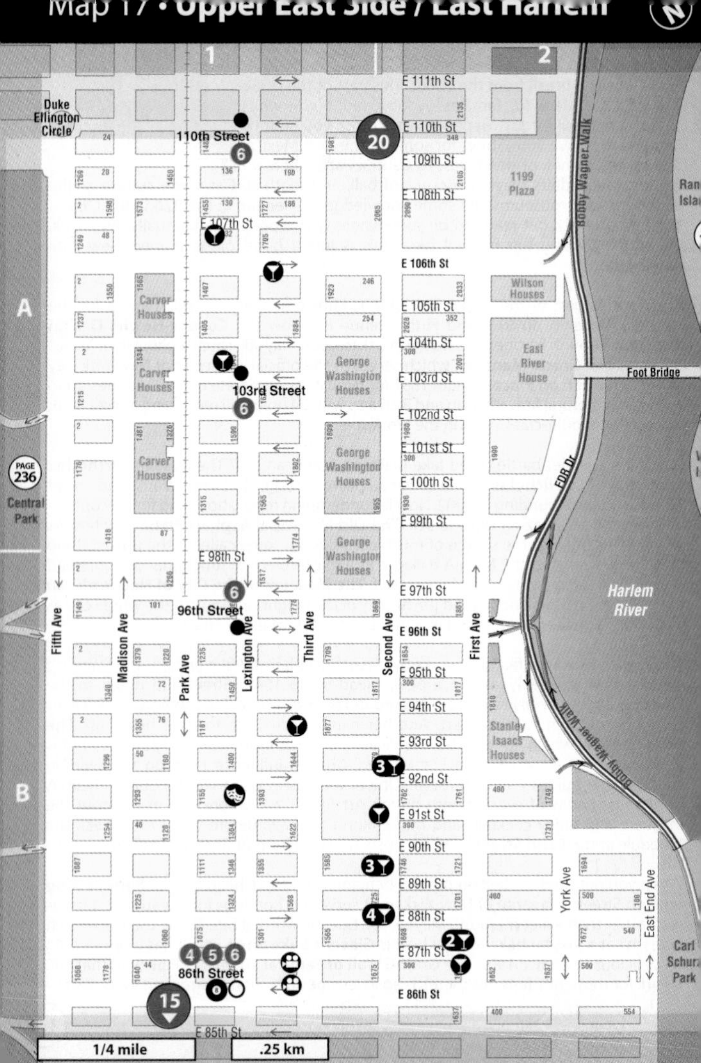

Duke Ellington Circle
110th Street
E 111th St
E 110th St
E 109th St
E 108th St
E 107th St
E 106th St
E 105th St
E 104th St
E 103rd St
103rd Street
E 102nd St
E 101st St
E 100th St
E 99th St
E 98th St
E 97th St
96th Street
E 96th St
E 95th St
E 94th St
E 93rd St
E 92nd St
E 91st St
E 90th St
E 89th St
E 88th St
E 87th St
86th Street
E 86th St
E 85th St
1199 Plaza
Bobby Wagner Walk
Wilson Houses
East River House
Foot Bridge
Carver Houses
George Washington Houses
Stanley Isaacs Houses
FDR Dr
Harlem River
PAGE 236
Central Park
Fifth Ave
Madison Ave
Park Ave
Lexington Ave
Third Ave
Second Ave
First Ave
York Ave
East End Ave
Carl Schurz Park
1/4 mile
.25 km

To party like rockstars of the '70s art world, head over to **Elaine's** for a drink. Watch the big game at **Kinsale**. Then, escape the beer-filled Upper East Side bars with a stop for a cozy drink at **Auction House** or some Latin music at **FB Lounge** before ending the night with some drunken frat fun at **The Big Easy** or **Aces and Eights**.

Bars

- **Aces And Eights** • 1683 1st Ave [88th St]
  212-860-4020
  Come to play lots and lots of beer pong and darts.
- **Auction House** • 300 E 89th St [Second Ave]
  212-427-4458
  Stylish lounge…or at least stylish for the Upper East Side.
- **BB&R** • 1720 2nd Ave [89th St]
  212-987-5555
  Seriously just want to watch the game? Come here.
- **Big Easy** • 1768 2nd Ave [E 92nd St]
  212-348-0879
  Cheap college dive. Beer Pong anyone?
- **Blondies Sports Bar** • 1770 2nd Ave [93rd St.]
  212-410-3300
  Watch sports every night of the week.
- **Cavatappo Wine Bar** •
  1728 2nd Ave [E 90th St]
  212-426-0919
  Jewel box-sized spot to sip wine and nibble appetizers.
- **East End Bar and Grill** •
  1664 1st Ave [E 87th St]
  212-348-3783
  Mellow Irish hang out.
- **Elaine's** • 1703 2nd Ave [E 88th St]
  212-534-8103
  Party with Elaine like a '70s art star.
- **FB Lounge** • 172 E 106th St [Lexington Ave]
  212-348-3929
  Live Latin jazz, Afrocaribbean, and world beats.
- **Kinsale Tavern** • 1672 3rd Ave [E 94th St]
  212-348-4370
  Right-off-the-boat Irish staff. Good beers.
- **Marty O'Brien's** • 1696 2nd Ave [E 88th St]
  212-722-3889
  Where kilted firefighters go to enjoy pints on St. Paddy's.
- **Pat O'Briens** • 1701 2nd Ave [88th St.]
  212-410-2013
  A refuge for Boston fans with cheap beer specials.
- **Phil Hughes** • 1682 1st Ave [E 88th St]
  212-722-9415
  An honest-to-god dive bar on the UES.
- **Puerto Rico USA Bar** •
  124 E 107th St [Lexington Ave]
  212-410-1170
  Friendly dive complete with domino table.
- **Rathbones Pub** •
  1702 2nd Ave [E 88th St]
  212-369-7361
  Your basic Manhattan pub.
- **Reif's Tavern** • 302 E 92nd St [2nd Ave]
  212-426-0519
  Dive-o-rama since 1942.
- **SpaHa Lounge** •
  1634 Lexington Ave [E 104th St]
  212-860-0800
  Good happy hour. Lamest name ever.
- **Tool Box** • 1742 2nd Ave [E 91st St]
  212-348-1288
  Perhaps the only official gay bar on the UES.

Billiards

- **East Side Billiard Club** •
  163 E 86th St [Lexington Ave]
  212-831-7665
  Go for the pool, not the atmosphere.

Movie Theaters

- **AMC Loews Orpheum 7** •
  1538 3rd Ave [E 87th St]
  212-876-2111
  The Upper East Side's premier multiplex.
- **City Cinemas East 86th Street** •
  210 E 86th St [Third Ave]
  212-744-1999
  It wouldn't be our first choice.

Theaters/Performing Arts

- **92nd Street Y** •
  1395 Lexington Ave [E 92nd St]
  212-415-5500
  Check out the terrific Lyrics and Lyricists series.

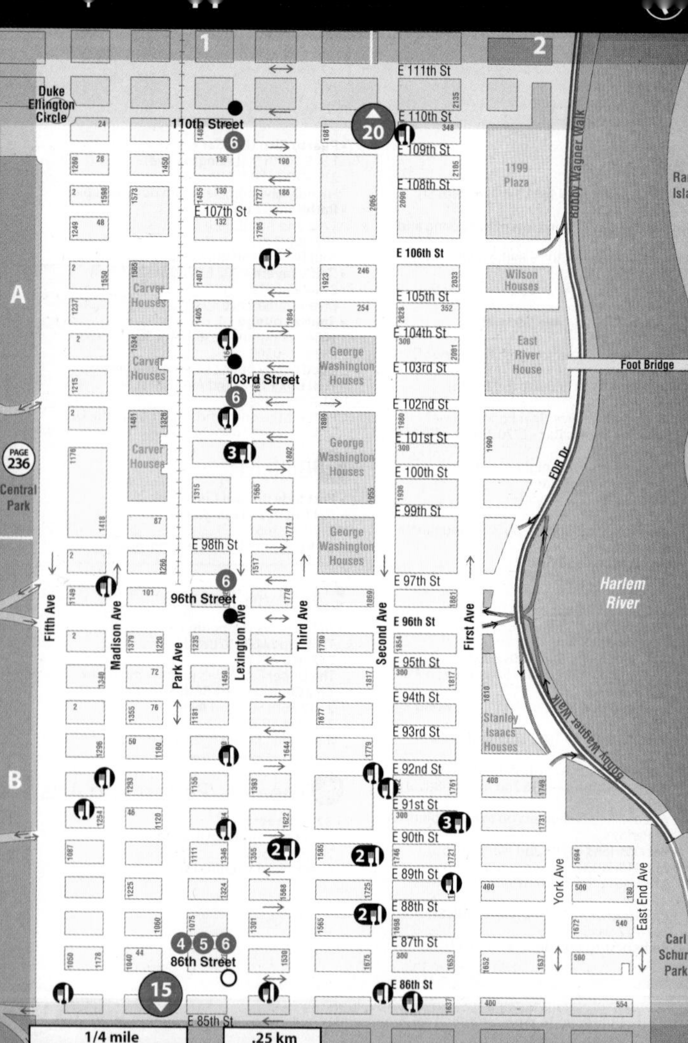
1
2
A
B
Duke Ellington Circle
110th Street
103rd Street
96th Street
86th Street
E 111th St
E 110th St
E 109th St
E 108th St
E 107th St
E 106th St
E 105th St
E 104th St
E 103rd St
E 102nd St
E 101st St
E 100th St
E 99th St
E 98th St
E 97th St
E 96th St
E 95th St
E 94th St
E 93rd St
E 92nd St
E 91st St
E 90th St
E 89th St
E 88th St
E 87th St
E 86th St
E 85th St
Fifth Ave
Madison Ave
Park Ave
Lexington Ave
Third Ave
Second Ave
First Ave
York Ave
East End Ave
FDR Dr
Bobby Wagner Walk
1199 Plaza
Wilson Houses
East River House
Foot Bridge
Carver Houses
George Washington Houses
Stanley Isaacs Houses
Harlem River
Central Park
PAGE 236
Carl Schurz Park
20
15
1/4 mile
.25 km

For brunch, the Upper East Side's signature meal, there's no place like **Sarabeth's**. If you want to spend the money on a good steak, head to the **Parlor Steakhouse**. Other gems: Awesome Italian is **Sfloglia**, cozy Turkish is **Peri Ela**, tasty Mexican is **El Paso**, no-menu Puerto Rican is **La Fonda Boricua**, and unique Alsatian is **Cafe D'Alsace**.

Restaurants

- **Café D'Alsace** • 1695 2nd Ave [E 88th St] 212-722-5133 • $$$$ Chic Alsatian bistro with NYC's only known beer sommelier.
- **Cafe Sabarsky** • 1048 5th Ave [E 86th St] 212-288-0665 • $$$ Beautiful wood-paneled surroundings for sipping Viennese coffee.
- **Cavatappo Grill** • 1712 1st Ave [E 89th St] 212-987-9260 • $$$$$ Northern Italian standout with loyal neighborhood following.
- **Chef Ho's Peking Duck Grill** • 1720 2nd Ave [E 89th St] 212-348-9444 • $$$ Creative gourmet-ish Chinese cuisine. Try the Banana Chicken—delicious!
- **El Paso Taqueria** • 1642 Lexington Ave [E 104th St] 212-831-9831 • $ Fantastic Mexican. Try the chilaquiles and spicy guacamole.
- **Elaine's** • 1703 2nd Ave [E 88th St] 212-534-8103 • $$$$ Ignore the naysayers! Great food and fun center-of-it-all vibe.
- **Ithaka** • 308 E 86th St [Second Ave] 212-628-9100 • $$$ Fish grilled to perfection. Live music too.
- **Itzocan Bistro** • 1575 Lexington Ave [101st St] 212-423-0255 • $$ Mexi-French-fusion.
- **Joy Burger Bar** • 1567 Lexington Ave [100th St] 212-289-6222 • $ Burgers that, yes, bring joy to your mouth.
- **La Fonda Boricua** • 169 E 106th St [Lexington] 212-410-7292 • $$ Tasty Puerto Rican home-cookin'. No menus, just point.
- **Moustache** • 1621 Lexington Ave [102nd St] 212-828-0030 • $$ Middle Eastern surrounded by Mexican.
- **Naruto Ramen** • 1596 3rd Ave [90th St] 212-289-7803 • $$ Sip Japanese soup at the cramped counter.
- **Nina's Argentinian Pizzeria** • 1750 2nd Ave [E 91st St] 212-426-4627 • $$ Make reservations for delish gourmet pizza.
- **One Fish Two Fish** • 1399 Madison Ave [97th St] 212-369-5677 • $$ Good enough seafood without the pretentiousness.
- **Papaya King** • 179 E 86th St [Third Ave] 212-369-0648 • $ Dishing out damn good dogs since 1932.
- **Parlor Steakhouse** • 1600 3rd Ave [90th St] 212-423-5888 • $$$$ Sink your teeth into an authentic filet mignon worth the dough.
- **Peri Ela** • 1361 Lexington Ave [E 90th St] 212-410-4300 • $$ Classy Turkish restaurant.
- **Piatto D'Oro I** • 349 E 109th St [Second Ave] 212-828-2929 • $$$ East Harlem Italian.
- **Pinocchio** • 1748 1st Ave [E 91st St] 212-828-5810 • $$$$$ Itty bitty sleeper Italian with rave reviews and loyal fans.
- **Pintaile's Pizza** • 26 E 91st St [Fifth Ave] 212-722-1967 • $$ Tasty thin-crust stuff.
- **Pio Pio** • 1746 1st Ave [E 91st St] 212-426-5800 • $$ The Matador chicken combo will feed the whole family.
- **Sabora Mexico** • 1744 1st Ave [E 90th St] 212-289-2641 • $$ Small, home-cooked, cheap and delicious.
- **Sala Thai** • 1718 2nd Ave [89th St] 212-410-5557 • $$ Take out the most underrated Thai food on the UES.
- **Sarabeth's** • 1295 Madison Ave [E 92nd St] 212-410-7335 • $$$ Good upper class breakfast, if you can get in.
- **Sfoglia** • 1402 Lexington Ave [E 92nd St] 212-831-1402 • $$$$ Exquisite and experimental Italian by 92nd Street Y.
- **Tokubei 86** • 314 E 86th St [2nd Ave] 212-628-5334 • Long time UES friendly Japanese pub with sushi.
- **Yo In Yo Out** • 1569 Lexington Ave [100th St] 212-987-5350 • $$ French trifecta: crepes, croissants, and coffee.
- **Zebu Grill** • 305 E 92nd St [Second Ave] 212-426-7500 • $$$$$ Candlelit Brazilian bistro with exposed brick and earthy wooden tables.

Looking for more? http://www.notfortourists.com/nyc/map17/restaurants

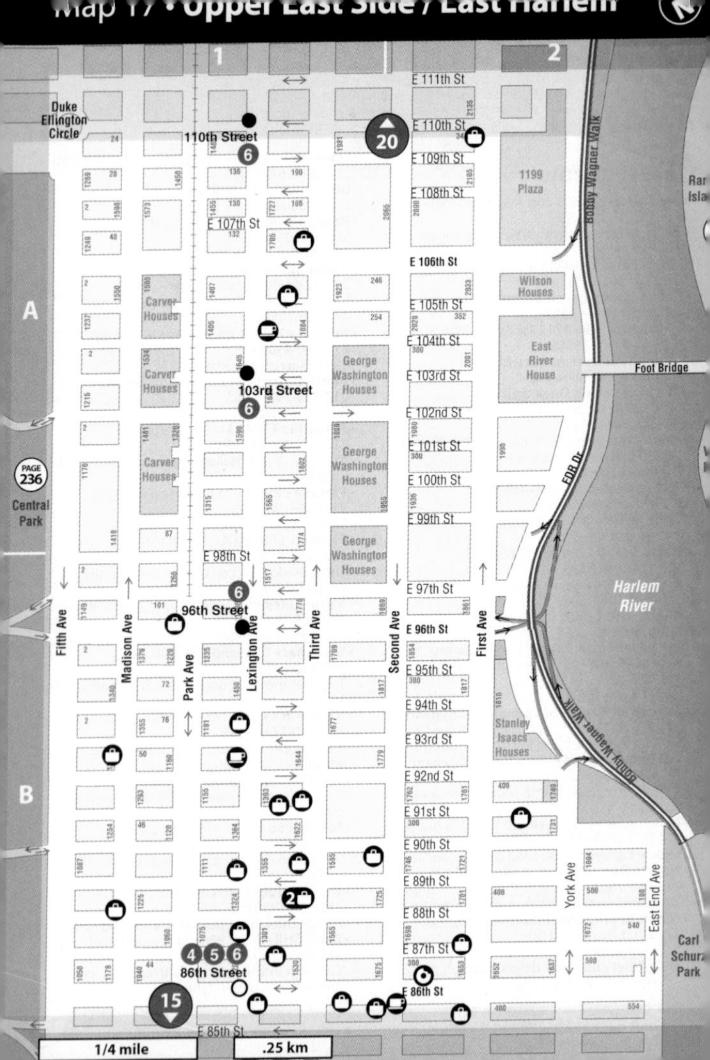

Duke Ellington Circle
110th Street
E 111th St
E 110th St
E 109th St
E 108th St
E 107th St
E 106th St
E 105th St
E 104th St
E 103rd St
E 102nd St
E 101st St
E 100th St
E 99th St
E 98th St
E 97th St
E 96th St
E 95th St
E 94th St
E 93rd St
E 92nd St
E 91st St
E 90th St
E 89th St
E 88th St
E 87th St
E 86th St
E 85th St
103rd Street
96th Street
86th Street
1199 Plaza
Wilson Houses
East River House
Foot Bridge
Carver Houses
George Washington Houses
Stanley Isaacs Houses
Bobby Wagner Walk
FDR Dr
Harlem River
Central Park
PAGE 236
Fifth Ave
Madison Ave
Park Ave
Lexington Ave
Third Ave
Second Ave
First Ave
York Ave
East End Ave
Carl Schurz Park
1/4 mile
.25 km

Bagels, Coffee, & Shopping

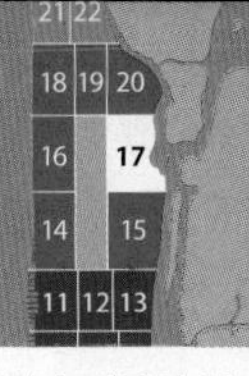

Stop to feed your mind at The Corner Bookstore before heading over to Eli's Vinegar Factory for an overpriced but delicious bag of groceries. Then fuel up on coffee at M Rohrs or East Harlem Cafe. Before heading home, go to the shop at Cooper-Hewitt. For runners, Super Runners Shop is a must-stop.

Bagels

- **Tal Bagels** • 333 E 86th St [Second Ave]
  212-427-6811
  Pretty good. Lots of cream cheese options.

Coffee

- **Crumbs** • 1418 Lexington Ave [93rd St]
  212-360-7200
  Double whammy: coffee and cupcakes.
- **East Harlem Cafe** •
  1651 Lexington Ave [E104th St]
  212-996-2080
  Best coffee in the 'hood.
- **M Rohrs** • 310 E 86th St [2nd Ave]
  212-396-4456
  Best coffeehouse on the UES. Beans by the pound.

Shopping

- **Best Cellars** • 1291 Lexington Ave [E 97th St]
  212-426-4200
  Lots of wines under $20 and daily tastings.
- **Blacker & Kooby** • 1204 Madison Ave [88th St]
  212-369-8308
  Good selection of stationery, pens, & art supplies.
- **The Children's General Store** •
  168 E 91st St [Lexington Ave]
  212-426-4479
  Toys, games, crafts, and all things kids love.
- **Corner Bookstore** • 1313 Madison Ave [93rd St]
  212-831-3554
  Tiny, old-school shop. Great selection.
- **Coup de Coeur** • 1628 3rd Ave [E 91st St]
  212-410-9720
  Stylish boutique on not-so-stylish stretch of Third Avenue.
- **Eli's Vinegar Factory** • 431 E 91st St [First Ave]
  212-987-0885
  Gourmet market with prepared (and expensive) foods.
- **Glaser's Bake Shop** • 1670 1st Ave [E 87th St]
  212-289-2562
  Best black-and-white cookies for more than a century.
- **Goliath RF** • 175 E 105th St [Third Ave]
  212-360-7683
  Super cool urban sneaker emporium.
- **Gourmet Garage** • 1245 Park Ave [E 96th St]
  212-348-5850
  Not really gourmet, but better than the average market.
- **Housing Works Thrift Shop** •
  1730 2nd Ave [E 90th St]
  212-722-8306
  Uptown outpost of our favorite thrift shop.
- **Kitchen Arts & Letters** •
  1435 Lexington Ave [E 93rd St]
  212-876-5550
  Fine selection of food and wine books.
- **La Tropezienne** • 2131 1st Ave [E 110th St]
  212-860-5324
  Excellent French bakery in El Barrio.
- **MAD Vintage Couture & Designer Resale** •
  167 E 87th St [Lexington Ave]
  212-427-4333
  Former art gallery turned boutique.
- **Milano Market Place** • 1582 3rd Ave [88th St]
  212-996-6681
  Gem of an Italian market.
- **Mister Wright** • 1593 3rd Ave [E 90th St]
  212-722-4564
  Best liquor store on the UES. Huge selection.
- **Orva** • 155 E 86th St [Lexington Ave]
  212-369-3448
  Ladies' discount department store.
- **Pickles, Olives Etc** • 1647 1st Ave [E 86th St]
  212-717-8966
  Pickle barrel-sized shop worth a visit.
- **Rincon Musical** • 1936 3rd Ave [E 107th St]
  212-828-8604
  Latino music headquarters. Always blastin' the tunes.
- **Schaller & Weber** • 1654 2nd Ave [E 86th St]
  212-879-3047
  A relic of old Yorkville with countless German meats.
- **Shatzi The Shop** • 243 E 86th St [Third Ave]
  212-289-1830
  The saving grace of strip mall-ish, chain-hogged 86th Street.
- **Super Runners Shop** •
  1337 Lexington Ave [E 89th St]
  212-369-6010
  Think before you buy running shorts that are too tight.
- **Wankel's Hardware & Paint** •
  1573 3rd Ave [E 88th St]
  212-369-1200
  The best hardware store around.

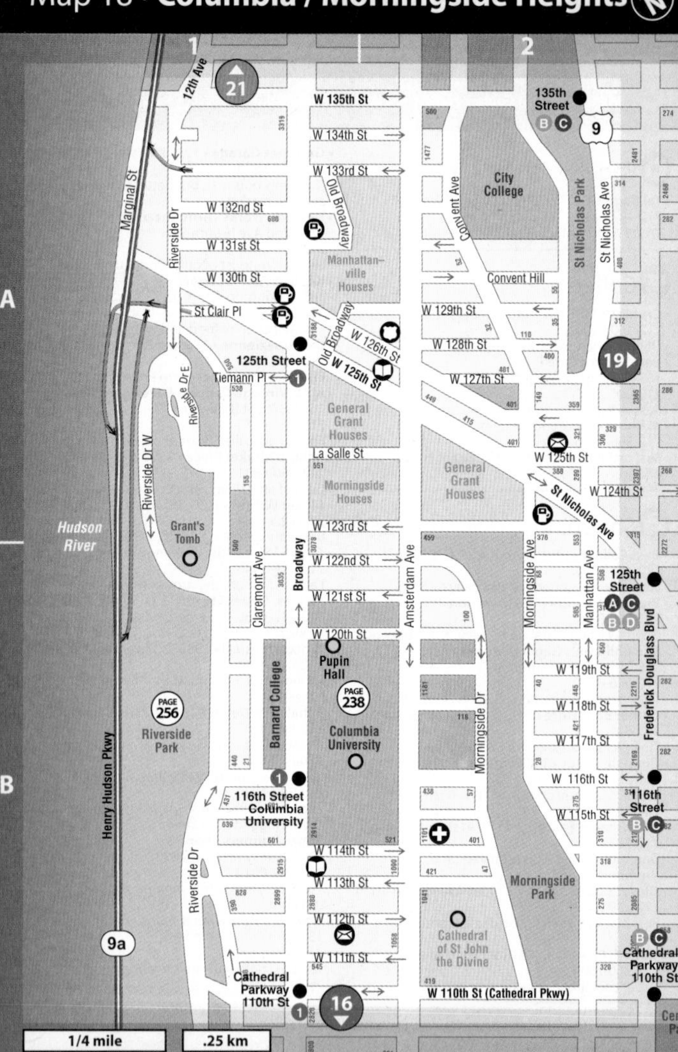

W 135th St
W 134th St
W 133rd St
W 132nd St
W 131st St
W 130th St
St Clair Pl
W 129th St
W 128th St
W 127th St
W 126th St
W 125th St
La Salle St
W 124th St
W 123rd St
W 122nd St
W 121st St
W 120th St
W 119th St
W 118th St
W 117th St
W 116th St
W 115th St
W 114th St
W 113th St
W 112th St
W 111th St
W 110th St (Cathedral Pkwy)
12th Ave
Marginal St
Riverside Dr
Riverside Dr E
Riverside Dr W
Old Broadway
Tiemann Pl
Claremont Ave
Broadway
Amsterdam Ave
Convent Ave
Convent Hill
Morningside Ave
Morningside Dr
Manhattan Ave
St Nicholas Ave
St Nicholas Park
Frederick Douglass Blvd
Henry Hudson Pkwy
City College
Manhattanville Houses
General Grant Houses
Morningside Houses
Grant's Tomb
Riverside Park
Barnard College
Pupin Hall
Columbia University
Morningside Park
Cathedral of St John the Divine
Hudson River
135th Street
125th Street
116th Street Columbia University
Cathedral Parkway 110th St
116th Street
Cathedral Parkway 110th St
Central Park
1/4 mile
.25 km

Until the late 19th century, Morningside Heights was mostly undeveloped farmland. Then in 1895, **Columbia University** moved from midtown Manhattan to 116th and Broadway, the site of a former insane asylum. The rest is history. Columbia and Morningside Heights, which occupies the area of New York squeezed in between the Upper West Side and Harlem, are now forever linked for better or worse. Smack dab in the center of Morningside Heights at 116th Street between Broadway and Amsterdam is the gorgeous main campus of Columbia. A stroll through here quickly replenishes the soul and provides a nice escape from the chaotic city. Just watch out for the freshmen rushing to and from class.

Like many neighborhoods in other cities dominated by an elite university, Morningside Heights had been historically mischaracterized as being a Gilbraltar of culture within a barren, dangerous part of town. But the stereotypes from the '70s and '80s couldn't be further from the truth. The Morningside Heights area is one of the safer areas of New York City. Morningside Park still provides a clear line between the Columbia and residential side of town, but because of the skyrocketing rents that also came with the '90s, the lines between the two have increasingly blurred. Over the years, the relationship between the community and the nearby affluent campus has ebbed and flowed with the university's plans for expansion, land disputes, and greater gentrification.

Not all development has had mixed consequences. In 2008, the **Cathedral of St. John the Divine** reopened after prolonged renovations following a fire in 2001. The wait was worth it; the world's largest Anglican church and fourth largest church in the world in an awe-inspiring display of architecture, scholarship, and local, national, and world history. Built around the same time as the University (in the same lot once belonging to an asylum), St. John the Divine provides a link between the neighborhood and the millennia of history that seemingly preceded it.

If American history and nature is more your style, the neighborhood features grounds arguably just as hallowed. While corny jokes from grade school should tell you who's buried in **Grant's Tomb**, the mausoleum of the head of the Union Army, the 18th President of the United States and the 19th First Lady is a national landmark under the supervision of the National Park Service. Following an extensive renovation in the early '90s, Grant's Tomb is now one of the best places in the neighborhood to get in touch with nature due to its size, proximity to Riverside Park, and supervision by U.S. Park Services.

Right across the street from Grant's Tomb is **Riverside Church**, a nexus point of American social history, where Martin Luther King Jr., Nelson Mandela, and Kofi Annan have all given famous speeches. An interdenominational church with longstanding ties to the city's black residents, Riverside Church is one of the bully pulpits of African-American and civil rights discussion. Dr. King, most famously, denounced the Vietnam war here.

W 135th St
W 134th St
W 133rd St
W 132nd St
W 131st St
W 130th St
St Clair Pl
W 129th St
W 128th St
W 127th St
W 126th St
W 125th St
La Salle St
W 124th St
W 123rd St
W 122nd St
W 121st St
W 120th St
W 119th St
W 118th St
W 117th St
W 116th St
W 115th St
W 114th St
W 113th St
W 112th St
W 111th St
W 110th St (Cathedral Pkwy)
12th Ave
Marginal St
Riverside Dr
Old Broadway
Manhattanville Houses
City College
Convent Ave
Convent Hill
St Nicholas Park
St Nicholas Ave
135th Street
125th Street
Tiemann Pl
Riverside Dr E
Riverside Dr W
General Grant Houses
Morningside Houses
Grant's Tomb
Hudson River
Claremont Ave
Broadway
Amsterdam Ave
Morningside Ave
Manhattan Ave
Frederick Douglass Blvd
Barnard College
Columbia University
Riverside Park
Henry Hudson Pkwy
116th Street Columbia University
Morningside Dr
Morningside Park
Cathedral of St John the Divine
Cathedral Parkway 110th St
116th Street
Central Park
PAGE 256
PAGE 238
1/4 mile
.25 km

Since outsiders rarely head uptown, neighborhood nightlife mostly consists of grad students avoiding dissertations in beer bars (**1020 Bar**), undergrads avoiding papers with heavier drinking (**The Heights Bar & Grill**), and residents avoiding it all in dives (**Patrick Ryan's**). Columbia will regularly bring in word-class operas at the **Miller Theater**.

Bars

- **1020 Bar** • 1020 Amsterdam Ave [W 110th St]
  212-531-3468
  Columbia dive with super cheap beer.
- **Cafe Amrita** • 301 W 110th St [Central Park W]
  212-222-0683
  Caffeinated Columbia students, snacks, wine, beer.
- **Cotton Club** • 656 W 125th St [St Clair Pl]
  212-663-7980
  Good, fun swingin' uptown joint.
- **The Heights Bar & Grill** •
  2867 Broadway [W 111th St]
  212-866-7035
  Hang out on the rooftop with Columbia students.
- **Lerner Hall** • 2920 Broadway [W 115th St]
  212-854-5800
  Columbia student union features coffee, conventions, and wacky parties.
- **Max Caffe** •
  1262 Amsterdam Ave [W 122nd St]
  212-531-1210
  Low-key date place. Wine, good food, and sweet patio.
- **Nectar Bar** •
  2235 Frederick Douglass Blvd [W 120th St]
  212-961-9622
  Classy wine bar. A Cotton Club era throwback.
- **Patrick Ryan's** • 3155 Broadway [Tiemann Pl]
  212-537-7660
  New ownership provides ridiculously cheap drink specials.
- **Perk's** • 553 Manhattan Ave [W 123rd St]
  212-666-8500
  Live music every Wednesdays and Thursdays.
- **Showman's Cafe** •
  375 W 125th St [Morningside Ave]
  212-864-8941
  Live jazz. In Harlem. That's all you need to know.

Theaters/Performing Arts

- **Manhattan School of Music** •
  120 Claremont Ave [W 122nd St]
  212-749-2802
  Classics played by students and guest artists.
- **Miller Theater–Columbia University** •
  2960 Broadway [W 116th St]
  212-854-7799
  Making chamber music hip for the college kiddies.

W 135th St
W 134th St
W 133rd St
Old Broadway
W 132nd St
W 131st St
W 130th St
St Clair Pl
Marginal St
12th Ave
Riverside Dr
Manhattan-ville Houses
City College
Convent Ave
Convent Hill
St Nicholas Park
St Nicholas Ave
135th Street
W 129th St
W 128th St
W 127th St
W 126th St
W 125th St
125th Street
Tiemann Pl
Riverside Dr E
General Grant Houses
La Salle St
Morningside Houses
Riverside Dr W
Grant's Tomb
Hudson River
W 124th St
St Nicholas Ave
W 123rd St
W 122nd St
W 121st St
W 120th St
Claremont Ave
Broadway
Morningside Ave
Manhattan Ave
125th Street
W 119th St
W 118th St
W 117th St
W 116th St
W 115th St
Frederick Douglass Blvd
Barnard College
PAGE 238
Columbia University
PAGE 256
Riverside Park
Henry Hudson Pkwy
Morningside Dr
116th Street Columbia University
116th Street
W 114th St
W 113th St
W 112th St
W 111th St
Morningside Park
Cathedral of St John the Divine
Cathedral Parkway 110th St
W 110th St (Cathedral Pkwy)
Cathedral Parkway 110th St
9a
9
21
19
16
1/4 mile
.25 km

The Columbia kids have many long-standing quick favorites such as the giant slices of **Koronet Pizza** or the quick Middle Eastern food of **Amir's**. For something more relaxed, try Ethiopian at **Massawa**, brunch time at **Kitchenette**, or the dangerously delicious meat emporium of **Dinosaur BBQ**. Italian lovers get their fix at cozy **Max SoHa** and the wonderful **Pisticci**.

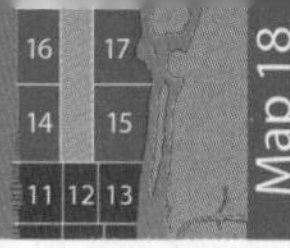

Restaurants

- **Ajanta** • 1237 Amsterdam Ave [121st St]
  212-316-6776 • $$
  Morningside Heights' prime Indian lunch/dinner place.
- **Amir's Falafel** • 2911 Broadway [W 113th St]
  212-749-7500 • $
  A for price. B- for quality.
- **Bistro Ten 18** • 1018 Amsterdam Ave [110th St]
  212-662-7600 • $$$
  Excellent uptown American bistro.
- **Campo** • 2888 Broadway [113th]
  212-864-1143 • $$$
  Italian by day, hip and cozy undergrad hangout at night.
- **Community Food and Juice** •
  2893 Broadway [W 113th St]
  212-665-2800 • $$$
  Columbia foodies dig this place. And so should you.
- **Deluxe Diner** • 2896 Broadway [W 113th St]
  212-662-7900 • $$
  Hip diner with good brunch and happy hour.
- **Dinosaur Bar-B-Que** •
  646 W 131st St [Broadway]
  212-694-1777 • $$$
  Not just for Syracuse fans. Head WAY uptown.
- **Havana Central** • 2911 Broadway [W 113th St]
  212-662-8830 • $$$
  The old West End gone Cuban. Bring earplugs.
- **The Heights Bar & Grill** •
  2867 Broadway [W 111th St]
  212-866-7035 • $$
  Columbia students can't drink all the time so they eat here.
- **Hungarian Pastry Shop** •
  1030 Amsterdam Ave [W 111th St]
  212-866-4230 • $
  Exactly what it is—and excellent.
- **Kitchenette** • 1272 Amsterdam Ave [123rd St]
  212-531-7600 • $$
  Cozy and good for everything.
- **Koronet Pizza** • 2848 Broadway [W 111th St]
  212-222-1566 • $
  Just one slice. Really. That's all you'll need.
- **Le Monde** • 2885 Broadway [W 112th St]
  212-531-3939 • $$
  French bistro pub with a nice bar.
- **Massawa** • 1239 Amsterdam Ave [W 121st St]
  212-663-0505 • $$
  Neighborhood Ethiopian joint.
- **Max SoHa** • 1274 Amsterdam Ave [123rd St]
  212-531-2221 • $$
  The Italian genius of Max, uptown.
- **Mill Korean** • 2895 Broadway [W 113th St]
  212-666-7653 • $$
  Good Korean for Columbia kids.
- **Miss Mamie's Spoonbread Too** •
  366 W 110th St [Manhattan Ave]
  212-865-6744 • $$
  Soul food spectacular.
- **New York** • 1270 Amsterdam Ave [123rd St]
  212-280-0705 • $
  Best place for brunch in Morningside Heights.
- **P + W Sandwich Shop** •
  1030 Amsterdam Ave [W 111th St]
  212-222-2245 • $
  Fresh sliced deli meats.
- **Panino Sportivo** •
  1231 Amsterdam Ave [W 121st St]
  212-662-2066 • $$
  Gooooaaaal on the TV. And pricey Italian sandwiches.
- **Pinnacle** • 2937 Broadway [115th St]
  212-662-1000 • $
  Proximity to campus has only made pizza/sandwiches more popular.
- **Pisticci** • 125 La Salle St [Broadway]
  212-932-3500 • $$
  Wonderful, friendly Italian. A true gem.
- **Presidential Pizza** •
  357 W 125 St [St Nicholas Ave]
  212-222-7744 • $
  Grab a handful of napkins for 125th Street's best slice.
- **Sezz Medi'** • 1260 Amsterdam Ave [122nd St]
  212-932-2901 • $$
  Popular brick oven pizza.
- **Symposium** • 544 W 113th St [Amsterdam]
  212-865-1011 • $$
  Traditional underground (literally) Greek fare.
- **Terrace in the Sky** •
  400 W 119th St [Morningside Dr]
  212-666-9490 • $$$$$
  Expensive rooftop terrace French for when the parents are in town.
- **Tom's Restaurant** • 2880 Broadway [112th St]
  212-864-6137 • $
  Yes. This is the Seinfeld diner. Can we go now?
- **V&T Pizzeria** •
  1024 Amsterdam Ave [W 110th St]
  212-666-8051 • $
  Columbia pizza and pasta. Family friendly if you're into that.

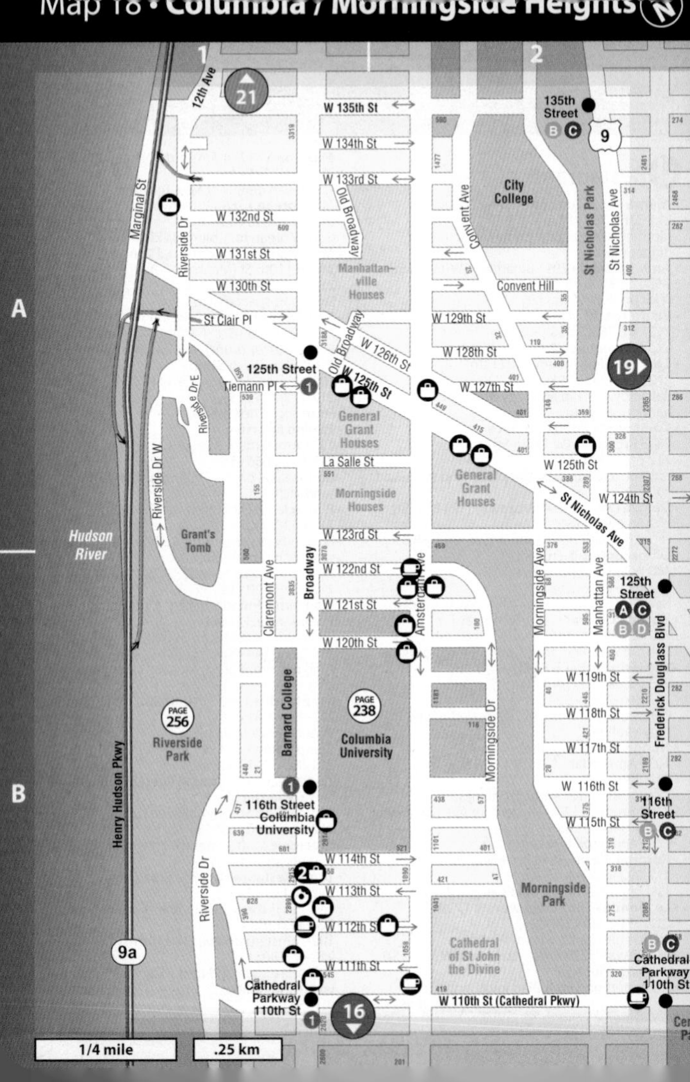

W 135th St
W 134th St
W 133rd St
W 132nd St
W 131st St
W 130th St
St Clair Pl
W 129th St
W 128th St
W 127th St
W 126th St
W 125th St
W 124th St
W 123rd St
W 122nd St
W 121st St
W 120th St
W 119th St
W 118th St
W 117th St
W 116th St
W 115th St
W 114th St
W 113th St
W 112th St
W 111th St
W 110th St (Cathedral Pkwy)
La Salle St
Tiemann Pl
12th Ave
Marginal St
Riverside Dr
Riverside Dr E
Riverside Dr W
Old Broadway
Broadway
Claremont Ave
Amsterdam Ave
Convent Ave
Convent Hill
Morningside Ave
Morningside Dr
Manhattan Ave
St Nicholas Ave
St Nicholas Park
Frederick Douglass Blvd
Henry Hudson Pkwy
Hudson River
City College
Manhattanville Houses
General Grant Houses
Morningside Houses
Grant's Tomb
Riverside Park
Barnard College
Columbia University
Morningside Park
Cathedral of St John the Divine
135th Street
125th Street
116th Street
116th Street Columbia University
Cathedral Parkway 110th St
PAGE 256
PAGE 238
21
19
16
9
9a
1/4 mile
.25 km

Bagels, Coffee, & Shopping

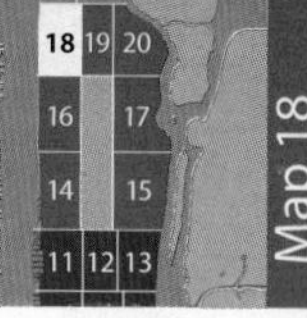

The newly-expanded **Book Culture** is a world-class academic bookstore. **Ricky's** provides a resource for style needs, and few dimestores are quite as expansive as **El Mundo**. Coffee on the go at **Oren's** or sit and talk Nietzsche at **Hungarian Pastry Shop**. Groceries and free samples at the 24-hour **Westside Market**. Or everything at the massive **Fairway**.

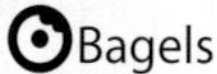

Bagels

- **Nussbaum & Wu** • 2897 Broadway [113th St]
  212-280-5344
  Fine but it's worth the walk to Absolute.

Coffee

- **Cafe Amrita** • 301 W 110th St [Central Park W]
  212-222-0683
  Study (or update your blog) while you caffeinate.
- **Hungarian Pastry Shop** •
  1030 Amsterdam Ave [W 111th St]
  212-866-4230
  Professors and grad students love to read here.
- **Max Caffe** • 1262 Amsterdam Ave [122nd St]
  212-531-1210
  Great spot to hang out. Open at 8 am.
- **Oren's Daily Roast** • 2882 Broadway [112th St]
  212-749-8779
  Hip staff pours superior java at local mini-chain.

Shopping

- **Amsterdam Liquor Mart** •
  1356 Amsterdam Ave [W 126th St]
  212-222-1334
  Stock up on your way to that beer pong party.
- **Appletree Market** •
  1225 Amsterdam Ave [120th St]
  212-865-8840
  One of the better grocery options for Columbia kids.
- **Aunt Meriam's** • 435 W 125th St [Morningside]
  212-531-0322
  Hard to find African-American artifacts.
- **Book Culture** • 536 W 112th St [Amsterdam]
  212-865-1588
  Excellent bookstore servicing Columbia/ Barnard students.
- **C-Town** • 560 W 125th St [Old Broadway]
  212-662-2388
  No-frills market way cheaper than your local bodega.
- **Citarella** • 461 W 125th St [Amsterdam Ave]
  212-874-0383
  Wealthy foodies love this place.
- **Clinton Supply** • 1256 Amsterdam Ave [W 122nd St]
  212-222-8245
  Random hardware stuff for your new dorm or apartment.
- **Columbia Hardware** •
  2905 Broadway [W 113th St]
  212-662-2150
  Where the smart kids get their hammers.
- **Fairway Market** • 2328 12th Ave [W 133rd St]
  212-234-3883
  So big. So good. So New York.
- **Franklin and Lennon Paint Co** •
  537 W 125 St [Broadway]
  212-864-2460
  Long-standing outlet with biggest selection of paint and supplies.
- **Hartley Pharmacy** •
  1219 Amsterdam Ave [120th St]
  212-749-8480
  Mom & Pop pharmacy with staff that knows you personally.
- **M2M Asian Market** • 2935 Broadway [115th St]
  212-280-4600
  Sushi, soba, Asian groceries. Perfect for a quick stop.
- **Mondel Chocolates** • 2913 Broadway [114th St]
  212-864-2111
  Mom-and-pop candy shop with great chocolates.
- **Ricky's** • 2906 Broadway [112th St]
  212-280-2861
  If a drug store can be hip…
- **Samad's Gourmet** • 2867 Broadway [111th St]
  Hard to find Middle Eastern and world delicacies.
- **Sea & Sea Fish Market** •
  310 St Nicholas Ave [W 125th St]
  212-222-7427
  Fish and more fish. They'll fry it up for you!
- **Vino Fino** • 1250 Amsterdam Ave [122nd St]
  212-222-0388
  Lots of tastings and friendly owners.
- **Westside Market** • 2840 Broadway [110th St]
  212-222-3367
  Bordering on gourmet shopping for Columbia U.

Map 19 • Harlem (Lower)

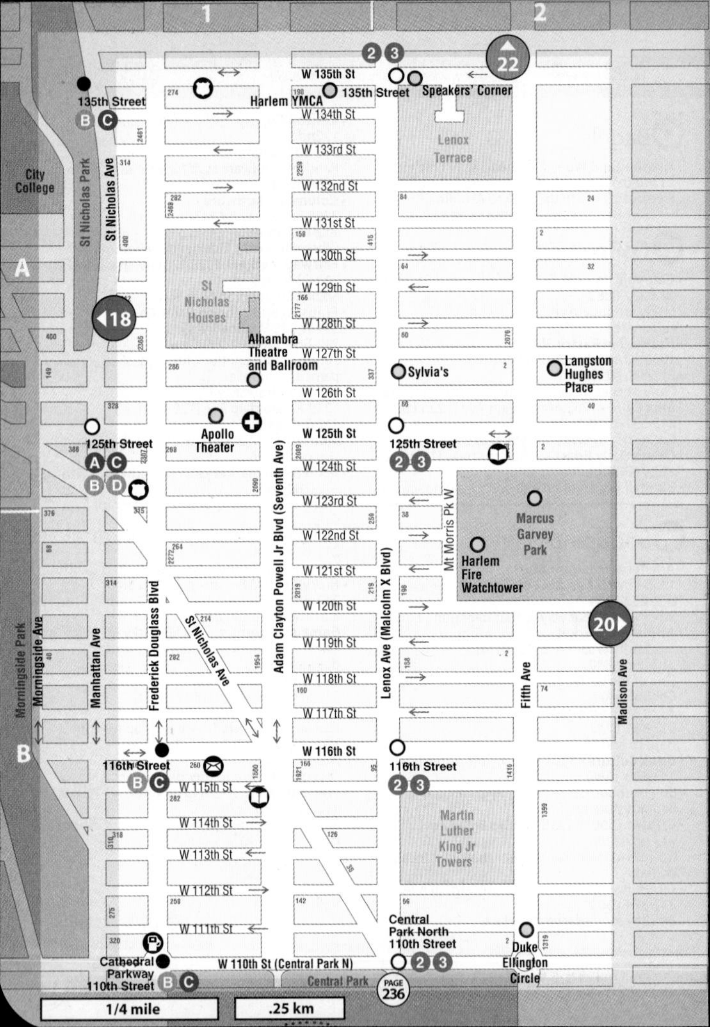

W 135th St
135th Street
Harlem YMCA
Speakers' Corner
135th Street
W 134th St
Lenox Terrace
W 133rd St
City College
St Nicholas Park
St Nicholas Ave
W 132nd St
W 131st St
W 130th St
St Nicholas Houses
W 129th St
W 128th St
Alhambra Theatre and Ballroom
W 127th St
Sylvia's
Langston Hughes Place
W 126th St
Apollo Theater
W 125th St
125th Street
125th Street
W 124th St
Adam Clayton Powell Jr Blvd (Seventh Ave)
Mt Morris Pk W
Marcus Garvey Park
W 123rd St
W 122nd St
Harlem Fire Watchtower
W 121st St
Lenox Ave (Malcolm X Blvd)
W 120th St
Frederick Douglass Blvd
St Nicholas Ave
W 119th St
Morningside Park
Morningside Ave
Manhattan Ave
W 118th St
Fifth Ave
Madison Ave
W 117th St
W 116th St
116th Street
116th Street
W 115th St
W 114th St
Martin Luther King Jr Towers
W 113th St
W 112th St
W 111th St
Central Park North 110th Street
Duke Ellington Circle
Cathedral Parkway 110th Street
W 110th St (Central Park N)
Central Park

PAGE 236

1/4 mile
.25 km

Neighborhood Overview

New Yorkers below 96th Street rarely venture above the park for more than a chicken-and-waffles feast or an Amateur Night ticket. Well, the joke's on them. Harlem is a thriving neighborhood in every sense of the word—great community spirit, great street life, great architecture, great arts and culture…pretty much great everything. The lifeline of this neighborhood is 125th Street, a thoroughfare known for the Apollo Theater, a zillion stores, and players strutting their stuff. With some of the tastiest grub in town, bargains lining the streets, and locals who keep it real, Harlem is a nabe for New Yorkers who like it a little gruff.

For better or for worse, Harlem is changing. Bill Clinton keeps his office on 125th Street. Chi-chi cupcake cafes push uptown. And chic French bistros hold shop next to grubby bodegas. Even as American Apparel wrangles itself a spot across from the Apollo, the nabe retains a sense of gritty pride. 125th Street crawls with vendors selling everything from fur vests to coco helado. A random TV in the wall next door to the Apollo plays Soul Train on repeat. Storefront churches fill Sunday mornings with Gospel ballads. Just journey uptown to check it out, and leave the credit card at home—125th is still a cash-only kind of street.

A mind-boggling number of writers, artists, and civil rights leaders made names for themselves in Harlem, and the community doesn't want anyone to forget it. At the tip-top of Central Park, **Duke Ellington** sits at an oversized grand piano; the statue was erected in 1997. Shockingly, this young memorial was the first one to be dedicated to an African-American in New York City. The Morris Historical District houses **Marcus Garvey Park**, renamed after the famous civil rights leader in 1973. On a more literary note, visit Langston Hughes Place, the street where the poet lived. Look for the ivy-covered building halfway down the block, but just snap a photo. The home went on the market in 2009. Then, check out his first residence at the still-operating **Harlem YMCA**. The facilities became an oasis for black visitors and artists during the Harlem Renaissance, when many of New York's hotels, theaters and restaurants were segregated. The list of short-term residents reads like an artsy walk of fame, with Hughes, Ralph Ellison, Claude McKay, and James Baldwin all calling the 135th Street location home.

Food, music, and entertainment happily collide in Harlem. The Apollo Theatre is easily the area's most notable landmark, with everyone from Ella Fitzgerald to the Jackson Five kicking off their careers on that stage. The 70-year-old Amateur Night show still runs on Wednesdays, just prep for a line. Even more musical greats—Billie Holiday, Bessie Smith—haunted the **Alhambra Theatre and Ballroom**. If it had been around, we like to think they all would have chowed at **Sylvia's**, a soul food institution that has dished out piping hot fried chicken, waffles and mashed potatoes since 1962.

Stroll the residential blocks for a complete view of changing Harlem. Sure, brownstones sell for upwards of a million dollars, but row-houses with shattered windows and planked doors remain. Harlem is a neighborhood in flux, but it's not the Upper West Side. That means old-school New York tactics still apply. Walk fast, with purpose and with a sense of direction (even if you managed to get lost in the very easy-to-understand grid).

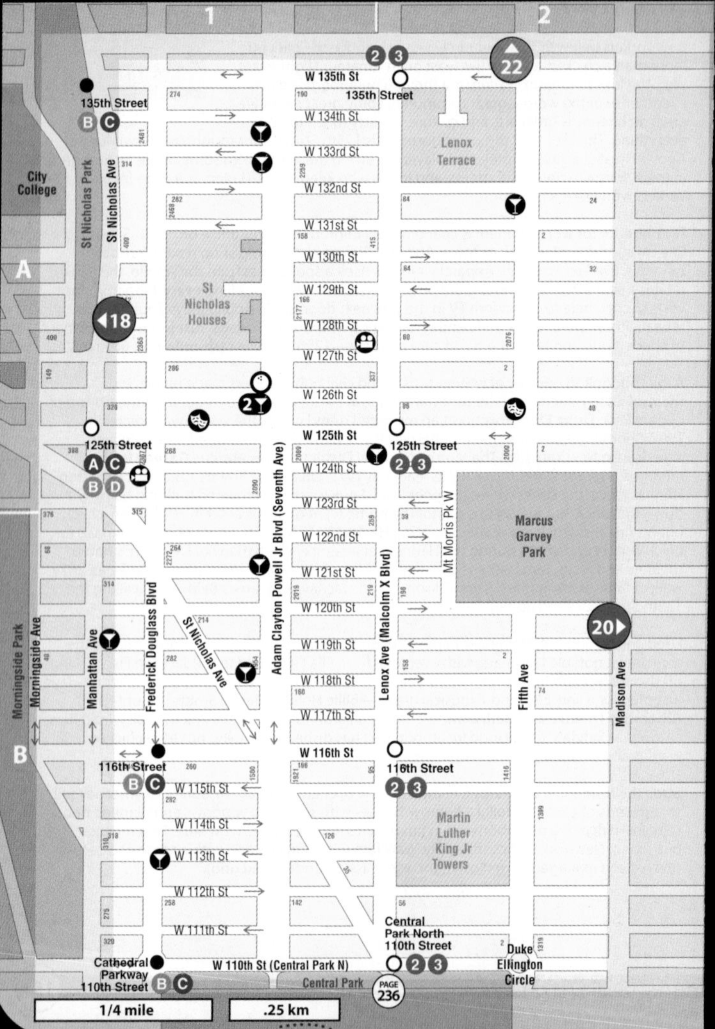

1
2
22
18
20
A
B
W 135th St
135th Street
W 134th St
W 133rd St
W 132nd St
W 131st St
W 130th St
W 129th St
W 128th St
W 127th St
W 126th St
W 125th St
125th Street
W 124th St
W 123rd St
W 122nd St
W 121st St
W 120th St
W 119th St
W 118th St
W 117th St
W 116th St
116th Street
W 115th St
W 114th St
W 113th St
W 112th St
W 111th St
W 110th St (Central Park N)
Central Park North 110th Street
Cathedral Parkway 110th Street
City College
St Nicholas Park
St Nicholas Ave
St Nicholas Houses
Lenox Terrace
Marcus Garvey Park
Martin Luther King Jr Towers
Mt Morris Pk W
Adam Clayton Powell Jr Blvd (Seventh Ave)
Lenox Ave (Malcolm X Blvd)
Frederick Douglass Blvd
Manhattan Ave
Morningside Ave
Morningside Park
Fifth Ave
Madison Ave
Duke Ellington Circle
Central Park
1/4 mile
.25 km

PAGE 236

Nightlife

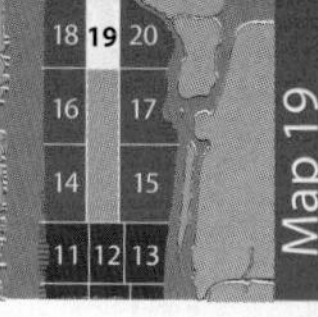

Dive bars, underground jazz, and live music spectacles mesh for a diverse scene. Catch a show at the landmark **Apollo Theater** (Harlem residents, bring proof of address for a discount); sip fancy cocktails at **67 Orange Street**; or slip into the **Lenox Lounge** for classic jazz. Watch indie movies (a lot about Harlem) at **Maysles Cinema**.

Bars

- **67 Orange Street** •
  2082 Frederick Douglass Blvd [113th St]
  212-662-2030
  Classy cocktail bar with speakeasy style.
- **The Den** • 2150 5th Ave [W 132nd St]
  212-234-3045
  Welcome addition to the Harlem scene.
- **Gospel Uptown** •
  2110 Adam Clayton Powell Jr Blvd [126th St]
  212-865-1841
  The Gospel version of the Hard Rock Café, in a good way.
- **Lenox Lounge** • 288 Lenox Ave [W 124th St]
  212-427-0253
  Old-time Harlem hangout; bar in the front, jazz in the back room.
- **Minton's Playhouse** •
  208 W 118 St [Adam Clayton Powell]
  212-864-8346
  Live jazz almost every night.
- **Moca Bar & Grill** •
  2210 Frederick Douglass Blvd [W 119th St]
  212-665-8081
  Serving up hip hop, classics, and R&B.
- **Paris Blues** •
  2021 Adam Clayton Powell Jr Blvd [121st St]
  212-864-9110
  Nothing fancy, just a solid bar.
- **PJ's** •
  2256 Adam Clayton Powell Jr Blvd [W 133rd St]
  212-862-1511
  Everyone loves Tom!
- **Seville Lounge** • 2121 7th Ave [W 126th St]
  212-864-8624
  Reliable neighborhood vibe.
- **Shrine Bar & Restaurant** •
  2271 Adam Clayton Powell Jr Blvd [134th St]
  212-690-7807
  Drink for cheap while Harlem and Columbia bands play.

Bowling

- **Harlem Lanes** •
  2116 Adam Clayton Powell Jr Blvd [W 126th St]
  212-678-2695
  Finally, bowling above 96th Street. Hooray!

Movie Theaters

- **AMC Magic Johnson Harlem 9** •
  2309 Frederick Douglass Blvd [W 124th St]
  212-665-6923
  Owned by Magic. Best choice for Upper Manhattan.
- **Maysles Cinema** •
  343 Malcolm X Blvd [127th St]
  212-582-6050
  Amazing indies and documentaries from local film-makers.

Theaters/Performing Arts

- **Apollo Theater** •
  253 W 125th St [Frederick Douglass Blvd]
  212-531-5300
  Where booing is not only allowed, it's encouraged!
- **National Black Theatre** •
  2031 5th Ave [E 126th St]
  212-722-3800
  No, they don't do Neil Simon here.

W 135th St
135th Street
W 134th St
W 133rd St
W 132nd St
W 131st St
W 130th St
W 129th St
W 128th St
W 127th St
W 126th St
W 125th St
125th Street
W 124th St
W 123rd St
W 122nd St
W 121st St
W 120th St
W 119th St
W 118th St
W 117th St
W 116th St
116th Street
W 115th St
W 114th St
W 113th St
W 112th St
W 111th St
W 110th St (Central Park N)
Central Park North 110th Street
Cathedral Parkway 110th Street
Central Park
Duke Ellington Circle
City College
St Nicholas Park
St Nicholas Ave
St Nicholas Houses
Lenox Terrace
Marcus Garvey Park
Martin Luther King Jr Towers
Mt Morris Pk W
Morningside Park
Morningside Ave
Manhattan Ave
Frederick Douglass Blvd
Adam Clayton Powell Jr Blvd (Seventh Ave)
Lenox Ave (Malcolm X Blvd)
Fifth Ave
Madison Ave

18
20
22
PAGE 236

1/4 mile
.25 km

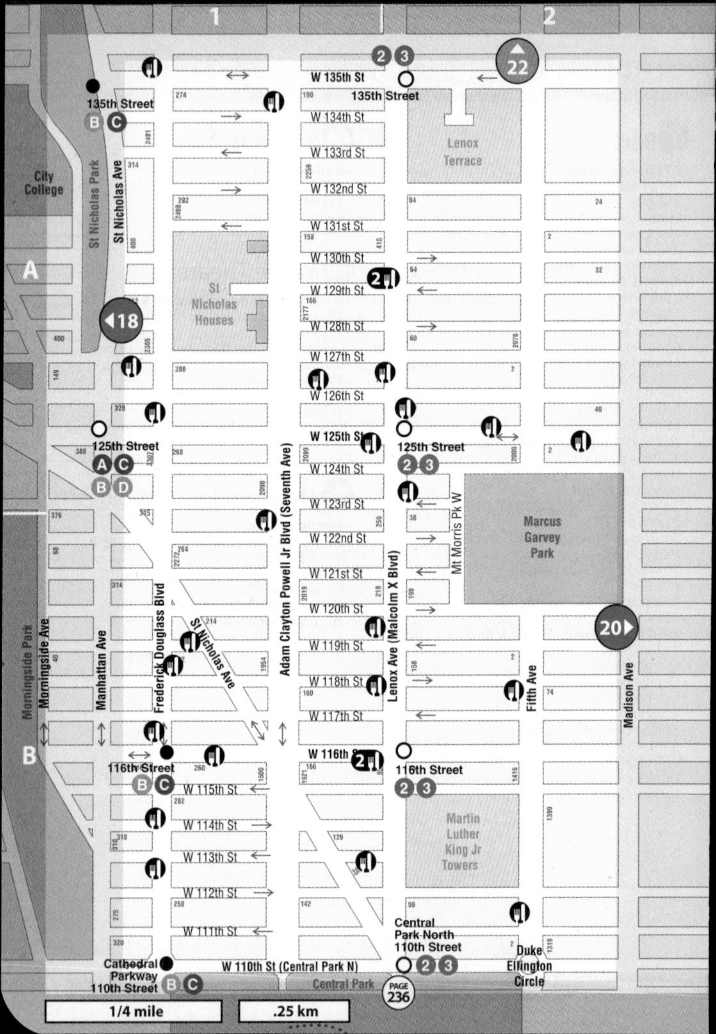

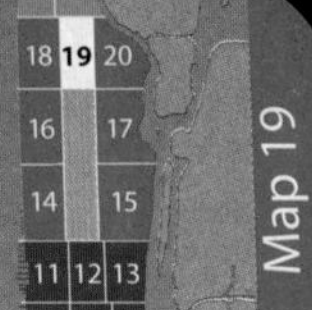

Don't give soul food all of the credit; Harlem dining is increasingly global. Kick off the morning at **Il Caffe Latte** with steaming lattes and breakfast wraps. Settle in at **Patisserie des Ambassades** for French-Senegalese entrees. For straight up Senegalese, try **Africa Kine**. Head to **Amy Ruth's** or **Sylvia's** when home-style cooking beckons.

Restaurants

- **African Kine Restaurant** • 256 W 116th St [Frederick Douglass Blvd] 212-666-9400 • $ Senegalese with nice little dining room.
- **Amy Ruth's** • 113 W 116th St [Lenox Ave] 212-280-8779 • $$ Soul food, incredible fried chicken.
- **Billie's Black** • 271 W 119th St [St Nicholas] 212-280-2248 • $$ Good food + live entertainment.
- **Cafe Veg** • 2291 7th Ave [134th St] 212-491-3223 • $$ A veggie oasis in Harlem.
- **Chez Lucienne** • 308 Malcolm X Blvd [125th St] 212-289-5555 • $$ Cozy little French bistro. Authentic and affordable!
- **Fishers of Men II** • 159 W 126th St [7th Ave] 212-678-4268 • $ Sequel to the East side store: fried fish, plus franks.
- **Harlem BBQ** • 2367 Frederick Douglass Blvd [127th St] 212-222-1922 • $$ Football-sized frozen cocktails and entire $6 chickens to-go.
- **Il Caffe Latte** • 189 Lenox Ave [119th Street] 212-222-2241 • $ Fresh sandwiches, massive $3 lattes and a stellar Latin wrap.
- **Island Salad** • 22 E 125 St [5th Ave] 212-860-3000 • $ A healthy food oasis.
- **Jacob's Restaurant** • 373 Malcolm X Blvd [W 129th St] 212-866-3663 • $ Soul food and salad by the pound for cheap.
- **Le Baobab** • 120 W 116th St [Lenox Ave] 212-864-4700 • $ Satisfying Senegalese complete with TV in French.
- **Lolita's Cafe** • 57 Lenox Ave [113th St] 212-222-6969 • $$ Cheap and cozy neighborhood Mexican joint.
- **Manna's Soul Food and Salad Bar** • 2331 Frederick Douglass Blvd [125th St] 212-749-9084 • $$ Pile a buffet plate with everything from oxtail to collard greens.
- **Melba's** • 300 W 114th St [Frederick Douglass] 212-864-7777 • $$$ Upscale soul food.
- **Mobay** • 17 W 125 St [5th Ave] 212-876-9300 • $$$ Throwdown Caribbean soul food at this Food Network fave.
- **Native** • 101 W 118th St [Lenox Ave] 212-665-2525 • $ Excellent soul food.
- **Ottomanelli Brothers** • 1325 5th Ave [111th St] 212-828-8900 • $$ Solid Italian food comes to Harlem.
- **Papaya King** • 121 W 125th St [Lenox Ave] 212-678-4268 • $ Dawgs for all you dawgs.
- **Patisserie Des Ambassades** • 2200 Frederick Douglass Blvd [119th St] 212-666-0078 • $ Great breakfast pastries. Senegalese food too.
- **Piatto D'Oro II** • 1 E 118th St [Fifth Ave] 212-722-7220 • $$ Classic Italian offspring of East 109th Street locale.
- **Strictly Roots** • 2058 Adam Clayton Powell Jr Blvd [W 123rd St] 212-864-8699 • $$ Cheap and filling Caribbean food. Oh yeah, it's vegan too.
- **Svntn Below** • 2163 Frederick Douglass Blvd [W 117th St] 212-749-2569 • $$$ Fancy pants restaurant complete with bottle service.
- **Sylvia's** • 328 Lenox Ave [W 126th St] 212-996-0660 • $$$ An institution. Not overrated.
- **Tonnie's Minis** • 264 Lenox Ave [123rd St] 212-831-5292 • $ New York's cupcake obsession pushes uptown.
- **Trattoria Amici** • 381 Lenox Ave [129th St] 212-828-8040 • $$ Casual Italian American, free delivery, top-notch Tiramisu.
- **Yvonne Yvonne** • 301 W 135th St [Frederick Douglass Blvd] 212-862-1223 • $ Good jerk chicken, ribs, etc from a steam table.
- **Zoma** • 2084 Frederick Douglass Blvd [W 113th St] 212-662-0620 • $$ Tasty Ethiopian in a tasteful setting.

Map 19 • Harlem (Lower)

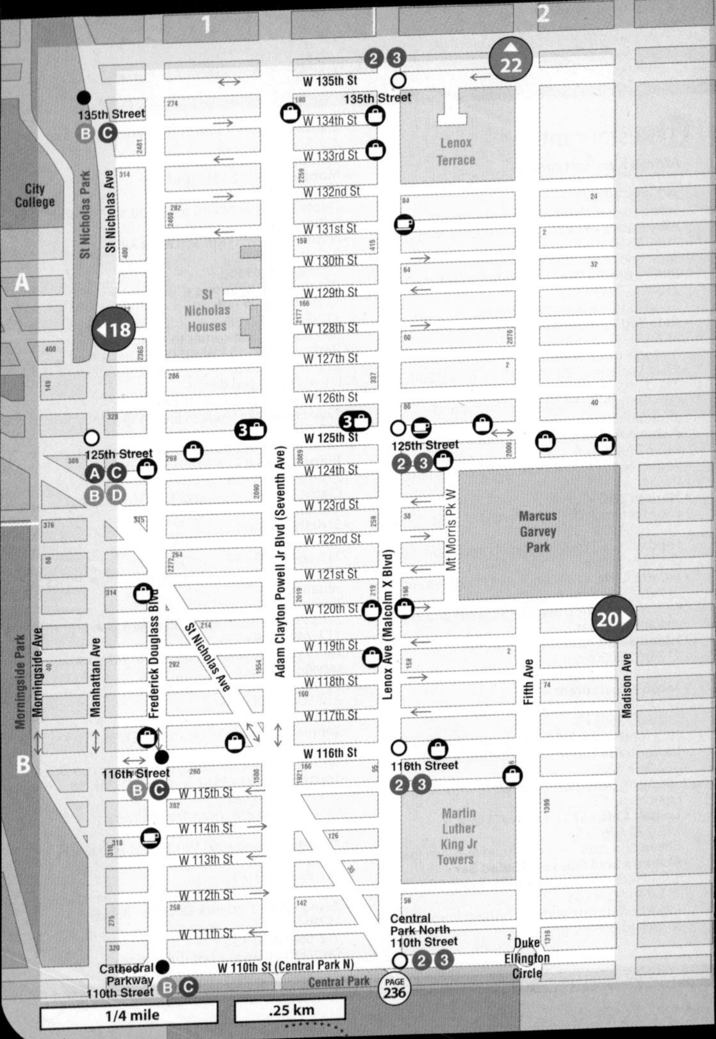

W 135th St
135th Street
2 3
22
W 134th St
W 133rd St
Lenox Terrace
W 132nd St
W 131st St
W 130th St
W 129th St
W 128th St
W 127th St
W 126th St
W 125th St
125th Street
W 124th St
W 123rd St
W 122nd St
W 121st St
W 120th St
W 119th St
W 118th St
W 117th St
W 116th St
116th Street
W 115th St
W 114th St
W 113th St
W 112th St
W 111th St
W 110th St (Central Park N)
Central Park North 110th Street
Central Park
PAGE 236
Duke Ellington Circle
Cathedral Parkway 110th Street
135th Street
B C
City College
St Nicholas Park
St Nicholas Ave
St Nicholas Houses
18
125th Street
A C
B D
116th Street
Marcus Garvey Park
Mt Morris Pk W
20
Martin Luther King Jr Towers
Morningside Park
Morningside Ave
Manhattan Ave
Frederick Douglass Blvd
Adam Clayton Powell Jr Blvd (Seventh Ave)
Lenox Ave (Malcolm X Blvd)
Fifth Ave
Madison Ave
1/4 mile
.25 km

With everything from **Champ's** to **M.A.C.** cosmetics, 125th Street anchors Harlem shopping. **H&M** stocks the same trendy threads as everywhere else, without the long lines. **Gem**, a two-story department store that looks like a spruced up garage sale, rules for apartment needs. Street vendors fill any other gaps. Everything you want is here, guaranteed.

Coffee

- **La Perle Noir Cafe** • 420 Lenox Ave [131st St]
  212-234-1777
  Bustling cafe with a neighborhood feel and free Wi-Fi.
- **Society Coffee & Juice** •
  2104 Frederick Douglass Blvd [W 114th St]
  212-222-3323
  Cool litte cafe. Nice design.
- **Starbucks** • 77 W 125th St [Lenox Ave]
  917-492-2454
  Use the bathroom. Then head to the closest indie shop.

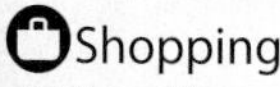

Shopping

- **467 Lenox Liquors** • 467 Lenox Ave [133rd St]
  212-234-7722
  Standard liquor store, sans bullet-proof glass.
- **Atmos** • 203 W 125th St [Adam Clayton Powell]
  212-666-2242
  Palace of popular urban streetwear.
- **BBraxton** • 1400 5th Ave [115th St]
  212-369-3094
  Exceptional grooming for exceptional men.
- **The Brownstone** • 2032 5th Ave [Madison]
  212-996-7980
  Clothing boutique featuring local designers.
- **Carol's Daughter** • 24 W 125th St [5th Ave]
  212-828-6757
  Nature-inspired skin care presented with love.
- **Champs** • 208 W 125th St [Seventh Ave]
  212-280-0296
  Sports, street shoes, and wear. For losers too.
- **Dr Jay's Harlem NYC** •
  256 W 125th St [Frederick Douglass Blvd]
  212-665-7795
  Urban fashions is just what the doctor ordered.
- **Friendly Cleaners** •
  471 W 125th St [Amsterdam Ave]
  212-316-3471
  Reliable staff for wash & fold, and dry cleaning.
- **Gem** • 126 W 125 St [Lenox Ave]
  212-932-3848
  Kind of like Kmart, but crappier.
- **Grandma's Place** • 84 W 120th St [Lenox Ave]
  212-360-6776
  Harlem toy store. Your grandkid will probably love it.
- **H&M** • 125 W 125th St [Lenox Ave]
  212-665-8300
  Sort-of-hip, disposable fashion.
- **Harlem Underground Clothing** •
  20 E 125th St [Fifth Ave]
  212-987-9385
  Embroidered Harlem t-shirts.
- **Harlem Vintage** •
  2235 Frederick Douglass Blvd [W 121st St]
  212-866-9463
  Excellent wine shop. Best in Harlem.
- **Hats by Bunn** • 2283 7th Ave [W 134th]
  212-694-3590
  Cool caps.
- **Hue-Man** •
  2319 Frederick Douglass Blvd [W 125th St]
  212-665-7400
  African-American books.
- **Jimmy Jazz** • 132 W 125th St [Lenox Ave]
  212-665-4198
  Urban designers with a range of sizes.
- **M•A•C** • 202 W 125th St [7th Ave]
  212-665-0676
  Beauty products in many colors and shades.
- **Make My Cake** •
  121 St Nicholas Ave [116th St]
  212-932-0833
  Red. Velvet. Cheesecake. Bonus: In-store WiFi.
- **Malcolm Shabazz Harlem Market** •
  58 W 116th St [Lenox Ave]
  212-987-8131
  An open-air market for all your daishiki needs.
- **N Boutique** • 171 Lenox Ave [W 118th St]
  212-961-9100
  Hip boutique with fashion, apothecary, jewelry, and home accessories.
- **Paragon Department Store** •
  488 Lenox Ave [135th St]
  212-926-9470
  It's like a compulsive hoarder decided to sell everything.
- **Settepani** • 196 Lenox Ave [W 120th St]
  917-492-4806
  Lovely baked goods.
- **United Hardware** •
  2160 Frederick Douglass Blvd [W 117th St]
  212-666-7778
  Good for basic tools; that's about all.

Major Deegan Expwy
87
E 134th St
E 135th St
RR Bridge
Lincoln Ave
Alexander Ave
Bruckner Blvd
E 132nd St
Abraham Lincoln Housing
Abraham Lincoln Housing
THE BRONX
PAGE 226
E 132nd St
Third Ave Bridge
Willis Ave
E 131st St
Harlem River
E 130th St
Harlem River Dr
Willis Ave Bridge
A
E 129th St
Keith Haring "Crack is Wack" Mural
E 128th St
E 127th St
Metro North Harlem 125th St
E 126th St
125th Street
Triborough Bridge
E 125th St (Dr Martin Luther King Jr Blvd)
E 124th St
Harlem Fire Watchtower
E 123rd St
Paladino Ave
Marcus Garvey Park
Sen R Wagner Sr Houses
Sen R Wagner Sr Houses
Ronald McNair Pl
E 122nd St
Harlem Courthouse
Sylvan Pl
E 121st St
E 120th St
19
E 119th St
E 118th St
Fifth Ave
Madison Ave
Park Ave
Lexington Ave
Third Ave
E 117th St
Second Ave
First Ave
Pleasant Ave
Bobby Wagner Walk
E 116th St
Pete Pascale Pl
Church of Our Lady of Mt Carmel
B
116th Street
E 115th St
Sen R Taft Houses
Sen R Taft Houses
JW Johnson Housing
JW Johnson Housing
Jefferson Houses
Jefferson Houses
E 114th St
Thomas Jefferson Swimming Pool
Jefferson Park
FDR Dr
E 112th St
E 111st St
110th Street
E 110th St
17
Duke Ellington Circle
1/4 mile
.25 km

El Barrio, also known as Spanish Harlem or East Harlem (just don't call it "SpaHa"), is a neighborhood that is alive with history and culture—Puerto Rican, African-American, Mexican, Italian, Dominican...it's really one of the most diverse neighborhoods in the city. It's not uncommon to find people playing congas on the street or riding tricked out bicycles with Puerto Rican tunes blasting from their radios. You can feel a real sense of community in the bodegas and on the streets as residents chat up their neighbors and warmly greet one another with "Papi" or "Mami." In the summer locals crowd into **Thomas Jefferson Park** and the abundant community gardens provide residents with the perfect chill out spots. Exploring this neighborhood is highly recommended.

But it's not all pretty. East Harlem has been through some tough times in the past few decades to say the least. And unfortunately, to a lot of New Yorkers, it is still a place to avoid. **Keith Haring's "Crack is Wack" Mural** is a symbol of the urban decay in the 1970s and '80s when drugs, poverty, and violence ravaged the neighborhood. Burnt-out buildings were the norm and social problems skyrocketed. Today concrete housing projects dominate the landscape (some very unique like **Taino Towers**) with a few vacant lots here and there, but crime is way down and rents are creeping up.

In recent years the neighborhood has rapidly changed with new condos sprouting up everywhere (some even with doormen), a growing Mexican population moving in (check out 116th Street between Second and Third for amazing food and groceries), and even a touch of suburbia with the gigantic **Costco** that opened in 2009.

Before the Puerto Rican migration, Italians used to call East Harlem home. In the 1930s there were tens of thousands of immigrants from Southern Italy living here. The Italian legacy has almost entirely disappeared with the last of the great bakeries closing a few years ago. Today there are only a few remnants left including the gorgeous **Church of Our Lady of Mount Carmel** (the first Italian church in New York), the **Virgen del Carmen Shrine**, and restaurants like **Rao's** and **Patsy's Pizza**.

Underneath the Metro-North viaduct is another remnant of the old neighborhood, the historic public market **La Marqueta**. Established by Mayor LaGuardia in 1936, this place was the hub of shopping activity for decades with over 500 vendors. Now it only has a few businesses left selling Puerto Rican delicacies like bacalao. Hopefully it will be revived by the city in the near future. In the meantime, locals pack the public plaza (that looks more like a cage) between 115th and 116th Streets on Saturdays in the summer for live music and dancing.

To see the neighborhood in full party mode, head here for the second weekend in June when the Puerto Rican Day Parade is in full swing. On Sunday the parade strolls down Fifth Avenue, but on Saturday Third Avenue and 116th Street come alive for a full-on Puerto Rican party—live music, barbecues on the sidewalk, and lots of Nuyorican pride.

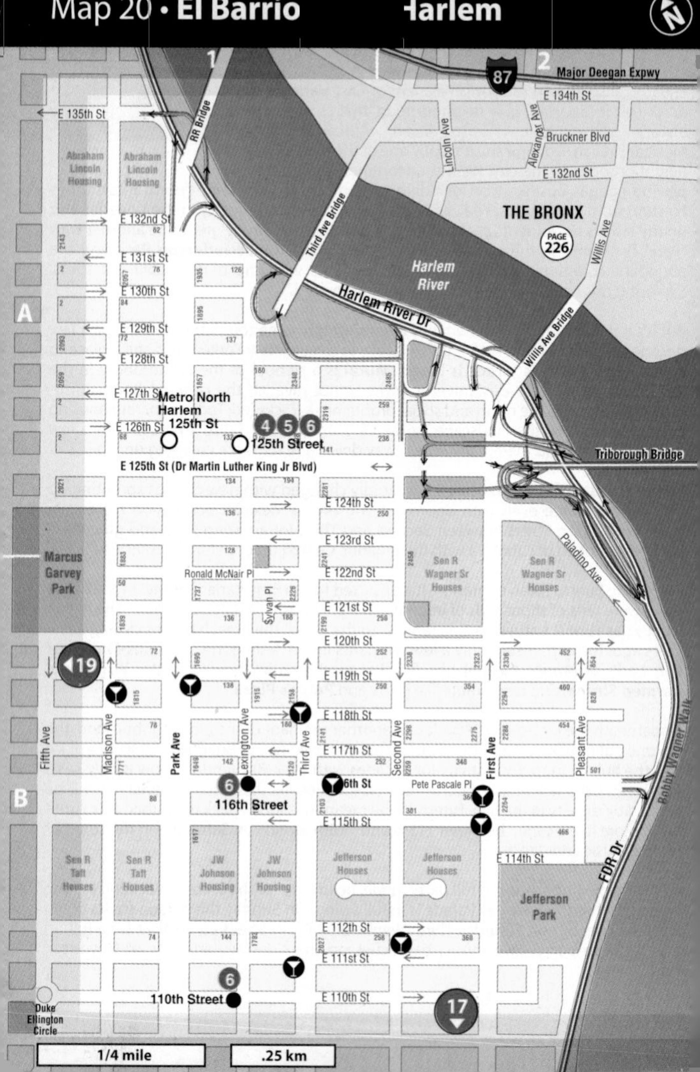
Major Deegan Expwy
87
E 134th St
Bruckner Blvd
E 132nd St
Lincoln Ave
Alexander Ave
THE BRONX
PAGE 226
Willis Ave
Harlem River
Harlem River Dr
Third Ave Bridge
Willis Ave Bridge
RR Bridge
E 135th St
Abraham Lincoln Housing
Abraham Lincoln Housing
E 132nd St
E 131st St
E 130th St
E 129th St
E 128th St
E 127th St
Metro North Harlem 125th St
E 126th St
125th Street
E 125th St (Dr Martin Luther King Jr Blvd)
Triborough Bridge
E 124th St
E 123rd St
E 122nd St
Ronald McNair Pl
Sylvan Pl
E 121st St
E 120th St
E 119th St
E 118th St
E 117th St
116th St
116th Street
Pete Pascale Pl
E 115th St
E 114th St
E 112th St
E 111st St
E 110th St
110th Street
Marcus Garvey Park
Sen R Wagner Sr Houses
Sen R Wagner Sr Houses
Paladino Ave
Sen R Taft Houses
Sen R Taft Houses
JW Johnson Housing
JW Johnson Housing
Jefferson Houses
Jefferson Houses
Jefferson Park
Fifth Ave
Madison Ave
Park Ave
Lexington Ave
Third Ave
Second Ave
First Ave
Pleasant Ave
FDR Dr
Bobby Wagner Walk
Duke Ellington Circle
19
17
1/4 mile
.25 km

Camaradas is your one-stop hot spot for drinks and live entertainment from old-school DJs to Latin grooves. **Mojitos** has a friendly bar to knock back a few drinks. **Raggs** is a proud local joint with a pool table and jukebox while **The Duck** plays country music and women dance on the bar.

Bars

- **Amor Cubano** • 2018 3rd Ave [111th St]
  212-996-1220
  The house band always has this place grooving.
- **Café Creole** • 2167 3rd Ave [E 118th St]
  212-876-8838
  Live entertainment: Jazz, etc.
- **Camaradas** • 2241 1st Ave [E 115th St]
  212-348-2703
  Ececltic live music and tasty bar food. Great vibe.
- **The Duck** • 2171 2nd Ave [112th St]
  212-831-0000
  Uptown country dive. Weird as it sounds.
- **Madison Cigar Lounge** •
  1825 Madison Ave [E 118th St]
  212-828-1625
  Walk-in humidor, private cigar lockers, and exclusive tastings.
- **Mojitos** • 227 E 116th St [Third Ave]
  212-828-8635
  Good Mexican happy hour destination.
- **Orbit East Harlem** • 2257 1st Ave [E 116th St]
  212-348-7818
  Drinks, Latin music, and late night adventures.
- **Ragg's Pub** • 101 E 119th St [Park Ave]
  212-534-9681
  Great little cop bar in the shadow of the Metro-North viaduct.

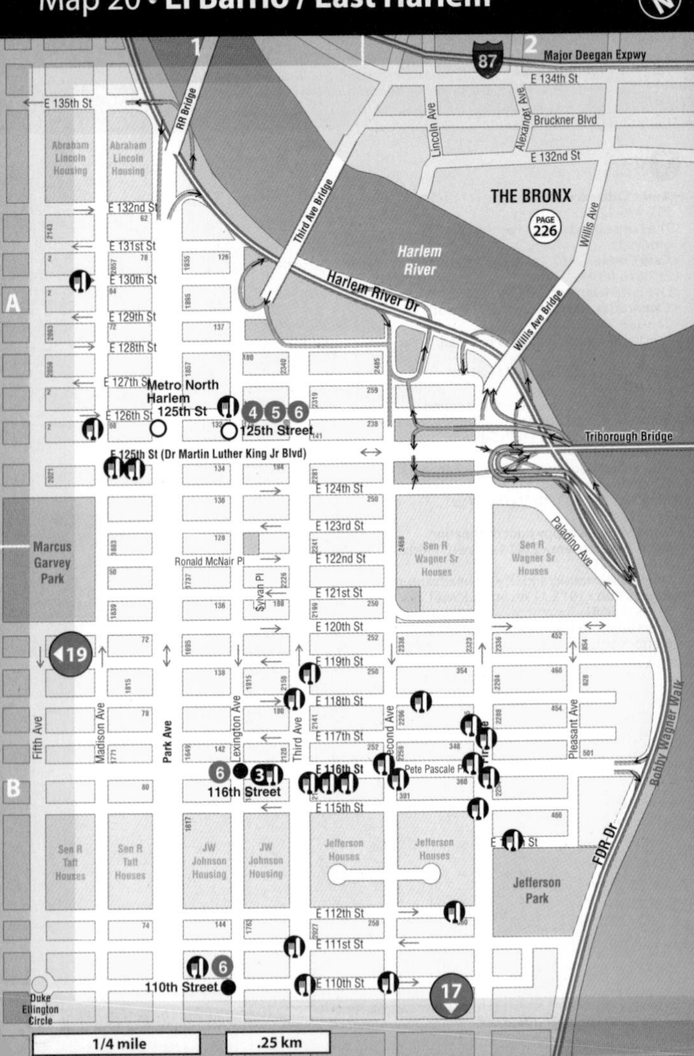

Major Deegan Expwy
87
E 134th St
E 135th St
RR Bridge
Lincoln Ave
Alexander Ave
Bruckner Blvd
E 132nd St
Abraham Lincoln Housing
Abraham Lincoln Housing
THE BRONX
PAGE 226
Third Ave Bridge
Willis Ave
Harlem River
Harlem River Dr
Willis Ave Bridge
E 132nd St
E 131st St
E 130th St
E 129th St
E 128th St
E 127th St
Metro North Harlem 125th St
E 126th St
125th Street
Triborough Bridge
E 125th St (Dr Martin Luther King Jr Blvd)
E 124th St
E 123rd St
Marcus Garvey Park
Ronald McNair Pl
E 122nd St
Sen R Wagner Sr Houses
Sen R Wagner Sr Houses
Paladino Ave
Sylvan Pl
E 121st St
E 120th St
19
E 119th St
E 118th St
Fifth Ave
Madison Ave
Park Ave
Lexington Ave
Third Ave
Second Ave
E 117th St
Pleasant Ave
Bobby Wagner Walk
E 116th St
Pete Pascale Pl
116th Street
E 115th St
Sen R Taft Houses
Sen R Taft Houses
JW Johnson Housing
JW Johnson Housing
Jefferson Houses
Jefferson Houses
Jefferson Park
FDR Dr
E 112th St
E 111st St
110th Street
E 110th St
17
Duke Ellington Circle
1/4 mile
.25 km

Patsy's pizza really is the "original" New York thin-crust pizza. The slices from the take-out window are the best in NYC. Unless you know the Mayor, **Rao's** is another New York restaurant you'll never see the inside of. 116th Street is a budget culinary wonderland. Try **Taco Mix**, **Sandy**, or **El Nuevo Caridad**.

Restaurants

- **A Taste of Seafood** •
  59 E 125th St [Madison Ave]
  212-831-5584 • $
  Fried fish sandwiches on white bread. Lord, have mercy!
- **Amor Cubano** • 2018 3rd Ave [111th St]
  212-996-1220 • $$
  Good Cuban food. Great live music.
- **Café Creole** • 2167 3rd Ave [E 118th St]
  212-876-8838 • $$
  Okra gumbo, jambalaya, and good veggie options.
- **Camaradas** • 2241 1st Ave [E 115th St]
  212-348-2703 • $$
  Spanish/Puerto Rican/tapas/music. Nice!
- **Casa de los Tacos** • 2277 1st Ave [E 116th St]
  212-860-7389 • $
  Try an especial de la casa.
- **Charlie's Place** • 1960 Madison Ave [125th St]
  212-410-0277 • $$
  Harlem's first sushi bar.
- **Cuchifritos** • 168 E 116th St [Lexington Ave]
  212-876-4846 • $
  Puerto Rican fried treats.
- **El Nuevo Caridad** • 2257 2nd Ave [E 116th St]
  212-860-8187 • $
  Dominican baseball stars approve of this chicken.
- **El Paso Taqueria** • 237 E 116th St [3rd Ave]
  212-860-9753 • $$
  Great Mexican with fantastic daily specials.
- **El Tapatio Mexican Restaurant** •
  209 E 116th St [Third Ave]
  212-876-3055 • $$
  Tiny but good.
- **Fishers of Men** • 32 E 130th St [Madison Ave]
  212-828-4447 • $
  Anything deep fried tastes good. Especially this seafood.
- **Golden Crust** •
  2085 Lexington Ave [E 126th St]
  212-722-5253 • $
  It's all about the patties.
- **Green Apple BBQ** • 362 E 112th St [1st Ave]
  212-410-6915 • $$
  Pretty solid ribs and sides like collard greens.
- **L&T Coffee Shop** • 2265 1st Ave [E 116th St]
  212-348-4485 • $
  Meet locals at the counter of this basic diner.
- **La Corsa** • 123 E 110th St [Park Ave]
  212-860-1133 • $
  Pizza. Good grandma slices.
- **Manna's** • 51 E 125th St [Madison Ave]
  212-360-4975 • $
  Soul food buffet by the pound.
- **Mojitos** • 227 E 116th St [Third Ave]
  212-828-8635 • $$
  Live music Thursday, Friday and Saturday.
- **Orbit East Harlem** • 2257 1st Ave [E 116th St]
  212-348-7818 • $$$
  Dinner, brunch, music, etc. A little pricey.
- **Patsy's Pizzeria** • 2287 1st Ave [E 118th St]
  212-534-9783 • $$
  The original thin-crust pizza. Best take-out slices in NY.
- **Pee Dee Steakhouse** •
  2006 3rd Ave [E 110th St]
  212-996-3300 • $
  Grilled meats for cheap.
- **Polash Indian Cuisine Restaurant** •
  2179 3rd Ave [E 119th St]
  212-410-0276 • $$
  Surprisingly solid uptown Indian Restaurant.
- **Rao's** • 455 E 114th St [First Ave]
  212-722-6709 • $$$$$
  An Italian institution, but you'll never get in.
- **Ricardo Steakhouse** •
  2145 2nd Ave [E 110th St]
  212-289-5895 • $$
  Steak, bar, outside patio with upscale vibe and valet parking.
- **Sandy Restaurant** • 2261 2nd Ave [E 116th St]
  212-348-8654 • $$
  Neighborhood Dominican joint. Try the lechon asado.
- **Taco Mix** • 236 E 116 St [Third Ave]
  212-831-8147 • $
  The best tacos in El Barrio. Go for the al pastor.
- **Treichville West African Cuisine** •
  339 E 118th St [Second Ave]
  212-369-7873 • $$
  It's all about the dish thiebou djeun. Open very late.

Major Deegan Expwy
87
E 134th St
E 135th St
Bruckner Blvd
Lincoln Ave
Alexander Ave
E 132nd St
RR Bridge
Abraham Lincoln Housing
Abraham Lincoln Housing
THE BRONX
PAGE 226
Willis Ave
Third Ave Bridge
E 132nd St
E 131st St
E 130th St
Harlem River
Harlem River Dr
E 129th St
E 128th St
Willis Ave Bridge
E 127th St
Metro North Harlem 125th St
E 126th St
125th Street
Triborough Bridge
E 125th St (Dr Martin Luther King Jr Blvd)
E 124th St
E 123rd St
Marcus Garvey Park
Ronald McNair Pl
E 122nd St
Sen R Wagner Sr Houses
Sen R Wagner Sr Houses
Paladino Ave
Sylvan Pl
E 121st St
E 120th St
E 119th St
E 118th St
E 117th St
Fifth Ave
Madison Ave
Park Ave
Lexington Ave
Third Ave
Second Ave
First Ave
Pleasant Ave
Bobby Wagner Walk
E 116th St
Pete Pascale Pl
116th Street
E 115th St
Sen R Taft Houses
Sen R Taft Houses
JW Johnson Housing
JW Johnson Housing
Jefferson Houses
Jefferson Houses
E 114th St
Jefferson Park
FDR Dr
E 112th St
E 111th St
110th Street
E 110th St
Duke Ellington Circle
1/4 mile
.25 km

Casablanca Meat Market is always packed. And for good reason with excellent homemade sausages. For do-it-yourself projects **The Demolition Depot** is a gold mine. Latin music fans swear by **Casa Latina Music Store**. There's even a touch of suburbia in East Harlem with the recent opening of **Costco**.

Shopping

- **115 R & P Beer Distributors** •
  77 E 115th St [Park Ave]
  212-828-5511
  Beer at a good price if you buy in bulk.
- **American Outlet Superstore** •
  2226 3rd Ave [E 121st]
  212-987-6459
  Everything for your apartment
- **Capri Bakery** • 186 E 116th St [Third Ave]
  212-410-1876
  Spanish El Barrio bakery.
- **Casa Latina Music Store** •
  151 E 116th St [Lexington Ave]
  212-427-6062
  El Barrio's oldest record store.
- **Casablanca Meat Market** •
  125 E 110th St [Park Ave]
  212-534-7350
  The line out the door every Saturday says it all.
- **Costco** • 517 E 117 St [Pleasant Ave]
  212-896-5873
  Giving Long Islanders another reason to drive into the city.
- **The Demolition Depot** •
  216 E 125th St [Third Ave]
  212-860-1138
  Amazing selection of architectural salvage.
- **Don Paco Lopez Panaderia** •
  2129 3rd Ave [E 116th St]
  212-876-0700
  Mexican bakery famous for Three Kings Day cake.
- **Eagle Tile & Home Center** •
  2254 2nd Ave [E 115th]
  212-423-0333
  Update the tile in your kitchen or bathroom
- **Goodwill Thrift Shop** •
  2231 3rd Ave [122nd St]
  212-410-0973
  A few floors of used stuff (some of it pretty good).
- **Gothic Cabinet Craft** •
  2268 3rd Ave [E 123rd St]
  212-410-3508
  Real wood furniture. Cheap in price not quality.
- **Heavy Metal Bike Shop** •
  2016 3rd Ave [E 110 St]
  212-410-1144
  Pedal to the metal for repairs and parts.
- **La Marqueta** • 1607 Park Ave [E 112th St]
  212-534-4900
  A couple Puerto Rican food stalls. Still waiting to be revived.
- **Lore Upholstery Shop** •
  2201 3rd Ave [E 120th St]
  212-534-1025
  Well known by Madison Avenue clientele, Reupholster your sidewalk/dumpster chair.
- **Mi Barrio Meat Market** •
  1875 Lexington Ave [E 117th St]
  866-463–0695
  Traditional butcher shop with Mexican specialties.
- **Mi Mexico Lindo Bakery** •
  2267 2nd Ave [E 116th St]
  212-996-5223
  Grab a tray at this old-school bakery.
- **Motherhood Maternity** •
  163 E 125th St [Lexington Ave]
  212-987-8808
  Casual wear for soon-to-be mommies.
- **Pathmark** • 160 E 125th St [Lexington Ave]
  212-722-9155
  Huge supermarket. One of the only ones to sell fresh food.
- **R&S Strauss Auto** • 2005 3rd Ave [E 110th St]
  212-410-6688
  Power steering fluid and windshield wipers 'til 9 pm!
- **Raices Dominican Cigars** •
  2250 1st Ave [E 116th St]
  212-410-6824
  Hand-rolled cigars. With a smoking room!
- **Raskin Carpet** • 2246 3rd Ave [E 122nd St]
  212-369-1100
  Long time East Harlem store has Santa at Xmas.
- **Savoy Bakery** • 170 E 110th St [3rd Ave]
  212-828-8896
  Lots of tasty sponge cakes.
- **SpaHa Cafe** • 1872 Lexington Ave [E 116th St]
  212-427-1767
  Pretty decent coffee and baked goods.
- **Third Avenue Liquors** • 2030 3rd Ave [112th St]
  212-876-6994
  Giant selection. Clean. But behind glass of course.
- **VIM** • 2239 3rd Ave [E 122nd St]
  212-369-5033
  Street wear—jeans, sneakers, tops—for all.
- **Young's Fish Market** • 2004 3rd Ave [110th St]
  212-876-3427
  Get it fresh or fried.

W 160th St
W 159th St
W 158th St
W 157th St
157th Street
W 156th St
W 155th St
155th Street
Macombs Dam Br
W 154th St
W 153rd St
W 152nd St
W 151st St
W 150th St
W 149th St
W 148th St
W 147th St
W 146th St
W 145th St
145th Street
W 144th St
W 143rd St
W 142nd St
W 141st St
W 140th St
W 139th St
W 138th St
137th Street City College
W 137th St
W 136th St
W 135th St
135th Street
W 134th St
EDW M Morgan
Riverside Dr
Edgecombe Ave
Harlem River Dr
Audubon Terrace
American Academy of Arts and Letters
Hispanic Society Museum
Trinity Church Cemetery's Graveyard of Heroes
Trinity Cemetery
Church of the Intercession
St Nicholas Ave
St Nicholas Pl
Bailey House
Jackie Robinson Park
Henry Hudson Pkwy
Hudson River
Riverside Park
Broadway
Amsterdam Ave
Convent Ave
Church of the Crucifixion
Bradhurst Ave
Frederick Douglass Blvd
Hamilton Heights Historic District
Hamilton Ter
Hamilton Pl
Hamilton Grange National Memorial
St Nicholas Park
City College
St Nicholas Ter
Ped Bridge
North River Water Pollution Control Plant & Riverbank State Park
12th Ave
1/4 mile
.25 km

Hamilton Heights doesn't quite feel like Manhattan. A stew of college students, neo-gothic architecture and vibrant Dominican culture brings a foreign flavor to the upper, upper west side of the island. Like everywhere above the park, Columbia University's expansion threatens to throw gentrification into double-time. Even in the face of rising rent, however, Alexander Hamilton's former country estate still seems vaguely bucolic. Gently sloping parks, free museums and striking brownstones anchor the neighborhood. Street vendors dish out spicy tacos and wrap juicy tamales. Winding streets lined with row houses tempt anyone to stroll for hours. Sandwiched between the Hudson and St. Nicholas Park, this section of the country's most chaotic city offers much needed respite from the concrete and steel.

Counting landmarked buildings in Hamilton Heights is like keeping track of nuns in Rome. The number is staggering, but none are as striking as **City College's** white and brick neo-gothic buildings. Turrets, towers and gargoyles practically litter the historic college's campus. For classic New York, mosey up to the **Hamilton Heights Historic District**, just north of City College. Trademark row houses line the streets where Alexander Hamilton's original home sat. **Hamilton Grange National Memorial** is now hanging out in St. Nicholas Park. The Bailey House is one of the coolest houses in Manhattan, and probably the only one built on a circus fortune. It was the home of P.T. Barnum's partner James Bailey. For crazy concrete church design, nothing beats the whacked out **Church of the Crucifixtion**.

Central Park gets all of the fanfare, but uptown green space is hillier and virtually tourist-free. Sure, the park service built Riverbank State Park to appease residents after the city dumped a sewage plant along the river, but the state rolled out the red carpet. The facilities, set inside the more expansive Riverside Park, boast a roller skating rink, running track and soccer field. Skip the gym fees, and swim laps at the indoor pool, which costs a paltry $2 to enter. The **Trinity Cemetery Graveyard of Heroes** feels almost otherworldly, with enough rolling paths for a rural European plot. Several Astors, Charles Dickens' son and John James Audubon are all buried here. St. Nicholas Park is worth a daytime visit just for its spacious lawns, but don't miss Hamilton Grange. The National Park Service restored the building after moving it to the park in 2009.

In a city where museums charge $20 just to elbow strangers for a glimpse of a Botticelli, the **Hispanic Society of America Museum and Library** seems nearly miraculous. Admission is free to the museum and reference library, which showcases the arts and cultures of Spain, Portugal, and Latin America. Browse the society's prints, paintings and artifacts, but linger in **Audubon Terrace**. The square-city block plot was named for the famous naturalist, John James Audubon, who once farmed in Washington Heights. The land became a cultural center in 1904 and also houses the **American Academy of Arts and Letters**. Years of neglect left the terrace looking drab, but a new glass structure linking the Academy of Arts and Letters and the Hispanic Society signals a welcome rejuvenation.

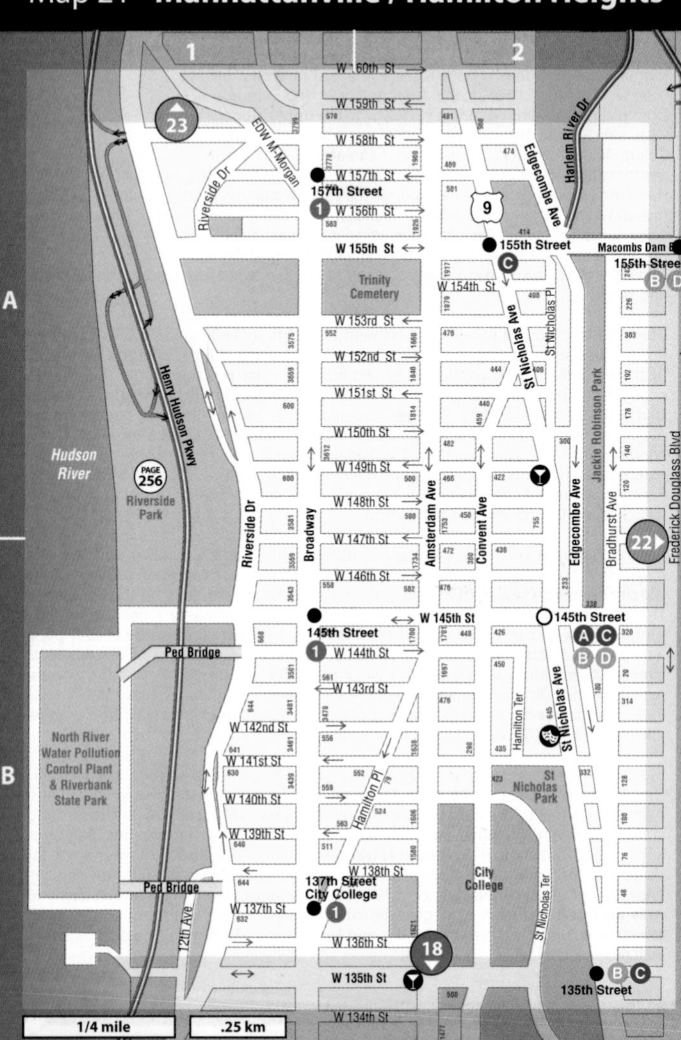

Hudson River
Riverside Park
Henry Hudson Pkwy
North River Water Pollution Control Plant & Riverbank State Park
Ped Bridge
Ped Bridge
12th Ave
Riverside Dr
EDW M Morgan
Broadway
Amsterdam Ave
Convent Ave
St Nicholas Ave
St Nicholas Pl
Edgecombe Ave
Harlem River Dr
Jackie Robinson Park
Bradhurst Ave
Frederick Douglass Blvd
Hamilton Ter
Hamilton Pl
St Nicholas Ter
Trinity Cemetery
St Nicholas Park
City College
Macombs Dam Br
W 160th St
W 159th St
W 158th St
W 157th St
W 156th St
W 155th St
W 154th St
W 153rd St
W 152nd St
W 151st St
W 150th St
W 149th St
W 148th St
W 147th St
W 146th St
W 145th St
W 144th St
W 143rd St
W 142nd St
W 141st St
W 140th St
W 139th St
W 138th St
W 137th St
W 136th St
W 135th St
W 134th St
157th Street
155th Street
145th Street
137th Street City College
135th Street
PAGE 256
1/4 mile
.25 km

Despite its downtown drink prices, the dim and crowded **St. Nick's Pub** might be the best jazz bar anywhere in the world. For a side of art with your drink, look to **La Pregunta Cafe**, a cool art space with a full bar and food.

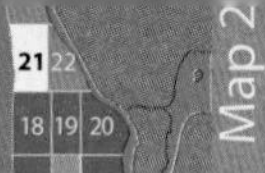

Bars

- **La Pregunta Arts Cafe •**
  1528 Amsterdam Ave [135th St]
  347-591-6387
  Cool art space with a full bar and food. Dig it!
- **St Nick's Pub •**
  773 St Nicholas Ave [W 149th St]
  212-283-9728
  Amazing vibe, go for African Saturday nights.

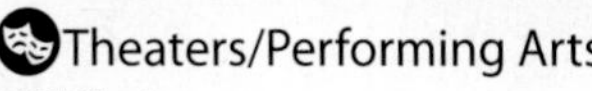

Theaters/Performing Arts

- **HSA Theater •**
  645 St Nicholas Ave [W 141st St]
  212-868-4444
  The Harlem School of the Arts.

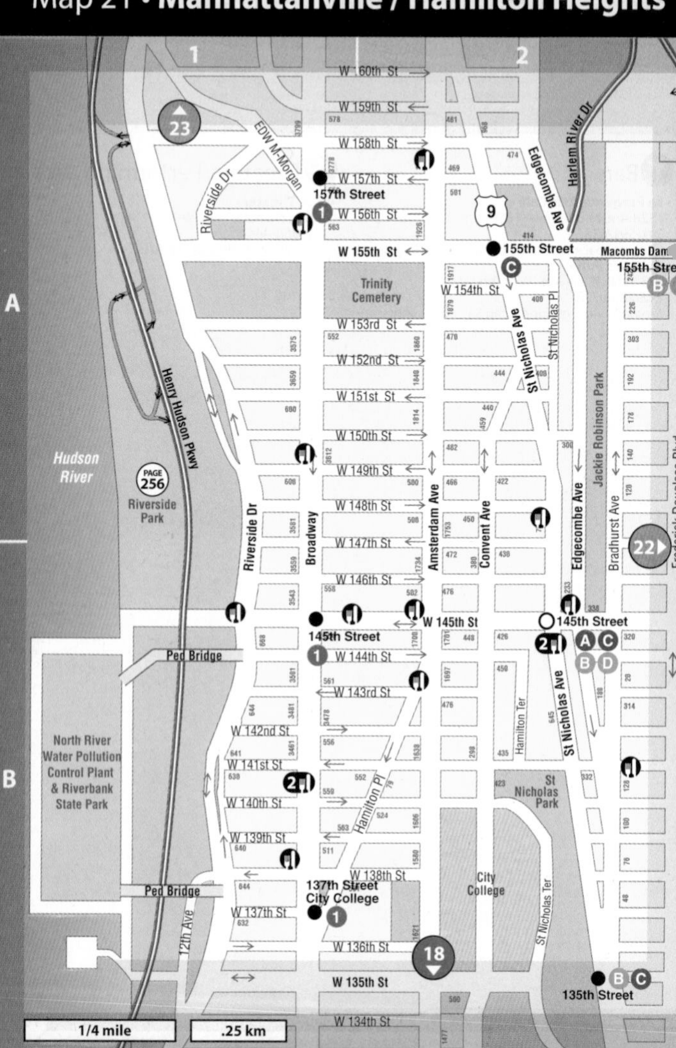

W 160th St
W 159th St
W 158th St
W 157th St
157th Street
W 156th St
W 155th St
155th Street
Macombs Dam
155th Street
W 154th St
Trinity Cemetery
W 153rd St
W 152nd St
W 151st St
W 150th St
W 149th St
W 148th St
W 147th St
W 146th St
W 145th St
145th Street
W 144th St
W 143rd St
W 142nd St
W 141st St
W 140th St
W 139th St
W 138th St
137th Street City College
W 137th St
W 136th St
W 135th St
135th Street
W 134th St
EDW M Morgan
Riverside Dr
Edgecombe Ave
Harlem River Dr
St Nicholas Ave
St Nicholas Pl
Jackie Robinson Park
Bradhurst Ave
Frederick Douglass Blvd
Henry Hudson Pkwy
Hudson River
Riverside Park
Broadway
Amsterdam Ave
Convent Ave
Hamilton Ter
Hamilton Pl
St Nicholas Park
St Nicholas Ter
City College
12th Ave
Ped Bridge
North River Water Pollution Control Plant & Riverbank State Park
PAGE 256
1/4 mile
.25 km

Authenticity reigns in Hamilton Heights. Meander up Broadway for your pick of taquerias and Dominican eats. **Picante** boasts some of the best sit-down Mexican. Cheap Middle Eastern can be found at **Queen Sheeba**. For ambience, look west. **The River Room of Harlem** claims sweeping views of the Hudson.

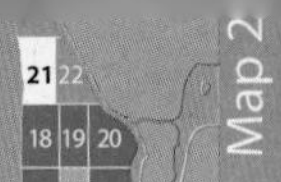

Restaurants

- **Devin's Fish & Chips** • 747 St Nicholas Ave [W 147th St] 212-491-5518 • $ Greasy goodness just steps from St. Nick's Pub. Recommended.
- **Ecuatoriana Restaurant** • 1685 Amsterdam Ave [143rd St] 212-491-4626 • $$ Legit Ecuadorian fare, sans guinea pig.
- **El Toro Partido** • 3431 Broadway [140th St] 212-281-1587 • $$ Better-now-than-later Mexican.
- **Famous Fish Market** • 684 St Nicholas Ave [W 145th St] 212-491-8323 • $ Deep fried and from the sea.
- **Jesus Taco** • 501 W 145th St [Amsterdam Ave] 212-234-3330 • $ Tacos and burgers.
- **Jimbo's Hamburger Palace** • 528 W 145th St [Amsterdam Ave] 212-926-0338 • $ Cheap, fast, easy burgers.
- **La Oaxaquena Restaurant** • 1969 Amsterdam Ave [157th St] 212-283-7752 • $ One of the best in a parade of taquerias.
- **New Caporal Fried Chicken** • 3772 Broadway [W 157th St] 212-862-8986 • $ A neighborhood institution. With shrimp too!
- **Paul's Pies** • 3409 Broadway [138th St] 212-234-7878 • $ Bare-bones pies, whole or by the slice.
- **Picante** • 3424 Broadway [139th St] 212-234-6479 • $$ Arguably Manhattanville's best Mexican, plus affordable margs.
- **Queen Sheeba** • 317 W 141st St [Frederick Douglass Blvd] 212-862-6149 • $ Cafeteria style Middle Eastern that's friendly on the wallet.
- **Raw Soul** • 348 W 145th St [Edgecombe Ave] 212-491-5859 • $$ All raw food, all the time.
- **The River Room** • 679 Riverside Dr [145th St] 212-491-1500 • $$$ Swank entrees, sweeping views and live jazz.
- **Sunshine Kitchen** • 695 St Nicholas Ave [W 145th St] 212-368-4972 • $ Delicious curried goat.
- **Tonalli Cafe Bar** • 3628 Broadway [149th St] 212-926-0399 • $$ Bring your own Chianti for an Italian feast.

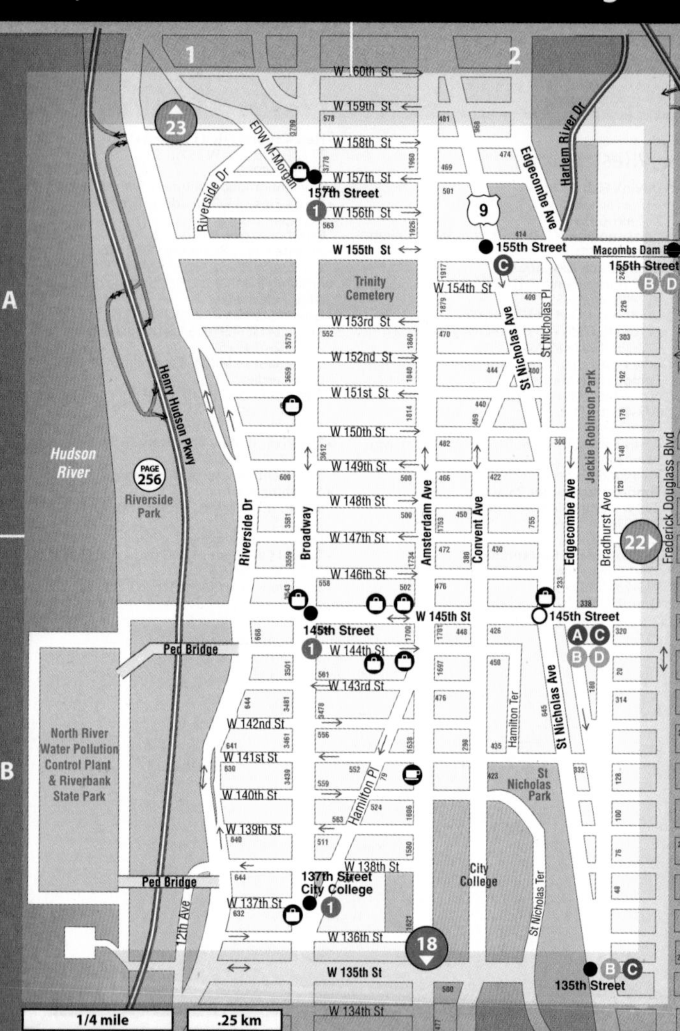
1
2
A
B
23
W 160th St
W 159th St
W 158th St
W 157th St
W 156th St
W 155th St
W 154th St
W 153rd St
W 152nd St
W 151st St
W 150th St
W 149th St
W 148th St
W 147th St
W 146th St
W 145th St
W 144th St
W 143rd St
W 142nd St
W 141st St
W 140th St
W 139th St
W 138th St
W 137th St
W 136th St
W 135th St
W 134th St
EDW M Morgan
Riverside Dr
157th Street
9
Edgecombe Ave
Harlem River Dr
155th Street
Macombs Dam Bridge
155th Street
Trinity Cemetery
St Nicholas Ave
St Nicholas Pl
Jackie Robinson Park
Henry Hudson Pkwy
Hudson River
PAGE 256
Riverside Park
Broadway
Amsterdam Ave
Convent Ave
Bradhurst Ave
Frederick Douglass Blvd
22
145th Street
Ped Bridge
North River Water Pollution Control Plant & Riverbank State Park
Hamilton Ter
Hamilton Pl
St Nicholas Park
137th Street City College
City College
St Nicholas Ter
12th Ave
18
135th Street
1/4 mile
.25 km

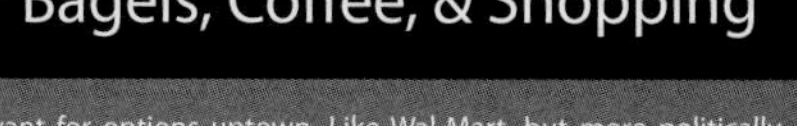

Bagels, Coffee, & Shopping

You won't want for options uptown. Like Wal-Mart, but more politically correct, **El Mundo** stocks everything. Grab gifts for you and everyone you know at **SOH-Straight out of Harlem Creative Outlet**. Or just browse Broadway for mom-and-pop storefronts.

Coffee

- **Café One** • 1619 Amsterdam Ave [139th St]
  212-690-0060
  Free wifi, quality pastries and reliable java.

Shopping

- **The Adventist Care Center** •
  528 W 145th St [Amsterdam Ave]
  646-281-4264
  Thrift store with a great selection of hats.
- **B-Jays USA** • 540 W 143rd St [Hamilton Pl]
  212-694-3160
  Every sneaker under the sun.
- **El Mundo** • 3791 Broadway [W 158th St]
  212-368-3648
  Cheap homegoods and discounted brand name apparel.
- **Felix Supply** • 3650 Broadway [W 150th St]
  212-283-1988
  Stock up on basics near Trinity Cemetery.
- **Foot Locker** • 3549 Broadway [W 146th St]
  212-491-0927
  Get your sneakers from a fake referee.
- **Reliable Wine & Liquor Shop** •
  3375 Broadway [W 137th St]
  212-926-2888
  For wine, sometimes reliable is all you need.
  Unique gifts and crafts.
- **Sweet Chef Southern Style Bakery** •
  122 Hamilton Pl [141st St]
  212-862-5909
  Killer sweet potato pies and banana pudding.
- **Unity Liquors** •
  708 St Nicholas Ave [W 146th St]
  212-491-7821
  Right by the subway, where all liquor stores should be.
- **VIM** • 508 W 145th St [Amsterdam Ave]
  212-491-1143
  Street wear—jeans, sneakers, tops—for all.

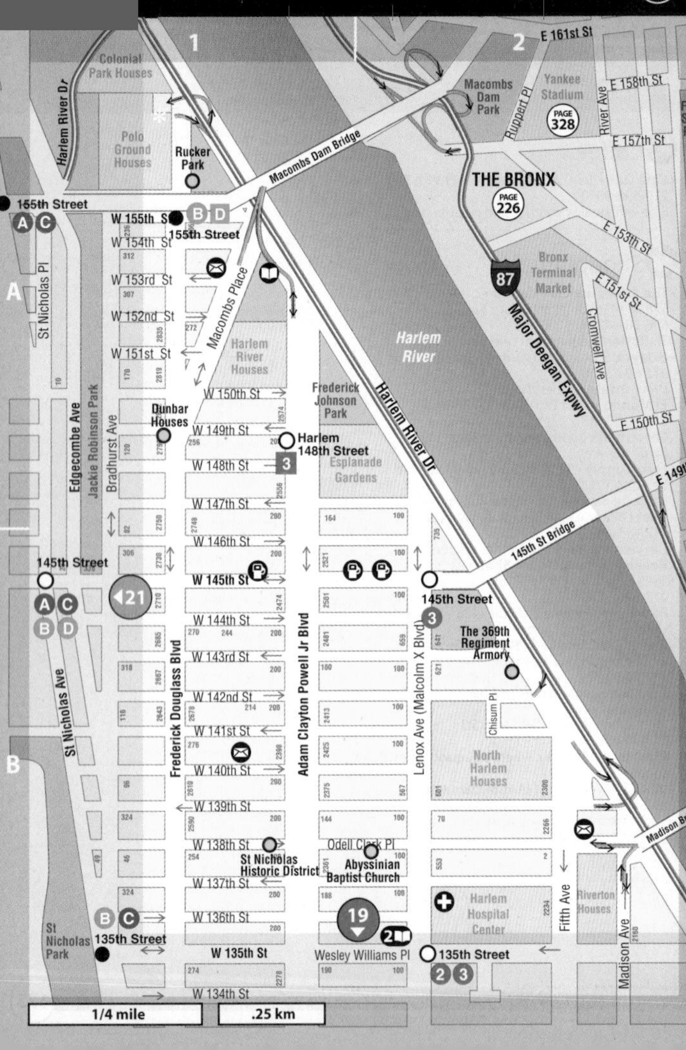
Colonial Park Houses
Harlem River Dr
Polo Ground Houses
Rucker Park
Macombs Dam Bridge
Macombs Dam Park
Ruppert Pl
Yankee Stadium
PAGE 328
River Ave
E 161st St
E 158th St
E 157th St
THE BRONX
PAGE 226
155th Street
W 155th St
155th Street
W 154th St
W 153rd St
W 152nd St
W 151st St
Macombs Place
Harlem River Houses
E 153th St
Bronx Terminal Market
87
E 151st St
Major Deegan Expwy
Cromwell Ave
Harlem River
St Nicholas Pl
Edgecombe Ave
Jackie Robinson Park
Bradhurst Ave
W 150th St
Frederick Johnson Park
Dunbar Houses
W 149th St
Harlem 148th Street
W 148th St
Esplanade Gardens
Harlem River Dr
E 150th St
E 149th
W 147th St
W 146th St
145th St Bridge
145th Street
W 145th St
145th Street
W 144th St
The 369th Regiment Armory
W 143rd St
St Nicholas Ave
Frederick Douglass Blvd
Adam Clayton Powell Jr Blvd
Lenox Ave (Malcolm X Blvd)
W 142nd St
W 141st St
Chisum Pl
North Harlem Houses
W 140th St
W 139th St
W 138th St
Odell Clark Pl
Madison Bri
St Nicholas Historic District
Abyssinian Baptist Church
W 137th St
Harlem Hospital Center
Fifth Ave
Riverton Houses
W 136th St
St Nicholas Park
135th Street
W 135th St
Wesley Williams Pl
135th Street
Madison Ave
W 134th St
1/4 mile
.25 km

Neighborhood Overview

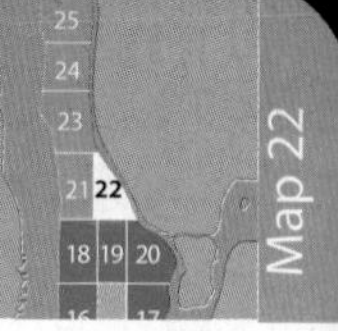

At first glance, upper Harlem lacks character. Generic buffets and 99-cent stores line Lenox, one of the nabe's anchor streets. 145th street sprawls with suburban gas stations and an entrance to the 145th Street Bridge. High rises dot the uptown skyline. But this 20-block triangle sandwiched between St. Nicholas and the Harlem River is the lifeline of black culture in New York. Everyone from starving artists to self-made millionaires have called upper Harlem home, and a visit to the **Schomburg Center for Research** reveals the neighborhood's significant impact. Not surprisingly, gentrification is a sensitive point of controversy, but for now, the culture remains intact. Old churches maintain a sense of community. Heavenly soul food attracts locals and tourists. Historic districts preserves the neighborhood's past. Upper Harlem has it all—you just have to dig a little.

History buffs, perk up. A stroll through upper Harlem is one of Manhattan's most jam-packed walks. Start at 135th Street and Lenox, or "Speaker's Corner," an intersection where back in the day anyone shouted their concerns and critiques of current events. Most famously, Marcus Garvey presented his views on race at this corner. The Harlem Hellfighters, an all-black military unit that fought in World War I and World War II, housed their headquarters at the imposing **369th Regiment Armory**. The building still operates as a sustainment brigade, but an obelisk outside honors the soldiers. Long before the Hellfighters, Ethiopian traders protested segregation policies by founding the **Abyssinian Baptist Church** in 1808. After 203 years, the congregation only moved once, in 1923, to its striking neo-Gothic building.

Classic row houses, historic churches, and apartment complexes define upper Harlem's architecture. Most notably, the Rockefeller family built the **Dunbar Houses** in 1926 to provide affordable housing in Harlem. Instead of families, the complex attracted writers, artists, musicians and poets, including W.E.B. DuBois, the first African-American to graduate from Harvard. Similarly ambitious residents moved in to the **St. Nicholas Historic District**. Sometimes called "Strivers' Row," Stanford White designed the houses, where many upwardly mobile residents lived. Note the original "Walk your Horses" signs (there aren't any carriage rides in the neighborhood).

From libraries to basketball courts, Harlem's cultural options are distinct. **Rucker Park** is home to famously intense pickup games. Kareem Abdul-Jabbar, Kobe Bryant, and hundreds of exceedingly talented locals have dribbled on those courts. Swing by to try your hand or just enjoy the show. The Schomburg Center for Research in Black Culture focuses on preserving the history of people of African descent worldwide. The center's dizzying array of artifacts, prints, images and manuscripts includes more than 100,000 items. For a more low-key library experience, visit the **Countee Cullen Regional Branch Library**. At the turn of the century, Madame C.J. Walker lived at this same address. The "richest woman in Harlem" earned her fortune by selling hair care products tailored for African-American women.

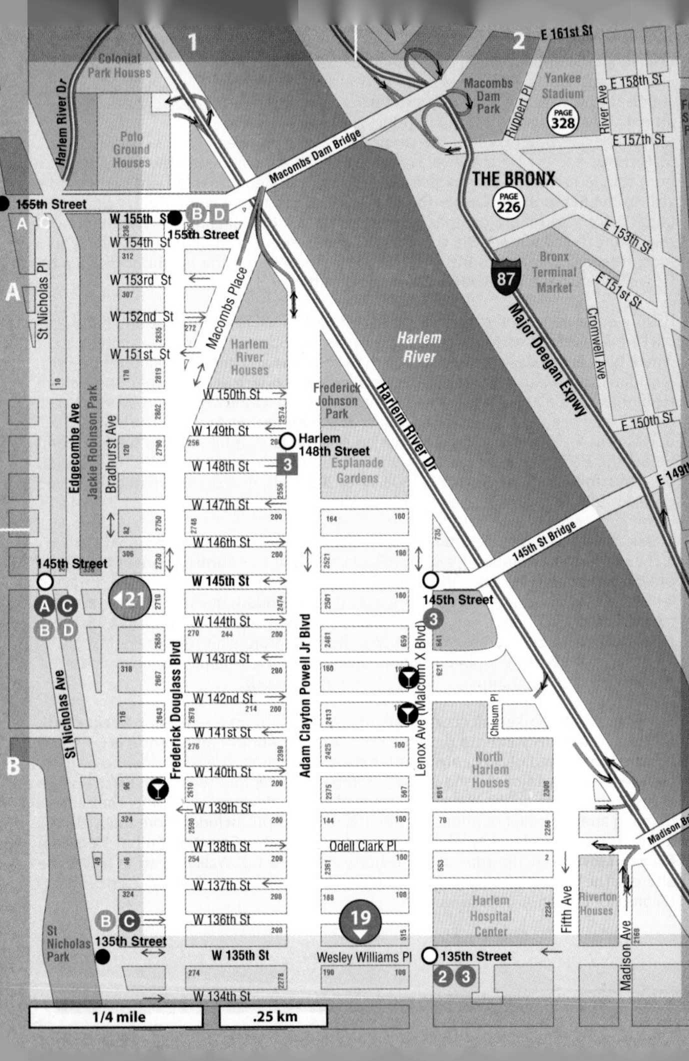

1
2
Colonial Park Houses
Polo Ground Houses
Harlem River Dr
Macombs Dam Bridge
Macombs Dam Park
Yankee Stadium
PAGE 328
THE BRONX
PAGE 226
E 161st St
E 158th St
E 157th St
E 153th St
E 151st St
E 150th St
E 149th St
Ruppert Pl
River Ave
Cromwell Ave
Bronx Terminal Market
87
Major Deegan Expwy
Harlem River
155th Street
W 155th St
155th Street
W 154th St
W 153rd St
W 152nd St
W 151st St
W 150th St
W 149th St
W 148th St
W 147th St
W 146th St
W 145th St
W 144th St
W 143rd St
W 142nd St
W 141st St
W 140th St
W 139th St
W 138th St
W 137th St
W 136th St
W 135th St
W 134th St
Macombs Place
Harlem River Houses
Frederick Johnson Park
Harlem 148th Street
Esplanade Gardens
Harlem River Dr
145th St Bridge
145th Street
145th Street
St Nicholas Pl
Edgecombe Ave
Jackie Robinson Park
Bradhurst Ave
St Nicholas Ave
Frederick Douglass Blvd
Adam Clayton Powell Jr Blvd
Lenox Ave (Malcolm X Blvd)
Chisum Pl
North Harlem Houses
Odell Clark Pl
Wesley Williams Pl
Harlem Hospital Center
Riverton Houses
Fifth Ave
Madison Ave
Madison Bri
St Nicholas Park
135th Street
135th Street
21
19
A
B
1/4 mile
.25 km

Dive bars and live music round out the nightlife scene above 135th Street. Swill anything in a bottle at **A Touch of Dee**, a retro-ish corner bar that attracts locals. For a schizophrenic mix of jazz, dancing, karaoke, and pool, **Real's Lounge** is top-notch. **Londel's Supper Club** has classic jazz on Fridays and Saturdays.

Bars

- **A Touch of Dee •**
  657 Malcolm X Blvd [W 143rd St]
  212-283-9456
  Friendly '70s shrine full of old-timers.
- **Londel's Supper Club •**
  2620 Frederick Douglass Blvd [W 140th St]
  212-234-6114
  Great live music on Friday & Saturdays.
- **Real's Lounge •**
  695 Lenox Ave [145th St]
  917-346-2706
  An unlikely live music hub.

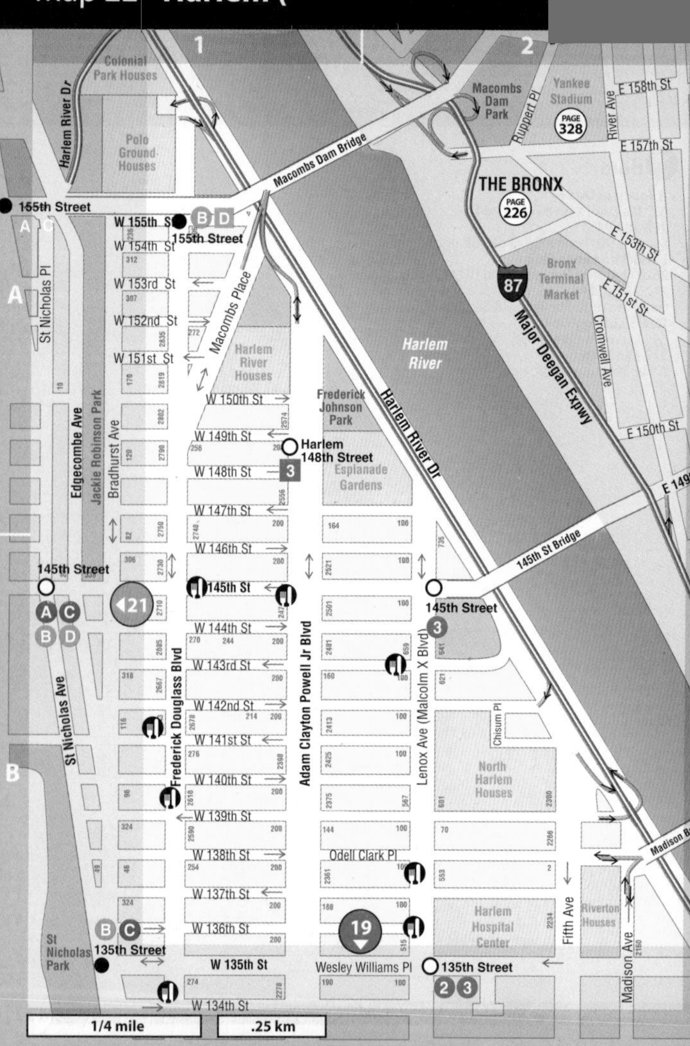
Colonial Park Houses
Harlem River Dr
Polo Ground Houses
Macombs Dam Bridge
Macombs Dam Park
Ruppert Pl
Yankee Stadium
PAGE 328
River Ave
E 158th St
E 157th St
THE BRONX
PAGE 226
155th Street
W 155th St
155th Street
W 154th St
W 153rd St
W 152nd St
W 151st St
Macombs Place
E 153th St
Bronx Terminal Market
E 151st St
87
Major Deegan Expwy
Cromwell Ave
Harlem River
St Nicholas Pl
Harlem River Houses
Frederick Johnson Park
Harlem River Dr
W 150th St
W 149th St
Harlem 148th Street
W 148th St
Espianade Gardens
E 150th St
E 149th St
Edgecombe Ave
Jackie Robinson Park
Bradhurst Ave
W 147th St
W 146th St
145th St Bridge
145th Street
145th St
145th Street
21
W 144th St
W 143rd St
W 142nd St
W 141st St
W 140th St
W 139th St
W 138th St
W 137th St
W 136th St
W 135th St
W 134th St
St Nicholas Ave
Frederick Douglass Blvd
Adam Clayton Powell Jr Blvd
Lenox Ave (Malcolm X Blvd)
Chisum Pl
North Harlem Houses
Odell Clark Pl
Harlem Hospital Center
Fifth Ave
Riverton Houses
Madison Ave
Madison Br
19
St Nicholas Park
135th Street
Wesley Williams Pl
135th Street
1/4 mile
.25 km

The parade of routine delis on Lenox hides some of Manhattan's tastiest eats. **Miss Maude's Spoonbread** dishes out calorically foolish comfort food. **Sherman's BBQ** is a classic rib shack that always hits the spot. For fried fishy take-out goodness, hit up the window service at **O'Fishole Seafood**.

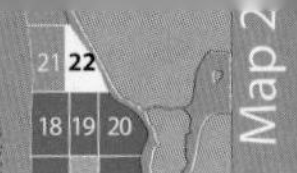

Restaurants

- **Cheesesteak Factory** • 2496 Adam Clayton Powell Jr Blvd [145th St] 212-690-1111 • $ Don't confuse this sandwich shop with its suburban doppelganger.
- **Grini's Grill and Restaurant** • 100 W 143rd St [Lenox Ave] 212-694-6274 • $ This "tapas bar" actually serves heaping plates of meat and rice.
- **Londel's Supper Club** • 2620 Frederick Douglass Blvd [W 140th St] 212-234-6114 • $$$ Good Southern with live music on the weekend.
- **Lowe's Eatery** • 101 W 136 St [Lenox Ave] 212-690-1713 • $ Unassuming Caribbean soul food.
- **Mama Tina's** • 2649 8th Ave [141st St] 212-368-2820 • $ Decent pizza for late-night pangs.
- **Miss Maude's Spoonbread Too** • 547 Lenox Ave [W 138th St] 212-690-3100 • $$ Harlem food for the soul.
- **O'Fishole Seafood** • 274 W 145th St [8th Ave] 212-234-2601 • $$ Jimbo's, the burger place, does fish; equally greasy and delicious.
- **Sherman's BBQ** • 2509 Frederick Douglass Blvd [134th St] 917-478-2073 • $$ Classic rib shack that's open late. Usually to 3 am.

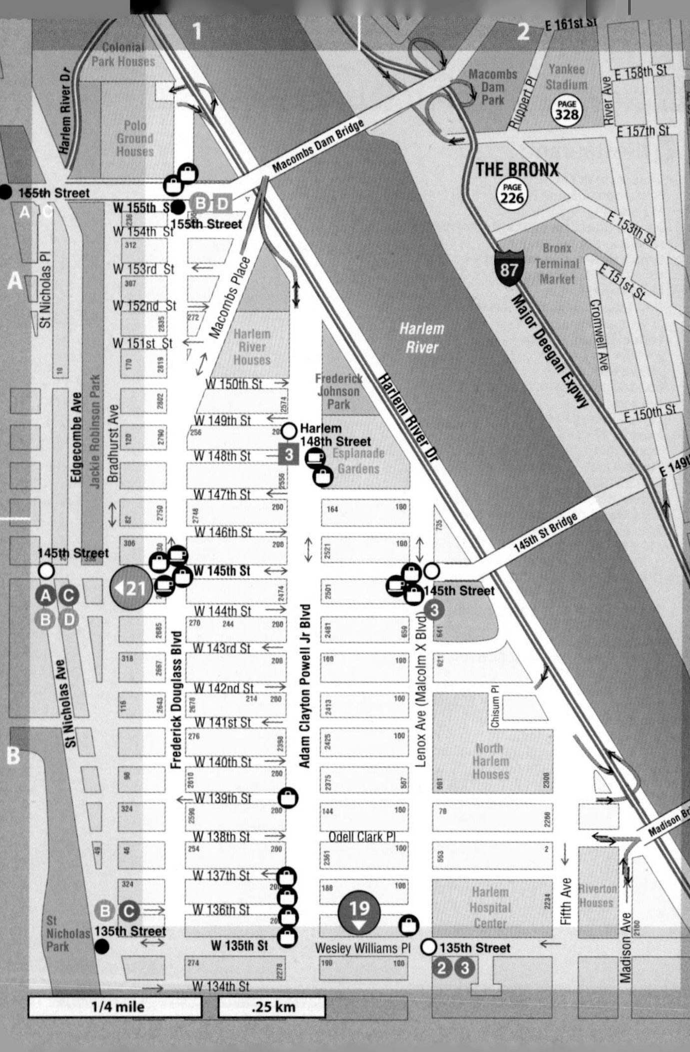

1
2
A
B
Colonial Park Houses
Polo Ground Houses
Harlem River Dr
Macombs Dam Bridge
Macombs Dam Park
Yankee Stadium
PAGE 328
Ruppert Pl
River Ave
E 161st St
E 158th St
E 157th St
THE BRONX
PAGE 226
E 153th St
E 151st St
E 150th St
E 149th St
Bronx Terminal Market
87
Major Deegan Expwy
Cromwell Ave
Harlem River
155th Street
W 155th St
W 154th St
W 153rd St
W 152nd St
W 151st St
W 150th St
W 149th St
W 148th St
W 147th St
W 146th St
W 145th St
W 144th St
W 143rd St
W 142nd St
W 141st St
W 140th St
W 139th St
W 138th St
W 137th St
W 136th St
W 135th St
W 134th St
Macombs Place
Harlem River Houses
Frederick Johnson Park
Harlem 148th Street
Esplanade Gardens
St Nicholas Pl
Edgecombe Ave
Jackie Robinson Park
Bradhurst Ave
145th Street
145th St Bridge
Frederick Douglass Blvd
Adam Clayton Powell Jr Blvd
Lenox Ave (Malcolm X Blvd)
St Nicholas Ave
Chisum Pl
North Harlem Houses
Odell Clark Pl
Wesley Williams Pl
135th Street
St Nicholas Park
Harlem Hospital Center
Fifth Ave
Riverton Houses
Madison Ave
Madison Bri
1/4 mile
.25 km

Bagels, Coffee, & Shopping

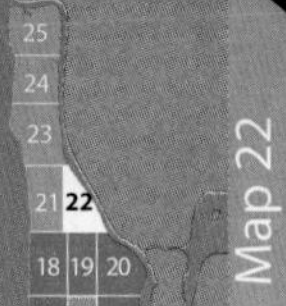

Wandering Lenox and 145th streets will unearth everything from cheap, expansive supermarkets like **Pathmark** and **Associated** to niche sneaker shops like **Sneaker Q**. **Make My Cake** has sugary cupcakes, cheesecakes and regular cakes.

Coffee

- **Dunkin' Donuts** • 110 W 145th St [Lenox Ave]
  212-234-3440
  Decent coffee served in gigantic Styrofoam cups.
- **Dunkin' Donuts** •
  2730 Frederick Douglass Blvd [W 145th St]
  212-862-0635
  Decent coffee served in gigantic Styrofoam cups.
- **Starbucks** •
  301 W 145th St [Frederick Douglass Blvd]
  212-690-7835
  One of the few coffee spots around here.
- **T & J Bakery** •
  2541 Adam Clayton Powell Jr Blvd [W 148th St]
  212-234-5662
  Amazing baked goods. And coffee too.

Shopping

- **Associated** •
  2927 Frederick Douglass Blvd [W 155th St]
  212-368-1300
  Basic supermarket that fills a void.
- **B Oyama Homme** • 2330 7th Ave [W 137th St]
  212-234-5128
  Fashion for men.
- **Baskin-Robbins** •
  2730 Frederick Douglass Blvd [W 145th St]
  212-862-0635
  Do they still have 31 flavors?
- **Denim Library** • 2326 7th Ave [W 137th St]
  212-281-2380
  Experts in denimology.
- **Harlem Discount Liquors** •
  2302 Adam Clayton Powell Jr Blvd [W 135th St]
  212-234-5958
  Do you need to know more than "discount" and "liquor"?
- **Luis Liquor** • 108 W 145th St [Lenox Ave]
  212-694-6619
  Perfect grab-and-go shop near the subway.
- **Make My Cake** •
  2380 Adam Clayton Powell Jr Blvd [W 139th St]
  212-234-2344
  Freshly baked cakes from a Southern family recipe.
- **Met Food** •
  2541 Adam Clayton Powell Jr Blvd [W 147th St]
  212-862-0239
  No-frills market way cheaper than your local bodega.
- **Montgomery's** • 2312 7th Ave [W 136th St]
  212-690-2166
  Featuring one-of-a-kind fashions.
- **New York Public Library Shop** •
  515 Lenox Ave [W 136th St]
  212-930-0869
  Shop specializing in Black history and culture.
- **Pathmark** •
  300 W 145th St [Frederick Douglass Blvd]
  212-281-3158
  No-frills market that gets the job done.
- **Sneaker Q** • 693 Lenox Ave [142nd St]
  212-491-9179
  Get your kicks at this Lenox storefront.
- **T & J Bakery** •
  2541 Adam Clayton Powell Jr Blvd [W 148th St]
  212-234-5662
  Pies, cakes, muffins…just go.

Map 23 • Washington Heights

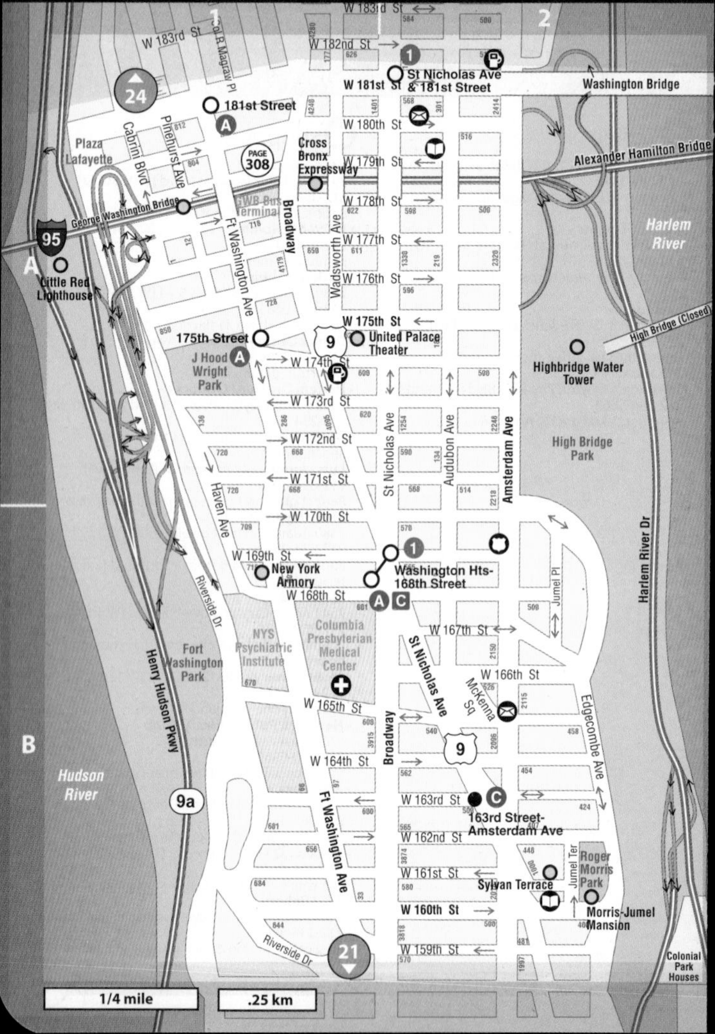

PAGE 308
24
21

Washington Heights is a veritable United Nations of immigrant stories. Irish settlers moved up north in the 1900s. After World War I, European Jews called this hilly stretch of Manhattan home. Now, the 'hood swings to an undeniable merengue beat. The largely Dominican sliver of northern Manhattan probably claims more authenticity than any Punta Cana all-inclusive. Street vendors whip up delectable chimichurris, a sort of Dominican hamburger. Broadway houses a seemingly limitless number of chicken-and-rice eateries. English almost feels like a second language. As with all of Manhattan, this swath of delis and pollerias sees change in the future. Hipsters searching for cheap rent keep hiking uptown, and higher end Dominican fusion eateries are breaking into the restaurant scene. It looks like everyone knows that all you have to do is take the A train even farther than Harlem.

Some of Manhattan's most storied buildings live far uptown, and The Heights are no exception. Most notable is the **Morris-Jumel Mansion**, a hilltop home that looks like it belongs in Gone With the Wind, not Gotham. British Colonel Roger Morris built the abode in 1765, but George Washington famously stationed his headquarters here in the fall of 1776. After the Revolutionary War, Morris left the estate, which stretched up from Harlem. If that's not impressive enough, note that Washington also took John Adams, Thomas Jefferson, and John Quincy Adams to dine there in 1790. The museum is open for visits, but beware: There have been rumors of hauntings. For a less ghostly architecture tour, check out the two-block historic district of **Sylvan Terrace**. This stretch of wooden row houses lines the skinny street leading up to the mansion. Although the turn-of-the-century homes underwent a few incarnations—from wooden to faux brick to stucco—they are now largely restored to their original condition. Another turn of the century creation, the **New York Armory**, had a similar rebirth. The armory first served as a training center for the National Guard in 1909. It rose to fame as a center for track and field competitions until the 1980s, when it became a homeless shelter. Now, the armory has been restored and functions again as a track and field center.

This skinny expanse of Manhattan boasts some of the country's top transportation accomplishments. Construction began in 1948 for the **Cross Bronx Expressway**, one of the country's first highways to forge through such a densely populated urban area. Heading west into Fort Lee, NJ, the **George Washington Bridge** is the only 14-lane suspension crossing in the country. Hikers, bikers and skaters can skip the pricey tolls and enjoy views of Palisades Interstate Park in New Jersey. The best part about the bridge: **The Little Red Lighthouse** that rests underneath. The charmingly out-of-place tower only operated between 1921 and 1948, but it earned fame from the 1942 children's book The Little Red Lighthouse and the Great Gray Bridge, by Hildegarde Swift and Lynd Ward.

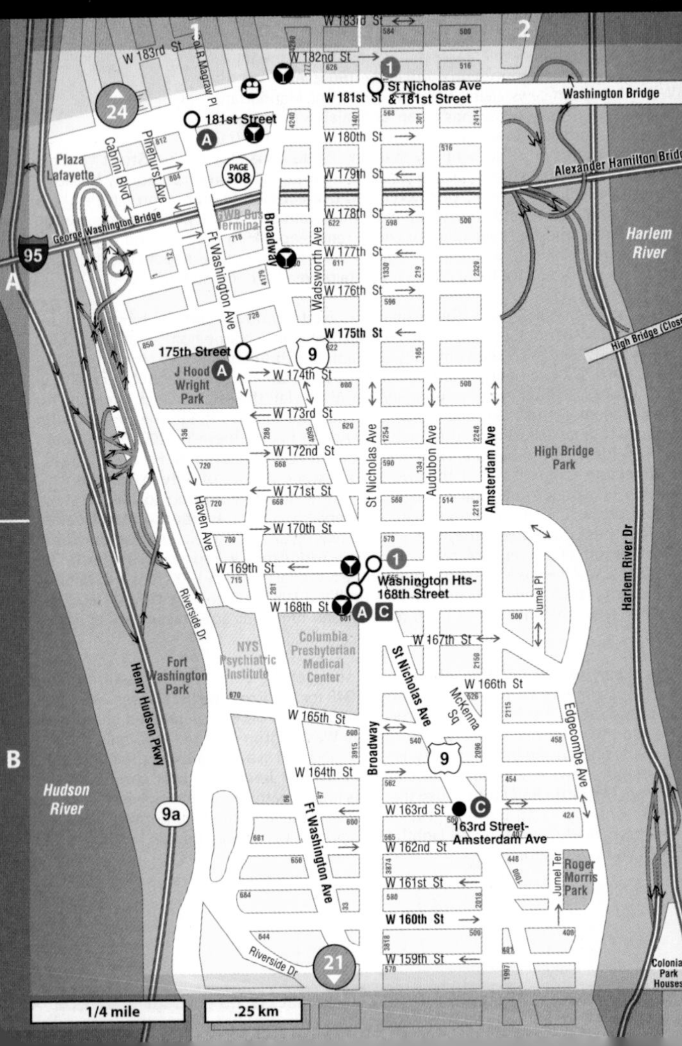

W 183rd St
W 182nd St
W 181st St
St Nicholas Ave & 181st Street
181st Street
Washington Bridge
W 180th St
Plaza Lafayette
Cabrini Blvd
Pinehurst Ave
Col R Magraw Pl
PAGE 308
W 179th St
Alexander Hamilton Bridge
George Washington Bridge
GWB Bus Terminal
Broadway
W 178th St
Harlem River
95
W 177th St
Wadsworth Ave
Ft Washington Ave
W 176th St
W 175th St
High Bridge (Closed)
175th Street
9
J Hood Wright Park
W 174th St
W 173rd St
W 172nd St
St Nicholas Ave
Audubon Ave
Amsterdam Ave
High Bridge Park
W 171st St
Haven Ave
W 170th St
W 169th St
Washington Hts-168th Street
W 168th St
Riverside Dr
Jumel Pl
Harlem River Dr
W 167th St
NYS Psychiatric Institute
Columbia-Presbyterian Medical Center
Fort Washington Park
Henry Hudson Pkwy
W 166th St
McKenna Sq
W 165th St
Edgecombe Ave
W 164th St
Hudson River
9a
W 163rd St
163rd Street-Amsterdam Ave
W 162nd St
Roger Morris Park
Jumel Ter
W 161st St
W 160th St
W 159th St
Riverside Dr
Colonial Park Houses
24
21
1/4 mile
.25 km

From hopping gay bars to suave wine lounges, The Heights nightlife scene won't leave you wanting. Groove to salsa and Reggaeton at **No Parking** or duck into **Coogan's** for a pint.

Bars

- **Coogan's** • 4015 Broadway [W 169th St]
  212-928-1234
  Join doctors, professors and off-duty cops for a cold one.
- **No Parking** • 4168 Broadway [W 177th St]
  212-923-8700
  The Heights gets a gay bar.
- **Plum Pomidor** • 603 W 168th St [Broadway]
  212-781-3333
  Live jazz Mondays, mediocre Italian food.
- **The Red Room Vinoteca** •
  1 Bennett Ave [181st and 184th]
  917-975-2690
  Dionysus would be proud.
- **Reynold's Cafe** • 4241 Broadway [W 180th St]
  212-923-8927
  Drink Guinness. Speak Spanish.

Movie Theaters

- **Coliseum Cinemas** •
  701 W 181st St [Broadway]
  212-740-1545
  We love Washington Heights, but not its movie theater.

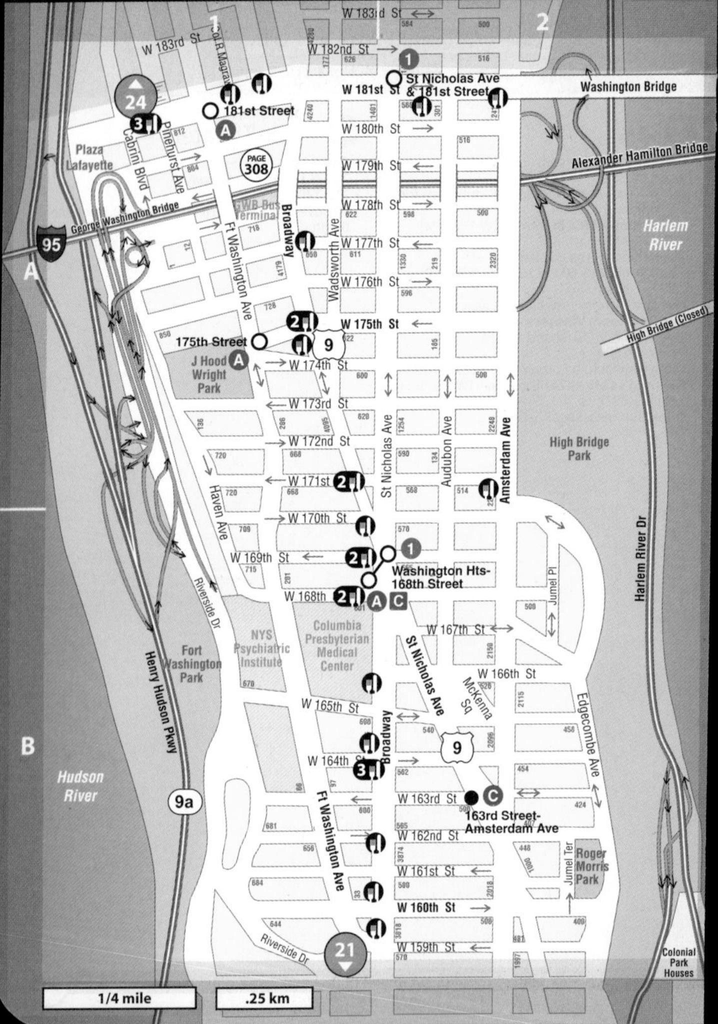

Map 23 • Washington Heights

W 183rd St
W 182nd St
W 181st St
W 180th St
W 179th St
W 178th St
W 177th St
W 176th St
W 175th St
W 174th St
W 173rd St
W 172nd St
W 171st St
W 170th St
W 169th St
W 168th
W 167th St
W 166th St
W 165th St
W 164th St
W 163rd St
W 162nd St
W 161st St
W 160th St
W 159th St
Col R Magraw
181st Street
St Nicholas Ave & 181st Street
Washington Bridge
Alexander Hamilton Bridge
Plaza Lafayette
Cabrini Blvd
Pinehurst Ave
PAGE 308
GWB Bus Terminal
George Washington Bridge
95
Broadway
Wadsworth Ave
Ft Washington Ave
Harlem River
High Bridge (Closed)
175th Street
9
J Hood Wright Park
St Nicholas Ave
Audubon Ave
Amsterdam Ave
High Bridge Park
Haven Ave
Washington Hts-168th Street
Jumel Pl
Harlem River Dr
Riverside Dr
NYS Psychiatric Institute
Columbia Presbyterian Medical Center
Fort Washington Park
Henry Hudson Pkwy
Mckenna Sq
Edgecombe Ave
Hudson River
9a
163rd Street-Amsterdam Ave
Jumel Ter
Roger Morris Park
Colonial Park Houses
1/4 mile
.25 km

Dominican eats dominate the foodie scene up here; **Restaurant Margot** is easily one of the best. Hit up **El Malecon** for unsurpassed roast chicken. When variety beckons **Tawaa Indian** and **Sushi Yu** dish up tasty alternatives. Cheap margaritas—no need for passport—at **Agave Azul**. good luck choosing from the **Hudson View** menu (btw, there is no view).

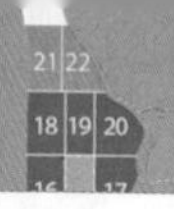

Restaurants

- **181 Cabrini** • 854 W 181st St [Cabrini Blvd]
  212-923-2233 • $$
  Seasonal American bistro.
- **Agave Azul** • 839 W 181st St [Cabrini Blvd]
  212-740-5222 • $$
  After-work margaritas.
- **Aqua Marina** • 4060 Broadway [W 171st St]
  212-928-0070 • $
  OK Uptown Italian.
- **Caridad Express** •
  554 W 181st St [Audubon Ave]
  212-927-9729 • $
  Vegetarians: enter at your own risk.
- **Carrot Top Pastries** •
  3931 Broadway [W 165th St]
  212-927-4800 • $
  Baked goods and coffee too!
- **Coogan's** • 4015 Broadway [W 169th St]
  212-928-1234 • $$
  Where med students and cops go.
- **Dallas BBQ** • 3956 Broadway [W 166th St]
  212-568-3700 • $$
  When you can't get to Virgil's.
- **El Conde Steak House** •
  4139 Broadway [W 175th St]
  212-781-3231 • $$$
  Big slabs of MEAT.
- **El Malecon** • 4141 Broadway [W 175th St]
  212-927-3812 • $
  Dominican—fabulous roast chicken.
- **El Ranchito** • 4129 Broadway [W 175th St]
  212-928-0866 • $$
  Central America in New York!
- **Empire Szechuan** •
  4041 Broadway [W 170th St]
  212-568-1600 • $$
  Take a guess at what they serve.
- **Fibe Bistro** • 4055 Broadway [170th Street]
  212-781-7690 • $$$
  Eclectic mix of seafood, small plates and Mexican.
- **Flaco's Pizza** • 3876 Broadway [162nd Street]
  212-923-3733 • $
  Chowing on this cheap, delish pizza won't keep you flaco.
- **Hudson View Restaurant** •
  770 W 181st St [Fort Washington Ave]
  212-781-0303 • $$
  Ch ch ch choices.
- **Jimmy Oro Restaurant** •
  711 W 181st St [Broadway]
  212-795-1414 • $
  Chinese/Spanish. Huge variety.
- **Joa** • 3908 Broadway [W 164th St]
  212-543-0922 • $$
  Rare find: A cheap, quick meal that isn't Dominican.
- **Parrilla** • 3920 Broadway [W 164th St]
  212-543-9500 • $$
  Argentinean with cool-ass grill.
- **Reme Restaurant** •
  4021 Broadway [W 169th St]
  212-923-5452 • $
  New York comfort food at this typical diner.
- **Restaurant Margot** •
  3822 Broadway [159th St]
  212-781-8494 • $$
  Arguably, The Heights' very best Dominican.
- **Restaurante Ecuatoriano Genesis** •
  511 W 181st St [Amsterdam Ave]
  212-923-3030 • $$
  Yummy South American cuisine a block from the 1 train.
- **Silver Palace Chinese Restaurant** •
  3844 Broadway [160th Street]
  212-927-8000 • $$
  Standard storefront Chinese fare.
- **Sushi Yu** • 827 W 181st St [Pinehurst]
  212-781-8833 • $
  Raw fish for when you need to take a plantain break.
- **Tabouli** • 3915 Broadway [164th Street]
  212-927-1100 • $
  Settle in with some shawarma or relax over a hookah.
- **Taino Restaurant** •
  2228 Amsterdam Ave [W 171st St]
  212-543-9035 • $$
  Neighborhood Latino with entertaining men constantly arguing outside.
- **Tawaa** • 4005 Broadway [168th Street]
  212-795-3374 • $$
  Score free delivery on spicy vindaloo.
- **Tipico Dominicano** •
  4177 Broadway [W 177th St]
  212-781-3900 • $
  Family place to watch the game. Goooooaal!
- **University Deli** • 603 W 168th St [Broadway]
  212-568-3838 • $
  Standard deli fare, with a large doctor clientele.

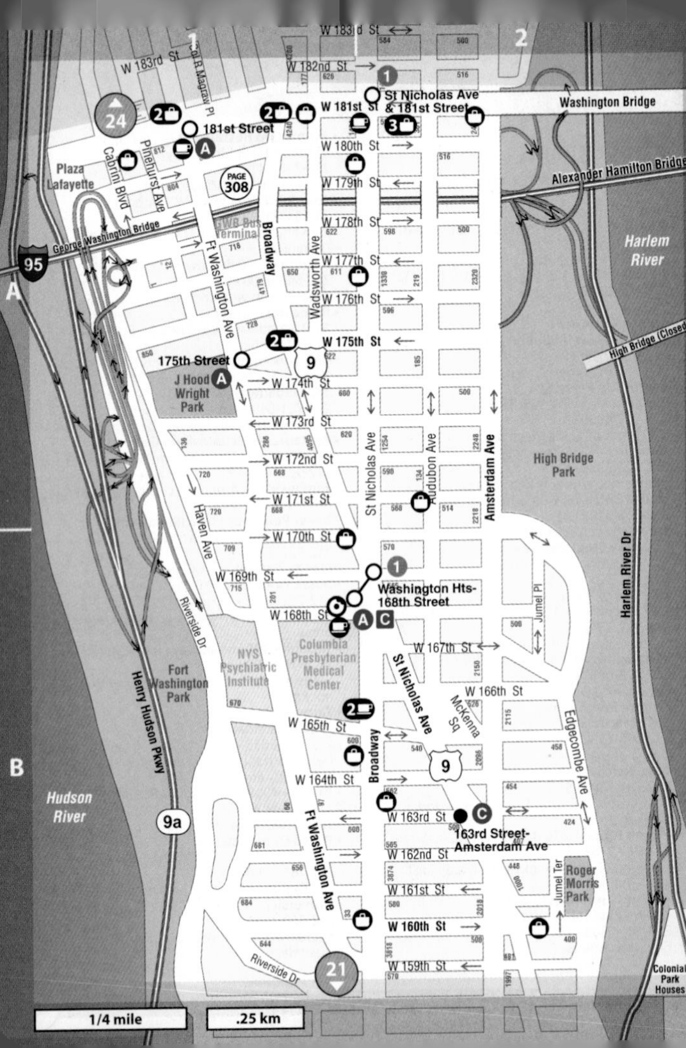

W 183rd St
W 182nd St
W 181st St
St Nicholas Ave & 181st Street
Washington Bridge
181st Street
W 180th St
Plaza Lafayette
Cabrini Blvd
Pinehurst Ave
Col R Magaw Pl
PAGE 308
W 179th St
Alexander Hamilton Bridge
W 178th St
GWB Bus Terminal
Broadway
George Washington Bridge
95
Ft Washington Ave
Wadsworth Ave
W 177th St
Harlem River
W 176th St
A
W 175th St
High Bridge (Closed)
175th Street
9
J Hood Wright Park
W 174th St
W 173rd St
W 172nd St
St Nicholas Ave
Audubon Ave
Amsterdam Ave
High Bridge Park
W 171st St
Haven Ave
W 170th St
W 169th St
Washington Hts-168th Street
W 168th St
Jumel Pl
Riverside Dr
NYS Psychiatric Institute
Columbia Presbyterian Medical Center
W 167th St
Harlem River Dr
Fort Washington Park
St Nicholas Ave
W 166th St
McKenna Sq
Henry Hudson Pkwy
W 165th St
Edgecombe Ave
Broadway
B
W 164th St
Hudson River
W 163rd St
163rd Street-Amsterdam Ave
9a
Ft Washington Ave
W 162nd St
Roger Morris Park
Jumel Ter
W 161st St
W 160th St
Riverside Dr
W 159th St
21
24
1
2
Colonial Park Houses
1/4 mile
.25 km

Broadway's chaos anchors this nabe's shopping options. Stroll the street for a mind-boggling number of hardware stores, check out oodles of vendors at **La Plaza de las Americas**, and score free delivery on groceries at **Liberato.** For a taste of Russia, check out **Moscow on the Hudson**. It's all here.

Bagels

- **Mike's Bagels** • 4003 Broadway [W 168th St]
  212-928-2300
  More like Bob's than Murray's.

Coffee

- **Dunkin' Donuts** •
  1416 St Nicholas Ave [W 181st St]
  212-928-1900
  Decent coffee served in gigantic Styrofoam cups.
- **Jou Jou** • 603 W 168th St [Broadway]
  212-781-2222
  Open 24 hours!
- **Jou Jou Café** • 3959 Broadway [166th Street]
  212-740-8081
  Serving your soup, sandwich and espresso needs all day and night.
- **Starbucks** • 803 W 181st St [Ft Washington]
  212-927-4272
  Fuel up and take a break from 181st.
- **X Caffe** • 3952 Broadway [W 165th St]
  212-543-1999
  Hip and comfortable.

Shopping

- **3841 Hardware** • 3841 Broadway [W 160th St]
  212-927-9320
  No name required at this classic, Broadway tool supply shop.
- **Bravo Supermarket** •
  1331 St Nicholas Ave [W 177th St]
  212-927-1331
  Clean and well-supplied.
- **Carrot Top Pastries** •
  3931 Broadway [W 165th St]
  212-927-4800
  Top carrot cake, muffins, chocolate cake, rugalach, and more.
- **Chung Haeum** • 566 W 181st St [Audubon Ave]
  212-928-8235
  Best store ever. All local artists at affordable prices.
- **Fever** • 1387 St Nicholas Ave [W 180th St]
  212-781-6232
  For ladies, at night.
- **FootCo** • 1422 St Nicholas Ave [W 181st St]
  212-928-3330
  Sneakers galore.
- **Fort Washington Bakery and Deli** •
  808 W 181st St [Fort Washington Ave.]
  212-795-1891
  Damn good looking cookies.
- **Goodwill Industries** •
  512 W 181st St [Amsterdam Ave]
  212-923-7910
  Everything and anything for cheaper.
- **Jennifer Ouellette** • 854 W 181st St [Cabrini]
  212-927-7451
  Hollywood-worthy hair accessories.
- **Jumel Terrace Books** •
  426 W 160th St [Jumel Terrace]
  212-928-9525
  African-American and mostly out of print books.
- **La Bella** • 4033 Broadway [169th St]
  212-927-2023
  Time for that bi-weekly pedicure.
- **La Plaza de Las Americas** •
  Broadway & W 175th St
  Outdoor street vendor market.
- **Liberato** • 3900 Broadway [163rd Street]
  212-927-8250
  Get your fruits and veggies delivered—free!
- **Modell's** • 606 W 181st St [St Nicholas Ave]
  212-568-3000
  Lots and lots of sporting goods.
- **Moscow on the Hudson** •
  801 W 181st St [Fort Washington Ave]
  212-740-7397
  Comrades, this place is Russian culinary heaven.
- **Nunez Hardware** • 4147 Broadway [175th St]
  212-927-8518
  Scavenge for tools at this old-school, stocked-to-bursting shop.
- **Santana Banana** • 661 W 181st St [Wadsworth]
  212-568-4096
  Leather shoes for men and women who are into leather.
- **Total Beauty Supplies, Ltd.** •
  650 W 181st St [Wadsworth Ave]
  212-923-6139
  Bad hair days are over.
- **Tribeca** • 655 W 181st St [Wadsworth Ave]
  212-543-3600
  Trendy store for women. Good soundtrack.
- **Vargas Liquor Store** • 114 Audubon Ave [W 171st St]
  212-781-5195
  Convenient for paper-bag-drinking in Highbridge Park, if that's your thing.

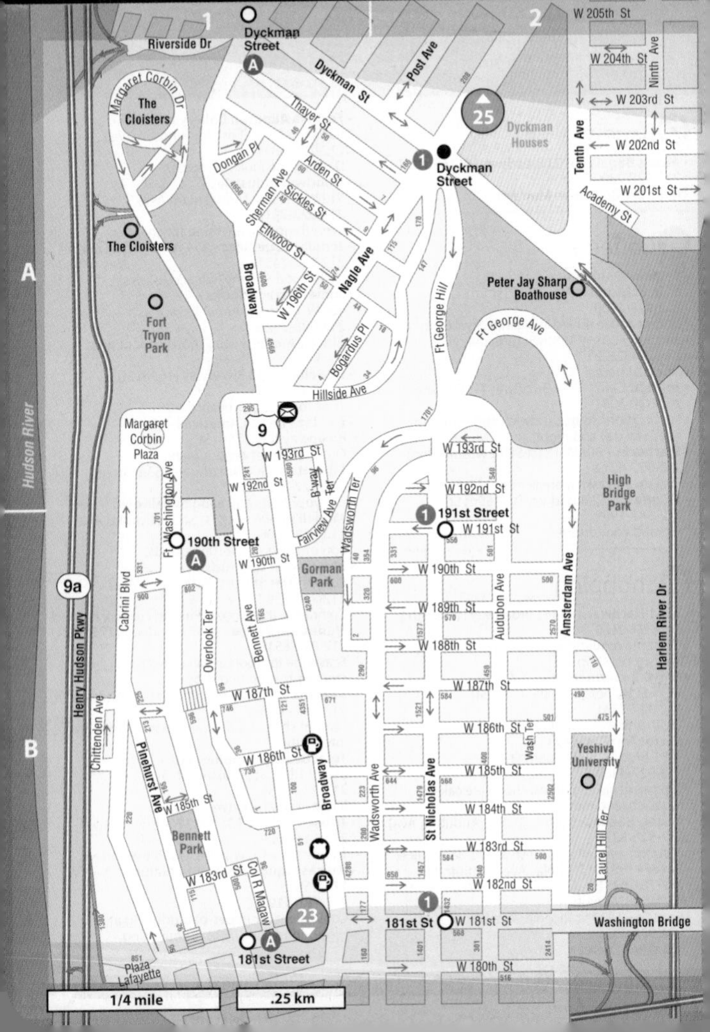

1
2
A
B

Riverside Dr
Dyckman Street
Dyckman St
Post Ave
Thayer St
Margaret Corbin Dr
The Cloisters
Dongan Pl
Arden St
Sherman Ave
Sickles St
Ellwood St
Nagle Ave
W 196th St
Broadway
Bogardus Pl
Hillside Ave
Fort Tryon Park
Fort George Hill
Ft George Ave
Dyckman Houses
Peter Jay Sharp Boathouse
Tenth Ave
Ninth Ave
W 205th St
W 204th St
W 203rd St
W 202nd St
W 201st St
Academy St
Hudson River
Margaret Corbin Plaza
W 193rd St
W 192nd St
B'way Ter
Fairview Ave
Wadsworth Ter
191st Street
W 191st St
190th Street
Ft Washington Ave
W 190th St
Gorman Park
W 189th St
W 188th St
W 187th St
W 186th St
W 185th St
W 184th St
W 183rd St
W 182nd St
W 181st St
W 180th St
Cabrini Blvd
Overlook Ter
Bennett Ave
Audubon Ave
Amsterdam Ave
High Bridge Park
Harlem River Dr
Henry Hudson Pkwy
9a
9
Chittenden Ave
Pinehurst Ave
Bennett Park
Col R Magaw Pl
Wadsworth Ave
St Nicholas Ave
Wash Ter
Yeshiva University
Laurel Hill Ter
181st St
181st Street
Washington Bridge
Plaza Lafayette
23
25

1/4 mile
.25 km

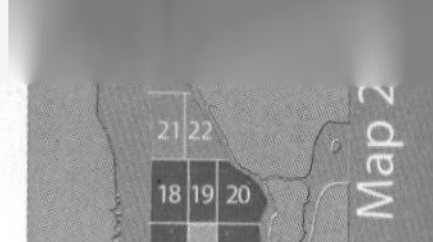

Sandwiched between two colossal parks, this northern Manhattan neighborhood gets its name from the park that runs along Broadway and the Hudson River, Fort Tryon Park. Fort George is the name of the last fort of its sort (pardon the tongue twister) which was built in 1776 at the intersection of Audubon Avenue and 192nd Street. Today it's also known locally as "Hudson Heights." Name debates aside; this area possesses many hidden qualities. For starters, it hosts people of various ethnicities and backgrounds. The space surrounding Fort Tryon Park and Yeshiva University is predominantly Jewish, but east of Broadway begins to feel more south-of-the-border and Caribbean. Second, the streets, some of them pretty steep, offer pedestrians pleasant strolls. And last but not least, if you speak to the locals, they'll tell you that they wouldn't live anywhere else. The reason? Well, this place has quieter streets and bigger spaces for less, great chunks of green land, and great spots for your chillin' necessities on any given day of the week. And if you ever feel like leaving this land of greatness, downtown Manhattan is just 30 minutes away.

Built in 1935 by Frederick Law Olmsted Jr., son of the architect of Central Park, and gifted to the city of New York by John D. Rockefeller in 1917, **Fort Tryon Park** is the 67-acre chunk of green that never goes unnoticed. 1995 was a good year for this site because it was then that it became part of the New York Restoration Project, founded by Bette Midler, who switched Beaches for Parks (we're kidding, Bette) and under which the park went through a much needed restoration (thanks, Bette). The historic architecture of this site has offered generations of visitors areas of recreation, gardens to contemplate and grass lawns to spread colorful picnic blankets. If the basket is empty park goers can always go to the New Leaf Restaurant, an upscale restaurant and a landmark within a landmark. If they are feeling "cultural" then we suggest paying **The Cloisters** a visit. The building, an extension of the Metropolitan Museum of Art, offers a feast to the eye thanks to its magnificent architecture (with elements from four medieval French cloisters), stained-glass windows, tapestries and gardens for the horticultural enthusiast. Don't miss the Medieval Festival that takes place here every year. Visitors can experience the Middle Ages way of life and even dance, sing and talk like back in the day. Wardererel!

At the edge of the Harlem River stands the **Peter Jay Sharp Boathouse**. Reminiscent of the old New York boating life, this structure is the first new community boathouse in New York City in nearly 100 years. It opened its doors in 2004 to offer the community rowing lessons and regattas. To reach the boathouse go to Tenth Avenue and Dyckman and walk south on the Lillian Goldman Walkway. Just before you get there, you'll pass by the restored Swindler Cove Park, a nice spot from which to stare at the ducks or contemplate the river. If you decide to continue south on the walkway, the only way out is through the bridge that connects to 155th Street in Harlem. You've been warned.

Zysman Hall is the name of what was Yeshiva University's Main Building, back in 1928 when it was completed. Today Zysman Hall, designed by Charles B. Meyers Associates, is home to YU's High School for Boys. Once inside, don't expect to be greeted by a tour guide. The guard will most likely escort you to the door. Instead, stick to admiring the building from the outside since it features a Byzantine style that reflects the Jewish approach to architecture. If you feel the need to stock up on kosher goodies, now is the time—cross the street and visit the delis, restaurants and bodegas that carry them.

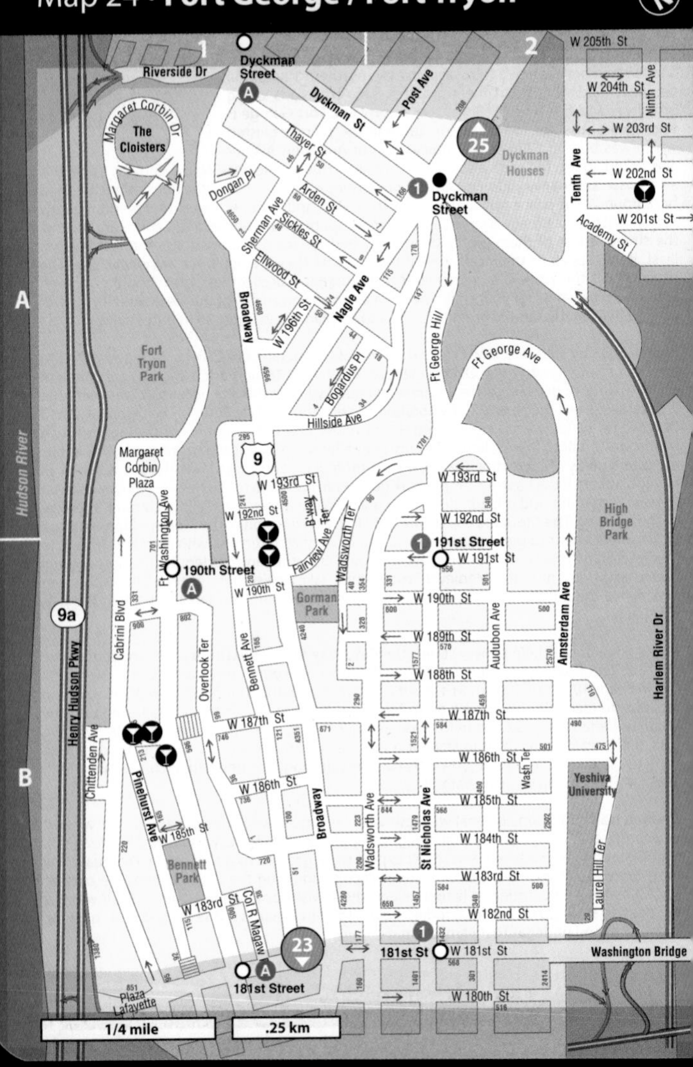

Dyckman Street
Riverside Dr
The Cloisters
Margaret Corbin Dr
Dyckman St
Post Ave
Thayer St
Dongan Pl
Arden St
Sherman Ave
Sickles St
Ellwood St
W 196th St
Broadway
Nagle Ave
Dyckman Street
Dyckman Houses
Ft George Hill
Ft George Ave
Bogardus Pl
Hillside Ave
Fort Tryon Park
Margaret Corbin Plaza
W 193rd St
W 192nd St
B'way Ter
Fairview Ave
Wadsworth Ter
191st Street
W 191st St
190th Street
W 190th St
Gorman Park
Ft Washington Ave
Cabrini Blvd
Overlook Ter
Bennett Ave
W 189th St
W 188th St
W 187th St
W 186th St
W 185th St
W 184th St
W 183rd St
W 182nd St
181st St
W 181st St
W 180th St
Audubon Ave
Amsterdam Ave
High Bridge Park
Harlem River Dr
Wash Ter
Yeshiva University
Laurel Hill Ter
Washington Bridge
Henry Hudson Pkwy
Hudson River
Chittenden Ave
Pinehurst Ave
Bennett Park
Col R Magaw
181st Street
Plaza Lafayette
Wadsworth Ave
St Nicholas Ave
W 205th St
W 204th St
W 203rd St
W 202nd St
W 201st St
Ninth Ave
Tenth Ave
Academy St
1/4 mile
.25 km

OK. There isn't a ginormous selection of bars but don't leave the neighborhood just yet. Get some drinks and placate the late-afternoon hunger at **Bleu Evolution**. **The Monkey Room** is ideal for game nights or late night drinks. Hit the dance floor in absolute Caribbean fashion at **Arka Lounge**. For a good neighborhood bar, try **Locksmith Wine Bar**.

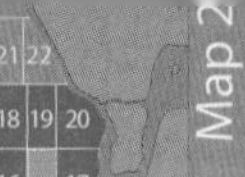

Bars

- **Arka Lounge** • 4488 Broadway [West 192 St]
  212-567-9425
  Caribbean club scene.
- **Bleu Evolution** •
  808 W 187th St [Ft Washington Ave]
  212-928-6006
  Have a drink in the lounge.
- **Locksmith Wine Bar** •
  4463 Broadway [W 192nd St]
  212-304-9463
  Friendly spot to grab a glass of wine or beer.
- **The Monkey Room** •
  589 Fort Washington Ave [W 187th St]
  212-543-9888
  Tiny like a capuchin.
- **Next Door by 107 West** •
  813 W 187th St [Fort Washington Ave]
  212-543-2111
  Half-price bottles of organic wine on Thursdays. Awesome!
- **Umbrella Bar & Lounge** •
  440 W 202nd St [9th Ave]
  212-942-5921
  Hispanic dance club.

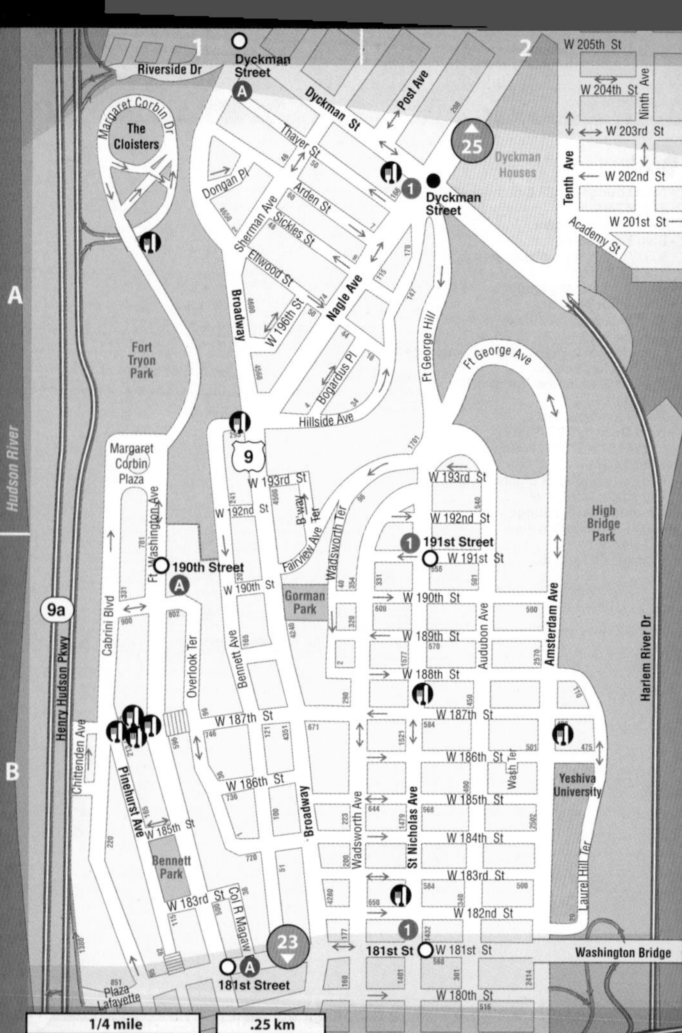

Dyckman Street
Riverside Dr
Margaret Corbin Dr
The Cloisters
Dyckman St
Post Ave
Thayer St
Dongan Pl
Arden St
Sherman Ave
Sickles St
Ellwood St
Nagle Ave
Broadway
W 196th St
Bogardus Pl
Hillside Ave
Ft George Hill
Ft George Ave
Dyckman Houses
Dyckman Street
W 205th St
W 204th St
Ninth Ave
W 203rd St
Tenth Ave
W 202nd St
W 201st St
Academy St
Fort Tryon Park
Hudson River
Margaret Corbin Plaza
W 193rd St
W 192nd St
B'way Ter
Fairview Ave
Wadsworth Ter
W 193rd St
W 192nd St
191st Street
W 191st St
High Bridge Park
Ft Washington Ave
190th Street
W 190th St
Gorman Park
W 190th St
9a
Cabrini Blvd
Overlook Ter
Bennett Ave
W 189th St
Audubon Ave
Amsterdam Ave
W 188th St
Harlem River Dr
Henry Hudson Pkwy
W 187th St
W 187th St
Chittenden Ave
W 186th St
Wash Ter
Pinehurst Ave
W 186th St
Broadway
Yeshiva University
W 185th St
Wadsworth Ave
W 185th St
St Nicholas Ave
W 184th St
Bennett Park
Laurel Hill Ter
W 183rd St
W 183rd St
Col R Magaw
W 182nd St
181st St
W 181st St
Washington Bridge
181st Street
Plaza Lafayette
W 180th St
1/4 mile
.25 km

New Leaf Restaurant at Fort Tryon Park is a must. Find great Indian cuisine at **Kismat**. Enjoy a real Caribbean meal at **La Casa Del Mofongo** or go Dominican at **Rancho Jubilee**. The Mexican food can't be beat at **Tacos El Paisa**. For perfect falafel make your way to **Golan Heights**.

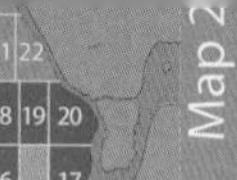

Restaurants

- **107 West •**
  811 W 187th St [Ft Washington Ave]
  212-923-3311 • $$
  Salads, burgers, chicken…you get the idea.
- **809 Sangria Bar & Grill •**
  112 Dyckman St [Nagle Ave]
  212-304-3800 • $$$
  Dominican grilled meat-a-thon.
- **Bleu Evolution •**
  808 W 187th St [Ft Washington Ave]
  212-928-6006 • $$
  Uptown bohemian. Calm.
- **Golan Heights •**
  2553 Amsterdam Ave [W 187th St]
  212-795-7842 • $
  Tasty Israeli falafel and shawarma. Popular for lunch.
- **Kismat** • 603 Fort Washington Ave [187 St]
  212-795-863 • $$
  Throw your taste buds a surprise party.
- **La Casa del Mofongo •**
  1447 St Nicholas Ave [182 St]
  212-740-1200 • $$
  The obvious: have the mofongo.
- **New Leaf Restaurant & Bar •**
  1 Margaret Corbin Dr [Henry Hudson Pkwy]
  212-568-5323 • $$$$
  Uptown haven for a fancier dinner or brunch.
- **Next Door by 107 West •**
  813 W 187th St [Fort Washington Ave]
  212-543-2111 • $$
  Organic specialties served in a warm atmosphere.
- **Rancho Jubilee** • 1 Nagle Ave [Hillside Ave]
  212-304-0100 • $$
  Like a portal to the DR (Dominican Republic).
- **Tacos El Paisa •**
  1548 St Nicholas Ave [W 188th St]
  917-521-0972 0• $
  Fantastic hole-the-wall Mexican.

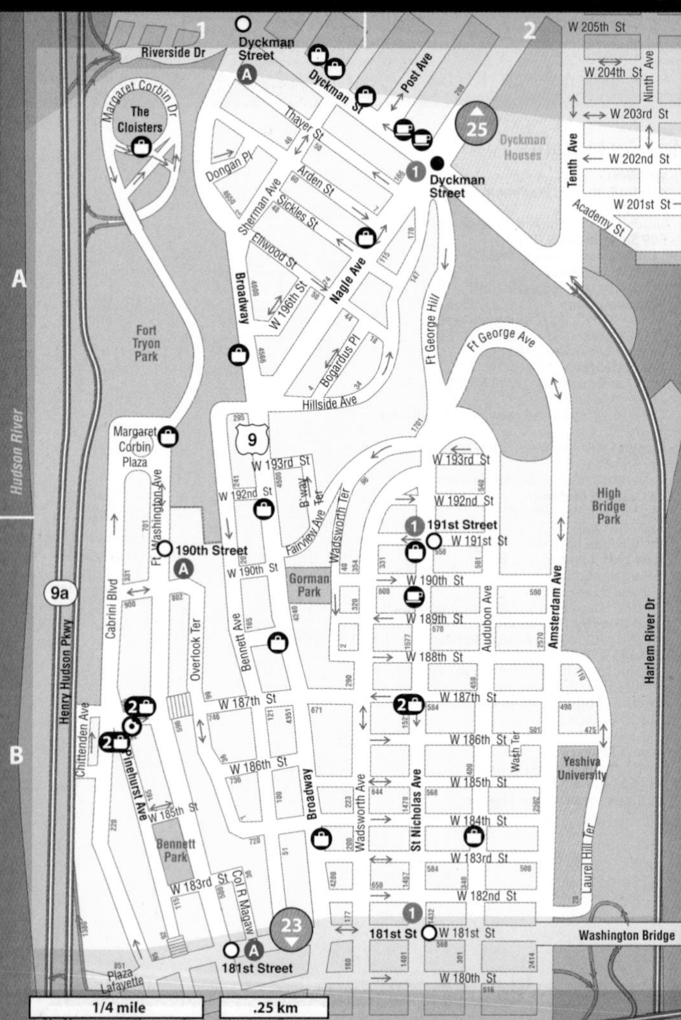

Dyckman Street
Riverside Dr
Margaret Corbin Dr
The Cloisters
Dyckman St
Post Ave
Thayer St
Dongan Pl
Arden St
Sherman Ave
Sickles St
Ellwood St
Nagle Ave
Broadway
W 196th St
Bogardus Pl
Hillside Ave
Ft George Hill
Ft George Ave
Dyckman Houses
Dyckman Street
W 205th St
W 204th St
Ninth Ave
W 203rd St
Tenth Ave
W 202nd St
W 201st St
Academy St
Fort Tryon Park
Hudson River
Margaret Corbin Plaza
W 193rd St
W 192nd St
B'way Ter
Fairview Ave
Wadsworth Ter
191st Street
W 191st St
190th Street
Ft Washington Ave
W 190th St
Gorman Park
Cabrini Blvd
Overlook Ter
Bennett Ave
W 189th St
W 188th St
Audubon Ave
Amsterdam Ave
High Bridge Park
Harlem River Dr
Henry Hudson Pkwy
9a
9
W 187th St
W 186th St
Wash Ter
Chittenden Ave
Pinehurst Ave
W 185th St
Yeshiva University
Broadway
Wadsworth Ave
St Nicholas Ave
W 184th St
Bennett Park
W 183rd St
Col R Magaw
Laurel Hill Ter
W 182nd St
181st St
W 181st St
Washington Bridge
181st Street
W 180th St
Plaza Lafayette
1/4 mile
.25 km

Home to one-of-a-kind shops like **Gideons Bakery** for kosher sweets and **Food Palace** for caviar and other Russian goodies. Buy your furry friend a treat and a makeover at **Critter Outfitter**. Get gourmet edibles at **Frank's Market** or practice rhyme by buying wine from **Vines on Pine**.

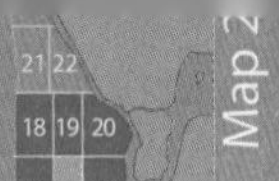

Bagels

- **Gideons Bakery** •
  810 W 187th St [Fort Washington Ave]
  212-927-9262
  Get there early. These bagels go fast.

Coffee

- **Dunkin' Donuts** •
  1599 St Nicholas Ave [W 190th St]
  212-568-1039
  Decent coffee served in gigantic Styrofoam cups.
- **Jimbo's Coffee Shop** •
  117 Dyckman St [Nagle Ave]
  212-942-9769
  Standard NYC diner.
- **La Sala 78** • 111 Dyckman St [Nagle Ave]
  212-304-0667
  Enjoy some art with your latte.

Shopping

- **Apex Supply** • 4580 Broadway [W 196th St]
  212-304-0808
  Where eggshell is considered a color.
- **Associated** •
  592 Fort Washington Ave [W 187th St]
  212-543-0721
  No-frills market way cheaper than your local bodega.
- **Century Hardware** •
  4309 Broadway [W 184th St]
  212-927-9000
  Experts in nuts and bolts.
- **The Cloisters Museum Store** •
  Ft Tryon Park [Margaret Corbin Dr]
  212-650-2277
  Dark Age trinkets.
- **Critter Outfitter** •
  210 Pinehurst Ave [187th St]
  212-928-0342
  Pet stuff galore!
- **Fine Fare** • 1617 St Nicholas Ave [191st St]
  212-543-3008
  Decent supermarket. "Fine" may be stretching it.
- **Food Palace** • 4407 Broadway [189th St]
  212-928-3038
  Your local Russian supermarket.
- **Foot Locker** • 146 Dyckman St [Sherman Ave]
  212-544-8613
  No lockers. But lots of sneakers.
- **Frank's Gourmet Market** •
  807 W 187th St [Fort Washington Ave]
  212-795-2929
  Best food shopping around. 15 types of olives.
- **Gideons Bakery** •
  810 W 187th St [Fort Washington Ave]
  212-927-9262
  Kosher sugar coma.
- **J&P Discount Liquors** •
  377 Audubon Ave [W 184th St]
  212-740-4027
  Who doesn't like cheaper liquor?
- **La Salle Gourmet** • 117 Nagle Ave [Sickles St]
  212-567-2390
  Deli with ice cream open 24 hours.
- **Libreria Caliope** •
  170 Dyckman St [Sherman Ave]
  212-567-3511
  Spanish and English books.
- **Metropolitan Museum of Art Bookshop-Cloisters Branch** •
  799 Fort Washington Ave [Margaret Corbin Dr]
  212-650-2277
  Art books.
- **NHS Hardware** •
  1539 St Nicholas Ave [W 187th St]
  212-927-3549
  Get into the DIY spirit.
- **Radio Shack** •
  180 Dyckman St [Vermilyea Ave]
  212-304-0364
  Official post-nuclear war survivor, w/ Keith Richards and cockroaches.
- **Sanchez Liquors** •
  4500 Broadway [W 192nd St]
  212-544-9350
  Look for the sign that says "S'wine."
- **Vines on Pine** • 209 Pinehurst Ave [187th St]
  212-928-0342
  One-of-a-kind selections.

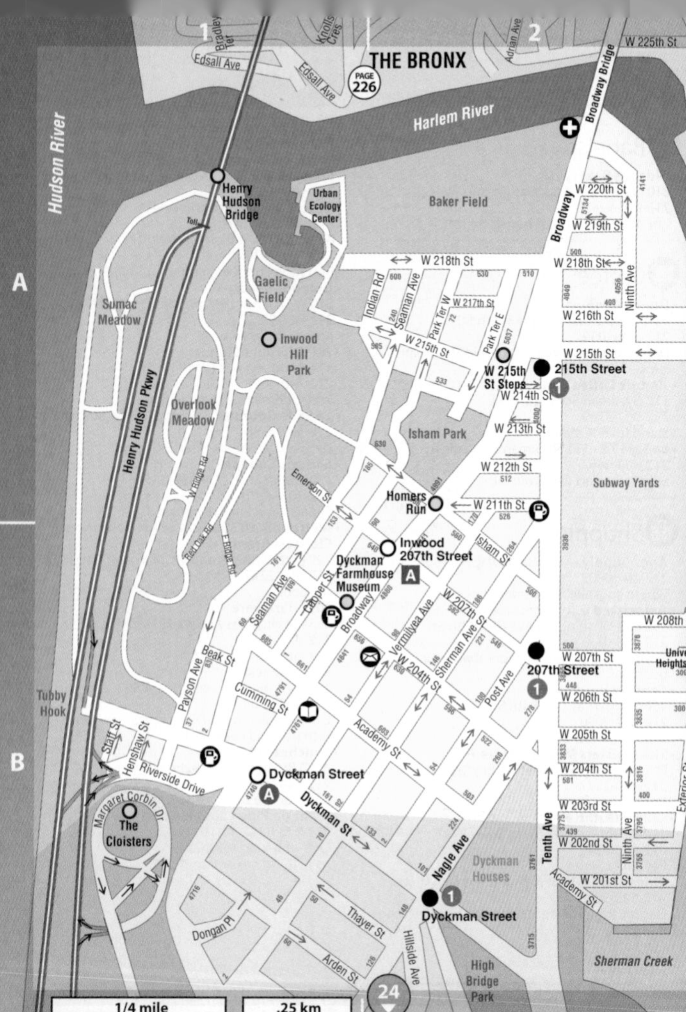

THE BRONX
PAGE 226
Harlem River
Hudson River
Henry Hudson Bridge
Urban Ecology Center
Baker Field
Gaelic Field
Sumac Meadow
Inwood Hill Park
Overlook Meadow
Henry Hudson Pkwy
Isham Park
Subway Yards
215th Street
W 215th St Steps
Homers Run
Inwood 207th Street
Dyckman Farmhouse Museum
207th Street
Tubby Hook
Dyckman Street
The Cloisters
Dyckman Street
Dyckman Houses
High Bridge Park
Sherman Creek
Broadway
Broadway Bridge
Tenth Ave
Ninth Ave
Nagle Ave
Riverside Drive
Margaret Corbin Dr
1/4 mile
.25 km
24

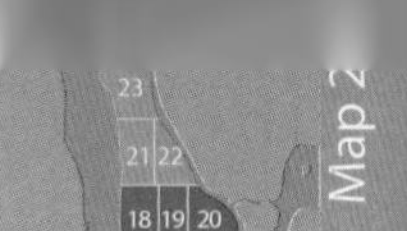

Newsflash: Inwood is in Manhattan. Be prepared to say this every time you talk about this neighborhood because most mortals can't seem to point it out on the map. Located on the northernmost tip of the island, this hill-surrounded neighborhood has something for everyone.

There are few places in Manhattan where you can get affordable housing AND fit all your belongings in something bigger than a shoebox. Indeed Inwood is one of the best-kept housing secrets in New York. West of Broadway offers views, pathways, quiet streets, and artsy cafes. Parking is tricky, but possible—worst-case scenario would be leaving your four-wheeler in one of the many parking lots around the area, which are very affordable. Living on this side is pricier because of the aforementioned perks and well, because it's right next to **Inwood Hill Park**. Cross Broadway to the east side and you'll find the air is filled with free bachata, especially during the summer. The grass might be greener on the other side, but this predominantly Dominican area hosts even cheaper housing alternatives.

160 acres of green are at your disposal thanks to Inwood Hill Park, which stretches along the Hudson from Dyckman Street to the northern tip of Manhattan. This major city lung and the last remaining forestland in the island, features oaks, wildflowers, paved paths, and play areas. Take your kids or nephews to **Emerson Playground** on a sunny day, brag about hiking through real woods without leaving the city, let your dog play with its kin at **Homer's Run** or challenge your significant other to a tennis match. Don't forget to hit the Farmers Market on any given Saturday to stock up on organic produce and local foods. It'll be there even if the weather's crappy.

You probably think that the little house on the hill at Broadway and 204th is a landscape mistake, but this visual delight known as the **Dyckman Farmhouse Musuem** (c. 1784) was originally part of several hundred acres of farmland owned by the Dyckman family. Today, it's a reminder of how much the city's tentacles have grown. On weekends expect to find seniors sitting on the benches by the farmhouse's garden (don't forget to say hi! Or hola!).

The **Henry Hudson Bridge** connects Manhattan and The Bronx through a two-level, 7-lane structure. With thousands of vehicles crossing back and forth each day, drivers and passengers can take a minute to admire the lavish engineering efforts. The $3 toll gets you to the other side and views of the Hudson River and the Harlem Ship Canal.

If you're feeling adventurous, in a Rocky sort-of-way, then climb the **West 215th Steps**. All 111 of them (yep, we counted). Pedestrians bump into Park Terrace East going up, to find a few rare species: actual houses with driveways.

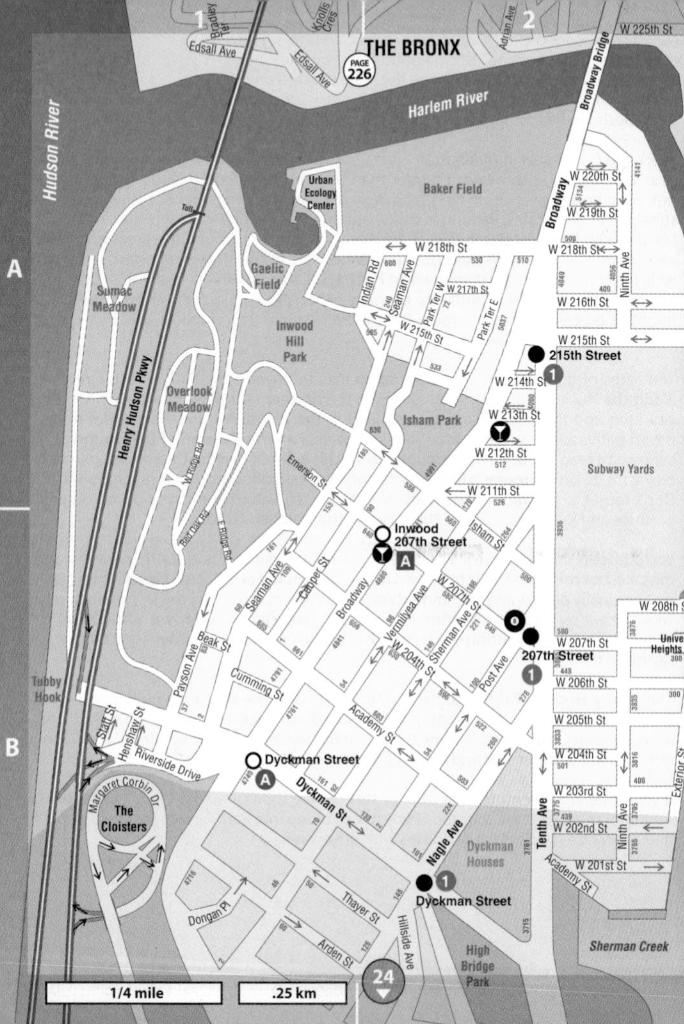
THE BRONX
PAGE 226
Harlem River
Hudson River
Broadway Bridge
W 225th St
Edsall Ave
Bradley Ter
Knolls Cres
Adrian Ave
Urban Ecology Center
Baker Field
Broadway
W 220th St
W 219th St
W 218th St
Ninth Ave
W 216th St
W 215th St
215th Street
W 214th St
W 213th St
W 212th St
W 211th St
Subway Yards
Sumac Meadow
Gaelic Field
Inwood Hill Park
Overlook Meadow
Isham Park
Henry Hudson Pkwy
Indian Rd
Seaman Ave
Park Ter W
W 217th St
Park Ter E
Emerson St
W Ridge Rd
Red Oak Rd
E Bridge Rd
Inwood 207th Street
Isham St
W 207th St
W 208th St
Univer Heights
207th Street
Payson Ave
Beak St
Cumming St
Seaman Ave
Cooper St
Vermilyea Ave
Sherman Ave
Post Ave
W 204th St
Academy St
W 206th St
W 205th St
W 204th St
W 203rd St
W 202nd St
W 201st St
Exterior St
Tenth Ave
Tubby Hook
Staff St
Henshaw St
Riverside Drive
Dyckman Street
Dyckman St
Nagle Ave
Dyckman Houses
Margaret Corbin Dr
The Cloisters
Dyckman Street
Thayer St
Dongan Pl
Arden St
Hillside Ave
High Bridge Park
Sherman Creek
1/4 mile
.25 km
24

Well, if you refuse to take the 1 or A trains south for more exciting options, then dive into **Piper's Kilt** of Inwood for some beers and wings. **Irish Eyes** has lots of old-school character and is as local as you can get.

Bars

- **Irish Eyes** • 5008 Broadway [W 213th St]
  212-567-9072
  Knock on the window if the light is on.
- **Piper's Kilt** • 4944 Broadway [W 207th St]
  212-569-7071
  A bit more spiffed up than it used to be.

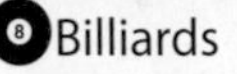

Billiards

- **Post Billiards Café** • 154 Post Ave [W 207th St]
  212-569-1840
  When you need to play way way uptown.

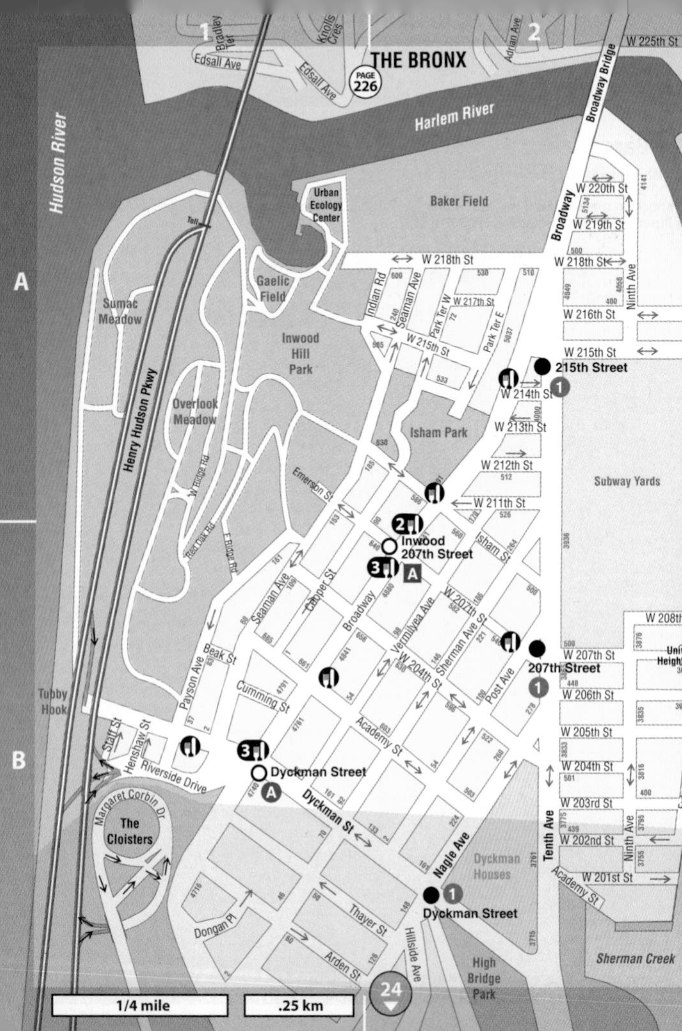
THE BRONX
PAGE 226
Harlem River
Hudson River
Broadway Bridge
W 225th St
Edsall Ave
Bradley Ter
Knolls Cres
Adrian Ave
Baker Field
Urban Ecology Center
Gaelic Field
Sumac Meadow
Inwood Hill Park
Overlook Meadow
Henry Hudson Pkwy
Toll
Broadway
W 220th St
W 219th St
W 218th St
W 217th St
W 216th St
W 215th St
215th Street
W 214th St
W 213th St
W 212th St
W 211th St
Ninth Ave
Indian Rd
Seaman Ave
Park Ter W
Park Ter E
Isham Park
Subway Yards
Emerson St
W Bridge Rd
Red Oak Rd
E Bridge Rd
Inwood 207th Street
Isham St
W 207th St
Cooper St
Vermilyea Ave
Sherman Ave
W 208th St
University Heights
207th Street
W 206th St
W 205th St
W 204th St
W 203rd St
W 202nd St
W 201st St
Payson Ave
Beak St
Cumming St
W 204th St
Post Ave
Academy St
Tubby Hook
Staff St
Henshaw St
Riverside Drive
Dyckman Street
Dyckman St
Margaret Corbin Dr
The Cloisters
Nagle Ave
Dyckman Houses
Tenth Ave
Dyckman Street
Thayer St
Dongan Pl
Arden St
Hillside Ave
High Bridge Park
Sherman Creek
1/4 mile
.25 km
24

Get brunch at **Garden Cafe** or go to Park View Cafe for great bagels with a view. Go calorie crazy at **Elsa La Reina del Chicharron** for the best pork rinds in town. Sushi lovers go to **Mama Sushi** and Italian cuisine aficionados go to **Il Sole** or **La Estufa**. Practice your Spanish at **Mamajuana Cafe**.

Restaurants

- **Capitol Restaurant** •
4933 Broadway [W 207th St]
212-942-5090 • $$
Nice neighborhood diner.
- **Daniel's Fruit-opia** •
510 W 207th St [10th Avenue]
212-304-0029 • $
Who knew fruit shakes could be addictive?
- **Elsa La Reina Del Chicharron** •
4840 Broadway [204th St]
212-304-1070 • $
It's worth the coronary bypass.
- **Garden Café** • 4961 Broadway [Isham St]
212-544-9480 • $$
Homestyle brunch for less than 10 bucks.
- **Grandpa's Brick Oven Pizza** •
4973 Broadway [Isham St]
212-304-1185 • $$
Personal brick oven pies and catering.
- **Guadalupe** • 597 W 207th St [Broadway]
212-304-1083 • $$
High class Mexican.
- **Il Sole** • 233 Dyckman St [Seaman Ave]
212-544-0406 • $$
Neighborhood Italian.
- **La Estufa** • 5035 Broadway [W 215th St]
212-567-6640 • $$
This Italian can't be beat north of 14th street.
- **Mama Sushi** • 237 Dyckman St [Broadway]
212-544-0003 • $
As good as uptown sushi gets.
- **Mamajuana Cafe** •
247 Dyckman St [Seaman Ave]
212-304-0140 • $$$
Tasty Nuevo Latino cuisine.
- **Park Terrace Bistro** •
4959 Broadway [Isham St]
212-567-2828 • $$
One of the great hidden gems of the city. Moroccan fare.
- **Park View Cafe and Restaurant** • 219 Dyckman St [Broadway]
212-544-9024 • $$
Brunch bliss.
- **Pizza Haven** • 4942 Broadway [207 St]
212-569-3720 • $
They bring-a the pizza.

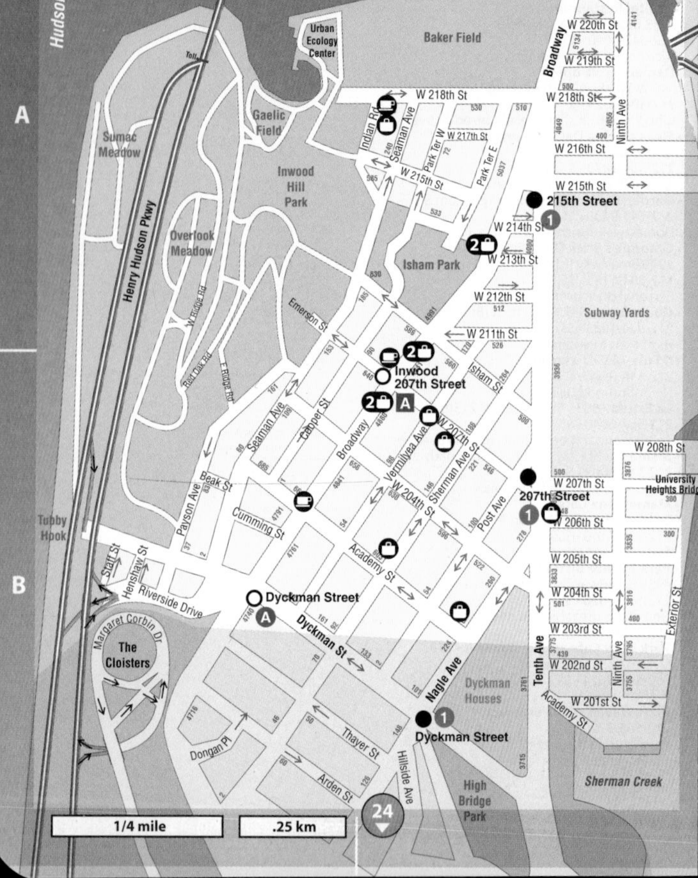

THE BRONX
PAGE 226
Bradley Terr
Knolls Cres
Adrian Ave
Edsall Ave
W 225th St
Broadway Bridge
Harlem River
Hudson River
Urban Ecology Center
Baker Field
Broadway
W 220th St
W 219th St
W 218th St
Gaelic Field
Sumac Meadow
Inwood Hill Park
Indian Rd
Seaman Ave
Park Ter W
W 217th St
Park Ter E
W 216th St
Ninth Ave
W 215th St
215th Street
W 214th St
W 213th St
Isham Park
Overlook Meadow
Henry Hudson Pkwy
W Ridge Rd
Emerson St
W 212th St
W 211th St
Subway Yards
Inwood 207th Street
Isham St
Red Oak Rd
E Ridge Rd
Seaman Ave
Cooper St
Broadway
Vermilyea Ave
W 207th St
Sherman Ave
W 208th St
University Heights Bridge
W 207th St
207th Street
W 206th St
Beak St
Payson Ave
Cumming St
W 204th St
Post Ave
W 205th St
Tubby Hook
Staff St
Henshaw St
Riverside Drive
Academy St
Dyckman Street
W 204th St
W 203rd St
Exterior St
Margaret Corbin Dr
The Cloisters
Dyckman St
Nagle Ave
Tenth Ave
W 202nd St
Ninth Ave
Dyckman Houses
Academy St
W 201st St
Dyckman Street
Thayer St
Dongan Pl
Arden St
Hillside Ave
High Bridge Park
Sherman Creek
1/4 mile
.25 km
24

Entertainment

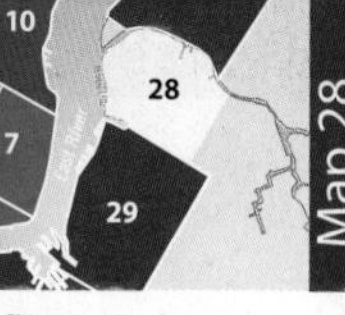

The Pencil Factory remains the nightlife favorite of a certain demographic; Polish dance clubs cater to another. Where **Wedel's** churns out fancy Polish chocolates, legions of Manhattan Avenue meat markets slash out infinite slabs of bloody flesh. **The Thing's** got everything you never thought would merit a thrift store. Best Polish food? Answer: **Lomzynianka**.

Nightlife

- **Alligator Lounge II** • 113 Franklin St [Greenpoint Ave]
- **Black Rabbit** • 91 Greenpoint Ave [Franklin St]
- **Blackout** • 916 Manhattan Ave [Kent St]
- **Coco 66** • 66 Greenpoint Ave [Franklin St]
- **The Diamond** • 43 Franklin St [Calyer St]
- **Enid's** • 560 Manhattan Ave [Driggs Ave]
- **Europa** • 98 Meserole Ave [Manhattan Ave]
- **The Habitat** • 988 Manhattan Ave [Huron St]
- **The Manhattan Inn** • 632 Manhattan Ave [Nassau Ave]
- **The Mark Bar** • 1025 Manhattan Ave [Green St]
- **Matchless** • 557 Manhattan Ave [Driggs Ave]
- **Palace Café** • 206 Nassau Ave [Russell St]
- **Pencil Factory** • 142 Franklin St [Greenpoint Ave]
- **Pit Stop Bar** • 152 Meserole Ave [McGuinness Blvd]
- **Red Star** • 37 Greenpoint Ave [West St]
- **Shayz Lounge** • 130 Franklin St [Milton St]
- **TBD Bar** • 224 Franklin St [Green St]
- **Tommy's Tavern** • 1041 Manhattan Ave [Freeman St]
- **Van Gogh's Radio Lounge** • 147 Franklin St [Java St]
- **Warsaw** • 261 Driggs Ave [Eckford St]

Restaurants

- **Acapulco** • 1116 Manhattan Ave [Clay St]
- **Ashbox** • 1154 Manhattan Ave [Ash St]
- **Brooklyn Ice Cream Factory** • 97 Commercial St [Box St]
- **Brooklyn Label** • 180 Franklin St [Java St]
- **Christina's** • 853 Manhattan Ave [Noble St]
- **Divine Follie Café** • 929 Manhattan Ave [Kent]
- **Eat** • 124 Meserole Ave [Leonard St]
- **Enid's** • 560 Manhattan Ave [Driggs Ave]
- **Erb** • 681 Manhattan Ave [Norman Ave]
- **Five Leaves** • 18 Bedford Ave [Nassau Ave]
- **Fresca Tortilla** • 620 Manhattan Ave [Nassau]
- **God Bless Deli** • 818 Manhattan Ave [Calyer]
- **Kam Loon** • 975 Manhattan Ave [India St]
- **Kestane Kebab** • 110 Nassau Ave [Eckford St]
- **Kyoto Sushi** • 161 Nassau Ave [Diamond St]
- **La Brique** • 645 Manhattan Ave [Bedford Ave]
- **La Taverna** • 946 Manhattan Ave [Java St]
- **Lamb & Jaffy** • 1073 Manhattan Ave [Eagle St]
- **Lokal** • 905 Lorimer St [Nassau Ave]
- **Lomzynianka** • 646 Manhattan Ave [Nassau]
- **Manhattan 3 Decker** • 695 Manhattan Ave [Norman Ave]
- **Ott** • 970 Manhattan Ave [India St]
- **Peter Pan Doughnuts** • 727 Manhattan Ave [Norman Ave]
- **Pio Pio Riko** • 996 Manhattan Ave [Huron St]
- **Relax** • 68 Newell St [Nassau Ave]
- **Sapporo Haru** • 622 Manhattan Ave [Nassau]
- **Schmook's Pizza** • 86 Nassau Ave [Manhattan]
- **Thai Café** • 925 Manhattan Ave [Kent St]
- **Valdiano** • 659 Manhattan Ave [Bedford Ave]

Shopping

- **Alter** • 109 Franklin St [Greenpoint Ave]
- **Angel Street Thrift Shop** • 67 Guernsey St [Norman Ave]
- **Brouwerij Lane** • 78 Greenpoint Ave [Franklin]
- **Cracovia Liquors** • 150 Nassau Ave [Newell St]
- **Dalaga** • 150 Franklin St [Greenpoint Ave]
- **Dandelion Wine** • 153 Franklin St [Java St]
- **The Garden** • 921 Manhattan Ave [Kent St]
- **Hayden-Harnett** • 211 Franklin St [Freeman]
- **Kill Devil Hill** • 170 Franklin St [Java St]
- **Maria's Deli** • 136 Meserole Ave [Eckford St]
- **Old Hollywood** • 110 Meserole Ave [Manhattan Ave]
- **Open Air Modern** • 606 Manhattan Ave [Nassau Ave]
- **Permanent Records** • 181 Franklin St [Huron]
- **Photoplay** • 928 Manhattan Ave [Kent St]
- **Pop's Popular Clothing** • 7 Franklin St [Meserole Ave]
- **Steve's Meat Market** • 104 Nassau Ave [Leonard]
- **The Thing** • 1001 Manhattan Ave [Huron St]
- **Wedel** • 772 Manhattan Ave [Meserole Ave]
- **Word** • 126 Franklin St [Milton St]

Map 29 • Williamsburg

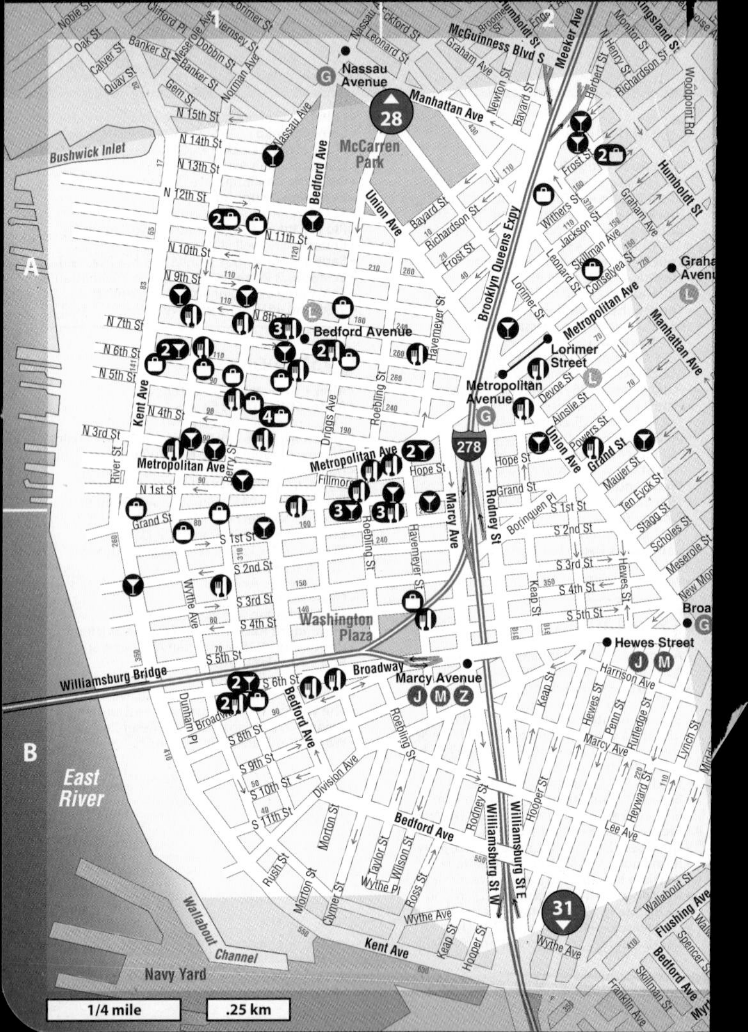

Nassau Avenue
McCarren Park
Bedford Avenue
Lorimer Street
Metropolitan Avenue
Marcy Avenue
Hewes Street
Washington Plaza
Williamsburg Bridge
Bushwick Inlet
East River
Wallabout Channel
Navy Yard
Brooklyn Queens Expy
Kent Ave
Bedford Ave
Metropolitan Ave
Grand St
Broadway
Union Ave
Manhattan Ave
Marcy Ave
Rodney St
Williamsburg St W
Williamsburg St E

1/4 mile
.25 km

You want it, it's here. Carnivores flock to **Peter Luger** and **Fette Sau**, beer-lovers throw 'em back at **Spuyten Duyvil** and **Radegast**, while **Barcade** gives joystick junkies their fix. Live music? **Glasslands**, **Zebulon**, **Pete's Candy Store**, or **Music Hall** should do it for ya. And if you want to listen at home, stop by **Earwax**, **Academy Annex**, or **Soundfix**.

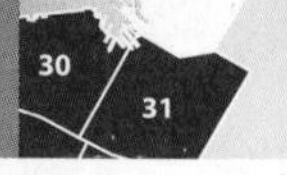

Nightlife

- **Barcade** • 388 Union Ave [Ainslie St]
- **Bembe** • 81 S 6th St [Berry St]
- **Berry Park** • 4 Berry St [N 14th St]
- **Bruar Falls** • 245 Grand St [Roebling St]
- **Clem's** • 264 Grand St [Roebling St]
- **Daddy's** • 437 Graham Ave [Frost St]
- **East River Bar** • 97 S 6th St [Berry St]
- **Glasslands Gallery** • 289 Kent Ave [S 2nd St]
- **Greenpoint Tavern** • 188 Bedford Ave [N 7th]
- **Hotel Delmano** • 82 Berry St [N 9th St]
- **Huckleberry Bar** • 588 Grand St [Lorimer St]
- **Iona** • 180 Grand St [Bedford Ave]
- **Knitting Factory Brooklyn** • 361 Metropolitan Ave [Havemeyer St]
- **Larry Lawrence** • 295 Grand St [Havemeyer]
- **The Levee** • 212 Berry St [Metropolitan Ave]
- **Music Hall of Williamsburg** • 66 N 6th St [Kent]
- **Nita Nita** • 146 Wythe Ave [N 8th St]
- **Pete's Candy Store** • 709 Lorimer St [Richardson]
- **Public Assembly** • 70 N 6th St [Wythe Ave]
- **Radegast Hall** • 113 N 3rd St [Berry St]
- **Rose** • 345 Grand St [Havemeyer St]
- **Spuyten Duyvil** • 359 Metropolitan Ave [Havemeyer St]
- **Trash** • 256 Grand St [Roebling St]
- **Turkey's Nest** • 94 Bedford Ave [N 12th St]
- **Union Pool** • 484 Union Ave [Rodney St]
- **Zebulon** • 258 Wythe Ave [N 3rd St]

Restaurants

- **Acqua Santa** • 556 Driggs Ave [N 7th St]
- **Baci & Abbracci** • 204 Grand St [Driggs Ave]
- **Bakeri** • 150 Wythe Ave [N 8th St]
- **Banh Mi** • 172 Bedford Ave [N 7th St]
- **Blackbird Parlour** • 197 Bedford Ave [N 6th St]
- **Bozu** • 296 Grand St [Havemeyer St]
- **The Brooklyn Star** • 33 Havemeyer St [N 8th]
- **Diner** • 85 Broadway [Berry St]
- **Dressler** • 149 Broadway [Bedford Ave]
- **DuMont** • 432 Union Ave [Devoe St]
- **Egg** • 135 N 5th St [Bedford Ave]
- **Fette Sau** • 354 Metropolitan Ave [Roebling St]
- **Fiore** • 284 Grand St [Roebling St]
- **Juliette** • 135 N 5th St [Bedford Ave]
- **La Superior** • 295 Berry St [S 2nd St]
- **Le Barricou** • 533 Grand St [Union Ave]
- **Marlow & Sons** • 81 Broadway [Berry St]
- **Northside Bakery** • 149 N 8th St [Bedford Ave]
- **Oasis** • 161 N 7th St [Bedford Ave]
- **Peter Luger Steak House** • 178 Broadway [Driggs Ave]
- **Relish** • 225 Wythe St [N 3rd St]
- **Roebling Tea Room** • 143 Roebling St [Metropolitan Ave]
- **Rye** • 247 S 1st St [Roebling St]
- **Shachi's** • 197 Havemeyer St [S 4th St]
- **Teddy's Bar and Grill** • 96 Berry St [N 8th St]
- **Vinnie's** • 148 Bedford Ave [N 9th St]
- **Walter Foods** • 253 Grand St [Roebling St]
- **Yola's Café** • 524 Metropolitan Ave [Union Ave]
- **Zenkichi** • 77 N 6th St [Wythe Ave]

Shopping

- **Academy Annex** • 96 N 6th St [Wythe Ave]
- **Amarcord** • 223 Bedford Ave [N 4th St]
- **Beacon's Closet** • 88 N 11th St [Wythe Ave]
- **Bedford Cheese Shop** • 229 Bedford Ave [N 5th]
- **The Brooklyn Kitchen** • 100 Frost St [Meeker]
- **Buffalo Exchange** • 504 Driggs Ave [N 9th St]
- **Built By Wendy** • 46 N 6th St [Kent Ave]
- **Earwax Records** • 218 Bedford Ave [N 5th St]
- **Emily's Pork Store** • 426 Graham Ave [Withers]
- **Future Perfect** • 115 N 6th St [Berry St]
- **KCDC Skateshop** • 90 N 11th St [Wythe Ave]
- **Marlow & Daughters** • 95 Broadway [Berry St]
- **The Mini-Market** • 218 Bedford Ave [N 5th St]
- **Roulette** • 188 Havemeyer St [S 3rd St]
- **Savino's Quality Pasta** • 111 Conselyea St [Manhattan Ave]
- **Sodafine** • 119 Grand St [Berry St]
- **Sound Fix Records** • 44 Berry St [N 11th St]
- **Spoonbill & Sugartown** • 218 Bedford Ave [N 5th St]
- **Sprout** • 44 Grand St [Kent Ave]
- **Spuyten Duyvil Grocery** • 132 N 5th St [Bedford]
- **Treehouse** • 430 Graham Ave [Frost St]
- **Two Jakes** • 320 Wythe Ave [Grand St]
- **Ugly Luggage** • 214 Bedford Ave [N 5th St]
- **Uva Wines** • 199 Bedford Ave [N 5th St]
- **Whisk** • 231 Bedford Ave [N 3rd St]

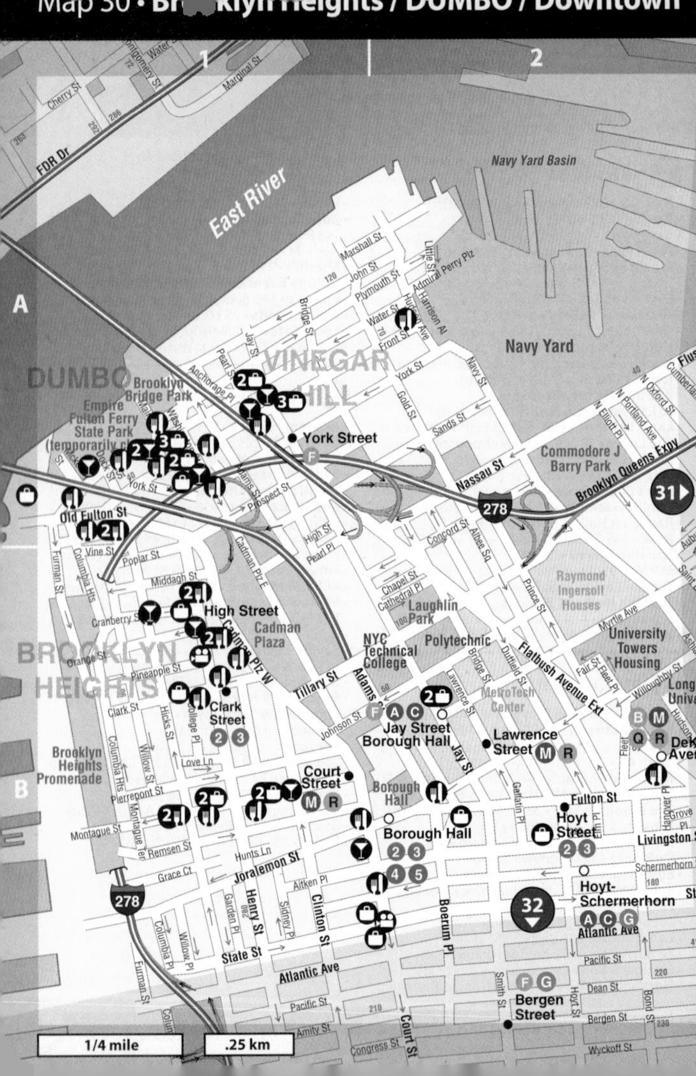
1
2
A
B
East River
Navy Yard Basin
Navy Yard
DUMBO
VINEGAR HILL
Brooklyn Bridge Park
Empire Fulton Ferry State Park (temporarily c
Commodore J Barry Park
Raymond Ingersoll Houses
University Towers Housing
Cadman Plaza
Laughlin Park
NYC Technical College
Polytechnic
MetroTech Center
BROOKLYN HEIGHTS
Brooklyn Heights Promenade
Borough Hall
York Street
High Street
Clark Street
Jay Street Borough Hall
Lawrence Street
Court Street
Borough Hall
Hoyt Street
Hoyt-Schermerhorn
Bergen Street
DeKalb Ave
FDR Dr
Cherry St
Water St
Montgomery St
Marginal St
Old Fulton St
Furman St
Columbia Hts
Vine St
Poplar St
Middagh St
Cranberry St
Orange St
Pineapple St
Clark St
Hicks St
Willow St
College Pl
Love Ln
Pierrepont St
Montague St
Montague Ter
Remsen St
Hunts Ln
Grace Ct
Joralemon St
Garden Pl
Henry St
Sidney Pl
Clinton St
Aitken Pl
State St
Atlantic Ave
Pacific St
Amity St
Congress St
Court St
Boerum Pl
Columbia Pl
Willow Pl
Smith St
Hoyt St
Bond St
Dean St
Bergen St
Wyckoff St
Schermerhorn St
Livingston St
Fulton St
Elm Pl
Gallatin Pl
Jay St
Lawrence St
Bridge St
Duffield St
Flatbush Avenue Ext
Fair St
Fleet Pl
Fleet St
Willoughby St
Myrtle Ave
Hanover Pl
Grove Pl
Hudson Ave
Ashland Pl
Saint Edwards St
Auburn Pl
Prince St
Albee Sq
Concord St
Chapel St
Cathedral Pl
Tillary St
Adams St
Johnson St
Cadman Plz W
Cadman Plz E
High St
Pearl Pl
Prospect St
York St
Dock St
Washington St
Main St
Anchorage Pl
Pearl St
Jay St
Bridge St
Marshall St
John St
Plymouth St
Water St
Front St
York St
Gold St
Navy St
Sands St
Nassau St
Hudson Ave
Little St
Admiral Perry Plz
Harrison Al
Brooklyn Queens Expy
N Elliott Pl
N Portland Ave
N Oxford St
Cumberland
Flushing
278
31
32
1/4 mile
.25 km

Entertainment

Old-world **Henry's End** is at the top of our list for food, but also check out ultrahip **Superfine**, good slices at **Fascati**, and posh gastropub **Jack the Horse**. For culture, **St. Ann's** is the place. For chocolate, two words: **Jacques Torres**. When Tim and Jason move in together, they accessorize at **West Elm**. The **Pavilion** is one our our favorite small movie theaters.

Movie Theaters

- **Pavilion Brooklyn Heights** • 70 Henry St [Orange St]
- **Regal Court Street Stadium 12** • 108 Court St [State St]

Nightlife

- **68 Jay Street Bar** • 68 Jay St [Front St]
- **Eamonn's** • 174 Montague St [Clinton St]
- **Galapagos Art Space** • 16 Main St [Water St]
- **Henry Street Ale House** • 62 Henry St [Cranberry St]
- **Jack the Horse Tavern** • 66 Hicks St [Cranberry St]
- **O'Keefe's** • 62 Court St [Livingston St]
- **reBar** • 147 Front St [Pearl St]
- **Speak Low** • 81 Washington St [York St]
- **St Ann's Warehouse** • 38 Water St [Dock St]
- **Water Street Bar** • 66 Water St [Main St]

Restaurants

- **Bubby's** • 1 Main St [Plymouth St]
- **DUMBO General Store** • 111 Front St [Adams St]
- **Fascati Pizzeria** • 80 Henry St [Orange St]
- **Five Front** • 5 Front St [Old Fulton St]
- **Five Guys** • 138 Montague St [Henry St]
- **Grimaldi's** • 19 Old Fulton St [Doughty St]
- **Hale & Hearty Soup** • 32 Court St [Remsen St]
- **Heights Café** • 84 Montague St [Hicks St]
- **Henry's End** • 44 Henry St [Middagh St]
- **Iron Chef House** • 92 Clark St [Monroe Pl]
- **Jack the Horse Tavern** • 66 Hicks St [Cranberry St]
- **Junior's Restaurant** • 386 Flatbush Avenue Ext [St Johns Pl]
- **Lantern Thai** • 101 Montague St [Hicks St]
- **Miso** • 40 Main St [Front St]
- **Morton's the Steakhouse** • 399 Adams St [Willoughby St]
- **Noodle Pudding** • 38 Henry St [Middagh St]
- **Park Plaza Restaurant** • 220 Cadman Plaza W [Clark St]
- **Pete's Downtown** • 2 Water St [Old Fulton St]
- **Queen Ristorante** • 84 Court St [Livingston St]
- **Rice** • 81 Washington St [York St]
- **River Café** • 1 Water St [Old Fulton St]
- **Siggy's Good Food** • 76 Henry St [Orange St]
- **Superfine** • 126 Front St [Pearl St]
- **Sushi Gallery** • 71 Clark St [Henry St]
- **Teresa's** • 80 Montague St [Hicks St]
- **Toro Restaurant** • 1 Front St [Old Fulton St]
- **Vinegar Hill House** • 72 Hudson Ave [Water St]

Shopping

- **Almondine Bakery** • 85 Water St [Main St]
- **Barnes & Noble** • 106 Court St [State St]
- **Bridge Fresh Market** • 68 Jay St [Water St]
- **Brooklyn Ice Cream Factory** • 1 Water St [Old Fulton St]
- **Cranberry's** • 48 Henry St [Cranberry St]
- **Design Within Reach** • 76 Montague St [Hicks St]
- **Egg Organics** • 68 Jay St [Water St]
- **Halcyon** • 57 Pearl St [Water St]
- **Half Pint** • 55 Washington St [Front St]
- **Heights Prime Meats** • 59 Clark St [Henry St]
- **Housing Works-Brooklyn Thrift Shop** • 122 Montague St [Henry St]
- **Jacques Torres Chocolate** • 66 Water St [Main]
- **Lassen & Hennigs** • 114 Montague St [Henry]
- **Macy's** • 422 Fulton St [Hoyt St]
- **Modell's** • 360 Fulton St [Red Hook Ln]
- **Montague Street Video** • 138 Montague St [Clinton St]
- **Peas & Pickles** • 55 Washington St [Front St]
- **Pomme** • 81 Washington St [York St]
- **powerHouse Arena** • 37 Main St [Water St]
- **Recycle-A-Bicycle** • 35 Pearl St [Plymouth St]
- **Sid's Hardware & Homecenter** • 345 Jay St [Myrtle Prom]
- **Stewart/Stand** • 165 Front St [Jay St]
- **Super Runners Shop** • 123 Court St [State St]
- **Tango** • 145 Montague St [Henry St]
- **TKTS Booth** • 1 Metrotech Center [Johnson St]
- **West Elm** • 75 Front St [Main St]

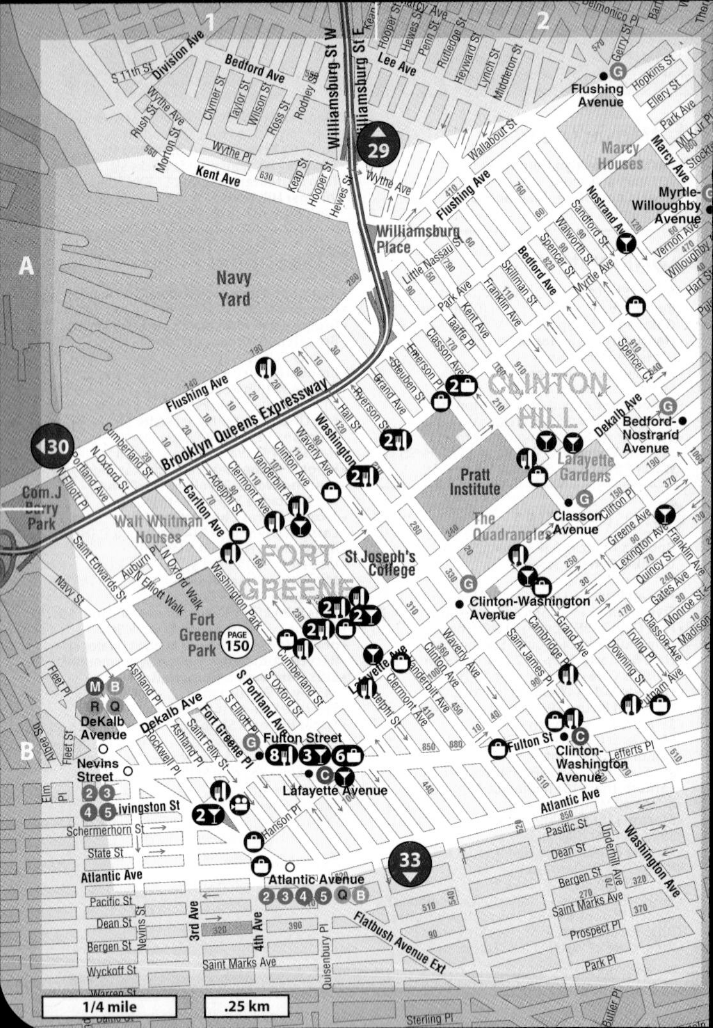

Navy Yard
Williamsburg Place
Clinton Hill
Fort Greene
Pratt Institute
The Quadrangles
Lafayette Gardens
St Joseph's College
Fort Greene Park
PAGE 150
Walt Whitman Houses
Marcy Houses
Com.J Barry Park
Brooklyn Queens Expressway
Flushing Avenue
Myrtle-Willoughby Avenue
Bedford-Nostrand Avenue
Classon Avenue
Clinton-Washington Avenue
Fulton Street
Lafayette Avenue
DeKalb Avenue
Nevins Street
Atlantic Avenue
Flushing Ave
Kent Ave
Wythe Ave
Division Ave
Bedford Ave
Lee Ave
Myrtle Ave
Dekalb Ave
Fulton St
Atlantic Ave
Washington Ave
Flatbush Avenue Ext
Livingston St
Schermerhorn St
State St
Pacific St
Dean St
Bergen St
Saint Marks Ave
Wyckoff St
Warren St
Prospect Pl
Park Pl
Sterling Pl
3rd Ave
4th Ave
1/4 mile
.25 km

Entertainment

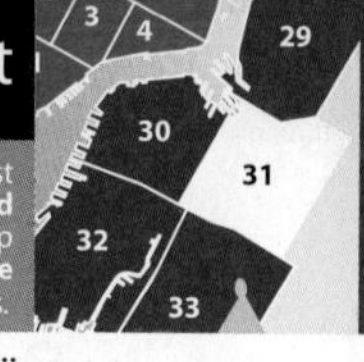

Choice Greene & **Greene Grape's** great gourmet food selections have just raised rents here. Otherwise, head for cool eats and Afro beats at **Grand Dakar**, friendly French at **Chez Oskar**, pre-BAM hipness at **No. 7**, killer cheap Mexican at **Castro's**, posh Italian at **Locanda**, and short rib heaven at **Smoke Joint**. **Frank's**, **Moe's**, **The Alibi**, and **Rope** are all good local watering holes.

Movie Theaters

- **BAM Rose Cinemas** • 30 Lafayette Ave [St Felix St]

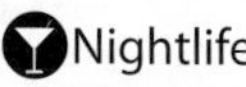

Nightlife

- **The Alibi** • 242 Dekalb Ave [Vanderbilt Ave]
- **BAMcafé** • 30 Lafayette Ave [Ashland Pl]
- **Brooklyn Masonic Temple** • 317 Clermont Ave [Lafayette Ave]
- **Brooklyn Public House** • 247 Dekalb Ave [Vanderbilt Ave]
- **Der Schwarze Kolner** • 710 Fulton St [S Oxford St]
- **Frank's Cocktail Lounge** • 660 Fulton St [S Elliott Pl]
- **Grand Dakar** • 285 Grand Ave [Clifton Pl]
- **Moe's** • 80 Lafayette Ave [S Portland Ave]
- **Navy Yard Cocktail Lounge** • 200 Flushing Ave [Waverly Ave]
- **Project Parlor** • 742 Myrtle Ave [Sanford St]
- **Rope** • 415 Myrtle Ave [Clinton Ave]
- **Rustik** • 471 Dekalb Ave [Franklin Ave]
- **Sputnik** • 262 Taaffe Pl [DeKalb Ave]
- **Stonehome Wine Bar** • 87 Lafayette Ave [S Portland Ave]
- **Sweet Revenge** • 348 Franklin Ave [Lexington Ave]
- **Thomas Beisl** • 25 Lafayette Ave [Ashland Pl]

Restaurants

- **67 Burger** • 67 Lafayette Ave [S Elliott Pl]
- **abistro** • 154 Carlton Ave [Myrtle Ave]
- **Bati** • 747 Fulton St [S Portland Ave]
- **Black Iris** • 228 Dekalb Ave [Clermont Ave]
- **Cafe Lafayette** • 99 S Portland Ave [Fulton St]
- **Castro's Restaurant** • 511 Myrtle Ave [Grand]
- **Chez Lola** • 387 Myrtle Ave [Clermont Ave]
- **Chez Oskar** • 211 Dekalb Ave [Adelphi St]
- **Choice Market** • 318 Lafayette Ave [Grand]
- **Five Spot** • 495 Myrtle Ave [Ryerson St]
- **The General Greene** • 229 Dekalb Ave [Clerrmont Ave]
- **Habana Outpost** • 757 Fulton St [S Portland]
- **Ici** • 246 Dekalb Ave [Vanderbilt Ave]
- **Il Porto** • 37 Washington Ave [Flushing Ave]
- **Kif** • 219 Dekalb Ave [Adelphi St]
- **Kush** • 17 Putnam Ave [Grand Ave]
- **Locanda Vini & Olii** • 129 Gates Ave [Cambridge Pl]
- **Luz** • 177 Vanderbilt Ave [Myrtle Ave]
- **Madiba** • 195 Dekalb Ave [Carlton Ave]
- **Maggie Brown** • 455 Myrtle Ave [Washington]
- **Night of the Cookers** • 767 Fulton St [S Oxford]
- **No. 7** • 7 Greene Ave [Fulton St]
- **Olea** • 171 Lafayette Ave [Adelphi St]
- **Scopello** • 63 Lafayette Ave [S Elliott Pl]
- **The Smoke Joint** • 87 S Elliot Pl [Lafayette Ave]
- **Soule** • 920 Fulton St [Washington Ave]
- **Thomas Beisl** • 25 Lafayette Ave [Ashland Pl]
- **Umi Nom** • 433 Dekalb Ave [Classon Ave]
- **Yamashiro** • 466 Myrtle Ave [Washington Ave]

Shopping

- **Bargains R Us** • 976 Fulton St [Grand Ave]
- **Bespoke Bicycles** • 64 Lafayette Ave [S Elliott]
- **Blue Bass Vintage** • 431 Dekalb Ave [Classon]
- **Brooklyn Flea** • 176 Lafayette Ave [Clermont]
- **Cake Man Raven Confectionary** • 708 Fulton St [Hanson Pl]
- **Choice Greene** • 214 Greene Ave [Grand Ave]
- **Dope Jams** • 580 Myrtle Ave [Classon Ave]
- **Gnarly Vines** • 350 Myrtle Ave [Carlton Ave]
- **Green in BKLYN** • 432 Myrtle Ave [Clinton]
- **The Greene Grape** • 765 Fulton St [S Oxford]
- **Greene Grape Provisions** • 753 Fulton St [S Portland Ave]
- **Greenlight Bookstore** • 686 Fulton St [S Portland Ave]
- **Lit Fuse Cyclery** • 409 Willoughby Ave [Walworth St]
- **Malchijah Hats** • 225 Dekalb Ave [Clermont]
- **The Midtown Greenhouse Garden Center** • 115 Flatbush Ave [Hanson Pl]
- **Olivino** • 905 Fulton St [Clinton Ave]
- **Pratt Institute Bookstore** • 550 Myrtle Ave [Emerson Pl]
- **Sister's Community Hardware** • 900 Fulton St [Washington Ave]
- **Target** • 139 Flatbush Ave [Atlantic Ave]
- **Thirst Wine Merchants** • 187 Dekalb Ave [Carlton Ave]
- **White Elephant Gallery** • 572 Myrtle Ave [Classon Ave]
- **Yu Interiors** • 15 Greene Ave [Cumberland St]

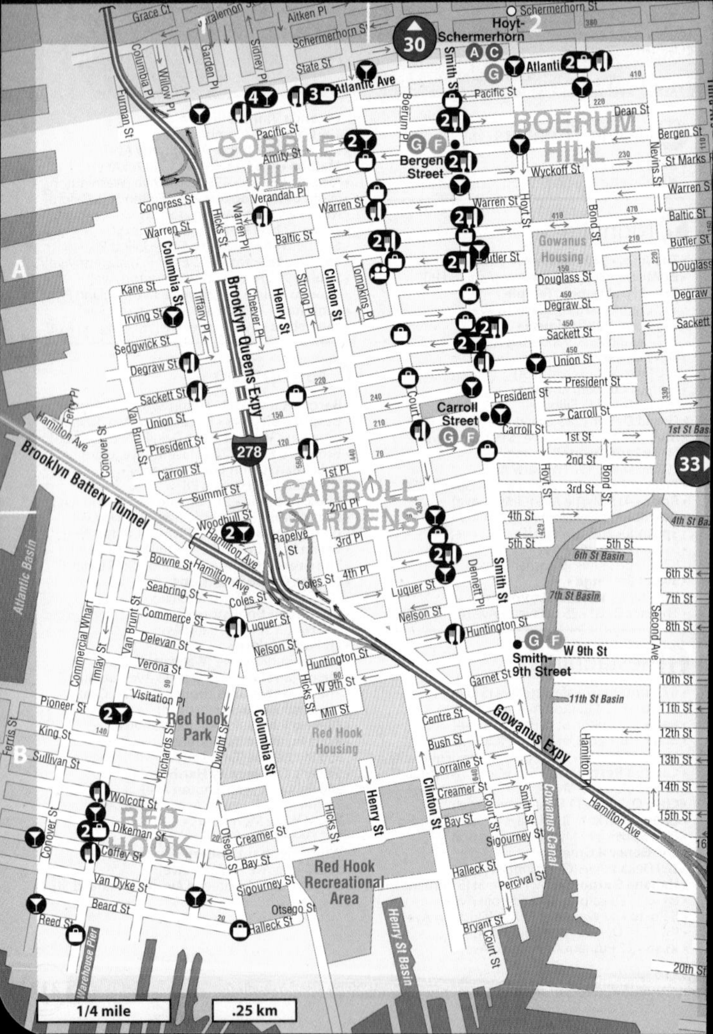

COBBLE HILL
BOERUM HILL
CARROLL GARDENS
RED HOOK
Hoyt-Schermerhorn
Bergen Street
Carroll Street
Smith-9th Street
Brooklyn Queens Expy
278
Brooklyn Battery Tunnel
Gowanus Expy
Gowanus Canal
Gowanus Housing
Red Hook Park
Red Hook Housing
Red Hook Recreational Area
Atlantic Basin
Henry St Basin
Warehouse Pier
1st St Basin
4th St Basin
6th St Basin
7th St Basin
11th St Basin
30
33
Grace Ct
Aitken Pl
Schermerhorn St
State St
Atlantic Ave
Pacific St
Amity St
Dean St
Bergen St
St Marks
Wyckoff St
Verandah Pl
Congress St
Warren St
Baltic St
Butler St
Douglass St
Degraw St
Sackett St
Union St
President St
Carroll St
1st St
2nd St
3rd St
4th St
5th St
6th St
7th St
8th St
W 9th St
10th St
11th St
12th St
13th St
14th St
15th St
20th St
Kane St
Irving St
Sedgwick St
Summit St
Woodhull St
Rapelye St
1st Pl
2nd Pl
3rd Pl
4th Pl
Luquer St
Nelson St
Huntington St
Garnet St
Bowne St
Seabring St
Commerce St
Delevan St
Verona St
Visitation Pl
Pioneer St
King St
Sullivan St
Wolcott St
Dikeman St
Coffey St
Van Dyke St
Beard St
Reed St
Creamer St
Bay St
Sigourney St
Otsego St
Halleck St
Centre St
Bush St
Lorraine St
Percival St
Bryant St
Mill St
Coles St
Hamilton Ave
Furman St
Columbia Pl
Willow Pl
Garden Pl
Sidney Pl
Boerum Pl
Smith St
Hoyt St
Bond St
Nevins St
Columbia St
Hicks St
Warren Pl
Tiffany Pl
Cheever Pl
Henry St
Strong Pl
Clinton St
Tompkins Pl
Court St
Dennett Pl
Van Brunt St
Conover St
Ferry Pl
Commercial Wharf
Imlay St
Richards St
Dwight St
Ferris St
Second Ave
1/4 mile
.25 km

Nightlife? Head for **Boat** (jukebox), **Brooklyn Inn** (classic), **Brooklyn Social** (cool), or **Sunny's** (dive). Restaurants? Hit **Alma** (Mexican), **Char No. 4** (hip), **Ferdinando's** (Sicilian), **Frankie's** (brunch), **Po** (Italian), and **Quercy** (French). Shopping? **D'Amico's** (coffee), **Stinky** (cheese), **Staubitz** (meat), **Swallow** (beautiful stuff), and **Sahadi's** (imports). Full yet?

32
33
Prospe

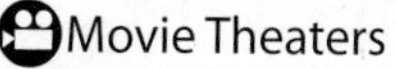

Movie Theaters

- **Cobble Hill Cinemas** • 265 Court St [Butler St]

Nightlife

- **Abilene** • 442 Court St [3rd Pl]
- **Bar Great Harry** • 280 Smith St [Sackett St]
- **Black Mountain** • 415 Union St [Hoyt St]
- **Boat** • 175 Smith St [Wyckoff St]
- **Botanica** • 220 Conover St [Coffey St]
- **Brazen Head** • 228 Atlantic Ave [Court St]
- **Brooklyn Inn** • 148 Hoyt St [Bergen St]
- **Brooklyn Social** • 335 Smith St [Carroll St]
- **Building on Bond** • 112 Bond St [Pacific St]
- **Clover Club** • 210 Smith St [Baltic St]
- **Cody's** • 154 Court St [Dean St]
- **Downtown Bar & Grill** • 160 Court St [Amity]
- **Floyd** • 131 Atlantic Ave [Henry St]
- **Fort Defiance** • 365 Van Brunt St [Dikeman St]
- **Gowanus Yacht Club** • 323 Smith St [President]
- **Henry Public** • 329 Henry St [Atlantic Ave]
- **home/made** • 293 Van Brunt St [Pioneer St]
- **The Jakewalk** • 282 Smith St [Sackett St]
- **Jalopy** • 315 Columbia St [Hamilton Ave]
- **Kili** • 81 Hoyt St [State St]
- **Last Exit** • 136 Atlantic Ave [Henry St]
- **Montero's Bar and Grill** • 73 Atlantic Ave [Hicks]
- **Moonshine** • 317 Columbia St [Hamilton Ave]
- **PJ Hanley's** • 449 Court St [4th Pl]
- **Red Hook Bait & Tackle** • 320 Van Brunt St [Pioneer St]
- **Rocky Sullivan's** • 34 Van Dyke St [Dwight St]
- **Sugar Lounge** • 147 Columbia St [Irving St]
- **Sunny's** • 253 Conover St [Reed St]
- **Waterfront Ale House** • 155 Atlantic Ave [Clinton]

Restaurants

- **Alma** • 187 Columbia St [Degraw St]
- **Atlantic Chip Shop** • 129 Atlantic Ave [Henry]
- **Bar Tabac** • 128 Smith St [Dean St]
- **Bedouin Tent** • 405 Atlantic Ave [Bond St]
- **Bocca Lupo** • 391 Henry St [Warren St]
- **Buttermilk Channel** • 524 Court [Huntington]
- **Caserta Vecchia** • 221 Smith St [Butler St]
- **Chance** • 223 Smith St [Butler St]
- **Char No. 4** • 196 Smith St [Baltic St]
- **Chestnut** • 271 Smith St [Degraw St]
- **DeFonte's Sandwich Shop** • 379 Columbia St [Luquer St]
- **Ferdinando's Focacceria** • 151 Union St [Hicks]
- **Fragole** • 394 Court St [Carroll St]
- **Frankie's 457** • 457 Court St [Luquer St]
- **The Good Fork** • 391 Van Brunt St [Coffey St]
- **The Grocery** • 288 Smith St [Sackett St]
- **Hadramout** • 172 Atlantic Ave [Clinton St]
- **Hanco's** • 85 Bergen St [Smith St]
- **Hope & Anchor** • 347 Van Brunt St [Wolcott]
- **Joya** • 215 Court St [Warren St]
- **Ki Sushi** • 122 Smith St [Dean St]
- **Lucali** • 575 Henry St [Carroll St]
- **Po** • 276 Smith St [Sackett St]
- **Quercy** • 242 Court St [Baltic St]
- **Saul** • 140 Smith St [Bergen St]
- **Sherwood Café/Robin des Bois** • 195 Smith St [Warren St]
- **South Brooklyn Pizza** • 451 Court St [4th Pl]
- **Watty & Meg** • 248 Court St [Kane St]

Shopping

- **A Cook's Companion** • 197 Atlantic Ave [Court]
- **American Beer Distributors** • 256 Court St [Kane St]
- **Blue Marble** • 420 Atlantic Ave [Bond St]
- **Butter** • 389 Atlantic Ave [Bond St]
- **Caputo's Fine Foods** • 460 Court St [3rd Pl]
- **D'Amico Foods** • 309 Court St [Degraw St]
- **Dear Fieldbinder** • 198 Smith St [Baltic St]
- **Enamoo** • 109 Smith St [Pacific St]
- **Environment337** • 337 Smith St [Carroll St]
- **Erie Basin** • 388 Van Brunt St [Dikeman St]
- **Exit 9** • 127 Smith St [Dean St]
- **Fairway** • 480 Van Brunt St [Reed St]
- **Fish Tales** • 191 Court St [Wyckoff St]
- **Flight 001** • 132 Smith St [Dean St]
- **G Esposito & Sons** • 357 Court St [President]
- **Ikea** • 1 Beard St [Otsego St]
- **Malko Karkanni Bros.** • 174 Atlantic [Clinton]
- **Mazzola Bakery** • 192 Union St [Henry St]
- **Metal and Thread** • 398 Van Brunt St [Coffey]
- **Sahadi Importing Company** • 187 Atlantic Ave [Court St]
- **Smith & Vine** • 268 Smith St [Douglass St]
- **Staubitz Meat Market** • 222 Court St [Baltic]
- **Stinky** • 261 Smith St [Degraw St]
- **Swallow** • 361 Smith St [2nd St]

PROSPECT HEIGHTS

PARK SLOPE

WINDSOR TERRACE

Atlantic Avenue

Pacific Street

Bergen Street

7th Avenue

Grand Army Plaza

Union Street

4th Avenue-9th Street

7th Avenue

15th Street-Prospect Park

Prospect Avenue

Brooklyn Botanic Garden

Prospect Park

Flatbush Ave

Atlantic Ave

Pacific St

Dean St

Bergen St

St Mark's Pl

Prospect Pl

Park Pl

Sterling Pl

St Johns Pl

Lincoln Pl

Berkeley Pl

Union St

President St

Carroll St

Garfield Pl

1st St

2nd St

3rd St

4th St

5th St

6th St

7th St

8th St

9th St

10th St

11th St

12th St

13th St

14th St

15th St

16th St

17th St

18th St

Warren St

Baltic St

Butler St

Douglass St

Degraw St

Sackett St

Third Ave

Fourth Ave

Fifth Ave

Sixth Ave

Seventh Ave

Eighth Ave

Carlton Ave

Vanderbilt Ave

Washington Ave

Grand Ave

Underhill Ave

Butler Pl

Plaza St E

Grand Army Plz

Quisenbury Pl

Whitwell Pl

Denton Pl

Polhemus Pl

Fiske Pl

Montgomery Pl

Prospect Park W

Prospect Park SW

West Dr

East Dr

W Lake Dr

Prospect Expy

Prospect Ave

Windsor Pl

Webster Pl

Jackson Pl

Calder Pl

Tenth Ave

Howard Pl

Fuller Pl

Sherman St

11th Ave

Hamilton Ave

State St

1st St Basin

4th St Basin

Nevins St

1/4 mile

.25 km

As if 7th and 5th Avenues didn't have enough already, now 4th (**Sheep Station**, **Cherry Tree**, etc.) gets into the act. Top food abounds—**Applewood**, **Franny's**, **Blue Ribbon**, **Stone Park**—as does great nabe hangouts **Beast**, **The Gate**, and **Flatbush Farm**. For live acts, head to **Barbes**, **Southpaw**, and **Union Hall**.

Nightlife

- **Bar Toto** • 411 11th St [6th Ave]
- **Barbes** • 376 9th St [6th Ave]
- **Beast** • 638 Bergen St [Vanderbilt Ave]
- **Beer Table** • 427 7th Ave [14th St]
- **The Bell House** • 149 7th St [3rd Ave]
- **Black Horse Pub** • 568 5th Ave [16th St]
- **Buttermilk Bar** • 577 5th Ave [16th St]
- **Canal Bar** • 270 3rd Ave [President St]
- **Cherry Tree** • 65 4th Ave [Bergen St]
- **Commonwealth** • 497 5th Ave [12th St]
- **Cornelius** • 565 Vanderbilt Ave [Pacific St]
- **Draft Barn** • 530 3rd Ave [13th St]
- **Flatbush Farm** • 76 St Marks Ave [6th Ave]
- **Freddy's Bar and Backroom** • 485 Dean St [6th Ave]
- **The Gate** • 321 5th Ave [3rd St]
- **Great Lakes** • 284 5th Ave [1st St]
- **Hank's Saloon** • 46 3rd Ave [Atlantic Ave]
- **Issue Project Room** • 232 3rd St [3rd Ave]
- **littlefield** • 622 Degraw St [4th Ave]
- **Loki Lounge** • 304 5th Ave [2nd St]
- **O'Connor's** • 39 5th Ave [Bergen St]
- **Pacific Standard** • 82 4th Ave [St Marks Pl]
- **Park Slope Ale House** • 356 6th Ave [5th St]
- **Patio Lounge** • 179 5th Ave [Berkeley Pl]
- **Puppet's Jazz Bar** • 481 5th Ave [11th St]
- **Soda** • 629 Vanderbilt Ave [Prospect Pl]
- **Southpaw** • 125 5th Ave [Sterling Pl]
- **Starlite Lounge** • 1084 Bergen St [Flatbush]
- **Tavern on Dean** • 755 Dean St [Underhill Ave]
- **Union Hall** • 702 Union St [5th Ave]
- **Washington Commons** • 748 Washington Ave [Park Pl]

Restaurants

- **12th Street Bar and Grill** • 1123 8th Ave [11th St]
- **Al Di La Trattoria** • 248 5th Ave [Carroll St]
- **Applewood** • 501 11th St [7th Ave]
- **Beast** • 638 Bergen St [Vanderbilt Ave]
- **Belleville** • 332 5th Ave [3rd St]
- **Blue Ribbon Brooklyn** • 280 5th Ave [1st St]
- **Brooklyn Fish Camp** • 162 5th Ave [Douglass St]
- **Cheryl's Global Soul** • 236 Underhill Ave [Lincoln Pl]
- **ChipShop** • 383 5th Ave [6th St]
- **Convivium Osteria** • 68 5th Ave [St Marks Pl]
- **Flatbush Farm** • 76 St Marks Ave [6th Ave]
- **Franny's** • 295 Flatbush Ave [Prospect Pl]
- **Gen Restaurant** • 659 Washington Ave [St Marks Ave]
- **Ghenet** • 348 Douglass St [4th Ave]
- **Hanco's** • 350 7th Ave [10th St]
- **Jpan Sushi** • 287 5th Ave [1st St]
- **La Taqueria** • 72 7th Ave [Berkeley Pl]
- **Moim** • 206 Garfield Pl [7th Ave]
- **Nana** • 155 5th Ave [Lincoln Pl]
- **Rawstar Vegan Live Cuisine** • 687 Washington Ave [Prospect Pl]
- **Rose Water** • 787 Union St [6th Ave]
- **Scalino** • 347 7th Ave [10th St]
- **Sheep Station** • 149 4th Ave [Douglass St]
- **Smiling Pizzeria** • 323 7th Ave [9th St]
- **Stone Park Cafe** • 324 5th Ave [3rd St]
- **Taro Sushi** • 446 Dean St [5th Ave]
- **Tom's** • 782 Washington Ave [Sterling Pl]
- **The V-Spot** • 156 5th Ave [Degraw St]
- **Watana** • 420 7th Ave [14th St]

Shopping

- **Beacon's Closet** • 92 5th Ave [Warren St]
- **Bierkraft** • 191 5th Ave [Union St]
- **Bklyn Larder** • 228 Flatbush Ave [Bergen St]
- **Blue Apron Foods** • 814 Union St [7th Ave]
- **Blue Marble Ice Cream** • 186 Underhill Ave [St Johns Pl]
- **Brooklyn Superhero Supply** • 372 5th Ave [5th St]
- **Clay Pot** • 162 7th Ave [Garfield Pl]
- **Cog and Pearl** • 190 5th Ave [Berkeley Pl]
- **Dixon's Bicycle Shop** • 792 Union St [7th Ave]
- **Grab** • 438 7th Ave [15th St]
- **Gureje** • 886 Pacific St [Underhill Ave]
- **JackRabbit Sports** • 151 7th Ave [Garfield Pl]
- **Leaf and Bean** • 83 7th Ave [Berkeley Pl]
- **Loom** • 115 7th Ave [President St]
- **Matter** • 227 5th Ave [President St]
- **Pie Shop** • 211 Prospect Park West [16th St]
- **Rare Device** • 453 7th Ave [16th St]
- **Razor** • 329 5th Ave [4th St]
- **Russo's Fresh Mozzarella** • 363 7th Ave [11th]
- **Stitch Therapy** • 335 5th Ave [4th St]
- **Under The Pig Collectibles** • 355 5th Ave [5th St]
- **United Meat Market** • 219 Prospect Park West [16th St]

HOBOKEN
Hoboken Historical Museum
Hoboken North Ferries
to Pier 78 38th St
Elysian Park
JFK Stadium
Columbus Park
Willow Terrace
Stevens Institute of Technology
Frank Sinatra's Childhood House Location
Church Square Park
Stevens Park
Hudson River
Pier A Park
Hoboken Terminal
PAGE 286
Hoboken South Ferries
To Pier 78 38th St
To Pier 11 Wall St
Hoboken
Hoboken - PATH, NJ Transit, Light Rail
PAGE 298
PATH
35
1/4 mile
.25 km
14th St
Viaduct
13th St
12th St
11th St
10th St
9th St
8th St
7th St
6th St
5th St
4th St
3rd St
2nd St
1st St
Newark St
Hudson Pl
Observer Hwy
Palisade Ave
S Wing Viaduct
Paterson Plank Rd
Paterson St
Newark Ave
Manila Ave
Luis M Marin Blvd
Harrison St
Jackson St
Monroe St
Madison St
Jefferson St
Adams St
Grand St
Clinton St
Willow Ave
Park Ave
Garden St
Bloomfield St
Washington St
Court St
Hudson St
Castle Point Ter
River St
Sinatra Dr

It's only a short trip from the Village by PATH or ferry, but Hoboken feels more like an upscale college town. The salty longshoremen have moved on to that great pier in the sky, or at least to a members-only social club in town, leaving the waterfront to parkland, luxury condos, and many, many yuppies. Best bets for explorers are the raw clams at **Biggies**, and beer and brats at **Helmer's**.

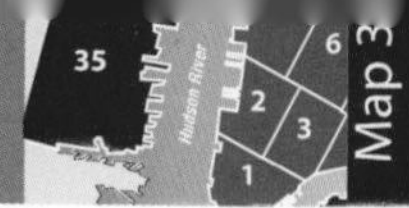

Landmarks

- **Elysian Park** • n/a
- **Frank Sinatra's Childhood House Location** • 415 Monroe St [4th St]
- **Hoboken Historical Museum** • 1301 Hudson St [13th St]
- **Hoboken Terminal** • 1 Hudson Pl [River St]
- **Willow Terrace** • 6th & 7th St b/w Willow Ave & Clinton St

Nightlife

- **City Bistro** • 56 14th St [Washington St]
- **Leo's Grandezvous** • 200 Grand St [2nd St]
- **Maxwell's** • 1039 Washington St [10th St]
- **Oddfellows** • 80 River St [Warren St]

Restaurants

- **Amanda's** • 908 Washington St [9th St]
- **Arthur's Tavern** • 237 Washington St [2nd St]
- **Baja** • 104 14th St [Washington St]
- **Bangkok City** • 335 Washington St [3rd St]
- **Biggie's Clam Bar** • 318 Madison St [3rd St]
- **Brass Rail** • 135 Washington St [1st St]
- **Far Side Bar & Grill** • 531 Washington St [5th St]
- **Gaslight** • 400 Adams St [4th St]
- **Helmer's** • 1036 Washington St [10th St]
- **Hoboken Gourmet Company** • 423 Washington St [4th St]
- **Karma Kafe** • 505 Washington St [5th St]
- **La Isla** • 104 Washington St [1st St]
- **Oddfellows Restaurant** • 80 River St [Warren St]
- **Robongi** • 520 Washington St [5th St]
- **Sushi Lounge** • 200 Hudson St [2nd St]
- **Trattoria Saporito** • 328 Washington St [3rd St]
- **Zafra** • 301 Willow Ave [3rd St]

Shopping

- **Big Fun Toys** • 602 Washington St [6th St]
- **City Paint & Hardware** • 130 Washington St [1st St]
- **Galatea** • 1224 Washington St [12th St]
- **Hoboken Farmboy** • 127 Washington St [1st St]
- **Kings Fresh Ideas** • 325 River St [3rd St]
- **Lisa's Italian Deli** • 901 Park Ave [9th St]
- **Peper** • 1028 Washington St [10th St]
- **Sparrow Wine and Liquor** • 1224 Shipyard Ln [12th St]
- **Sparrow Wine and Liquor** • 126 Washington St [1st St]
- **Tunes New & Used CDs** • 225 Washington St [2nd St]
- **Yes I Do** • 312 Washington St [3rd St]

34
17th St
16th St
15th St
14th St
13th St
18th St
Hoboken Ave
New Jersey Tpke
Coles St
Jersey Ave
Erie Ave
Grove St
78
Holland Tunnel
Hudson-Bergen Light Rail
Washington Blvd
North Blvd
Provost St
Newport Pkwy
11th St
10th St
9th St
Pavonia Ave
8th St
7th St
6th St
5th St
4th St
3rd St
2nd St
1st St
City Park
Hamilton Park
Hamilton Pl
Mc Williams Pl
Luis Munoz Marin Blvd
Court St
Mall Dr
Newport Center Mall
Newport
Pavonia/ Newport
Newport Ferries
River Dr
Division St
Brunswick St
Monmouth St
Manila Ave
Mary Benson Park
Thomas Gangemi Dr
PATH
PAGE 286
Harborside Ferries
Harsimus Cove
Metro Dr
Newark Ave
Maxwell St
Bay St
Christopher Columbus Dr
Powerhouse
Harborside
Harborside Shopping Complex
Warren St
Morgan St
Washington St
Grove Street
Steuben St
Wayne St
Mercer St
Montgomery St
York St
Bright St
Colden St
Varick St
Van Vorst Park
Barrow St
City Hall
PAGE 298
Exchange Place
Exchange Pl
Colgate
Colgate Ferry
Grand St
Greene St
Hudson St
Canal St
Hudson-Bergen Light Rail
Jersey Ave
Marin Blvd
Van Vorst St
Sussex St
Morris St
Essex St
Dudley St
Liberty Harbor Ferries
Hudson River
1/4 mile
.25 km
A
B

Jersey City has a siren song that lures dissatisfied New Yorkers to its mall-studded shores. First it came for the artists, then for our young families and yuppies. Next it came for our offices and suburbanites. Maybe you should start hanging out at **Marco and Pepe's** right now and be done with it. **White Mana's** is a bona fide landmark, after all, and we love **Morgan's** octopus platter, **Ibby's** falafel, and **Light Horse's** vibe.

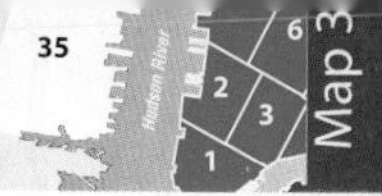

Landmarks

- **Colgate Clock** • 30 Hudson St [Essex St]
- **Harborside Shopping Complex** • n/a
- **Powerhouse** • 344 Washington St [Bay St]
- **White Mana** • 470 Tonnele Ave [Bleecker St]

Movie Theaters

- **AMC Loews Newport Center 11** • 30 Mall Dr W [Thomas Gangemi Dr]

Nightlife

- **Hamilton Park Ale House** • 708 Jersey Ave [10th St]
- **Lamp Post Bar and Grille** • 382 2nd St [Brunswick St]
- **LITM** • 140 Newark Ave [Grove St]
- **The Merchant** • 279 Grove St [Montgomery St]
- **PJ Ryan's** • 172 1st St [Luiz Munoz Marin Blvd]
- **White Star** • 230 Brunswick St [Pavonia Ave]

Restaurants

- **Amelia's Bistro** • 187 Warren St [Essex St]
- **Beechwood Cafe** • 290 Grove St [Mercer St]
- **Ibby's** • 303 Grove St [Wayne St]
- **Iron Monkey** • 97 Greene St [York St]
- **It's Greek to Me** • 194 Newark Ave [Jersey Ave]
- **Kitchen Café** • 60 Sussex St [Greene St]
- **Komegashi** • 103 Montgomery St [Warren St]
- **Komegashi Too** • 99 Pavonia Ave [River Dr S]
- **Light Horse Tavern** • 199 Washington St [Morris St]
- **Madame Claude** • 364 4th St [Brunswick St]
- **Marco and Pepe** • 289 Grove St [Mercer St]
- **Medina Restaurant** • 287 Grove St [Mercer St]
- **Morgan Seafood** • 2801 John F Kennedy Blvd [Sip Ave]
- **Presto's Restaurant** • 199 Warren St [Morris St]
- **Rosie Radigans** • 10 Exchange Pl, Lobby [Hudson St]
- **Saigon Café** • 188 Newark Ave [Jersey Ave]
- **Sri Ganesh** • 809 Newark Ave [Liberty Ave]
- **White Mana** • 470 Tonnele Ave [Bleecker St]

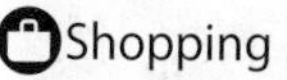

Shopping

- **Harborside Shopping Complex** • Exchange Pl
- **Newport Center Mall** • 30 Mall Dr W [Thomas Gangemi Dr]
- **Patel Snacks** • 785 Newark Ave [Herpert Pl]

Westchester
Woodlawn
Van Cortlandt Golf Course
Woodlawn Cemetery
Jerome Ave
Van Cortlandt Park
Mosholu Golf Course
Wave Hill
Riverdale Park
Riverdale
Kings-Bridge Heights
Harris Park
Marble Hill
Henry Hudson Bridge
Mosholu Pkwy
Norwood
Bedford Park
New York Botanical Garden
Fordham University
Bronx Park
Bronx Zoo
Belmont
East Tremont
Tremont
University Heights
University Heights Bridge
Major Deegan Expy
Webster Ave
Bronx River Pkwy
White Plains Rd
Wakefield
E 233rd St
Baychester Ave
Seton Falls Park
Williamsbridge
Gun Hill Rd
Boston Rd
BRONX
Bronx and Pelham Expwy
Morris Park
Williams Bridge Rd
E Tremont Ave
Parkchester
Westchester
Cross Bronx Expy
New England Thwy
Hutchinson River Pkwy
Shore Rd
Pelham Bay Park
Hunters Island
Rodman Neck
Eastchester
Co-Op City
Haften Park
Baychester
Bruckner Expy
Pelham Bay
St Raymond's Cemetery
Ferry Point Park
Castle Hill
Castle Hill Ave
Locombe Ave
Clason Point
Soundview
Sound View Park
Bronx River
Bronx Whitestone Bridge
West Farms
Sheridan Expy
Crotona Park
Claremont Park
Claremont Village
Morrisania
Boston Rd
Third Ave
Grand Concourse
Morris Heights
Washington Bridge
Hamilton Bridge
Henry Hudson Pkwy
Hudson River
E 161 St
Yankee Stadium
Macombs Dam Bridge
E 149th St
Longwood
St Mary's Park
Mott Haven
Westchester Ave
Bruckner Blvd
Bruckner Expy
Hunts Point
Riker's Island
145 St Bridge
Madison Ave Bridge
3rd Ave Bridge
Willis Ave Bridge
Port Morris
Triborough Bridge
Park Ave
QUEENS
MANHATTAN

Don't be afraid of the Boogie Down Bronx. Decades of entrenched poverty and poor urban planning once frayed many neighborhoods, but the borough today is no longer the burning wreck your parents warned you about years ago.

Communities

Belmont's Arthur Avenue **3** is still an authentic Little Italy even though many businesses now belong to Albanians. Woodlawn **9** is home to many Irish immigrants and it's got the pubs to prove it. With 15,372 units, towering Co-op City **13** is rightly called a city within the city; it even has its own mall! The Mott Haven **14** and Longwood **15** historic districts boast beautiful homes, but "The Hub" **16** features the grand architecture of the past conveniently filled with the discount shopping of today. For antiques, visit the cobblestone corridor of Bruckner Boulevard **17** at Alexander Avenue. Some of the city's grandest homes sit in the wooded environs of Riverdale **4**, while City Island **12** resembles nothing so much as a New England fishing village crossed with a New Jersey suburb.

Culture

The New York Botanical Garden **8** and the Bronx Zoo **10** are justly famous, well worth whatever effort it may take to get there. For a beautiful view of the Hudson and the Palisades beyond, choose the botanical garden and historic estate Wave Hill **5** or the quirky Hall of Fame for Great Americans **2** featuring 98 bronze busts of notable citizens in a grand outdoor colonnade. Explore your inner Goth at historic Woodlawn Cemetery **7** or Poe Cottage **18**, the American poet's final home. The recently expanded Bronx Museum of the Arts **20** is the best place to check out contemporary work from artists of African, Asian, and Latin American descent.

Sports

Well, the new stadium is here **1**, and, as predicted, it's overblown, with seats a million miles from the field, and mostly charmless. Get the cheapest ticket you can find and just spend the game walking around the concourses, which have the best views of the field. Van Cortlandt Park **6** offers playgrounds, ball fields, tennis and basketball courts, hiking trails, stables for horseback riding, and one of golf's classic courses, "Vanny."

Nature

The restoration of the Bronx River **19** coincides with the improvement of green spaces throughout the borough. Pelham Bay Park **11** is the city's largest at 2,764 acres, offering many recreational opportunities in addition to the Thomas Pell Wildlife Sanctuary, two nature centers, and immensely popular Orchard Beach.

Food

Belmont:

- Dominick's, 2335 Arthur Ave, 718-733-2807—Famous, old-school Italian-American where there are no menus and no set prices.
- Full Moon, 602 East 187th St, 718-584-3451—Wonderful pizza and calzones.
- Roberto Restaurant, 603 Crescent Ave, 718-733-9503—Classic fare, rumored to be the best around.
- Arthur Avenue Retail Market, 2344 Arthur Ave—Get all the right ingredients for home-cooked Italian meals.

City Island:

- Johnny's Reef, 2 City Island Ave, 718-885-2090—Local favorite for fresh, inexpensive seafood.

Riverdale:

- Riverdale Garden, 4574 Manhattan College Pkwy, 718-884-5232—Upscale American and Continental food in a beautiful setting.
- An Beal Bocht, 445 West 238th St, 718-884-7127—Café/bar/coffee shop hangout for the hip, young, and Irish.
- S&S Cheesecake, 222 West 238th St, 718-549-3888—Forget Junior's, this is the city's best.

The Hub:

- In God We Trust, 441 E 153rd St, 718-401-3595—A café within a dry goods shop serving authentic Ghanaian food.

University Heights:

- African-American Restaurant, 1987 University Ave, 718-731-8595—24-hour diner serving soul food alongside traditional Ghanaian specialties.
- Ebe Ye Yie, 2364 Jerome Ave, 718-563-6064—Hearty Ghanaian meals.

Concourse Village:

- The Feeding Tree, 892 Gerard Ave, 718-293-5025—Delicious Jamaican food close to Yankee Stadium.

Kingsbridge:

- El Economico, 5589 Broadway, 718-796-4851—Home-style Puerto Rican meals.

Pelham Bay:

- Louie & Ernie's, 1300 Crosby Ave, 718-829-6230—Their thin-crust pizza is the best in the borough.

Bruckner Boulevard:

- Rinconcito Mexicano, 381 East 138th St, 718-401-8314—A great little place for tortas and tacos

Landmarks

1 Yankee Stadium
2 Hall of Fame for Great Americans
3 Arthur Avenue
4 Riverdale
5 Wave Hill
6 Van Cortlandt Park
7 Woodlawn Cemetery
8 New York Botanical Garden
9 Woodlawn
10 Bronx Zoo
11 Pelham Bay Park
12 City Island
13 Co-op City
14 Mott Haven
15 Longwood
16 The Hub
17 Bruckner Boulevard
18 Poe Cottage
19 Bronx River
20 Bronx Museum of the Arts

N
MANHATTAN
West Side Expy
West Village
Stuyvesant Town
Holland Tunnel
East River
Manhattan Ave
Sunnyside
Greenpoint Ave
495
Long Island Expy
278
Maspeth
SoHo
East Village
FDR Dr
Greenpoint
9A
Hudson River
Chinatown
Williamsburg Bridge
Metropolitan Ave
Grand Ave
TriBeCa
Battery Park City
Lower East Side
Northside
Manhattan Bridge
Williamsburg
Financial District
Brooklyn Bridge
Vinegar Hill
QUEENS
Bushwick
Flushing Ave
Brooklyn-Queens Expy
Myrtle Ave
Brooklyn Battery Tunnel
Fort Greene
Bushwick
Broadway
Jackie Robinson Pkwy
Brooklyn Heights
Governors Island
Atlantic Ave
Cobble Hill
Boerum Hill
Bedford-Stuyvesant
BQE
Clinton St
Carroll Gardens
Atlantic Ave
Red Hook
Crown Heights
Kings Hwy
Park Slope
Eastern Pkwy
Pitkin Ave
Brownsville
East New York
Empire Blvd
Prospect Park
Prospect Expy
Linden Blvd
Wingate
27
Rockaway Pkwy
Gowanus Expy
4th Ave
Green-Wood Cemetery
Linden Blvd
39th St
Holy Cross Cemetery
Nostrand Ave
Utica Ave
Remsen Ave
Starrett City
278
Sunset Park
Ocean Ave
Ave D
Canarsie
Flatbush
Fort Hamilton Pkwy
Flatbush
Farragut
Flatlands Ave
Bay Ridge
Borough Park
47th St
Seaview Ave
Ave J
Flatlands
Canarsie Park
Dyker Heights
Midwood
Fourth Ave
16th Ave
Washington Cemetery
Coney Island Ave
Ocean Pkwy
Flatbush Ave
Bay Ridge Pkwy
65th St
Marine Park
Jamaica Bay
Bensonhurst
Ave P
Ave U
Mill Basin
Bergen Beach
86th St
Dyker Beach Park
Fort Hamilton
Ocean Parkway
Kings Hwy
Verrazano-Narrows Bridge
Cropsey Ave
Bath Beach
Bay Pkwy
Stillwell Ave
Ave U
Ocean Ave
Nostrand Ave
Gerritsen Ave
Marine Park
Belt
Floyd Bennett Field
27
Ave X
Lower Bay
Bensonhurst Park
Gravesend
Sheepshead Bay
Flatbush Ave
Shore/Belt Pkwy
Drier-Offerman Park
Manhattan Beach
Sea Gate
Neptune Ave
Brighton Beach
Manhattan Beach Park
Surf Ave
Coney Island
Rockaway Inlet
Rockaway

Until "The Great Mistake of 1898," Brooklyn was its own thriving city. Today, the Borough of Kings could still make a damn fine city all on its own. Although Manhattan will most likely overshadow Brooklyn for all of eternity, in recent years Brooklyn has begun to receive more than its fair share of attention. As Manhattan loses its neighborhood flavor while rents continue to soar, Brooklyn's popularity is at an all-time high. Scores of recent college grads, immigrants, ex-Manhattanites, and even celebrities are calling Brooklyn home. Along with the residential boom, Brooklyn has bloomed into a cultural and entertainment mecca, with top-notch restaurants, a thriving art and film scene, and plenty of unique shops. Throw in a bunch of cool bars, mind-blowing cultural diversity, and some of the city's best urban parks, and you get what may be the best place to live on the planet. At press time, we hear the behemoth and uber-controversial Atlantic Yards will break ground in the next year. We'll believe it when we see it. Right now, chalk one up for the little guys—Brooklyn will remain Brooklyn for at least a little while longer.

Communities

As the largest borough by population (over 2.5 million!), Brooklyn holds a special place as one of the nation's most important urban areas. As many as one in four people can trace their roots here! In Brooklyn, you can find pretty much any type of community—for better or for worse. As gentrification marches deeper into Brooklyn, the borough is changing fast. Neighborhoods most likely to see their first baby boutiques open soon include Red Hook, East Williamsburg, Prospect-Lefferts Gardens, and Crown Heights.

The first thing you notice when looking at Brooklyn on a map is the sheer size of it. Yet much of Brooklyn is largely unknown to most New Yorkers. Yes, Brooklyn Heights, Williamsburg, and Park Slope are nice communities that are fun to explore. However, if you've never ventured further out into Brooklyn than the obligatory trip to Coney Island, you're missing some fantastic neighborhoods. For instance, Bay Ridge **4** has beautiful single-family homes along its western edge, a killer view of the Verrazano Bridge, and a host of excellent shops and restaurants. Dyker Heights **6** is composed of almost all single-family homes, many of which go all-out with Christmas light displays during the holiday season. Brighton Beach **8** continues to be a haven for many Russian expatriates. The quiet, tree-lined streets of both Ocean Parkway **10** and Midwood **11** can make one forget all about the hustle and bustle of downtown Brooklyn, or downtown anywhere else for that matter. Finally, Bedford-Stuyvesant **12** has a host of cool public buildings, fun eateries, and beautiful brownstones.

Sports

No, the Dodgers are never coming back. This is still hard for many older Brooklynites to accept and accounts for much of the nostalgia that is still associated with the borough. If you can get beyond the fact that Ebbets Field is now a giant concrete housing complex, then you will enjoy spending a fine summer evening watching the Cyclones at Coney Island. Kensington Stables in Prospect Park provides lessons for wannabe equestrians. If you can never let go, then join the Brooklyn Kickball League to relive the happier moments of your childhood.

Attractions

There are plenty of reasons to dislike Coney Island **7**, imminent redevelopment notwithstanding, but they're simply not good enough when you stack them up against the Cyclone, the Wonder Wheel, Nathan's, Totonno's, the beach, the freaks, and *The Warriors*. Close by is the Aquarium **13**. Nature trails, parked blimps, views of the water, and scenic marinas all make historical Floyd Bennett Field **9** a worthwhile trip. For more beautiful views, you can check out Owl's Point Park **3** in Bay Ridge, or the parking lot underneath the Verrazano-Narrows Bridge **5** (located right off the Shore Parkway). The Verrazano might not be New York's most beautiful bridge, but it's hands-down the most awe-inspiring. Both Green-Wood Cemetery **2** and Prospect Park **1** provide enough greenery to keep you happy until you get to Yosemite. Finally, Brooklyn Heights **14** is the most beautiful residential neighborhood in all of New York. Don't believe us? Go stand on the corner of Willow and Orange Streets.

Food

Here are some restaurants in some of the outlying areas of Brooklyn: See pages 210 to 221 for other Brooklyn eateries.
Bay Ridge: Tuscany Grill, 8620 Third Ave, 718-921-5633—The gorgonzola steak is a must.
Coney Island: Totonno Pizzeria Napolitano, 1524 Neptune Ave, 718-372-8606—Paper-thin pizza. Bizarre hours.
Midwood: DiFara's Pizzeria, E 15th St & Ave J, 718-258-1367—Dirty, cheap, disgusting…awesome!
Sunset Park: Nyonya, 5223 Eighth Ave, 718-633-0808—Good quality Malaysian.
Sheepshead Bay: Randazzo's Clam Bar, 2017 Emmons Avenue, 718-615-0010—Essential summer dining.

Landmarks

1 Prospect Park
2 Green-Wood Cemetery
3 Owl's Point Park
4 Bay Ridge
5 Verrazano-Narrows Bridge
6 Dyker Heights
7 Coney Island
8 Brighton Beach
9 Floyd Bennett Field
10 Ocean Parkway
11 Midwood
12 Bedford-Stuyvesant
13 New York Aquarium
14 Brooklyn Heights

MANHATTAN
Flushing Bay
Whitestone Bridge
Throgs Neck Bridge
Triborough Bridge
College Point
Whitestone
Cross Island Pkwy
LaGuardia Airport
Steinway
East Elmhurst
Flushing
Bayside
Douglaston
Queensboro Bridge
Astoria
Grand Central Pkwy
Astoria Blvd
Whitestone Expy
Northern Blvd
Utopia Pkwy
Clearview Expy
Francis Lewis Blvd
Long Island City
Jackson Heights
Flushing Meadows
Auburndale
Long Island Expy
Woodside
Corona
Kissena Park
Queens Blvd
Sunnyside
Queens Expy
Elmhurst
Fresh Meadows
Floral Park
Brooklyn Queens Expy
Van Wyck Expy
Main St
Queens Village
Grand Ave
Maspeth
Forest Hills
Hillside Ave
Hollis
Metropolitan Ave
Jamaica
Kew Gardens
Jamaica Ave
Bushwick
Forest Park
QUEENS
Cambria Heights
Broadway
Richmond Hill
South Jamaica
Woodhaven
Merrick Blvd
St Albans
Jackie Robinson Pkwy
Atlantic Ave
Springfield Blvd
Ozone Park
Laurelton Pkwy
Conduit Ave
Rockaway Blvd
Springfield Gardens
Laurelton
Belt Pkwy
Kings Hwy
Rosedale
BROOKLYN
Linden Blvd
Cross Bay Blvd
Howard Beach
John F Kennedy International Airport
AirTrain
Rockaway Pkwy
Gateway National Recreation Area
Broad Channel
Far Rockaway
Somerville
Beach Channel Dr
Cross Bay Veterans Memorial Bridge
Jamaica Bay
Marine Parkway Bridge
Rockaway Beach
Atlantic Ocean
Lower New York Bay
Roxbury
Belle Harbor
Breezy Point
Rockaway Point

Local publications declared Queens the next big thing years ago. We'll go on record: Queens will never be cool. But it will have affordable rents, easy subway access, cheap bars, and fantastic restaurants by the bushel. If that's not enough for you, have fun living in Jersey City, suckers!

Communities

From the stately Tudor homes of Forest Hills **28** gardens to the hip-hop beat of Jamaica Avenue **11**, Queens has it all. Eastern Queens tends towards suburbia, while the communities along the borough's southern border often include active industrial districts. All things Asian can be found in Flushing **20**, the city's largest Chinatown. Sunnyside **21** and Woodside **22** are home to Irish and Mexican immigrants alike, making it easy to find a proper pint and a fabulous taco on the same block. Jackson Heights' **6** 74th Street is Little India, while 82nd Street holds South and Central American businesses. Corona **23** blends old-school Italian-American delis with Latino dance clubs. Elmhurst **24** has attracted Asian, Southeast Asian, and South American immigrants to set up shop on its crowded streets. Island Broad Channel **12** feels like a sleepy village, while the Rockaways **13** offer the only surfing beaches in the city.

Culture

Fans of contemporary art have long known P.S.1 **4** is the place to be, especially during its summer weekend WarmUp parties. Then head over to the Sculpture Center **31**, to see what new exhibit they've cooked up for us. The Noguchi Museum **3**, dedicated to the work of the Japanese-American sculptor, and neighboring Socrates Sculpture Park **2**, a waterfront space with changing exhibitions, are less known. The Fischer Landau Center **25** is almost entirely unknown despite its world-class collection of modern art. Movie buffs should look for repertory screenings at the American Museum of the Moving Image **5**. The delightfully kitschy Louis Armstrong House **26** is a must-see for jazz lovers. In Flushing Meadows-Corona Park, the New York Hall of Science **8** beckons the geeky kid in all of us with its hands-on exhibits while the Queens Museum of Art's **9** scale model of the entire city will wow even the most jaded New Yorkers.

Sports

In 2009, the Mets inaugurated a brand new place to make memories of exquisite disappointment, Jackie Robinson...err, sorry, kids...Citi Field. Enjoy the ersatz Ebbets Field façade. Feel free to root for the visiting team if you like—Mets supporters are far more subdued than their Yankee rivals. The U.S. Open takes place right across the street at the National Tennis Center **7**. See girls gone wild when our local ladies, The Queens of Pain, compete in the Gotham Girls Roller Derby league. Get out of that cruddy OTB and see the ponies live at the Aqueduct Racetrack **14**. Hitch a ride to Rockaway Beach **13** for swimming and surfing or paddle out in a kayak on loan from the Long Island City Community Boathouse **27**. Astoria Pool **1** is the city's largest with room for 3,000 swimmers. For bowling, all-night Whitestone Lanes **18** is the place to be.

Nature

Gantry State Park's **29** spacious piers attract strollers and urban fishermen alike with panoramic views of the Manhattan skyline, and a major park expansion is currently underway. The Jamaica Bay Wildlife Refuge **15** in Gateway National Recreation Area is internationally known for bird-watching. The Queens Zoo **19** is small but interesting, housing only animals native to North America. Flushing Meadows-Corona Park **30** is designed for active recreation, but Alley Pond Park **16** and Forest Park **17** have wooded trails perfect for wandering.

Food

Entire books have been written on where to eat in Queens (none as good as NFT, natch!), so these are just a handful of suggestions:
Corona: Leo's Latticini (a.k.a. Mama's), 46-02 104th St, 718-898-6639—Insanely good Italian sandwiches that pair well with dessert from the Lemon Ice King, 52-02 108th Street, 718-699-5133, just a few blocks away.
Forest Hills: Salut, 63-42 108th St, 718-275-6860—Order lots of lamb at this Kosher Uzbek gem.
Sunnyside: De Mole, 45-02 48th Ave, 718-392-2161—BYOB with fresh, simply prepared Mexican food.
Bayside: Uncle Jack's, 39-40 Bell Blvd, 718-229-1100—Mayor Bloomberg's favorite steakhouse serves up fine flesh.
Flushing: Spicy and Tasty, 39-07 Prince Street, 718-359-1601—The name of this Sichuan place is entirely accurate.
Woodside:

- Spicy Mina, 64-23 Broadway, 718-205-2340—Authentic Bangladeshi/Indian food superior to the blander fare of 74th Street.
- Sripaphai, 64-13 39th Ave, 718-899-9599—Easily the best Thai food in the city.
- La Flor, 53-02 Roosevelt Ave, 718-426-8023—Fantastic neighborhood café with Mexican-inflected dishes.

Elmhurst: Minangasli, 86-10 Whitney Ave, 718-429-8207—Delicious, inexpensive Indonesian fare.

Landmarks

1 Astoria Pool
2 Socrates Sculpture Park
3 Noguchi Museum
4 P.S.1 Art Museum
5 American Museum of the Moving Image
6 Jackson Heights
7 US Open/National Tennis Center
8 Hall of Science
9 Queens Museum of Art
10 Citi Stadium
11 Jamaica
12 Broad Channel
13 The Rockaways
14 Aqueduct Racetrack
15 Jamaica Bay Wildlife Refuge
16 Alley Pond Park
17 Forest Park
18 Whitestone Lanes
19 Queens Zoo
20 Flushing
21 Sunnyside
22 Woodside
23 Corona
24 Elmhurst
25 Fischer Landau Center
26 Louis Armstrong House
27 Long Island City Community Boathouse
28 Forest Hills
29 Gantry State Park
30 Flushing Meadows-Corona Park

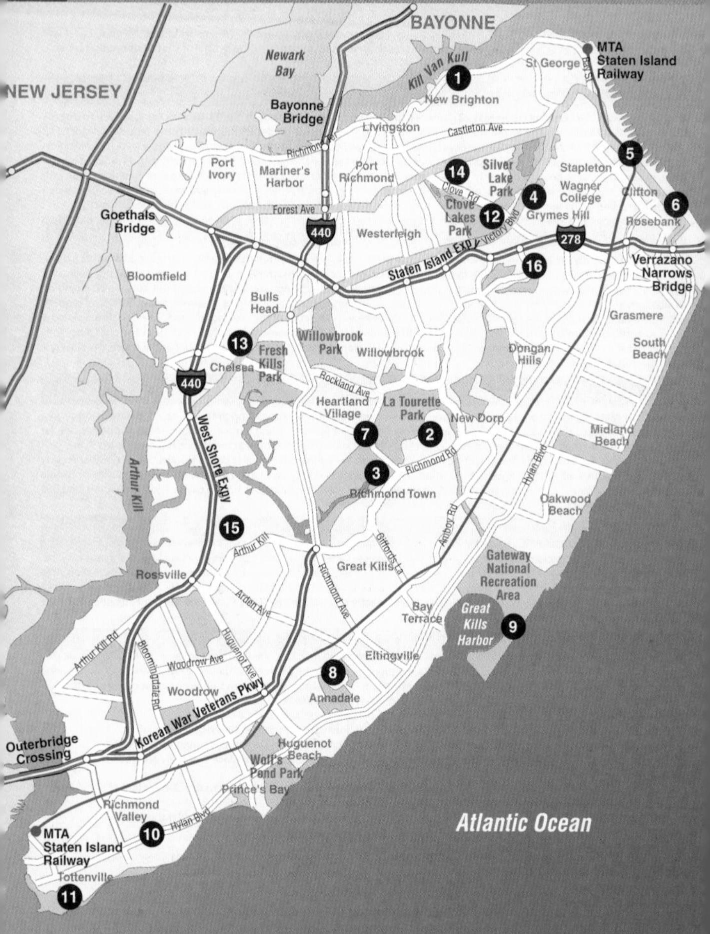

BAYONNE
Newark Bay
NEW JERSEY
Kill Van Kull
1
New Brighton
St George
Bay St
MTA Staten Island Railway
Bayonne Bridge
Livingston
Castleton Ave
Richmond Ter
Port Ivory
Mariner's Harbor
Port Richmond
14
Silver Lake Park
Stapleton
Wagner College
5
Clifton
6
Clove Rd
Clove Lakes Park
12
4
Grymes Hill
Rosebank
Goethals Bridge
Forest Ave
440
Westerleigh
Victory Blvd
278
Staten Island Expy
16
Verrazano Narrows Bridge
Bloomfield
Bulls Head
Grasmere
Willowbrook Park
Willowbrook
13
Fresh Kills Park
Chelsea
Dongan Hills
South Beach
440
Rockland Ave
Heartland Village
La Tourette Park
New Dorp
7
2
Midland Beach
West Shore Expy
Arthur Kill
3
Richmond Rd
Richmond Town
Hylan Blvd
Oakwood Beach
15
Amboy Rd
Arthur Kill Rd
Giffords La
Gateway National Recreation Area
Great Kills
Rossville
Richmond Ave
Arden Ave
Bay Terrace
Great Kills Harbor
9
Arthur Kill Rd
Huguenot Ave
Bloomingdale Rd
Woodrow Ave
Eltingville
8
Woodrow
Korean War Veterans Pkwy
Annadale
Outerbridge Crossing
Huguenot Beach
Wolf's Pond Park
Prince's Bay
Richmond Valley
Hylan Blvd
10
MTA Staten Island Railway
Atlantic Ocean
Tottenville
11

Staten Island, of thee we sing! Don't let the sight of yabbos with fake tans and gelled hair hold you back from exploring, lest you miss out on heaps of excellent pizza, the wildflower meadows at Mount Loretto, the windows on the past at Historic Richmond Town, the small-town charm of minor league baseball at St. George, and the striking design of the Chinese Scholars' Garden at Snug Harbor. It's high time you pulled your head out of your borough and hitched a ride on the ferry, if only to eat at one of SI's "holy trinity" of pizzerias.

Culture

1 **Snug Harbor Cultural Center**, 1000 Richmond Ter, 718-448-2500. A former sailors' home transformed to a waterfront arts complex, Snug Harbor's 83 acres include classrooms, studio spaces, performance venues, galleries, three museums, and a truly noteworthy botanical garden. Call to learn about cultural events and exhibits on site.

2 **Jacques Marchais Museum of Tibetan Art**, 338 Lighthouse Ave, 718-987-3500. A world-class collection of Tibetan art, courtesy of former New York art collector Edna Coblentz, who had the surprising French pseudonym Jacques Marchais.

3 **Historic Richmondtown**, 441 Clark Ave, 718-351-1611. Get back to old-timey times visiting restored homes from the 17th to the 19th centuries, most populated by costumed guides. Great for kids and adults who want to learn how to churn butter/forge metal.

4 **Wagner College**, 1 Campus Rd, 718-390-3100. Wagner's tranquil hilltop location rewards visitors with beautiful views of the serene surroundings, but its best feature is the planetarium.

5 **Staten Island Village Hall**, 111 Canal St. Last remaining village hall building in Staten Island, a reminder of the borough's rural past.

6 **Alice Austen House**, 2 Hylan Blvd, 718-816-4506. Alice Austen was an early twentieth-century amateur photographer, and now she's got a museum and a ferry boat named after her. Go figure. Some of her 8,000 images are on view at her house, which has a great view of lower New York Harbor.

Nature

7 **The Staten Island Greenbelt**, 200 Nevada Ave, 718-667-2165. This 2,500-acre swath of land (comprising several different parks) in the center of the island contains a golf course, a hospital, a scout camp, several graveyards, and plenty of wooded areas that remain relatively undeveloped and can be accessed only by walking trails. A good starting point is High Rock Park. Panoramic views abound.

8 **Blue Heron Park**, 222 Poillon Ave, 718-967-3542. This quiet, 147-acre park has a fantastic Nature Center and plenty of ponds, wetlands, and streams to explore. Noted for bird-watching, hence the name.

9 **Great Kills Park**, 718-987-6790. Part of the Gateway National Recreation Area, Great Kills boasts clean beaches, a marina, and a nature preserve.

10 **Mount Loretto Unique Area**, 6450 Hylan Blvd, 718-482-7287. Flourishing wetlands, grasslands, and beaches all rolled into one serenely beautiful waterfront park. Mysterious sculptures dot the beach.

11 **Conference House Park**, 7455 Hylan Blvd, 718-984-0415. The historic house is worth a look, but watching the sunset from the restored waterfront pavilion is a must. You'll also find NYC's very own "South Pole" on the beach here.

12 **Clove Lakes Park**, Clove Rd and Victory Blvd, 311. Who needs Central Park? Check out these romantic rowboats on the lake in season.

13 **Fresh Kills Park**, off Route 440. Former landfill, now a park. Sorta. They're working on it. Free tours by appointment.

Other

14 **110/120 Longfellow Road**. Celebrate one of the greatest American films without having to schlep to Sicily. This address is where the Corleone family held court in *The Godfather*.

15 **Ship Graveyard**, at Arthur Kill Rd and Rossville Ave. These ships of the damned make a perfect backdrop for Goth photo shoots.

16 **Staten Island Zoo**, 614 Broadway, 718-442-3100. Kids will go wild here, near the stunning Clove Lakes Park. Be sure to bring them to the vampire bat feedings.

Food

Snug Harbor:
RH Tugs, 1115 Richmond Ter, 718-447-6369. Standard bar food, but views of Kill Van Kull mean lots of hot tug and tanker action.

Tompkinsville:
New Asha, 322 Victory Blvd Ave, 718-420-0649. Great Sri Lankan food on the cheap. Spicy!

Port Richmond:
Denino's, 524 Port Richmond Ave, 718-442-9401. Some of the best pizza in town. Afterward, cross the street to Ralph's Famous for Italian ices.

Dongan Hills:
Lee's Tavern, 60 Hancock St, 718-667-9749. Great bar with great pizza—get the fresh mozzarella.

Grant City:
Nunzio's, 2155 Hylan Blvd, 718-667-9647. More great pizza. Notice a theme here?

Tottenville:
Gentile's, 5266 Arthur Kill Rd, 718-966-9005. Classic red sauce Italian-American dishes big enough for three.

Egger's Ice Cream Parlor, 7437 Amboy Rd, 718-605-9335. Old time ice cream and sweets. Kids love it.

Killmeyer's Old Bravarian Inn, 4254 Arthur Kill Rd, 718-984-1202. Historic German beer garden and eats. Jå!

Castleton Corners

Joe & Pats, 1758 Victory Blvd, 718-981-0887. Completing SI's "Holy Trinity" of pizza.

Driving In / Through Staten Island

To visit Staten Island, one must either drive/take a bus/take a cab over the Verrazano Bridge ($11 toll) from Bay Ridge, Brooklyn, or catch the ferry from Lower Manhattan. If you elect to do the latter, you'll find myriad buses departing from the St. George side of the ferry as well as the terminal of the Staten Island Railway, ready to whisk you all the way down to Tottenville and back with one swipe of the Metrocard (literally—it's free to get on and off anyplace other than St. George and Tompkinsville). To reach New Jersey via Staten Island, take the Verrazano to the Staten Island Expressway (Route 278) to Route 440 to the Outerbridge Crossing, and you're almost halfway to Princeton or the Jersey shore. However...the Staten Island Expressway often gets jammed. Two scenic, though not really quicker, alternatives: one, take Hylan Boulevard all the way south to almost the southwest tip of Staten Island, and then cut up to the Outerbridge Crossing; two, take Richmond Terrace around the north shore and cross to New Jersey at the Goethals Bridge. Remember, neither is really faster, but at least you'll be moving.

General Information

Battery Park Parks Conservancy: 212-267-9700
Websites: www.lowermanhattan.info
www.bpcparks.org
www.bpcdogs.org

Overview

The closest thing to suburbia around here. Welcome to Battery Park City—a master-planned community reminiscent of *Pleasantville*. Originally the brainchild of Nelson Rockefeller, this urban experiment transformed a WTC construction landfill into a 92-acre planned enclave on the southwestern tip of Manhattan. As space in Manhattan continues to disappear into the stratosphere (literally, the only way to build is up), the idea of BPC requires a doubletake. It's about making public spaces (about 30% of those 92 acres) work within private entities. Imagine taking Central Park, cutting it up, and saying, "Here, your neighborhood can have a chunk of it, and that street down there, and that street over there, too." Admit it: walking among private, commercial spaces day in and day out is enough to make anyone claustrophobic (thank you, Financial District). In BPC you walk through spacious parks with weird statues and brick pavers all on your way to work, the grocery store, the gym, or the movie theater. BPC will have you asking: "What's outside Battery Park City?"

Those looking for all-night eateries and party spots should pass it up, but if you've got kids this is the place for you. Many NY families—roughly 25,000 people—occupy the 40% of BPC that's dedicated residential space, including a future-forward "green" building, the Solaire. Robert F. Wagner Jr. and Rector are good choices for a picnic; The Esplanade or South Cove to walk along the Hudson; Nelson A. Rockefeller to play frisbee; North Cove to park your yacht; Teardrop Park for the kids.

Seeing: Amazing sculptures by Bourgeois, Otterness, Puryear, Dine, and Cragg. Inspired architecture: Stuyvesant High School, Siah Armajani's Tribeca Bridge, Kevin Roche's Museum of Jewish Heritage, Caesar Pelli's Winter Garden, and the World Financial Center. If you like things nice, neat, and compartmentalized, this 'hood is for you. If you do need a drink here, however, the Rise Bar at the Ritz is the place to do it—killer views!

Bagels

- **Pick A Bagel** • Embassy Suites • 102 North End Ave [Vesey St]

Banks

BA • Bank of America (ATM) • 3 World Financial Center [Vesey St]
BA • Bank of America (ATM) • 4 World Financial Ctr [Vesey St]
CH • Chase • 325 North End Ave [Vesey St]
CH • Chase • 331 South End Ave [Albany St]
HS • HSBC (ATM) • NY Mercantile Exchange • 1 N End Ave [Vesey St]

Car Rental

- **Avis Gateway Plaza** • 345 South End Ave [Albany St]

Coffee

- **Au Bon Pain** • WFC • 200 Liberty St [West St]
- **Cosi** • 200 Vesey St [West St]
- **Financier Patisserie** • 3 World Financial Center [W Side Hwy]
- **Starbucks** • 250 Vesey St [W Side Hwy]

Community Gardens

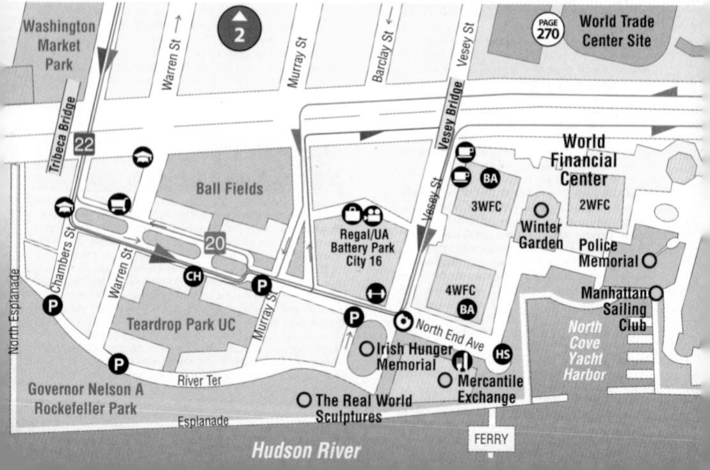

Gyms

- **Battery Park Swim & Fitness Center** • 375 South End Ave [Liberty St]
- **Liberty Club MCB** •200 Rector Pl [South End Ave]
- **NYSC** • 102 North End Ave [Vesey St]

Landmarks

- **The Irish Hunger Memorial** • Vesey St & North End Ave
- **Manhattan Sailing Club** • North Cove (Liberty St & North End Ave)
- **Mercantile Exchange** • 1 North End Ave [Vesey St]
- **Museum of Jewish Heritage** • 36 Battery Pl [Little West St]
- **Police Memorial** • Liberty St & South End Ave
- **The Real World Sculptures** • Rockefeller Park
- **Skyscraper Museum** • 39 Battery Pl [Little West St]
- **Winter Garden** • 37 Vesey St [Church St]

Liquor Stores

- **Bulls & Bears Winery** • 309 South End Ave [Albany St]

Movie Theaters

- **Regal Battery Park Stadium 11** • Embassy Suites • 102 North End Ave [Vesey St]

Nightlife

- **Rise Bar** • Ritz Carlton • 2 West St [Little West St]

Parking

Pet Shops

- **Le Pet Spa** • 300 Rector Pl [South End Ave]

Restaurants

- **Gigino at Wagner Park** • 20 Battery Pl [Washington St]
- **Grill Room** • WFC • 225 Liberty St [W Side Hwy]
- **Picasso Pizza** • 303 South End Ave [Albany St]
- **PJ Clarke's** • 4 World Financial Ctr [Vesey St]
- **Samantha's Fine Foods** • 235 South End Ave [Rector Pl]
- **Steamer's Landing** • 375 South End Ave [Liberty St]

Schools

- **PS 89** • 201 Warren St [Clinton St]
- **Stuyvesant High** • 345 Chambers St [North End Ave]

Shopping

- **DSW Shoe Warehouse** • 102 North End Ave [Vesey]

Supermarkets

- **Gourmet Heaven** • 450 North End Ave [Chambers St]
- **Gristedes** • 315 South End Ave [Albany St] 24
- **Gristedes** • 71 South End Ave [W Thames St]

Video Rental

- **Video Room** • 300 Rector Pl [South End Ave]

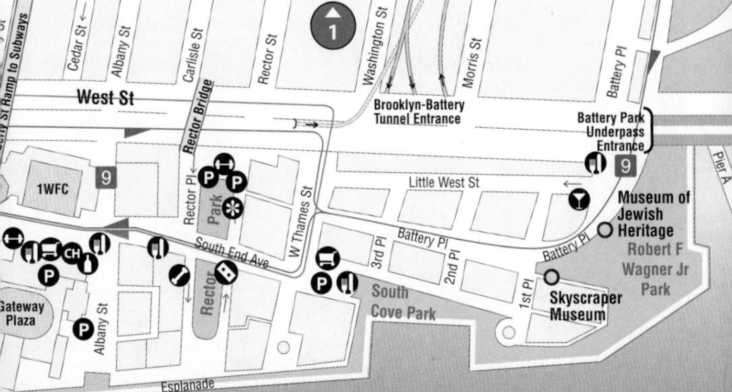

General Information

Website:	www.centralparknyc.org
Central Park Conservancy:	212-310-6600
Shakespeare in the Park:	212-539-8750

Overview

For continued mental health that doesn't require a therapist, look no further than a mind-clearing walk through New York's blessed Central Park. Leave stressful car noise and concrete behind to find relative quiet and soft ground. Wandering aimlessly through the 843 acres (worth more than an estimated $528 billion), you'll discover many isolated corners and hiding places, despite the fact that 25 million people visit every year. On any given day, you'll see people disco roller-skating, playing jazz, juggling, walking their dogs, running, making out, meditating, playing softball, whining through soccer practice, getting married, picnicking, and playing chess.

Designed by Frederick Law Olmsted and Calvert Vaux in the 1850s, Central Park has a diverse mix of attractions. The Central Park Conservancy (www.centralparknyc.org) leads walking tours, and you can always hail a horse-drawn carriage or bike taxi for a ride through the park if you want to look like a true tourist.

Practicalities

Central Park is easily accessible by subway, since the A C B D N R Q W 1 2 3 trains all circle the park. Parking along CPW is harder, so try side streets. Unless you're heading to the park for a big concert, a softball game, or Shakespeare in the Park, walking or hanging out (especially alone!) in the park at night is not recommended.

Nature

If you think people-watching in Times Square is good, wait until you check out the avian eye candy around here. More than 275 species of birds have been spotted in Central Park. The Ramble **27** is a good place to see them. There are an amazing number of both plant and animal species that inhabit the park, including the creatures housed in its two zoos **4** & **8.** In 2009, three rabid raccoon sightings vexed dog-walkers on both sides of the park and marked the disease's first surge in six years. A good source of information on all of the park's flora and fauna is schoolteacher Leslie Day's website, www.nysite.com/nature/index.htm.

Architecture & Sculpture

Central Park was designed to thrill visitors at every turn. The Bethesda Fountain **11,** designed by Emma Stebbins, is one of the main attractions of the park. Don't miss the view of Turtle Pond from Belvedere Castle **16** (home of the Central Park Learning Center). The Arsenal **5** is a wonderful ivy-clad building that houses the Parks Department headquarters. The original Greensward plan for Central Park is located in the Arsenal's third-floor conference room—if there isn't a meeting going on, you might be able to sneak a peek. Two of the most notable sculptures in the park are Alice in Wonderland **15** and the Obelisk **19**. Oh, and one other tiny point of interest…the Metropolitan Museum of Art **24** also happens to be in the park.

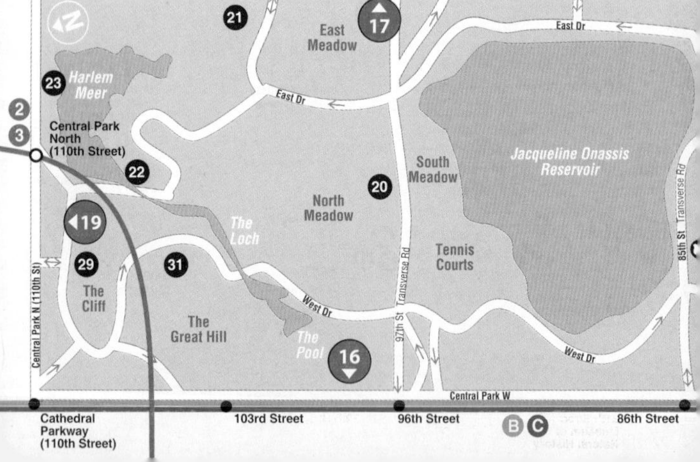

Open Spaces

New Yorkers covet space. Since they rarely get it in their apartments, they rely on large open areas such as Strawberry Fields **10**, the Great Lawn **26**, and Sheep Meadow **28.** The Ramble **27** and the Cliff **29** are still heavily forested and are good for hiking around, but don't go near them after dark. When it snows, you can find great sledding on Cedar Hill **30**, which is otherwise perfect for picnicking and sunbathing.

Performance

In warmer weather, Central Park is a microcosm of the great cultural attractions New York has to offer. The Delacorte Theater **18** is the home of Shakespeare in the Park, a New York tradition begun by famous director Joseph Papp. SummerStage **9** is now an extremely popular concert venue for all types of music, including the occasional killer rock concert. Opera companies and classical philharmonics also show up in the park frequently, as does the odd mega-star (Beastie Boys, Diana Ross, etc.). If you crave something truly outlandish, try the loinclothed Thoth, a self-proclaimed emotional hermaphrodite who plays the violin and sings in his own language, under the Angel Tunnel by the Bethesda Fountain **11**.

Sports

Rollerblading and roller skating are very popular (not just at the Roller Skating Rink **7**—see www.centralparkskate.com, www.cpdsa.org, www.skatecity.com), as is jogging, especially around the reservoir (1.57 mi). The Great Lawn **26** boasts beautiful softball fields. Central Park has 30 tennis courts (if you make a reservation, you can walk right on to the clay court with tennis shoes only—212-280-0205), fishing at Harlem Meer, gondola rides and boat rentals at the Loeb Boathouse **13**, model boat rentals at the Conservatory Water **14**, chess and checkers at the Chess & Checkers House **25**, two ice-skating rinks **1** & **22**, croquet and lawn bowling just north of Sheep Meadow **28**, and rock-climbing lessons at the North Meadow Rec Center **20**. You will also see volleyball, basketball, skateboarding, bicycling, and many pick-up soccer, frisbee, football, and kill-the-carrier games to join. During heavy snows, bust out your snowboard, cross-country skis, or homemade sled. Finally, Central Park is where the NYC Marathon ends each year.

Landmarks

1 Wollman Rink
2 Carousel
3 The Dairy
4 Central Park Zoo
5 The Arsenal
6 Tavern on the Green
7 Roller Skating Rink
8 Children's Zoo
9 SummerStage
10 Strawberry Fields
11 Bethesda Fountain
12 Bow Bridge
13 Loeb Boathouse
14 Model Boat Racing
15 Alice in Wonderland
16 Belvedere Castle
17 Shakespeare Gardens
18 Delacorte Theater
19 The Obelisk
20 North Meadow Recreation Center
21 Conservatory Garden
22 Lasker Rink
23 Dana Discovery Center
24 Metropolitan Museum of Art
25 Chess & Checkers House
26 The Great Lawn
27 The Ramble
28 Sheep Meadow
29 The Cliff
30 Cedar Hill
31 The Great Hill

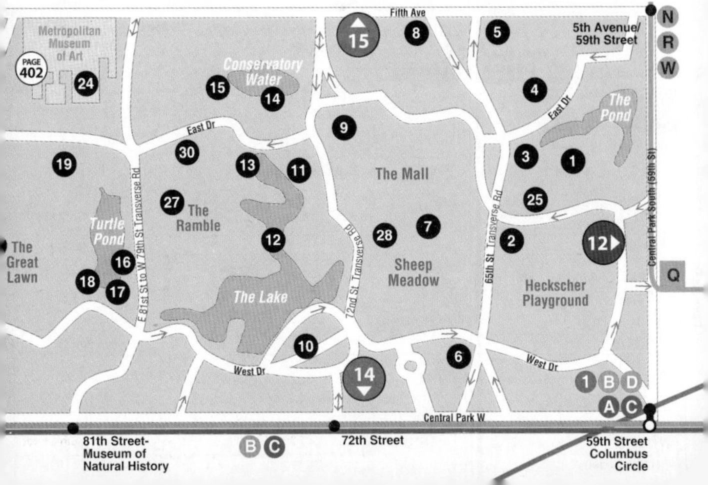

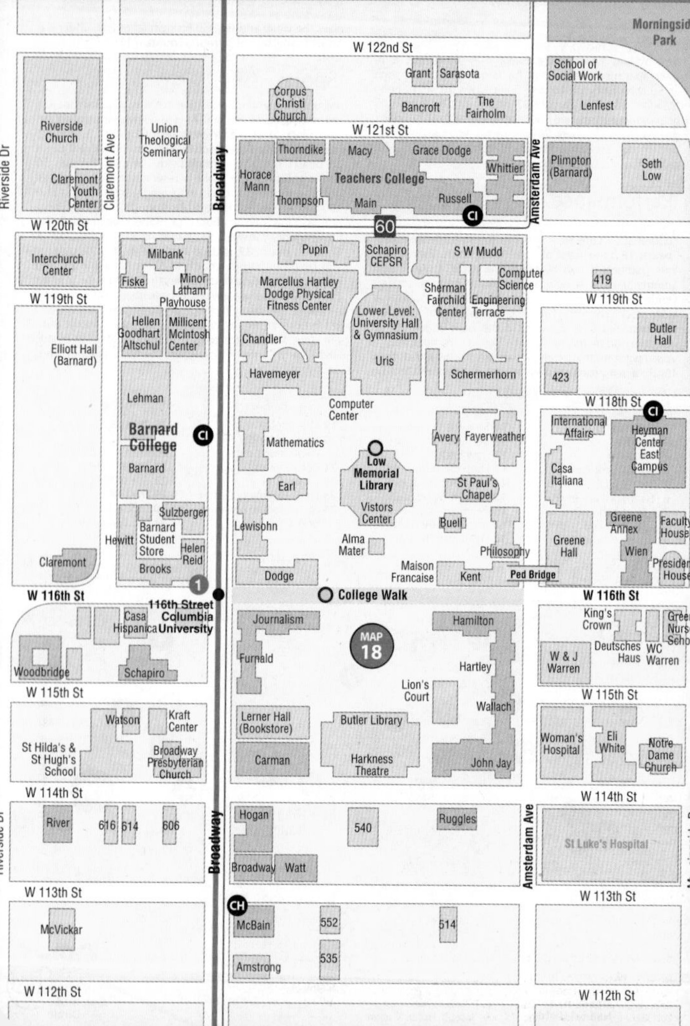

Morningside Park
W 122nd St
Grant
Sarasota
Corpus Christi Church
Bancroft
The Fairholm
School of Social Work
Lenfest
W 121st St
Riverside Church
Union Theological Seminary
Claremont Youth Center
Riverside Dr
Claremont Ave
Broadway
Thorndike
Macy
Grace Dodge
Horace Mann
Teachers College
Whittier
Thompson
Main
Russell
Amsterdam Ave
Plimpton (Barnard)
Seth Low
W 120th St
60
CI
Interchurch Center
Milbank
Fiske
Minor Latham Playhouse
Pupin
Schapiro CEPSR
S W Mudd
Computer Science
419
W 119th St
Marcellus Hartley Dodge Physical Fitness Center
Sherman Fairchild Center
Engineering Terrace
W 119th St
Lower Level: University Hall & Gymnasium
Hellen Goodhart Altschul
Millicent McIntosh Center
Elliott Hall (Barnard)
Chandler
Butler Hall
Havemeyer
Uris
Schermerhorn
423
Lehman
Computer Center
W 118th St
Barnard College
International Affairs
Heyman Center East Campus
Mathematics
Avery
Fayerweather
Low Memorial Library
Casa Italiana
Barnard
Earl
St Paul's Chapel
Vistors Center
Sulzberger
Barnard Student Store
Lewisohn
Buell
Greene Annex
Faculty House
Hewitt
Helen Reid
Alma Mater
Greene Hall
Philosophy
Wien
President House
Claremont
Brooks
Maison Francaise
Dodge
Kent
Ped Bridge
1
W 116th St
116th Street Columbia University
College Walk
W 116th St
Casa Hispanica
Journalism
Hamilton
King's Crown
Woodbridge
Schapiro
MAP 18
Furnald
Hartley
Deutsches Haus
W & J Warren
WC Warren
W 115th St
Lion's Court
W 115th St
Watson
Kraft Center
Lerner Hall (Bookstore)
Butler Library
Wallach
St Hilda's & St Hugh's School
Broadway Presbyterian Church
Carman
Harkness Theatre
John Jay
Woman's Hospital
Eli White
Notre Dame Church
W 114th St
W 114th St
River
616
614
606
Hogan
540
Ruggles
St Luke's Hospital
Broadway
Watt
W 113th St
W 113th St
CH
McVickar
McBain
552
514
535
Amstrong
W 112th St
W 112th St

General Information

NFT Map:	18
Morningside Heights:	2960 Broadway & 116th St
Medical Center:	601 W 168th St
Phone:	212-854-1754
Website:	www.columbia.edu
Students Enrolled:	23,813
Endowment:	Market value as of June 30, 2005 $5.191 billion

Overview

Yearning for those carefree days spent debating nihilism in the quad and wearing pajamas in public? Look no further than a quick trip to the Ivy League haven of Columbia University. Unlike the other collegiate institutions that pepper Manhattan's real estate, Columbia actually *has* a campus. The main campus, located in Morningside Heights, spans six blocks between Broadway and Amsterdam Avenues. Most of the undergraduate classes are held here, along with several of the graduate schools. Other graduate schools, including the Law School and School of International and Public Affairs, are close by on Amsterdam Avenue. The main libraries, Miller Theater, and St. Paul's Chapel are also located on the Morningside Heights campus. You can even get your intramural fix on a few fields for frisbee-throwing and pick-up soccer games.

Founded in 1754 as King's College, Columbia University is one of the country's most prestigious academic institutions. The university is well known for its core curriculum, a program of requirements that gives students an introduction to the most influential works in literature, philosophy, science, and other disciplines. It also prepares them for the rigors of those pesky dinner parties.

After residing in two different downtown locations, Columbia moved to its present campus (designed by McKim, Mead, and White) in 1897. Low Library remains the focal point of the campus as does the Alma Mater statue in front—a landmark that continues to inspire student superstitions (find the hidden owl and you might be the next valedictorian) thanks to a thwarted plot to blow it up by the radical Weather Underground in the '60s. Students line the stairs in front of the library on sunny days, eating lunch and chatting with classmates. Columbia even has its own spooky network of underground tunnels (third largest in the world) that date back to the old Morningside mental asylum and were utilized by students and police during the 1968 strike.

Town/gown relations in Morningside Heights are complicated, and getting more so by the day. While Columbia students consistently show local businesses the money, it's not enough to keep community members from freaking every time the university discusses new construction projects. The most famous of these struggles came in response to Columbia's plans to build a gymnasium in Morningside Park. Contentious proposals, approved in 2009, for a 17-acre expansion into Manhattanville (the area north of 125th Street) by 2030 still cause tension and fear of evictions, and the debate between the university and old-time residents continues.

Columbia's medical school is the second oldest in the nation, and the world's first academic medical center. The school is affiliated with the Columbia-Presbyterian Medical Center in Washington Heights and encompasses the graduate schools of medicine, dentistry, nursing, and public health. Columbia is the only Ivy League university with a journalism school, which was founded at the bequest of Joseph Pulitzer in 1912. (The prize is still administered there.) The school is also affiliated with Barnard College, Jewish Theological Seminary, Teachers College, and Union Theological Seminary.

Numerous movies have been filmed on or around the campus including *Ghostbusters*, *Hannah and Her Sisters*, and *Spiderman I* and *II*. Most recently, Patrick Dempsey was spotted promoting that 2008 chick flick you forgot about, Made of Honor.

Notable alums and faculty include artists James Cagney, Art Garfunkel, Georgia O'Keeffe, Rodgers and Hammerstein, Paul Robeson, and Twyla Tharp; critic Lionel Trilling; baseball player Lou Gehrig; and writers Isaac Asimov, Joseph Heller, Carson McCullers, Eudora Welty, Zora Neale Hurston, and Herman Wouk. Business alumni include Warren Buffet, Alfred Knopf, Joseph Pulitzer, and Milton Friedman, while government officials Madeline Albright, Dwight Eisenhower, Alexander Hamilton, Robert Moses, Franklin Delano Roosevelt, and Teddy Roosevelt all graced the university's classrooms. In the field of law, Benjamin Cardozo, Ruth Bader Ginsburg, Charles Evans Hughes, and John Jay called Columbia home, and Stephen Jay Gould, Margaret Mead, and Benjamin Spock make the list of notable science alumni.

Tuition

Columbia undergraduate tuition for 2009-2010 was $37,470 for the year, plus $9,980 for dorms and food, and another $2,100 for books and miscellaneous fees. We suggest: Shacking up with your Aunt Agatha on the Upper West Side for the duration.

Sports

The Columbia Marching Band plays "Roar, Lion, Roar" after every touchdown, but their instruments remain tragically roarless most of the time. The Lions almost set the record for straight losses by a major college football team when they dropped 44 consecutive games between 1983 and 1988. Not much has changed—their 2-8 record in 2008 was par for the course. The Lions play their mostly Ivy League opponents at Lawrence A. Wein Stadium (Baker Field), located way up at the top of Manhattan.

Columbia excels in other sports including crew, fencing, golf, tennis, and sailing (silver spoon not included). The university is represented by 29 men's and women's teams in the NCAA Division I. It also has the oldest wrestling team in the country.

Culture on Campus

The ire evoked by its controversial immigration speech, when students stormed the stage, pales when compared to Columbia's 2007 invitation to Iranian president Mahmoud Ahmadinejad to participate in a debate. Good or bad, it created much hype and put the campus in the spotlight for a day or two. Columbia does, however, feature plenty of other less volatile dance, film, music, theater, lectures, readings, and talks. Venues include: the Macy Gallery at the Teacher's College, which exhibits works by a variety of artists, including faculty and children's artwork; the fabulous Miller Theatre at 2960 Broadway, which primarily features musical performances and lectures; the student-run Postcrypt Art Gallery in the basement of St. Paul's Chapel; the Theatre of the Riverside Church for theatrical performances from their top-rated graduate program; and the Wallach Art Gallery on the 8th floor of Schermerhorn Hall, featuring art and architecture exhibits. Check the website for a calendar of events. And bring your rubber bullets, just in case.

Phone Numbers

Morningside Campus	212-854-1754
Medical Center	212-305-2500
Visitors Center	212-854-4900
Public Affairs	212-854-2037
University Development and Alumni Relations	877-854-ALUM(2586)
Library Information	212-854-3533
Graduate School of Architecture, Planning, and Preservation	212-854-3414
School of the Arts	212-854-2875
Graduate School of Arts and Sciences	212-854-4737
School of Dental and Oral Surgery	212-305-6726
School of Engineering	212-854-2993
School of General Studies	212-854-2772
School of International and Public Affairs	212-854-5406
Graduate School of Journalism	212-854-8608
School of Law	212-854-2640
School of Nursing	212-305-5756
School of Public Health	212-305-4797
School of Social Work	212-851-2300

Overview

East River Park is a long, thin slice of land, sandwiched between the FDR Drive and the East River, and running from Montgomery Street up to 12th Street. Built in the late 1930s as part of the FDR Drive, the park's recent refurbishments have made its sporting facilities some of the best Manhattan has to offer. The East River Esplanade, a walkway encircling many parts of the East Side, is a constant work-in-progress. The overall plan is to someday create one continuous green stretch from Maine to Florida, part of the highly ambitious East Coast Greenway project (www.greenway.org). But first we'll see if we can get East River Park to stretch as far as the UN. (Initial city plans are aiming to grow the park from Battery Park to Harlem.) The Parks Department plans to complete renovation on the Esplanade (between Delancey and 8th Street) by Fall 2010 – just two seasons behind its initial spring prediction. Not too shabby!

Attractions

No one would ever mistake East River Park for Battery Park, but to its credit, the city has made great improvements, cleaning and buffing it 'til it almost shines. The park comes alive in the summer and on weekends, when hundreds of families barbecue in the areas between the athletic fields, blaring music and eating to their hearts' content. Others take leisurely strolls or jogs along the East River Esplanade, which offers dramatic views of the river and Brooklyn. Many have turned the park's unused areas into unofficial dog runs, places for pick-up games of ultimate frisbee or soccer, and sunbathing areas. And aside from bathing beauties, you'll even find fishermen waiting patiently for striped bass (not that we have to tell you, but nothing caught in the East River should be eaten—while the water quality has improved dramatically, it's still full of pollutants).

Sports

The sports facilities at East River Park have undergone heavy reconstruction. The park now includes facilities for football, softball, basketball, soccer, tennis, and even cricket. Thankfully, many of the fields have been resurfaced with a resilient synthetic turf—a smart move given the amount of use the park gets by all the different sports leagues.

Facilities

There are three bathroom facilities located in the park—one at the tennis courts, one at the soccer/track field, and one up in the northern part of the

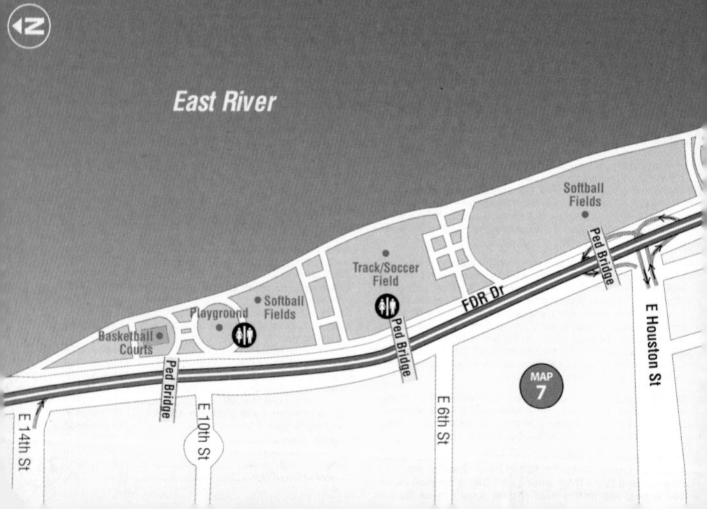

Lighting Schedule (for updates/changes, check www.esbnyc.com)

January • Martin Luther King, Jr. Day
January • March of Dimes
January–February • Lunar New Year
February 14 • Valentine's Day
February • President's Day
February • Westminster Kennel Club
February • Swisspeaks Festival for Switzerland
February • World Cup Archery Championship
March 17 • St. Patrick's Day
March • Greek Independence Day
March • Equal Parents Day/ Children's Rights
March • Wales/St. David's Day
March • Oscar Week in NYC
March • Colon Cancer Awareness
March • Red Cross Month
March–April • Spring/Easter Week
April • Earth Day
April • Child Abuse Prevention
April • National Osteoporosis Society
April • Rain Forest Day
April • Israel Independence Day
April • Dutch Queen's Day
April • Tartan Day
May • Muscular Dystrophy
May • Armed Forces Day
May • Memorial Day
May • Police Memorial Day
May • Fire Department Memorial Day
May • Haitian Culture Awareness
June 14 • Flag Day
June • Portugal Day
June • NYC Triathlon
June • Stonewall Anniversary/ Gay Pride
July 4 • Independence Day
July • Bahamas Independence Day
July • Bastille Day
July • Peru Independence
July • Columbia Heritage & Independence
August • US Open
August • Jamaica Independence Day
August • India Independence Day
August • Pakistan Independence Day
September • Mexico Independence Day
September • Labor Day
September • Brazil Independence Day
September • Pulaski Day
September • Race for the Cure
September • Switzerland admitted to the UN
September • Qatar Independence
September • Fleet Week/Support our Servicemen and Servicewomen/ Memorial for 9/11
September • Feast of San Gennaro
October • Breast Cancer Awareness
October • German Reunification Day
October • Columbus Day
October 24 • United Nations Day
October • Big Apple Circus
October • Pennant/World Series win for the Yankees
October • Pennant/World Series win for the Mets [Ha!]
October • NY Knicks Opening Day
October–November • Autumn
October • Walk to End Domestic Violence
November • NYC Marathon
November • Veterans' Day
November • Alzheimer's Awareness
December • First night of Hanukkah
December • "Day Without Art/Night Without Lights"/AIDS Awareness
December–January 7 (with interruptions) • Holiday Season

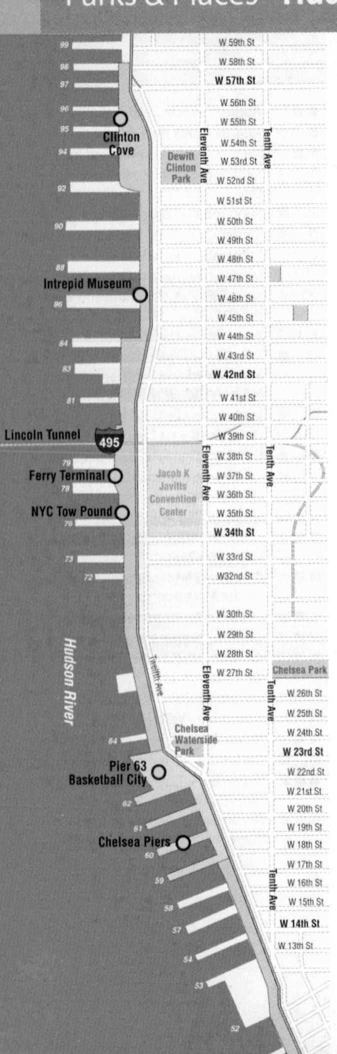

General Information

Hudson River Park Trust:	212-627-2020
Websites:	www.hudsonriverpark.org www.friendsofhudsonriverpark.org

Overview

It's up for debate whether Hudson River Park is a beacon for downtown joggers or a Bermuda triangle that pilots should fly away from. In a matter of months, this western stretch of green torpedoed into infamy when two planes and a helicopter crash-landed off the banks of the park. Most famously, the U.S. Airways "Miracle on the Hudson" skidded to a safe water landing in early 2009. Seven months later, a helicopter and a small plane collided in nearly the same spot and killed nine people.

Of course, we'd rather talk about the park's safer aerial acrobatics, like the trapezes and half-pipes that define this 550-acre, $330 million park development along the south and southwest coastline of Manhattan. Stretching from Battery Place to West 59th, Hudson River Park rivals Midtown's 800 acres of public lawn and is quickly becoming downtown's Central Park.

As part of the New York State Significant Coastal Fish and Wildlife Habitat, 400 acres of the total 550 thrive as estuarine sanctuary. This means the seventy fish species (there are fish in the Hudson?) and thirty bird species on the waterfront won't go belly up or beak down with all the marine preservation. Thanks to this effort, you'll be able to enjoy the winter flounder, white perch, owls, hawks, and songbirds for generations to come. (That's fantastic! Bob, tell them what else they've won…) What downtown, nature-loving, organic-eating savers of the planet have won is in what they've lost. As a mandate, office buildings, hotels, casino gambling boats, and manufacturing plants are prohibited from the HRP, as are residences (sorry, no water-front property next to your yacht) and jet skis (better to leave them in the Caymans). The Intrepid aircraft carrier/sea-air-space museum has reopened; check it out, especially during Fleet Week each year (usually the week of Memorial Day, in May). You'll get to see teeming Navy personnel and much more modern vessels, some of which absolutely dwarf the Intrepid itself. A sight not to be missed.

Art

From exhibition to permanent collection, HRP takes its culture cue from the surrounding downtown art scene of TriBeCa, SoHo, and Chelsea. You were probably one of the thousands waiting in line to see *Ashes and Snow*, Gregory Colbert's rendition of the interactions between animals and humans took form in the temporary Nomadic Museum on Pier 54. Or maybe you checked out Malcolm Cochran's *Private Passage* on Clinton Cove (55th–57th St). Similar to your late-night antics, you peered into a gigantic wine bottle. There, from portholes carved on the sides, you could see the interior of the stateroom of the Queen Mary. Or, hearkening back to an early time, the *Shadow of the Lusitania*. Justen Ladda recreated the shadow of the famous ship on the south side of Pier 54 (also home to reconstructed historic ships, not just their shadows), its original docking place, with glass and planters. Jutting out where Pier 49 used to sit is one of the park's more somber exhibits, the New York City AIDS memorial. Dedicated on World AIDS Day in 2008 after 14 years of fundraising and planning, the 42-foot-long memorial is both a striking accomplishment and a sober nod to those whose lives have been lost to the disease. A more permanent piece in HRP: *Salinity Gradient* in TriBeCa. Paver stones spanning 2000 feet take the shape of Hudson marine creatures. Striped bass included. Not impressed? HRP Trust hired different designers for each segment of the five-mile park, with only the esplanade and waterfront railing as universal pieces. Check out the landscape design of each segment.

Attractions

Season-specific events are held year-round at HRP. During the summer, experience fight-night basics on Pier 54 for Rumble on the River with live blood splattering with each KO. Sundays in the summer host Moon Dances on Pier 25 with free dance lessons before live New York bands play. Wednesday and Fridays in the summer boast River Flicks on Pier 54 and Pier 25 with throwback films like *The Goonies*. Pier of Fear is mainly a Halloween party for the kiddies, but if you're still down with dressing up as the *Scream* guy, hey, no one will stop you. Nature centers are next on the list of HRP's formidable repertoire of attractions.

Sports

Think of sports in terms of piers. You already know about ritzy Chelsea Piers, but soon enough "Pier 40" or "Pier 63" will also become vernacular to sports freaks. And there are far less expensive piers beyond CP. Most crucial to athletic-minded souls, a five-mile running/biking/blading path that threads through the piers. It's a miniature divided highway—smooth, simple, and super crowded during peak times (early evening and weekends). You'll find sunbathing lawns throughout (the most sport some will ever do). Pier 40: three and a half ball fields. Area south of Houston: three tennis courts. Mini-golf. Batting cages. Skateboard park. Beach volleyball. Trapeze lessons. Pier 40, CP, Pier 63, Pier 96: free kayaking. Those are the highlights; for more that's up your particular sports alley, check out the website.

How to Get There

Hmmm. How to most efficiently make your way through all the concrete to the shoreline? The 1 and A C E between Chambers and 59th Streets will get you the closest. Go west 'til you hit water. You're there.

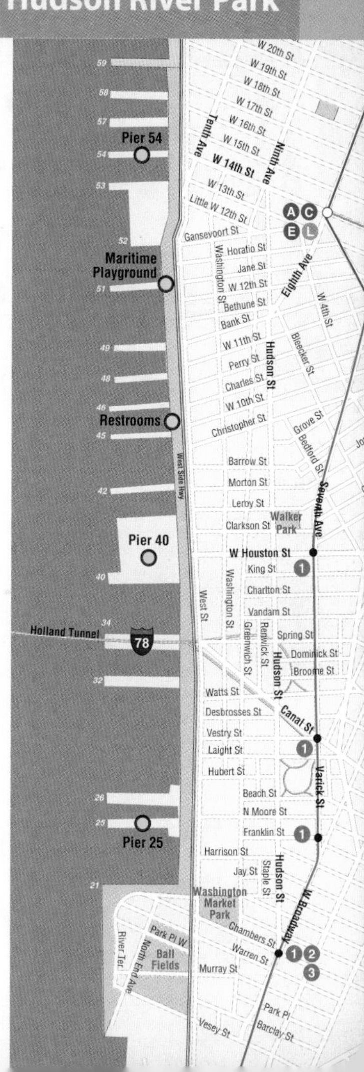

Parks & Places • **Javits Center**

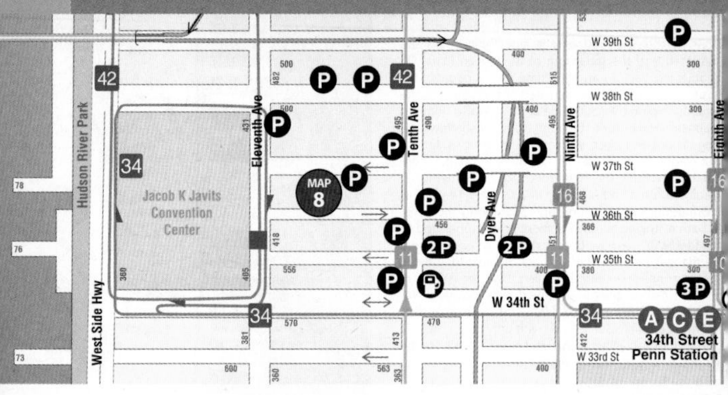

LEVEL ONE

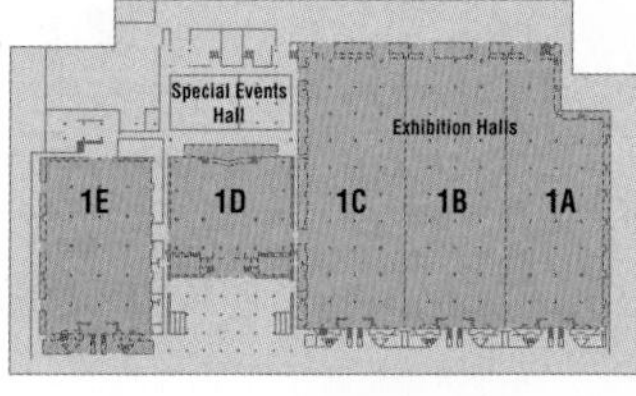

LEVEL THREE

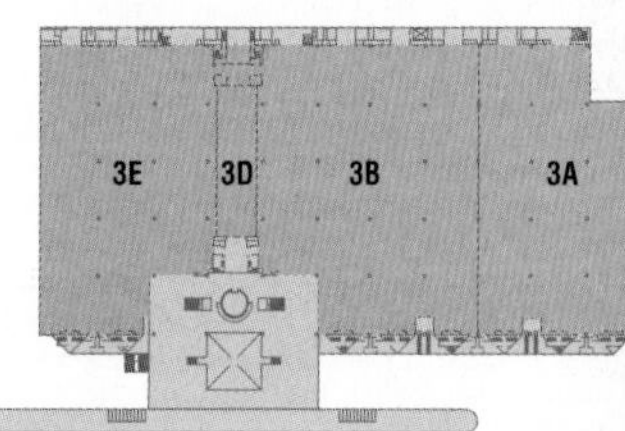

LEVEL TWO

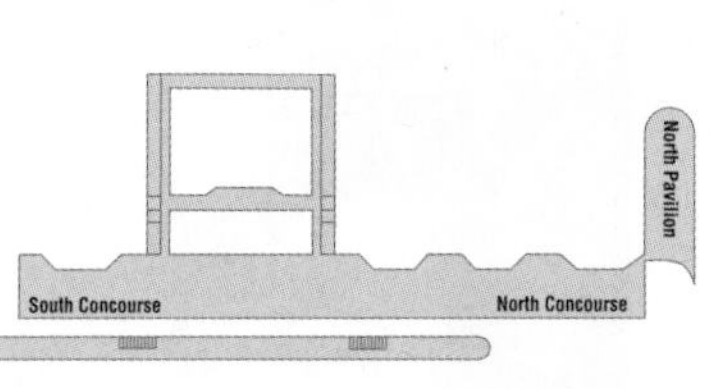

LEVEL FOUR

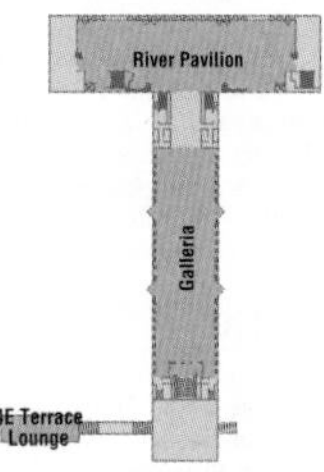

General Information

NFT Map:	8
Address:	655 W 34th St
Website:	www.javitscenter.com
Phone Number:	212-216-2000
Fax Number:	212-216-2588

Overview

This massive glass-and-steel behemoth of a convention hall next to the Hudson River was officially built to house big trade shows, conventions and expositions, but clearly its true purpose is to annoy anyone who has to go there. Located between 34th and 38th streets, the James Ingo Freed design has been sitting in the middle of nowhere sans subway link for an appalling 25 years. Dissatisfaction with the convention center has brewed for a number of years, with complaints ranging from the aesthetic (big ugly box) to the practical (lack of space). Various plans have been proposed over the years to expand the center up or over the adjoining west side rail yards, and overhaul the building's facade. The Javits even got dragged into the Jets stadium fiasco, but seems to have emerged with some concrete progress towards a revamping: in late-2006, ground was broken on an expansion that would more than double the size of the Center. Shockingly, the election of a new governor (Spitzer), and resignation of a governor due to prostitution allegations (Spitzer again) has resulted in a re-evaluation of the plans. When discovered that most of the $1.6 billion budget would go towards fixing—not expanding—the project was essentially nixed.

What is most important to know about the Javits, and most other convention centers in the world, is that they are essentially soulless, dehumanizing spaces with crappy bathrooms, horrific food, nowhere to sit, and filled (generally) with absolutely slimy, soulless, moronic sales and marketing people; it just depends on which industry is in town that moment as to what exact breed you're getting. Even the presence of cool sports cars (i.e. the Auto Show each Easter week) can't overcome a feeling, after spending even two hours in this convention center, of an absolute black nihilism. Surely someone's come up with something better? Perhaps all trade shows should simply be outdoors in Southern California in the spring—at least, that's our vote.

ATMs

CH • Chase • Level One
CH • Chase • Level Three

Services

Coat/Luggage Check
Concierge Services
FedEx Kinko's Office and Print Center
First Aid
Hudson News
Information
Lost and Found
Mailboxes Etc
Shoeshine
Wi-Fi (hourly, daily, and show plans available)

Food

The food at the Javits Center is, of course, rapaciously expensive, and, if you're exhibiting, usually sold out by 2:30 in the afternoon. Our suggestion is to look for people handing out Chinese food menus and have them deliver to your booth. (And yes, they take credit cards. And yes, it's bad Chinese food.)

Level 1
Boar's Head Deli
Caliente Cab Company
Carvel Ice Cream Bakery
Feast of the Dragon
Gourmet Coffee Bar
Market Fair/Korean Deli Buffet
Nathan's
Villa Cucina Italiana
Villa Pizza

Level 3
The Bakery
Boar's Head Deli
Carvels
Caliente Cab Company
Dai Kichi Sushi
The Dining Car
Feast of the Dragon
Go Gourmet
The Grille
Villa Pizza

North Concourse
New York Pretzel
Panini

How to Get There—Mass Transit

Until they extend that 7 train, there's no direct subway access to the center. The closest subway stop is at 34th Street/Penn Station, but even that's a good 4- to 5-block hike away. You can also take the buses from the 42nd Street 42 and 34th Street 34 subway stops, which will both drop you off right outside the center.

There are also numerous shuttle buses that run to various participating hotels and other locales free of charge for convention goers. Schedules and routes vary for each convention, so ask at the information desk on the first floor.

From New Jersey, the NY Waterway operates ferries from Weehawken, Hoboken, and Jersey City that ship you across the Hudson River to 39th Street and Twelfth Avenue in 15 minutes or less, dropping you just one block from the Javits Center. The ferries leave every 15–30 minutes during peak hours. Call 1-800-53-FERRY or go to www.nywaterway.com for a schedule and more information.

Lincoln Center / Columbus Circle

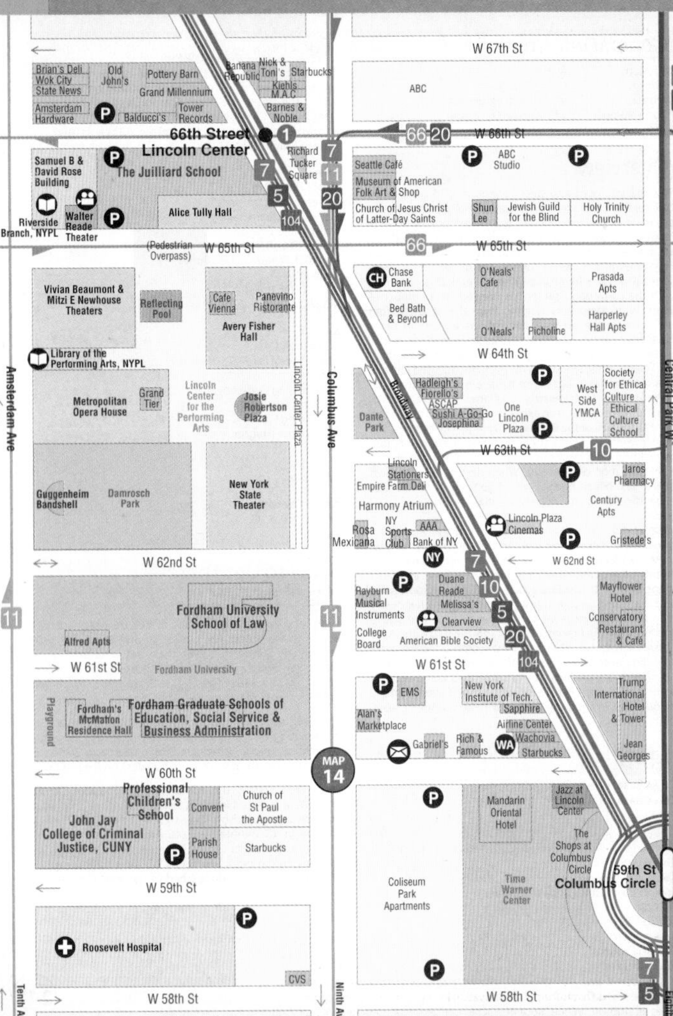

General Information

NFT Map: 14
Website: .... www.lincolncenter.org
General Information: 212-546-2656 (212-LINCOLN)
Customer Service: 212-875-5456
Alice Tully Hall: 212-875-5050
Avery Fisher Hall: 212-875-5030
The Chamber Music Society: 212-875-5775
Film Society of Lincoln Center: 212-875-5610
Guided Tours: 212-875-5350
Jazz at Lincoln Center: 212-258-9800
The Julliard School: 212-799-5000
Lincoln Center Theater: 212-362-7600
The Metropolitan Opera House: 212-362-6000
New York City Ballet: 212-870-5500
New York City Opera: 212-870-5630
New York Philharmonic: 212-875-5656
New York State Theater: 212-870-5570
Parking Garage: 212-874-9021
Walter Reade Theater: 212-875-5600

Ticket Purchase Phone Numbers

Alice Tully Hall: 212-721-5050
Avery Fisher Hall: 212-721-5030
CenterCharge: 212-721-6500
Film Society of Lincoln Center: 212-496-3809
MovieFone, Walter Reade Theater: 212-777-FILM
TeleCharge, Lincoln Center Theater: 212-239-6200
Ticketmaster, New York State Theater: 212-307-4100
Ticketmaster, Met & Ballet: 212-362-6000

Overview

Sometimes, the typical dinner-and-drinks can color only so many nights before you crave a more…let's say, cultured experience. Cue Lincoln Center. As one of Manhattan's most romantic spots, its stages have felt soft pirouettes of ballet slippers from the NYC Ballet, vibrations from sopranos in the Metropolitan Opera, and tap-tap-tap from the soles of trumpet-players. Culture, indeed. This four-square-block area borders on cultural obscenity. Better leave dinner-and-drinks to the pre-show. Now, thanks to the new Donald and Barbara Zucker Box Office that doles out discounted seats every day, even us peasants get to savor the famously expensive center's shows (and keep those dinner reservations). However, visual aesthetic doesn't start and stop onstage. Lincoln Center also showcases some of the city's signature art and architectural gems: Henry Moore's *Reclining Figure* is the centerpiece of the reflecting pool, and Marc Chagall's murals grace the foyer of the Metropolitan Opera House. Philip Johnson's Plaza Fountain anchors the entire center, creating an intimate space where New Yorkers can go to forget about their appallingly high rents and pretend they're in the scene from *Moonstruck* where Cher and Nicholas Cage meet to see *La Bohème*. For a more modern fairy tale, visit the gorgeously renovated Alice Tully Hall. Now you can go see a show amongst the grey hairs in a hip, airy space where you can grab a drink in the café on the ground floor. Goodbye musty 1960s, hello bright new world! Now, we really can't wait until the whole Lincoln Center renewal project is completed this year (yes, we're still being optimistic on that date).

Who Lives Where

A mecca of tulle, tin, and strings, Lincoln Center houses companies upon troupes upon societies. Matching the performing group to the building means you won't end up watching *Swan Lake* when you should be listening to Mozart. The most confusing part about Lincoln Center is that "Lincoln Center Theater" is two theaters—the Vivian Beaumont and the Mitzi E. Newhouse theaters. Jazz at Lincoln Center moved into the Frederick P. Rose Hall in the AOL/Time Warner Center.

American Ballet Theater — Metropolitan Opera House
Chamber Music Society — Alice Tully Hall
Film Society of Lincoln Center — Walter Reade Theater
Jazz at Lincoln Center — Frederick P. Rose Hall
Julliard Orchestra & Symphony — Alice Tully Hall
Metropolitan Opera Company — Metropolitan Opera House
Lincoln Center Theater — Vivian Beaumont Theater and Mitzi E. Newhouse Theater
Mostly Mozart Festival — Avery Fisher Hall
New York City Ballet — New York State Theater
New York City Opera — New York State Theater
New York Philharmonic — Avery Fisher Hall
School of American Ballet — Samuel B. and David Rose Building

Columbus Circle

Hooray! Something that isn't completely soulless in Columbus Circle! Cue: the Museum of Arts and Design, which opened up on the south side of the circle in 2008. Definitely check out its sublime permanent collection, its excellent temporary exhibits, and its cool design shop. Other than that, head for the Whole Foods or Lincoln Center. This mothership, inside one of the closest things to a shopping mall in NYC, anchors the Time Warner Center and the Mandarin Oriental Hotel, which, by the way, has pillows on which your out-of-town guests will not sleep, unless they own a small kingdom. Ditto for eating at Per Se ($250 per person, plus drinks). Other highlights for us common folk include Thomas Keller's Bouchon Bakery, the uptown outpost of TriBeCa's cool Landmarc restaurant, a Borders bookstore, and the Samsung UnStore, where you can check your email for free. The Trump International Hotel and Tower soars nearby. Nougatine, of Jean-Georges fame, features as its premier lunch spot…ahh…the other reason you go to Columbus Circle.

How to Get There

Lincoln Center is right off Broadway and only a few blocks north of Columbus Circle, which makes getting there easy. The closest subway is the 66th Street 1 stop, which has an exit right on the edge of the center. It's also an easy walk from the trains that roll into Columbus Circle. If you prefer above-ground transportation, the 5 7 10 11 66 104 bus lines all stop within one block of Lincoln Center. There is also a parking lot underneath the complex.

1. 31 Union Sq. W.
   Residence Hall
2. Albert and Vera List Academic Center
   6 E. 16th St.
3. 8 E. 16th St./ 79 Fifth Ave.
4. 25 E. 13th St.
5. 65 Fifth Ave.
6. 80 Fifth Ave.
7. Fanton Hall/Welcome Center
   72 Fifth Ave.
8. Arnhold Hall
   55 W. 13th St.
9. 118 W. 13th St.
   Residence Hall
10. 2 W. 13th St.
11. 70 Fifth Ave.
12. 68 Fifth Ave.
13. Shelia C. Johnson Design Center
    66 Fifth Ave.
14. Loeb Hall
    135 E. 12th St.
15. Alvin Johnson/
    J.M. Kaplan Building
    66 W. 12th St.
16. Eugene Lang College
    65 W. 11th St.
17. 64 W. 11th St.
18. 5 W. 8th St.
    Marlton House

General Information

NFT Maps:	5 & 6
Phone:	212-229-5600
Website:	www.newschool.edu
Enrollment:	9,300

Overview

The graffiti logoed New School, formerly The New School for Social Research, is a legendary progressive university located around Greenwich Village, housing eight major divisions, a world-renowned think tank and the backdrop for Project Runway. Founded in 1919 as a refuge for intellectual nonconformists (including historian Charles Beard, philosopher John Dewey, and several former Columbia professors), The New School credits its philosophy the fusing of American intellectual rigor and European critical thought.

The university annually enrolls 9,300 students within eight undergraduate and graduate divisions, including Parsons The New School for Design, Milano The New School for Management and Urban Policy, Eugene Lang College The New School for Liberal Arts, Mannes College The New School for Music, The New School for Drama, The New School for General Studies, The New School for Social Research, and The New School for Jazz and Contemporary Music.

The current New School for Social Research, formerly the Graduate Faculty of Political and Social Science, formerly the University in Exile was a division founded as haven for dismissed teachers from totalitarian regimes in Europe. Original members included psychologist Erich Fromm and political philosopher Leo Strauss. Quite a lineage with which more recent graduates as Sufjan Stevens and Marc Jacobs have to contend.

Tuition

Tuition for undergraduates is more than $38,000 and at least $12,000 for dorm food and a cramped Manhattan apartment. See website for details.
http://www.newschool.edu/tuition/06/parsons.html

Culture on Campus

Parsons is always showcasing something or other, from student shows to MoMa-presented conferences to fine arts lectures. The John L. Tischman Auditorium is the egg-shaped art deco venue for the masses. The quad courtyard, between buildings on 12th and 13th Streets, is the closest thing to a college campus. Otherwise, there's the city.

Transportation

All the subways that Union Square has to offer! N, Q, R, W, 4, 5, 6 and the L.

General Phone Numbers

Student Financial Services (Mannes) 212-580-0210
Career Development 212-229-1324
Counseling Services 212-229-1671
Financial Aid 212-229-8930
Food Services 212-229-5161
Health Education 212-229-5687
Health Services 212-598-4796
HEOP 212-229-8996
Student Housing 212-229-5459
Intercultural Support 212-229-8996
International Student Services 212-229-5592
International Student Services (Mannes) ... 212-580-0210
Student Ombuds 212-229-8996
Registrar 212-229-5620
Registration (Mannes) 212-580-0210
Student Development 212-229-5687
Student Financial Services 212-229-8930
Student Rights & Responsibilites 212-229-5349
Fogelman Library 212-229-5307
Gimbel Library 212-229-8914
Scherman Library 212-580-0210

Residence Hall Phone Numbers

Loeb Hall 212-229-1167
Marlton House 212-473-7014
Union Square 212-229-5343
William Street 646-414-0216
13th Street 646-414-2671
Security (24 Hours) 212-229-7001

Academic Phone Numbers

The New School for General Studies 212-998-8040
Milano The New School for Management and Urban Policy 212-998-3011
Parsons The New School for Design 212-998-6060
Eugene Lang College The New School for Liberal Arts 212-263-7300
The New School for Social Research 212-998-7200
Mannes College The New School for Music 212-998-7200
The New School for Drama 212-998-0100
The New School for Jazz and Contemporary Music 212-998-1800

Parks & Places • New York University

General Information

NFT Map: 6
Phone: 212-998-1212
Website: www.nyu.edu
Enrollment: 50,917

Overview

Founded in 1831, the nation's largest private university sprawls throughout Manhattan, though its most recognizable buildings border Washington Square. Total enrollment is just over 50,000, about 20,000 of whom are undergraduates, and all of whom are more culturally savvy than any 10 other generic college students.

The expansion of NYU during recent years has not been welcomed by local residents. Some Village folks blame NYU's sprawl for higher rents and diminished quirkiness. On the other hand, the students are a financial boom for businesses in the area, and many historical buildings (such as the row houses on Washington Square) are owned and kept in good condition by the university.

NYU comprises fourteen colleges, schools, and faculties, including the well-regarded Stern School of Business, the School of Law, and the Tisch School of Arts. It also has a school of Continuing and Professional Studies, with offerings in publishing, real estate, and just about every other city-centric industry you could imagine. 34,944 people applied to NYU for undergraduate school last year; just over 28% were accepted. And listen up, boys, 61% of those enrolled last year were female.

Unfortunately, the Chick-fil-A within the Weinstein Hall dining facility closed a few years ago. We're still in mourning.

Tuition

Tuition for undergraduates is over $37,000, and over $12,000 for "room and board." Time for daddy to break out the Gold Card, n'est-ce pas?

Sports

NYU isn't big on athletics. They don't have a football team. (Where would they play anyway?) It does have a number of other sports teams, though. The school competes in Division III and its mascot is the Bobcat, although all of their teams are nicknamed the Violets. Go figure.

Culture on Campus

The Grey Art Gallery usually has something cool (www.nyu.edu/greyart), and the new Skirball Center for the Performing Arts hosts live performances (www.skirballcenter.nyu.edu). NYU doesn't host nearly as many events as decent liberal arts schools in the middle of nowhere. Why bother? It's in Greenwich Village, surrounded by some of the world's best rock and jazz clubs, and on the same island as 700+ art galleries, thousands of restaurants, and tons of revival and new cinema. This is both the blessing and the curse of NYU—no true "campus," but situated in the middle of the greatest cultural square mileage in the world.

Transportation

NYU runs its own campus transportation service for students, faculty, staff, and alumni with school ID cards. They run 7 am to 2 am weekdays and 10 am to 2 am weekends.

Route A: 200 Water St (South Street Seaport) to 715 Broadway (near 4th St), stopping at the Lafayette and Broome Street dorms on the way.
Route B: Woolworth Building to 715 Broadway, passing through the same areas as Route A.
Route C: 715 Broadway loop, passing through SoHo, NoHo, and the East Village.
Route D: 715 Broadway loop through the West Village via the Greenwich Street dorm.
Route E: Midtown Center (SCPS near 42nd St and Fifth Ave) to 715 Broadway, stopping at the NYU Medical Center on the east side and passing through the Gramercy Park area.

General Phone Numbers

Gould Welcome Center: 212-998-INFO (4636)
NYU Protection and Transportation Services 212-998-2222
Undergraduate Admissions: 212-998-4500
Financial Aid: 212-998-4444
University Registrar: 212-998-4800
University Employment Office: 212-998-1250
Student Health Services: 212-443-1000
Kimmel Center for University Life: 212-998-4900
Bobst Library: 212-998-2500
Coles Sports Center: 212-998-2020
NYU Card: 212-443-CARD (2273)

Academic Phone Numbers

All undergraduate programs: 212-998-4500
Summer Session: 212-998-2292
Dental School: 212-998-9800
Steinhardt School of Education: 212-998-5000
Ehrenkranz School of Social Work: 212-998-5910
Gallatin School of Individualized Study: 212-998-7370
Graduate School of Arts & Science: 212-998-8040
Graduate Computer Science: 212-998-3011
Law School: 212-998-6060
School of Medicine: 212-263-7300
School of Continuing and Professional Studies Degree Program: 212-998-7200
School of Continuing and Professional Studies Real Estate Institute: 212-998-7200
School of Continuing and Professional Studies Non-Credit Program: 212-998-7171
Stern School of Business: 212-998-0100
Tisch School of the Arts: 212-998-1800
Wagner School of Public Service: 212-998-7414

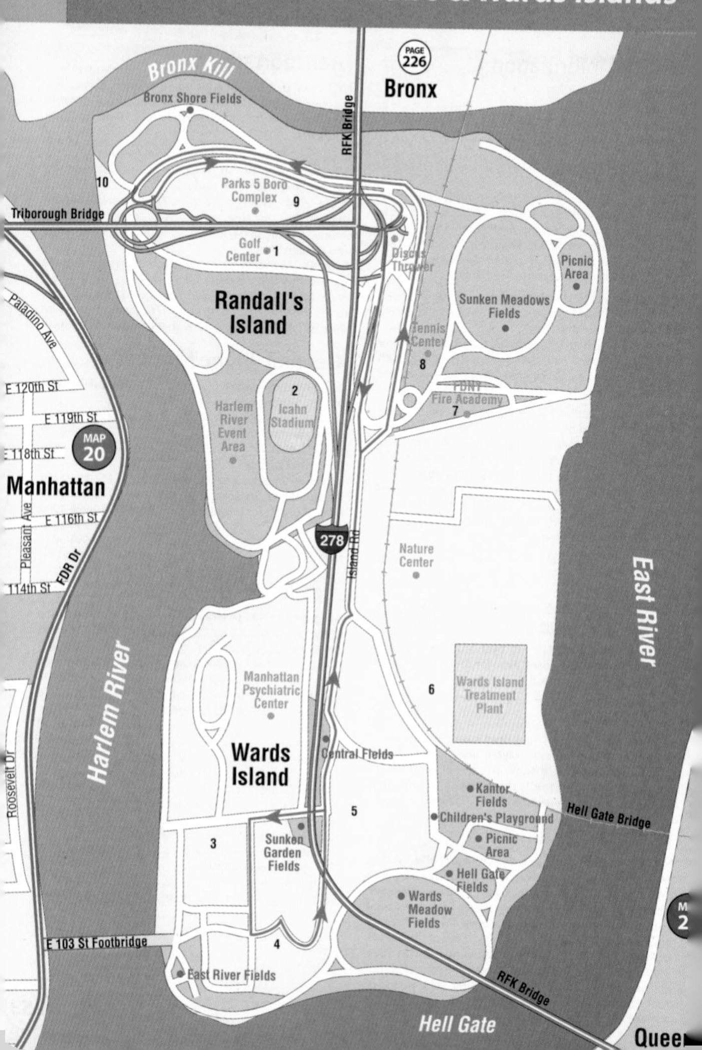
Bronx Kill
PAGE 226
Bronx
Bronx Shore Fields
RFK Bridge
10
Parks 5 Boro Complex
9
Triborough Bridge
Golf Center
1
Discus Thrower
Picnic Area
Sunken Meadows Fields
Randall's Island
Tennis Center
8
Paladino Ave
E 120th St
2
FDNY Fire Academy
7
Harlem River Event Area
Icahn Stadium
E 119th St
MAP 20
E 118th St
Manhattan
E 116th St
Pleasant Ave
278
Island Rd
Nature Center
FDR Dr
114th St
East River
Manhattan Psychiatric Center
Harlem River
6
Wards Island Treatment Plant
Wards Island
Central Fields
Roosevelt Dr
Kantor Fields
5
Children's Playground
Hell Gate Bridge
3
Sunken Garden Fields
Picnic Area
Hell Gate Fields
Wards Meadow Fields
E 103 St Footbridge
4
East River Fields
RFK Bridge
Hell Gate

General Information

Randall's Island Sports Foundation: 212-830-7722; www.risf.org

Overview

If landfills, minimal food options, and a treacherous mix of the Harlem and East Rivers called "Hell Gate" don't entice you over the Triborough Bridge, you probably have good instincts.

But put Randall's & Wards Islands' sullied past aside, and its 440 acres of public park space just across the bridge will surprise you. Conceived by Robert Moses, the two landfill-connected islands have undergone a major overhaul since 1999 and boast some of the city's top athletic fields and parks. Look to the Randall's Island Sports Foundation, which operates the greenspace, to keep progress humming. The foundation kicked off the park's renovation by replacing Downing Stadium with the state-of-the-art Icahn Track & Field Stadium in 2004. Since then, the RISF resorted 66 fields, built new waterfront bike and pedestrian paths, and even has a green energy plan in the works. In 2007, local activists put the kibosh on an eight-year-old plan to build a fancy suburban-style water park. Maybe the island has some bad ju-ju: Hell Gate, where the Harlem and East Rivers meet, has caused hundreds of ships to sink.

No mater what, we hope future plans bring in more food facilities. Currently, the only culinary options are a smattering of food trucks near the Icahn Stadium and the golf center's snack bar. One suggestion: Make a Whole Foods pit stop before enjoying a chill, weekend afternoon in the park.

How to Get There

By Car: Take the Triborough Bridge, exit left to Randall's Island. There's a $5.50 toll to get on the island with your car. It's free to leave!

By Subway/Bus: From Manhattan: take the 4 5 6 train to 125th Street, then transfer on the corner of 125th Street and Lexington Avenue for the 35 bus to Randall's Island. There's a bus about every 40 minutes during the day. From Queens: take the [illegible] from 61st Street-Woodside.

By Foot: A pedestrian footbridge at 103rd Street was built by Robert Moses in the '50s to provide Harlem residents access to the recreational facilities of the parks after then-City Council President Newbold Morris criticized the lack of facilities in Harlem. Today, the bridge is open only during summer daylight hours. See timetable on map.

1 **Randall's Island Golf Center** • 212-427-5689 • The golf center on Randall's Island has a driving range open year-round with 80 heated stalls, along with two 18-hole mini-golf courses, nine batting cages, a snack bar, and a beer garden. A weekend shuttle service is available every hour on the hour, 10 am–5 pm from Manhattan (86th Street and Third Avenue) and costs $10 round-trip. Summer hours are 6 am–11 pm Tuesday–Sunday and 11 am–11 pm on Mondays, with off-season hours from 8 am–8 pm Tuesday–Sunday and 1 pm–8 pm on Mondays.

2 **Icahn Track & Field Stadium** • 212- 860-1899 x101• Named for financier Carl Icahn, the 10,000-seat stadium is the only state-of-the-art outdoor track and field venue in New York City with a 400-meter running track and a regulation-size soccer field.

3 **Supportive Employment Center** • 212-534-3866

4 **Charles H. Gay Shelter Care Center for Men** • Volunteers of America - Greater New York • 212-369-8900 • www.voa-gny.org

5 **Odyssey House Drug Rehab Center** • Mabon Building • 212-426-6677

6 **DEP Water Pollution Control Plant** • 718-595-6600 • www.ci.nyc.ny.us/html/dep/html/drainage.html

7 **Fire Department Training Center** •

The NYC Fire Academy is located on 27 acres of landfill on the east side of Randall's Island. In an effort to keep the city's "bravest" in shape, the academy utilizes the easily accessible 68 acres of parkland for physical fitness programs. The ultra-cool training facility includes 11 Universal Studios–like buildings for simulations training, a 200,000 gallon water supply tank, gasoline and diesel fuel pumps, and a 300-car parking lot. In addition, the New York Transit Authority installed tracks and subway cars for learning and developing techniques to battle subway fires and other emergencies. It's really too bad they don't sell tickets and offer tours!

8 **Tennis Center** • 212- 427-6150 • 11 outdoor courts. Indoor courts heated for winter use.

9 **Robert Moses Building** • We're sure many an urban planning student has made a pilgrimage here.

10 **NYPD** • They launch cool-looking police boats from here.

General Information

Website:
www.nycparks.org or www.riversideparkfund.org

Riverside Park Administrator:
(212) 408-0264

79th Street Boat Basin - Public Marina:
(212) 496-2105

Overview

If Sally Struthers taught you anything about saving the world and you still can't get to that darned developing country, your ticket to heaven awaits at Riverside Park. Pick a program and you're saved: Sponsor a Bench or Sponsor a Tree. Yes, apparently crabapple (or "crab apple" otherwise risking the tongue twister, "crap-abble") and London plane trees need your desperate help. For years, they've been subject to the cruelty of noxious gases from passing cars and dogs' territorial marks, but you, even you, cannot justify lovesick children carving hearts and initials in their bark. You may even remember those poor, diseased-looking trees, like cobras shedding their skins, bark peeling to reveal a lighter inner bark. Light bulb on yet? Those are London plane trees (no diseases involved). And don't forget those benches suffering the wrath of a million deadweights, as they stop to rest their walking feet. Surely, even Sally herself doesn't discriminate against the most deserving.

After you've sponsored your new friend, revel in the four miles of pure, parkalicious plain. Spanning from 72nd to 158th Street, Riverside Park was designed in 1875 by Frederick Law Olmsted. It was expanded and adapted for active recreational use during the early 20th Century without losing too much of its charm. In 1980, the New York City Landmarks Preservation Commission crowned Riverside Park between 72nd and 125th a "scenic landmark."

Things to do along 300 acres of green goodness: Walk. Run. Cycle. Skate. Kayak. Play ball, any ball. (Especially tennis on those gorgeous red clay courts). Throw in a couple of dog walkers, and sure as sugar, you've got yourself a bona fide park (see Hudson River Park, Battery Park City, Central Park for reference).

Sights & Sounds

North waterfront between 147th and 152nd streets: It's a looker. To excite the secret Oscar slave in you, head to the Crabapple Grove at 91st for a self-guided tour of *You've Got Mail*, where Tom Hanks finally met Meg Ryan (as if they didn't know each other the whole time). While you're there, check out the Garden for All Seasons. You can take a guess at what kind of garden that is. Whistle not wet? Take a gander at the American elms that surreptitiously line Riverside Drive. Remember what it's like to have trees—real trees—where you live. Or, if you're so over the tree thing, the Soldiers' and Sailors' Monument at 89th gives homage to Civil War heroes from New York and gives you +1 in preparing for that all-important tavern trivia game. Same goes for Grant's Tomb at 122nd, an intriguing monument, especially with Jazz Mobile (an offshoot of T-Mobile and Jazz at Lincoln Center…) strumming serious beats on a lazy summer day. Who knew the key to heaven's gates was in your backyard?

Swing a Ring

Located at Riverside Park's Hudson Beach (W 105th St), Swing a Ring is a unique fitness apparatus that exists only in New York City (lucky us) and Santa Monica. There's a set for adults and a set for ankle-biters. It's free, permanent, open year-round, and virtually indestructible (read: won't be destroyed by wayward youth with too much spare time on their hands). Each May there's a "Swing a Ring Day" celebration featuring expert instruction for adults and youngsters. For more information about the rings and special events, visit www.swingaring.com. Once you try it, you'll never stop swinging! (Well, not until the big guy with the lycra bicycle shorts wants a turn.) For those whose swinging only extends to an ice cold Corona with a passable burger to wash it down, the tables at the Hudson Beach Café, overlooking the swing set, offer a scenic (and more sedentary) view of the action.

Practicalities

Take the 1 2 3 train to any stop between 72nd and 157th and it's just a short walk west to Riverside Park. Or just drive along Riverside Drive and park (no pun intended). And hey, be safe. Don't hang out there alone after dark.

Think Your Apartment is Cool?

Guess again, you Village Vamps and NoHo Stars. Ain't nothin' beats living on a houseboat at the 79th Street Boat Basin. But will Zabar's deliver?

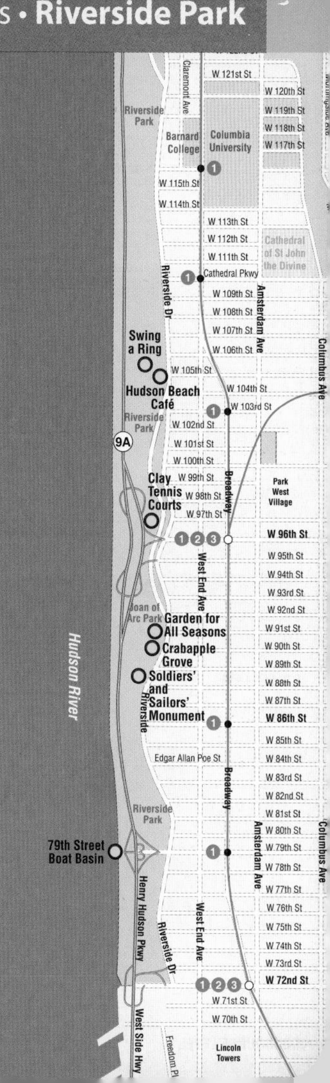

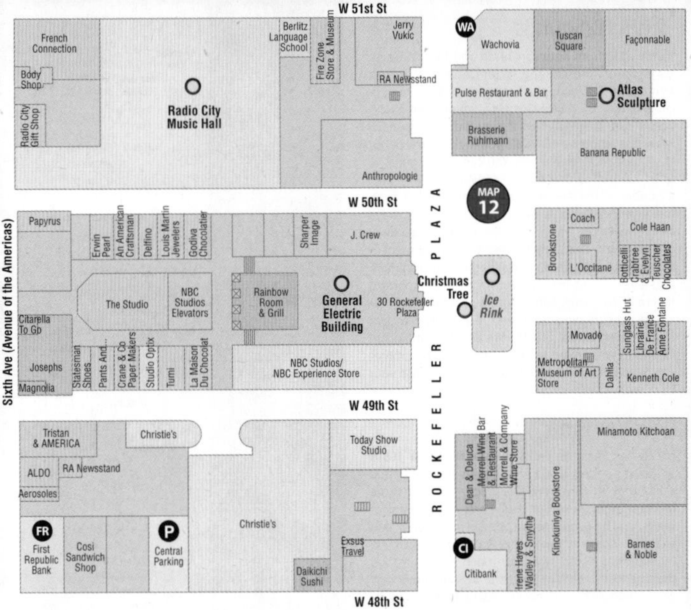

W 51st St
French Connection
Body Shop
Radio City Gift Shop
Radio City Music Hall
Berlitz Language School
Fire Zone Store & Museum
Jerry Vukic
RA Newsstand
Anthropologie
WA
Wachovia
Tuscan Square
Façonnable
Pulse Restaurant & Bar
Atlas Sculpture
Brasserie Ruhlmann
Banana Republic
MAP 12
W 50th St
Papyrus
Erwin Pearl
An American Craftsman
Delfino
Louis Martin Jewelers
Godiva Chocolatier
Sharper Image
J. Crew
The Studio
NBC Studios Elevators
Rainbow Room & Grill
General Electric Building
30 Rockefeller Plaza
Christmas Tree
Ice Rink
Citarella To Go
Josephs
Magnolia
Statesman Shoes
Pants And...
Crane & Co Paper Makers
Studio Optix
Tumi
La Maison Du Chocolat
NBC Studios/ NBC Experience Store
Brookstone
Coach
Cole Haan
L'Occitane
Botticelli
Crabtree & Evelyn
Teuscher Chocolates
Movado
Sunglass Hut
Librairie De France
Anne Fontaine
Metropolitan Museum of Art Store
Dahlia
Kenneth Cole
Sixth Ave (Avenue of the Americas)
ROCKEFELLER PLAZA
W 49th St
Tristan & AMERICA
Christie's
ALDO
RA Newsstand
Aerosoles
Today Show Studio
FR
First Republic Bank
Cosi Sandwich Shop
P
Central Parking
Christie's
Exsus Travel
Daikichi Sushi
Dean & Deluca
Morrell Wine Bar & Restaurant
Morrell & Company Wine Store
Kinokuniya Bookstore
Minamoto Kitchoan
CI
Citibank
Irene Hayes Wadley & Smythe
Barnes & Noble
W 48th St

STREET LEVEL

FR
First Republic ATM
Liberty Deli
Subway
Starbucks
Splendid Dry Cleaners
GNC
Kodak/Alpha Photo
Manchu WOK
The Grill at All About Food
Two Boots
Tossed
Mendy's Kosher Deli
Cucina & Co
Rock Center Café
United States Postal Service
Hallmark
Value Drug
Waldenbooks
FL
Its Easy
Ben & Jerry's
Auntie Anne's
FR
Yummy Sushi
NR Wireless
Godiva Chocolatier
Eshave
Starbucks
Ice Rink
Ice Skate House
Dahlia
Sbarro
RA Newsstand
Eddie's Shoe Repair
Franco Hair Salon Colorgroup
AT&T
Pret A Manger
Hale & Hearty
Value Drugs
Maui Wowi
Electronics Boutique
RA Newsstand
Swarovski
Sea Grill
UPS Store
Salon Vijin
Gary's Top Shoe

CONCOURSE LEVEL

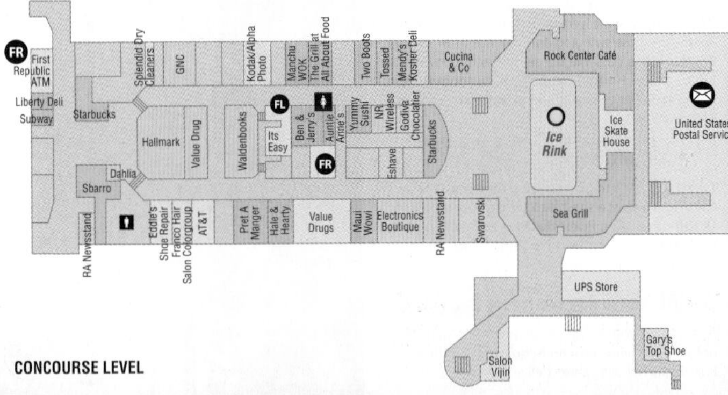

General Information

NFT Map:	12
Phone:	212-632-3975
Website:	www.rockefellercenter.com
Rink Phone:	212-332-7654
Rink Website:	www.therinkatrockcenter.com
NBC Tour Phone:	212-664-3700
Top of the Rock:	www.topoftherocknyc.com

Overview

Perhaps you've been blinded five streets away by 25,000 Swarovski crystals. Or maybe you've glimpsed a gargantuan King Kong of a tree shooting seventy feet in the air and wondered how on earth such vegetation could grow in concrete. Regardless, you fall for antics, arrive in bewilderment at Rockefeller Center, and stay for the ice-skating rink, services at St. Patrick's, and the Rockettes at Radio City Music Hall.

When there's not a huge pine tree to distract you, you'll note that Rockefeller Center occupies three square blocks with a slew of retail, dining, and office facilities. Midtown corporate just ain't the same without its magic. Embodying the Art Deco architecture of the era, the center's legacy began during the Great Depression.

The Top of the Rock Observation Deck, first opened more than 70 years ago by John D. Rockefeller, has finally reopened to the masses. Enjoy jaw dropping, 360-degree views of the skyline.

Today, the Associated Press, General Electric, and NBC call Rock their 9–5. (You've seen Dean & Deluca on TV during the *Today Show*'s outdoor broadcasts.) And "30 Rock" has *Saturday Night Live* and *Late Night with Jimmy Fallon*. Not bad for a tree-hugger, huh?

Where to Eat

How hungry are you? Rock Center isn't a prime dining destination, but you won't starve if you find yourself in the area. For cheaper fare, try places down in the Concourse such as Pret A Manger or Two Boots. For fancier (read: overpriced) food, try the Sea Grill (overlooking the skating rink). The food isn't straight out of *Gourmet*—you're paying for the view. Tuscan Square (16 W 51st St) offers pretty decent Italian, though prices are a bit inflated here as well. To sate your sweet tooth, Magnolia Bakery operates a midtown location here. (Although, if you're paying homage to a certain Bradshaw, we think you deserve to battle the crazed Sex and the City fans in the West Village.) Many restaurants in Rockefeller Center are open on Saturdays, but aside from the "nice" restaurants, only a few open their doors on Sundays. By far your best option is to walk north to 54th St and Fifth Ave and chow down at the Hallo Berlin food stand. Wurst and sausage here will be far better than anything you get in the center itself, and will cost you half as must. Just sayin'.

Where to Shop

For all the mall-lovers out there, Rockefeller Center has its own underground version—heck, there's even a Sharper Image and a Brookstone! For original, non-commercialized goods, check out these stores in Rockefeller Center and the surrounding area:

FireZone Store and Museum • 50 Rockefeller Plaza • Official seller of FDNY merchandise.
Kinokuniya Bookstore • 10 W 49th St • Japanese-language and Asian-themed, English-language books.
Minamoto Kitchoan • 608 Fifth Ave • Authentic Japanese pastries and cakes.
La Maison Du Chocolat • 30 Rockefeller Plaza • French chocolates.
Librairie De France • 610 Fifth Ave • Foreign bookseller, including French-language texts, children's books, travel guides, and maps.
Teuscher Chocolates • 620 Fifth Ave • Swiss chocolates.

And for the practical parts of your life: Dahlia (flowers), Eddie's Shoe Repair, Kodak/Alpha Photo, and Splendid Dry Cleaners. They're all located near the entrance to the Sixth Avenue subway (B D F V). A US Post Office is on the Eastern end of Concourse near the rink and UPS is in the area perpendicular to the Sea Grill. But they, like many of the stores in the Concourse, are closed on weekends. Unless you work in Rockefeller Center, it's not likely that you'll need to use them anyway.

The Rink

To practice your double loop: The rink opens Columbus Day weekend and closes early April to make way for the Rink Bar. Skating hours are 9 am–10:30 pm Monday–Thursday, 8:30 am–midnight Friday/Saturday, and 8:30 am–10 pm on Sundays. Skating prices range from $24.50 to $26.50 for adults, depending on the day you visit. (Weekends and holidays are the most expensive times to skate.) The skating rate for children ranges from $19.50 to $21.50 per session. Skate rentals are included in the cost. Lessons are available for $30 during the week and $35 during the weekend—call 212-332-7655 for more information. With hefty skating rates and a crowded rink, better to shoot for an early weekday morning or afternoon, or very early on the weekend. (Or maybe go to Bryant Park and glide for free.)

Overview

Once upon a time, Roosevelt Island was much like the rest of New York—populated by criminals, the sick, and the mentally ill. The difference was that they were the residents of the island's various mental institutions, hospitals, and jails, but these days this slender tract of land between Manhattan and Queens has become prime real estate for families and UN officials.

The 147-acre island, formerly known as "Welfare Island" because of its population of outcasts and the poor, was renamed for Franklin D. Roosevelt in 1973, when the island began changing its image. The first residential housing complex opened in 1975. Some of the old "monuments" remain, including the Smallpox Hospital and the Blackwell House (one of the oldest farmhouses in the city), while the Octagon Building, formerly a 19th-century mental hospital known for its deplorable conditions, has been turned into luxury condos (so yes, you're still in New York). Several more large buildings near the tramway have also been completed, and a few new shops are underneath these buildings.

The island's northern tip is a popular destination for fishermen with iron gullets. It's also the home of a lighthouse designed by James Renwick, Jr., of St. Patrick's Cathedral fame. The two rehab/convalescent hospitals on the island don't offer emergency services, so if you're in need of medical attention right away, you're out of luck. The island's main drag, Main Street (where did they come up with the name?), resembles a cement-block college campus circa 1968. Just south, closer to the tram, is a newly developed stretch of condos that are fetching top dollar. Two of these buildings are residences for Memorial Sloan-Kettering Cancer Center and Rockefeller and Cornell University employees.

Perhaps the best way to experience the island is to spend a little while on the local shuttle bus that runs the length of the island. You'll see a wonderful mix of folks, some crazy characters, and have a chance to grill the friendly bus drivers about all things Roosevelt Island. Trust us.

How to Get There

Roosevelt Island can be reached by the F train, but it's much more fun to take the tram. Plus, your-out-of town friends will love that this is the tram Tobey Maguire saved as Spiderman in the first movie. You can board it with a Metrocard (including an unlimited!) at 60th Street and Second Avenue in Manhattan—look for the big hulking mass drifting through the sky. It takes 4 minutes to cross and runs every 15 minutes (every 7 minutes during rush hour) 6 am–2 am, Sunday through Thursday, and 'til 3:30 am on Fridays and Saturdays. To get there by car, take the Queensboro Bridge and follow signs for the 21st Street-North exit. Go north on 21st Street and make a left on 36th Avenue. Go west on 36th Avenue and cross over the red Roosevelt Island Bridge. The only legal parking is at Motorgate Plaza at the end of the bridge at Main Street.

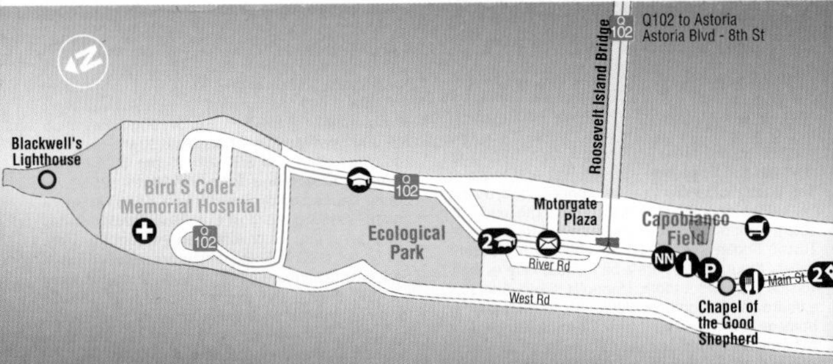

Banks
NN • New York National • 619 Main St

Coffee
• **Starbucks** • 455 Main St

Hospitals
• **Coler Goldwater–Coler Campus (No ER)** • 900 Main St [West Rd]
• **Coler Goldwater–Goldwater Campus (No ER)** • 1 Main St [River Rd]

Landmarks
• **Blackwell House** • 591 Main St
• **Blackwell's Lighthouse** • North tip of Roosevelt Island
• **Chapel of the Good Shepherd** • 543 Main St
• **Smallpox Hospital** • Near south tip of Roosevelt Island
• **Tramway** • 346 Main St [2nd Av]

Libraries
• **Roosevelt Island** • 524 Main St [East Rd]

Liquor Stores
• **Grog Shop** • 605 Main St

Post Offices
• **Roosevelt Island** • 694 Main St [River Rd]

Restaurants
• **Trellis** • 549 Main St

Schools
• **Lillie's International Christian** • 851 Main St
• **MS 271 Building (M271)** • 645 Main St
• **PS 217 Roosevelt Island** • 645 Main St

Supermarkets
• **Gristedes** • 686 Main St [River Rd]

Video Rental
• **Liberty Roosevelt Island** • 544 Main St [East Rd]
• **Roosevelt Island Video** • 544 Main St

Subways
F ....Roosevelt Island

Bus Lines
Q 102 ....Main St / East and West Rds

Parking

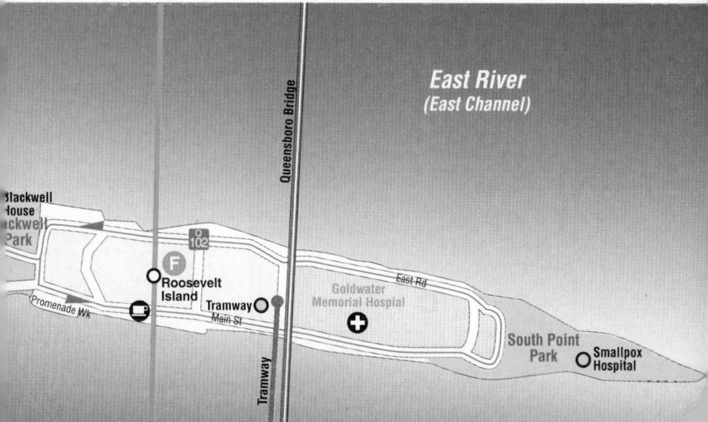

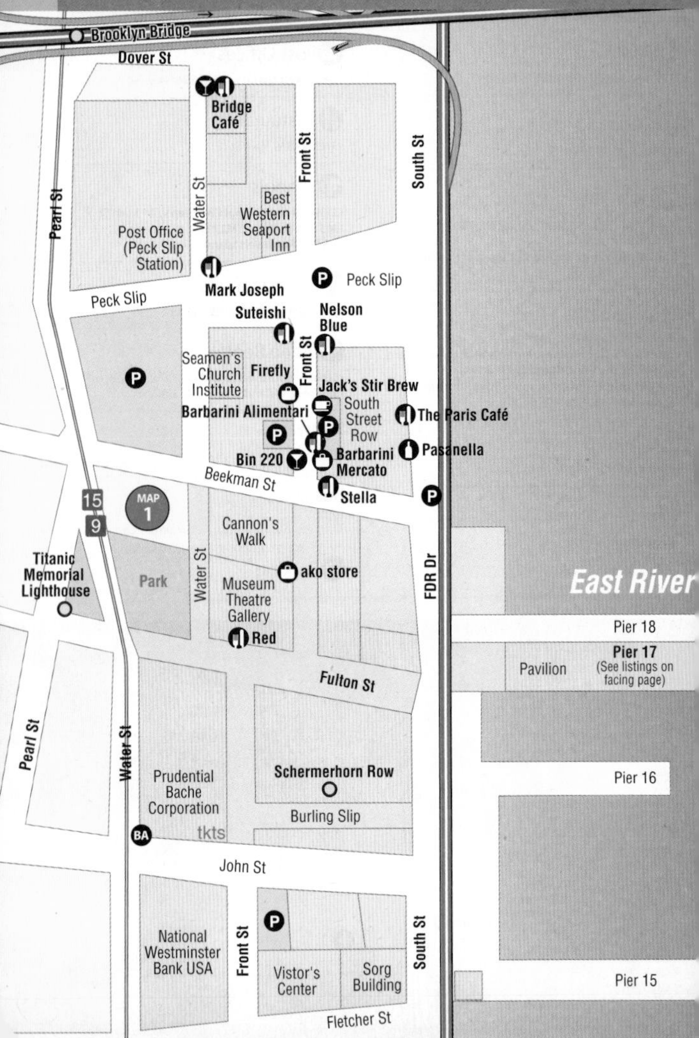
Brooklyn Bridge
Dover St
Bridge Café
Pearl St
Water St
Front St
South St
Best Western Seaport Inn
Post Office (Peck Slip Station)
Mark Joseph
Peck Slip
Peck Slip
Suteishi
Nelson Blue
Seamen's Church Institute
Firefly
Jack's Stir Brew
Barbarini Alimentari
South Street Row
The Paris Café
Pasanella
Bin 220
Barbarini Mercato
Beekman St
Stella
MAP 1
15
9
Titanic Memorial Lighthouse
Park
Cannon's Walk
ako store
Museum Theatre Gallery
Red
FDR Dr
East River
Pier 18
Pier 17 (See listings on facing page)
Pavilion
Fulton St
Schermerhorn Row
Prudential Bache Corporation
Burling Slip
tkts
BA
Pier 16
John St
National Westminster Bank USA
Vistor's Center
Sorg Building
Pier 15
Fletcher St

General Information

NFT Maps:	1 & 3
Phone:	212-SEAPORT
Phone (museum):	212-748-8600
Museum:	12 Fulton St www.southstseaport.org Hours vary by season. Visit the website or call for information.
Retail:	www.southstreet seaport.com
Hours:	Mon–Sat: 10 am–9 pm Sun: 11 am–8 pm

Overview

It's historic! Except for the stupid mall, of course. And all the f***ing chain stores everywhere. But at least there's the totally cool fish market at nights...oh wait, that moved to the Bronx. So what's left?

Ironically, it's not the old stuff that's the most interesting part of the seaport any more (although walking the cobblestone streets, having a drink at the city's oldest bar at the **Bridge Café**, and simply staring out at the Brooklyn and Manhattan Bridges from the **Promenade** are all great things to do). Instead, it's the wonderful new set of shops and restaurants that populate **Front Street** between Peck Slip and Beekman Street.

Where to start? By far our favorite stop is friendly and crowded **Nelson Blue**, with its crisp, clean New Zealand cuisine. It can get crowded early evenings with Wall Streeters, but off-times and weekends it's a perfect respite from walking the pavement. **Suteishi**, right across the street, does excellent sushi rolls, while **Barbarini Alimentari** gives great Italian take-out (just-opened **Barbarini Mercato** next door is a great little greens/cheese/charcuterie market, one of a whole slew that have opened up in every up-and-coming 'nabe in NYC).

Hip threads can be found at **ako store**, fun kid stuff (including clothes) can be found at **firefly**, and a gourmet cuppa joe can be sipped at **Jack's Stir Brew**. Have a glass of wine at **Bin 220** and then snag some seafood at posh **Stella**. You really can't go wrong down here now—this is a MAJOR change from five, and especially ten years ago.

Of course, there are some longer-standing places that should still be explored—including brunch at 19th-century spot **Bridge Café**, drinks at former fishmonger hangout **Paris Café**, succulent steaks at **Mark Joseph**, and satisfyingly above-average Mexican at mainstay **Red**.

The next wave for the Seaport was shaping up to be all the empty fish market stalls on **South Street**. Cool liquor store **Pasanella** is riding the wave down here, but unfortunately, a few other businesses have opened and closed already. It remains to be seen if the South Street can support another wave of hipness now that Front Street is saturated, or if it will get converted to even more tourist crapola à la Pier 17 mall, or—most likely given the state of the economy—nothing much of anything will happen for the next 12 months or so. But the infrastructure exists—wouldn't it be nice if the city just said "Hey, let's have a big permanent market with cool stalls like Reading Terminal Mall in Philadelphia or the Ferry Building in San Francisco."

Well, we all have dreams.

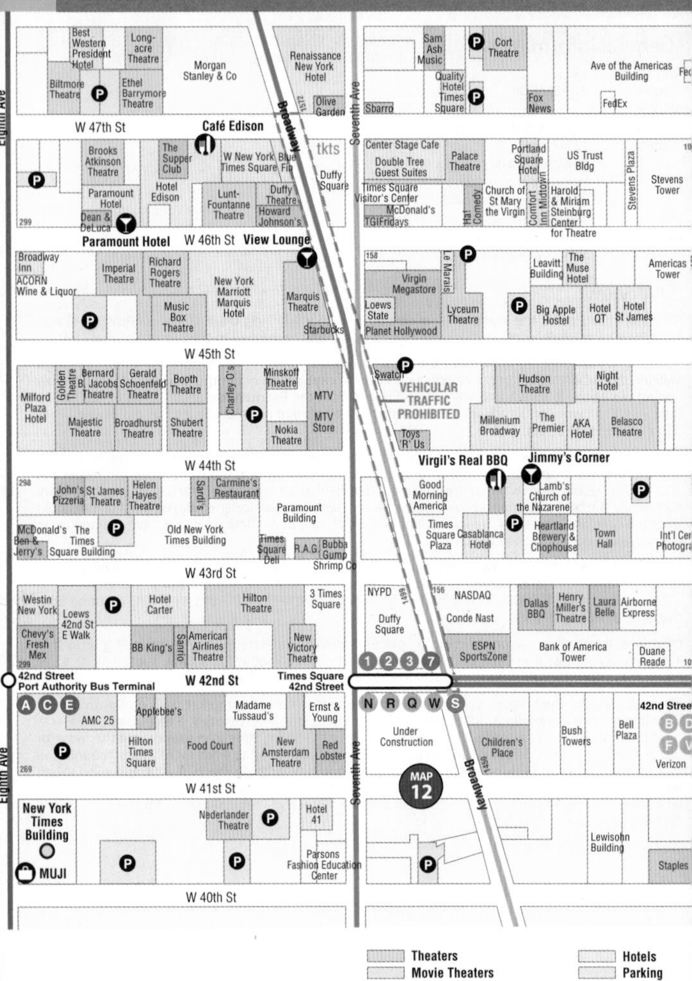

Theaters
Movie Theaters
Theme Restaurants/Stores
Hotels
Parking

General Information

NFT Map: 12
Website: www.timessquare.com
www.timessquarenyc.org
Transit: Take the 1 2 3 7 N Q R W and S trains to get to the center of everything at the 42nd Street/Times Square stop.

Overview

Is Times Square cool? Well, if you're not sure what our answer is, then close the book and read the title again. ***NOT*** for tourists, remember? Between the sheer mass of humanity and idiotic "attractions" such as the Bubba Gump Shrimp Company, the ESPN Zone, and, of course, the Hard Rock Café, spending any significant amount of time here will definitely turn your brain into strawberry Jell-o.

But all is not lost, faithful travelers. There are a few places, mostly on the edges of the madness (really, it's always the edge of things anyway, isn't it?), that are worth checking out, while your family is waiting on line for the Toys-R-Us ferris wheel or attempting to convince themselves that Chevy's serves good Mexican food.

In May 2009, the city began a pilot program whereby Broadway between 42nd and 47th streets would be closed to all but pedestrian traffic. In 2010, they announced it would become a permanent feature.

Sights

Our new favorite sight in the area is the new **New York Times Building**, on the corner of 43rd Street and Eighth Avenue, across from the heinous Port Authority Bus Terminal (can we please just drop a bomb on that and be done with it?). Designed by Renzo Piano, it's a brilliant architectural addition to the area, has several "green" building components, and also houses a hip **MUJI** (620 Eighth Ave) store.

Aside from standing in the middle of Times Square one warm summer night after dropping something mind-expanding, the only other suggestion we have is to have a drink once (once is enough) at the Marriott's **View Lounge** (1535 Broadway), which is a 360-degree rotating bar at the top of the Marriott. Overpriced drinks, nice view, you've done it, now it's time to leave.

Restaurants

About every fifth restaurant in NYC serves good food; the percentage goes way down in Times Square. There are still a few gems, though—including **Virgil's Real Barbeque** (152 W 44th St) (quite good food, although they rush you out like you're in Chinatown), the 24-hour French haven **Maison** (1700 Broadway, off the map) (an excellent beer selection as well), another French destination in **Marseille** (630 Ninth Ave, off the map), and the now-Michelin-starred Italian **Insieme** (777 Seventh Ave, off the map). For cheap and honest deli fare, you can't do better than the old-school **Café Edison** (228 W 47th St).

Nightlife

Fortunately, there is something decent to do here now—the **Iridium Jazz Club** (off the map) moved down to 1650 Broadway from Lincoln Center a few years ago. Les Paul jammed here every Monday before dying of pneumonia in 2009 at 94, but major acts like Pharoah Sanders still blow in occasionally. For a drink, the bar at the **Paramount Hotel** (235 W 46th St) is cool (merci, Monsieur Starck), though (of course) not cheap. Our recommendation: head a few blocks north to the **Russian Vodka Room** (265 W 52nd St, off the map) for a singular experience. You won't remember it, but you'll have fun doing it. And finally, for people who say the old Times Square is gone forever, stop in for a shot, a beer, and some lively conservation with the locals at **Jimmy's Corner** (140 W 44th St)—every neighborhood should have a bar like this.

Everything Else

There isn't. Go to the Village. Doesn't matter which one. Just get the hell out of here.

MAP 9
MAP 10
MAP 6
Duane Reade
ABC Carpet & Home
G-Star Raw
Environment Furniture
At Home
Andy's Deli
Sleepy's
Ann Sacks Tile & Home
Djoniba Dance & Drum Center
Alkit Camera
Old Town Bar and Grill
Park Avalon
Chase
Japonais
Butai
Los Dos Molinos
Paul & Jimmy's
Pete's Tavern
E 18th St
Paragon Sporting Goods
Broadway
Goodburger
Radio Shack
Chipotle
Geox
Petco
Cingular Wireless
North Fork Bank
Barnes & Noble
Sephora
Union Bar
Rothman's
CVS
Green Cafe
W Hotel - Olive's - Underbar
Zurich North America
Pierre Loti
The House
Inn at Irving Place
Cibar
Pure Food & Wine
Lillie's
Mandler's The Original Sausage Co
Verizon Wireless
Caesar's Pizza
Pret
Tisserie
E 17th St
Starbucks
Dogmatic
McDonald's
Republic
Heartland Brewery
Puma
Union Square Cafe
Blue Water Grill
Green Market / Farmer's Market
Green Market / Farmer's Market Mon, Wed, Fri & Sat
Union Sq W
Union Sq E (Park Ave)
Trevi Deli
Union Sq Theatre
Liquor Store
Barocco Kitchen
Sunny's Nails
NY Film Academy
Maoz
The Children's Place
Yama
Washington Irving High School
Irving Pl
E 16th St
Chat 'n' Chew
University Marketplace
Coffee Shop
Toasties Juice Bar
Children's Place
NYU Dorm
Park Bar
ComZone Copy
American Eagle Outfitters
Union Square Park
Zen Palate
The Cottage
Oasis Day Spa
The Vitamin Shoppe
Flushing Savings Bank
Babies R Us
Century Center for the Performing Arts
Lee Strasberg Theatre Institute
Fillmore at Irving Plaza
Darryl Roth Theatre
DR2
Galaxy Global Eatery
E 15th St
Amalgamated Bank of New York
Staples
Diesel
Starbucks
3 Square
Food Emporium
Vineyard Theatre
Link Bar & Lounge
New York Sports Clubs
GNC
Beth Israel Medical Center
Au Bon Pain
FedEx
Food Emporium
Game Stop
Haagen-Dazs
Eye to Eye Vision Center
Con Edison
Apple Bank
14 St - Union Square
N R Q W
E 14th St
4 5 6 L
Whole Foods
Trader Joe's
The Mentronome
Japan Exp
Taco Bell
Wendy's
Tavalon Tea
Bank of America
Duane Reade
West Coast Pizza
University Pl
Strawberry
1. Whole Foods Forever 21
2. Filene's Basement
3. DSW
ShoeMania
University Locksmith & Hardware
Bank of America
Max Brenner
Cosi
Broadway
Walgreens
NYU Dorm
PC Richard & Son
NYU Dorm
Fourth Ave
Regal Union Square Stadium 14
E 13th St
Crunch
Washington Mutual Bank
Forbidden Planet
Peridance Center
Bowlmor Lanes
The Strand

General Information

NFT Maps: 6, 9, & 10

Overview

Want to find the real pulse of Manhattan? Head straight to Union Square where thousands of people surge through here everyday to hang out on the steps, shop at the excellent farmers market, and watch the city roll on by. Part of the charm is that there's no real attraction here. There's a park with some benches, a statue, a dog run, the aforementioned market, and that's about it. After 9-11 New Yorkers congregated here to console each other and remember the perished. Since that fateful day, Union Square has become the de facto living room of Downtown. Between New School and NYU kids rushing to class, crazy street entertainers, lost tourists, and locals just trying to get to work, this place is always jumping. Historical note: The first ever Labor Day celebration took place here, so next time you're sitting in the park enjoying your lunch from the **Whole Food**'s salad bar, give thanks that the legal days of working 14-hour shifts are long over. At least for some of us.

Shopping

Unfortunately like the rest of Manhattan, the area around Union Square has slowly been transformed into a giant outdoor mall. You've got chain stores galore flanking the park, but if you look very carefully, you'll find a couple of good shopping options in these parts. High on the list is **The Strand** (828 Broadway), the iconic bookstore that keeps on chugging along (thank goodness). There's also **Forbidden Planet** (840 Broadway), a comic book nerd's heaven. For the sports nuts **Paragon Sporting Goods** (867 Broadway) is the place to get any kind of racquet, ball, or bat you can think of. And if your feet need some new duds, hike over to **Shoemania** (853 Broadway) where the selection will overwhelm you as much as the in-your-face staff. If you must choose a big name, the **Barnes & Noble** (33 E 17th) at the north end of the park has an amazing magazine selection and of course an incredible selection of NFTs. But the main draw is the **Union Square Farmers Market**—going strong for over thirty years this is the best place in the city to stock up on produce, cheese, baked goods, and meat. Fantastic.

Restaurants

For a true splurge make reservations at **Union Square Café** (21 E 16th St). Despite the 1980s décor, the food is truly wonderful (or so we hear…we're still trying to get a table). For a quick bite that won't break the bank, **Republic** (37 Union Sq W) serves up noisy noodles. To eat really cheap you can't beat **Maoz** (38 Union Sq E) for fast food vegetarian or **Dogmatic** (26 E 17th St) for a tasty sausage sandwich. Or do what the locals do and make a trip to the **Whole Food**'s (4 Union Sq E) salad bar section. In the warmer months you can sit in the park, but on colder days walk up to the second floor cafeteria and enjoy an amazing view of the city.

Nightlife

Ready for a stiff drink? **Old Town Bar and Restaurant** (45 E 18th St) is the prime choice. It has character, cheap cocktails, and the crowd isn't totally lame (yeah, it's that tough of a neighborhood to find a decent bar). Just west of the square is **Park Bar** (15 E 15th St), a perfect place to meet up for an after work blind date—it's small enough to force conversation with your new friend. Or try **Lillie's** (13 E 17th St) just up the block if you have a Irish-Victorian bar décor fetish. You'll know what we're talking about the second you walk in. If you like your bowling alleys with fancy cocktails and a doorman, then **Bowlmor** (110 University Pl) will do you just fine. And for live music, the **Filmore at Irving Plaza** (17 Irving Pl) is a staple on the New York rock scene.

Just Plain Weird

See that giant smoking magic wand clocky thingy on the south side of the square? It's actually got a name—*The Mentronome*. Installed in 1999, artists Andrew Ginzel and Kristen Jones created something that's supposed to inspire reflection on the pace of time in the city…or something like that. Unfortunately, every time we glance up at it, we feel even more on edge than we already are. The clock just keeps moving faster and faster and faster and faster and faster… so much for finding any peace and quiet in this part of town.

Just Off The Map

Unlike Dick Cheney, NFT does not condone torture in any way. But we will submit to it on occasion by braving the ridiculous mobs at **Trader Joe's** (142 E 14th St) . It's worth a few bruises and scratches to save a few bucks on Wasabi-Ginger Almonds and Organic Fair Trade Italian Coffee. Ditto for the "Two Buck Chuck" (that actually costs $2.99) at their wine shop (138 E 14th St). You can get a month's supply of wine here for the cost of one $38 bottle of average vino at your neighborhood restaurant – and TJ delivers. We'll drink to that.

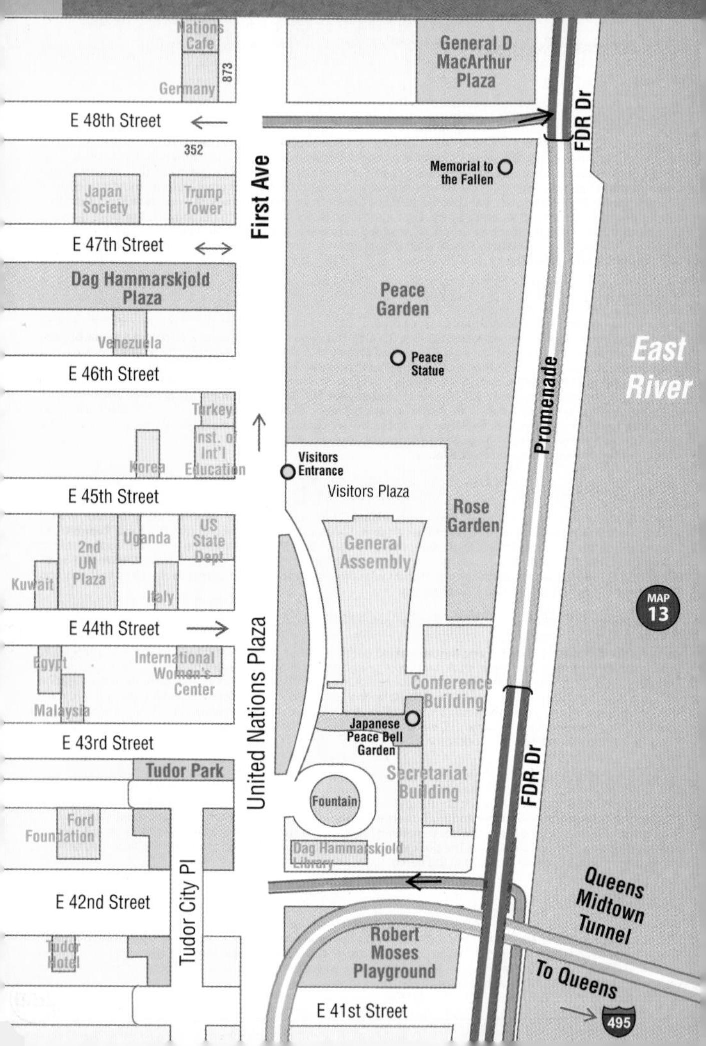
Nations Cafe
Germany
873
General D MacArthur Plaza
E 48th Street
FDR Dr
352
Memorial to the Fallen
Japan Society
Trump Tower
First Ave
E 47th Street
Dag Hammarskjold Plaza
Venezuela
Peace Garden
East River
Peace Statue
E 46th Street
Turkey
Inst. of Int'l Education
Korea
Promenade
Visitors Entrance
Visitors Plaza
E 45th Street
Rose Garden
US State Dept
Uganda
2nd UN Plaza
General Assembly
Kuwait
Italy
MAP 13
E 44th Street
Egypt
International Women's Center
Malaysia
Conference Building
United Nations Plaza
Japanese Peace Bell Garden
E 43rd Street
Tudor Park
Secretariat Building
FDR Dr
Fountain
Ford Foundation
Dag Hammarskjold Library
Tudor City Pl
E 42nd Street
Queens Midtown Tunnel
Robert Moses Playground
Tudor Hotel
To Queens
E 41st Street
495

General Information

NFT Map:	13
Address:	First Ave b/w 42nd & 48th Sts
Phone:	212-963-TOUR(8687)
Website:	www.un.org
Guided Tour Hours:	9:30 am–4:45 pm (10 am–4:30 pm on weekends) except Thanksgiving Day, Christmas Day, New Year's Day, and weekends during January and February.
Guided Tour Admission:	$13 for adults, $9 for seniors, $8.50 for students under 30, and $7 for children ages 5–14.

Overview

The United Nations Headquarters building, that giant domino teetering on the bank of the East River, opened its doors in 1951. It's here that the 191 member countries of the United Nations meet to fulfill the UN's mandate of maintaining international peace, developing friendly relations among nations, promoting development and human rights, and getting all the free f*#%ing parking they want. The UN is divided into bodies: the General Assembly, the Security Council, the Economic and Social Council, the Trusteeship Council, the Secretariat, and the International Court of Justice (located in the Hague). Specialized agencies like the World Health Organization (located in Geneva) and the UN Children's Fund (UNICEF) (located in New York) are part of the UN family.

The United Nations was founded at the end of World War II by world powers intending to create a body that would prevent war by fostering an ideal of collective security. New York was chosen to be home base when John D. Rockefeller Jr. donated $8.5 million to purchase the 18 acres the complex occupies. The UN is responsible for a lot of good—its staff and agencies have been awarded nine Nobel Peace Prizes over the years. However, the sad truth is the United Nations hasn't completely lived up to the goals and objectives of its 1945 charter. (This situation isn't helped by the bloated US doing all it can to undermine many initiatives.) Scandals involving the Oil-for-Food Program and alleged abuses by UN troops have certainly not boosted the UN's reputation recently. However, with a new secretary general in place, there is hope that the UN can finally function as a positive global force in a world that desperately needs guidance.

This place is definitely worth a visit. The UN Headquarters complex is an international zone complete with its own security force, fire department, and post office (which issues UN stamps). It consists of four buildings: the Secretariat building (the 39-story tower), the General Assembly building, the Conference building, and the Dag Hammarskjöld Library. Once you clear what feels like airport security, you'll find yourself in the visitors' lobby where there are shops, a coffee shop, and a scattering of topical small exhibits that come and go. The guided tour is your ticket out of the lobby and into important rooms like the Security Council Chambers and the impressive and inspiring General Assembly Hall. Sometimes tour groups are allowed to briefly sit in on meetings, but don't expect to spy Ban Ki-moon, the new Secretary-General, roaming the halls. Take a stroll through the Peace Bell Garden (off limits to the public, but it can be seen from the inside during the guided tour). The bell, a gift from Japan in 1954, was cast from coins collected by children from 60 different countries. A bronze statue by Henry Moore, *Reclining Figure: Hand*, is located north of the Secretariat Building. The UN grounds are especially impressive when the 500 prize-winning rose bushes and 140 flowering cherry trees are in bloom.

UN Headquarters is undergoing for a massive $3 billion renovation. The project is estimated to be completed in 2013 or around the same time the UN finally ends world poverty. We can still dream, right?

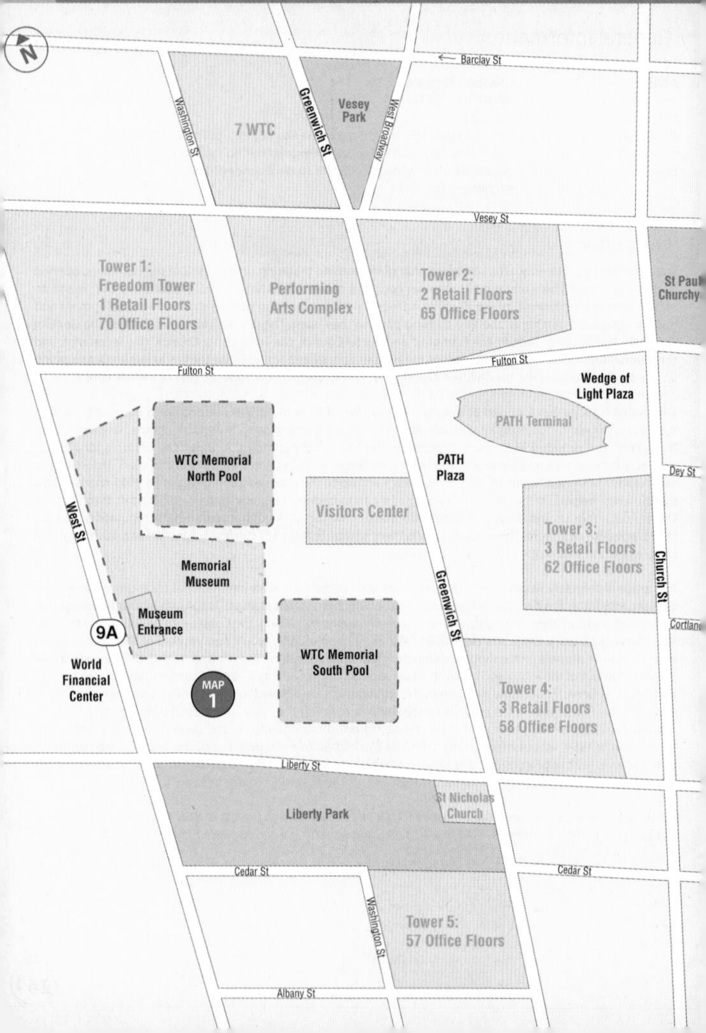

N
Barclay St
Washington St
7 WTC
Greenwich St
Vesey Park
West Broadway
Vesey St
Tower 1:
Freedom Tower
1 Retail Floors
70 Office Floors
Performing
Arts Complex
Tower 2:
2 Retail Floors
65 Office Floors
St Paul
Churchy
Fulton St
Fulton St
Wedge of
Light Plaza
PATH Terminal
WTC Memorial
North Pool
PATH
Plaza
Dey St
Visitors Center
West St
Tower 3:
3 Retail Floors
62 Office Floors
Church St
Memorial
Museum
Greenwich St
Museum
Entrance
9A
Cortland
WTC Memorial
South Pool
World
Financial
Center
MAP
1
Tower 4:
3 Retail Floors
58 Office Floors
Liberty St
St Nicholas
Church
Liberty Park
Cedar St
Cedar St
Washington St
Tower 5:
57 Office Floors
Albany St

As we mark a decade since 9/11, it's tough to not want to call your buddies over, borrow some hammers, and start filling the void still apparent in the Financial District.

Construction crews finally broke ground on the first large-scale projects in late 2006: the Freedom Tower (or officially 1 World Trade Center) and September 11th Memorial. To clear the area for a $2.2 billion transit hub designed by Santiago Calatrava (that keeps getting scaled back) to connect Manhattan and New Jersey and a dozen subway lines, relocating power lines is on the agenda as well. This year, these construction feats should be visually apparent, and even more so in 2010, since projected completion hovers around 2013. You can call your buddies mid-2013 when construction stalls. Because we all know it will.

Why has it taken this long? Numerous groups vied to make their vision of the rebuilding of the World Trade Center site become reality. The Port Authority originally built the buildings, and just before September 11th, they were leased to Larry Silverstein. As leaseholder, he had the right to collect insurance and redevelop the site. Created by Governor Pataki, the Lower Manhattan Development Corporation was assigned the task of overseeing the development of the site. The families of victims and the rest of the public have been vocal in expressing their desires for the rebuilding project as well.

In the fall of 2002, the LMDC selected a single design from more than 400 submissions. Studio Daniel Libeskind's proposal, *Memory Foundations*, achieved the nearly impossible task of getting the approval of the LMDC, Port Authority, city, and state of New York. Despite the Libeskind design being accepted as the official master plan, Silverstein hired architect David Childs. Feuds over designs dissolved late in the year, and Libeskind and Childs emerged with an amicable compromise, changing the arrangement of the buildings and parks on the ground and altering the look of the Freedom Tower.

What will it look like? The spire-like Freedom Tower will climb roughly 1,800 feet in the sky. Its footprint will match the footprints of the Twin Towers at 200 by 200 feet. Boasting 2.6 million square feet of office space, restaurants, an observation deck, and broadcasting facilities for the Metropolitan Television Alliance, it will be environmentally sound and ultra-safe. If it ever gets built, that is.

And the memorial? Michael Arad designed *Reflecting Absence* as waterfalls flowing into the sunken "footprints" of the twin towers, cascading onto the names etched in stone of those who died there. The plans also include a visitor's center designed by Norwegian firm Snohetta.

Debate still rages regarding many aspects of the project, from the height and look of the other towers to how many streets will be allowed to run through the site (many were de-mapped when the WTC was originally built). Also raging are class-action lawsuits alleging inadequate protection against toxins for workers. And with the economy still in the dumps, construction projects across the city have been put on hold. Stay tuned.

Transit has been restored to pre–September 11th order, with all subway lines resuming service to the area, along with PATH service to the newly constructed PATH station.

Useful Websites

- Lower Manhattan Info provides current details about construction and future plans for the WTC site and the surrounding area: www.lowermanhattan.info
- The World Trade Center Health Registry will track the health survey of thousands of people directly exposed to the events of 9/11: www.nyc.gov/html/doh/html/wtc/index.html
- The findings of the National Commission on Terrorist Attacks Upon the United States (the 9/11 Commission): www.9-11commission.gov
- "New York New Visions" is a coalition of several groups looking at different options for rebuilding the area: www.nynv.aiga.org
- The New York Skyscraper Museum continues to add information about the WTC and downtown NYC in general; they also contributed to the historical panels placed on the viewing wall around the site: www.skyscraper.org
- A second 9/11 families group: www.911families.org

W 34th St
34th Street
Penn Station
W 33rd St
J A Farley
Post Office
Penn
Station/
MSG
West Side
Rail Yards
W 31st St
W 30th St
Hudson
River
Park
W 29th St
W 28th St
Chelsea Park
Penn
Station
South
Houses
W 27th St
West Side Hwy
W 26th St
Eleventh Ave
Tenth Ave
Ninth Ave
Eighth Ave
W 25th St
9a
MAP
8
W 24th St
Chelsea
Waterside
Park
W 23rd St
23rd Street
W 22nd St
Hudson
River
Gallery
District
CHELSEA
W 21st St
Chelsea Piers
W 20th St
W 19th St
Chelsea Grasslands
W 18th St
W 17th St
10th Avenue Square
W 16th St
Chelsea
Market
Chelsea Market Public Art
W 15th St
Diller - Von Furstenberg
Sundeck & Water Feature
MEATPACKING
DISTRICT
8th
Avenue
W 14th St
14th Street
W 13th St
Washington Grasslands
Gansevoort Woodland
Little W 12th St
Gansevoort St
Hudson St
Gansevoort Plaza
MAP
5
Eighth Ave
W 4th St
Greenwich
Horatio St
Jane St
Washington St
Greenwich St
W 12th St
WEST
VILLAGE
Stairs
Elevator
Section 1
Section 2
Under Construction
Section 3
Pending development

General Information

NFT Maps: 5 & 8

Overview

Welcome to New York's newest, and instantly one of its coolest, parks. Open from 7 am to long after sunset and built on top of a disused portion of freight rail elevated train tracks, The High Line is at once both an escape from the sturm und drang of the city's streets and a celebration of Manhattan's west side, especially its architecture.

What's more, it's obvious that the presence of the High Line itself, stretching from the uber-hip Meatpacking District north into the heart of Chelsea's glut of hundreds of art galleries, is going to have a huge impact on further architectural and cultural development in the area. More and more folks are simply going to take the extra two-block schlep from the nearest subway stop (8th Avenue's A/C/E/L) to check out the park, its surrounding buildings, and the ever-increasing number of cultural, gastronomic, and nightlife options directly underneath (and above!) it.

One major example of new architectural work can simply be seen by looking UP when you're on the High Line; namely Polshek Partnerships' brilliant **Standard Hotel**, which straddles the High Line just south of 14th Street. The hotel sports a posh restaurant as well as a beer garden, both directly underneath the High Line. Two other stunning architectural gems visible from the High Line (looking west) are Frank Gehry's only New York building, Barry Diller's **IAC Headquarters**, and Jean Nouvel's new **condo building** right across the street. The IAC is one of the most wonderfully luminescent buildings in all of New York, and Nouvel's façade of hundreds of differently-sized panes of glass will become an instant classic. Of course, the work on the High Line itself, by architects Diller Scofidio + Renfro and landscape architects James Corner Field Operations, is simply amazing. The 10th Avenue Square area, with amphitheater-style seating and a living-room-window view of the northbound traffic of Tenth Avenue, is a favorite as well as a perfect place for a picnic (a picnic that can be perfectly constructed using wonderful **Chelsea Market** food vendors).

While weekend days during summer on the High Line is already a madhouse, we recommend an early-morning or evening stroll during spring and fall. The cityscape views at night are stunning; early morning is quiet and generally cool, until the sun moves above the skyscrapers to the east of the park.

Essentially, however, there is no bad time to visit the High Line. The views will be great no matter what time of day it is, and fantastic food options are always waiting for you, including hip **Cookshop (Map 8)**, French haven **La Luncheonette (Map 8)**, neighborhood standby **Red Cat (Map 8)**, Jean-Georges Vongerichten's **Spice Market (Map 5)**, warm **Italian Bottino (Map 8)**, and all-night Chelsea institution **Empire Diner (Map 8)**. Want cheaper fare? Hit greasy spoon **Hector's (Map 5)** or wait for one of the gourmet trucks to pull up around the corner from the Ganesvoort stairs, or go DIY by buying food at **Chelsea Market (Map 8)**.

At night, you can hang around to rock out at **The High Line Ballroom (Map 8)**, or drink at pubs **The Half King (Map 8)**, **Brass Monkey (Map 5)**, or the Standard's **Biergarten (Map 5)**, or, better yet, walk the streets of the West 20s in search of gallery openings (read: free wine and cheese). No matter how you slice it, a visit to the High Line will only make you happier. We promise.

Airline	Phone	JFK	EWR	LGA
Aer Lingus	800-474-7424	■		
Aeroflot	800-340-6400	■		
Aerolineas Argentinas	800-333-0276	■		
Aeromexico	800-237-6639	■		
Aerosvit Ukranian	212-661-1620	■		
Air Canada	888-247-2262	■	■	■
Air China	800-982-8802	■		
Air France	800-237-2747	■	■	
Air India	212-751-6200	■	■	
Air Jamaica	800-523-5585	■	■	
Air Plus Comet	877-999-7587	■	■	
Air Tahiti Nui	866-835-9286	■		
Air Tran	800-247-8726		■	■
Alaska Airlines	800-426-0333		■	
Alitalia	800-223-5730	■	■	
ANA (All Nippon)	800-235-9262	■	■	■
Allegro	800-903-2779	■		
American (domestic)	800-433-7300	■	■	■
American (international)	800-433-7300	■	■	■
American Eagle	800-433-7300	■	■	■
Asiana	800-227-4262	■		
ATA	800-435-9282		■	■
Austrian Airlines	800-843-0002	■		
Avianca	800-284-2622	■		
Azteca	212-289-6400	■	■	■
Biman Bangladesh	212-808-4477	■		
British Airways	800-247-9297	■	■	

Airline	Phone	JFK	EWR	LGA
BWIA	800-538-2942	■		
Cathay Pacific	800-233-2742	■	■	
Chautauqua	800-428-4322		■	■
China Airlines	800-227-5118	■		
China Eastern	866-588-0825	■		
Colgan	800-428-4322			■
Comair	800-354-9822	■	■	■
Constellation	866-484-2299	■		
Continental (domestic)	800-523-3273	■	■	■
Continental (international)	800-231-0856		■	
Copa Airlines	800-359-2672	■		
Corsair (seasonal)	800-677-0720	■		
Czech Airlines	800-223-2365	■	■	
Delta (domestic)	800-221-1212	■	■	■
Delta (international)	800-241-4141	■	■	■
Delta Connection	800-325-5205	■		
Delta Express	800-235-9359	■	■	■
Egyptair	800-334-6787	■		
El Al	800-223-6700	■	■	
Emirates	800-777-3999	■		
EOS	888-357-3677	■		
Etihad	888-8ETIHAD	■		
Eurofly	800-459-0581	■		
Eva Airways	800-695-1188		■	
Finnair	800-950-5000	■		
Frontier Airlines	800-432-1359		■	■
Iberia	800-772-4642	■		

Airline	Phone	JFK	EWR	LGA
Icelandair	800-223-5500	■		
Israir	877-477-2471	■		
Japan Airlines	800-525-3663	■		
Jet Blue	800-538-2583	■	■	■
KLM	800-374-7747	■	■	
Korean Air	800-438-5000	■		
Kuwait Airways	800-458-9248	■		
Lacsa	800-225-2272	■		
Lan Chile	800-735-5526	■		
Lan Ecuador	866-526-3279	■		
Lan Peru	800-735-5590	■		
LOT Polish	212-852-0240	■	■	
LTU	866-266-5588	■		
Lufthansa	800-645-3880	■	■	
Malaysia	800-582-9264		■	
Malev Hungarian	800-223-6884	■		
MaxJet	888-435-9626	■		
Mexicana	800-531-7921	■		
Miami Air (charter)	305-871-3300	■	■	
Midwest Express	800-452-2022		■	■
North American	800-371-6297	■		
Northwest (domestic)	800-225-2525	■	■	■
Northwest (international)	800-447-4747	■		■
Olympic	800-223-1226	■		
Qantas	800-227-4500	■	■	
Royal Air Maroc	800-344-6726	■		
Royal Jordanian	212-949-0050	■		

Airline	Phone	JFK	EWR	LGA
SAS	800-221-2350		■	
Saudi Arabian Airlines	800-472-8342	■		
Silverjet	877-359-7458		■	
SN Brussels	516-622-2248	■		
South African Airways	800-722-9675	■	■	■
Spirit	800-772-7117			■
Sun Country	800-359-6786	■		
Swiss Airlines	877-359-7947	■	■	
TACA	800-535-8780	■		
TAM	888-235-9826	■		
Tap Air Portugal	800-221-7370		■	
Thai Airways	800-426-5204	■		
Travel Spain	800-817-6177	■		
Turkish	800-874-8875	■		
United Airlines (domestic)	800-241-6522	■	■	■
United Airlines (intern'l)	800-241-6522	■	■	■
United Express	800-241-6522		■	■
US Airways	800-428-4322	■	■	■
USA3000	877-872-3000		■	
Uzbekistan	212-245-1005	■		
Varig	800-468-2744	■		
Virgin Atlantic	800-862-8621	■	■	

Transit • JFK Airport

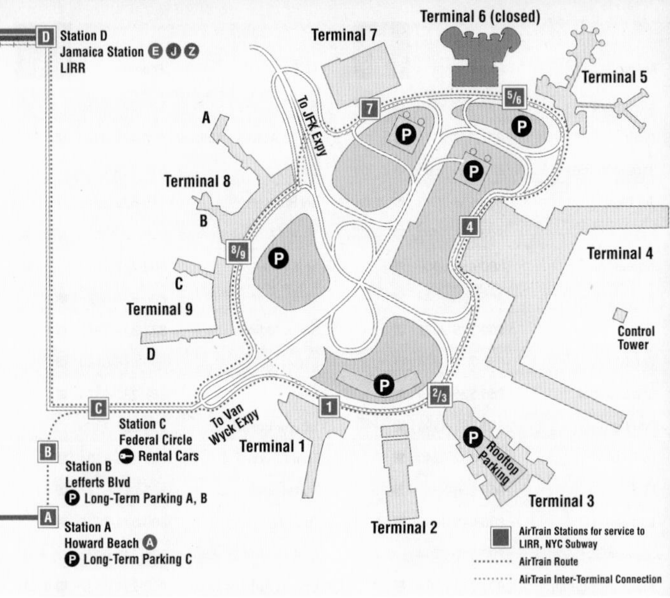

Airline	Terminal
Aer Lingus	4
Aeroflot	1
Aerolineas Argentinas	4
Aero Gal	4
Aero Mexico	1
Aerosvit Ukrainian	4
Air Berlin	8
Air Canada	7
Air China	1
Air Europa	4
Air France	1
Air India	4
Air Jamaica	4
AirPlus Comet	1
Air Tahiti Nui	4
Alitalia	1
Allegro (seasonal)	4
American	8
American Eagle	8
ANA	7
Asiana	4
Austrian Airlines	1
Avianca	4
Azteca	4
Biman Bangladesh	4
British Airways	7
Caribbean	4
Cathay Pacific	7
Cayman Airways	1
China Airlines	1
China Eastern	1
Comair	3
Copa Airlines	4
Czech Airlines	4
Delta	3
Egypt Air	4
El Al	4
Emirates	4
Etihad	4
Eurofly	4
Finnair	8
Flyglobespan	4
Iberia	7
Icelandair	7
Japan Airlines	1
Jet Airways	8
Jetblue(San Juan)	4
JetBlue Airways	5
KLM	4
Korean Air	1
Kuwait Airways	4
Lacsa	4
Lan Chile	4
Lan Ecuador	4
Lan Peru	4
LOT	4
Lufthansa	1
Malev Hungarian	8
Mexicana	8
Miami Air (charter)	4
North American	4
Northwest	4
Olympic	1
Pakistan	4
Qantas	7
Qatar	4
Royal Air Maroc	1
Royal Jordanian	4
Saudi Arabian Airlines	1
Singapore	4
South African	4
SN Brussels Airlines	8
Sun Country	4
Swiss International	4
TACA International	4
TAM	4
Travel Span	4
Turkish	1
United Airlines	7
US Airways/ America West	7
US Helicopter	3
Uzbekistan	4
Virgin American	4
Virgin Atlantic	4
XL Airways	4

General Information

Address: JFK Expy
Jamaica, NY 11430
Phone: 718-244-4444
Lost & Found: 718-244-4225
Website: www.kennedyairport.com
AirTrain: www.airtrainjfk.com
AirTrain Phone: 718-570-1048
Long Island Rail Road: www.mta.info/lirr

Overview

Ah, JFK. It's long been a nemesis to Manhattanites due to the fact that it's the farthest of the three airports from the city. Nonetheless, more than 32 million people go through JFK every year. A $9.5 billion expansion and modernization program will transform the airport, with JetBlue taking about $900 million of that for its gigantic, 26-gate, new HQ to address the ten million of you who, in spite of JFK's distance, wake up an hour earlier to save a buck.

JetBlue's new Terminal 5 rises just behind the landmark TWA building, which you should check out if you have time to kill after getting up an hour earlier. Its bubbilicious curves make this 1960s gem a glam spaceship aptly prepared to handle any swanky NY soiree. Top that, Newark.

Rental Cars (On-Airport)

The rental car offices are all located along the Van Wyck Expressway near the entrance to the airport. Just follow the signs.

1 • **Avis** • 718-244-5406 or 800-230-4898
2 • **Budget** • 718-656-6010 or 800-527-0700
3 • **Dollar** • 718-656-2400 or 800-800-4000
5 • **Enterprise** • 718-659-1200 or 800-RENT-A-CAR
4 • **Hertz** • 718-656-7600 or 800-654-3131
6 • **National** • 718-632-8300 or 800-CAR-RENTAL

Hotels

Crown Plaza JFK • 151-20 Baisley Blvd • 718-489-1000
Comfort Inn JFK • 144-36 153rd Ln • 718-977-0001
Double Tree Club Hotel • 135-40 140th St • 718-276-2188
Holiday Inn JFK Airport • 144-02 135th Ave • 718-659-0200
Ramada Plaza Hotel • Van Wyck Expy • 718-995-9000
Ramada Plaza Hotel • Van Wyck Expy • 718-995-9000
Best Western JFK Airport • 144-25 153rd Lane • 718-977-2100
Courtyard by Marriott JFK Airport • 145-11 North Conduit Ave. • 718-848-2121
Days Inn • 144-26 153rd Court • 718-527-9025
Fairfield Inn by Marriott • 156-08 Rockaway Blvd. • 718-977-3300
Hampton Inn • 144-10 135th Avenue • 718-322-7500
Hilton Garden Inn • 148-18 134th Street • 718-322-4448
Holiday Inn Express Kennedy Airport • 153-70 South Conduit Ave • 718-977-3100
Howard Johnson Express Inn at JFK Airport • 153-95 Rockaway Blvd • 718-723-6700
JFK Inn • 154-10 South Conduit Ave • 718-723-5100
Sheraton JFK Airport Hotel • 132-26 South Conduit Ave • 718-322-7190

G Washington Bridge
Cross Bronx Expy
Throgs Neck Expy
BRONX
NEW JERSEY
Bruckner Expy
Throgs Neck Bridge
Whitestone Bridge
Hudson River
Henry Hudson Pkwy
MANHATTAN
RFK Bridge
Flushing Bay
Grand Central Pkwy
LaGuardia Airport
Whitestone Expy
Central Park
FDR Dr
East River
Astoria Blvd
Northern Blvd
Clearview
Lincoln Tunnel
57th St
Queensboro Bridge
34th St
Midtown Tunnel
Queens Blvd
West St
Long Island Expy
Holland Tunnel
Brooklyn-Queens Expy
Woodhaven Blvd
QUEENS
Williamsburg Bridge
Metropolitan Ave
Manhattan Bridge
Brooklyn Bridge
Brooklyn-Battery Tunnel
Broadway
Atlantic Ave
Jamaica Ave
Van Wyck Expy
Flatbush Ave
N Conduit Ave
Rockaway
Prospect Expy
Prospect Park
Green-Wood Cemetery
BROOKLYN
Cross Bay Blvd
Airtrain
JFK Airport
Ocean Pkwy
Ocean Ave
Belt Pkwy
Floyd Bennett Field
Jamaica Bay
Lower Bay
ROCKAWAY BEACH
Rockaway Inlet

Car Services & Taxis

All County Express • 914-381-4223 or 800-914-4223
Classic Limousine • 631-567-5100 or 800-666-4949
Dial 7 Car & Limo Service • 212-777-7777 or 800-777-8888
Super Saver by Carmel • 800-922-7635 or 212-666-6666
Tel Aviv Limo Service • 800-222-9888 or 212-777-7777

Taxis from the airport to anywhere in Manhattan cost a flat $45 + tolls and tip, while fares to the airport are metered + tolls and tip. The SuperShuttle (800-258-3826) will drop you anywhere between Battery Park and 227th, including all hotels, for $13–$22, but be warned it could end up taking a while, depending on where your fellow passengers are going. Nevertheless, it's a good option if you want door-to-door service and have a lot of time to kill, but not a lot of cash.

How to Get There—Driving

You can take the lovely and scenic Belt Parkway straight to JFK, as long as it's not rush hour. The Belt Parkway route is about 30 miles long, even though JFK is only 15 or so miles from Manhattan. You can access the Belt by taking the Brooklyn-Battery Tunnel to the Gowanus (the best route) or by taking the Brooklyn, Manhattan, or Williamsburg Bridges to the Brooklyn-Queens Expressway to the Gowanus. If you're sick of stop-and-go highway traffic and prefer using local roads, take Atlantic Avenue in Brooklyn and drive east until you hit Conduit Avenue. Follow this straight to JFK—it's direct and fairly simple. You can get to Atlantic Avenue from any of the three downtown bridges (look at one of our maps first!). From midtown, you can take the Queens Midtown Tunnel to the Long Island Expressway to the Van Wyck Expressway South (there's never much traffic on the LIE, of course…). From uptown, you can take the Robery F. Kennedy Bridge to the Grand Central Parkway to the Van Wyck Expressway S. JFK also has two new AM frequencies solely devoted to keeping you abreast of all of the airport's endeavors that may affect traffic. Tune into 1630AM for general airport information and 1700AM for construction updates en route to your next flight. It might save you a sizeable headache.

How to Get There—Mass Transit

This is your chance to finish *War and Peace*. Replacing the free shuttle from the subway is the AirTrain, which will make your journey marginally smoother, but also make your wallet a little lighter. Running 24/7, you can board the AirTrain from the subway on the A line at either the Howard Beach stop or the E, J and Z lines at the Sutphin/Archer Ave-Jamaica Station stop. The ride takes around 15–25 minutes, depending on which airport terminal you need.

A one-way ride on the AirTrain sets you back $5, so a ride on the subway and then hopping the AirTrain will be a total of $7.25. If you're anywhere near Penn Station and your time is valuable, the LIRR to Jamaica will cost you $5.75 off-peak, $8 during peak times and $3.50 on weekends using a MTA CityTicket. The AirTrain portion of the trip will still cost you an additional $5 and round out your travel time to less than an hour.

If you want to give your MetroCard a workout, you can take the E or the F to the Turnpike/Kew Gardens stop and transfer to the Q10. Another possibility is the 3 or 4 to New Lots Avenue, where you transfer to the B15 to JFK. The easiest and most direct option is to take a New York Airport Service Express bus (718-875-8200) from either Grand Central Station, Penn Station, or the Port Authority for $15, or you can hop on the Trans-Bridge Bus Line (800-962-9135) at Port Authority for $12. Since the buses travel on service roads, Friday afternoon is not an advisable time to try them out.

Parking

Daily rates for the Central Terminal Area lots cost $3 for the first half-hour, $6 for up to one hour, $3 for every hour after that, up to $33 per day. Long-term parking costs $18 for the first 24-hours, then $6 in each 8-hour increment thereafter. Be warned, though—many of the ongoing construction projects at JFK affect both their short-term and long-term lots, so be sure to allow extra time for any unpleasant surprises. For updated parking availability, call 718-244-4080.

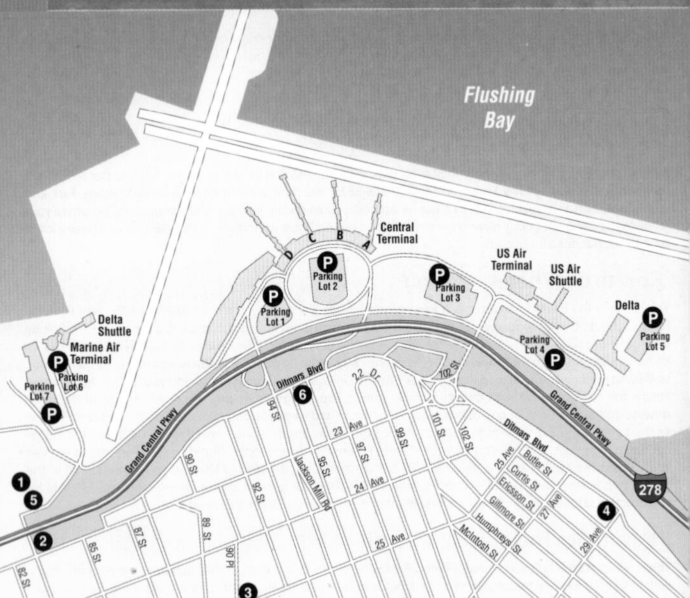

Airline	Terminal
Air Canada	A
American	D
American Eagle	C
Colgan	US Airways
Comair	Delta
Continental	A
Continental Express	A
Delta	Delta
Delta Connection	Delta
Delta Shuttle	Marine
Frontier Airlines	A/B
JetBlue Airways	B
Midwest	B
Northwest	Delta
Southwest	B
Spirit	B
United	C
United Express	C
US Airways	US Airways
US Airways Express	US Airways
US Airways Shuttle	US Airways Shuttle

General Information

Address: LaGuardia Airport
Flushing, NY 11371

Recorded Information: 718-533-3400

Lost & Found: 718-533-3988

Police: 718-533-3900

Website: www.laguardiaairport.com

Overview

The reason to fly from LaGuardia (affectionately known as LGA on your baggage tags) is that it is geographically the closest airport to Manhattan and thus a cheap(er) cab ride when your delayed flight touches down at 1 in the morning. The reason not to fly to and from here is that there is no subway line (HELLO, city officials!) and the check-in areas are just too darn small to accommodate the many passengers and their many bags that crowd the terminals at just about every hour of the day. Food is not a great option, so eat before you leave home. If you must dine, there are 5 Au Bon Pains throughout the terminals—find them as they are the most palatable choice available.

How to Get There—Driving (or directing your cabbie)

LaGuardia is mere inches away from Grand Central Parkway, which can be reached from both the Brooklyn-Queens Expressway (BQE) or from the Robert F. Kennedy Bridge. From Lower Manhattan, take the Brooklyn, Manhattan, or Williamsburg Bridges to the BQE to Grand Central Parkway E. From Midtown Manhattan, take FDR Drive to the Robert F. Kennedy Bridge to Grand Central. A potential alternate route (and money-saver) would be to take the 59th Street Bridge to 21st Street in Queens. Once you're heading north on 21st Street, you can make a right on Astoria Boulevard and follow it all the way to 94th Street, where you can make a left and drive straight into LaGuardia. This alternate route is good if the FDR and/or the BQE is jammed, although that probably means that the 59th Street Bridge won't be much better.

How to Get There—Mass Transit

Alas, no subway line goes to LaGuardia (although there SHOULD be one running across 96th Street in Manhattan, through Astoria, and ending at LaGuardia—but that's another story). The closest the subway comes is the 7 E F G R Jackson Heights/ Roosevelt Avenue/74th Street stop in Queens, where you can transfer to the Q33 or Q47 bus bus to LaGuardia. Sound exciting? Well, it's not. A better bus to take is the 60, which runs across 125th Street to the airport. An even better bet would be to pay the extra few bucks and take the New York Airport Service Express Bus ($12 one-way, 718-875-8200) from Grand Central Station. It departs every 20–30 minutes and takes approximately 45 minutes; also catch it on Park Avenue between 41st and 42nd Streets, Penn Station, and the Port Authority Bus Terminal. The improbably named SuperShuttle Manhattan is a shared mini-bus that picks you up anywhere within the city limits ($13–$22 one-way, 212-258-3826). If you want a taxi, search for the "hidden" cab line tucked around Terminal D as the line is almost always shorter than the others.

How to Get There—Really

Plan ahead and call a car service to guarantee that you won't spend the morning of your flight fighting for a taxi. Nothing beats door to door service. Allstate Car and Limousine: 212-333-3333 ($30 in the am & $38 in the pm + tolls from Union Square); LimoRes: 212-777-7171 ($30 + tolls from Union Square; best to call in the morning); Dial 7: 212-777-7777 ($30 in the am & $40 in the pm + tolls from Union Square), Carmel: 212-666-6666 ($31 + tolls to LGA, $28–$35 + tolls from LGA).

Parking

Daily parking rates at LaGuardia cost $3 for the first half-hour, $6 for up to one hour, $3 for every hour thereafter, and up to $33 per day. Long-term parking is $33 per day for the first two 24 hour periods, and $6 for each subsequent 8 hour period. (though only in Lot 3). You can use cash, credit card, or E-Z Pass to pay. Another option is independent parking lots, such as The Crowne Plaza (104-04 Ditmars Blvd, 718-457-6300 x295), Clarion Airport Parking (Ditmars Blvd & 94th St, 718-335-6713) and AviStar (23rd Ave & 90th St, 800-621-PARK). They run their own shuttle buses from their lots, and they usually charge $14–$17 per day. If all the parking garages onsite are full, follow the "P" signs to the airport exit and park in one of the off-airport locations.

Rental Cars

1 **Avis** • LGA	800-230-4898
2 **Budget** • 83-34 23rd Ave	800-527-0700
3 **Dollar** • 90-05 25th Ave	800-800-4000
4 **Enterprise** • 104-04 Ditmars Blvd	718-457-2900
5 **Hertz** • LGA	800-654-3131
6 **National** • Ditmars Blvd & 95th St	800-227-7368

Hotels

Airway Inn • 82-20 Astoria Boulevard • 718-565-5100

Clarion • 94-00 Ditmars Blvd • 718-335-1200

Courtyard • 90-10 Grand Central Pkwy • 718-446-4800

Crowne Plaza • 104-04 Ditmars Blvd • 718-457-6300

Eden Park Hotel • 113-10 Corona Ave • 718-699-4500

Holiday Inn • 37-10 114th Street • 718-651-2100

Howard Johnson • 135-33 38th Avenue • 718-461-3888

LaGuardia Airport Hotel • 100-15 Ditmars Boulevard • 888-307-7555

LaGuardia Marriott • 102-05 Ditmars Blvd • 718-565-8900

Lexington Marco LaGuardia Hotel • 137-07 Northern Boulevard • 718-445-3300

Paris Suites • 109-17 Horace Harding Expy • 718-760-2820

Sheraton • 135-20 39th Ave • 718-460-6666

Skyway Motel at LaGuardia • 102-10 Ditmars Boulevard • 718-899-6900

Wyndham Garden • 100-15 Ditmars Blvd • 718-426-1500

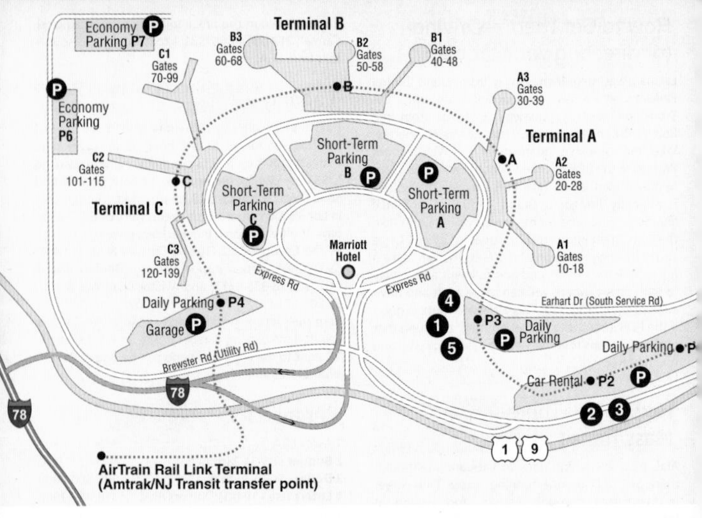

Airline	Terminal
Air Canada	A
Air France	B
Air India	B
Alaska Airlines	A
Alitalia	B
American (domestic)	A
American (international)	A/B*
American Eagle	A
British Airways	B
Casino Express (charter)	A
Comair Terminal	B
Continental Express Terminal	A
Continental	C
Delta	B
Delta Express	B
El Al	B
Eva Airways	B
Express Jet – Continental	C
Jet Airways	B
Jet Blue	A
Open Skies Terminal	B
US Airways Terminal	A
US Airways Express Terminal	A

Airline	Terminal
KLM Royal Dutch Airlines	B
L'Avion	B
LoT Polish	B
Lufthansa	B
Malaysia	B
Miami Air (Charter)**	B
Midwest	A
Northwest	B
Porter	B
Qantas	A
Qatar	B
SAS	B
Singapore Airlines	B
Swiss International Air Lines	B
TAP Portugal	B
United (domestic)	A
United (international)	A/B*
United Express	A
Virgin Atlantic	B
West Jet	A

* Departs Terminal A, arrives Terminal B.

** Charter Airlines: For departure/arrival information, contact the airline or travel agent.

General Information

Address:	10 Toler Pl, Newark, NJ 07114
Phone:	888-EWR-INFO
Police/Lost & Found:	973-961-6230
Airport Information:	973-961-6000
Transportation Info:	800-AIR-RIDE (247-7533)
Radio Station:	530 AM
Website:	www.newarkairport.com

Overview

Newark Airport is easily the nicest of the three major metropolitan airports. The monorail that connects the terminals and the parking lots, the AirTrain link from Penn Station, and the diverse food court (in Terminal C), make it the city's preferred point of departure and arrival. There are also plenty of international departures, making it a great second option to the miserable experience of doing JFK.

If your flight gets delayed or you find yourself with time on your hands, check out the d-parture spa in Terminals B or C to unwind, or, if you're feeling carnivorous after your screaming match with airline personnel, Gallagher's Steakhouse (Terminal C).

How to Get There–Driving

The route to Newark Airport is easy—just take the Holland Tunnel or the Lincoln Tunnel to the New Jersey Turnpike South. You can use either Exit 14 or Exit 13A. If you want a cheaper and slightly more scenic (from an industrial standpoint) drive, follow signs for the Pulaski Skyway once you exit the Holland Tunnel. It's free, it's one of the coolest bridges in America, and it leads you to the airport just fine. If possible, check a traffic report before leaving Manhattan—sometimes there are viciously long tie-ups, especially at the Holland Tunnel. It's always worth it to see which outbound tunnel has the shortest wait.

How to Get There–Mass Transit

If you're allergic to traffic, try taking the AirTrain service from Penn Station. It's run by Amtrak ($25–$48 one-way) and NJ Transit Airtrain ($15 one-way). If you use NJ Transit, choose a train that runs on the Northeast Corridor or North Jersey Coast Line with a scheduled stop for Newark Airport. If you use Amtrak, choose a train that runs on the Northeast Corridor Line with a scheduled stop for Newark Airport. The cheapest option is to take the PATH train ($1.75) to Newark Penn Station then switch to NJ Transit bus #62 ($1.25), which hits all the terminals. Just be alert at night since the area around Newark Penn Station can be a bit shady. You can also catch direct buses departing from Port Authority Bus Terminal (with the advantage of a bus-only lane running right out of the station and into the Lincoln Tunnel), Grand Central Terminal, and Penn Station (the New York version) on Olympia for $14. The SuperShuttle will set you back $13–$22, and a taxi from Manhattan will cost you around $50.

How to Get There–Car Services

Car services are always the simplest option, although they're a bit more expensive for Newark Airport than they are for LaGuardia. Allstate Car and Limousine: 212-333-3333 ($44 in the am & $52 in the pm + tolls from Union Square); Tri-State: 212-777-7171 ($43 + tolls from Union Square; best to call in the morning); Dial 7: 212-777-7777 ($44 in the am & $49 in the pm + tolls from Union Square).

Parking

Short term parking is $3 for every half-hour, up to $33 per day." Long-term parking rates are $3 for the first half-hour, $6 for up to one hour, $3 for every hour after that, $24 per day for the P1 and P3 lots, and $27 per day for the P4 lot. The P6 parking lot is much farther away and only serviced by a shuttle bus. Lot P6 costs $18 for first 24 hours, $6 for each 8-hour period or part thereafter. There are some off-airport lots that you can sometimes score for $18 per day, especially if you have a business card. Most of them are on the local southbound drag of Route 1 & 9. Valet parking costs $40 per day, $20 for each additional 12 hours.

Rental Cars

1 • **Avis**	800-230-4898
2 • **Budget**	800-527-0700
3 • **Dollar**	866-434-2226
4 • **Hertz**	800-654-3131
5 • **National**	800-227-7368
6 • **Enterprise** (Off-Airport)	800-325-8007

Hotels

Marriott (On-Airport) • 973-623-0006
Courtyard Marriott • 600 Rte 1 & 9 S • 973-643-8500
Hilton • 1170 Spring St • 908-351-3900
Howard Johnson • 20 Frontage Rd • 973-344-1500
Sheraton • 128 Frontage Rd • 973-690-5500
Hampton Inn • 1128-38 Spring St • 908-355-0500
Best Western • 101 International Wy • 973-621-6200
Holiday Inn North • 160 Frontage Rd • 973-589-1000
Days Inn • 450 Rte 1 South • 973-242-0900
Ramada Inn • 1 Haynes Ave • 973-824-4000
Wyndham Garden Hotel •
550 US Route 9 • 973-824-4000

Free Harlem River Crossings

- A Broadway Bridge
- B University Heights Bridge
- C Washington Bridge
- D A Hamilton Bridge
- E Macombs Dam Bridge
- F 145th St Bridge
- G Madison Ave Bridge
- H 3rd Ave Bridge
- I Willis Ave Bridge

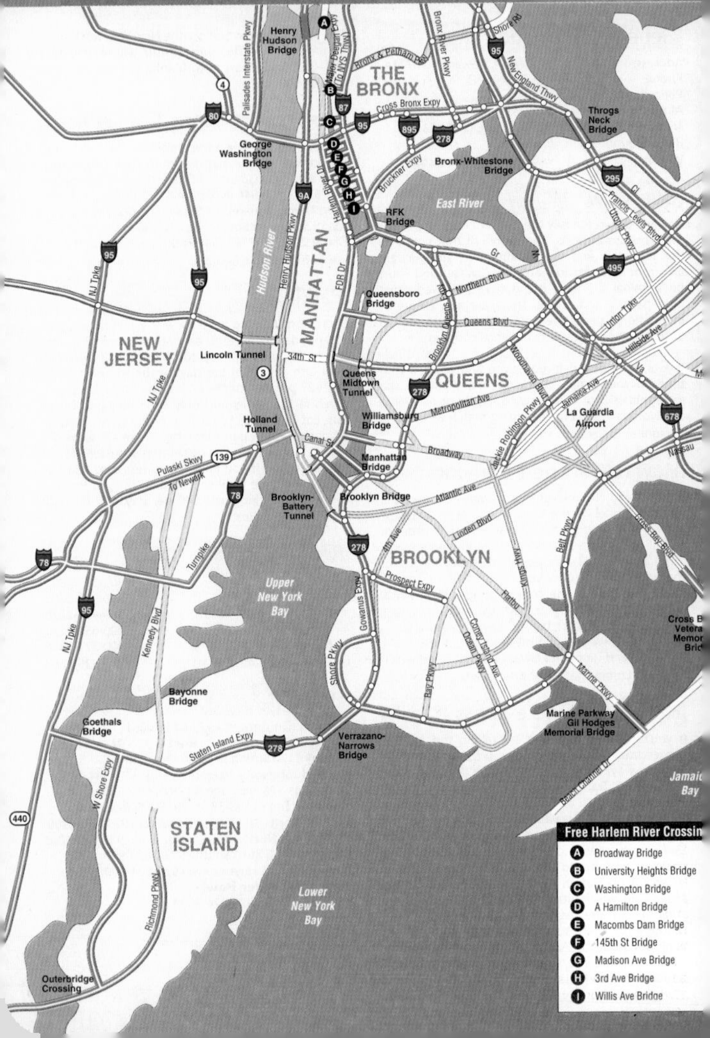

General Information

Port Authority of NY and NJ:	www.panynj.gov
DOT:	www.ci.nyc.ny.us/html/dot/home.html • 212-NEW-YORK
MTA:	www.mta.info
EZPass:	www.e-zpassny.com • 800-333-TOLL
Transportation Alternatives:	www.transalt.org
Best overall site:	www.nycroads.com

Overview

Since NYC is an archipelago, it's no wonder there are so many bridges and four major tunnels. Most of the bridges listed in the chart below are considered landmarks, either for their sheer beauty or because they were the first of their kind at one time. The traffic-jammed Holland Tunnel, finished in 1927, was the first vehicular tunnel connecting New Jersey and New York. King's Bridge, built between Manhattan and the Bronx in 1693, was sadly demolished in 1917. Highbridge, the oldest existing bridge in NYC (built in 1843), is no longer open to vehicles or pedestrians. Brooklyn Bridge, built in 1883, is the city's oldest functioning bridge, still open to vehicles and pedestrians alike, and is considered one of the most beautiful bridges ever built.

The '70s was a decade of neglect for city bridges. Inspections in the '80s and maintenance and refurbishment plans in the '90s/'00s have made the bridges stronger and safer than ever before. On certain holidays when the weather permits, the world's largest free-flying American flag flies from the upper arch of the New Jersey tower on the George Washington Bridge. The Williamsburg Bridge has been completely rebuilt and is almost unrecognizable from its pre-renovation form, especially the pedestrian pathways. The Triborough has been renamed the "RFK" Bridge, just to confuse everyone immensely.

		Toll/E-Z Pass Peak/E-Z Pass off-peak	# of lanes	Pedestrians/bicyclists?	# of vehicles/day (in thousands)	Original cost (in millions)	Engineer	Main span	Operated by	Opened to traffic
1	Geo. Washington Bridge	8.00/8.00/6.00 (inbound only)	14	yes	300	59	Othmar H. Ammann	4,760'	PANYNJ	10/25/31
2	Lincoln Tunnel	8.00/8.00/6.00 (inbound only)	6	no	120	75	Othmar H. Ammann Ole Singstad	8,216'	PANYNJ	12/22/37
3	Holland Tunnel	8.00/8.00/6.00 (inbound only)	4	no	100	54	Clifford Holland/ Ole Singstad	8,558'	PANYNJ	11/13/27
4	Verrazano-Narrows Bridge	* 11.00/9.14	12	no	190	320	Othmar H. Ammann	4,260'	MTA	11/21/64
5	Brooklyn-Battery Tunnel	5.50/4.57	4	no	60	90	Ole Singstad	9,117'	MTA	5/25/50
6	Brooklyn Bridge	free	6	yes	140	15	John Roebling/ Washington Roebling	1,595.5'	DOT	5/24/1883
7	Manhattan Bridge	free	4	yes	150	31	Leon Moisseiff	1,470'	DOT	12/31/09
8	Williamsburg Bridge	free	8	yes	140	24.2	Leffert L. Buck	1,600'	DOT	12/19/03
9	Queens-Midtown Tunnel	5.50/4.57	4	no	80	52	Ole Singstad	6,414'	MTA	11/15/40
10	Queensboro Bridge	free	10	yes	200	20	Gustav Lindenthal	1,182'	DOT	3/30/09
11	Robert F. Kennedy Bridge	5.50/4.57	8/ 6/8	yes	200	60.3	Othmar H. Ammann	1,380'	MTA	7/11/36
12	Henry Hudson Bridge	3.00/2.09	7	no	75	5	David Steinman	840'	MTA	12/12/36
13	Whitestone Bridge	5.50/4.57	6	no	110	20	Othmar H. Ammann	2,300'	MTA	4/29/39
14	Throgs Neck Bridge	5.50/4.57	6	no	100	92	Othmar H. Ammann	1,800'	MTA	1/11/61
15	Cross Bay Veterans Memorial Bridge	2.75/1.71	6	yes	20	29	n/a	3,000'	MTA	5/28/70
16	Marine Parkway Gil Hodges Memorial Bridge	2.75/1.71	4	yes	25	12	Madigan and Hyland	540'	MTA	7/3/37
17	Bayonne Bridge	8.00/8.00/6.00	4	yes	20	13	Othmar H. Ammann	5,780'	PANY/NJ	11/13/31
18	Goethals Bridge	8.00/8.00/6.00	4	no	75	7.2	Othmar H. Ammann	8,600'	PANY/NJ	6/29/28
19	Outerbridge Crossing	8.00/8.00/6.00	4	no	80	9.6	Othmar H. Ammann	750'	PANY/NJ	6/29/28

* $9.00/$8.00 with EZPass to Staten Island ($6.40/4.80 for registered Staten Island residents with EZPass), $2.25 with three or more occupants—cash only. Free to Brooklyn.

Transit • Ferries, Marinas & Heliports

Ferries/Boat Tours, Rentals & Charters

Name	*Contact Info*
Staten Island Ferry	311 • www.siferry.com This free ferry travels between Battery Park and Staten Island. On weekdays it leaves every 15–30 minutes 12 am–11:30 pm. On weekends, it leaves every hour 1:30 am–11:30 am and every half-hour at all other times.
NY Waterway	800-53-FERRY • www.nywaterway.com The largest ferry service in NY, NYWaterway offers many commuter routes (mostly from New Jersey), sightseeing tours. However, recent financial troubles have them closing many commuter lines.
NY Water Taxi	212-742-1969 • www.nywatertaxi.com Available for commuting, sightseeing, charter, and shuttles to Yankees and Mets games. Commuter tickets range between $4.50 and $6 and tours cost $20 to $25. For chartered trips or tours, call for a quote.
Sea Streak	800-BOAT-RIDE • www.seastreakusa.com Catamarans that go pretty fast from the Highlands in NJ to Wall Street and E 34th Street.
Circle Line Sightseeing Cruises	212-269-5755 • www.circleline42.com Circle Line offers many sightseeing tours, including a visit to Ellis Island (departs from Pier 16 at South Street Seaport—$11 for adults, $4.50 for kids)
Circle Line Downtown	www.circlelinedowntown.com (blurb & info missing)
Spirit of New York	212-727-7735 • www.spiritcruises.com Offers lunch and dinner cruises. Prices start at $43. Leaves from Pier 62 at Chelsea Piers. Make a reservation at least one week in advance, but the earlier the better.
Loeb Boathouse	212-517-2233 • www.thecentralparkboathouse.com You can rent rowboats from March through October at the Lake in Central Park, open seven days a week, weather permitting. Boat rentals cost $12 for the first hour and $3 for every additional 15 minutes (rentals also require a $30 cash deposit). The boathouse is open 10 am–5 pm, but the last boat goes out at 4:30 pm. Up to four people per boat. No reservations needed.
World Yacht Cruises	212-630-8100 or 800-498-4271 • www.worldyacht.com These fancy, three-hour dinner cruises start at $89.88 per person. The cruises depart from Pier 81 (41st Street) and require reservations. The cruise boards at 6 pm, sails at 7 pm, and returns at 10 pm. There's also a Sunday brunch cruise April–December that costs $61.85 per person.

Marinas/Passenger Ship Terminal

Name	*Contact Info*	*Map*
MarineMax Manhattan	212-336-7873 • www.marinemax.com Dockage at Chelsea Piers. They offer daily, weekly, and seasonal per-foot rates (there's always a waiting list).	8
NY Skyports Inc	212-686-4546 Located on the East River at E 23rd Street. Transient dockage costs $3 per foot.	10
79th St Marina	212-496-2105 This city-operated dock is filled with long-term houseboat residents. It's located at W 79th Street and the Hudson River. Open from May to October.	14
Dyckman Marina	212-496-2105 Transient dockage on the Hudson River at 348 Dyckman Street	25
Manhattan Cruise Terminal	212-246-5450 • www.nycruise.com If *Love Boat* re-runs aren't enough and you decide to go on a cruise yourself, you'll leave from the Manhattan Cruise Terminal. W 55th Street at 12th Avenue. Take the West Side Highway to Piers 88-92.	11
North Cove Yacht Harbor	212-786-1200 • www.thenorthcove.com A very, very fancy place to park your yacht in Battery Park City.	p. 234

Helicopter Services

Name	*Contact Info*	*Map*
Helicopter Flight Services	212-355-0801 • www.heliny.com For a minimum of $129, you can hop on a helicopter at the Downtown Manhattan Heliport at Pier 6 on the East River on weekdays, or at the W 30th Street Heliport on weekends and spend 15 minutes gazing down on Manhattan. Reservations are recommended, and there's a minimum of two passengers per flight.	3, 8
Liberty Helicopter Tours	212-967-6464 • www.libertyhelicopters.com Leaves from the heliport at W 30th Street and 12th Avenue (9 am–9 pm) or the Downtown Manhattan Heliport at Pier 6 on the East River (9 am–6:30 pm). Prices start at $69, and reservations are needed only when boarding at the Seaport. Flights depart every 5–10 minutes. Minimum of four passengers per flight.	3, 8

General Information

E-ZPass Information:	800-333-TOLL, www.e-zpassny.com
Radio Station Traffic Updates:	1010 WINS on the 1s for a 5 boroughs focus and 880 on the 8s for a suburbs focus
DOT Website:	www.ci.nyc.ny.us/html/dot/html/motorist/motorist.html
Real-Time Web Traffic Info:	www.metrocommute.com

Driving in Manhattan

Avoid it. Why drive when you can see the city so well on foot or by bus? (We don't count the subway as seeing the city, but rather as a cultural experience in and of itself.) We know that sometimes you just *have* to drive in the city, so we've made you a list of essentials.

- Great auto insurance that doesn't care if the guy who hit you doesn't have insurance and doesn't speak any English.
- Thick skin on driver, passengers, and car. Needed for the fender benders and screamed profanity from the cabbies that are ticked anyone but cabbies are on the road.
- Meditation CD to counteract cardiac arrest–inducing "almost" accidents.
- NFT. But we know you would never leave home without it.
- E-ZPass. Saves time and lives. Maybe not lives, but definitely time and some money.
- New York State license plates. Even pedestrians will curse you out if you represent anywhere other than the Empire State, especially NJ or CT or Texas.
- A tiny car that can fit into a spot slightly larger than a postage stamp or tons of cash for parking garages.
- Patience with pedestrians—they own the streets of New York. Well, co-own them with the cabbies, sanitation trucks, cops, and fire engines.

The following are some tips that we've picked up over the years:

Hudson River Crossings

In the Bridge or Tunnel battle, the Bridge almost always wins. The George Washington Bridge is by far the best Hudson River crossing. It's got more lanes and better access than either tunnel with a fantastic view to boot. If you're going anywhere in the country that's north of central New Jersey, take it. However, inbound traffic on the George can back up for hours in the morning because they don't have enough toll booth operators to handle all those nuts who don't have E-ZPass. The Lincoln Tunnel is decent inbound, but check 1010 AM (WINS) if you have the chance—even though they can be horribly inaccurate and frustrating. Avoid the Lincoln like the plague during evening rush hour (starts at about 3:30 pm). If you have to take the Holland Tunnel outbound, try the Broome Street approach, but don't even bother between 5 and 7 pm on weekdays.

East River Crossings

Brooklyn

Pearl Street to the Brooklyn Bridge is the least-known approach. Only the Williamsburg Bridge has direct access (i.e. no traffic lights) to the northbound BQE in Brooklyn, and only the Brooklyn Bridge has direct access to the FDR Drive in Manhattan. Again, listen to the radio if you can, but all three bridges can be disastrous as they seem to be constantly under construction (or, in a fabulous new twist, having one lane closed by the NYPD to for some unknown (terrorism?) reason). The Williamsburg is by far the best free route into North Brooklyn, but make sure to take the outer roadway to keep your options open in case the BQE is jammed. Your best option to go anywhere else in Brooklyn is usually the Brooklyn-Battery Tunnel, which can be reached from the FDR as well as the West Side Highway. Fun fact: The water you pass was so dirty in the '50s that it used to catch fire. The tunnel is not free ($5.50), but if you followed our instructions you've got E-ZPass anyway ($4.57). The bridges from south to north can be remembered as B-M-W, but they are not as cool as the cars that share the initials.

Queens

There are three options for crossing into Queens by car. The Queens Midtown Tunnel is usually miserable, since it feeds directly onto the parking lot known as the Long Island Expressway. The 59th Street Bridge (known as the Queensboro to mapmakers) is the only free crossing to Queens. The best approach to it is First Avenue to 57th Street (after that, follow the signs) or to 59th Street if you want to jump on the outer roadway that saves a ton of time and only precludes easy access to Northern Boulevard. If you're in Queens and want to go downtown in Manhattan, you can take the lower level of the 59th Street Bridge since it will feed directly onto Second Avenue, which of course goes downtown. The Triborough Bridge (RFK) is usually the best option (especially if you're going to LaGuardia, Shea, Astoria for Greek food, or Flushing for dim sum). The FDR to the Triborough is good except for rush hour—then try Third Avenue to 124th Street.

Harlem River Crossings

The Triborough (RFK) ($5.50) will get you to the Bronx in pretty good shape, especially if you are heading east on the Bruckner towards 95 or the Hutchinson (which will take you to eastern Westchester and Connecticut). To get to Yankee Stadium, take the Willis or the Macomb's Dam (which are both free). When you feel comfortable maneuvering the tight turns approaching the Willis, use it for all travel to Westchester and Connecticut in order to save toll money. The Henry Hudson Bridge ($3.00) will take you up to western Westchester along the Hudson, and, except for the antiquated and completely unnecessary toll plaza, is pretty good. It wins the fast and pretty prize for its beautiful surroundings. The Cross-Bronx Expressway will take years off your life. Avoid it at all costs.

Manhattan's "Highways"

There are two so-called highways in Manhattan—the Harlem River Drive/FDR Drive/East River Drive (which prohibits commercial vehicles) and the Henry Hudson Parkway/West Side Highway/Joe Dimaggio Highway. The main advantage of the FDR is that it has no traffic lights, while the West Side Highway has lights from Battery Park up through 57th Street. The main disadvantages of the FDR are (1) the potholes and (2) the narrow lanes. If there's been a lot of rain, both highways will flood, so you're out of luck (but the FDR floods first). Although the West Side Highway can fly, we would rather look at Brooklyn and Queens than Jersey, so the FDR wins.

Driving Uptown

The 96th Street transverse across Central Park is usually the best one, although if there's been a lot of rain, it will flood. If you're driving on the west side, Riverside Drive is the best route, followed next by West End Avenue. People drive like morons on Broadway, and Columbus jams up in the mid 60s before Lincoln Center and the mid 40s before the Lincoln Tunnel but it's still the best way to get all the way downtown without changing avenues. Amsterdam is a good uptown route if you can get to it. For the east side, you can take Fifth Avenue downtown to about 65th Street, whereupon you should bail out and cut over to Park Avenue for the rest of the trip. Do NOT drive on Fifth Avenue below 65th Street within a month of Christmas, and check the parade schedules before attempting it on weekends throughout the year. The 96th Street entrance to the FDR screws up First and Third Avenues going north and the 59th Street Bridge screws up Lexington and Second Avenues going downtown. Getting stuck in 59th Street Bridge traffic is one of the most frustrating things in the universe because there is absolutely no way out of it.

Driving in Midtown

Good luck! Sometimes Broadway is best because everyone's trying to get out of Manhattan, jamming up the west side (via the Lincoln Tunnel) and the east side (via the 59th Street Bridge and the Queens Midtown Tunnel). Friday nights at 9:30 pm can be a breeze, but from 10 pm to midnight, you're screwed as shows let out. The "interior" of the city is the last place to get jammed up—it's surprisingly quiet at 8 am. At 10 am, however, it's a parking lot. Those who plan to drive in Midtown on weekends from about March–October should check parade schedules for Fifth AND Sixth avenues.

The demarcation of several "THRU Streets" running east-west in Midtown has been with the city for a couple of years and folks are finally getting the hang of it. Still, it may screw you up. See the next page for more information.

Driving in the Village

People get confused walking in the village, so you can imagine how challenging driving can be in the maze of one ways and short streets. Beware. If you're coming into the Village from the northwest, 14th Street is the safest crosstown route heading east. However, going west, take 13th Street. Houston Street is under construction at a number of points along its length but it has the great benefit of direct access to FDR Drive, both getting onto it and coming off of it. If you want to get to Houston Street from the Holland Tunnel, take Hudson Street to King Street to the Avenue of the Americas to Houston Street (this is the **only** efficient way to get to the Village from the Holland Tunnel). First Avenue is good going north and Fifth Avenue is good going south. Washington Street is the only way to make any headway southbound and Hudson Street is the only way to make any headway northbound in the West Village.

Driving Downtown

Don't do it unless you have to. Western TriBeCa is okay and so is the Lower East Side—try not to "turn in" to SoHo, Chinatown, or the Civic Center. Canal Street is a complete mess during the day (avoid it), since on its western end, everyone is trying to get to the Holland Tunnel, and on its eastern end, everyone is mistakenly driving over the Manhattan Bridge (your only other option when heading east on Canal is to turn **right** on Bowery!). Watch the potholes! Chatham Square (the confluence of Bowery, Catherine, East Broadway, Oliver, St. James, Park Row, Worth, and Mott) is due for another major "reorg" starting summer 2009; that should be fun, no?

DMV Locations in Manhattan

If you're going to the DMV to get your first NY license (including drivers with other states' licenses), you'll need extensive documentation of your identity. The offices have a long list of accepted documents, but your best bet is a US passport and a Social Security card. If you don't have these things, birth certificates from the US, foreign passports, and various INS documents will be okay under certain conditions. Do not be surprised if you are turned away the first time. This trip requires great amounts of patience. Plan on spending three to six hours here. We're not kidding. This is not a lunch-hour errand.

Greenwich Street Office
11 Greenwich St
New York, NY 10004
(Cross Streets Battery Park Pl & Morris St)
M–F 8:30 am–4 pm
212-645-5550 or 718-966-6155

Harlem Office
159 E 125th St, 3rd Fl
New York, NY 10035
(Lexington and Third)
M, T, W & F 8:30 am–4 pm, Thursday 10 am–6 pm
212-645-5550 or 718-966-6155

Herald Square Office
1293-1311 Broadway, 8th Fl
New York, NY 10001
(Between W 33 & W 34th Sts)
* To exchange an out-of-state license for a New York license, you must go to License X-Press.
M–F 8:30 am–4 pm
212-645-5550 or 718-966-6155

Manhattan
License X-Press Office*
300 W 34th St
New York, NY 10001
(Between Eighth & Ninth aves)
*Service limited to license and registration renewals and out-of-state exchange. You can't get your snowmobile or boat license here, but you can surrender your license plate. Oh, and no permit renewals.
M–F 8:30 am–4 pm
212-645-5550 or 718-966-6155

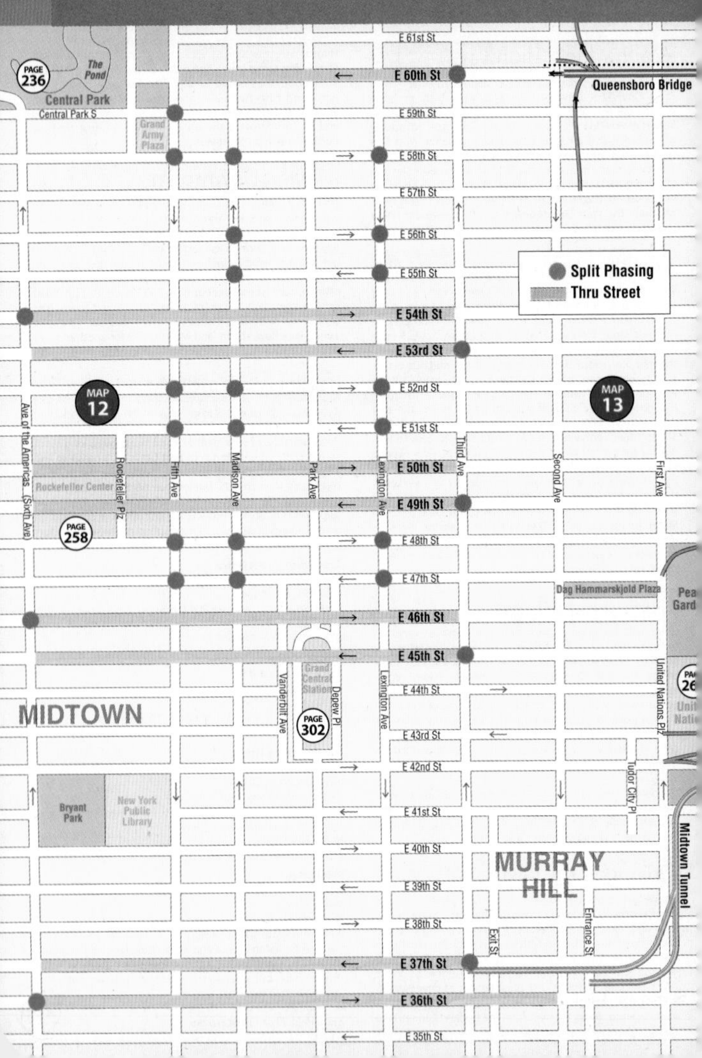

PAGE 236
The Pond
Central Park
Central Park S
Grand Army Plaza
E 61st St
E 60th St
Queensboro Bridge
E 59th St
E 58th St
E 57th St
E 56th St
E 55th St
Split Phasing
Thru Street
E 54th St
E 53rd St
E 52nd St
MAP 12
MAP 13
E 51st St
Ave of the Americas (Sixth Ave)
Rockefeller Center
Rockefeller Plz
Fifth Ave
Madison Ave
Park Ave
Lexington Ave
Third Ave
Second Ave
First Ave
E 50th St
E 49th St
PAGE 258
E 48th St
E 47th St
Dag Hammarskjold Plaza
E 46th St
E 45th St
Grand Central Station
Vanderbilt Ave
Depew Pl
PAGE 302
Lexington Ave
E 44th St
United Nations Plz
MIDTOWN
E 43rd St
E 42nd St
Tudor City Pl
Bryant Park
New York Public Library
E 41st St
E 40th St
MURRAY HILL
Midtown Tunnel
E 39th St
E 38th St
Exit St
Entrance St
E 37th St
E 36th St
E 35th St

General Information

NFT Maps: 12 & 13
DOT Website: www.nyc.gov/html/dot/html/motorist/streetprog.shtml
DOT Phone: 311

Overview

In the tradition of "don't block the box" and other traffic solutions (such as randomly arresting political protesters), the city introduced "THRU Streets," a program initially tested in 2002, as a permanent fixture in Midtown in 2004. The plan was implemented on some crosstown streets in Midtown in order to reduce travel times, relieve congestion, and provide a safer environment for pedestrians and cyclists. They are still working on cleaning up the exhaust fume issue, for those concerned about said environment.

On certain streets, cars are not allowed to make turns between Sixth and Third Avenues (with the exception of Park Avenue). The regulations are in effect between 10 am and 6 pm on weekdays. The affected streets are:

36th & 37th Streets
45th & 46th Streets
49th & 50th Streets
53rd & 54th Streets
60th Street (between Third and Fifth Avenues)

The good news is that turns from 59th Street are permitted. Oh joy.

The above streets are easily identifiable by big, purple "THRU Streets" signs. With everything that's going on in midtown Manhattan though, you'd be forgiven for missing a sign (by us, not by the NYPD). If you happen to unwittingly find yourself on a THRU Street and can't escape on Park Avenue, you're going to have to suck it up until you get to Sixth Avenue or Third Avenue, depending on the direction you're heading. If you attempt to turn before the designated avenue, you'll find yourself with an insanely expensive ticket. Of course, if you're trying to drive crosstown, it's in your best interests to take one of these streets.

Both sides of almost every non-THRU Street in this grid have been stuck with "No Standing Except Trucks Loading and Unloading" regulations, supposedly creating up to 150 spaces for truck loading (if you were ever stuck behind a truck in morning rush hour on a THRU Street in 2004, you would rejoice at this news). Additionally, one side of each non-THRU street has been "daylighted" for 80–100 feet in advance of the intersection. We are not exactly sure how they came up with the term "daylighted," but the DOT tells us it allows space for turning vehicles.

According to the DOT, THRU Streets are working—since the program began, travel times have fallen by 25% (as people have decided to emigrate to New Zealand) and vehicle speeds have increased by an average of 33% (from 4 mph to 5.3 mph). The THRU Streets combined now carry 4,854 vehicles per hour (up from 4,187), which means that each of the THRU Streets accommodates an average of 74 additional vehicles per hour.

Split Signal Phasing

Another traffic innovation in Midtown is "split signal phasing," which allows pedestrians to cross the street without having to worry about vehicles turning in their path at about 40 non-THRU Street intersections in this same grid. Of course, this system assumes that both pedestrians and drivers follow the rules of the road. In spite of the disregard that most New Yorkers display for crossing signals, the number of pedestrian accidents in the eight-month trial period (compared to the eight months prior to implementation) fell from 81 to 74. The number of cycling accidents fell from 30 to 17. Accidents not related to pedestrians or bikes fell from 168 to 102. We don't know if this accounts for accidents caused by drivers who became confused by the pretty purple signs. We have to admit that something must be working—though there would be no accidents if no one ever left their house…

Now if the DOT and NYPD could get traffic to flow smoothly onto bridges and into tunnels, they might actually be onto something. They can save you 1.5 minutes getting crosstown, just don't try leaving the city. Ever.

Information

Department of Transportation (DOT): 311 (24 hours) or 212-NEW-YORK (Out-of-state)
TTY Hearing-Impaired: 212-504-4115
Website: www.ci.nyc.ny.us/html/dot/
Parking Violations Help Line: 311
TTY Automated Information for the Hearing Impaired: 718-802-8555
Website: www.ci.nyc.ny.us/finance (parking ticket info)

Standing, Stopping and Parking Rules

In "No Stopping" areas, you **can't** wait in your car, drop off passengers, or load/unload.

In "No Standing" areas, you **can't** wait in your car or load/unload, but you **can** drop off passengers.

In "No Parking" areas, you **can't** wait in your car or drop off passengers, but you **can** load/unload.

NYC has just enacted a "no idling" law. That means, when you're doing one of the three illegal things mentioned above, shut your car off, so at least you only get one ticket, not two!

Parking Meter Zones

On holidays when street cleaning rules are suspended (see calendar), the "no parking" cleaning regulations for metered parking are also suspended. You can park in these spots but have to pay the meters. Also, metered spots are still subject to rules not suspended on holidays (see below). On MLH (major legal holidays), meter rules are suspended (so no need to feed the meter).

Meters

At a broken meter, parking is allowed only up to one hour. Where a meter is missing, parking is still allowed for the maximum time on the posted sign (an hour for a one-hour meter, two hours for a two-hour meter, etc.).

Instead of old-fashioned individual meters, muni-meters have spread like a virus throughout NYC. The machines let you purchase time-stamped slips which you stick in your windshield to show you paid. These machines accept coins, parking cards, and some (we wish it was all!) accept credit cards (for example, the machines in the theater district). In the case of a non-functional muni-meter, the one-hour time limit applies.

The DOT sells parking cards that come in $20, $50, and $100 denominations and can be used in muni-meters, municipal parking lots, and some single-space meters (look for a yellow decal). The cards can be purchased through the DOT website (www.nyc.gov/html/dot/home.html), by calling 311 (or 212-NEW-YORK if you're calling from outside the city), or by going to the Staten Island Ferry Terminal or one of the two City Stores.

As of spring 2006, you don't have to pay meters on Sunday, even if the signs say you do (unless the law changes again with the political winds).

Signs

New York City Traffic Rules state that one parking sign per block is sufficient notification. Check the entire block and read all signs carefully before you park. Then read them again.

If there is more than one sign posted for the same area, the more restrictive sign takes effect (of course). If a sign is missing on a block, the remaining posted regulations are the ones in effect.

The Blue Zone

The Blue Zone is a "No Parking" (Mon–Fri, 7 am–7 pm) area in Lower Manhattan. Its perimeter has been designated with blue paint; however, there are no individual "Blue Zone" signs posted. Any other signs posted in that area supersede Blue Zone regulations. Confused yet?

General

- All of NYC was designated a Tow Away Zone under the State's Vehicle & Traffic Law and the NYC Traffic Rules. This means that any vehicle parked or operated illegally, or with missing or expired registration or inspection stickers, may, and probably will, be towed.
- On major legal holidays, stopping, standing, and parking are permitted except in areas where stopping, standing, and parking rules are in effect seven days a week (for example, "No Standing Anytime").
- It is illegal to park in a spot where SCR are in effect, even if the street cleaner has already passed. If you sit in your car, the metermaid will usually let you stay
- Double-parking of passenger vehicles is illegal at all times, including street-cleaning days, regardless of location, purpose, or duration. Everyone, of course, does this anyway. If everyone is double parked on a certain block during street cleaning, the NYPD probably is not ticketing. However, leave your phone number in the window in case the person you blocked in feels vindictive and demand that a cop write you a ticket.
- It is illegal to park within 15 feet of either side of a fire hydrant. The painted curbs at hydrant locations do not indicate where you can park. Isn't New York great? Metermaids will tell you that each cement block on the sidewalk is five feet, so make sure you are three cement blocks from the hydrant (2.5 will not do).
- If you think you're parked legally in Manhattan, you're probably not, so go and read the signs again.
- Cops will now just write you parking tickets and mail them to you if you are parked in a bus stop; so you won't even know it's happening unless you're very alert.
- There is now clearly an all-out effort to harass everyone who is insane enough to drive and/or park during the day in downtown Manhattan. Beware.

Alternate Side Parking Suspension Calendar 2010–2011 (Estimated*)

2010 Holiday	*Date*	*Day*	*Rules*
Labor Day	Sept 6	Mon	MLH
Rosh Hashanah	Sept 8	Wed	ASP
Idul-Fitr	Sept 10	Fri	ASP
Yom Kippur	Sept 17	Fri	ASP
Succoth	Sept 22	Wed	ASP
Shemini Atzereth	Sept 29	Wed	ASP
Simchas Torah	Sept 30	Thur	ASP
Columbus Day	Oct 11	Mon	ASP
All Saints Day	Nov 1	Mon	ASP
Election Day	Nov 2	Tue	ASP
Diwali	Nov 5	Fri	ASP
Veterans Day	Nov 11	Thur	ASP
Idul-Adha	Nov 17	Wed	ASP
Thanksgiving Day	Nov 25	Thur	MLH
Immaculate Conception	Dec 8	Wed	ASP
Christmas Day	Dec 25	Sat	MLH
2011 Holiday	*Date*	*Day*	*Rules*
New Year's Day	*Jan 1*	*Sat*	*MLH*
MLK Birthday	*Jan 17*	*Mon*	*ASP*
Chinese New Year	*Feb 3*	*Thurs*	*ASP*
Lincoln's Birthday (Observed)	*Feb 11*	*Fri*	*ASP*
Purim	*Feb 17*	*Thurs*	*ASP*
President's Day (Washington's Birthday)	*Feb 21*	*Mon*	*ASP*
Ash Wednesday	*Mar 9*	*Wed*	*ASP*
Passover (1st-2nd Day)	*Apr 18-19*	*Mon-Tue*	*ASP*
Passover (7th-8th Day)	*Apr 25-26*	*Mon-Tue*	*ASP*
Holy Thursday	*Apr 21*	*Thurs*	*ASP*
Holy Thursday (Orthodox)	*Apr 21*	*Thu*	*ASP*
Good Friday	*Apr 22*	*Fri*	*ASP*
Good Friday (Orthodox)	*Apr 22*	*Fri*	*ASP*
Memorial Day	*May 30*	*Mon*	*MLH*
Solemnity of the Ascension	*Jun 2*	*Thurs*	*ASP*
Shavuot	*Jun 8-9*	*Wed-Thurs*	*ASP*
Independence Day	*July 4*	*Mon*	*MLH*
Feast of the Assumption	*Aug 15*	*Mon*	*ASP*
Idul-Fitr	*Aug 30*	*Tue*	*ASP*
Labor Day	*Sept 5*	*Mon*	*MLH*
Rosh Hashanah	*Sept 30*	*Fri*	*ASP*
Yom Kippur	*Oct 7*	*Fri*	*ASP*
Columbus Day	*Oct 10*	*Mon*	*ASP*
Succoth	*Oct 13*	*Thurs*	*ASP*
Shemini Atzereth	*Oct 19*	*Wed*	*ASP*
Simchas Torah	*Oct 20*	*Thurs*	*ASP*
Diwali	*Oct 21*	*Fri*	*ASP*
All Saints Day	*Nov 1*	*Tues*	*ASP*
Idul-Adha	*Nov 6*	*Sun*	*ASP*
Election Day	*Nov 8*	*Tues*	*ASP*
Veterans Day	*Nov 11*	*Fri*	*ASP*
Thanksgiving Day	Nov 24	Thurs	MLH
Immaculate Conception	*Dec 8*	*Thurs*	*ASP*
Christmas Day	Dec 25	Sun	MLH

*** Note: We go to press before the DOT issues its official calendar. However, using various techniques, among them a Ouija Board, a chainsaw, and repeated phone calls to said DOT, we think it's pretty accurate. Nonetheless, caveat parkor.**

- **Street Cleaning Rules** (SCR)
  Most SCR signs are clearly marked by the "P" symbol with the broom through it. Some SCR signs are the traditional 3-hour ones ("8 am–11 am" etc.) but many others vary considerably. Check the times before you park. Then check them again.
- **Alternate Side Parking Suspended** (ASP)
  "No Parking" signs in effect one day a week or on alternate days are suspended on days designated ASP; however, all "No Stopping" and "No Standing" signs remain in effect.
- **Major Legal Holiday Rules in Effect** (MLH)
  "No Parking" and "No Standing" signs that are in effect fewer than seven days a week are suspended on days designated MLH in the above calendar.
- If the city finds that a neighborhood keeps its streets clean enough, it may lessen the number of street cleaning days, or even eliminate them all together. So listen to your mother and don't litter.

Tow Pounds

Manhattan
Pier 76 at W 38th St & Twelfth Ave
open 24 hours: Monday 7 am–Monday 5 am
212-971-0771 or 212-971-0772

Bronx
745 E 141st St b/w Bruckner Expy & East River
Open Monday-Friday: 8 am-10 pm, Saturday: 8 am-3 pm, Sunday: Closed
718-585-1385 or 718-585-1391

Brooklyn
Brooklyn Navy Yard; corner of Sands St & Navy St
Open Monday-Friday 8 am-10 pm, Saturday 8 am-3 pm, and on the second Sunday of each month from 11 am-6 pm.
718-694-0696

Queens
Under the Kosciusko Bridge at 56th Rd & Laurel Hill Blvd
Open Monday-Friday from 8 am-10 pm, Saturday from 8 am-3 pm, and closed on Sunday; 718-786-7122, 718-786-7123, or 718-786-7136

Find out if your car was towed (and not stolen or disintegrated): 718-422-7800 or 718-802-3555 (TTY)

http://nycserv.nyc.gov/NYCServWeb/NYCSERVMain

Once you've discovered that your car has indeed been towed, your next challenge is to find out which borough it's been towed to. This depends on who exactly towed your car—the DOT, the Marshal, etc. Don't assume that since your car was parked in Manhattan that they will tow it to Manhattan—always call first.

So you've located your car, now come the particulars: If you own said towed car, you're required to present your license, registration, insurance, and payment of your fine before you can collect the impounded vehicle. If you are not the owner of the car, you can usually get it back with all of the above, if your last name matches the registration (i.e. the car belongs to a relative or spouse); otherwise, you'll need a notarized letter with the owner's signature authorizing you to take the car. The tow fee is $185, plus a $70 execution fee, plus $10–$15 for each day it's in the pound. If they've put a boot on it instead, it's still $185. You can pay with cash or debit card; if you own the car, you can also pay by credit card or certified check. We recommend bringing a wad of cash and a long Russian novel for this experience.

General Information

New York City:	718-217-LIRR
Nassau County:	516-822-LIRR
Suffolk County:	631-231-LIRR
TTY Information (Hearing Impaired):	718-558-3022
Group Travel and Tours:	718-558-7498 (M–F 8 pm–4 pm)
Mail & Ride:	800-649-NYNY
MTA Police Eastern Region:	718-558-3300 or 516-733-3900
Lost & Found (M-F 7:20 am-7:20 pm):	212-643-5228
Ticket Refunds (M-F 8 am-4 pm):	718-558-3488
Ticket Machine Assistance:	877-LIRR-TSM
Hamptons Reserve Service:	718-558-8070
Website:	www.mta.info/lirr

Overview

The Long Island Railroad is the busiest railroad in North America. It has eleven lines with 124 stations stretching from Penn Station in midtown Manhattan, to the eastern tip of Long Island, Montauk Point. An estimated 81 million people ride the LIRR every year. If you enjoy traveling on overcrowded trains with intermittent air-conditioning, then the LIRR is for you. If you are going anywhere on Long Island and you don't have a car, the LIRR is your best bet. Don't be surprised if the feeling of being in a seedy bar creeps over you during evening rush—those middle-aged business men like their beer en route. Despite a recent movement to ban the sale of alcohol on LIRR station platforms and trains, for now, it's still legal to get your buzz on.

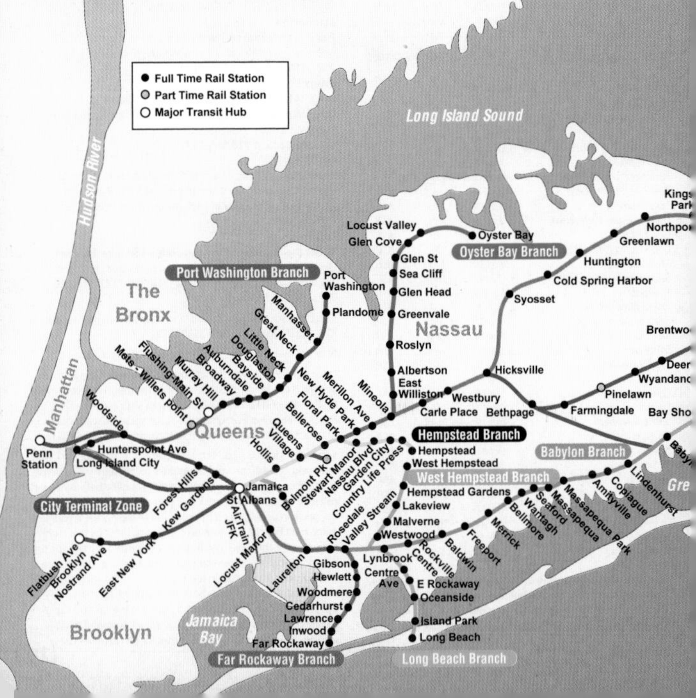

If you're not a regular LIRR user, you might find yourself taking the train to Shea Stadium for a Mets game (Port Washington Branch), Long Beach for some summer surfing (Long Beach Branch), or to Jamaica to transfer to the AirTrain to JFK (tip—the subway is cheaper). For the truly adventurous, take the LIRR all the way out to the Hamptons beach house you are visiting for the weekend (Hamptons Reserve seating is available during the summer for passengers taking 6 or more trips). Bring a book as it is a long ride.

Fares and Schedules

Fares and schedules can be obtained by calling one of the general information lines, depending on your area. They can also be found on the LIRR website. Make sure to buy your ticket before you get on the train at a ticket window or at one of the ticket vending machines in the station. Otherwise it'll cost you an extra $6 or more depending on your destination. As it is a commuter railroad, the LIRR offers weekly and monthly passes, as well as ten-trip packages for on- or off-peak hours. The LIRR's CityTicket program offers discounted one-way tickets for $3.50

Pets on the LIRR

Trained service animals accompanying passengers with disabilities are permitted on LIRR trains. Other small pets are allowed on trains, but they must be confined to closed, ventilated containers.

Bikes on the LIRR

You need a permit ($5) to take your bicycle onto the Long Island Railroad. Pick one up at a ticket window or online at the LIRR website.

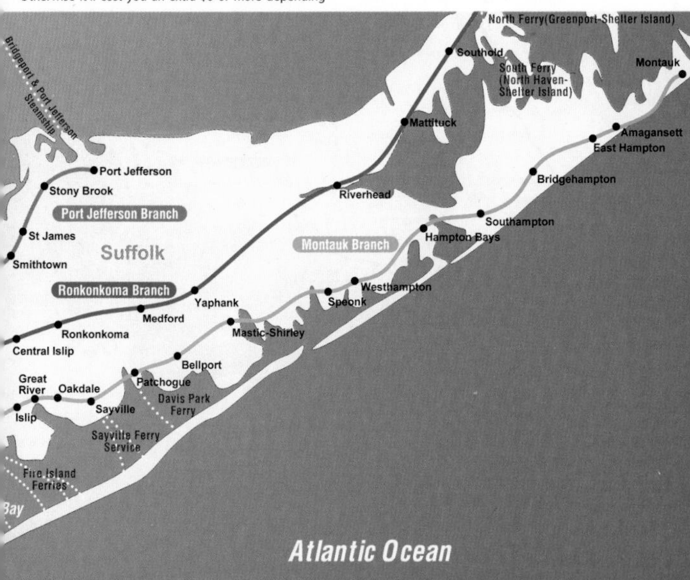

Key
Rail Station
Wheelchair or ADA Accessible station
Major transit hub
Rail Station
Connecting rail service
© 2004 Metropolitan Transportation Authority
Design: Michael Hertz Associates, NYC
Amtrak to Albany
Poughkeepsie
HUDSON LINE
DUTCHESS
HARLEM LINE
New Hamburg
Beacon
Breakneck Ridge
Cold Spring
PUTNAM
Garrison
Manitou
Peekskill
WESTCHESTER
Cortlandt
Hudson River
Croton-Harmon
Ossining
Scarborough
Philipse Manor
Tarrytown
Irvington
Ardsley-on-Hudson
Dobbs Ferry
Hastings-on-Hudson
Greystone
Glenwood
Yonkers
Ludlow
Riverdale
Spuyten Duyvil
Marble Hill
University Hts
Morris Hts
Yankees-E 153 St
Harlem-125 St
NEW YORK
Grand Central Terminal
Penn Station
PATH
Wassaic
Tenmile River
Dover Plains
Harlem Valley-Wingdale
Appalachian Trail
Pawling
Patterson
NEW YORK CONNECTICUT
Southeast
Brewster
Croton Falls
Purdy's
Golden's Bridge
Katonah
Bedford Hills
Mount Kisco
Chappaqua
Pleasantville
Hawthorne
Mt Pleasant
Valhalla
North White Plains
White Plains
Hartsdale
Scarsdale
Crestwood
Tuckahoe
Bronxville
Mt Vernon West
Fleetwood
Wakefield
Woodlawn
Williams Bridge
Botanical Garden
Fordham
Tremont
Melrose
THE BRONX
Danbury Branch
Danbury
Bethel
Redding
Branchville
Cannondale
Wilton
Merritt 7
New Canaan Branch
New Canaan
Talmadge Hill
Springdale
Glenbrook
LITCHFIELD
Housatonic River
NEW HAVEN
FAIRFIELD
Waterbury Branch
Waterbury
Naugatuck
Beacon Falls
Seymour
Ansonia
Derby-Shelton
New Haven-Union Station
New State
Milford
Stratford
Bridgeport
Bridgeport & Port Jefferson Steamboat Co.
NEW HAVEN LINE
Fairfield
Southport
Green's Farms
Westport
East Norwalk
South Norwalk
Rowayton
Darien
Noroton Heights
Stamford
Old Greenwich
Riverside
Cos Cob
Greenwich, CT
Port Chester, NY
Rye
Harrison
Mamaroneck
Larchmont
New Rochelle
Pelham
Mt Vernon East
Long Island Sound
NASSAU
QUEENS
BROOKLYN

General Information

NYC Phone:	212-532-4900
All other areas:	800-METRO-INFO
Website:	www.mta.info/mnr
Lost and Found (Grand Central):	212-340-2555
MTA Inspector General:	800-MTA-IG4U

Overview

Metro-North is an extremely accessible and efficient railroad with three of its main lines (Hudson, Harlem, and New Haven) originating in Grand Central Station in Manhattan (42nd St & Park Ave). Those three lines east of the Hudson River, along with two lines west of the Hudson River that operate out of Hoboken, NJ (not shown on map), form the second-largest commuter railroad system in the US. Approximately 250,000 commuters use the tri-state Metro-North service each day for travel between New Jersey, New York, and Connecticut. Metro-North rail lines cover roughly 2,700 square miles of territory. The best thing about Metro-North is that it lands you at Grand Central Station, one of the city's finest pieces of architecture. On weekdays, sneak into the land of platforms via the North Passage, accessible at 47th & 48th Streets. At least for now, it's still legal to have an after work drink on Metro-North. During happy hour (starting somewhere around 3 pm), hit the bar car or buy your booze in advance on the platform at Grand Central. It might make you feel better about being a wage slave. But beware of having too happy of an hour as the bathrooms can be stinky and not all cars have them.

Fares and Schedules

Fare information is available on Metro-North's extraordinarily detailed website (along with in-depth information on each station, full timetables, and excellent maps) or at Grand Central Station. The cost of a ticket to ride varies depending on your destination so you should probably check the website before setting out. Buy advance tickets on MTA's WebTicket site for the cheapest fares. If you wait until you're on the train to pay, it'll cost you an extra $4.75–$5.50. Monthly and weekly rail passes are also available for commuters. Daily commuters save 50% on fares when they purchase a monthly travel pass.

Hours

Train frequency depends on your destination and the time of day that you're traveling. On weekdays, peak-period trains east of the Hudson River run every 20–30 minutes; off-peak trains run every 30–60 minutes; and weekend trains run hourly. Hours of operation are approximately 5 am to 3 am. Don't miss the last train out as they leave on time and wait for no one.

Bikes on Board

If you're planning on taking your two-wheeler onboard, you'll need to apply for a bicycle permit first. An application form can be found on the Metro-North website at http://mta.info/mnr/html/mnrbikepermit.htm. The $5 permit fee and application can either be mailed into the MTA, or processed right away at window 27 at Grand Central Terminal.

Common sense rules for taking bikes on board include: no bikes on escalators, no riding on the platform, and board the train after other passengers have boarded. Unfortunately there are restrictions on bicycles during peak travel times. Bicycles are not allowed on trains departing from Grand Central Terminal 7 am–9 am and 3:01 pm–8:15 pm. Bikes are not permitted on trains arriving at Grand Central 5 am–10 am and 4 pm–8 pm. Don't even think about taking your bike with you on New Year's Eve, New Year's Day, St. Patrick's Day, Mother's Day, eve of Rosh Hashanah, eve of Yom Kippur, eve of Thanksgiving, Thanksgiving Day, Christmas Eve, or Christmas Day—they're not allowed. The Friday before any long weekend is also a no-no. There's a limit of two bikes per carriage, and four bikes per train at all times. Unfortunately, the same restrictions are not imposed on passengers with 4 Vera Bradley overnight bags heading off to the country house, but that is another story.

Riders of folding bikes do not require a permit and do not have to comply with the above rules, provided that the bike is folded at all times at stations and on trains.

Pets

Only seeing-eye dogs and small pets, if restrained or confined, are allowed aboard the trains.

One-Day Getaways

Metro-North offers "One-Day Getaway" packages on its website. Packages include reduced rail fare and discounted entry to destinations along MNR lines including Bruce Museum ($17.75), Dia:Beacon ($29.50), Hudson River Museum/Andrus Planetarium ($13.75), Maritime Aquarium at Norwalk ($29.25), Mohegan Sun Casino ($43.25), New York Botanical Garden ($19.75), and Nyack ($14.50). WebTicket saves passengers 5% of the fare. The website also suggests one-day hiking and biking excursions.

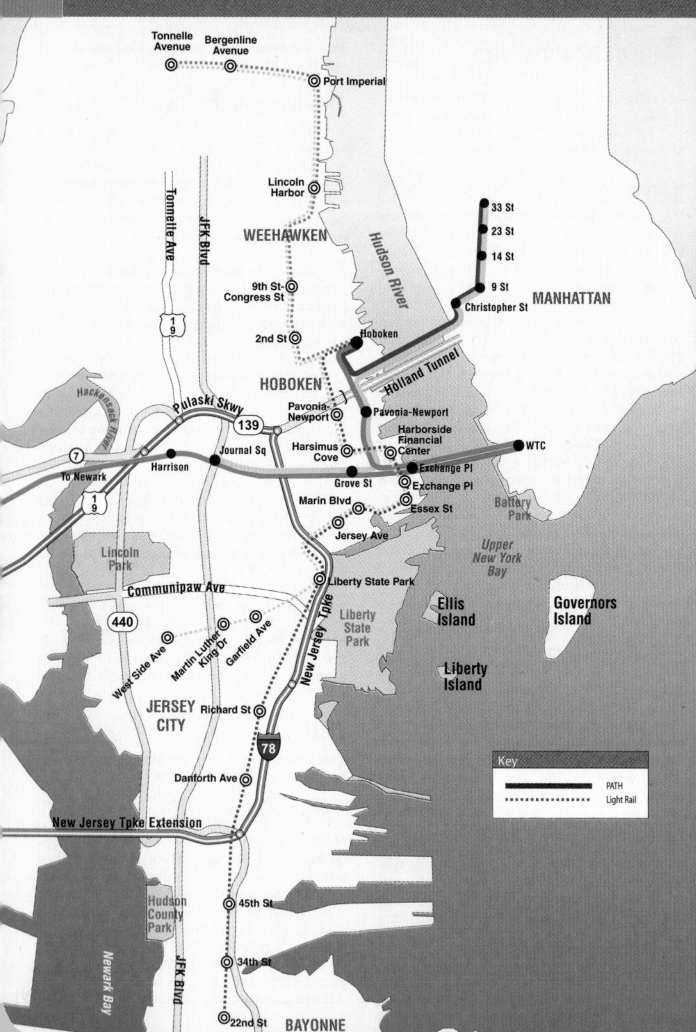
Tonnelle Avenue
Bergenline Avenue
Port Imperial
Lincoln Harbor
WEEHAWKEN
Hudson River
Tonnelle Ave
JFK Blvd
9th St-Congress St
2nd St
Hoboken
HOBOKEN
Holland Tunnel
33 St
23 St
14 St
9 St
Christopher St
MANHATTAN
Pavonia-Newport
Pavonia-Newport
Harborside Financial Center
Harsimus Cove
WTC
Exchange Pl
Exchange Pl
Grove St
Marin Blvd
Essex St
Jersey Ave
Battery Park
Hackensack River
Pulaski Skwy
139
7
To Newark
Harrison
Journal Sq
1 9
Lincoln Park
Communipaw Ave
440
Liberty State Park
Upper New York Bay
Ellis Island
Governors Island
Liberty State Park
Liberty Island
West Side Ave
Martin Luther King Dr
Garfield Ave
New Jersey Tpke
JERSEY CITY
Richard St
78
Danforth Ave
New Jersey Tpke Extension
Key
PATH
Light Rail
Hudson County Park
45th St
34th St
22nd St
Newark Bay
JFK Blvd
BAYONNE

PATH Train

General Information
Website: www.panynj.gov/path
Phone: 800-234-7284
Police/Lost & Found: 201-216-6078

Overview

The PATH (Port Authority Trans-Hudson Corp.) is an excellent small rail system that services Newark, Jersey City, Hoboken, and Manhattan. There are a few basic lines that run directly between 33rd Street (Herald Square) in Manhattan & Hoboken, 33rd Street & Jersey City, and Newark & the WTC. Transfers between the lines are available at most stations. The PATH can be quite useful for commuters on the west side of Manhattan when the subway isn't running, say, due to a sick passenger or mysterious police investigation. Additionally, you can catch the PATH to Newark and then either jump in a cheap cab or take New Jersey Transit one stop to Newark Airport. It's a more economical option than taking a car all the way in from Manhattan, and you can take it back to the Village late at night when you've finished seeing a show at Maxwell's in Hoboken.

Check the front or the sides of incoming trains to determine their destination. Don't be fooled by the TV screens installed at stations; they occasionally announce the time of the next arrival, but as their main purpose is low-quality advertising, they are often incorrect. Also, don't assume that if a Journal Square train just passed through, the next train is going to Hoboken. Often there will be two Journal Square trains in a row, followed by two Hoboken trains. During the weekend, PATH service can be excruciatingly slow and confusing, and is best only endeavored with a seasoned rider.

Fares

The PATH costs $1.75 one-way. Regular riders can purchase 10-trip, 20-trip, and 40-trip QuickCards, which reduce the fare per journey to $1.20–$1.36. The fare for seniors (65+) is $1 per ride. You can also use pay-per-ride MTA MetroCards for easy transition between the PATH and subway.

Hours

The PATH runs 24/7 (although a modified service operates between 11pm–6am, M–F, and 7:30pm–9 am, S, S, & H). Daytime service is pretty consistent, but the night schedule for the PATH is a bit confusing, so make sure to look at the map. You may be waiting underground for up to a half an hour. During off hours the train runs on the same track through the tunnel. This allows for maintenance to be completed on the unused track.

Hudson-Bergen Light Rail

General Information
Website: http://www.mylightrail.com/
Phone: 800-772-2222

Overview

Even though it's called the Hudson-Bergen Light Rail system (HBLR, operated by NJ Transit), it actually only serves Hudson county. Bergen County residents are still waiting for their long promised connection. The HBLR has brought about some exciting changes (a.k.a. "gentrification") in Jersey City, though Bayonne remains (for the moment) totally, well…Bayonne. Currently there are 23 stops (with at least one more stop planned in Bayonne) in the system, including service to Jersey City, Hoboken, Weehawken, and Union City. Transfer at the Hoboken stop for the PATH into Manhattan.

Fares

The Light Rail is $1.90 per trip; reduced fare is 95 cents. Ten-trip tickets are $16.25, monthly passes cost $58, and monthly passes with parking are $93. Unless you have a monthly pass, you need to validate your ticket before boarding at a Ticket Validating Machine (TVM). Once validated, tickets are only valid for 90 minutes, so don't buy too far in advance. The trains and stations have random fare inspection and the fine for fare evasion is $100.

Hours

Light rail service operates between 5 am and 1:30 am. Times are approximate, check the website for exact schedules on each line.

Bikes on Board

Bikes are allowed (no permit or fee required) on board during off-peak times—weekdays from 9:30 am to 4 pm and 7 pm to 6 am, and all day Saturday, Sunday, and NJ state holidays. Bicycles have to be accompanied on the low-floor vestibule section of each rail car.

Pets

Small pets are allowed, as long as they're confined to a carry container. Service animals are permitted at all times.

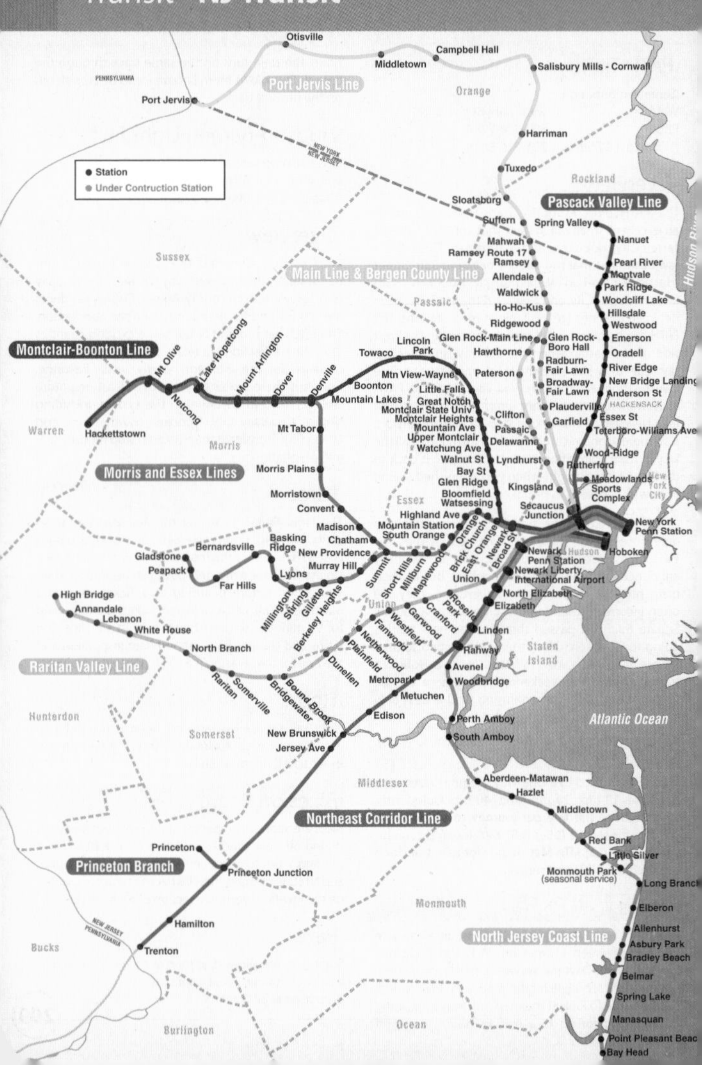

Station
Under Contruction Station
Port Jervis Line
Main Line & Bergen County Line
Pascack Valley Line
Montclair-Boonton Line
Morris and Essex Lines
Raritan Valley Line
Northeast Corridor Line
Princeton Branch
North Jersey Coast Line
Otisville
Middletown
Campbell Hall
Salisbury Mills - Cornwall
Port Jervis
Harriman
Tuxedo
Sloatsburg
Suffern
Mahwah
Ramsey Route 17
Ramsey
Allendale
Waldwick
Ho-Ho-Kus
Ridgewood
Glen Rock-Main Line
Glen Rock-Boro Hall
Hawthorne
Radburn-Fair Lawn
Paterson
Broadway-Fair Lawn
Plauderville
Clifton
Garfield
Passaic
Delawanna
Lyndhurst
Rutherford
Kingsland
Secaucus Junction
Spring Valley
Nanuet
Pearl River
Montvale
Park Ridge
Woodcliff Lake
Hillsdale
Westwood
Emerson
Oradell
River Edge
New Bridge Landing
Anderson St
Essex St
Teterboro-Williams Ave
Wood-Ridge
Meadowlands Sports Complex
New York Penn Station
Hoboken
Hackettstown
Mt Olive
Netcong
Lake Hopatcong
Mount Arlington
Dover
Denville
Mountain Lakes
Boonton
Towaco
Lincoln Park
Mtn View-Wayne
Little Falls
Great Notch
Montclair State Univ
Montclair Heights
Mountain Ave
Upper Montclair
Watchung Ave
Walnut St
Bay St
Glen Ridge
Bloomfield
Watsessing
Mt Tabor
Morris Plains
Morristown
Convent
Madison
Chatham
Summit
Highland Ave
Mountain Station
South Orange
Orange
Brick Church
East Orange
Newark Broad St
Newark Penn Station
Newark Liberty International Airport
North Elizabeth
Elizabeth
Linden
Rahway
Avenel
Woodbridge
Perth Amboy
South Amboy
Aberdeen-Matawan
Hazlet
Middletown
Red Bank
Little Silver
Monmouth Park (seasonal service)
Long Branch
Elberon
Allenhurst
Asbury Park
Bradley Beach
Belmar
Spring Lake
Manasquan
Point Pleasant Beac
Bay Head
Gladstone
Peapack
Far Hills
Bernardsville
Basking Ridge
Lyons
Millington
Stirling
Gillette
Berkeley Heights
Murray Hill
New Providence
Short Hills
Millburn
Maplewood
Union
Roselle Park
Cranford
Garwood
Westfield
Fanwood
Netherwood
Plainfield
Dunellen
Bound Brook
Bridgewater
Somerville
Raritan
North Branch
White House
Lebanon
Annandale
High Bridge
Metropark
Metuchen
Edison
New Brunswick
Jersey Ave
Princeton
Princeton Junction
Hamilton
Trenton
Pennsylvania
New York
New Jersey
Orange
Rockland
Sussex
Passaic
Warren
Morris
Essex
Hudson
Union
Hunterdon
Somerset
Middlesex
Monmouth
Bucks
Burlington
Ocean
Staten Island
New York City
Hackensack
Hudson River
Atlantic Ocean

General Information

Address:	1 Penn Plz E Newark, NJ 07105
Phone:	973-275-5555 or 800-772-2222
Website:	www.njtransit.com
Quik-Tik (monthly passes):	866-QUIK-TIK
Emergency Hotline:	973-378-6565
Newark Lost and Found:	973-491-8792
Hoboken Lost and Found:	201-714-2739
New York Lost and Found:	212-630-7389
AirTrain:	973-961-6230
Atlantic City Terminal:	609-343-7174

Overview

NJ Transit carries hundreds of thousands of New Jersey commuters to New York every morning and returns them to their suburban enclaves at the end of the day. The trains are usually clean (and immune to the weirdness that plagues the LIRR), but some lines (like the Pascack Valley Line) seem to just creep along, which can be problematic when you're trying to make a transfer before reaching the Big Apple. But with many new stations, including the renovated transfer station at Secaucus, and an expanded Light Rail system (see PATH page), NJ Transit is staying competitive with all other modes of transportation into and out of the city. NJ Transit also runs an AirTrain to Newark Airport. As the rails have been prone to power loss and broken switches lately, NJ Transit won't be competing with Japanese rail systems any time soon, but riding their rails generally beats waiting in traffic at the three measly Hudson River automobile crossings. NJ Transit also offers bus lines to Hoboken and Newark for areas not served by train lines. The newest station will be the Meadowlands Stop on the Pascack Valley line. You'll be able to get off and check out a game or that crazy-ass Xanadu project.

Secaucus Transfer Station

The three-level train hub at Secaucus is celebrating its fifth birthday! The station cost around $450 million and took 14 years to complete. The building is dedicated to Democratic New Jersey Senator Frank R. Lautenberg, who was responsible for securing the federal funds necessary for construction. The former Secaucus Transfer Station is now officially known as the Frank R. Lautenberg Station at Secaucus Junction (which, if you want to get technical, is not actually a junction). We're certain that most commuters will adopt this name whenever referring to the station, or maybe they'll just call it "Secaucus."

For riders, the biggest advantage of the new station is that they no longer have to travel out to Hoboken to get to Penn Station. (Secaucus is just an 8-minute ride from Penn Station.) The Secaucus hub connects ten of NJ Transit's 11 rail lines, and also offers service to Newark Airport, downtown Newark, Trenton, and the Jersey Shore.

Fares and Schedules

Fares and schedules can be obtained at Hoboken, Newark, Penn Station, on NJ Transit's website, or by calling NJ Transit. If you wait to pay until you're on the train, you'll pay an extra five bucks for the privilege. NJ Transit also offers discounted monthly, weekly, weekend, and ten-trip tickets for regular commuters.

Pets

Only seeing-eye dogs and small pets in carry-on containers are allowed aboard the trains and buses.

Bikes

You can take your bicycle onboard a NJ Transit train only during off-peak hours (weekdays from 9:30 am–4 pm, and from 7 pm–5 am) and during all hours on the weekends. Bikes are not allowed on board most holidays, or the Fridays prior to any holiday weekend; however, a folding frame bicycle can be taken onboard at any time. Most NJ Transit buses participate in the "Rack 'n' Roll" program, which allows you to load your bike right on to the front of the bus.

Overview

Phone: 800-USA-RAIL
Website: www.amtrak.com

General Information

Amtrak is our national train system, and while it's not particularly punctual or affordable, it *will* take you to many major northeastern cities in half a day or less. Spending a few hours on Amtrak also makes you want to move to Europe where France is now running trains at 357 mph (as opposed to 35 mph in the US). But if you plan a trip at the last minute and miss the requisite advance on buying airline tickets or want to bring liquids with you with checking baggage, you might want to shop Amtrak's fares. Bonus: Amtrak allows you to talk on cell phones in most cars and has plugs for laptop computers at your seat.

Amtrak was created by the federal government in 1971. Today, Amtrak services 500+ stations in 46 states (Alaska, Hawaii, South Dakota, and Wyoming sadly do not have the pleasure of being serviced by Amtrak). While not being as advanced as the Eurail system, Amtrak serves over 24 million passengers a year, employs 19,000 people, still has the same décor it did in the early 1970s, and provides "contract-commuter services" for several state and regional rail lines.

Red Caps (station agents) are very helpful, especially for passengers traveling with children and strollers. The only problem is finding an available one!

Amtrak in New York

In New York City, Amtrak runs out of Pennsylvania Station, an eyesore currently located underneath Madison Square Garden. We treat the station like our annoying little brother, calling it Penn for short and avoiding it when we can. But don't despair—chances are the city you'll wind up in will have a very nice station, and, if all goes well, so will we, once the front half of the Farley Post Office is converted to a "new" Penn Station. Warning: If you hop in a cab to get to Amtrak, specify that you want to be dropped off at Eighth Avenue and 33rd Street in order to avoid LIRR and Madison Square Garden foot traffic. Don't let the cabbie argue with you, especially if you have luggage. He is just trying to make his life easier.

Popular Destinations

Many New Yorkers use Amtrak to get to Boston, Philadelphia, or Washington DC. Of course, these are the New Yorkers who are traveling on an expense account or fear the Chinatown bus service. Amtrak also runs a line up to Montreal and through western New York state (making stops in Buffalo, Rochester, Albany, etc.) Check Amtrak's website for a complete listing of all Amtrak stations.

Going to Boston

Amtrak usually runs 18 trains daily to Boston. One-way fares cost $59–$101, and the trip, which ends at South Station in downtown Boston, takes about four-and-a-half hours door-to-door. For $117 one-way, you can ride the high speed Acela ("acceleration" and "excellence" combined into one word, though perhaps "expensive" would have been more appropriate) and complete the journey in three to three-and-a-half hours—if there are not track problems.

Going to Philadelphia

About 40 Amtrak trains pass through Philadelphia every day. One-way tickets cost about $45–$60 on a regular Amtrak train; if you're really in a hurry, you can take the special "Metroliner" service for $87, which will get you there in an hour and fifteen minutes, or the Acela for $81, which takes about one hour from station to station. The cheapest rail option to Philly is actually to take NJ Transit to Trenton and then hook up with Eastern Pennsylvania's excellent SEPTA service—this will take longer, but will cost you under $25. Some commuters take this EVERY day. Thank your lucky stars you're probably not one of them.

Going to Washington DC

(Subtitle: *How Much is Your Time Worth?*)
Amtrak runs over 40 trains daily to DC and the prices vary dramatically. The cheapest trains cost $69 one-way and take just under four hours. The Acela service costs more than double at $125-$146 one-way, and delivers you to our nation's capital in less than three hours (sometimes). Worth it? Only you can say. Depending on what time of day you travel, you may be better off taking the cheaper train when the Acela will only save you 30 minutes.

A Note About Fares

While the prices quoted above for Boston, Philly, and DC destinations tend to remain fairly consistent, fare rates to other destinations, such as Cleveland, Chicago, etc., can vary depending on how far in advance you book your seat. For "rail sales" and other discounts, check www.amtrak.com. Military IDs will save you a bundle, so use them if you have them. Occasionally (or rarely), Amtrak offers discounts that can be found on their website under "Hot Deals."

Baggage Check (Amtrak Passengers)

A maximum of three items may be checked up to thirty minutes before departure. Up to three additional bags may be checked for a fee of $10 (two carry-on items allowed). No electronic equipment, plastic bags, or paper bags may be checked. See the "Amtrak Policies" section of their website for details.

General Information

NFT Map:	9
Address:	Seventh Ave & 33rd St
General Information (Amtrak):	800-872-7245
MTA Subway Stops:	1 2 3 A C E
MTA Bus Lines:	4 10 16 34
Train Lines:	LIRR, Amtrak, NJ Transit
LaGuardia Airport Bus Service:	NY Airport Service, 212-875-8200, $12
JFK Airport Bus Service:	NY Airport Service, 212-875-8200, $15
Passengers per day:	600,000

Overview

Penn Station, designed by McKim, Mead & White (New York's greatest architects), is a Beaux-Arts treasure, filled with light and... oh wait, that's the one that was torn down. Penn Station is essentially a basement, complete with well-weathered leather chairs, unidentifiable dust particles, and high-cholesterol snack food. Its claim to fame is that it is the busiest Amtrak station in the country. If the government gods are with us, the plan to convert the eastern half of the Farley Post Office (also designed by McKim, Mead & White) next door to an above-ground, light-filled station will come to fruition. With bureaucracy at hand, we aren't holding our collective breath. Until then, Penn Station will go on servicing 600,000 people per day in the rat's maze under Madison Square Garden.

Penn Station services Amtrak, the LIRR, and NJ Transit trains. Amtrak, which is surely the worst national train system of any first-world country, administers the station. How is it that the Europeans have bullet trains and it still takes 3 or more hours to get from NYC to DC? While we're hoping the new station proposal will come through, will it help the crazed LIRR commuters struggling to squish down stairwells to catch the 6:05 to Ronkonkoma? We can only hope.

Dieters traveling through Penn Station should pre-pack snacks. The fast food joints are just too tempting. Donuts and ice cream and KFC, oh my! Leave yourself time to pick up some magazines and a bottle of water for your train trip. It may turn out to be longer than you think.

The plus side to Penn is that it's easy to get to from just about anywhere in the city via subway or bus. If you are just too ritzy to take the MTA (or you have an abundance of baggage), have your cab driver drop you off anywhere surrounding the station except for Seventh Avenue—it is constantly jammed with tour buses and cabs trying to drop off desperately late passengers.

Terminal Shops

On the LIRR Level

Food & Drink

Auntie Anne's Soft Pretzels
Blimpie
Caruso's Pizza
Carvel
Cinnabon
Colombo Frozen Yogurt
Europan Café
Haagen Dazs
Hot & Crusty
Hot Dog Stand
KFC
Knot Just Pretzels
Le Bon Café
McDonald's
Nedick's
Pizza Hut
Primo! Cappuccino
Rose Pizza and Pasta
Salad Chef/Burger Chef
Tim Horton's
Seattle Coffee Roasters
Soup King
Soup Man/Smoothie King (2)
Starbucks
Subway
TGI Friday's
Tracks Raw Bar & Grill

Other

Carlton Cards
Dreyfus Financial Center
Duane Reade
GNC
Hudson News (4)
K-Mart
Petal Pusher
Penn Books
Perfumania
Soleman—Shoe repair, locksmith
Verizon Wireless

On the Amtrak Level

Food & Drink

Auntie Anne's Soft Pretzels (2)
Baskin Robbins
Deli
Don Pepi Pizza
Houlihan's Restaurant & Bar
Nathan's/Carvel
Kabooz's Bar and Grille
Krispy Kreme Doughnuts
Penn Sushi
Pizza Hut
Primo! Cappuccino (3)
Roy Rogers
Soup Man/Smoothie King/
Sodutto Ice Cream
Tim Horton's
Zaro's Bread Basket (2)

Other

Book Corner
Duane Reade
Elegance
Gifts & Electronics
GNC
Hudson News (3)
Joseph Lawrence Jewelers
New York New York
Shoetrician—Shoe repair and shine
Tiecoon
The Petal Pusher
Staples
Tourist Information Center
Verizon Wireless

There is a Wachovia 24-hour ATM and a PNC Bank ATM located on the Amtrak level. There is a Bank of America 24-hour ATM and a 24-hour HSBC ATM located on the LIRR level, in addition to the generic (money-thieving) ATMs located in several stores throughout the station.

Temporary Parcel/Baggage Check

The only facility for storing parcels and baggage in Penn Station is at the Baggage Check on the Amtrak level (to the left of the ticket counter). There are no locker facilities at Penn Station. The Baggage Check is open from 5:15 am until 10 pm and costs $4.50 per item for each 24-hour period.

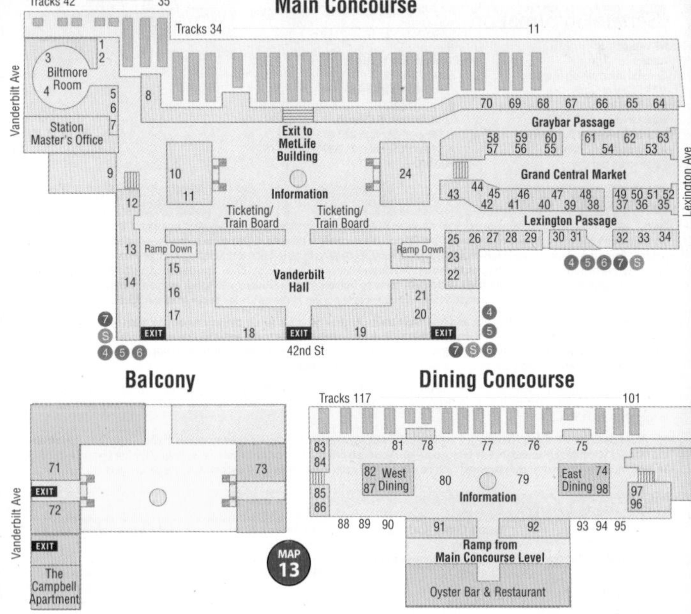

Main Concourse

1. Central Watch Band
2. Grand Central Racquet
3. Eddie's Service Shop
4. Dahlia
5. Eddie's Shoeshine & Repair
6. Papyrus
7. Junior's Brooklyn NYC
8. Starbucks
9. New York Transit Museum
10. Zaro's Bakery
11. Chase Bank
12. Pylones
13. Posman Books
14. Rite Aid
15. The Bewerage Bar
16. Francesco's Hair Salon, Barber Shop & Day Spa
17. Hot & Crusty
18. Banana Republic
19. Kenneth Cole
20. Brooklyn Industries
21. Super Runners Shop
22. Financier
23. Papyrus
24. Hudson News
25. Swatch
26. Capital One Bank
27. L'occitane
28. Grand Central Optical
29. The Art Of Shaving
30. Tumi
31. LittleMissMatched
32. Joon Jewelry
33. La Crasia
34. Pink Slip
35. Starbucks
36. Aveda
37. InnaSense
38. Tea & Honey Store
39. Mac
40. Tia's Place
41. Origins
42. Cursive
43. Forever Silver
44. Pescatore
45. Dishes At Home
46. Li-La Chocolates
47. Oren's Daily Roast Coffees & Teas
48. Penzeys Spices
49. Zaro's Bread Basket
50. Wild Edibles
51. Murray's Real Salami
52. Bread Corrado Pastry
53. Greenwich Produce
54. Ceriello
55. Murray's Cheese
56. German Royal Hams - Koglin
57. Greenwich Produce
58. O & Co
59. Grande Harvest Wines
60. Cobbler Shine
61. Toto
62. Joe - Art Of Coffee
63. GNC
64. Rosetta Stone
65. Tibet Kailash
66. D-Line Jewelry
67. Windhorse
68. The Soap Bar
69. Selen Design
70. Zaro's Bakery
71. Michael Jordan's The NYC Steakhouse
72. Dipriani Dolce
73. Charlie Palmer's Metrazur

Dining Concourse

74. Zaro's Bread Basket
75. Eddie's Shoeshine
76. Golden Krust
77. Hudson News
78. New York Pretzel
79. Caffe Pepe Rosso
80. Dishes
81. Dahlia
82. Ciao Bella Gelato
83. Paninoteca Italiana
84. Chirping Chicken
85. Eata Pita
86. Feng Shui Chinese Cuisine
87. Hale & Hearty Soups
88. Mendy's Dairy & Appetizing
89. Mendy's Kosher Delicatessen
90. Masa's
91. Junior's
92. Zocalo
93. Central Market Grill
94. The Manhattan Chili
95. Brother Jimmy's BBQ
96. Two Boots Pizzeria
97. Cafe Spice Express
98. Magnolia Bakery

General Information

NFT Map:	13
Address:	42nd St & Park Ave
General Information:	212-340-2210
Lost and Found:	212-340-2555
Website:	www.grandcentralterminal.com
MTA Subway Stops:	4 5 6 7 S
MTA Bus Lines:	1 2 3 4 42 98 101 102 104 Q32
Other Rail Lines:	Metro-North
Newark Airport Bus Service:	Olympia, 877-8-NEWARK, $14
LaGuardia Airport Bus Service:	NY Airport Express, 718-875-8200, $12
JFK Airport Bus Service:	NY Airport Express, 718-875-8200, $15

Overview

Grand Central Terminal, designed in the Beaux-Arts style by Warren & Wetmore, is by far the most beautiful of Manhattan's major terminals, and it is considered one of the most stunning terminals in the world. Its convenient location in the heart of Midtown and its refurbishments only add to its intrinsic appeal. The only downside is that the station will only get you on a train as far north as Dutchess County or as far east as New Haven via Metro-North—in order to head to the Island or Jersey, you'll have to hoof it over to GCT's architecturally ugly stepsister Penn Station.

If you ever find yourself underestimating the importance of the Grand Central renovations (begun in 1996 with continued work and maintenance today), just take a peek at the ceiling toward the Vanderbilt Avenue side—the small patch of black shows how dirty the ceiling was previously. And it was really dirty…

Diners have any number of choices from Michael Jordan's The Steak House NYC or Metrazur (for those seeking fine dining) to the food court on the lower level (perfect for commuters or those intent on saving a few bucks). After hitting the raw stuff at Oyster Bar, go right outside its entrance to hear a strange audio anomaly: If you and a friend stand in opposite corners and whisper, you'll be able to hear each other clearly. You can even do some grocery shopping in the Grand Central Market on the east side of the main concourse. Alternatively, folks looking to hit the sauce may do so in 1920s grandeur in The Campbell Apartment near the Vanderbilt Avenue entrance.

By far the coolest food option, however, is Grand Central Market, located between the east passages of the terminal as you head out towards Lexington Avenue. Instead of paying for overpriced food, build your own bread-meat-cheese extravaganza, or take home fresh fish or perfected butchered meat to cook at home later on. Our favorite vendors: Murray's Cheese, Murray's Real Salami, Wild Edibles, and Dishes at Home.

Grand Central Station offers three tours: the hour-long LaSalle Tour (212-340-2345, $50 for small groups, $5/person for groups over 10, payment required in advance), the Municipal Arts Society Tour (212-935-3960, $10 suggested donation), and the Grand Central Partnership Tour (212-883-2420, free). Grand Central's website also offers a printer-friendly walking tour guide for visitors who want to wander on their own.

ATMs

Chase
Numerous generic (money-thieving) ATMs at stores throughout the station.

East Dining

Brother Jimmy's BBQ
Café Spice
Central Market Grill
Golden Krust Patties
Jaques-Imo's to Geaux
Little Pie Company
Caffé Pepe Rosso
Two Boots
Zaro's Bread Basket
Zócalo Bar and Restaurant

West Dining

Dishes
Ciao Bella Gelateria
Chirping Chicken
Eata Pita
Feng Shui
Hale and Hearty Soups
Junior's
Masa Sushi
Mendy's Kosher Dairy
Mendy's Kosher Delicatessen
New York Pretzel
Paninoteca Italiana

General Information

NFT Map: 11
Address: 41st St & Eighth Ave
General Information: 212-564-8484
Kinney Garage: 212-502-2341
Website: www.panynj.gov/CommutingTravel/bus/html/pa.html
Subway: A C E Port Authority
1 2 3 7 N R Q W S Times Square
MTA Bus Lines: 10 11 16 20 27 42 104
Newark Airport Bus Service: Olympia, 212-964-6233, $13
LaGuardia Airport Bus Service: NY Airport Express, 718-875-8200, $12
JFK Airport Bus Service: NY Airport Express, 718-875-8200, $15

Overview

Devised as a solution to New York City's horrendous bus congestion, the Port Authority Bus Terminal was completed in 1950. The colossal structure consolidated midtown Manhattan's eight, separate, interstate bus stations into one convenient drop-off and pick-up point. Back in the day the Port Authority held the title of "largest bus terminal in the world," but for now we'll have to be content with merely the biggest depot in the United States. The Port Authority is located on the north and south sides of W 41st Street (b/w Eighth Ave & Ninth Ave) in a neighborhood that real-estate agents haven't yet graced with an official name. How about Greyhound Gardens?

There are plenty of things to do should you find that you've got some time to kill here. Send a postcard from the post office, donate blood at the blood bank on the main floor, use the refurbished bathrooms, bowl a few frames and have a cocktail at Leisure Time Bowl, or eat fancy French food at the ambitious sit-down restaurant, Metromarche, located in the south wing (they're really trying to class up the joint). There are also many souvenir carts, newsstands, and on-the-go restaurants, as well as a statue of beloved bus driver Ralph Kramden located outside of the south wing. The grungiest area of the terminal is the lower bus level, which is dirty and exhaust-filled, best visited just a few minutes before you need to board your bus. The chart on the right shows which bus companies run out of the Port Authority and provides a basic description of their destinations.

If you can, avoid interstate bus rides from the Port Authority on the busiest travel days of the year. The lines are long, the people are cranky, and some of the larger bus companies hire anyone who shows up with a valid bus operator's license and their very own bus (apparently, easier to obtain than you might think). The odds of having a disastrous trip skyrocket when the driver is unfamiliar with the usual itinerary.

On Easter Sunday, Christmas Eve, or Thanksgiving, one can see all the angst-ridden sons and daughters of suburban New Jersey parents joyfully waiting in cramped, disgusting corridors for that nauseating bus ride back to Leonia or Morristown or Plainfield or wherever. A fascinating sight.

Terminal Shops

South Wing—Lower Bus Level
Green Trees
Hudson News

South Wing—Subway Mezzanine
Au Bon Pain
Hudson News
Music Explosion

South Wing—Main Concourse
Metromarche
Au Bon Pain
Auntie Anne's
Casa Java
Deli Plus
Duane Reade
GNC
Jamba Juice
Hudson News
Hudson News Book Corner
Marrella Men's Hair Stylist
NY Blood Center
Radio Shack
Ruthie's Hallmark
Stop 'n Go Wireless
Strawberry
US Postal Service
Villa Pizza
World's Fare Restaurant Bar
Zaro's Bakery

South Wing—Second Floor
Café Metro
Drago Shoe Repair
Bank of America
Hudson News Book Corner
Kelly Film Express
Leisure Time Bowling Center
McAnn's Pub
Mrs Fields Bakery Café
Munchy's Gourmet
Sak's Florist
Sweet Factory

South Wing—Fourth Floor
First Stop-Last Stop Café
Hudson News

North Wing-Lower Bus Level
Snacks-N-Wheels

North Wing—Subway Mezzanine
Bank of America (ATM)
Green Trees
Hudson News

North Wing—Main Concourse
Continental Airlines
Hudson News
Mrs Fields Cookies

North Wing—on 42nd Street
Big Apple Café

North Wing—Second Floor
Bank of America (ATM)
Hudson News
Jay's Hallmark Bookstore
Tropica Juice Bar
USO

North Wing—Third Floor
Hudson News
Tropica Juice Bar

Bus Company	*Phone*	*Area Served*
Academy Bus Transportation	800-442-7272	Serves New York City, including Staten Island, Wall Street, Port Authority, and New Jersey, including Hoboken www.academybus.com
Adirondak New York & Pine Hill Trailways	800-776-7548	Serves all of New York State with coach connections throughout the US. www.trailwaysny.com
Capitol Trailways	800-333-8444	Service between Pennsylvania, Virginia, New York State, and New York City. www.capitoltrailways.com
Carl Bieber Bus	800-243-2374	Service to and from Port Authority and Wall Street in New York and Reading, Kutztown, Wescosville, Hellertown, and Easton, Pennsylvania. www.biebertourways.com
Coach USA	800-522-4514	Service between New York City and W Orange, Livingston, Morristown, E Hanover, Whippany, and Floram Park, New Jersey. www.coachusa.com
DeCamp Bus	800-631-1281	Service between New York City and New Jersey, including the Meadowlands. www.decamp.com
Greyhound Bus	800-231-2222	Serves most of the US and Canada. www.greyhound.com
Gray Line Bus	800-669-0051	Service offered throughout the US and Canada. www.grayline.com
Lakeland Bus	973-366-0600	Service between New York and New Jersey. www.lakelandbus.com
Martz Group	800-233-8604	Service between New York and Pennsylvania. www.martzgroup.com
New Jersey Transit	973-275-5555	Serves New York, New Jersey, and Philadelphia. www.njtransit.com
NY Airport Service	212-875-8200	Service between Port Authority and Kennedy and LaGuardia airports. www.nyairportservice.com
Olympia Trails	877-894-9155	Provides express bus service between Manhattan and Newark Airport. Makes stops all over New York City, including Penn Station, Grand Central, and many connections with hotel shuttles. www.olympiabus.com
Peter Pan Lines	800-343-9999	Serves the East, including Boston, New Hampshire, Maine, Philly, DC. Also goes to Canada. www.peterpanbus.com
Rockland Coaches (NY)	845-356-0877	Services New York's Port Authority, GW bridge, 44th Street, and 8th Street to and from most of Bergen County and upstate New York. www.coachusa.com/rockland
ShortLine Bus	800-631-8405	Serves the New York City airports, Atlantic City, and the Hudson Valley. www.shortlinebus.com
Suburban	732-249-1100	Offers commuter service from Central New Jersey to and from Port Authority and Wall Street. Also services between the Route 9 Corridor and New York City. www.coachusa.com/suburban
Susquehanna Trailways	800-692-6314	Service to and from New York City and Newark (Greyhound Terminal) and Summerville, New Jersey, and many stops in Central Pennsylvania, ending in Williamsport and Lock Haven. www.susquehannabus.com
Trans-Bridge Lines	610-868-6001 800-962-9135	Offers service between New York, Pennsylvania and New Jersey, including Newark and Kennedy airports. transbridgelines.com
Red & Tan Hudson County (NJ)	908-354-3330	Serves New York City and Hudson County, New Jersey. www.coachusa.com/redandtan

General Information

NFT Map:	23
Address:	4211 Broadway & 178th St
Phone:	800-221-9903 or 212-564-8484
Website:	www.panynj.gov/bus-terminals/ gwbbs-about-station.htmll
Subway:	A (175th St), A 1 (181st St)
Buses:	100 98 5 4 3 ?

Overview

Change is coming slowly to the George Washington Bridge Bus Terminal, though we can hope it will never lose its "lived-in" charm. The Port Authority has cleaned the station up a bit, added some needed signage, and improved the lighting, but any place with pigeons routinely wandering through the indoors can never be too chic. Hit some downtime before your bus arrives and your entertainment options are limited to people-watching, opening a new bank account, or placing bets at OTB. If you luck out and the weather's nice, though, the view of the bridge upstairs is pretty sweet.

Stores

Lower Level:
Bridge Stop Newsstand
HealthPlus Healthcare
Subway Pedestrian Walkway
NJT T Ticket Vending Machines
Port of Calls/Retail Pushcarts

Concourse:
ATM
Bridge Stop Newsstand
Dentists—Howard Bloom, DDS; Steve Kaufman DDS
E-Z Visions Travel
Food Plus Café
GW Books and Electronics
HealthPlus Healthcare
Neighborhood Trust Federal Credit Union
New York National Bank
Off-Track Betting
Pizza Palace
Terminal Barber Shop
Washington Heights Optical

Street Level:
Blockbuster Video
Rite-Aid Pharmacy
Urban Pathways—Homeless Outreach Office
Port Authority Business Outreach Center (179th St underpass)

Bus Companies

Air Brook •
800-800-1990 • airbrook.com
To Atlantic City (Tropicana)

Astro-Eastern Bus Company •
201-865-2230
Trips to Florida (purchase tickets on the upper level).

Express Bus Service •
973-742-4700 • expressbusservice.com
To Elmwood Park, Englewood, Fort Lee, Hackensack, Paramus, Paterson, River Edge, and Teaneck (all stops on Route 4).

New Jersey Transit •
973-275-5555
To 60th St, Bergenfield, Bogota, Cliffside Park, Coytesville, Dumont, Edgewater (including Edgewater Commons Mall), Englewood, Englewood Cliffs, West Englewood, Fair Lawn (including the Radburn section), Fairview, Fort Lee, Glen Rock, Guttenberg, Hackensack (including NJ Bus Transfer), Hoboken, North Hackensack (Riverside Square), Irvington, Jersey City, Kearney, Leonia, Maywood, Newark, North Bergen, Paramus (including the Bergen Mall and Garden State Plaza), Paterson (including Broadway Terminal), Ridgewood, Rochelle Park, Teaneck (including Glenpointe and Holy Name Hospital), Union City, Weehawken, and West New York.

Red & Tan/Coach USA •
908-354-3330 • coachusa.com/redandtan
To Alpine, Bergenfield, Blauvelt, Bradlees Shopping Center, Closter, Congers, Creskill, Demarest, Dumont, Emerson, Englewood, Englewood Cliffs, Grandview, Harrington Park, Haverstraw, Haworth, Hillsdale, Linwood Park, Montvale, Nanuet, (including Nanuet Shopping Mall), Nauraushaun, New City, New Milford, Northvale (including Northvale Industrial Park), Norwood, Nyack, Oradell, Orangeburg, Palisades, Park Ridge, Pearl River, Piermont, Rivervale, Rockland Lake, Rockland Psych Center, Rockleigh (including Rockleigh Industrial Park), South Nyack, Sparkill, Spring Valley, Stony Point, Tappan, Tenafly, Upper Nyack, Valley Cottage, West Haverstraw, Westwood, and Woodcliff Lake.

Saddle River Tours •
973-777-1900 • saddlerivertours.com
To Atlantic City

Vanessa Express • 201-453-1970
To Cliffside Park, Jersey City, North Bergen, Union City, and West New York.

General Information

NFT Map: 3
Websites: www.chinatown-bus.com
www.chinatown-bus.org

Overview

There are several inexpensive bus lines running from Chinatown in New York City to the respective Chinatowns in Boston, Philadelphia, Washington DC, Richmond, and Atlanta. If you're lucky, you'll catch a kung-fu movie on board, but be prepared for an '80s "classic" like *Turner & Hooch*. Tickets usually cost $15–20 each way, and can be purchased online or in person at pick-up locations.

Cheaper than planes and trains, the Chinatown buses have become extraordinarily popular. They are in such demand that Greyhound and Trailways have lowered their online fares to compete. That said, Chinatown buses are an infinitely more adventurous mode of transportation. The odds are high that you'll experience at least one problem during the course of your trip including, but not limited to, poor customer service, unmarked bus stops, late departures, less than ideal bus conditions, and hucking or spitting from other passengers. More pertinent problems include cancelled or delayed trips without warning, breakdowns, fires, broken bathrooms (or none at all), stolen luggage, and drop-offs on the side of the road near the highway because bus companies don't have permission to deliver passengers to central transportation hubs. Conversely, service has improved greatly in the past few years, and many people have enjoyed dirt-cheap, hassle-free experiences on the Chinatown buses. It's probably not the best choice for families, but anyone else should give it a try.

A few tips to make your trip easier: 1) MAKE SURE YOU GET ON THE RIGHT BUS. We cannot emphasize this enough. Do not be embarrassed to ask everyone on the bus which city they're going to. 2) Do not sit anywhere near the bathroom. You will smell the intense, probably illegal, cleaning products for the first half of the ride, and your fellow passengers' business for the second half. 3) If the bus isn't full, it's perfectly fine to take your luggage onboard with you if you're worried about theft. This is an especially good idea when leaving the New York stations. 4) Arrive at least 30 minutes ahead of time. Trust us. This will save you a chaotic sprint under the Manhattan Bridge while you jump on the wrong bus. Yes, it has happened even to NFT experts. 5) To Boston we prefer Lucky Star over Fung Wah, just because it's usually a little less crowded, but both do the job just fine.

Another newer option that's a step above Chinatown buses (but still really cheap) are Bolt Bus (www.boltbus.com) and Megabus (www.megabus.com). Check the website for more details, but both leave from the vicinity of Penn Station and travel to Boston, DC, Philly, and even Toronto. And they have Wi-Fi connections so you can surf the NFT website on board. Try that on a Chinatown bus.

Bus Companies

Fung Wah Transportation Inc. •
212-925-8889 • www.fungwahbus.com
- To Boston every hour on the hour between 7 am–10 pm. From **139 Canal Street** to South Station: one-way $15, round trip $30.

Lucky Star Bus Transportation •
617-426-8801 • www.luckystarbus.com.
- To Boston every hour 7 am–10 pm. From **69 Chrystie St** to South Station: one-way $15, round trip $30.

Boston Deluxe •
917-662-7552 or 646-773-3816 • www.bostondeluxe.com
- To Boston at 9 am, 12:30 pm, and 6 pm. From **1250 Broadway & 32nd St** or **88 E Broadway** to 175 Huntington Ave: one-way $15, round trip $30.
- To Hartford at 8:30 am, 12:30 pm, and 5:30 pm. From the same pick-up points to 365 Capital Ave: one-way $15, round trip $30.

Washington Deluxe • 866-BUS-NY-DC • www.washny.com
- To Washington several times a day; From **34th St & 8th Ave**. Additional departures from **Delancey & Allen Sts**, and several locations in **Williamsburg** to various locations in DC. Schedule varies by day of the week, so it's recommended that you check the website for info. $40 round-trip and $25 each way on Saturdays.

Dragon Deluxe •
800-475-1160 or 212-966-5130 • www.dragondeluxe.com
- To Washington DC six times a day between 7:30 am and 11:30 pm. From **153 Lafayette St** or **Broadway & W 32nd St-Herald Square** to 14th & L Sts: one-way $20, round trip $35.
- To Baltimore six times a day between 7:30 am and 11:30 pm. From the same pick-up points to 5600 O'Donnell St: one-way $20, round trip $35.
- To Albany at 7:30 am and 5:30 pm. From the same pick-up points to Madison Ave (between the New York State Museum and Empire State Plaza): one-way $25, round trip $45
- To Woodbury Commons at 7:30 am and 5:30 pm. From the same pick-ups points to Woodbury Commons: one-way $15, round trip $30.

Eastern Travel • 212-244-6132 • www.easternshuttle.com
- To Washington DC 6–12 times a day between 7:30 am and 7:30 pm; From **88 E Broadway**, **430 7th Ave at W 34th St,** or **5 Times Square (in front of the Ernst &Young Building)** to 715 H Street in Washington DC: one-way $20, round trip $35.
- To Baltimore 6–12 times a day between 7:30 am and 7:30 pm. From same pickup-point to 5501 O'Donnell St Cut Off: one-way $20, round trip $35.

New Century Travel • 215-627-2666 • www.2000coach.com
- To Philadelphia every hour between 7 am and 11 pm. From **88 E Broadway** or **5994 8th Ave, Williamsburg** (7 am only) to 55 N 11th St: one-way $12, round trip $20.
- To DC eight times between 7 am and 11 pm; From **88 E Broadway** to 513 H St NW: one-way $20, round trip $35.
- To Richmond at 5 pm and 1 am. From **88 E Broadway** to 2808 W Broad St: one-way $40, round-trip $60.

Today's Bus • 212-343-3281 • www.todaysbus.com
- To Philadelphia every hour between 7:15 am and 11 pm. From **88 E Broadway** to 1041 Race St: one-way $12, round trip $20.
- To DC 14 times a day between 7:15 am and 11 pm. From **88 E Broadway** to 610 I St NW: one-way $20, round trip $35.
- To Norfolk, VA, at 6 pm. From **13 Allen St** to 649 Newton Rd: one-way $25, round trip $40.
- To Richmond, VA, at 5 pm. From **88 E Broadway** to 5215 W Broad St: one-way $40, round trip $60.
- To Atlanta, GA, at 8 pm. From **109 E Broadway** to 5150 Buford Hwy NE: one-way $90, round trip $170.

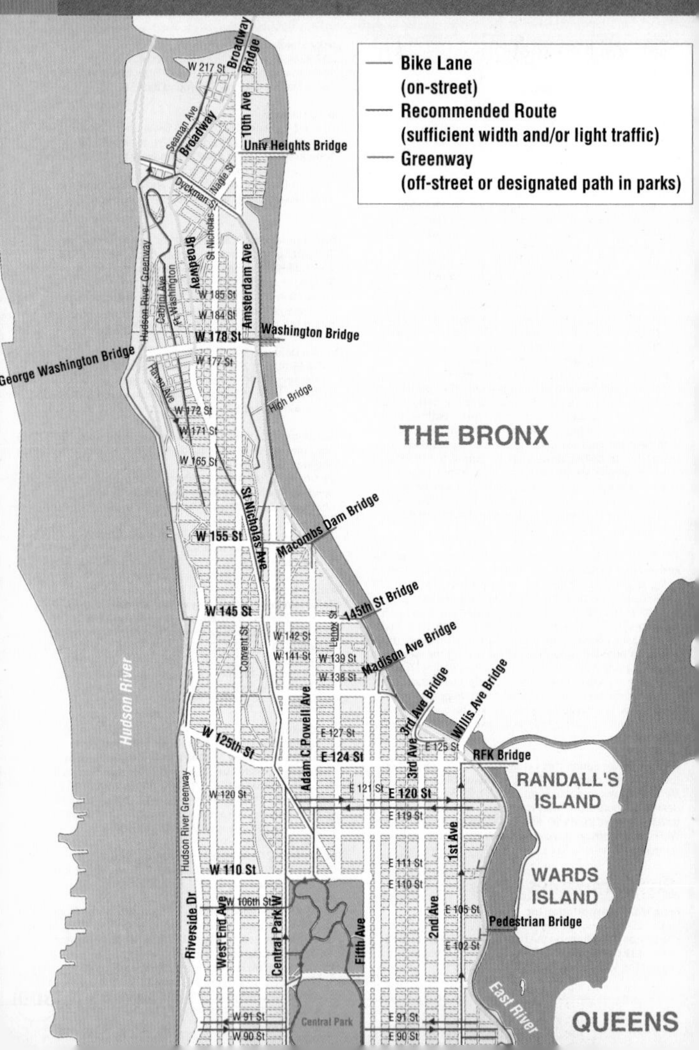

Bike Lane
(on-street)
Recommended Route
(sufficient width and/or light traffic)
Greenway
(off-street or designated path in parks)
THE BRONX
Hudson River
RANDALL'S ISLAND
WARDS ISLAND
QUEENS
East River
Central Park
George Washington Bridge
Washington Bridge
High Bridge
Univ Heights Bridge
Broadway Bridge
Macombs Dam Bridge
145th St Bridge
Madison Ave Bridge
3rd Ave Bridge
Willis Ave Bridge
RFK Bridge
Pedestrian Bridge
Hudson River Greenway
W 217 St
Seaman Ave
Broadway
10th Ave
Dyckman St
Nagle St
St Nicholas
Amsterdam Ave
Cabrini Ave
Ft Washington
W 185 St
W 184 St
W 178 St
W 177 St
Haven Ave
W 172 St
W 171 St
W 165 St
St Nicholas Ave
W 155 St
W 145 St
Convent St
W 142 St
W 141 St
Lenox St
W 139 St
W 138 St
Adam C Powell Ave
W 125th St
E 127 St
E 124 St
E 125 St
3rd Ave
W 120 St
E 121 St
E 120 St
E 119 St
1st Ave
W 110 St
E 111 St
E 110 St
2nd Ave
E 105 St
E 102 St
Riverside Dr.
West End Ave
W 106th St
Central Park W
Fifth Ave
W 91 St
W 90 St
E 91 St
E 90 St

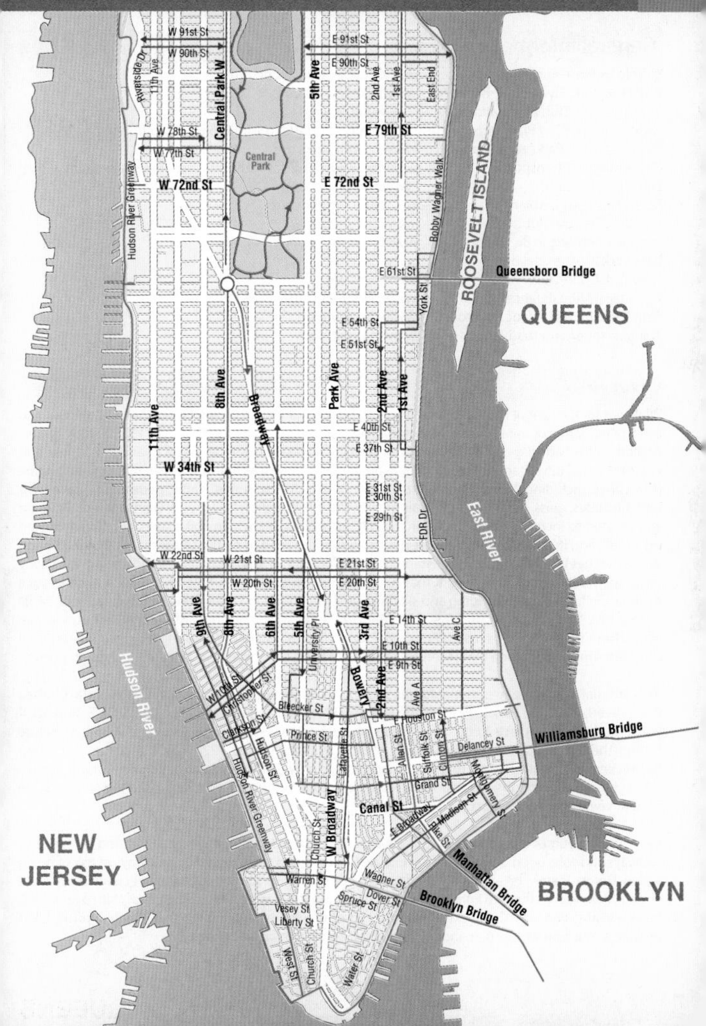
W 91st St
W 90th St
Riverside Dr
11th Ave
Central Park W
E 91st St
E 90th St
5th Ave
2nd Ave
1st Ave
East End
W 78th St
W 77th St
E 79th St
Central Park
Hudson River Greenway
W 72nd St
E 72nd St
Bobby Wagner Walk
ROOSEVELT ISLAND
E 61st St
Queensboro Bridge
York St
QUEENS
E 54th St
E 51st St
8th Ave
Broadway
Park Ave
2nd Ave
1st Ave
11th Ave
E 40th St
E 37th St
W 34th St
E 31st St
E 30th St
E 29th St
FDR Dr
East River
W 22nd St
W 21st St
E 21st St
W 20th St
E 20th St
9th Ave
8th Ave
6th Ave
5th Ave
University Pl
3rd Ave
E 14th St
Ave C
E 10th St
E 9th St
Hudson River
W 10th St
Christopher St
Bleecker St
Bowery
2nd Ave
Ave A
E Houston St
Clarkson St
Prince St
Lafayette St
Allen St
Suffolk St
Clinton St
Delancey St
Williamsburg Bridge
Hudson St
Hudson River Greenway
Grand St
Montgomery St
W Broadway
Canal St
E Broadway
Madison St
Pike St
Church St
NEW JERSEY
Warren St
Wagner St
Manhattan Bridge
Dover St
Spruce St
Brooklyn Bridge
BROOKLYN
Vesey St
Liberty St
West St
Church St
Water St

General Information

Bicycle Defense Fund:	www.bicycledefensefund.org
Bike New York, Five Borough Bike Tour:	www.bikenewyork.org
Century Road Club Association (CRCA):	www.crca.net
Department of City Planning:	www.nyc.gov/html/dcp/html/bike/home.shtml
Department of Parks & Recreation:	www.nycgovparks.org
Department of Transportation:	www.nyc.gov/html/dot/html/bicyclists/bikemain.shtml
Empire Skate Club:	www.empireskate.org
Fast & Fabulous Lesbian & Gay Bike Club:	www.fastnfab.org
Five Boro Bicycle Club:	www.5bbc.org
League of American Bicyclists:	www.bikeleague.org
New York Bicycle Coalition:	www.nybc.net
New York Cycle Club:	www.nycc.org
NYC Streets Renaissance:	www.nycstreets.org
Time's Up! Bicycle Advocacy Group:	www.times-up.org
Transportation Alternatives:	www.transalt.org

Overview

While not for the faint of heart, biking and skating around Manhattan can be one of the most efficient and exhilarating forms of transportation. Transportation Alternatives estimates that over 130,000 New Yorkers hop on a bike each day—an all-time high for the city. Manhattan is relatively flat, and the fitness and environmental advantages of using people power are incontrovertible. However, there are also some downsides, including, but not limited to: psychotic cab drivers, buses, traffic, pedestrians, pavement with potholes, glass, debris, and poor air quality. In 1994, the Bicycle Network Development Program was created to increase bicycle usage in the NYC area. Since then, many bike lanes have been created on streets and in parks (see map on previous page). These tend to be the safest places to ride, though they often get blocked by parked or standing cars. Central Park is a great place to ride, as are the newly developed paths from Battery Park that run along the Hudson River. East River Park is another nice destination for recreational riding and skating—just not after dark! In addition to bicycle rentals, Pedal Pusher Bike Shop (1306 Second Ave, 212-288-5592) offers recorded tours of Central Park, so you can learn about the park and exercise at the same time. There is also talk of creating a city wide bike rental program similar to the one that recently launched in Paris. Let's hope that New York jumps on board!

Recreational skating venues in Manhattan include Wollman and Lasker Rinks in Central Park, Chelsea Piers, Riverbank State Park (679 Riverside Drive at 145th St), and Rivergate Ice Rink (401 E 34th St). If you're looking for a place to get your skates sharpened to your own personal specifications before hitting the ice, contact Westside Skate & Stick (174 Fifth Ave, 212-228-8400), a custom pro shop for hockey and figure skaters that's by appointment only. For more information on skating venues throughout the boroughs, check out www.skatecity.com. For organized events, visit the Empire Skate Club at www.empireskate.org.

Bikes are sometimes less convenient than skates. Where skates can be tucked in a bag and carried onto subways, indoors, or on buses, bikes have to be locked up on the street and are always at risk of being stolen. Unfortunately, bike racks are hard to come by in NYC, so you may need to get creative on where to park. Always lock them to immovable objects and don't skimp on a cheap bike lock. With over 40,000 bikes a year stolen in NYC, the extra cost for a top-of-the-line bike lock is worth it. On the upside, bikes provide a much faster, less demanding form of transportation around the city.

Crossing the Bridges by Bike

Crossing the Brooklyn, Manhattan, or Williamsburg Bridges by bike is a great way for Brooklynites to commute to work (unless, of course, it's really windy and cold out). Riding across these bridges also makes for a great weekend outing for Manhattanites and Brooklynites alike. All bridges afford amazing views of the Manhattan and Brooklyn skylines. In the fall of 2003, the DOT estimated that nearly 4,000 cyclists crossed the East River bridges each day. It just isn't healthy to stay underground so much, so gear up and give it a go.

Brooklyn Bridge

Separate bicycle and pedestrian lanes run down the center of the bridge, with the bicycle lane on the north side and the pedestrian lane on the south. Cyclists should beware of wayfaring tourists taking photographs. We do not recommend rollerblading across the bridge—the wooden planks make for quite a bumpy ride. The bridge is quite level and, aside from the tourists and planks, fairly easy to traverse.

Brooklyn Access: Stairs to Cadman Plz E and Prospect St, ramp to Johnson & Adams Sts
Manhattan Access: Park Row and Centre St, across from City Hall Park

Manhattan Bridge

The last of the Brooklyn crossings to be outfitted with decent pedestrian and bike paths, the Manhattan Bridge bike and pedestrian paths are on separate sides of the bridge. The walking path is on the south side, and the bike path is on the north side of the bridge. The major drawback to walking across the Manhattan Bridge is that you have to climb a steep set of stairs on the Brooklyn side (not the best conditions for lugging around a stroller or suitcase). Fortunately, the bike path on the north side of the bridge is ramped on both approaches. However, be careful on Jay Street when accessing the bridge in Brooklyn due to the dangerous, fast-moving traffic.

Brooklyn Access: Jay St & Sands St
Manhattan Access: Bike Lane–Canal St & Forsyth St
Pedestrian Lane–Bowery, just south of Canal St

Williamsburg Bridge

The Williamsburg Bridge has the widest pedestrian/bike path of the three bridges to Brooklyn. The path on the north side, shared by cyclists and pedestrians, is 12 feet wide. The southern path, at eight feet wide, is also shared by bikers and walkers. Now that both sides of the bridge are always open to pedestrians and bikes, this is one of the best ways to get to and from Brooklyn. As a bonus fitness feature, the steep gradient on both the Manhattan and Brooklyn sides of the bridge gives bikers and pedestrians a good workout.

Brooklyn Access: North Entrance–Driggs Ave, right by the Washington Plz
South Entrance–Bedford Ave b/w S 5th & S 6th Sts
Manhattan Access: Delancey St & Clinton St/Suffolk St

George Washington Bridge

Bikers get marginalized by the pedestrians on this crossway to New Jersey. The north walkway is for pedestrians only, and the south side is shared by pedestrians and bikers. Cyclists had to fight to keep their right to even bike on this one walkway, as city officials wanted to institute a "walk your bike across" rule to avoid bicycle/pedestrian accidents during construction. The bikers won the battle but are warned to "exercise extra caution" when passing pedestrians.

Manhattan Access: W 178th St & Fort Washington Ave
New Jersey Access: Hudson Ter in Fort Lee

Robert F. Kennedy Bridge

Biking is officially prohibited on this two-mile span that connects the Bronx, Queens, and Manhattan. Unofficially, people ride between the boroughs and over to Wards Island all the time. The bike path is quite narrow, compared to the paths on other bridges, and the lighting at night is mediocre at best. The tight path sees less pedestrian/cycling traffic than other bridges, which, paired with the insufficient lighting, gives the span a rather ominous feeling after dark. If you're worried about safety, or keen on obeying the laws, the 103rd Street footbridge provides an alternative way to reach Wards Island sans car. This pedestrian pass is open only during the warmer months, and then only during daylight hours. See page 297 for more information about the footbridge schedule.

Bronx Access: 133rd St & Cypress Ave

Manhattan Access: Ramps--124/126th Sts & First Ave Stairs–Second Ave and 124/126 Sts

Queens Access: 26th St & Hoyt Ave (beware of extremely steep stairs).

Queensboro Bridge

The north outer roadway of the Queensboro Bridge is open exclusively to bikers, 24/7, except for the day of the New York Marathon. More than 2,500 cyclists and pedestrians per day traverse the bridge. Bikers complain about safety issues on the Manhattan side of the bridge: With no direct connection from Manhattan onto the bridge's West Side, bikers are forced into an awkward five-block detour to get to Second Avenue, where they can finally access the bridge.

Manhattan Entrance: 60th St, b/w First Ave & Second Ave

Queens Entrance: Queens Plz & Crescent St

Bike Rentals (and Sales)

Cadence Cycling • 174 Hudson St • 212-226-4400 • Map 2
Canal Street Bicycles • 417 Canal St • 212-334-8000 • Map 2
Gotham Bikes • 112 W Broadway • 212-732-2453 • Map 2
Bike Works • 106 Ridge St • 212-388-1077 • Map 4
Chari & Co. • 175 Stanton St • 212-475-0102 • Map 4
Dah Bike Shop • 134 Division St • Map 4
Frank's Bike Shop • 533 Grand St • 212-533-6332 • Map 4
The Hub Station • 73 Morton St • 212-965-9334 • Map 5
West Village Waterfront Bike Shop • 391 West St • 212-414-2453 • Map 5
Bfold 224 • E 13th St • 212-529-7247 • Map 6
Bicycle Habitat • 244 Lafayette St • 212-431-3315 • Map 6
Metro Bicycles • 332 E 14th St • 212-228-4344 • Map 6
NYC Velo • 64 2nd Ave • 212-253-7771 • Map 6
Track Star NYC • 231 Eldridge St • 212-982-2553 • Map 6
Busy Bee Bikes • 437 E 6th St • 212-228-2347 • Map 7
Continuum Cycles • 199 Avenue B • 212-505-8785 • Map 7
Landmark Bicycles • 136 E 3rd St • 212-674-2343 • Map 7
Recycle-A-Bicycle • 75 Avenue C • 212-475-1655 • Map 7
Larry's Bicycles Plus • 1690 2nd Ave • Map 17
Bike and Roll • 557 12th Ave • 212-260-0400 • Map 8
City Bicycles & Hobby • 315 W 38th St • 212-563-3373 • Map 8
Enoch's Bike Shop • 480 10th Ave • 212-582-0620 • Map 8
A Bicycle Shop • 163 W 22nd St • 212-691-6149 • Map 9
Chelsea Bicycles • 130 W 26th St • 212-727-7278 • Map 9
Metro Bicycles • 546 Avenue of the Americas • 212-255-5100 • Map 9
Paragon Sporting Goods • 867 Broadway • 212-255-8036 • Map 9
Sid's Bikes • 151 W 19th St • 212-989-1060 • Map 9
Manhattan Velo • 141 E 17th St • 212-253-6788 • Map 10

Sid's Bikes • 235 E 34th St • 212-213-8360 • Map 10
Spokesman Cycles • 34 Irving Pl • 212-995-0450 • Map 10
Liberty Bicycles • 846 9th Ave • 212-757-2418 • Map 11
Manhattan Bicycle Shop • 791 9th Ave • 212-262-0111 • Map 11
Metro Bicycles • 360 W 47th St • 212-581-4500 • Map 11
Ferrara Cycle Shop • 6304 20th Ave • 718-232-6716 • Map 12
Conrad's Bike Shop • 25 Tudor City Pl • 212-697-6966 • Map 13
Bay Ridge Bicycle World • 8916 3rd Ave • 718-238-1118 • Map 14
Bicycle Renaissance • 430 Columbus Ave • 212-362-3388 • Map 14
Eddie's Bicycles • 480 Amsterdam Ave • 212-580-2011 • Map 14
Toga Bikes • 110 West End Ave • 212-799-9625 • Map 14
Bicycles NYC • 1400 3rd Ave • 212-794-2929 • Map 15
Bike Heaven • 348 E 62nd St • 212-230-1919 • Map 15
NYC Wheels • 1603 York Ave • 212-737-3078 • Map 15
Pedal Pushers • 1306 2nd Ave • 212-288-5592 • Map 15
Champion Bicycles • 896 Amsterdam Ave • 212-662-2690 • Map 16
Innovation Bike Shop • 105 W 106th St • 212-678-7130 • Map16
Metro Bicycles • 231 W 96th St • 212-663-7531 • Map16
Metro Bicycles • 1311 Lexington Ave • 212-427-4450 • Map 17
ModSquad Cycles • 2119 Frederick Douglass Blvd • 212-865-5050 • Map19
Heavy Metal Bike Shop • 2016 3rd Ave • 212-410-1144 • Map 20
Junior Bicycle Shop • 1820 Amsterdam Ave • 212-690-6511 • Map 21
Mani's Bicycle Shop • 8 Bennett Ave • 212-927-8501 • Map 23
Victor's Bike Repair • 4125 Broadway • 212-740-5137 • Map 23
Tread Bike Shop • 250 Dyckman St • 212-544-7055 • Map 25

Bikes and Mass Transit

Surprisingly, you can take your bike on trains and some buses—just make sure it's not during rush hour and you are courteous to other passengers. The subway requires you to carry your bike down staircases, use the service gate instead of the turnstile, and board at the very front or back end of the train. To ride the commuter railroads with your bike, you may need to purchase a bike permit. For appropriate contact information, see transportation pages.

Amtrak: Train with baggage car required.
LIRR: $5 permit required.
Metro-North: $5 permit required.
New Jersey Transit: No permit required.
PATH: No permit required.
New York Water Taxi: No fee or permit required
NY Waterway: $1 fee.
Staten Island Ferry: Enter at lower level.
Bus companies: Call individual companies.

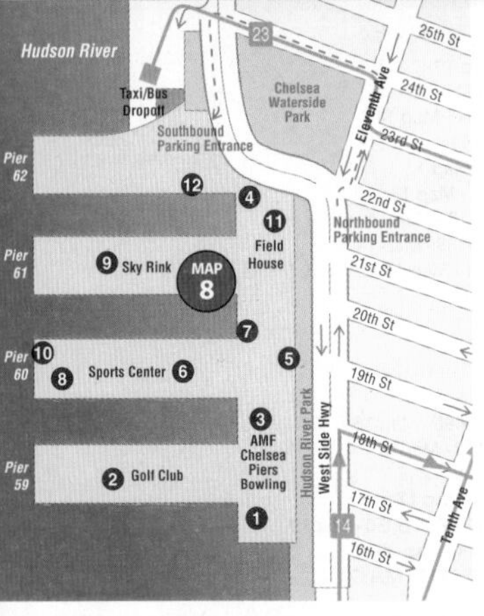

General Information

NFT Map: 8
Website: www.chelseapiers.com

Overview

Opened in 1910 as a popular port for trans-Atlantic ships, Chelsea Piers found itself neglected and deteriorating by the 1960s. In 1992, Roland W. Betts (fraternity brother of George W. Bush) began the plan to renovate and refurbish the piers as a gargantuan 28-acre sports and entertainment center. In 1995, Chelsea Piers re-opened its doors to the public at a final cost of $120 million—all private money. The only help from the state was a very generous 49-year lease. By 1998, Chelsea Piers was the third most popular attraction in New York City, after Times Square.

How to Get There

Unless you live in Chelsea, it's a real pain to get to the Piers. The closest subway is the C E to 23rd Street and Eighth Avenue, and then it's still a three-avenue block hike there. If you're lucky, you can hop a 23 bus on 23rd Street and expedite the last leg of your journey. L train commuters should get off at the Eighth Avenue stop and take the 14 bus across to the West Side Highway where you'll be dropped off at 18th Street.

If you drive, entering from the south can be a little tricky. It's pretty well signed, so keep your eyes peeled. Basically you exit right at Eleventh Avenue and 22nd Street, turn left onto 24th Street, and then make a left onto the West Side Highway. Enter Chelsea Piers the same way you would if you were approaching from the north. Parking costs $14 for the first hour, $18 for two, $22 for three. Street parking in the West 20s is an excellent alternative in the evenings after 6 pm.

Facilities

Chelsea Piers is amazing. There are swimming pools, ice-skating rinks, a bowling alley, spa, restaurants, shops, batting cages—you name it. So, what's the catch? Well, it's gonna cost ya. Like Manhattan rents, only investment bankers can afford this place.

1 **Chelsea Brewing Company** • 212-336-6440. Microbrewery and restaurant. Try the amber ale, wings, nachos, and cheesy fries—all excellent.

2 **The Golf Club at Chelsea Piers** • 212-336-6400. Aside from potentially long wait times, the 250-yard driving range with 52 heated stalls and automated ball-feed (no buckets or bending over!) is pretty awesome. $25 buys you 90 balls (peak) or 147 balls (off-peak). If you don't bring your own, club hire is $4/one club, $5/two, $6/three, or $12/ten. Before 5 pm on weekdays, you can whack all the balls you want for an hour for $20 plus free club rental.

3 **300 New York** • 212-835-BOWL. A very schmancy 40-lane bowling alley equipped with video games and bar. $8/game plus $6 shoe rental.

4 **Ruthy's Bakery & Café** • 212-336-6333. Pastries and sandwiches.

5 **New York Presbyterian Sports Medicine Center** • 212-366-5100. Performance physical therapy.

6 **The Spa at Chelsea Piers** • 212-336-6780. It's not Canyon Ranch. A basic 50-minute massage is $105, a basic 50-minute facial is $105. They also have a range of scrubs, wraps, polishes, manicures, pedicures, and waxes.

7 **College Sports Television** • Street-level broadcast center accessible to the public with interactive events and activities for college sports fans.

8 **The Sports Center** • 212-336-6000. A very expensive, monster health club with a 10,000-square-foot climbing wall, a quarter-mile track, a swimming pool, and enough fitness equipment for a small army in training. If you have to ask how much the membership is, you can't afford it.

9 **Sky Rink** • 212-336-6100. Two 24/7 ice rinks mainly used for classes, training, and bar mitzvahs.

10 **The Lighthouse** • 212-336-6144. 10,000-square-foot event space for private gatherings catered by Abigail Kirsch.

11 **The Field House** • 212-336-6500. The Field House is an 80,000-square-foot building with a 23-foot climbing wall, a gymnastics training center, four batting cages, two basketball courts, and two indoor soccer fields. A season (ten games plus playoffs) of league soccer costs $230/person, league basketball costs $185/person, rock-climbing costs $18/class, and gymnastics costs $28/class.

12 **Spirit Cruise** • 866-483-3866; www.spiritofnewyork.com. Ships run out of Chelsea Piers and Weehawken, NJ. Dinner cruises are approximately $70/person, and if you're having a big function, you can rent the entire boat

Unfortunately, but not surprisingly, there are no golf courses on the island of Manhattan. Thankfully, there are two driving ranges where you can at least smack the ball around until you can get to a real course, as well as a golf simulator at Chelsea Piers that lets you play a full round "at" various popular courses (Pebble Beach, St. Andrews, etc.). NYC has a number of private and public courses throughout the outer boroughs and Westchester; however, they don't even come close to satisfying the area's huge demand for courses.

Golf Courses	*Borough*	*Address*	*Phone*	*Par*	*Fee*
Mosholu Golf Course	Bronx	3700 Jerome Ave	718-655-9164	9 holes, par 30	Weekend fees $17.75/early, twilight/$39.50 morning and afternoon - weekday fees $16.75-$28, non-residents add $8.
Pelham/Split Rock Golf	Bronx	870 Shore Rd	718-885-1258	18 holes, par 71	Weekend fees $17.75/early, twilight/$39.50 morning and afternoon - weekday fees $16.75-$28, non-residents add $8.
Van Cortlandt Golf Course	Bronx	Van Cortlandt Pk S & Bailey Ave	718-543-4595	18 holes, par 70	M–F/$16.75–$28; weekend $17.75/early, twilight; $39.50/ morning and afternoon; non-resident add $8.
Marine Park Golf Club	Brooklyn	2880 Flatbush Ave	718-338-7149	18 holes, par 72	Weekend fees $17/early, twilight/$38 morning and afternoon–weekday fees $16–$27, non-residents add $7
Dyker Beach Golf Course	Brooklyn	86th St & Seventh Ave	718-836-9722	18 holes, Par 71	Weekend fees $17/early, twilight/$38 morning and afternoon; weekday fees $16–$27, non-residents add $8
Golf Simulator	New York	Chelsea Piers Golf Club	212-336-6400		$45/hour (see previous Chelsea Piers page)
LaTourette Golf Course	Staten Island	1001 Richmond Hill Rd	718-351-1889	18 holes, par 72	M–F/$16.75–$28; weekend $17.75/early, twilight; $39.50/morning and afternoon; non-resident add $8.
Silver Lake Golf Course	Staten Island	915 Victory Blvd	718-442-4653	18 holes, par 69	M–F/$16.75–$28; weekend $17.75/early, twilight; $39.50/morning and afternoon; non-resident add $8.
South Shore Golf Course	Staten Island	200 Huguenot Ave	718-984-0101	18 holes, par 72	M–F/$16.75–$28; weekend $17.75/early, twilight; $39.50/morning and afternoon; non-resident add $8.
Clearview Golf Course	Queens	202-12 Willets Point Blvd	718-229-2570	18 holes, par 70	Weekend fees $17.75/early, twilight/$39.50 morning and afternoon–weekday fees $16.75–$28, non-residents add $8.
Douglaston Golf Course	Queens	63-20 Marathon Pkwy, Douglaston	718-224-6566	18 holes, par 67	Weekend fees $17.75/early, twilight/$39.50 morning and afternoon–weekday fees $16.75–$28, non-residents add $8.
Forest Park Golf Course	Queens	101 Forest Park Dr, Woodhaven	718-296-0999	18 holes, par 70	Weekend fees $17.75/early, twilight/$39.50 morning and afternoon–weekday fees $16.75–$28, non-residents add $8.
Kissena Park Golf Course	Queens	164-15 Booth Memorial Ave	718-939-4594	18 holes, Par 64	Weekend fees $17.75/early, twilight/$39.50 morning and afternoon–weekday fees $16.75–$28, non-residents add $8.

Driving Ranges		*Address*	*Phone*	*Fee*
Brooklyn Sports Center	Brooklyn	3200 Flatbush Ave	718-253-6816	$10 for 150 balls, $12 for 285 balls
Chelsea Piers: Pier 59	Manhattan	Pier 59	212-336-6400	$20 for 118 balls, $30 for 186 balls
Randall's Island Golf	Manhattan	1 Randalls Is Rd	212-427-5689	$12 for 119 balls
Center Golden Bear	Queens	232-01 Northern Blvd	718-225-9187	$10 for large bucket, $7.50 for small bucket

For swimming pools in Manhattan, you pretty much have two options: pay exorbitant gym fees or health club fees in order to use the private swimming facilities, or wait until the summer to share the city's free outdoor pools with openly urinating summer camp attendees. OK, so it's not that bad! Some YMCAs and YWCAs have nice indoor pools, and their fees are reasonable. And several of the same New York public recreation centers that have outdoor pools (and some that do not) have indoor pools for year-round swimming. Though plenty of kids use the pools, there are dedicated adult swim hours in the mornings, at lunch time, and in the evenings (pee-free if you get there early). Just don't forget to follow each pool's admittance ritual, strange as it may seem—the locker room attendants generally rule with an iron fist. And if you can wait the obligatory 30 minutes, there's an authentic local food court near the standout public pool in Red Hook (155 Bay St, Brooklyn).

Then there's the Hudson. Yes, we're serious. There are about eight races in the Hudson each year, and the water quality is tested before each race. New York City also has some great beaches for swimming, including Coney Island, Manhattan Beach, and the Rockaways. If you prefer your swimming area enclosed, check out the pool options in Manhattan:

Pools	*Address*	*Phone*	*Type*	*Fees*	*Map*
All Star Fitness Center	75 West End Ave	212-265-8200	Indoor	$16/day	14
Asphalt Green	555 E 90th St	212-369-8890	Indoor	$25/day	17
Asser Levy Recreation Center	E 23rd St & Asser Levy Pl	212-447-2020	Indoor, Outdoor	Outdoor free, Indoor $75/year	10
Athletic and Swim Club at Equitable Center	787 Seventh Ave	212-265-3490	Indoor	Call for fees	12
Bally Toal Fitness	139 W 32nd St	212-465-1750	Indoor	$25/day	9
Bally Toal Fitness	350 W 50th St	212-265-9400	Indoor	$25/day	11
Battery Park Swim & Fitness Center	375 South End Ave	212-321-1117	Indoor	Call for fees	p234
Chelsea Piers Sports Center	19th St & Hudson River Park	212-336-6000	Indoor	$75/year	8
Chelsea Recreation Center	430 W 25th St	212-255-3705	Indoor	$75/year	8
Excelsior Athletic Club	301 E 57th St	212-688-5280	Indoor	$25/day	7
Gravity Fitness Center at Le Parker Meridien	119 W 56th St	212-708-73400	Indoor	$50/day	12
Hamilton Fish Recreation Center	128 Pitt St	212-387-7687	Outdoor - Summer months	Free	4
Hansborough Recreation Center	35 W 134th St	212-234-9603	Indoor	$75/year	19
Highbridge	2301 Amsterdam Ave	212-927-2400	Outdoor - Summer months	Free	23
Jackie Robinson Pool	85 Bradhurst Ave	212-234-9606	Outdoor - Summer months	Free	21
John Jay	E 77th St & Cherokee Pl	212-794-6566	Outdoor - Summer months	Free	15
Lasker Pool	110th St & Lenox Ave	212-534-7639	Outdoor - Summer months	Free	19
Lenox Hill Neighborhood House	331 E 70th St	212-744-5022	Indoor	Call for fees	15
Manhattan Plaza Health Club	482 W 43rd St	212-563-7001	Indoor - Summer months	$35/day	11
Marcus Garvey Swimming Pool	13 E 124th St	212-410-2818	Outdoor - Summer months	Free	19
Millennium UN Plaza Hotel Health Club	1 United Nations Plaza	212-702-5016	Indoor	$30/day or $88/month	13
New York Health & Racquet Club	110 W 56th St	212-541-7200	Indoor	$50/day or $99/month	12
New York Health & Racquet Club	115 E 57th St	212-826-9650	Indoor	$50/day or $99/month	13
New York Health & Racquet Club	132 E 45th St	212-986-3100	Indoor	$50/day or $99/month	13
New York Health & Racquet Club	1433 York Ave	212-737-6666	Indoor	$50/day or $99/month	15
New York Health & Racquet Club	20 E 50th St	212-593-1500	Indoor	$50/day or $99/month	12
New York Health & Racquet Club	24 E 13th St	212-924-4600	Indoor	$50/day or $$99/month	6
New York Health & Racquet Club	39 Whitehall St	212-269-9800	Indoor	$50/day or $99/month	1
New York Health & Racquet Club	62 Cooper Sq	212-904-0400	Indoor	$50/day or $99/month	6
New York Sports Club	1601 Broadway	212-977-8880	Indoor	$25/day	12
New York Sports Club	1637 Third Ave	212-987-7200	Indoor	$25/day	17
New York Sports Club	614 Second Ave	212-213-5999	Indoor	$25/day	10
Recreation Center 54	348 E 54th St	212-754-5411	Indoor	$75/year	13
Recreation Center 59	533 W 59th St	212-397-3159	Indoor	$75/year	11
Reebok Sports Club NY	160 Columbus Ave	212-362-6800	Indoor	$188/month	14
Riverbank State Park	679 Riverside Dr	212-694-3600	Indoor - Summer months	$2/day	21
Sheltering Arms	Amsterdam & W 129 St	212-662-6191	Indoor, Outdoor	$75/year	18
Sheraton New York Health Club	811 Seventh Ave	212-621-8591	Indoor - Summer months	$40/day	12
Thomas Jefferson Park	2180 First Ave	212-860-1383	Outdoor - Summer months	Free	20
Tompkins Square Mini Pool	500 E 9th St	212-387-7685	Outdoor - Summer months	Free	7
Tony Dapolito Recreation Center	1 Clarkson St	212-242-5228	Indoor, Outdoor	$75/year	5
UN Plaza Health Club	1 UN Plz 41st Floor	212-702-5016	Indoor	$30/day or $88/month	13
West End Sports Club	75 West End Ave	212-265-8200	Indoor	$16/day	14
YMCA	1395 Lexington Ave	212-415-5700	Indoor	$30/day or $88/month	17
YMCA	180 W 135th St	212-281-4100	Indoor	$30/day or $88/month	19
YMCA	224 E 47th St	212-756-9600	Indoor	$30/day or $88/month	13
YMCA	344 E 14th St	212-780-0800	Indoor	$20/day	6

General Information

Manhattan Parks Dept: 212-360-8131 • Website: www.nycgovparks.org
Permit Locations: The Arsenal, 830 Fifth Ave & 64th St; Paragon Sporting Goods Store, 867 Broadway & 18th St

Overview

There are more tennis courts on the island of Manhattan than you might think, although getting to them may be a bit more than you bargained for. Most of the public courts in Manhattan are either smack in the middle of Central Park or are on the edges of the city—such as Hudson River Park (Map 5), East River Park (Map 7) and Riverside Park (Map 16). These courts in particular can make for some pretty windy playing conditions.

Tennis

Tennis	*Address*	*Phone*	*Type/ # of Cts./Surface*	*Map*
Coles Center, NYU	181 Mercer St	212-998-2045	Schools, 9 courts, Rubber	6
Midtown Tennis Club	341 Eighth Ave	212-989-8572	Private, 8 courts, Har-Tru	8
Manhattan Plz Racquet Club	450 W 43rd St	212-594-0554	Private, 5 courts, Cushioned Hard	11
Millennium UN Plaza Hotel Gym	2nd Ave & 44th St	212-758-1234	Private, 1 court, Supreme	13
River Club	447 E 52nd St	212-751-0100	Private, 2 courts, Clay	13
The Tennis Club	15 Vanderbilt Ave, 3rd Fl	212-687-3841	Private, 2 courts, Hard	13
Town Tennis Club	430 E 56th St	212-752-4059	Private, 2 courts, Clay, Hard	13
Rockefeller University	1230 York Ave	212-327-8000	Schools, 1 court, Hard	15
Sutton East Tennis Club	488 E 60th St	212-751-3452	Private, 8 courts, Clay, Available Oct–April.	15
Central Park Tennis Center	93rd St near West Dr	212-280-0205	Public, Outdoor, 26 Fast-Dry, 4 Hard	16
Riverside Park	Riverside Dr & W 96th St	212-469-2006	Public, Outdoor, 10 courts, Clay	16
PS 146 Ann M Short	421 E 106th St	n/a	Schools, 3 courts, Hard	17
Tower Tennis Courts	1725 York Ave	212-860-2464	Private, 2 courts, Hard	17
PS 125 Ralph Bunche	425 W 123rd St	n/a	Schools, 3 courts, Hard	18
Riverbank State Park	W 145th St & Riverside Dr	212-694-3600	Public, Outdoor, 1 court, Hard	21
F Johnson Playground	W 151st St & Seventh Ave	212-234-9609	Public, Outdoor, 8 courts, Hard	22
Fort Washington Park	Hudson River & 170th St	212-304-2322	Public, Outdoor, 10 courts, Hard	23
The Dick Savitt Tennis Center	575 W 218th St	212-942-7100	Private, 6 courts, Hard	25
Inwood Hill Park	207th St & Seaman Ave	212-304-2381	Public, Outdoor, 9 courts, Hard	25
Roosevelt Island Racquet Club	281 Main St	212-935-0250	Private, 12 courts, Clay	p260
Randall's Island	East & Harlem Rivers	212-860-1827	Public, Outdoor, 11 courts, Hard	p254
Randall's Island Indoor Tennis	Randall's Island Park	212-427-6150	Private, 4 courts, Hard Available Oct–April.	p254

Getting a Permit

The tennis season, according to the NYC Parks Department, lasts from April 7 to November 18. Permits are good for use until the end of the season at all public courts in all boroughs, and are good for one hour of singles or two hours of doubles play. Fees are:

Juniors (17 yrs and under) $10
Senior Citizen (62 yrs and over) $20
Adults (18–61 yrs) $100
Single-play tickets $7

When it comes to yoga, New York City has it better than other places in the country, where yoga is often confined to sweaty, ping-pong-table-inhabited back rooms in makeshift recreation centers. Luckily, New Yorkers have an array of charming, airy, sometimes even glossy studios in which to practice—as well as what seems to be an infinite variety of yoga styles to choose from. You can mellow out in meditation, relax in Restorative, practice Pranayama, kick-it Kundalini style, vie for the Vinyasa vibe, jive with Jivamukti, awaken your spirit with Ashtanga, investigate Iyengar, or bend it like Bikram—just to name a few. To get you started, here's a short list of places to try. Remember, it's always a good idea to contact studios in advance for information about their different approaches to classes, what branches of yoga they teach, class sizes, appropriate attire, cost, and schedules.

Word to the wise: You may want to begin with an introductory class wherever you land. Even seasoned yogis will want to familiarize themselves with the methods of each studio before jumping in headstand first.

Yoga	*Address*	*Phone*	*Website*	*Map*
Kula Yoga Project	28 Warren St, 4th Fl	212-945-4460	www.kulayoga.com	2
Dance New Amsterdam	280 Broadway	212-625-8369	www.dnadance.org/site	3
Virayoga	580 Broadway, Ste 1109	212-334-9960	www.virayoga.com	3
Yogaworks Soho	459 Broadway	212-965-0801	www.yogaworks.com	3
Integral Yoga Institute	227 W 13th St	212-929-0586	www.integralyogany.org	5
Mahayogi Yoga Mission	228 Bleeker St	212-807-8903	www.mahayogiyogamission.org	5
Practice Yoga West Village	240 W 14th St	212-255-7588	www.practiceyoga.com	5
Yamuna	132 Perry St	212-633-2143	www.yamunastudio.com	5
exhale Soho	68 Spring St	212-249-3000	www.exhalespa.com	6
Jivamukti Yoga School Downtown	841 Broadway	212-353-0214	www.jivamuktiyoga.com	6
Lila Yoga, Dharma and Wellness	302 Bowery	212-254-2130	www.lilawellness.com	6
New York Open Center	83 Spring St	212-219-2527	www.opencenter.org	6
OM Yoga Center	826 Broadway, 6th Fl	212-254-9642	www.omyoga.com	6
Three Jewels Yoga	61 Fourth Ave	212-475-6650	www.threejewels.org	6
Virayoga	580 Broadway	212-334-9960	www.virayoga.com	6
Ashtanga Yoga Shala	295 E 8th St	212-614-9537	www.ashtangayogashala.net	7
Ramakrishnananda Yoga Vedanta Mission	96 Ave B	646-436-7010	www.ramakrishnananda.com	7
Bikram Yoga NYC Flatiron	182 FIfth Ave	212-206-9400	www.bikramyoganyc.com	9
The Breathing Project	15 W 26th St	212-979-9642	www.breathingproject.org	9
Fluid Fitness	1026 Sixth Ave	212-278-8330	www.yogamovesgyro.com	9
Iyengar Yoga Institute of New York	150 W 22nd St	212-691-9642	www.iyengarnyc.org	9
Kundalini Yoga East	873 Broadway	212-982-5959	www.kundaliniyogaeast.com	9
Laughing Lotus	59 W 19th St, 3rd Fl	212-414-2903	www.laughinglotus.com	9
Manhattan Dahn Yoga Studio	830 Sixth Ave	212-725-3262	www.dahnyoga.com	9
Movements Afoot	151 W 30th St	212-904-1399	www.movementsafoot.com	9
Panetta Movement Center	214 W 29th St	212-239-0831	www.panettamovementcenter.com	9
Shambhala Meditation Center of New York	118 W 22nd St	212-675-6544	www.ny.shambhala.org	9
Sivananda Yoga Vedanta Center	243 W 24th St	212-255-4560	www.sivananda.org	9
Union Square Dahn Yoga Studio	37 Union Sq W	212-691-7799	www.dahnyoga.com	9
Universal Force Healing Center	7 W 24th St	917-606-1730	www.universalforceyoga.com	9
Yoga Works Downtown	138 Fifth Ave	212-647-9642	www.yogaworks.com	9
Dharma Mittra Yoga New York Center	297 Third Ave	212-889-8160	www.dharmayogacenter.com	10
New York Underground Fitness	440 W 57th St	212-957-4781	www.nyundergroundfitness.com	11
Sonic Yoga	754 Ninth Ave	212-397-6344	www.sonicyoga.com	11
Bikram Yoga NYC Midtown	797 Eighth Ave	212-245-2525	www.bikramyoganyc.com	12
BR Manhattan Dahn Yoga Studio	532 Madison Ave	212-935-5777	www.dahnyoga.com	12
exhale	150 Central Park S	212-249-3000	www.exhalespa.com	12
Healthy Tao	250 W 49th St	212-586-2100	www.healthytao.com	12
Prana Mandir Yoga Studio	4 W 43rd St	212-803-5446	www.pranamandir.com	12

Reflections Yoga	250 W 49th St	212-974-2288	www.reflectionsyoga.com	12
Yoga Works Midtown	160 E 56th St	212-935-9642	www.yogaworks.com	13
Bikram Yoga NYC Upper West Side	143 W 72nd St	212-724-7303	www.bikramyoganyc.com	14
Life In Motion	2744 Broadway	212-666-0877	www.lifeinmotion.com	14
Namaste Yoga	371 Amsterdam Ave	212-580-1778	www.namasteyogacenter.net	14
Practice Yoga Upper West Side	140 W 83rd St	212-724-4884	www.practiceyoga.com	14
Steps	2121 Broadway	212-874-2410	www.stepsnyc.com	14
World Yoga Center	265 W 72nd St	212-787-4908	www.worldyogacenter.com	14
Yoga Works Westside	37 W 65th St, 4th Fl	212-769-9642	www.yogaworks.com	14
Bikram Yoga NYC Upper East Side	173 E 83rd St	212-288-9642	www.bikramyoganyc.com	15
exhale	980 Madison Ave	212-249-3000	www.exhalespa.com	15
exhale at Manhattan House	200 E 66th St	212-249-3000	www.exhalespa.com	15
Jivamukti Yoga Center Uptown	853 Lexington Ave	646-290-8106	www.jivamuktiyoga.com	15
MonQi Fitness	201 E 67th St	212-327-2170	www.monqifitness.com	15
New York Yoga HOT	132 E 85th St	212-439-9642	www.newyorkyoga.com	15
Yoga Works Eastside	1319 Third Ave	212-650-9642	www.yogaworks.com	15
Park East Dahn Yoga Studio	168 E 66th St	212-249-0077	www.dahnyoga.com	15
Baby Om	250 Riverside Dr #25	212-615-6935	www.babyom.com	16
Life In Motion Yoga	2744 Broadway	212-666-0877	www.lifeinmotion.com	16
New York Yoga	1629 York Ave	212-717-9642	www.newyorkyoga.com	17
Riverside Church Wellness Center	490 Riverside Dr	212-870-6758	www.theriversidechurchny.org	18

Whether you're looking for a new hobby or need a new atmosphere in which to booze (that isn't your 300 sq. ft. apartment), a good pool-hall is a great way to get the job done. Or perhaps you simply enjoy a hearty game of 8-ball, and it's as simple as that; in any case, an eclectic mix of options dot the island of Manhattan.

If you're in search of a laid-back, nonsense-free setting, **SoHo Billiards (Map 6)** is best. It occupies a large space with a ton of tables, cheap rates and drinks, small crowds, and a low-key, local scene. **Fat Cat Billiards (Map 5)** is another great option if you're looking for a chill setting—located underground in a dim basement, it holds 20 tables and offers an hourly rate of $4.50 (not to mention the $2 Pabst). For those of you who tire of shiny balls and green felt, there are multiple Scrabble, checkers, and chess stations scattered about—and if that's not enough, there are nightly jazz and comedy performances in the performance room.

In what appears to be a new breed of pool hall, **Slate Resaurant Bar & Billiards (Map 9)** actually has a velvet rope outside, as if to suggest there's something legitimately exclusive about it. Alas, the SoHo House it's not, although there are two levels with plenty of tables, a clean and comfy lounge setting around the bar, plenty of top-shelf liquor—and extremely loud Top-40 hits blasting on the speakers. Accordingly, the staff can have a bit of an attitude, which is more bewildering than anything else. If you're uptown, head instead to the recently renovated **East Side Billiards and Bar (Map 16)**, where in addition to the 13 tables, you can also play ping-pong. Or ditch your friends and wander into the attached video game arcade, the largest of its kind outside of Times Square (so they say). On the other hand, if you don't have any friends to begin with, think about signing up for one of the East Side seasonal pool leagues—where you not only get to compete and socialize, but receive additional discounts. Last but not least is **Amsterdam Billiards Club (Map 6)**—Manhattan's swankiest billiards parlor. With its mahogany bar, multiple fireplaces, and extensive wine list, the club is best suited for corporate events and private parties (for 20 to 500 people). It also boasts the largest co-ed league in the country and offers lessons for all skill levels.

So what are you waiting for? Turn off the latest CSI spin-off (or whatever crap you're watching), get off the couch, and give yourself a real challenge—play some pool!

Billiards	*Address*	*Phone*	*Map*	*Fee*
Tropical 128	128 Elizabeth St	212-925-8219	3	$8 per hour per person; $12 per hour for 2 people
Fat Cat Billiards	75 Christopher St	212-675-6056	5	$5 per hour per player
Amsterdam Billiards and Bar	110 E 11th St	212-995-1314	6	$6 per person per hour
Pressure	110 University Pl	212-352-1161	6	$26 per hour
SoHo Billiards	298 Mulberry St	212-925-3753	6	$7 per hour per table
Slate Restaurant Bar & Billiards	54 W 21st St	212-989-0096	9	$17 per hour for two players
East Side Billiard Club	163 E 86th St	212-831-7665	16	$7.50 per hour per person
Post Billiards Café	154 Post Ave	212-569-1840	25	Weekdays, $8 per hour for 2 people; weekends 10 per hour for 2 people

If you want to go bowling in Manhattan, you have four solid options. Keep in mind that there's just about no way to bowl cheaply, so if you're struggling to keep a positive balance in your bank account, you may want to find another activity or head out to New Jersey.

The best priced bowling can be found just north of historic 125th Street at **Harlem Lanes (Map 19)**. Games start at $5.50 at this two floor, 24-lane alley. Other features include a café, a sports bar, a lounge, party room (available for children's birthday parties as well as adult gatherings), and an arcade. This alley also hosts singles nights, family bowling night, and a Sunday gospel brunch.

For those looking to affordably bowl lower down on the island, hit **Leisure Time Bowl (Map 12)** where you can pay per game ($7.50 weekdays, $9.50 nights and weekends) or per lane (starting at $50/hour). Connected to the Port Authority (remember this in case you have a long wait for a bus), Leisure Time has 30 lanes, a full bar and pub menu, and two game-rooms, with a new dance floor and lounge on the way. You can even make online reservations at www.leisuretimebowl.com (yes, bowling has hit the 21st century). At Chelsea Piers, you'll find the **300 New York (Map 8)**. Part of the massive AMF national chain of bowling alleys, 300 offers 40 lanes. On weekend nights, the center plays host to "Xtreme Bowling," a glow-in-the-dark "bowling party" featuring music, fog machines, and an "enhanced" rate of $8.75 per person per game. Bring your credit card to 300—you'll need it after a few short hours in the lanes.

Honestly, if you're looking for "extreme" glow-in-the-dark bowling, skip Chelsea Piers and go downtown to **Bowlmor Lanes (Map 6)**. On Monday nights, "Night Strike" is the place to be. $22 per person provides shoes and all the games you can bowl—assuming you can handle the sometimes long wait (not such a big deal since they offer free pool upstairs along with not-so-free cocktails in the lounge).

Finally, for the world's ultimate (hipster) bowling experience, head to **The Gutter (Map 29)** in Brooklyn—the borough's first new bowling alley in over fifty years. It's like a Stroh's ad from the 1980s (except the beer is fancier). It doesn't get any better than bowling on beautiful, old-school lanes and drinking tasty microbrews with your buddies. But The Gutter now has some serious competition, as sprawling **Brooklyn Bowl (Map 29)** has opened two blocks away. Featuring food by Blue Ribbon and live bands many nights, it's already become another great bowling option—and again, far better than anything in Manhattan.

Manhattan	*Address*	*Phone*	*Map*	*Fees*
300	Chelsea Piers, Pier 60	212-835-2695	8	$8.75/game/person. $5 for shoes.
Bowlmor Lanes	110 University Pl	212-255-8188	6	Su–Th: Before 5pm: $9.45/game; After 5pm $9.95/game; Fri-Sat: Before 5pm: $9.95/game; After 5pm: $10.95/game; Shoes: $6
Harlem Lanes	2116 Adam Clayton Powell Jr Blvd	212-678-2695	19	M–Th all day and Fr before 6pm: $5.50/game. Fr after 6 pm and weekends: $7.50/game. $4.50 shoes.
Leisure Time	625 Eighth Ave, 2nd Fl	212-268-6909	12	Weekdays: $7.50/person/game. Weeknights and weekends: $9.50/person/game.
Lucky Strike Lanes	624 W 42nd St	646-829-0170	11	$25 per lane per 1/2 hour, $4 shoes.

Brooklyn	*Address*	*Phone*	*Fees*
Brooklyn Bowl	61 Wythe Ave	718-963-3369	$25 per lane per 1/2 hour, $3.50 shoes.
Gil Hodges Lanes	6161 Strickland Ave, Marine Park	718-763-3333	$6.00-$8.00, $4.25 for shoes.
The Gutter	200 N 14th St, Williamsburg	718-387-3585	$6-$7/game/person, $2 for shoes.
Maple Lanes	1570 60th St, Borough Park	718-331-9000	$4.50–$6.50 per game, $4.25 shoes.
Melody Lanes	461 37th St, Sunset Park	718-832-2695	$5.50–$7.00 per game, $3.50 shoes.
Shell Lanes	1 Bouck Ct, Coney Island	718-336-6700	$3.25–$5.25 per game, $3.50 shoes.

Queens	*Address*	*Phone*	*Fees*
AMF 34th Avenue Lanes	69-10 34th Ave, Woodside	718-651-0440	$4–$6 per game, $4.75 for shoes
Astoria Bowl - Maric Lanes	19-45 49th St, Astoria	718-274-1910	$4 per game, $6 on weekends, $4 for shoes
Cozy Bowl	98-18 Rockaway Blvd, Ozone Park	718-843-5553	$3–$6 per game, $3.50 for shoes.
JIB Lanes	67-19 Parsons Blvd, Flushing	718-591-0600	$3.75 per game, $3.50 for shoes.
Whitestone Lanes	30-05 Whitestone Expy, Flushing	718-353-6300	$4.50-$7.50 per game, $4.50 shoes.

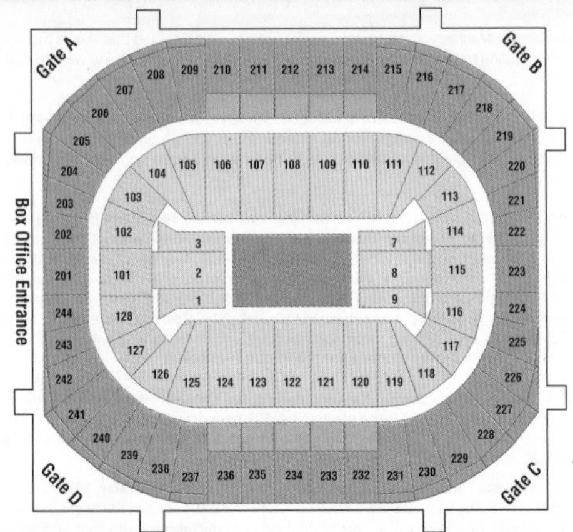

General Information

Address: 165 Mulberry St Newark, NJ 07102
Website: www.prucenter.com
Devils: www.devils.nhl.com
Nets: www.nba.com/nets
Seton Hall: www.shupirates.com
Ticketmaster: 800-745-3000, www.ticketmaster.com

Overview

Opened in October 2007, the Prudential Center (or "The Rock" to the media and fans) is a state of the art arena in downtown Newark. Yes, you heard that right, downtown Newark is now a prime destination for Devils, Nets, and Seton Hall basketball fans. The Rock is hands down a billion times better than the cold and charmless Izod Center which is sitting in the middle of the Meadowlands all alone and empty except for the occasional Doo Wop or Megadeth concert (no joke). Its future is as murky as a bucketful of Meadowlands swamp water. Meanwhile the future of New Jersey sports never looked better with the Prudential Center. With a capacity of 18,000 and all the bells and whistles of the modern sports going experience, Devils fans are loving this place. And at least for awhile, Nets fans will be watching their team play here too. The Nets are scheduled to move to Brooklyn sometime in the next few years, but don't hold your breath. The Rock is probably a temporary home, unless Brooklyn runs Ratner and his Arena/Atlantic Yards Project out on a rail.

How to Get There—Driving

From New York City take the George Washington Bridge or Lincoln Tunnel and follow signs to New Jersey Turnpike South. From the NJ Turnpike Southbound take Exit 15W onto I-280 westbound. Turn right on Exit 15 A towards Route 21 southbound. Turn right onto Rector Street. Turn left onto Broad Street southbound. Continue on Broad Street to Lafayette Street and make a left. Prudential Center will be on your left hand side. According to the website The Prudential Center "is one of the most easily accessible arenas in the country." There is lots of parking, but traffic can still be unpredictable. Always allow more time than you think you'll need. Highways surrounding the arena include 280, 78, NJ Turnpike, 1 & 9, 21, 22, Garden State Parkway, 80 and NJ 3.

How to Get There—Mass Transit

No need to get on a bus anymore at Port Authority thank goodness for Devils and Nets games. Just take NJ Transit to Broad Street Station, then switch to Newark Light Rail to Newark Penn Station, which is only two blocks west of the Prudential Center. Even easier is taking the PATH train to Newark Station. The arena is only a short walk away. Call or check the website for more details.

How to Get Tickets

The box office is open Monday to Saturday from 11 am to 6 pm and is closed Sunday, unless there is an event. To purchase tickets without going to the box office, call Ticketmaster at 800-745-3000, or visit their website. Or try stubhub.com the day of the game to find some good deals.

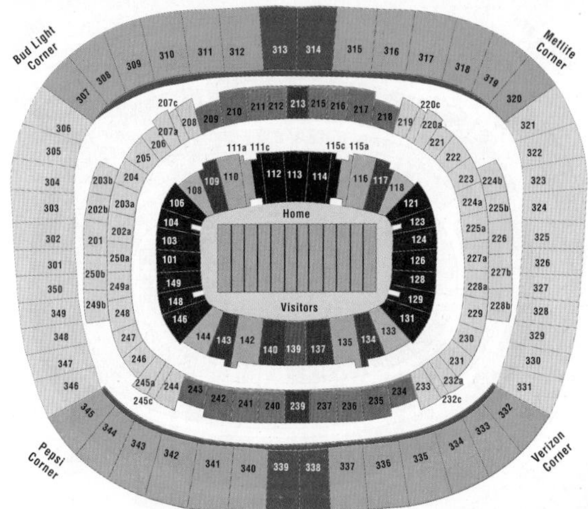

General Information

Address:	East Rutherford, NJ 07073
Phone:	201-935-3900
Giants:	www.giants.com
Jets:	www.newyorkjets.com
Red Bulls:	www.newyorkredbulls.com
Ticketmaster:	800-745-3000, www.ticketmaster.com

Overview

Well, well, how times have changed. Who's the top team moving into the brand-new "Meadowlands Stadium?" That's right—the JETS J-E-T-S JETS! How 'bout dem Jets, fans? Rex Ryan's team outdid itself in making the playoffs, then serving some serious whup-ass on the road in two playoff games in Cincinnati and San Diego, before finally falling to the uber-professional Colts in the AFC Championship Game.

Meanwhile, the Giants...were golfing, having failed to make the playoffs entirely. Of course, with the Giants having won a Super Bowl as recently as 2007, the claim can be made that there are two very good franchises about to move in to the new stadium. We'll see how we like it, but the fact remains that they spent a billion dollars to build it and guess what? Still no roof. So we'll be freezing our asses off in December again. But then again, maybe that's the way football is supposed to be...at least if you're a cheese-head.

How to Get There —Driving

Meadowlands Stadium is only five miles from the Lincoln Tunnel (closer to Midtown than Shea Stadium, even), but leave early if you want to get to the game on time—remember that the Giants and the Jets are a) sold out for every game and b) have tons of fans from both Long Island and the five boroughs. You can take the Lincoln Tunnel to Route 3 W to Route 120 N, or you can try either the Holland Tunnel to the New Jersey Turnpike N to Exit 16W, or the George Washington Bridge to the New Jersey Turnpike S to Exit 16W. Accessing the stadium from Exit 16W allows direct access to parking areas. Parking costs $15 for most events.

How to Get There–Mass Transit

On game days NJ Transit now runs trains directly to the stadium. The new stop is called Meadowland Sports Complex. Train service will begin about 3 ½ hours prior to a major event or football game. After events, trains will depart frequently from the Meadowlands for up to two hours.

How to Get Tickets

For the Jets and the Giants, scalpers and friends are the only options. For the Red Bulls and for concerts, you can call Ticketmaster or visit the website.

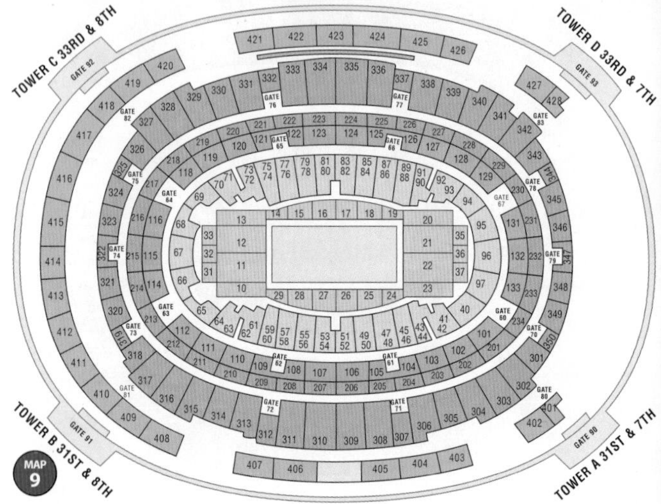

General Information

NFT Map:	9
Address:	4 Pennsylvania Plz New York, NY 10001
Phone:	212-465-6741
Website:	www.thegarden.com
Knicks:	www.nyknicks.com
Liberty:	www.nyliberty.com
Rangers:	www.newyorkrangers.com
Ticketmaster:	800-745-3000, www.ticketmaster.com

Overview

Once resembling the Doge's Palace in Venice (c.1900), the since-relocated Altoid 'tween Seventh and Eighth Avenues atop Penn Station remains one of the legendary venues in sport, becoming so almost solely by way of the sport of boxing. It now, for good and ill, houses the NBA's Knicks (catch Spike Lee and various supermodels courtside), NHL's Rangers, The Liberty of the WNBA, St. John's University's Red Storm, as well as concerts, tennis tournaments, dog shows, political conventions, and, for those of you with 2+ years of graduate school, monster truck rallies and "professional" wrestling. There's also The Theater at Madison Square Garden for more intimate shows. Check out MSG's website for a full calendar of events.

How to Get There–Mass Transit

MSG is right above Penn Station, which makes getting there very easy. You can take the A C E and 1 2 3 lines to 34th Street and Penn Station, or the N R Q W, B D F V, and PATH lines to 34th Street and 6th Avenue. The Long Island Rail Road also runs right into Penn Station.

How to Get Tickets

For single seats for the Knicks and the Rangers, you can try Ticketmaster, but a better bet would be to try the "standby" line (show up a half-hour before game time and wait). You can find some decent deals online at Craigslist, Stubhub, and ebay when the Knick are riding a losing streak (which definitely has been the case in recent years). The ubiquitous ticket scalpers surrounding the Garden are a good last resort for when your rich out-of-town friends breeze in to see a game. Liberty tickets (and tickets for other events) are usually available through Ticketmaster.

PAGE 230

General Information

Address:	123-01 Roosevelt Ave & 126th St Flushing, Queens
Shea Stadium/Citi Field Box Office:	718-507-TIXX
Website:	www.mets.com
Mets Clubhouse Shops:	11 W 42nd St & Roosevelt Field Mall, Garden City, LI
Ferry:	800-BOATRIDE or 732-872-2628

Overview

The t-shirts reading, "I'm Still Calling It Shea," were ready by the new stadium's opening, though given the financial crisis some of us have been referring to it as "Debit's Field" or "Two-Shea," but naming aside it's actually a pretty nice ballpark. Fans enter through The Jackie Robinson Rotunda, guaranteeing that young fans who know nothing of segregated baseball and separate drinking fountains will get a little lesson on civil rights as they read the inspiring quotes etched in the façade and pose for pictures next to Robert Indiana's sculpture of the number 42. Once inside you might get the feeling you're at a food court with a ball game going on in the background, but the selections are pretty good, including Shake Shack, Nathan's, Blue Smoke and El Verano Taquería. There are even some spots where you can get a decent sized beer on tap for $6 (at press time). You can buy nostalgic sports gear at "47" (named for the year Robinson broke into the majors) and women can buy their Mets bikinis and form-fitting jeans with a pair of eye-catching Mets logos on the butt at Touch by Alyssa Milano. There are about 14,000 fewer seats than at Shea, making affordable seating less available, but the Mets tier their ticket prices so that a weeknight game against a lousy team can be a pretty good deal, even if you have no view of the left field corner. The fence has got a few crazy angles in hopes that it'll help Jose Reyes hit more triples. Oh yes, and those people protesting nearby are the hard-working small business owners that the city is kicking out in order to improve the surroundings.

How To Get Tickets

You can order Mets tickets by phone through the Mets' box office, on the internet through the Mets' website, or at the Mets Clubhouse Shops (11 West 42nd St, the Manhattan Mall, and Roosevelt Field Mall in Garden City).

How To Get There—Driving

Yeah. Good luck trying to make the first pitch on a weekday night. But if you must, take the Robert F. Kennedy Bridge to the Grand Central Parkway; the Mid-Town Tunnel to the Long Island Expressway to the Grand Central; or the Brooklyn-Queens Expressway to the LIE to the Grand Central. If you want to try and avoid the highways, get yourself over to Astoria Boulevard in Queens, make a right on 108th Street, then a left onto Roosevelt Avenue.

How To Get There—Mass Transit

The good news is that the 7 train runs straight to Citi Field. The bad news is it's the only train that goes there. However, it will get you there and back (eventually), and the 7 is accessible from almost all the other train lines in Manhattan. Alternately, you can take the E, F, G, or R to Roosevelt Avenue and pick up the 7 there, saving about 30 minutes. Also, NY Water Taxi runs a ferry service (the "Mets Express") to Citi Field from the South Street Seaport, E 34th Street, and E 94th Street. The other option is the Port Washington LIRR from Penn Station, which stops at Citi Field on game days.

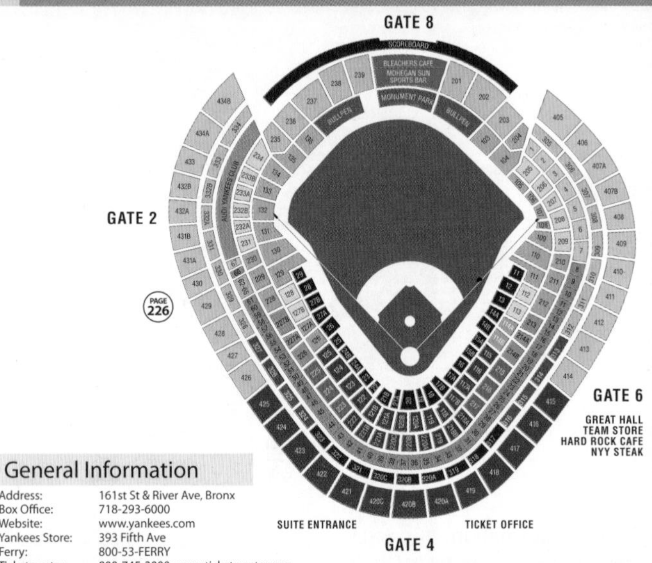

General Information

Address:	161st St & River Ave, Bronx
Box Office:	718-293-6000
Website:	www.yankees.com
Yankees Store:	393 Fifth Ave
Ferry:	800-53-FERRY
Ticketmaster:	800-745-3000; www.ticketmaster.com

Overview

New Yankee Stadium is here. And it's big. Very, very big. There's a lot of great amenities (the Lobel's Sliced Steak Sandwich Cart is far and away our favorite), but there's also a lot to complain about. In no particular order: seats cost more, most seats are farther away from the field, you can barely hear the crack of the bat, the stadium doesn't get as loud anymore, there is a stupid wire that runs across your field of vision on the first and third base lines on the upper levels, you have to pay extra to get into the outfield bar, you can't get in to one of the restaurants without a fancy seat, half the fancy seats are unsold so there is all this empty space where all the best seats are, the stadium floors are rough plain concrete and the ramps and staircases are so bare as to feel almost prison-like, you still can't bring a bag into the f***ing place… we could keep going. While the video screen is amazing, we'd prefer to actually watch the game LIVE by being CLOSE TO THE FIELD. And since the policy of not showing any play that is remotely controversial (i.e. interesting) on replay still seems to be in place, why go at all? Honestly, we're thinking of switching our allegiances; maybe we'll at least wait for Mo to retire and Jeter to get his 3,000 hit. At least the team is good; we say: enjoy watching them on TV.

While the rant above still applies regarding the stadium, we do have to congratulate the Yankees on winning it all again in 2009. The team itself is back with a vengeance, as free agent signings Mark Teixiera, CC Sabathia, and A.J. Burnett all paid off. We say sayonara and good luck to stalwarts Johnny Damon and Hideki Matsui; we'll see what Mr. Granderson does in 2010. Chances are: the Yankees probably won't suck.

How to Get There—Driving

Driving to Yankee Stadium from Manhattan isn't as bad as you might think. Your best bet is to take the Willis Avenue Bridge from either First Avenue or FDR Drive and get on the Major Deegan for about one mile until you spot the stadium exit. From the Upper West Side, follow Broadway up to 155th Street and use the Macombs Dam Bridge to cross over the river to the stadium (thus avoiding crosstown traffic). Parking (in contrast to ticket prices) is cheap, especially at lots a few blocks away from the stadium.

How to Get There—Mass Transit

Getting to the stadium by subway is easy. The 4 and D and the B (on weekdays) all run express to the stadium, and you can easily hook up with those lines at several junctions in Manhattan. And now you can take Metro-North, since the city built a dedicated station just for Yankee Stadium.

How to Get Tickets

You can purchase tickets by phone through Ticketmaster, at the box office or the Yankee store, or online through either Ticketmaster or the Yankees website. And of course the illegal scalpers who are all over the damned place.

Beyond the obvious crowd-pleasers, New York City landmarks are super-subjective. One person's favorite cobblestoned alley is some developer's idea of prime real estate. Bits of old New York disappear to differing amounts of fanfare and make room for whatever it is we'll be romanticizing in the future. Ain't that the circle of life? The landmarks discussed are highly idiosyncratic choices, and this list is by no means complete or even logical, but we've included an array of places, from world famous to little known, all worth visiting.

Coolest Skyscrapers

Most visitors to New York go to the top of the **Empire State Building (Map 9)**, but it's far more familiar to New Yorkers from afar—as a directional guide, or as a tip-off to obscure holidays (orange & white means it's time to celebrate ASPCA Day again!). If it's class you're looking for, the **Chrysler Building (Map 13)** has it in spades. Unfortunately, this means that only the "classiest" are admitted to the top floors. Other midtown highlights include the **Citicorp Center (Map 13)**, a building that breaks out of the boxy tower form, and the **GE Building (Map 12)**, one of the steepest-looking skyscrapers in the city. More neck-craning excitement can be found in the financial district, including the **Woolworth Building (Map 3)**, the **American International Building (Map 1)** at 70 Pine Street (with private spire rooms accessible only to the connected), **40 Wall Street (Map 1)**, the **Bankers Trust Company Building (Map 1)**, and **20 Exchange Place (Map 1)**. For a fine example of blending old, new, and eco-friendly architecture styles, check out the stunning **Hearst Tower (Map 12)**.

Best Bridges

The Brooklyn Bridge (Map 3) is undoubtedly the best bridge in New York—aesthetically, historically, and practically; you can walk or bike across on a wooden sidewalk high above the traffic. It's also worth walking across the George Washington Bridge (Map 23), though it takes more time than you'd expect (trust us). **The Henry Hudson Bridge (Map 25)** expresses the tranquility of that part of the island—view it from Inwood Hill Park to see its graceful span over to Spuyten Duyvil.

Great Architecture

The Beaux-Arts interior of **Grand Central Terminal (Map 13)** is full of soaring arches and skylights. Head to SoHo to see the **Little Singer Building (Map 6)** and other gorgeous cast-iron structures. You can find intricately carved faces and creatures on the tenement facades of the Lower East Side. **The Flatiron (Map 9)**, once among the tallest buildings in the city, remains one of the most distinctive. **The Lever House (Map 13)** and the **Seagram Building (Map 13)** redefined corporate architecture and are great examples of Modernism. Take the Ferry to **Ellis Island (Map 1)**, devoted solely to the immigrant experience, features domed ceilings and Guastavino tiled arches. **The Guggenheim (Map 17)** is one of New York's most unique and distinctive buildings (apparently there's some art inside, too). **The Cathedral of St. John the Divine (Map 18)** has a very medieval vibe and is the world's largest unfinished cathedral—a much cooler destination than the eternally crowded **St. Patrick's Cathedral (Map 12)**.

Great Public Buildings

Once upon a time, the city felt that public buildings should inspire civic pride through great architecture. Head downtown to view **City Hall (Map 3)** (1812), **Tweed Courthouse (Map 3)** (1881), **Jefferson Market Courthouse (Map 5)** (1877—now a library), the **Municipal Building (Map 3)** (1914), and a host of other courthouses built in the early 20th century. **The Old Police Headquarters (Map 3)**, now a posh condo, would be a more celebrated building if it wasn't located on a little-trafficked block of Centre Street in Little Italy/Chinatown. And what are the chances a firehouse built today would have the same charm as the **Great Jones Firehouse (Map 6)**? If the guys are around outside, they're happy to let you in to look around.

Outdoor Spaces

Central Park obviously. **Madison Square Park (Map 9)** is not as well known as many other central city parks, but it is home to the Shake Shack, where you can grab a burger, a shake, and a bit of peace and quiet on the grass. Newly renovated **Washington Square Park (Map 6)** has re-opened its gates to the NYU students, street performers, tourists, and pot dealers that love to gather there. There's all kinds of interesting folk around **Tompkins Square Park (Map 7)**, which makes it ideal for people watching. In addition to **Union Square (Map 9)** housing a bunch of great statues (Gandhi, Washington, Lincoln), it also hosts an amazing farmers market (Mon, Wed, Fri, and Sat) and is close to great shopping. You can dream all you want about having a picnic at **Gramercy Park (Map 10)**, but until you score a coveted key (or become friends with Julia Roberts), you'll have to admire the greenery from the sidewalk like the rest of us. **Bryant Park (Map 12)** attracts a chi-chi lunch crowd (it's a Wi-Fi hotspot) and hosts movies in the summer. Next door, people lounge on the **New York Public Library (Map 12)** steps and reminisce about their favorite scene from Ghostbusters, no doubt. **Rockefeller Center (Map 12)** tends to get overrun by tourists, but it's still deserving of a visit, especially to view the Art Deco styling. **The Cloisters (Map 24)** and **Inwood Hill Park (Map 25)** are great uptown escapes. Thanks to Stuyvesant Street's diagonal path, **St. Mark's-in-the-Bowery (Map 6)** gets a nice little corner of land in front for a park, which gives a hint of its rural past. Mountainous **Marcus Garvey Park (Map 19)** in Harlem is a good destination on Sundays when the famous drum circle is in full effect.

Lowbrow Landmarks

The **Chinatown Ice Cream Factory (Map 3)** is worth a slog through Chinatown crowds on a hot day. Just around the corner is **Doyers Street (Map 3)**, which retains the slight air of danger from its gang war past. **CBGB's (Map 6)** is gone, but punk spirit survives (somewhat) on the nearby street corner known as **Joey Ramone Place (Map 6)**. If you're in to old-time debauchery, there are tons of classic and historic New York bars including the **Bridge Café (Map 1)**, **McSorley's (Map 6)**, **Pete's Tavern (Map 10)**, the **White Horse Tavern (Map 5)**, **Chumley's (Map 5)**, the **Ear Inn (Map 5)**, and **Old Town Bar (Map 9)**.

Lame, Bad & Overrated Landmarks

Even the most cynical New Yorker would have to admit that **Times Square (Map 12)** is a unique place, but the truth is that it's no fun to compete for sidewalk space with tourists in search of dinner at the Bubba Gump Shrimp Company. Despite the fantastic summer concert series, **South Street Seaport (Map 1)** is essentially a lame mall with some old ships parked nearby. But if potential plans for a public market come to fruition, we'll gladly brave the tourists to visit every weekend. **Madison Square Garden (Map 9)** doesn't really deserve its status as a great sports arena. Aside from a few shining moments, the teams there usually stink, and the architecture is mostly banal. The worst part is that the gorgeous old Penn Station was torn down to make room for it. You can see pictures of the old station when you walk through the new **Penn Station (Map 9)**, which is famous not for its totally drab and depressing environs, but because of the sheer volume of traffic it handles. **The Cross-Bronx Expressway (Map 23)** gets a mention as the worst highway ever.

Underrated Landmarks

Many of these get overlooked because they are uptown. **Grant's Tomb (Map 18)** was once one of New York's most famous attractions, but these days it's mostly a destination for history buffs. **The City College (Map 21)** campus is quite beautiful, even though a few newer buildings muck things up. Farther north, **Sylvan Terrace (Map 23)** and the **Morris-Jumel Mansion (Map 23)**, a unique block of small row houses and a revolutionary war-era house, offer a truer glimpse of old New York than the Seaport or Fraunces Tavern. Memorialized in a beloved children's book, a visit to **The Little Red Lighthouse (Map 23)** will make you feel like you're on the coast of Maine and not actually standing under the George Washington Bridge.

Map 1 • Financial District

20 Exchange Place	20 Exchange Pl	Check out the cool facade with its bronze depictions of various modes of both ancient and modern transportation.
40 Wall St	40 Wall St	The tallest building in the world upon its completion in 1930…for a day, until the Chrysler went up. Oh, and Trump owns it.
Alexander Hamilton U.S. Custom House	1 Bowling Green • 212-514-3700	Stately Cass Gilbert building; check out the oval staircases.
American International Building	70 Pine St	Great Art Deco skyscraper.
American Stock Exchange	86 Trinity Pl • 212-306-1000	New York's other stock exchange.
Bankers Trust Company Building	14 Wall St	More neck-craning excitement from the NYC skyline!
Battery Maritime Building	10 South St • 212-312-3517	Ready-to-be-converted riverfront building.
Bowling Green	Broadway & State St	Watch the tourists take pics of the bull. New York's first park.
Bridge Café	279 Water St • 212-227-3344	The oldest bar in NYC. Great vibe, good food too.
Canyon of Heroes	Broadway b/w Bowling Green & City Hall Park	Markers in the sidewalk remember those honored with a ticker tape parade.
Charging Bull	Bowling Green Park	Rub his cojones for luck.
Cunard Building	25 Broadway • 212-363-9490	Former Cunard headquarters, former post office, currently a locked building with great ceiling mosaics.
Delmonico's Building	56 Beaver St • 212-509-1144	Once the site of THE restaurant in New York.
Equitable Building	120 Broadway • 212-490-0666	Its massiveness gave momentum to zoning laws for skyscrapers.
Federal Hall	26 Wall St • 212-825-6888	Where George the First was inaugurated.
Ferry to Ellis Island	Pier A & Battery Park	The main building features beautiful domed ceilings and Guastavino tiled arches.
The Federal Reserve Bank	33 Liberty St • 212-720-6130	Where *Die Hard* 3 took place.
The First JP Morgan Bank	23 Wall St	Still visibly scarred from an anarchist bombing in 1920.
India House	1 Hanover Square	Members-only club in historic, nautical-themed house. Secret bar to the left up the stairs. You're welcome.
Liberty Plaza	Trinity Pl & Cedar St	Cool urban park (benches included).
New York Stock Exchange	20 Broad St • 212-656-5168	Where Wall Street took place.
South Street Seaport	Fulton St & South St • 212-732-7678	Mall with historic ships as backdrop.
St Paul's Chapel & Cemetery	Broadway & Fulton St • 212-233-4164	Old-time NYC church and cemetery.

Standard Oil Building	26 Broadway	Sweeping wall of a building overlooking Bowling Green.
Staten Island Ferry	1 Whitehall St	Grab a tall boy on board and enjoy the view.
Trinity Church	74 Trinity Pl • 212-602-0848	Formerly the tallest building in New York.
Vietnam Veterans Plaza	Coenties Slip & Water St	A nice quiet spot to contemplate our faded dreams of empire.
World Trade Center Site	Church St & Vesey St	We still can't believe what happened.

Map 2 • TriBeCa

American Thread Building	260 W Broadway	Check out cool rounded front; watch out for tunnel traffic.
Cary Building	105 Chambers St	Cast-iron goodness on Chambers. We like it.
The Dream House	275 Church St • 212-925-8270	Cool sound + light installation by LaMonte Young. Closed during summer.
Duane Park	Duane St & Hudson St	One of the nicest spots in all of New York.
Fleming Smith Warehouse	451 Washington St	TriBeCa's most sublimely beautiful structure. Believe it.
Ghostbusters Firehouse	14 N Moore St	Are you the gatekeeper?
Harrison Street Row Houses	Harrison St & Greenwich St	Some old houses.
New York Law School	185 W Broadway • 212-431-2100	New York Law's new main building burns brightly on cold TriBeCa nights.
New York Telephone Company Building	140 W Broadway	Massive Art Deco gem still looms over now-fashionable TriBeCa.
No. 8 Thomas Street	8 Thomas St	Bizarre Venetian townhouse in the middle of downtown. Really.
One York Street	1 York St	Enrique Norten's postmodern offering is pretty damned good.
Powell Building	105 Hudson St	Carrere & Hastings gem w/ Nobu on the ground floor.
Textile Building	66 Leonard St	Henry J. Hardenbergh goodness in TriBeCa.
Washington Market Park	310 Greenwich St • 212-274-8447	One of the city's oldest marketplaces.

Map 3 • City Hall / Chinatown

87 Lafayette St	87 Lafayette St	Ex-firehouse designed in Chateau style by Napoleon LeBrun.
African Burial Ground	290 Broadway • 212-637-2019	Colonial burial ground for 20,000+ African-American slaves.
Brooklyn Bridge	Chambers St & Centre St	The granddaddy of them all. Walking toward Manhattan at sunset is as good as it gets.
Centre Market Place	Centre St & Broome St	Another great street we can't afford to live on.
Chatham Towers	170 Park Row	1960s poured-concrete apartment buildings overlooking Chatham Square. Nice windows.
Chinatown Arcade	48 Bowery	Hidden dirty hallway connecting Elizabeth to the Bowery.
Chinatown Fair	8 Mott St • 212-964-1542	Sneak out of the office to play Ms. Pac Man here.
Chinatown Ice Cream Factory	65 Bayard St • 212-608-4170	The best ice cream (ginger, black sesame, mango, red bean…), ever.
Chinatown Visitors Kiosk	Canal, Baxter, & Walker	Good meeting point. Just look out for the dragon.
City Hall	260 Broadway • 212-788-3000	Beautiful and slightly less barricaded than last year.
Columbus Park	67 Mulberry St • 212-408-0100	Former Five Points hub now operates as prime Chinatown hangout.
Confucius Plaza	Bowery & Division St	Confucius say: live here!
Criminal Courthouse	100 Centre St • 212-374-4423	Imposing.
Doyers Street (Bloody Angle)	Doyers St	One of the few angled streets in New York. Has a decidedly otherworldly feel.
Eastern States Buddhist Temple	64 Mott St • 212-966-6229	The oldest Chinese Buddhist temple on the east coast.
Eldridge Street Synagogue	12 Eldridge • St 212-219-0302	The first large-scale building by Eastern Euro immigrants in NY.
Foley Square	Worth St & Centre St	Now with bizarre black obelisk. Guiliani hated it.
Hall of Records/Surrogate's Court	Chambers St & Park Row	Great lobby and zodiac-themed mosaics.
Municipal Building	Chambers St & Park Row	Wonderful McKim, Mead & White masterpiece.
Museum of Chinese in America	215 Centre St • 212-619-4785	Beautiful new home designed by Maya Lin.
Not For Tourists	2 East Broadway • 212-965-8650	Where the sh** goes down!
Old New York Life Insurance Company	346 Broadway	Great narrow McKim, Mead & White with hand-wound clock and cool internal stairwells.
Old Police Headquarters	240 Centre St	A beautiful building in the center of the not so beautiful Little Italy/Chinatown area.
Shearith Israel Cemetery	55 St James Pl	Oldest Jewish cemetery in New York.

Super-Cool Cast Iron	Crosby St & Grand St	We want to live on the top floor of this building.
Thurgood Marshall US Courthouse	40 Centre St	Cass Gilbert masterpiece from 1935.
Tweed Courthouse	52 Chambers St	Great interior dome, but will we ever see it?
Woolworth Building	233 Broadway	A Cass Gilbert classic. The top half's being converted to condos.

Map 4 • Lower East Side

Angel Orensanz Theatre	172 Norfolk St • 212-529-7194	Performance space in ex-synagogue. Amazing.
Bialystoker Synagogue	7 Bialystoker Pl • 212-475-0165	The oldest building in NY to currently house a synagogue. Once a stop on the Underground Railroad.
Blue Condo	105 Norfolk St	Bernard Tschumi's odd masterpiece.
Gouverneur Hospital	Gouverneur Slip & Water St	One of the oldest hospital buildings in the world.
Lower East Side Tenement Museum	108 Orchard St • 212-982-8420	Great illustration of turn-of-the-century (20th, that is) life.

Map 5 • West Village

Bob Dylan's One-Time Apartment	161 W 4th St	Bob Dylan lived here in the '60s.
The Cage (basketball court)	320 Sixth Ave at W 4th St	Where everybody's got game…
Chumley's	86 Bedford St • 212-675-4449	Former speakeasy under renovation; let's hope it reopens soon!
The Ear Inn	326 Spring St • 212-226-9060	Second-oldest bar in New York; great space.
The High Line	Gansevoort to 20th St, west of Tenth Ave • 212-206-9922	Stunning elevated park; a testament to human creativity.
Jefferson Market Courthouse	425 Sixth Ave • 212-243-4334	Now a library.
Old Homestead	56 Ninth Ave • 212-242-9040	Said to be NY's oldest steakhouse, circa 1868.
Patchin Place	W 10th St b/w Sixth Ave & Greenwich Ave	Tiny gated enclave, once home to e.e. cummings.
Stonewall Inn	53 Christopher St • 212-488-2705	Site of a very important uprising in the late '60s.
Westbeth Building	Washington St & Bethune St • 212-989-4650	Cool multifunctional arts center.
White Horse Tavern	567 Hudson St • 212-243-9260	Another old, cool bar. Dylan Thomas drank here (too much).

Map 6 • Washington Square / NYU / NoHo / SoHo

376 Lafayette St	376 Lafayette St	Henry Hardenbergh's NoHo masterpiece, circa 1888.
The Alamo (The Cube)	Astor Pl & Fourth Ave	Give it a spin sometime…
Bayard-Condict Building	65 Bleecker St	Louis Sullivan's only New York building.
Bond Street Architecture	Bond St	Uber-futuristic condo projects by Herzog & de Meuron et al.
Brown Building of Science	23-29 Washington Pl	Site of the Triangle Shirtwaist Fire.
Colonnade Row	428 Lafayette St	Remains of a very different era.
Con Edison Building	145 E 14th St	Cool top.
Cooper Union	30 Cooper Sq • 212-353-4100	Great brownstone-covered building.
Cooper Union New Academic Building	41 Cooper Square	Supercool, futuristic, and eco-friendly architecture.
DeVinne Press Building	399 Lafayette St	Killer 1885 brick-and-glass masterpiece by Babb, Cook & Willard.
Former location of CBGB & OMFUG	315 Bowery	Club is gone, but its shell remains for the time being
Gem Spa	131 Second Ave • 212-995-1866	Magazine stand that serves fantastic egg creams.
Grace Church	802 Broadway • 212-254-2000	Another old, small, comfortable church.
Great Jones Firehouse	Great Jones St & Bowery	The coolest firehouse in NYC.
Joey Ramone Place	Bowery & E 2nd St	It's Joey Ramone's place. Period.
Little Singer Building	561 Broadway	Now houses Kate's Paperie; a fine building by Ernest Flagg.
Lombardi's	32 Spring St • 212-941-7994	Said to be the first pizzeria in the US, circa 1905.
Mark Twain House	14 W 10th St	Mark Twain lived here. It's also NYC's most haunted portal.
McSorley's	15 E 7th St • 212-474-9148	One of the oldest bars in Manhattan, and some would say one of the best. Others…
Milano's	51 E Houston	One of our favorite bars. An utter dump.
New Museum of Contemporary Art	235 Bowery • 212-219-1222	Brilliant white stacked cubes houses contemporary art and killer bookstore. Yah.

New York City Marble Cemetery	74 E 2nd St • 212-228-6401	Cool, but generally closed. But you can still see in.
Old Merchant's House	29 E 4th St • 212-777-1089	The merchant is now dead.
Prada	575 Broadway • 212-334-8888	Big, pretentious Rem Koolhaas-designed store. Worth a look.
The Public Theater	425 Lafayette St • 212-539-8500	Can you still get free condoms in the lobby?
Salmagundi Club	47 Fifth Ave • 212-255-7740	Cool building.
Site of the Weathermen Explosion	18 W 11th St • 718-549-3200	Townhouse where the Weathermen's plans to destroy Columbia's library went awry.
St Mark's-in-the-Bowery Church	131 E 10th St • 212-674-6377	Old church with lots of community ties.
The Strand	828 Broadway • 212-473-1452	Used mecca; world's messiest and best bookstore.
University Settlement House	184 Eldridge St • 212-674-9120	Providing a haven for lower east siders of all ages since 1886.
Wanamaker's	Broadway & E 8th St	Once the classiest department store in the city, now houses a Kmart.
Washington Mews	University Pl (entrance)	Where horses and servants used to live. Now coveted NYU space.
Washington Square Park	Washington Sq	Dime bag, anyone?

Map 7 • East Village

Charlie Parker House	151 Ave B	The Bird lived here. Great festival every summer in Tompkins Square.
General Slocum Monument	Tompkins Sq Park	Memorial to one of the worst disasters in NYC history.
Joe Strummer Mural	112 Avenue A	Ha, you think it's funny... turning rebellion into money?
Katz's Deli	205 E Houston St • 212-254-2246	Classic NY deli, interior hasn't changed in decades.
Nuyorican Poet's Café	E 3rd St • 212-780-9386	Where mediocre poets die of humiliation.
Pyramid Club	101 Ave A • 212-228-4888	Classic '80s and '90s club.
Russian and Turkish Baths	268 E 10th St • 212-674-9250	Sweat away all your urban stress.
St Brigid Roman Catholic Church	119 Avenue B	Historic Irish church spared demolition, still standing on Tompkins Square.
Tompkins Square Park	Ave A & E 9th St • 212-387-7685	Home to many.

Map 8 • Chelsea

Chelsea Market	75 Ninth Ave	Foodies flock here. So should you.
The Frying Pan	Pier 66 • 212-989-6363	Old ship makes for amazing party digs.
General Theological Seminary	175 Ninth Ave • 212-243-5150	Oldest seminary of the Episcopal Church; nice campus.
JA Farley	421 Eighth Ave • 212-330-3296	Another McKim, Mead & White masterpiece.
Jacob K Javits Convention Center	655 W 34th St • 212-216-2000	IM Pei's attempt to make sense out of New York. Love the location.
Maritime Hotel	363 W 16th St • 212-242-4300	Ahoy! Porthole office building now uber-cool hotel.
Starrett-Lehigh Building	601 W 26th St • 212-924-0505	One of the coolest factories/warehouses ever built.

Map 9 • Flatiron / Lower Midtown

Arnold Constable's Dry Good Store	855 Broadway	The mansard roof to end all mansard roofs.
Broadway Lord & Taylor	901 Broadway	Incredible detail on former Lord & Taylor outlet.
Chelsea Hotel	222 W 23rd St • 212-243-3700	The scene of many, many crimes.
Croisic Building	220 5th Ave	Just another outstanding NYC building. Circa 1912.
De Lamar Mansion	233 Madison Ave	Dutch sea captain's mansion now inhabited by Polish diplomats.
Empire State Building	34th St & Fifth Ave • 212-736-3100	The roof deck at night is unmatched by any other view of New York.
Flatiron Building	175 Fifth Ave • 212-633-0200	A lesson for all architects: design for the actual space.
Flower District	28th St b/w Sixth & Seventh Aves	Lots of flowers by day, lots of nothing by night.
Garment District	West 30s south of Herald Sq	Clothing racks by day, nothing by night. Gritty, grimy.
Hugh O'Neill's Dry Goods Store	655 Avenue of the Americas	Brilliant cast-iron from Mortimer Merritt.
Koreatown	W 32nd St b/w Broadway & Fifth Ave	Korean restaurants, bars, and shops. Bustling on the weekends.
Macy's	151 W 34th St • 212-695-4400	13 floors of wall-to-wall tourists! Sound like fun?
Madison Square Garden	4 Penn Plz • 212-465-6741	Crappy, uninspired venue for Knicks, Rangers, Liberty, and over-the-hill rock bands.
Madison Square Park	23rd St & Broadway • 212-538-1884	One of the most underrated parks in the city. Lots of great weird sculpture.
Metropolitan Life Insurance Co	1 Madison Ave • 212-578-3700	Cool top, recently refurbished.
Morgan Library	225 Madison Ave • 212-685-0008	See cool stuff the dead rich dude collected.

New York Life Insurance Company	51 Madison Ave	The gold roof? Your insurance premiums at work.
New York State Appellate Court	Madison Ave & E 25th St	Insanely ornate 1899 courthouse; where new lawyers get sworn in.
Old Town Bar	45 E 18th St	Classic NY pub housed in former speak-easy.
Penn Station	31st St & Eighth Ave	Well, the old one was a landmark, anyway…
Siegel-Cooper Department Store	616 Avenue of the Americas	Beaux-Arts retail madness. Now a f***in' Bed, Bath & Beyond.
Stern Brothers' Dry Goods Store	32 W 23rd St	Awesome ornate cast-iron; now houses Home Depot. Whatever.
Theodore Roosevelt Birthplace	28 E 20th St • 212-260-1616	Teddy was born here, apparently.
Tin Pan Alley	W 28th St b/w Sixth Ave & Broadway	Where all that old-timey music came from.
Union Square	14th St-Union Sq	Famous park for protests and rallys. Now bordered on all sides by chain stores.

Map 10 • Murray Hill / Gramercy

69th Armory	68 Lexington Ave	Event space, historic landmark, hookers at night.
Baruch College	55 Lexington Ave • 646-312-1000	Baruch's "vertical campus;" very cool unless you need an elevator quickly.
Curry Hill	Lexington Ave & E 28th St	Eat your way down Lexington in the 20s!
Friends Meeting House	15 Rutherford Pl • 212-475-0466	Quaker meeting house from 1861. No guns, please.
Gramercy Park	Irving Pl & E 20 St	New York's only keyed park. This is where the revolution will doubtlessly start.
Kips Bay Plaza	1st Ave & E 30th St	I.M. Pei does the superblock, 1960s-style. A tad brutalist.
Mayor James Harper Residence	4 Gramercy Park W	Cool wrought-iron madness from 1846.
National Arts Club	15 Gramercy Park S • 212-475-3424	One of two beautiful buildings on Gramercy Park South.
Pete's Tavern	129 E 18th St • 212-473-7676	Where O Henry hung out. And so should you, at least once.
Protestant Welfare Agencies Building	281 Park Ave S	Looming Gothic structure circa 1894. Worth a look.
The Players	16 Gramercy Park S	The other cool building on Gramercy Park South.
Sniffen Court	36th St & Third Ave	Great little space.
St. Vartan Park	1st Ave & E 35th St	Murray Hill kid/playground nexus.
Stuyvesant Town	1st Ave & E 20th St	Would you really want to live here? Really?
Tammany Hall/Union Sq Theater	100 E 17th St • 212-505-0700	Once housed NYC's Democratic political machine.

Map 11 • Hell's Kitchen

The Annex/Hell's Kitchen Flea Market	W 39th St & Dyer Ave • 212-243-5343	Old Chelsea Annex flea market is now located here.
Broadway Dance Center	322 W 45th St • 212-582-9304	The place for tap lessons.
Daily Show Studio	733 11TH Ave	Home of our favorite TV show. Thank you John Stewart.
Dewitt Clinton Park	11th Ave & W 52nd St	Where the neighborhood mutts meet to sniff butts.
Intrepid Sea, Air and Space Museum	12th Ave & W 46th St • 212-245-0072	Holy crap! An aircraft carrier in the middle of the Hudson River!
Restaurant Row	46th St b/w Eighth & Ninth Aves	Mingle with tourists during pre-theater dinners.
Theatre Row	W 42nd St b/w 9th & Dyer Aves	This is that "Broadway" place that everyone keeps talking about, isn't it?

Map 12 • Midtown

Algonquin Hotel	59 W 44th St • 212-840-6800	Where snark was invented.
Alwyn Court Apartments	182 W 58th St	100-year-old apartment building with awesomely detailed exterior.
American Radiator Building	40 W 40th St	Massive gold-and-black Art Deco gem looms over Bryant Park..
Austrian Cultural Forum	11 E 52nd St • 212-319-5300	Incredibly sleek sliver of a building.
Broadway Dance Center	221 W 57th St, 5th Fl • 212-582-9304	The place for tap lessons
Bryant Park	42nd St & Sixth Ave	Summer movies, winter ice-skating, hook-ups year round.
Carnegie Hall	881 7th Ave • 212-247-7800	Stock up on free cough drops in the lobby.
Diamond District	47th St b/w 5th and 6th Ave	Big rocks abound! Center of the world's diamond industry.
The Debt Clock	Sixth Ave & 44th St	How much the US has borrowed—we're totally screwed.

GE Building	30 Rockefeller Plaza	The tallest building at Rock Center.
Hearst Tower	300 W 57th St	It's green! It's mean! It's fit to be seen!
Little Brazil	W 46th St b/w 5th & 6th Ave	Small stretch of Brazilian businesses. Gisele not included.
Museum of Modern Art (MoMA)	11 W 53rd St • 212-708-9400	The renovation worked! Admire the beauty of architecture and art.
New York Public Library	Fifth Ave & 42nd St • 212-340-0849	A wonderful Beaux Arts building. Great park behind it. The Map Room rules.
New York Times Building	8th Ave & W 40th St	Renzo Piano's impressive new home for The Gray Lady.
Phyllis Harriman Mason Gallery	215 W 57th St • 212-247-4510	Midtown brilliance from Henry J. Hardenbergh; ASL pretty good, too.
Plaza Hotel	768 Fifth Ave • 212-759-3000	Now anyone can be Eloise with her own Plaza condo.
Rockefeller Center	600 Fifth Ave • 212-632-3975	Sculpture, ice skating, and a mall!
Royalton Hotel	44th St b/w Fifth Ave & Sixth Ave • 212-869-4400	Starck + Schrager = cool.
St Patrick's Cathedral	Fifth Ave & 50th St • 212-753-2261	NYC's classic cathedral.
Times Square	42nd St-Times Sq	It looks even cooler than it does on TV!
TKTS	Times Square & W 47th St	Get cheap Broadway tix underneath the cool looking stairs.
Villard House	457 Madison Ave	Killer brownstone palazzos by holy fathers McKim, Mead & White.
Ziegfeld Theatre	141 W 54th St •212-307-1862	Glorious 1969 movie palace. 1,100 seats and red carpeting.

Map 13 • East Midtown

Central Synagogue	123 E 55th St • 212-838-5123	NYC's oldest continuous use Jewish house of worship. Architectural gem.
Chanin Building	122 E 42nd St	Not the Chrysler, but still a way-cool Art Deco masterpiece.
Chrysler Building	405 Lexington Ave • 212-682-3070	The stuff of Art Deco dreams. Wish the Cloud Club was still there.
Citicorp Center	153 E 53rd St	How does it stand up?
Daily News Building	220 E 42nd St	Great Caesar's ghost! An Art Deco gem.
Grand Central Terminal	42nd St • 212-340-2583	Another Beaux Arts masterpiece by Warren and Wetmore. Ceiling, staircases, tiles, clock, Oyster Bar, all great.
Lipstick Building	885 3rd Ave	Philip Johnson does New York, deliriously (well).
The Lever House	390 Park Ave	A great example of architectural modernism, but even better, it's so fresh and so clean!
Seagram Building	375 Park Ave • 877-353-3377	Or, "how to be a modernist in 3 easy steps!"
St. Bartholomew's Church	109 E 50th St	Brilliant Byzantine-style church with great dome, performances, etc.
The Seven Year Itch	E 52nd St & Lexington Ave	Marilyn Monroe's lucky subway grate.
Sutton Place	Sutton Pl b/w 57th & 59th St	Quiet, exclusive little lane for the rich and sometimes famous.
Tudor City	Tudor City Place	3000 apartments in "American" Tudor style. Hmmmm.
United Nations	E 46th St & 1st Ave • 212-963-8687	The diplomatic version of the World Cup.
Waldorf Astoria	301 Park Ave • 212-355-3000	Great hotel, although the public spaces aren't up to the Plaza's.

Map 14 • Upper West Side (Lower)

American Museum of Natural History	Central Park W at 79th St 212-769-5100	Includes an outstanding planetarium and lots and lots of stuffed animals.
Ansonia Hotel	2109 Broadway • 212-724-2600	Truly unique residence on Broadway.
Apthorp	2201 Broadway	Huge, city-block-spanning condos complete with inner courtyard.
The Dakota	Central Park W & W 72nd St	Classic Central Park West apartment building, designed by Henry J Hardenbergh.
The Dorilton	Broadway & 71st St	Cool, weird arch. Flashy facade.
Hotel Des Artistes	1 W 67th St	$4,000,000 artist studios on CPW. Nice one.
Lincoln Center	70 Lincoln Center Plaza • 212-875-5456	A rich and wonderful complex. Highly recommended—movies, theater, music, opera.
The Majestic	115 Central Park W	Great brick by Chanin.
MLK Sculpture	122 Amsterdam Ave	Massive brutalist-but-cool square monument to MLK.

Museum of Natural History	Central Park W & 79th St • 212-769-5100	Includes the new planetarium and lots and lots of stuffed animals.
New York Historical Society	2 W 77th St • 212-873-3400	Oldest museum in New York City.
Rotunda at 79th St Boat Basin	W 79th St • 212-496-2105	Rotunda arcade arches great location.
The San Remo	Central Park W & 74th St • 212-877-0300	Emery Roth's contribution to the Upper West Side skyline.
West End Collegiate Church	West End Ave & W 77th St • 212-787-1566	Dutch/Flemish goodness from Robert Gibson, . circa 1892

Map 15 • Upper East Side (Lower)

Asia Society	725 Park Ave • 212-288-6400	Small-scale modernism.
Bemelmans Bar	35 E 76th St • 212-744-1600	Features lovely mural by creator of Madeline books, Ludwig Bemelmans.
Bernie Madoff Apartment	133 E 64th St	Madoff lived here, before he went to The Big House.
Breakfast at Tiffany's Apartment	169 E 71st St	Where Holly Golightly and "Fred" lived in *Breakfast at Tiffany's*.
Butterfield Market	1114 Lexington Ave • 212-288-7800	UES gourmet grocer circa 1915.
The Explorers Club	46 E 70th St • 212-628-8383	Indiana Joneses of the world hang out here. Some events open to the public.
Frank E Campbell Funeral Chapel	1076 Madison Ave • 212-288-3500	Undertaker to the famously deceased like Lennon and Joan Crawford.
Frick Collection	1 E 70th St • 212-288-0700	Lots of furniture.
The Jeffersons High-rise	185 E 85th St	We're movin' on up…to a dee-luxe apartment in the sky-hi.
The Lotos Club	5 E 66th St • 212-737-7100	Twain loved this private literary club. NFT is still waiting for an invite.
The Manhattan House	200 E 66th St	Seminal UES "white-brick" building.
The Metropolitan Club	1 E 60th St	1894 millionaire's clubhouse built by McKim, Mead & White.
Metropolitan Museum of Art	1000 Fifth Ave • 212-535-7710	The mother of all art musuems. Check out: temple, roof garden, Clyfford Still room, baseball cards.
Mount Vernon Hotel Museum and Garden	421 E 61st St • 212-838-6878	Nice old building.
New York Society Library	53 E 79th St • 212-288-6900	A 250-year-old library. Wow!
Parisian-style Chimneys	E 80th St & Park Ave	A touch of Paris on the UES.
Park East Synagogue	163 E 67th St • 212-737-6900	1890 Moorish-Jewish asymmetrical brilliance from Schneider & Herter.
Roosevelt Island Tram	E 59th St & 2nd Ave	As featured in Spider Man.
Temple Emanu-El	1 E 65th St • 212-744-1400	Way cool building.
Whitney Museum of American Art	945 Madison Ave • 212-570-3600	Always has something to talk about, like the controversial Biennial.
Zion-St Mark's Evangelical Lutheran Church	339 E 84th St • 212-288-0600	Last "Germantown" church (see the General Slocum memorials inside).

Map 16 • Upper West Side (Upper)

Broadway Mall Community Center	W 96th St & Broadway	Beaux-Arts home of The West Side Arts Coalition.
El Taller Latino Americano	2710 Broadway • 212-665-9460	Vibrant cultural hub for Latino art, music, and dance.
Fireman's Memorial	W 100th St & Riverside Dr	Memorial to fallen fire fighters.
Joan of Arc Memorial	Riverside Dr & W 93 St	Impressive statue erected in 1915.
Maurice Schinasi House	351 Riverside Dr	My name is Elmer J. Fudd, I own a mansion...
Pomander Walk	261 W 94th St	Great little hideaway.
Soldiers and Sailors Monument	Riverside Dr & 89th St	It's been seen in *Law & Order*, along with everything else in New York.
Straus Park	Broadway & W 106 St	Green respite just off the craziness of Broadway.

Map 17 • Upper East Side / East Harlem

92nd Street Y	1395 Lexington Ave • 212-415-5500	Community hub for film, theater, and interesting lectures.
Cooper-Hewitt National Design Museum	2 E 91st St • 212-849-8355	Great design shows; run by the Smithsonian.
El Museo del Barrio	1230 5th Ave • 212-831-7272	NYC's only Latino museum.
Glaser's Bake Shop	1670 First Ave • 212-289-2562	Best black-and-white cookies for more than a century.
Gracie Mansion	Carl Schulz Park & 88th St • 212-570-4751	Our own Buckingham Palace, and right above the FDR Drive.

Grafitti Wall of Fame	E 106th & Park Ave	This street art will blow you away.
Guggenheim Museum	1071 Fifth Ave • 212-423-3500	Wright's only building in NYC, but it's one of the best.
Henderson Place	East End Ave & E 86th St	Charming Queen Anne–style apartment houses circa 1881–82.
Islamic Cultural Center	1711 3rd Ave • 212-722-5234	Enormous and extraordinary mosque. Bustling on Fridays.
Jewish Museum	1109 Fifth Ave • 212-423-3200	Over 28,000 artifacts of Jewish culture and history.
Julia de Borgos Cultural Center	1680 Lexington Ave • 212-831-4333	Artistic and community hub of East Harlem.
Museum of the City of New York	Fifth Ave & 103rd St • 212-534-1672	Nice space, but we were excited when they were going to move to the Tweed Courthouse.
Old Municipal Asphalt Plant (Asphalt Green)	90th St & FDR Dr • 212-369-8890	Industrial architecture turned sports facility.
Papaya King	179 E 86th St • 212-369-0648	Dishing out damn good dogs since 1932.
Schaller & Weber	1654 Second Ave • 212-879-3047	A relic of old Yorkville with great German meats.
St Nicholas Russian Orthodox Cathedral	15 E 97th St	This UES cathedral, built in 1902, remains the center of Russian Orthodoxy in the US.

Map 18 • Columbia / Morningside Heights

Cathedral of St John the Divine	1047 Amsterdam Ave • 212-316-7540	Our favorite cathedral. Completely unfinished and usually in disarray, just the way we like it.
Columbia University	116th St & Broadway • 212-854-1754	A nice little sanctuary amid the roiling masses.
Grant's Tomb	122nd St & Riverside Dr • 212-666-1640	A totally underrated experience, interesting, great grounds.
Pupin Hall	550 W 120th St	Original site of the Manhattan Project.

Map 19 • Harlem (Lower)

Alhambra Theatre and Ballroom	2116 Adam Clayton Powell Blvd • 212-222-6940	Last Harlem dance hall.
Apollo Theater	253 W 125th St • 212-531-5300	The one and the only.
Duke Ellington Circle	110th St & Fifth Ave	Nice monument to a jazz great.
Harlem Fire Watchtower	Marcus Garvey Park	It's tall.
Harlem YMCA	180 W 135th St • 212-281-4100	Sidney Poitier, James Earl Jones, and Eartha Kitt have performed at this Y's "Little Theatre."
Langston Hughes Place	20 E 127th St • 212-534-5992	Where the prolific poet lived and worked 1947–1967.
Marcus Garvey Park	E 120-124th Sts & Madison Ave • 212-201-PARK	Appeallingly mountainous park.
Speaker's Corner	Lenox Ave & W 135 St	Famous soapbox for civil rights leaders, including Marcus Garvey.
Sylvia's	328 Lenox Ave • 212-996-0660	This restaurant is worth the trip.

Map 20 • El Barrio / East Harlem

Church of Our Lady of Mt Carmel	448 E 115th St • 212-534-0681	The first Italian parish in NYC.
Danny's Club	Pleasant Ave & E 114th St	Funky neighborhood fashion shop going strong for 30+ years.
Harlem Courthouse	170 E 121st St	One of the most impressive buildings in Manhattan.
Keith Haring "Crack is Wack" Mural	Second Ave & 127th St	Keith was right.
La Marqueta	1607 Park Ave • 212-534-4900	This public market used to be bustling; not so much anymore.
Taino Towers	3rd Ave & E 123rd St	Unique low-income housing development opened in 1979.
Thomas Jefferson Park	2180 First Ave • 212-860-1372	Green space with a giant pool and bbqs in the summer.

Map 21 • Manhattanville / Hamilton Heights

American Academy of Arts & Letters	633 W 155th St • 212-368-5900	New glass structure links it to the Hispanic Society.
Audubon Terrace	Broadway & W 155th St	Pleasant, if lonely, Beaux Arts complex. What's it doing here?
Bailey House	10 St Nicholas Pl	Romanesque revival mansion from PT Barnum's partner James Bailey.
Church of the Crucifixion	459 W 149th St	Whacked-out concrete church by Costas Machlouzarides, circa 1967.
Church of the Intercession	550 W 155th St • 212-283-6200	Cool Gothic church by Ralph Cram and friends.
City College	160 Convent Ave • 212-650-7000	Peaceful gothic campus.
Hamilton Grange National Memorial	287 Convent Ave • 212-368-9133	Elegant buildings on a serene street.

Hamilton Heights Historic District	W 141st b/w W 145th St & Convent Ave	Hamilton's old dig moved here from its original location and now facing the wrong way. Damn those Jeffersonians.
Hispanic Society Museum	613 W 155th St • 212-926-2234	Free museum (Tues–Sat) with Spanish masterpieces.
Trinity Church Cemetery's Graveyard of Heroes	3699 Broadway	Hilly, almost countryish cemetery.

Map 22 • Harlem (Upper)

The 369th Regiment Armory	2366 Fifth Ave	Home of the Harlem Hellfighters.
Abyssinian Baptist Church	132 Odell Clark Pl • 212-862-7474	NY's oldest black congregation.
The Dunbar Houses	Frederick Douglass Blvd & W 149th St	Historic multi-family houses.
Rucker Park	155th St & Frederick Douglass Blvd	Kareem Abdul-Jabbar's, and a ton of talented locals', Harlem court.
St Nicholas Historic District	202 W 138th St	Beautiful neo-Georgian townhouses.

Map 23 • Washington Heights

Cross Bronx Expressway	n/a	Worst. Highway. Ever.
George Washington Bridge	W 178th St	Try to see it when it's lit up. Drive down from Riverdale on the Henry Hudson at night and you'll understand.
Highbridge Water Tower	Highbridge Park	Now-defunct but totally cool water tower; try to get inside.
Little Red Lighthouse	under the George Washington Bridge • 212-304-2365	It's there, really!
Morris-Jumel Mansion	Edgecombe Ave & 161st St • 212-923-8008	The oldest building in New York, at least until someone changes it again.
New York Armory	216 Ft Washington Ave • 212-923-1803	World class running facility houses Track & Field Hall of Fame.
Sylvan Terrace	b/w Jumel Ter & St Nicholas Ave	The most un-Manhattanlike place in all the world.
United Palace Theater	4140 Broadway	First a movie theater, then a church, now Beck. Sweet.

Map 24 • Fort George / Fort Tryon

The Cloisters	Ft Tryon Park • 212-923-3700	The Met's storehouse of medieval art. Great herb garden, nice views.
Fort Tryon Park	Ft Washington Ave	A totally beautiful and scenic park on New York's north edge.
Peter Jay Sharp Boathouse	Swindler Cove Park • 917-865-3055	See the West Bronx by boat.
Yeshiva University Main Building (Zysman Hall)	Amsterdam Ave & W 187th St • 212-960-5224	Interesting Byzantine-style building.

Map 25 • Inwood

Dyckman House	4881 Broadway • 212-304-9422	Needs some work.
Emerson Playground	Isham St	Kids (and adults) love playing around on the iron wolf.
Henry Hudson Bridge	n/a	Affords a nice view from the Inwood Hill Park side.
Homer's Run	Isham St	Where dogs par-tay.
Inwood Hill Park	n/a	The last natural forest and salt marsh in Manhattan!
West 215th Street Steps	W 215th St	Elevation of sidewalk requires steps.

Battery Park City

The Irish Hunger Memorial	Vesey St & North End Ave	A memorial to the "The Great Irish Famine and Migration" to the US in the mid-1800s.
Manhattan Sailing Club	North Cove (Liberty St & North End Ave) • 212-786-3323	Membership required.
Mercantile Exchange	1 North End Ave	A great, big financial building in Battery Park.
Museum of Jewish Heritage	36 Battery Pl • 646-437-4200	A living memorial to the Holocaust.
Police Memorial	Liberty St & South End Ave	A fountain commemorating the career of a policeman and those killed in the line of duty.
The Real World Sculptures	n/a	Tom Otterness sculptures of a tiny, whimsical society. Cooler than Smurfs.
Skyscraper Museum	39 Battery Pl • 212-968-1961	The place to go to learn what's up in New York.
Winter Garden	37 Vesey St	A cavernous marble and glass atrium.

Roosevelt Island

Blackwell House	591 Main St	Fifth-oldest wooden house in New York City.
Blackwell's Lighthouse	n/a	Built by institutionalized 19th-century convicts, just like the rest of NYC.
Chapel of the Good Shepherd	543 Main St • 917-843-3338	1888 Chapel given as a gift to island inmates and patients.

Smallpox Hospital	n/a	New York City's only landmarked ruin.
Tramway	Tramway Plz	As featured in *Spider-Man*.

Map 26 • Astoria

Astoria Park and Pool	19th St & 23rd Dr • 718-626-8621	City's oldest and largest public pool surrounded by 65 acres of waterfront parkland.
Athens Square Park	30th Ave & 30th St	You'll love it as much as the kids.
Buzzer Thirty	38-01 23rd Ave • 646-523-8582	Community arts organization with an exhibition space.
The Greater Astoria Historical Society	35-20 Broadway • 718-278-0700	Preserving the past and future of Astoria.
Kaufman Astoria Studios	34-12 36th St • 718-706-5300	The US's largest studio outside of Los Angeles sits on a 13-acre plot with 8 sound stages.
Museum of the Moving Image	36-01 35th Ave • 718-784-4520	Learn about film and television, or catch screenings of classic films.
Socrates Sculpture Park	Broadway & Vernon Blvd • 718-956-1819	Cool, gritty sculpture park with events and films.

Map 27 • Long Island City

5 Pointz/Crane Street Studios	Jackson Ave & Crane St	7 train riders will see this graffiti-covered studio building from afar; PS1 visitors should take a closer look.
Center for the Holographic Arts	45-10 Court Sq • 718-784-5065	Promotes the art of holography and/or the holography of art.
The Chocolate Factory	5-49 49th Ave • 718-482-7069	Performance space for experimental theater.
Citicorp Building	1 Court Sq	This 48-story structure is the tallest New York building outside of Manhattan.
Fisher Landau Center for Art	38-27 30th St • 718-937-0727	Temporary exhibits plus a world-class permanent collection of contemporary art.
Gantry Plaza State Park	50-50 Second St • 718-786-6385	Waterfront park and piers with breathtaking skyline views.
Hunter's Point Historic District	45th Ave b/w 21st St & 23rd St	Well-preserved homes from LIC's first heyday in the late 1800s.
Local Project	21-36 44th Rd	Non-profit performance venue and gallery space.
Long Island City Courthouse	25-10 Court Sq • 718-298-1000	Built in 1876 and rebuilt in 1904, an architectural gem.
The Noguchi Museum	9-01 33rd Rd • 718-204-7088	Showcases Noguchi's work in a converted factory with a beautiful garden.
NY Center for Media Arts	45-12 Davis St	Exhibition space for emerging artists.
PS1 Contemporary Art Center	22-25 Jackson Ave • 718-784-2084	MoMA's contemporary art space, w/ dance parties every summer Saturday.
SculptureCenter	44-19 Purves St • 718-361-1750	An artist-run nonprofit and gallery supporting experimental sculpture since 1928.
Silvercup Studios	42-22 22nd St • 718-906-2000	Former bakery is now a busy film and television studio.
The Space	42-16 West St	Organization to encourage public arts in Long Island City.

Map 28 • Greenpoint

Newton Creek Sewage Treatment Plant	Greenpoint Ave & Provost St	Take a moment to contemplate all of the famous and beautiful peoples' shit floating around in here.

Map 29 • Williamsburg

Brooklyn Brewery	79 N 11th St • 718-486-7422	Connect with your beer by witnessing its birth; free samples also encourage closeness.
City Reliquary	370 Metropolitan Ave	Artifacts from New York's vast and rich history.
Williamsburg Bridge	S 5th St & Driggs St	Bridge of the chosen people—Jews and well-off hipsters.

Map 30 • Brooklyn Heights / DUMBO / Downtown

Brooklyn Borough Hall	209 Joralemon St • 718-802-3700	Built in the 1840s, this Greek Revival landmark was once employed as the official City Hall of Brooklyn.
Brooklyn Bridge	Adams St & East River	If you haven't walked over it at least twice yet, you're not cool.
Brooklyn Heights Promenade	n/a	The best place to really see Manhattan. It's the view that's in all the movies.
Brooklyn Historical Society	128 Pierrepont St • 718-222-4111	Want to really learn about Brooklyn? Go here.
Brooklyn Ice Cream Factory	Fulton Ferry Pier • 718-246-3963	Expensive, old-fashioned ice cream beneath the bridge.
Brooklyn Navy Yard	Waterfront	Nation's first navy yard employed 70,000 people during WWII. Today, it houses a diverse range of businesses.
Brooklyn Tabernacle	17 Smith St • 718-783-0942	Home of the award-winning Brooklyn Tabernacle Choir.
Empire-Fulton Ferry State Park	n/a	Stunning views of the bridge.

Fulton Street Mall	Fulton St b/w Flatbush Ave & Borough Hall Plz	The shopping experience, Brooklyn style. Hot sneakers can be had for a song.
Jetsons Building	110 York St	View this sculptural roof from the Manhattan Bridge at night when it's lit with colored lights.
Junior's Restaurant	386 Flatbush Ave • 718-852-5257	For the only cheesecake worth its curds and whey. (Free pickles, great if you're preggers.)
Manhattan Bridge	n/a	Connecting Brooklyn to that other borough.
New York Transit Museum	Boerum Pl & Schermerhorn St • 718-694-1600	Everything one can say about the MTA.

Map 31 • Fort Greene / Clinton Hill

Broken Angel	Quincy St b/w Downing St & Classon St	Crazy architectural home soon to be condos. Home of Dave Chappelle's *Block Party*.
Brooklyn Academy of Music	30 Lafayette Ave • 718-636-4100	America's oldest continuously operating performing arts center. Never dull.
Brooklyn Masonic Temple	317 Clermont Ave • 718-638-1256	Its vestrymen have included Robert E. Lee and Thomas J. (Stonewall) Jackson.
Ft Greene Park	DeKalb Ave & Washington Park	Liquor store proximity is a plus on a warm afternoon when you visit this welcome chunk of green.
Lafayette Avenue Presbyterian Church	85 S Oxford St • 718-625-7515	Nationally known church with performing arts; former Underground Railroad stop.
Long Island Rail Road Station	Hanson Pl & Flatbush Ave • 718-217-5477	A low red-brick building hosting more than 20 million passengers annually. A total craphole.
Pratt Institute Power Plant	200 Willoughby Ave • 718-636-3600	This authentic steam generator gets fired up a few times a year to impress the parents. Cool.
Steiner Studios	15 Washington Ave	Film studio in the Brooklyn Navy Yard. Spike Lee's *Inside Man* was recently shot here.
Williamsburg Savings Bank Building	1 Hanson Pl	Still the tallest building in the borough and when you're lost, a sight for sore eyes.

Map 32 • BoCoCa / Red Hook

Beard Street Pier	Foot of Van Brunt St on the water	Historic 19th century warehouses, now a cluster of shops and offices.
Brooklyn Clay Retort and Fire Brick Building	76 Van Dyke St	Red Hook's first official Landmark building dates to the mid-19th century.
Gowanus Canal	n/a	Brooklyn's answer to the Seine.
Phone Booth	Huntington St & Hamilton Ave	Where hookers, pimps, and dealers call mom for money.
Red Hook Park	Richards St & Verona St	Watch futbol and eat Central American street food every Saturday from spring through fall.
Red Hook Grain Terminal	n/a	Visit just to wonder what it's doing there.
Warren Place	Warren Pl	Public housing from the 1870s.

Map 33 • Park Slope / Prospect Heights / Windsor Terrace

Brooklyn Botanic Garden	900 Washington Ave • 718-623-7200	A beautiful and peaceful spot inside and out. Cherry blossoms in spring are awe inspiring.
Brooklyn Conservatory of Music	58 Seventh Ave • 718-622-3300	This Victorian Gothic brownstone hosts performances by its students and guest artists.
Brooklyn Public Library (Central Branch)	Grand Army Plz • 718-230-2100	The building looks like a book!
Grand Army Plaza	Flatbush Ave & Plaza St	Site of John H. Duncan's Soldiers' and Sailors' Memorial Arch.
New York Puppet Library	Grand Army Plz	The Memorial Arch at Grand Army Plaza has a funky theater at the top. A must-see (Summer Saturdays only).
Park Slope Food Co-op	782 Union St • 718-622-0560	These farm-fresh-veggies will do for those in search of their peck of dirt. Rinse.

Television

1	NY1 (24-Hour News)	www.ny1.com
2	WCBS (CBS)	www.wcbstv.com
4	WNBC (NBC)	www.wnbc.com
5	WNYW (FOX)	www.fox5ny.com
7	WABC (ABC)	www.7online.com
9	WWOR (My9)	www.my9ny.com
11	11 WPIX (PIX11)	www.wpix.com
13	WNET (PBS)	www.thirteen.org
21	WLIW (Long Island Public)	www.wliw.org
25	NYC TV (Public)	www.nyc.gov/media
31	WPXN (Ion)	www.ionline.tv
41	WXTV (Univision)	www.univision.com
47	WNJU (Telemundo)	www.telemundo.com
49	CPTV (Conn. Public)	www.cptv.org
50	WNJN (NJ Public)	www.njn.net
55	WLNY (Syndicated TV/Movies)	www.wlnytv.com
63	WMBC (Ethnic/Religious)	www.wmbctv.com

AM Stations

570	WMCA	Religious
620	WSNR	Talk/Ethnic)
660	WFAN	Sports/Mets/Giants Nets/Devils
710	WOR	Talk
770	WABC	Talk/Jets
820	WNYC	Talk
880	WCBS	News/Yankees
930	WPAT	Talk/Ethnic (NJ)
970	WNYM	Talk
1010	WINS	News
1050	WEPN	Sports/Jets/Knicks/ Rangers
1100	WHLI	Easy Listening
1130	WBBR	Talk/Bloomberg/ Islanders
1160	WVNJ	Talk
1190	WLIB	Gospel
1230	WFAS	Adult Standards
1240	WGBB	Mandarin Chinese
1280	WADO	Sports (en Espanol)/ Mets/Yankees/Jets
1330	WWRV	Religious (en Espanol)
1380	WKDM	Chinese (Mandarin)
1430	WNSW	Korean (NJ)
1460	WVOX	Talk
1480	WZRC	Cantonese
1520	WTHE	Gospel
1530	WJDM	Religious (en Espanol)
1560	WQEW	Radio Disney
1600	WWRL	Talk/NY Liberty
1660	WWRU	Korean

FM Stations

87.7	WNYZ	Christian/Talk
88.1	WCWP	College (LI)
88.3	WBGO	Jazz (NJ)
88.7	WRHU	College (LI)
88.9	WSIA	College
89.1	WFDU	College (NJ)
89.1	WNYU	College
89.5	WSOU	College/Rock (NJ)
89.9	WKCR	College/Jazz
90.3	WHCR	College
90.3	WHPC	College (LI)
90.7	WFUV	Adult Alternative
91.1	WFMU	Free-form! (NJ)
91.5	WNYE	Radio NY
92.3	WXRK	Top 40
93.1	WPAT	Latin (NJ)
93.5	WVIP	Caribbean
93.9	WNYC	Talk/Classical
94.7	WFME	Religious (NJ)
95.5	WPLJ (JACK)	Top 40
96.3	WXNY	Latin
96.7	WCTZ	Adult Contemporary
97.1	WQHT	Hip-Hop/R&B
97.9	WSKQ	Latin
98.3	WKJY	Adult Contemporary
98.7	WRKS	Urban Adult Contemporary
99.5	WBAI	Talk
100.3	WHTZ (Z-100)	Top 40
100.7	WHUD	Adult Contemporary
101.1	WCBS	Oldies
101.9	WRXP	Alternative Rock
102.7	WWFS	Adult Contemporary
103.1	WJUX	Christian
103.5	WKTU	Top 40/Dance (LI)
103.9	WFAS	Top 40
104.3	WAXQ	Classic Rock
105.1	WWPR	Hip-Hop/R&B
105.5	WDHA	Rock (NJ)
105.9	WQXR	Classical
106.7	WLTW	Adult Contemporary
107.1	WXPK	Adult Alternative
107.5	WBLS	Urban Adult Contemporary

Print Media

amNY	330 W 34th St, 17th Floor	212-239-5398	Free daily; pick it up at the subway.
Daily News	450 W 33rd St	212-210-2100	Daily tabloid; rival of the *Post*. Good sports.
El Diario	345 Hudson St, 13th Fl	212-807-4600	Daily; America's oldest Spanish-language newspaper.
L Magazine	20 Jay Street, Ste 207, Brooklyn	718-596-3462	Bi-weekly arts and events focus; free.
Metro NYC	44 Wall St	212-952-1500	Free daily; pick it up at the subway.
Newsday	235 Pinelawn Rd, Melville	631-843-2000	Daily; based in Long Island.
New York Magazine	444 Madison Ave, 4th Fl	212-508-0700	Broad-based upscale weekly.
New York Review of Books	1755 Broadway, 5th Fl	212-757-8070	Bi-weekly; intellectual lit review. Recommended.
New York Observer	915 Broadway, 9th Fl	212-755-2400	Weekly.
New York Post	1211 Avenue of the Americas	212-930-8000	Daily tabloid; known for its sensationalist headlines.
New York Press	333 Seventh Ave, 14th Fl	212-244-2282	Free weekly; mostly opinion/editorial.
New York Times	620 Eighth Ave	212-698-4637	Daily; one of the world's best-known papers.
The New Yorker	4 Times Square	212-286-5400	Weekly; intellectual news, lit, and arts.
Time Out New York	475 Tenth Ave, 12th Fl	646-432-3000	Weekly; the best guide to goings-on in the city.
The Onion	536 Broadway, 10th Fl	212-627-1972	Weekly; news satire & listings.
The Village Voice	36 Cooper Sq	212-475-3300	Free, alternative weekly.
Wall Street Journal	200 Liberty St	212-416-2000	Daily; famous financial paper.

Event	Location	Description
January		
• Winter Antiques Show	Park Ave at 67th St	Selections from all over the country.
• Three Kings Day Parade	El Museo del Barrio	Features a cast of hundreds from all over the city dressed as kings or animals—camels, sheep, and donkeys (early Jan).
• Outsider Art Fair	Corner of Lafayette & Houston	Art in many forms of media from an international set. $15 admits one for one day.
• National Boat Show	Jacob Javits Convention Center	Don't go expecting a test drive (early Jan).
• Chinese New Year	Chinatown	Features dragons, performers, and parades.
February		
• Empire State Building Run-Up	Empire State Building	Run until the 86th floor (0.2 miles) or heart seizure.
• The Art Show	Park Ave at 67th St	A very large art fair.
• Westminster Dog Show	Madison Square Garden	Fancy canines more well groomed than you.
• Seventh on Sixth Fall Fashion Show	Bryant Park	Weeklong celeb-studded event.
• NY Comic Con	Jacob Javits Center	Comic enthusiasts convene at the nerd mecca.
March		
• International Cat Show	Madison Square Garden	Fine felines.
• St Patrick's Day Parade	Fifth Avenue	Irish pride (March 17). We recommend fleeing.
• Orchid Show	Bronx River Parkway	Brought to you by the New York Botanical Garden.
• Ringling Brothers Circus	Madison Square Garden	Greatest Show on Earth (March–April).
• Whitney Biennial	Whitney Museum	Whitney's most important American art, every other year (March–June).
• Greek Independence Day Parade	Fifth Avenue	Floats and bands representing area Greek Orthodox churches and Greek federations and organizations (Late March).
• The Armory Show	West Side Piers	Brilliant best-of-galleries show—recommended.
• New Directors/New Films	MoMA	Film festival featuring new films by emerging directors.
April		
• Macy's Flower Show	Broadway and 34th St	Flowers and leather-clad vixens. Okay, just flowers really.
• Easter Parade	Fifth Avenue	Starts at 11 am, get there early (Easter Sunday).
• New York Antiquarian Book Fair	Park Ave at 67th St	170 international booksellers exhibition.
• New York International Auto Show	Jacob Javits Convention Center	Traffic jam.
• Spring Spectacular	Radio City Music Hall	The Rockettes in bunny costumes? (Easter week).
• New York City Ballet Spring Season	Lincoln Center	Features new and classical ballet (April–June).
• Taste of Chinatown	Chinatown	$1–$2 snack stands take over the streets.
May		
• Tribeca Film Festival	Various locations including Regal 16 at BPC, BMCC Chambers St, Battery Park	Festival includes film screenings, panels, lectures, discussion groups, and concerts (Early May).
• The Great Five Boro Bike Tour	Battery Park to Staten Island	Tour de NYC (first Sunday in May).
• Ninth Avenue International Food Festival	Ninth Ave from 37th to 57th Sts	Decent but overrated.
• Fleet Week	USS Intrepid	Boats and sailors from many navies (last week in May).
• New York AIDS Walk	Central Park	10K walk whose proceeds go toward finding a cure.
• Lower East Side Festival of the Arts	Theater for the New City, 155 First Ave	Celebrating Beatniks and Pop Art (last weekend in May).
• Spring Flower Exhibition	NY Botanical Garden, Bronx	More flowers.
• Cherry Blossom Festival	Brooklyn Botanic Garden	Flowering trees and Japanese cultural events. (late April–early May).
• Martin Luther King, Jr/ 369th Regiment Parade	Fifth Avenue	Celebration of equal rights (third Sunday in May).
• Thursday Night Concert Series	South Street Seaport	Free varied concerts (May–September).
• Affordable Art Fair	Midtown	Prices from $500 to no more than $10,000; worth a look if you're buying.

June

Event	Location	Description
• Puerto Rican Day Parade	Fifth Avenue	Puerto Rican pride.
• Metropolitan Opera Parks Concerts	Various locations	Free performances through June and July.
• Museum Mile Festival	Fifth Avenue	Museum open-house (second Sunday in June).
• Gay and Lesbian Pride Parade	Columbus Circle, Fifth Ave & Christopher St	Commemorates the 1969 Stonewall riots (last Sunday in June).
• New York Jazz Festival	Various locations	All kinds of jazz.
• JVC Jazz Festival	Various locations	Descends from the Newport Jazz Festival.
• Mermaid Parade	Coney Island	Showcase of sea-creatures and freaks—basically, Brooklynites.
• Feast of St Anthony of Padua	Little Italy	Patron saint of expectant mothers, Portugal, seekers of lost articles, shipwrecks, Tigua Indians, and travel hostesses, among other things (Saturday before summer solstice).
• Central Park SummerStage	Central Park	Free concerts, but get there very, VERY early. (June–August).
• Bryant Park Free Summer Season	Sixth Ave at 42nd St	Free music, dance, and film (June–August).
• Midsummer Night Swing	Lincoln Center	Performances with free dance lessons (June–July).
• Big Apple Barbecue Block Party	Madison Sq Park	Outdoor jazz, endless grilled meats. 'Nuff said.
• American Crafts Festival	Lincoln Center	Celebrating quilts and such.

July

Event	Location	Description
• Macy's Fireworks Display	East River	Independence Day's literal highlight (July 4).
• Washington Square Music Festival	W 4th St at LaGuardia Pl	Open-air concert (July–August).
• New York Philharmonic Concerts	Various locations	Varied programs (June-July).
• Summergarden	MoMA	Free classical concerts (July–August).
• Celebrate Brooklyn! Performing Arts Festival	Prospect Park Bandshell	Nine weeks of free outdoor events (July–August).
• Mostly Mozart	Lincoln Center	The name says it all (July–August).
• New York Shakespeare Festival	Delacorte Theater in Central Park	Two free plays every summer (June–September)—Zounds!
• Music on the Boardwalk	Coney Island	"Under the Boardwalk" not on the set list, presumably… (July–August).
• PS1 Warm Up	PS1 Contemporary Art Center	An assortment of musical performances every Saturday afternoon (July–August).
• Village Voice Siren Music Festival	Coney Island	Free outdoor show featuring renowned and emerging artists. For the alternative minded (July).

August

Event	Location	Description
• Harlem Week	Harlem	Black and Latino culture. The celebration lasts all month.
• Hong Kong Dragon Boat Festival	Flushing-Meadows Park Lake, Queens	Wimpy canoes need not apply.
• The Fringe Festival	Various locations, Lower East Side	Avant-garde theater.
• US Open Tennis Championships	USTA National Tennis Center, Flushing	Final Grand Slam event of the year (August–September).
• Howl Festival	Tompkins Square Park	Counter culture meets commerce: ah, we love the East Village! Recommended.
• Lincoln Center Out of Doors	Lincoln Center	Free outdoor performances throughout the month.

September

Event	Location	Description
• West Indian Day Carnival	Eastern Parkway from Utica—Grand Army Plaza, Brooklyn	Children's parade on Saturday, adult's parade on Labor Day (Labor Day Weekend).
• Richmond County Fair	441 Clarke Ave, Staten Island	Best agricultural competitions (Labor Day).
• Wigstock	Pier 54 b/w 12th–13th Sts, west side	Celebration of drag, glamour, and artificial hair (Labor Day Weekend). Each year is rumored to be the last…
• Feast of San Gennaro	Little Italy	Plenty of greasy street food (third week in September).
• Broadway on Broadway	Times Square	Sneak peek at old and new plays.

September—*continued*

Event	Location	Description
• Brooklyn BeerFest	N 11th St between Berry and Wythe, Brooklyn	Taste test of over 100 beers. Yum!
• Atlantic Antic	Brooklyn Heights	Multicultural street fair (last Sunday in September).
• New York City Opera Season	Lincoln Center	Popular and classical operas.

October

Event	Location	Description
• Race for the Mayor's Cup	NY Harbor	And the winner gets to find out what he's been drinking! (September–November)
• New York Film Festival	Lincoln Center	Features film premieres (early October).
• Fall Crafts Park Avenue	Seventh Regiment Armory on Park Avenue, b/w 66th and 67th Sts	Display and sale of contemporary American crafts by 175 of the nation's finest craft artists.
• Columbus Day Parade	Fifth Avenue	Celebrating the second person to discover America (Columbus Day).
• Halloween Parade	West Village	Brings a new meaning to costumed event (October 31).
• Halloween Dog Parade	East Village	"Awwww, they're so cuuuute!"
• Fall Antique Show	Pier 92	Look at old things you can't afford.
• Chrysanthemum and Bonsai Festival	NY Botanical Garden, Bronx	Even more flowers.
• Blessing of the Animals	St John the Divine, Morningside Heights	Where to take your gecko.
• Big Apple Circus	Lincoln Center	Step right up! (October–January)
• Hispanic Day Parade	Fifth Ave b/w 44th and 86th Sts	A celebration of Latin America's rich heritage (mid October).
• Open House NY	Various locations, all boroughs	Insider access to architecture and design landmarks (early October)—recommended.
• NY Underground Comedy	Various locations	Find undiscovered comedians before Comedy Festival Central does.
• DUMBO Art Under the Bridge Festival	Dumbo, Brooklyn	Over 600 artists open their studios to the public (late September/early October).

November

Event	Location	Description
• New York City Marathon	Verrazano to Central Park	26 miles of NYC air (first Sunday of November).
• Veteran's Day Parade	Fifth Ave from 42nd St to 79th St	Service at Eternal Light Memorial in Madison Square Park following the parade.
• Macy's Thanksgiving Day Parade	Central Park West at 79th St to Macy's	Santa starts the holiday season.
• The Nutcracker Suite	Lincoln Center	Christmas tradition (November–December).
• Singing Christmas Tree	South Street Seaport	Warning: might scare small children, family pets, and stoners (November–December).
• Christmas Spectacular	Radio City Music Hall	Rockettes star (November–January).
• A Christmas Carol	Madison Square Garden	Dickens by way of New York City (Nov–Jan).
• Origami Christmas Tree	Museum of Natural History	Hopefully not decorated with candles (Nov–Jan).

December

Event	Location	Description
• Christmas Tree Lighting Ceremony	Rockefeller Center	Most enchanting spot in the city, if you don't mind sharing it with about a million others.
• Messiah Sing-In	Call 212-333-5333	Handel would be proud.
• New Year's Eve Fireworks	Central Park	Hot cider and food available (December 31).
• New Year's Eve Ball Drop	Times Square	Welcome the new year with a freezing mob (Dec 31).
• Blessing of the Animals	Central Presbyterian Church	Where to take your other gecko (December 24).
• Menorah Lighting	Fifth Avenue	Yarmulke required.
• New Year's Eve Midnight Run	Central Park	5k for the brave.
• John Lennon Vigil	Strawberry Fields, Central Park	Anniversary of the singer/songwriter's death. (December 9).
• Alvin Ailey American Dance Theater	New York City Center	Dance at its best.
• Holiday Window Displays	Saks Fifth Avenue, Macy's, Lord & Taylor	A New York tradition.
• Small Press Book Fair	Small Press Center	Indie publishers and self-published authors.

"New York is the concentrate of art and commerce and sport and religion and entertainment and finance, bringing to a single compact arena the gladiator, the evangelist, the promoter, the actor, the trader and the merchant." —E. B. White

Useful Phone Numbers

Emergencies:	911
General City Information:	311
City Board of Elections:	212-VOTE-NYC
Con Edison:	800-752-6633
Time Warner Cable:	212-358-0900 (Manhattan); 718-358-0900 (Queens/ Brooklyn); 718-816-8686 (Staten Island)
Cablevision:	718-617-3500
Verizon:	xxx-890-1550 (add 1 and your local area code plus the seven digit number)
Police Headquarters:	646-610-5905
Public Advocate:	212-669-7200

Bathrooms

When nature calls, New York can make your life excruciatingly difficult. The city-sponsored public bathroom offerings, including dodgy subway restrooms and the sporadic experimentation with self-cleaning super porta-potties, leave a lot to be desired. Your best bet, especially in an emergency, remains bathrooms in stores and other buildings that are open to the public.

The three most popular bathroom choices for needy New Yorkers (and visitors) are Barnes & Noble, Starbucks, and any kind of fast food chain. Barnes & Noble bathrooms are essentially open to everyone (as long as you're willing to walk past countless shelves of books during your navigation to the restrooms). They're usually clean enough, but sometimes you'll find yourself waiting in line during the evening and weekends. Although Starbucks bathrooms are more prevalent, they tend to be more closely guarded (in some places you have to ask for a key) and not as clean as you'd like. Fast food restrooms are similarly unhygienic, but easy to use inconspicuously without needing to purchase anything.

For a comprehensive listing of bathrooms in NYC (including hours and even ratings), try www.allny.com (look under "NYC Bathroom Guide") and the Bathroom Diaries at www.thebathroomdiaries.com/usa/new+york.

If you're busting to go and there's no Barnes & Noble, Starbucks, or fast food joint in sight, consider the following options:

- **Public buildings**—including train stations (Grand Central, Penn Station) and malls (South Street Seaport, World Financial Center, Manhattan Mall, The Shops at Columbus Circle).
- **Government buildings**—government offices, courthouses, police stations.
- **Department stores**—Macy's, Bloomingdale's, Saks, etc.
- **Other stores**—Old Navy, Bed Bath & Beyond, FAO Schwartz, NBA store, The Strand, etc.
- **Supermarkets**—Pathmark, Food Emporium, D'Agostino, Gristedes, Key Food, etc. You'll probably have to ask, because the restrooms in supermarkets are usually way in the back amongst the employee lockers.
- **Diners**—they are in every neighborhood, and usually they are busy enough so that if you simply stride in and head towards the back (since that's where the bathroom is most of the time anyway) WITHOUT stopping, they probably won't notice. Works for us, usually.
- **Bars**—a good choice at night when most other places are closed. Try to choose a busy one so as not to arouse suspicion. Most bars have those intimidating signs warning you that the restrooms are for customers only!
- **Museums**—most are closed at night, and most require an entry fee during the day. How desperate are you?
- **Colleges**—better if you're young enough to look like a student.
- **Parks**—great during the day, closed at night.
- **Hotels**—you might have to sneak past the desk though.
- **Times Square visitors centers**—1560 Broadway and 810 Seventh Avenue.
- **Places of worship**—unpredictable hours, and not all have public restrooms.
- **Subways**—how bad do you have to go? Your best bets are express stops on the IND lines, for example, 34th Street and 6th Avenue. Some stations have locked bathrooms, with keys available at the booths.
- **Gyms**—i.e. places where you have a membership.
- **Outdoor public bathrooms**—the city tries these out from time to time—see if you can find one.

Websites

www.bridgeandtunnelclub.com • Musings and explorations of New York.
www.curbed.com • Keeps track of the daily developments in New York real estate.
www.downtownny.com • Info on everything downtown.
www.eatingintranslation.com • One guy eats his away through NYC.
www.eater.com • Restaurant gossip galore.
www.famousfatdave.com • The hungry cabbie!
www.fieldtrip.com/ny • Hundreds of suggestions for places to visit in the city.
www.forgotten-ny.com • Fascinating look at the relics of New York's past.
www.freenyc.net • Even cheapskates can have fun in the city.
www.gawker.com • A daily, guilty pleasure.
www.gothamist.com • Blog detailing various daily news and goings-on in the city.
www.hopstop.com • Get from here to there.
www.lowermanhattan.info • An excellent resource for information about what's happening in Lower Manhattan.
www.menupages.com • Menus for almost every restaurant in Manhattan.
www.metropolitanwalks.com • Interesting walking tours of NYC.
www.midtownlunch.com • Good eats for the office set.
www.myopenbar.com • Hooray for free booze!
www.newyork.craigslist.org • Classifieds for every area, including personals, apartments, musicians, jobs, and more.
www.notfortourists.com • The ultimate NYC website.
www.nyc.gov • New York City government resources.
www.nyc-grid.com • Photo blog of NYC, block by block.
www.nycsubway.org • Complete history and overview of the subways.
www.nycgo.com • The official NYC tourism site.
www.overheardinnewyork.com • Say what?
www.porkchop-express.com • Homage du pork by NFT freelancer.
www.scoutingny.com • A film scout chronicles the city.
www.theskint.com • Cool events listed daily.
www.vintagenytours.com • Tours by native New Yorkers.
www.vanishingnewyork.blogspot.com • Chronicling the loss of all the good stuff.

New York Timeline — a timeline of significant events in New York history (by no means complete)

1524: Giovanni de Verrazano enters the New York harbor.
1609: Henry Hudson explores what is now called the Hudson River.
1626: The Dutch purchase Manhattan and New Amsterdam is founded.
1647: Peter Stuyvesant becomes Director General of New Amsterdam.
1664: The British capture the colony and rename it "New York."
1754: King's College/Columbia founded.
1776: British drive colonial army from New York and hold it for the duration of the war.
1776: Fire destroys a third of the city.
1789: Washington takes the Oath of Office as the first President of the United States.
1801: Alexander Hamilton founds the *New-York Evening Post*, still published today as the *New York Post*.
1811: The Commissioners Plan dictates a grid plan for the streets of New York.
1812: City Hall completed.
1825: Completion of the Erie Canal connects New York City commerce to the Great Lakes.
1835: *New York Herald* publishes its first edition.
1835: Great Fire destroys 600 buildings and kills 30 New Yorkers.
1854: First Tammany Hall–supported mayor Fernando Woods elected
1859: Central Park opens.
1863: The Draft Riots terrorize New York for three days.
1868: Prospect Park opens.
1871: Thomas Nast cartoons and *New York Times* exposes lead to the end of the Tweed Ring.
1880: The population of Manhattan reaches over 1 million.
1883: Brooklyn Bridge opens.
1886: The Statue of Liberty is dedicated, inspires first ticker tape parade.
1888: The Blizzard of '88 incapacitates the city for two weeks.
1892: Ellis Island opens; 16 million immigrants will pass through in the next 32 years.
1897: Steeplechase Park opens, first large amusement park in Coney Island.
1898: The City of Greater New York is founded when the five boroughs are merged.
1904: The subway opens.
1906: First New Year's celebration in Times Square.
1911: Triangle Shirtwaist Fire kills 146, impels work safety movement.
1920: A TNT-packed horse cart explodes on Wall Street, killing 30; the crime goes unsolved.
1923: The Yankees win their first World Championship.
1929: Stock market crashes, signaling the beginning of the Great Depression.
1929: The Chrysler Building is completed.
1930: The Empire State Building is built, then tallest in the world.
1927: The Holland Tunnel opens, making it the world's longest underwater tunnel.
1931: The George Washington Bridge is completed.
1933: Fiorello LaGuardia elected mayor.
1934: Robert Moses becomes Parks Commissioner.
1939: The city's first airport, LaGuardia, opens.
1950: United Nations opens.
1955: Dodgers win the World Series; they move to LA two years later.
1963: Pennsylvania Station is demolished to the dismay of many; preservation efforts gain steam
1964: The Verrazano-Narrows Bridge is built, at the time the world's longest suspension bridge.
1965: Malcolm X assassinated in the Audubon Ballroom.
1965: Blackout strands hundreds of thousands during rush hour.
1969: The Stonewall Rebellion marks beginning of the gay rights movement.
1969: The Miracle Mets win the World Series.
1970: Knicks win their first championship.
1970: First New York City Marathon takes place.
1971: World Trade Center opens.
1975: Ford to City: Drop Dead.
1977: Thousands arrested for various mischief during a city-wide blackout.
1977: Ed Koch elected mayor to the first of three terms.
1987: The Giants win the Super Bowl, their first championship in over thirty years.
1987: Black Monday—stock market plunges.
1993: Giuliani elected mayor.
1993: A bomb explodes in the parking garage of the World Trade Center, killing 5.
1994: Rangers win the Stanley Cup after a 40-year drought.
2000: NFT publishes its first edition.
2000: Yankees win their 26th World Championship.
2001: The World Trade Center is destroyed in a terrorist attack; New Yorkers vow to rebuild.
2003: Tokens are no longer accepted in subway turnstiles.
2004: Yankees lose the LCS to the Boston Red Sox. We don't want to talk about it.
2005: Bloomberg sees his West Side Stadium proposal quashed.
2006: Ground is broken on the WTC memorial.
2007: Construction begins (again) on the Second Avenue subway line.
2008: Giants win Super Bowl XLII.
2009: Recession? What recession?

Essential New York Songs

"Sidewalks of New York" — Various, written by James Blake and Charles Lawlor, 1894
"Give My Regards to Broadway" — Various, written by George Cohan, 1904
"I'll Take Manhattan" — Various, written by Rodgers and Hart, 1925
"Puttin' on the Ritz" — Various, written by Irving Berlin, 1929
"42nd Street" — Various, written by Al Dubin and Harry Warren, 1932
"Take the A Train" — Duke Ellington, 1940
"Autumn in New York" — Frank Sinatra, 1947
"Spanish Harlem" — Ben E. King, 1961
"Car 54 Where Are You?" — Nat Hiken and John Strauss, 1961
"On Broadway" — Various, written by Weil/Mann/Leiber/Stoller, 1962
"Talkin' New York" — Bob Dylan, 1962
"Up on the Roof" — The Drifters, 1963
"59th Street Bridge Song" — Simon and Garfunkel, 1966
"I'm Waiting for My Man" — Velvet Underground, 1967
"Brooklyn Roads" — Neil Diamond, 1968
"Crosstown Traffic" — Jimi Hendrix, 1969
"Personality Crisis"— The New York Dolls, 1973
"New York State of Mind" — Billy Joel, 1976
"53rd and 3rd" — The Ramones, 1977
"Shattered" — Rolling Stones, 1978
"New York, New York" — Frank Sinatra, 1979
"Life During Wartime" — Talking Heads, 1979
"New York New York" — Grandmaster Flash and the Furious 5, 1984
"No Sleep Til Brooklyn" — Beastie Boys, 1987
"Christmas in Hollis" — Run-D.M.C., 1987
"New York" — U2, 2000
"I've Got New York" — The 6th's, 2000
"New York, New York" — Ryan Adams, 2001
"The Empty Page" — Sonic Youth, 2002
"New York" — Ja Rule f. Fat Joe, Jadakiss, 2004
"Empire State of Mind" — Jay-Z, 2009

Essential New York Movies

The Crowd (1928)
42nd Street (1933)
King Kong (1933)
Pride of the Yankees (1942)
Arsenic and Old Lace (1944)
Miracle on 34th Street (1947)
On the Town (1949)
On the Waterfront (1954)
The Blackboard Jungle (1955)
An Affair to Remember (1957)
The Apartment (1960)
Breakfast at Tiffany's (1961)
West Side Story (1961)
Barefoot in the Park (1967)
John & Mary (1969)
Midnight Cowboy (1969)
French Connection (1970)
The Out of Towners (1970)
Shaft (1971)
Mean Streets (1973)
Serpico (1973)
Godfather II (1974)
The Taking of Pelham One Two Three (1974)
Dog Day Afternoon (1975)
Taxi Driver (1976)
Saturday Night Fever (1977)
Superman (1978)
Manhattan (1979)
The Warriors (1979)
Fame (1980)
Escape From New York (1981)
Nighthawks (1981)
Ghostbusters (1984)
The Muppets Take Manhattan (1984)
After Hours (1985)
Crocodile Dundee (1986)
Wall Street (1987)
Moonstruck (1987)
Big (1988)
Bright Lights, Big City (1988)
Working Girl (1988)
Do the Right Thing (1989)
Last Exit to Brooklyn (1989)
When Harry Met Sally (1989)
A Bronx Tale (1993)
Kids (1995)
Men in Black (1997)
Bringing Out the Dead (1999)
The Royal Tenenbaums (2001)
Gangs of New York (2002)
Spider-Man (2002)
25th Hour (2003)
The Interpreter (2005)
Inside Man (2006)
The Devil Wears Prada (2006)
American Gangster (2007)
Sex and the City (2008)
New York I Love You (2009)
Whatever Works (2009)

Essential New York Books

A Tree Grows in Brooklyn, by Betty Smith
Coming of age story set in the slums of Brooklyn.

The Alienist by Caleb Carr
Great portrait of late-19th century New York complete with serial killer, detective, and Teddy Roosevelt.

The Bonfire of the Vanities, by Tom Wolfe
Money, class and politics undo a wealthy bond trader.

Bright Lights, Big City, by Jay McInerney
1980s yuppie and the temptations of the city.

Catcher in the Rye, by J. D. Salinger
Influential portrayal of teenage angst.

The Cricket in Times Square, by George Selden
Classic children's book.

The Death and Life of Great American Cities, by Jane Jacobs
Influential exposition on what matters in making cities work.

The Encyclopedia of New York City, by Kenneth T. Jackson, ed
Huge and definitive reference work.

Gotham: A History of New York City to 1898, by Edwin G. Burrows and Mike Wallace
Authoritative history of New York.

The Fuck-Up, by Arthur Nersesian
Scraping by in the East Village of the '80s.

Here is New York, by E. B. White
Reflections on the city.

House of Mirth, by Edith Wharton
Climbing the social ladder in upper crust, late 19th-century NY.

Knickerbocker's History of New York, by Washington Irving
Very early (1809) whimsical "history" of NY.

Manchild in the Promised Land, by Claude Brown
Autobiographical tale of growing up in Harlem.

The Power Broker, by Robert Caro
Biography of Robert Moses, you'll never look at the city the same way after reading it.

The Recognitions, by William Gaddis
Ever thought New Yorkers were phony? They are.

Washington Square, by Henry James
Love and marriage in upper-middle-class 1880s NY.

The Best of the Best

With all the culture the city has to offer, finding activities to amuse children is easy enough. From fencing classes to the funnest parks, our guide will provide you with great ideas for entertaining your little ones.

★ **Neatest Time-Honored Tradition:** The Central Park Carousel (830 Fifth Ave, 212-879-0244) features the largest hand-carved figures ever constructed and has been in residence in the park since 1950. $1 will buy you a memory to last forever. Open 10 am to 6 pm on weekdays and 10 am to 7 pm weekends, weather permitting.

★ **Coolest Rainy Day Activity:** The Children's Museum of the Arts (182 Lafayette St, 212-274-0986) offers activities for wee ones as young as 10 months, because its never too early to find out whether your child might be the next Picasso. Budding painters can use the open art studio; dramatic ones stage productions in the performing arts gallery; those who must touch everything delight in the creative play stations. Open Wed–Sun, 12–5 pm; Thurs, 12–6 pm.

★ **Sweetest Place to Get a Cavity:** Jacques Torres (350 Hudson St, 212-414-2462) where kids can watch cocoa beans turn into chocolate bars in the glass-encased factory-emporium. As if you needed another reason: Torres makes chocolate-covered Cheerios, and a host of other fun confections. Open Mon–Sat, 9 am–7 pm, Sun, 10 am–6 pm.

★ **Best Spots for Sledding:** Central Park's Pilgrim Hill and Cedar Hill. Kids pray for a snow day for the chance to try out this slick slope. BYO sled or toboggan.

★ **Funnest Park:** Hudson River Park Playground (Pier 51, Gansevoort St) With a beautiful view of the Hudson River, the park features several sprinklers, a winding "canal," and a boat-themed area complete with prow, mast, and captain's wheel.

★ **No Tears Hair Cuts:** Former Cozy's coiffer Jennifer Bilek (917-548-3643) offers professional in-home services, eliminating the fear of the unknown. She'll cut moms and dads, too…and offers "glamour parties" for girls ages 5–12.

★ **Best Halloween Costume Shopping:** Halloween Adventure (104 Fourth Ave, 212-673-4546) is the city's costume emporium that has every disguise you can possibly imagine, along with wigs, make-up supplies, and magic tricks to complete any child's dress-up fantasy. Open year-round.

★ **Best Place for Sunday Brunch:** There a billion places to take the kids to get pancakes and eggs on Sunday mornings, so why not try something totally different—dim sum in Chinatown! The kids will be entertained as carts of dumplings, pork buns, and unidentified foods constantly roll on by for non-stop eating fun. Try Mandarin Court, 88 Palace, or Dim Sum Go Go which are all located in Map 3 of the book.

Rainy Day Activities

- **American Museum of Natural History** (Central Park West at 79th St, 212- 769-5100) Fantastic for kids of all ages, with something to suit every child's interest. From the larger-than-life dinosaur fossils and the realistic animal dioramas to the out-of-this-world Hayden Planetarium, all attention will be rapt. The hands-on exhibits of the Discovery Room and the IMAX theater are also worth a visit. Open 10 am–5:45 pm daily.
- **Bowlmor Lanes** (110 University Pl, 212-255-8188) Great bowling alley with a retro décor that kids will love. Bumpers are available to cut down on those pesky gutter balls. Children are welcome every day before 5 pm and all day Sunday—a popular birthday spot.
- **Brooklyn Children's Museum** (145 Brooklyn Ave, 718-735-4400) The world's first museum for children (opened in 1899) engages kids in educational hands-on activities and exhibits. Kids can learn about life in New York in the Together in the City exhibit and find out why snakes are so slimy in the Animal Outpost.
- **Staten Island Children's Museum** (1000 Richmond Ter, 718-273-2060) Offers plenty of hands-on opportunities for kids to explore everything from pirate ships to the rainforest. There's also an outdoor play space (weather permitting). Birthday parties. The museum is open Tues–Fri, 12 pm–5 pm; Sat–Sun, 10 pm–5pm.
- **Children's Museum of Manhattan** (212 W 83rd St, 212-721-1234) As soon as you arrive at the museum, sign up for some of the day's activities. While you're waiting, check out the other exhibits in the museum. There's the Word Play area designed for the younger children in your group and the Time/Warner Media Center for the older set, where kids can produce their own television shows. The museum is open Tue–Sun, 10am–5pm.
- **Intrepid Sea Air Space Museum** (Pier 86, 46th St & 12th Ave, 212-245-0072) Tour the *Growler*, a real submarine that was once a top-secret missle command center, or take a virtual trip on one of the simulator rides. After you've taken a look at the authentic aircrafts on deck, visit the museum of the *Intrepid* to see an extensive model airplane collection and a Cockpit Challenge flight video game for those aspiring pilots. The museum is open Mon–Fri, 10 am–5 pm, and Sat–Sun 10 am–6pm .
- **Little Shop of Crafts** (711 Amsterdam Ave, 212-717-6636) Great space to bead/paint. Stay for hours.
- **Lower East Side Tenement Museum** (108 Orchard St, 212-431-0233) The museum offers insight into immigrant life in the late 19th and early 20th centuries by taking groups on tours of an historic tenement building on the Lower East Side. One tour called "Visit the Confino Family" is led by "Victoria Confino," a young girl dressed in authentic costume who teaches children about the lives of immigrants in the early 1900s. A great place to take your kids if they haven't already been there on a school field trip.
- **The Metropolitan Museum of Art** (1000 Fifth Ave, 212-535-7710) A great museum to explore with audio guides designed specifically for children. From the armor exhibits to the Egyptian Wing, the museum offers art exhibits from all historical periods.
- **Noguchi Museum** (9-01 33rd Rd at Vernon Blvd, Long Island City, 718-204-7088) This newly renovated museum that features the works of Japanese-American artist Isamu Noguchi offers interesting tours and hands-on workshops for toddlers to teens. The fees are nominal, but you must register beforehand.
- **The Museum of Modern Art** (11 W 53rd St, 212-708-9400) Besides the kid-friendly audio guides that help make this renowned museum enjoyable for tykes, MoMA has a lot of exciting weekend family programs that get kids talking about art and film. Lots of fun hands-on programs too. Registration is a must—these programs book up fast.
- **Sydney's Playground** (66 White St, 212-431-9125) A 6,000-square-foot indoor playground featuring a bouncy house, climbing play town, and a book nook. There's also a Womb Room, a quiet, dimly lit space with a view of the play area for moms who need to quiet baby while big brother plays.

Shopping Essentials

Kid's designer couture sounds like a recipe for disaster, with threats of grass stains, paint stains, and dirt lurking around every corner. But it exists and thrives in New York City, nonetheless (e.g. Julian & Sara). buybuyBaby has nursing rooms, which are very helpful. Here's a list of shops for the best party clothes and party gifts and everything in between:

- **American Girl Place** • 609 Fifth Ave • 877-AGPLACE• dolls
- **Bambini** • 1088 Madison Ave • 212-717-6742 • European clothing
- **Bellini** • 1305 Second Ave • 212-517-9233 • furniture
- **Bombalulus** • 101 W 10th St • 212-463-0897 • unique clothing & toys
- **Bonpoint** • 1269 Madison Ave • 212-722-7720 • 811 68th St • 212-879-0900 • pricey clothing
- **Books of Wonder** • 18 W 18th St • 212- 989-3270 • books
- **Boomerang Toys** • 173 West Broadway • 212-226-7650 • infant toys
- **Bu and the Duck** • 106 Franklin St • 212-431-9226 • vintage-inspired clothing/toys
- **buybuyBABY** • 270 Seventh Ave • 917-344-1555 • furniture/clothing/toys
- **Calypso Enfant & Bebe** • 426 Broome St • 212-966-3234 • hand-made clothing
- **Catimini** • 1125 Madison Ave • 212-987-0688 • French clothing
- **The Children's General Store** • Central Passage Grand Central Terminal • 212-682-0004 • toys
- **The Children's Place** • chain clothing store
  - 1460 Broadway • 212-398-4416
  - 901 Sixth Ave • 212-268-7696
  - 173 E 86th St • 212-831-5100
  - 22 W 34th St • 212-904-1190
  - 2183 Broadway • 917-441-9807
  - 36 E 16 St • 212-529-2201
  - 600 W 181 St • 212-923-7244
  - 1164 Third Ave • 212-717-7187
  - 248 W 125th St • 212-866-9616
  - 650 Sixth Ave • 917-305-1348
  - 163 E 125th St • 212-348-3607
  - 142 Delancey St • 212-979-5071
- **Dinosaur Hill** • 306 E 9th St • 212-473-5850 • toys & clothes
- **Disney Store** • 711 Fifth Ave • 212-702-4124 • Disney merchandise
- **Discovery Channel Store** • Grand Central Station (107 E 42nd St) • 212-808-9144 • educational toys
- **East Side Kids** • 1298 Madison Ave • 212-360-5000 • shoes
- **EAT Gifts** • 1062 Madison Ave • 212-861-2544 • toys & trinkets
- **Estella** • 493 Sixth Ave • 212-255-3553 • boutique clothing
- **FAO Schwarz** • 767 Fifth Ave • 212-644-9400 • toy land
- **Funky Fresh Children's Boutique** • 9 Clinton St • 212-254-5584 • unique clothing
- **GapKids/baby Gap** • chain clothing store
  - 1 Astor Pl • 212-253-0145
  - 11 Fulton St • 212-374-1051
  - 1535 Third Ave • 212-423-0033
  - 750 Broadway • 212-674-1877
  - 2300 Broadway • 212-873-2044
  - 734 Lexington Ave • 212-751-1543
  - 225 Liberty St • 212-945-4090
  - 1988 Broadway • 212-721-5304
  - 122 Fifth Ave • 917-408-5580
  - 250 W 57th St • 212-315-2250
  - 657 Third Ave • 212-697-3590
  - 680 Fifth Ave • 212-977-7023
  - 60 W 34th St • 212-760-1268
  - 1212 Sixth Ave • 212-730-1087
  - 1466 Broadway • 212-382-4500
- **Geppetto's Toy Box** • 10 Christopher St • 212 620-7511 • toys
- **Granny-Made** • 381 Amsterdam Ave • 212-496-1222 • hand-made sweaters
- **Greenstone's** • hats & clothing
  - 442 Columbus Ave • 212-580-4322
  - 1184 Madison Ave • 212-427-1665
  - 1410 Second Ave • 212-794-0530
- **Gymboree** • chain clothing store
  - 1049 Third Ave • 212- 688-4044
  - 2015 Broadway • 212- 595-7662
  - 1332 Third Ave • 212-517-5548
  - 2271 Broadway • 212- 595-9071
  - 1120 Madison Ave • 212-717-6702
- **Halloween Adventure** • 104 Fourth Ave • 212-673-4546 • costumes & magic tricks
- **Homefront Kids** • 202 E 29th St • 212-381-1969 • clothes, toys, and books
- **Jacadi** • expensive French clothing
  - 1296 Madison Ave • 212-369-1616
  - 787 Madison Ave • 212-535-3200
  - 1260 Third Ave • 212-717-9292
- **Jay Kos** • boys' clothing
  - 986 Lexington Ave • 212-327-2382
  - 475 Park Ave • 212-319-2770
- **Julian & Sara** • 103 Mercer St • 212-226-1989 • European clothing
- **Just for Tykes** • 83 Mercer St • 212-274-9121 • clothing & furniture
- **KB Toys**• 901 Sixth Ave • 212-629-5386 • chain toy store
- **Karin Alexis** • 2587 Broadway • 212-769-9550 • clothing & toys
- **Kidding Around** • 60 W 15th St • 212-645-6337 • toy store
- **Kidrobot** • 126 Prince St • 212-966-6688 • toy store
- **Leeper Kids** • Grand Central Station, Lexington Terminal • 212-499-9111 • pricey clothing & toys
- **Lester's** • 1534 Second Ave • 212-734-9292 • clothing
- **Lilliput** • pricey clothing
  - 240 Lafayette St • 212-965-9201
  - 265 Lafayette St • 212-965-9567
- **Little Eric** • 1118 Madison Ave • 212-717-1513 • shoes
- **Lucky Wang** • clothing
  - 82 7th Ave • 212-229-2900
  - 799 Broadway • 212-353-2850
- **Magic Windows** • 1186 Madison Ave • 212-289-0028 • clothing
- **Manhattan Dollhouse Shop** • 767 Fifth Ave (inside FAO Schwarz) • 877-DOLLHSE • dolls
- **Mary Arnold Toys** • 1010 Lexington Ave • 212-744-8510 • toys
- **Oilily** • 820 Madison Ave • 212-772-8686 • unique clothing
- **Peanut Butter and Jane** • 617 Hudson St • 212-620-7952 • clothing & toys
- **Penny Whistle Toys** • 448 Columbus Ave • 212-873-9090 • toys & trinkets
- **Planet Kids** • infant gear
  - 247 E 86th St • 212-426-2040
  - 2688 Broadway • 212-864-8705
- **Nintendo World** • 10 Rockefeller Plz • 646-459-0800 • games galore, including Pokemon
- **Promises Fulfilled** • 1592 Second Ave • 212-472-1600 • toys & trinkets
- **ShooFly** • 42 Hudson St • 212-406-3270 • shoes & accessories
- **Space Kiddets** • 26 E 22nd St • 212-420-9878 • girls' clothing
- **Spring Flowers** • shoes & clothes
  - 538 Madison Ave • 212-207-4606
  - 907 Madison Ave • 212-717-8182
  - 1050 Third Ave • 212-758-2669
- **Talbot's Kids and Babies** • clothing
  - 527 Madison Ave • 212-758-4152
  - 1523 Second Ave • 212-570-1630
- **Tannen's Magical Development Co**
  - 45 W 34th,Ste 608 • 212-929-4500 • magic shop
- **Tip Top Shoes** • 155 W 72nd St • 212-787-4960 • great sales for kids
- **The Scholastic Store** • 557 Broadway • 212-343-6166 • books & toys
- **Ibiza Kidz** • 61 Fourth Ave • 212-375-9984 fun clothing & shoes
- **Karin Alexis** • 2587 Broadway • 212-665-1565 • original clothing & gifts for tots
- **Tiny Doll House** • 314 E 78th St • 212-744-3719 • dolls
- **Toys R Us** • 1514 Broadway • 646-366-8800 • toy superstore •
- **West Side Kids** • 498 Amsterdam Ave • 212-496-7282 • toys
- **Yoya** • clothing
  - 636 Hudson St • 646-336-6844
  - 15 Gansevoort St • 212-242-5511
- **Z'baby** • clothing
  - 100 W 72nd St • 212-579-BABY
  - 996 Lexington Ave • 212-472-BABY
- **Zitomor** • 969 Madison Ave, 3rd Fl • 212-737-5560 • toys & books

Outdoor *and* Educational

They can't learn *everything* from the Discovery Channel.

- **Central Park Zoo** • 830 Fifth Ave • 212-439-6500 • Houses more than 1,400 animals, including some endangered species. Take a walk through the arctic habitat of the polar bears and penguins to the steamy tropical Rain Forest Pavilion. The Tisch Children's Zoo nearby is more suited for the younger crowd with its smaller, cuddlier animals.
- **Fort Washington Park** • W 155 St to Dyckman, at the Hudson River • 212-304-2365 • Call the Urban Park Rangers to arrange a tour of the little red lighthouse located at the base of the George Washington Bridge. The lighthouse affords some spectacular views—better than anything they'd see from atop Dad's shoulders. The park offers a "Junior Ranger Program" for kids, as well as a playground in Picnic Area "B."
- **Historic Richmond Town** • 441 Clarke Ave, Staten Island • 718-351-1611 • A 100-acre complex with over 40 points of interest and a museum that covers over three centuries of the history of Staten Island. People dressed in authentic period garb lead demonstrations and tours.
- **New York Botanical Garden** • Bronx River Parkway at Fordham Road, Bronx • 718-817-8777 • 250 acres and 50 different indoor and outdoor gardens and plant exhibits to explore. The Children's Adventure Garden changes each season, and kids can get down and dirty in the Family Garden. Keen young botanists can join the Children's Gardening Program and get their own plot to care for.

Classes

With all of their after-school classes and camps, the children of New York City are some of the most well-rounded (and programmed) in the country. Help them beef up their college applications with some fancy extracurriculars. It's never too early…

- **92nd Street Y After-School Programs** • 1395 Lexington Ave, 212-415-5500 • The center provides children of all ages with tons of activities, ranging from music lessons and chess to flamenco and yoga. 92nd St is known as "the Y to beat all Ys."
- **Abrons Arts Center/Henry Street Settlement** • 466 Grand St, 212-598-0400 • The Arts Center offers classes and workshops for children of all ages in music, dance, theater, and visual arts.
- **Archikids** • 472 16th St, 718-768-6123 • After-school classes and summer camp for children ages five and up that teach kids about architecture through hands-on building projects.
- **The Art Farm** • 419 E 91st St, 212-410-3117 • "Mommy & Me" art and music classes, baking courses, and small animal care for the very young.
- **Asphalt Green** • 555 E 90th St, 212-369-8890 • Swimming and diving lessons, gymnastics, team sports, and art classes. They've got it all for kids one and up.
- **Baby Moves** • 139 Perry St, 212-255-1685 • A developmental play space that offers classes for infants to six year-olds in movement, music, and play.
- **Church Street School for Music and Art** • 74 Warren St, 212-571-7290 • This community arts center offers a variety of classes in music and art involving several different media, along with private lessons and courses for parents and children.
- **Dieu Donné Papermill** • 433 Broome St, 212-226-0573 • Workshops in hand papermaking offered for children ages seven and up.
- **FasTracKids.** • 307 E 84th St, 212-737-3344 • The Studio offers hands-on courses in art, science, and yoga, with an emphasis on process and discovery.
- **Greenwich House Music School** • 46 Barrow St, 212-242-4770 • Group classes and private lessons in music and ballet for children of all ages.
- **Greenwich Village Center** • 219 Sullivan St, 212-254-3074 • Run by the Children's Aid Society, the center provides arts and after-school classes ranging from gymnastics to origami, as well as an early childhood program and nursery school.
- **Hamilton Fish Recreation Center** • 128 Pitt St, 212-387-7687 • The center offers free swimming lessons in two outdoor pools along with free after-school programs with classes like astronomy and photography.
- **Hi Art!** • 939 8th Ave, Studio 4A , 917-318-9499• For children ages 2–12, the classes focus on the exploration of art in museums and galleries in the city and giving kids the freedom to develop what they've seen into new concepts in a spacious studio setting.
- **Institute of Culinary Education** • 50 W 23rd St, 800-522-4610 • Hands-on cooking classes.
- **Irish Arts Center** • 553 W 51st St, 212-757-3318 • Introductory Irish step dancing classes for children five and up.
- **Jewish Community Center** • 334 Amsterdam Ave, 646-505-4444 • The center offers swimming lessons, team sports, and courses in arts and cooking. There's even a rooftop playground.
- **Kids at Art** • 431 E 73rd St, 212-410-9780 • Art program that focuses on the basics in a non-competitive environment for kids ages 2–11.
- **Marshall Chess Club** • 23 W 10th St, 212-477-3716 • Membership to the club offers access to weekend chess classes, summer camp, and tournaments for children ages five and up.
- **Tannen's Magic** • 45 W 34th St, Suite 608, 212-929-4500 • Private magic lessons for children eight and up on weekday evenings or group lessons of three to four teens on Monday nights. Their week-long summer sleep-away camp is also very popular.
- **The Techno Team** • 160 Columbus Ave, 212-501-1425 • Computer technology classes for children ages 3–12.
- **Trapeze School** • West St at Houston St, 917-797-1872 • Kids ages six and up can learn how to fly through the air with the greatest of ease.

Babysitting/Nanny Services

Baby Sitter's Guild • 60 E 42nd St, 212-682-0227
Barnard Babysitting Agency • 49 Claremont Ave, 212-854-2035
My Child's Best Friend • 239 E 73rd St, 212-396-4090
New York City Explorers • 244 Fifth Ave, 212-591-2619

Where to go for more info

www.gocitykids.com
www.ny.com/kids

Map 1 • Financial District

Claremont Prep	41 Broad St
Downtown Little School	15 Dutch St
High School for Economics and Finance	100 Trinity Pl
High School for Leadership & Public Service	90 Trinity Pl
Millennium High	75 Broad St
UCP of NYC	80 Maiden Ln
Wildcat Academy Charter	17 Battery Pl

Map 2 • TriBeCa

Adelphi University	75 Varick St
The Art Institute of New York City	75 Varick St
Borough of Manhattan Community College	199 Chambers St
College of New Rochelle DC-37 Campus	125 Barclay St
IS 289	201 Warren St
Metropolitan College of New York	75 Varick St
Montessori	53 Beach St
New York Academy of Art	111 Franklin St
New York Law	57 Worth St
PS 150	334 Greenwich St
PS 234 Independence	292 Greenwich St
St John's University	101 Murray St
Unity Center for Urban Technologies	121 Sixth Ave
Washington Market	55 Hudson St

Map 3 • City Hall / Chinatown

French Culinary Institute	462 Broadway
M298 Pace High	100 Hester St
MS 131 Dr Sun Yat Sen	100 Hester St
Murray Bergtraum High	411 Pearl St
New York Career Institute	11 Park Pl
Pace University	1 Pace Plz
PS 001 Alfred E Smith	8 Henry St
PS 124 Yung Wing	40 Division St
PS 130 Hernando DeSoto	143 Baxter St
Ross Global Academy Charter	52 Chambers St
St James	37 St James Pl
St Joseph	1 Monroe St
Transfiguration	29 Mott St
The Transfiguration Kindergarten	10 Confucius Pl

Map 4 • Lower East Side

Beth Jacob Parochial	142 Broome St
Collaborative Academy of Science, Technology & LA	220 Henry St
Dual Language & Asian Studies High	350 Grand St
Essex Street Academy (M294)	350 Grand St
Henry Street School for International Studies (M292)	220 Henry St
High School for History and Communication	350 Grand St
JHS 056 Corlears	220 Henry St
Little Star c/o Broome Day Care	151 Broome St
Lower Manhattan Arts Academy	350 Grand St
Mesivta Tifereth Jerusalem	141 East Broadway
New Design High	350 Grand St
PS 002 Meyer London	122 Henry St
PS 042 Benjamin Altman	71 Hester St
PS 110 Florence Nightingale	285 Delancey St
PS 126 Jacob Riis	80 Catherine St
PS 134 Henrietta Szold	293 East Broadway
PS 137 John L Bernstein	293 East Broadway
PS 184M Shuang Wen	293 East Broadway
Seward Park High	350 Grand St
University Neighborhood High	200 Monroe St
University Neighborhood Middle	220 Henry St
The Urban Assembly Academy of Government and Law	350 Grand St

Map 5 • West Village

Chelsea Career and Technical Education High	131 Sixth Ave
City Country	146 W 13th St
Elisabeth Irwin High	40 Charlton St
Empire State College–State University of New York	325 Hudson St
Food/Maritime Annex (M641)	250 W Houston St
Greenwich House Music School	46 Barrow St
Greenwich Village	490 Hudson St
Home Instruction (M501)	250 W Houston St
HS 560M City as School	16 Clarkson St
Joffrey Ballet	434 Sixth Ave
Little Red School House	272 Sixth Ave
Merce Cunningham Studio	55 Bethune St
The New School for Drama	151 Bank St
Notre Dame	327 W 13th St
Our Lady of Pompeii	240 Bleecker St
Pratt Institute	144 W 14th St
PS 003 The Charrette School	490 Hudson St
PS 41 Greenwich Village	116 W 11th St
PS 721 Manhattan Occupational Training	250 W Houston St
St Joseph	111 Washington Pl
St Luke's	487 Hudson St
Village Community	272 W 10th St

Map 6 • Washington Sq / NYU / NoHo / SoHo

Alfred Adler Institute	594 Broadway
Auxiliary Services	198 Forsyth St
Benjamin N Cardozo School of Law	55 Fifth Ave
Cascades HS for Teaching and Learning (M650)	198 Forsyth St
Cooper Union	30 Cooper Sq
Eugene Lang College	65 W 11th St
Gateway	236 Second Ave
Grace Church	86 Fourth Ave
Harvey Milk High	2 Astor Pl
Hebrew Union College	1 W 4th St
Institute of Audio Research	64 University Pl
La Salle Academy	44 E 2nd St
Legacy School for Intergrated Studies	34 W 14th St

Little Red School House	196 Bleecker St
Milano The New School for Management and Urban Policy	72 Fifth Ave
Nativity Mission	204 Forsyth St
The New School for Jazz and Contemporary Music	55 W 13th St
New School for Social Research	65 Fifth Ave
New York Eye and Ear Institute	310 E 14th St
New York University	22 Washington Sq N
NYU Graduate School of Arts and Science	5 Washington Sq N
NYU Leonard N Stern School of Business	44 W 4th St
NYU School of Law	40 Washington Sq S
NYU Shirley M Ehrenkranz School of Social Work	1 Washington Sq N
NYU Steinhardt School of Education	82 Washington Sq E
NYU Wagner	295 Lafayette St
Parsons School of Design	66 Fifth Ave
PS 751 Career Development Center	113 E 4th St
Satellite Academy High	198 Forsyth St
St Anthony	60 MacDougal St
St George Academy	215 E 6th St
St George Elementary	215 E 6th St
St Patrick	233 Mott St
Third Street Music School Settlement	235 E 11th St
Tisch School of Arts	721 Broadway
Tisch School of Arts–Dance	111 Second Ave

Map 7 • East Village

Bard High School Early College	525 E Houston St
Children's Workshop (M361)	610 E 12th St
Comelia Connelly Center for Education	220 E 4th St
East Side Community High	420 E 12th St
East Village Community	610 E 12th St
George Jackson Academy	104 St Marks Pl
Girls Preparatory Charter	333 E 4th St
Immaculate Conception	419 E 13th St
Lower East Side Prep	145 Stanton St
Manhattan Charter	100 Attorney St
Marte Valle Secondary	145 Stanton St
Mary Help of Christians	435 E 11th St
New Explorations into Science, Technology and Math	111 Columbia St
Our Lady of Sorrows	219 Stanton St
PS 015 Roberto Clemente	333 E 4th St
PS 019 Asher Levy	185 First Ave
PS 020 Anna Silver	166 Essex St
PS 034 F D Roosevelt	730 E 12th St
PS 063 William McKinley	121 E 3rd St
PS 064 Robert Simon	600 E 6th St
PS 140 Nathan Straus	123 Ridge St
PS 142 Amalia Castro	100 Attorney St
PS 188 The Island School	442 E Houston St
PS 363 Neighborhood	121 E 3rd St
PS 364 Earth School	600 E 6th St
PS 94M	442 E Houston St
St Brigid	185 E 7th St
Technology, Arts and Sciences Studio	185 First Ave
Tompkins Square Middle Extension	600 E 6th St
The Urban Assembly School of Business for Young Women	420 E 12th St

Map 8 • Chelsea

Bayard Rustin Educational Complex	351 W 18th St
Corlears	324 W 15th St
General Theological Seminary	175 Ninth Ave
Guardian Angel	193 Tenth Ave
Humanities Preparatory Academy	351 W 18th St
The James Baldwin School	351 W 18th St
The Lorge School	353 W 17th St
MS 260 Clinton School for Writers & Artists	320 W 21st St
NYC Lab HS- Collaborative Studies	333 W 17th St
NYC Lab MS-Collaborative Studies	333 W 17th St
NYC Museum School	333 W 17th St
PS 011 William T Harris	320 W 21st St
PS 033 Chelsea	281 Ninth Ave
St Columba	331 W 25th St
St Michael Academy	425 W 33rd St
Technical Career Institute	320 W 31st St

Map 9 • Flatiron / Lower Midtown

American Academy of Dramatic Arts	120 Madison Ave
Apex Technical	635 Sixth Ave
Assoc Metro Area Autistic Children	25 W 17th St
Ballet Tech	890 Broadway
The Chubb Institute	498 Seventh Ave
Community High	40 E 29th St
Fashion Institute of Technology	227 W 27th St
The Graduate Center (CUNY)	365 Fifth Ave
High School of Fashion Industries	225 W 24th St
Institute for Culinary Education	50 W 23rd St
John A Coleman	590 Sixth Ave
Learning Spring Elementary	254 W 29th St
Liberty High School Academy for Newcomers	250 W 18th St
Manhattan Village Academy	43 W 22nd St
NYU School of Continuing and Professional Studies	145 Fourth Ave
Pacific College of Oriental Medicine	915 Broadway
Phillips Beth Israel School of Nursing	776 Sixth Ave
Physical City High	55 E 25th St
Satellite Academy High	120 W 30th St
The School of Film And Television	39 W 19th St
Touro College	27 W 23rd St
Winston Preparatory	126 W 17th St
Xavier High	30 W 16th St

Map 10 • Murray Hill / Gramercy

The American Sign Language & English Dual Language High	225 E 23rd St
The American Sign Language & English Lower (M347)	225 E 23rd St
Baruch College	1 Bernard Baruch Wy
Baruch College Campus High	17 Lexington Ave
Churchill	301 E 29th St
Epiphany Elementary	234 E 22nd St
Friends Seminary	222 E 16th St
Health Prof & Human Svcs High	345 E 15th St
HS 413 School of the Future High	127 E 22nd St
Institute for Collaborative Education	345 E 15th St
Institute for Secondary Education	345 E 15th St
JHS 104 Simon Baruch	330 E 21st St
The Lee Strasberg Theater Institute	115 E 15th St
Manhattan Comprehensive Night and Day High	240 Second Ave
MS 255 Salk School of Science	319 E 19th St
New York Film Academy	100 E 17th St
Norman Thomas High	111 E 33rd St
NYSARC - NYC Chapter	200 Park Ave S
NYU Dental	345 E 24th St
NYU Medical Center	550 First Ave
PS 040 Augustus St-Gaudens	319 E 19th St
PS 116 Mary L Murray	210 E 33rd St
PS 226	345 E 15th St
The School of Visual Arts	209 E 23rd St
Stern College for Women of Yeshiva U	245 Lexington Ave
United Nations International	24 FDR Dr
Washington Irving High	40 Irving Pl

Map 11 • Hell's Kitchen

Alvin Ailey / Joan Weill Center for Dance	405 W 55th St
American Academy McAllister Institute	619 W 54th St
The Facing History School	525 W 50th St
Food and Finance High	525 W 50th St
High School for Environmental Studies	448 W 56th St
High School of Graphic Communication Arts	439 W 49th St
High School of Hospitality Management	525 W 50th St
Holy Cross	332 W 43rd St
Independence High (M544)	850 Tenth Ave
John Jay College	899 Tenth Ave
Manhattan Bridges High	525 W 50th St
Park West High	525 W 50th St
Professional Performing Arts High	328 W 48th St
PS 035	317 W 52nd St
PS 051 Elias Howe	520 W 45th St
PS 111 Adolph S Ochs	440 W 53rd St
PS 212 Midtown West	328 W 48th St
Sacred Heart of Jesus	456 W 52nd St
Urban Assembly School of Design & Construction	525 W 50th St
YWCA-Polly Dodge	538 W 55th St

Map 12 • Midtown

Berkeley College	3 E 43rd St
Circle in the Square Theatre	1633 Broadway
Coalition School for Social Change	220 W 58th St
Daytop Prep	54 W 40th St
The Family School West	308 W 46th St
Jacqueline Kennedy Onassis High	120 W 46th St
Katharine Gibbs	50 W 40th St
Laboratory Institute of Merchandising	12 E 53rd St
Landmark High	220 W 58th St
Lyceum Kennedy	225 W 43rd St
Practicing Law Institute	810 Seventh Ave
Repertory Company High	123 W 43rd St
St Thomas Choir	202 W 58th St
SUNY College of Optometry	33 W 42nd St
Wood Tobe-Coburn	8 E 40th St

Map 13 • East Midtown

Aaron	309 E 45th St
Amity Language Institute	124 E 40th St
The Beekman School	220 E 50th St
Cathedral High	350 E 56th St
High School of Art & Design	1075 Second Ave
Montessori Family School of Manhattan	323 E 47th St
Montessori School of New York	347 E 55th St
Neighborhood Playhouse	340 E 54th St
NY Institute of Credit	380 Lexington Ave
PS 059 Beekman Hill	228 E 57th St
Turtle Bay Music School	244 E 52nd St

Map 14 • Upper West Side (Lower)

Abraham Joshua Heschel High	20 West End Ave
American Musical and Dramatic Academy	2109 Broadway
The Anderson School	100 W 84th St
Art and Technology High	122 Amsterdam Ave
Beacon High	227 W 61st St
Beit Rabban Day	8 W 70th St
Blessed Sacrement	147 W 70th St
The Calhoun	433 West End Ave
The Calhoun Lower School	160 W 74th St
Collegiate	260 W 78th St
Ethical Culture-Fieldston	33 Central Park W
Fiorello H LaGuardia High	100 Amsterdam Ave
Fordham University	113 W 60th St
High School for Arts, Imagination & Inquiry	122 Amsterdam Ave
J G B Educ Services	15 W 65th St
JHS 044 William J O'Shea	100 W 77th St
Juilliard	60 Lincoln Ctr Plz
Law, Advocacy and Community Justice High	122 Amsterdam Ave
Louis D Brandeis High	145 W 84th St
Lucy Moses School For Music & Dance	129 W 67th St
M283 Manhattan Theatre Lab	122 Amsterdam Ave

Manhattan Day	310 W 75th St
Manhattan Hunter High School of Science	122 Amsterdam Ave
Mannes College of Music	150 W 85th St
Martin Luther King High	122 Amsterdam Ave
Metropolitan Montessori	325 W 85th St
MS 244 Columbus Middle	100 W 77th St
MS 245M The Computer School	100 W 77th St
New York Academy of Sciences	250 Greenwich St
New York Institute of Technology	1855 Broadway
Parkside	48 W 74th St
Professional Children's School	132 W 60th St
PS 009 Sarah Anderson	100 W 84th St
PS 087 William Sherman	160 W 78th St
PS 191 Amsterdam	210 W 61st St
PS 199 Jesse Straus	270 W 70th St
PS 243 Center	270 W 70th St
PS 811M Mickey Mantle	466 West End Ave
Robert Louis Stevenson	24 W 74th St
Rodeph Sholom	7 W 83rd St
Special Music School of America (M882)	129 W 67th St
Urban Assembly School for Media Studies	122 Amsterdam Ave
West End Day	255 W 71st St
York Prep	40 W 68th St

Map 15 • Upper East Side (Lower)

Abraham Lincoln	12 E 79th St
All Souls	1157 Lexington Ave
Allen-Stevenson	132 E 78th St
Birch Wathen Lenox	210 E 77th St
Brearly	610 E 83rd St
Browning	52 E 62nd St
Buckley	113 E 73rd St
Caedmon	416 E 80th St
Cathedral	319 E 74th St
Chapin	100 East End Ave
Dominican Academy	44 E 68th St
East Side Middle	1458 York Ave
Eleanor Roosevelt High	411 E 76th St
Ella Baker	317 E 67th St
Episcopal	35 E 69th St
Geneva School of Manhattan	583 Park Ave
Hewitt	45 E 75th St
Hunter College	695 Park Ave
JHS 167 Robert F Wagner	220 E 76th St
Kennedy Child Study Center	151 E 67th St
Loyola	980 Park Ave
Lycée Francais de New York	505 E 75th St
Manhattan High School for Girls	154 E 70th St
Manhattan International High	317 E 67th St
Martha Graham	316 E 63rd St
Marymount	1026 Fifth Ave
Marymount Manhattan College	221 E 71st St
The McCarton School	350 E 82nd St
New York School of Interior Design	170 E 70th St
NYU Institute of Fine Arts	1 E 78th St
PS 006 Lillie D Blake	45 E 81st St
PS 158 Bayard Taylor	1458 York Ave
PS 183 R L Stevenson	419 E 66th St
PS 290 Manhattan New School	311 E 82nd St
Queen Sofia Spanish Institute	684 Park Ave
Rabbi Arthur Schneier Park East Day	164 E 68th St
Ramaz	60 E 78th St
Ramaz Lower	125 E 85th St
Ramaz Middle	114 E 85th St
Regis High	55 E 84th St
Rockefeller University	1230 York Ave
Rudolf Steiner Lower	15 E 79th St
Rudolf Steiner Upper	15 E 78th St
Sotheby's Institute of Art	1334 York Ave
St Ignatius Loyola	48 E 84th St
St Jean Baptiste High	173 E 75th St
St Stephan of Hungary	408 E 82nd St
St Vincent Ferrer High	151 E 65th St
Talent Unlimited High	317 E 67th St
Town School	540 E 76th St
Ukrainian Institute of America	2 E 79th St
Urban Academy Lab High	317 E 67th St
Vanguard High	317 E 67th St
Weill Cornell Medical College	525 E 68th St

Map 16 • Upper West Side (Upper)

Abraham Joshua Heschel	270 W 89th St
Aichhorn	23 W 106th St
Alexander Robertson	3 W 95th St
The Anglo-American International	18 W 89th St
Ascension	220 W 108th St
Columbia Grammar and Prepatory	5 W 93rd St
De la Salle Academy	202 W 97th St
Dwight	291 Central Park W
Edward A Reynolds West Side High (M505)	140 W 102nd St
Holy Name of Jesus	202 W 97th St
JHS 054 Booker T Washington	103 W 107th St
Mandell Nursery-Kindergarten	127 W 94th St
Morningside Montessori	251 W 100th St
Mott Hall II	234 W 109th St
MS 246M Crossroads	234 W 109th St
MS 247M Dual Language Middle	32 W 92nd St
MS 250 West Side Collaborative	735 West End Ave
MS 256 Academic and Athletic Excellence	154 W 93rd St
MS 258 Community Action	154 W 93rd St
PS 038 Roberto Clemente	232 E 103rd St
PS 075 Emily Dickinson	735 West End Ave
PS 084 Lillian Weber	32 W 92nd St
PS 145 Bloomingdale	150 W 105th St
PS 163 Alfred E Smith	163 W 97th St
PS 165 Robert E Simon	234 W 109th St
PS 166 Richard Rodgers School of Arts and Technology	132 W 89th St

PS 333 Manhattan School for Children	154 W 93rd St
Riverside Early Learning Center	202 Riverside Dr
School for Young Performers	175 W 92nd St
The Smith School	131 W 86th St
Solomon Schechter High	1 W 91st St
St Agnes Boys	555 West End Ave
St Gregory the Great	138 W 90th St
Stephen Gaynor	148 W 90th St
The Studio School	124 W 95th St
Trinity	139 W 91st St
Upper Trevor Day	1 W 88th St
West Side Montessori	309 W 92nd St
Yeshiva Ketana of Manhattan	346 W 89th St

Map 17 • Upper East Side / East Harlem

Academy of Environmental Science Secondary High (M635)	410 E 100th St
Amber Charter	220 E 106th St
Ballet Academy East	1651 Third Ave
Bilingual Bicultural Mini	219 E 109th St
The Bilingual Bicultural School (M182)	219 E 109th St
Brick Church	62 E 92nd St
Central Park East I Elementary	1573 Madison Ave
Central Park East II (M964)	19 E 103rd St
Central Park East Secondary	1573 Madison Ave
Convent of the Sacred Heart	1 E 91st St
Cristo Rey High	112 E 106th St
Dalton	108 E 89th St
East Harlem Block	1615 Madison Ave
East Harlem School at Exodus House	309 E 103rd St
Harbor Science & Arts Charter	1 E 104th St
Heritage	1680 Lexington Ave
Horace Mann	55 E 90th St
Hunter College Elementary	71 E 94th St
Hunter College High	71 E 94th St
JHS 013 Jackie Robinson	1573 Madison Ave
La Scuola D'Italia Guglielmo M	12 E 96th St
Life Sciences Secondary	320 E 96th St
Lower Trevor Day	11 E 89th St
Manhattan Country	7 E 96th St
Mount Sinai School of Medicine	1 Gustave Levy Pl
MS 224 Manhattan East Center for Arts & Academics	410 E 100th St
National Academy School of Fine Arts	5 E 89th St
Nightingale-Bamford	20 E 92nd St
NY Center for Autism Charter	433 E 100th St
Our Lady of Good Counsel	323 E 91st St
Park East High	230 E 105th St
PS 050 Vito Marcantonio	433 E 100th St
PS 072	131 E 104th St
PS 083 Luis Munoz Rivera	219 E 109th St
PS 108 Angelo Del Toro	1615 Madison Ave
PS 146 Ann M Short	421 E 106th St
PS 169 Robert F Kennedy	110 E 88th St
PS 171 Patrick Henry	19 E 103rd St
PS 198 Isador and Ida Straus	1700 Third Ave
PS 77 Lower Lab	1700 Third Ave
Reece	180 E 93rd St
Richard R Green High School of Teaching (M570)	421 E 88th St
School of Cooperative Technical Education	321 E 96th St
Solomon Schechter	50 E 87th St
Spence	22 E 91st St
St Bernard's	4 E 98th St
St David's	12 E 89th St
St Francis de Sales	116 E 97th St
St Joseph Yorkville	420 E 87th St
Tag Young Scholars JHS (M012)	240 E 109th St
Tito Puente Educational Complex (M117)	240 E 109th St
The Trevor Day School	11 E 89th St
Young Women's Leadership High	105 E 106th St

Map 18 • Columbia / Morningside Heights

A Philip Randolph Campus High	443 W 135th St
Annunciation	461 W 131st St
Bank Street School for Children	610 W 112th St
Barnard College	3009 Broadway
Cathedral	1047 Amsterdam Ave
Columbia University	2960 Broadway
Computer School	370 W 120th St
The Cooke Center For Learning	475 Riverside Dr
Corpus Christi	535 W 121st St
High School for Math, Science and Engineering at City College	138 Convent Ave
IS 195 Roberto Clemente	625 W 133rd St
IS 223 Mott Hall	71 Convent Ave
IS 286 Renaissance Military	509 W 129th St
Jewish Theological Seminary of America	3080 Broadway
Kipp Infinity Charter	625 W 133rd St
Kipp S.T.A.R. College Preparatory (M726)	433 W 123rd St
Manhattan School of Music	120 Claremont Ave
Powell MS for Law & Social Justice	509 W 129th St
PS 036 Margaret Douglas	123 Morningside Dr
PS 125 Ralph Bunche	425 W 123rd St
PS 129 John H Finley	425 W 130th St
PS 161 Pedro A Campos	499 W 133rd St
PS 180 Hugo Newman	370 W 120th St
Riverside Church Week Day	490 Riverside Dr
The School at Columbia University	556 W 110th St
St Hilda's and St Hugh's	619 W 114th St
St Joseph's School of the Holy Family	168 Morningside Ave
Teachers College, Columbia University	525 W 120th St

Map 19 • Harlem (Lower)

Christ Crusader Academy	302 W 124th St
College of New Rochelle Rosa Parks Campus	144 W 125th St
Democracy Prep Charter	222 W 134th St
Fellowship of Learning	9 W 130th St
Frederick Douglass Academy II	215 W 114th St

Future Leaders Institute Charter	134 W 122nd St
Great Tomorrows USA	38 W 123rd St
Harlem Children's Zone/Promise Academy Charter M284	175 W 134th St
Harlem Children's Zone/Promise Academy II Charter	220 W 121st St
Harlem Episcopal	1330 Fifth Ave
Harlem Link Charter (M329)	134 W 122nd St
Harlem Renaissance High	22 E 128th St
Harlem Success Charter	34 W 118th St
Helene Fuld School of Nursing North	26 E 120th St
IS 275	175 W 134th St
JHS 088 Wadleigh	215 W 114th St
Kappa II	144 W 128th St
Mount Pleasant Christian Academy	126 W 119th St
Opportunity Charter	240 W 113th St
PS 076 A Philip Randolph	220 W 121st St
PS 092 Mary M Bethune Academy	222 W 134th St
PS 133 Fred R Moore	2121 Fifth Ave
PS 149 Sojourner Truth	41 W 117th St
PS 154 Harriet Tubman	250 W 127th St
PS 162	34 W 118th St
PS 175 Henry H Garnet	175 W 134th St
PS 185 John M Langston	20 W 112th St
PS 208 Alain L Locke	21 W 111th St
PS 241 Family Academy	240 W 113th St
PS 242M GP Brown Comp	134 W 122nd St
Rice High	74 W 124th St
School of the Arts (M3SA)	215 W 114th St
Sister Clara Mohammed	102 W 116th St
Sisulu-Walker Charter	125 W 115th St
St Aloysius	223 W 132nd St
St Benedict Day Nursery & Kindergarten	21 W 124th St
Thurgood Marshall Academy	200 W 135th St
Wadleigh Secondary School for the Performing and Visual Arts	215 W 114th St

Map 20 • El Barrio / East Harlem

Academy for Health/Sciences	2351 First Ave
All Saints	52 E 130th St
Bilingual 45 RCBS (M055)	2351 First Ave
Bilingual Bicultural Art School	160 E 120th St
Children's Storefront	70 E 129th St
The Choir Academy of Harlem	2005 Madison Ave
East Harlem Tech (M02P)	2351 First Ave
Harlem Day Charter	240 E 123rd St, 4th Fl
Highway Christian Academy	132 E 111th St
HS 435 Manhattan Center Math and Science	280 Pleasant Ave
Issac Newton JHS for Science & Math (M825)	260 Pleasant Ave
JHS John S Roberts	2351 First Ave
Kappa II (M317)	144 E 128th St
King's Academy	2345 Third Ave
Leadership Village Academy Charter	315 E 113th St
Manhattan Center for Science & Math	260 Pleasant Ave
Mount Carmel-Holy Rosary	371 Pleasant Ave
New York Prep (M03Q)	315 E 113th St
NY College of Podiatric Medicine	1800 Park Ave
Our Lady Queen of Angels	232 E 113th St
PS 007 Samuel Stern	160 E 120th St
PS 030 Hernandez/Hughes	144 E 128th St
PS 057 James W Johnson	176 E 115th St
PS 079 Horan	55 E 120th St
PS 096 Joseph Lanzetta	216 E 120th St
PS 101 Draper	141 E 111th St
PS 102 Jacques Cartier	315 E 113th St
PS 112 Jose Celso Barbosa	535 E 119th St
PS 138	144 E 128th St
PS 155 William Paca	319 E 117th St
PS 206 Jose Celso Babosa	508 E 120th St
River East (M037)	508 E 120th St
St Ann	314 E 110th St
St Paul	114 E 118th St
Urban Peace Academy (M695)	2351 First Ave

Map 21 • Manhattanville / Hamilton Heights

Boricua College	3755 Broadway
Childs' Memorial Christian Academy	1763 Amsterdam Ave
City College	Convent Ave b/w W 130th St & W 141st St
Dance Theatre of Harlem	466 W 152nd St
Harlem International Community	421 W 145th St
Harlem School of the Arts	645 St Nicholas Ave
HS 685 Bread & Roses Integrated Arts High	6 Edgecombe Ave
Kappa IV (M302)	6 Edgecombe Ave
M304 Mott Hall High	6 Edgecombe Ave
The Moore Learning Center	614 W 157th St
New Heights Academy Charter	1818 Amsterdam Ave
Our Lady of Lourdes	468 W 143rd St
PS 028 Wright Brothers	475 W 155th St
PS 153 Adam C Powell	1750 Amsterdam Ave
PS 192 Jacob H Schiff	500 W 138th St
PS 325	500 W 138th St
Shabak Christian/Daly Day	459 W 152 St
St Catherine of Genoa	508 W 153rd St

Map 22 • Harlem (Upper)

East Harlem Village Academy Charter (M709)	244 W 144th St
Frederick Douglass Academy	2581 Adam Clayton Powell Jr Blvd
PS 046 Arthur Tappan	2987 Frederick Douglass Blvd
PS 123 Mahalia Jackson	301 W 140th St
PS 194 Countee Cullen	244 W 144th St
PS 197 John Russwurm	2230 Fifth Ave
PS 200 James Smith	2589 Adam Clayton Powell Jr Blvd
Resurrection	282 W 151st St
St Charles Borromeo	214 W 142nd St
St Mark the Evangelist	55 W 138th St
Thurgood Marshall Academy Lower	276 W 151st St

Map 23 • Washington Heights

Columbia University Medical Center	630 W 168th St
Columbia University School of Dental and Oral Surgery	630 W 168th St
Columbia University School of Nursing	630 W 168th St
HS 552 Gregorio Luperon High	516 W 181st St
Incarnation Elementary	570 W 175th St
Interboro	260 Audubon Ave
IS 164 Edward W Stitt	401 W 164th St
Mailman School of Public Health	722 W 168th St
Mirabel Sisters IS 90	21 Jumel Pl
The Modern School	870 Riverside Dr
MS 319 Maria Teresa	21 Jumel Pl
MS 321 Minerva	21 Jumel Pl
MS 326 Writers Today & Leaders Tomorrow	401 W 164th St
MS 328	401 W 164th St
Patria (MS 324)	21 Jumel Pl
PS 004 Duke Ellington	500 W 160th St
PS 008 Luis Belliard	465 W 167th St
PS 115 Humboldt	586 W 177th St
PS 128 Audubon	560 W 169th St
PS 173	306 Ft Washington Ave
PS 210 21st Century Academy	4111 Broadway
St Rose of Lima	517 W 164th St
St Spyridon Parochial	120 Wadsworth Ave

Map 24 • Fort George / Fort Tryon

Business & Finance High	549 Audubon Ave
City College Academy of the Arts	4600 Broadway
Community Health Academy of the Heights	511 W 182nd St
Health Careers & Sciences High	549 Audubon Ave
IS 218 Salome Ukena	4600 Broadway
IS 528 Bea Fuller Rodgers	180 Wadsworth Ave
JHS 143 Eleanor Roosevelt	511 W 182nd St
Juan Bosch Public	12 Ellwood St
Law & Public Service High	549 Audubon Ave
Media & Communications High	549 Audubon Ave
Mesivta Rabbi Samson Raphael	8593 Bennett Ave
Middle School 322	4600 Broadway
Mother Cabrini High	701 Ft Washington Ave
Our Lady Queen of Martyrs	71 Arden St
PS 005 Ellen Lurie	3703 Tenth Ave
PS 048 PO Michael J Buczek	4360 Broadway
PS 132 Juan Pablo Duarte	185 Wadsworth Ave
PS 152 Dyckman Valley	93 Nagle Ave
PS 187 Hudson Cliffs	349 Cabrini Blvd
PS 189	2580 Amsterdam Ave
St Elizabeth	612 W 187th St
Washington Heights Expeditionary Learning	511 W 182nd St
Yeshiva Rabbi SR Hirsch	91 Bennett Ave
Yeshiva University	500 W 185th St
Yeshiva University High	2540 Amsterdam Ave

Map 25 • Inwood

Amistad Dual Language	4862 Broadway
Good Shepherd	620 Isham St
JHS 052 Inwood	650 Academy St
Manhattan Christian Academy	401 W 205th St
Muscota (M314)	4862 Broadway
Northeastern Academy	532 W 215th St
PS 018	4124 Ninth Ave
PS 098 Shorac Kappock	512 W 212t St
PS Intermediate School 278	407 W 219th St
PS/IS 278 (M278)	407 W 219th St
St Jude	433 W 204th St
St Matthew Lutheran	200 Sherman Ave

Battery Park City

PS 89	201 Warren St
Stuyvesant High	345 Chambers St

Roosevelt Island

Lillie's International Christian	851 Main St
MS 271 Building (M271)	645 Main St
PS 217 Roosevelt Island	645 Main St

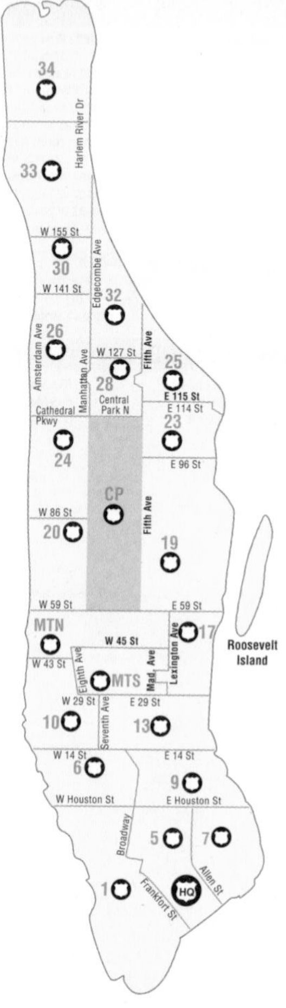

Important Phone Numbers

All Emergencies:	911
Non-Emergencies:	311
Terrorism Hot Line:	888-NYC-SAFE
Crime Stoppers:	800-577-TIPS
Crime Stoppers (Spanish):	888-57-PISTA
Sex Crimes Report Line:	212-267-RAPE
Crime Victims Hotline:	212-577-7777
Cop Shot:	800-COP-SHOT
Missing Persons Case Status:	646-610-6914
Missing Persons Squad:	212-473-2042
Operation Gun Stop:	866-GUNSTOP
Organized Crime Control Bureau Drug Line:	888-374-DRUG
Complaints (Internal Affairs):	212-741-8401
Website:	www.nyc.gov/nypd

Statistics	*2009*	*2008*	*2006*	*2005*	*2003*
Uniformed Personnel	39,787	37,838	37,038	39,110	37,200
Murders	471	523	597	540	596
Rapes	1,201	1,298	1,497	1,640	1,877
Robberies	18,533	22,355	23,556	24,417	25,890
Felony Assaults	16,644	16,230	17,124	17,336	18,717
Burglaries	19,318	20,685	22,950	23,997	29,120
Grand Larcenies	39,342	44,166	46,525	47,619	46,518
Grand Larcenies (cars)	10,672	12,481	15,731	17,865	23,144

Precinct		*Phone*	*Map*
1st Precinct	16 Ericsson Pl	212-334-0611	2
5th Precinct	19 Elizabeth St	212-334-0711	3
7th Precinct	19 1/2 Pitt St	212-477-7311	4
6th Precinct	233 W 10th St	212-741-4811	5
9th Precinct	130 Avenue C	212-477-7811	7
Mid-Town South	357 W 35th St	212-239-9811	8
10th Precinct	230 W 20th St	212-741-8211	9
13th Precinct	230 E 21st St	212-477-7411	10
Mid-Town North	306 W 54th St	212-760-8300	11
17th Precinct	167 E 51st St	212-826-3211	13
20th Precinct	120 W 82nd St	212-580-6411	14
19th Precinct	153 E 67th St	212-452-0600	15
24th Precinct	151 W 100th St	212-678-1811	16
23rd Precinct	162 E 102nd St	212-860-6411	17
26th Precinct	520 W 126th St	212-678-1311	18
28th Precinct	2271 Frederick Douglass Blvd	212-678-1611	19
32nd Precinct	250 W 135th St	212-690-6311	19
25th Precinct	120 E 119th St	212-860-6511	20
30th Precinct	451 W 151st St	212-690-8811	21
33rd Precinct	2207 Amsterdam Ave	212-927-3200	23
34th Precinct	4295 Broadway	212-927-9711	24
Central Park Precinct	86th St & Transverse Rd	212-570-4820	p236

Post Offices / Zip Codes

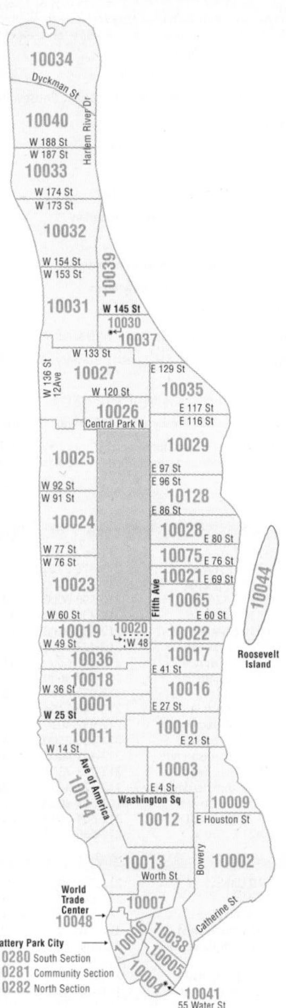

Branch	Address	Phone	Map
Canal Street	350 Canal St	212-925-3378	2
Church Street	90 Church St	212-330-5001	2
Chinatown	6 Doyers St	212-267-3510	3
Peck Slip	1 Peck Slip	212-964-1054	3
Knickerbocker	128 East Broadway	212-608-3598	4
Pitt Station	185 Clinton St	212-254-9270	4
Village	201 Varick St	212-645-0327	5
West Village	527 Hudson St	212-989-5084	5
Cooper	93 Fourth Ave	212-254-1390	6
Patchin	70 W 10th St	212-475-2534	6
Prince	124 Greene St	212-226-7868	6
Peter Stuyvesant	432 E 14th St	212-677-2112	7
Tompkins Square	244 E 3rd St	212-673-6415	7
James A Farley	421 Eighth Ave	212-330-2902	8
London Terrace	234 Tenth Ave	800-275-8777	8
Port Authority	309 W 15th St	212-645-0351	8
Empire State	19 W 33rd St	212-736-8282	9
Greeley Square	39 W 31st St	212-244-7055	9
Midtown	223 W 38th St	212-819-9604	9
Old Chelsea	217 W 18th St	212-675-0548	9
Station 138 (Macy's)	151 W 34th St	212-494-2688	9
Madison Square	149 E 23rd St	212-673-3771	10
Murray Hill	205 E 36th St	212-545-0836	10
Murray Hill Finance	115 E 34th St	212-689-1124	10
Radio City	322 W 52nd St	212-265-3672	11
Times Square	340 W 42nd St	212-502-0421	11
Bryant	23 W 43rd St	212-279-5960	12
Rockefeller Center	610 Fifth Ave	212-265-3854	12
Dag Hammarskjold	884 Second Ave	800-275-8777	13
Franklin D Roosevelt	909 Third Ave	800-275-8777	13
Grand Central Station	450 Lexington Ave	212-330-5722	13
Tudor City	5 Tudor City Pl	800-275-8777	13
Ansonia	178 Columbus Ave	212-362-1697	14
Columbus Circle	27 W 60th St	212-265-7858	14
Planetarium	127 W 83rd St	212-873-5698	14
Cherokee	1483 York Ave	212-517-8361	15
Gracie	229 E 85th St	212-988-6680	15
Lenox Hill	217 E 70th St	212-330-5561	15
Cathedral	215 W 104th St	212-662-0355	16
Park West	693 Columbus Ave	800-275-8777	16
Yorkville	1617 Third Ave	212-369-2747	17
Columbia University	534 W 112th St	800-275-8777	18
Manhattanville	365 W 125th St	212-662-1540	18
Morningside	232 W 116th St	800-275-8777	19
Oscar Garcia Rivera	153 E 110th St	212-860-1896	20
Triborough	167 E 124th St	212-534-0381	20
Hamilton Grange	521 W 146th St	212-281-1538	21
College Station	217 W 140th St	212-283-7096	22
Colonial Park	99 Macombs Pl	212-368-9849	22
Lincolnton	2266 Fifth Ave	212-281-9781	22
Audubon	511 W 165th St	212-568-2387	23
Sergeant Riayan A Tejeda	555 W 180th St	212-568-2690	23
Fort George	4558 Broadway	212-942-5266	24
Inwood Post Office	90 Vermilyea Ave	212-567-7821	25
Roosevelt Island	694 Main St	800-275-8777	p260

If you have to get to a hospital (especially in an emergency), it's best to go to the closest one. However, as a quick reference, the following is a list of the largest hospitals by neighborhood, complete with the name of its corresponding map. But no matter which hospital you drag yourself into, for heaven's sake make sure you have your insurance card.

Lower Manhattan: NYU Downtown Hospital • William & Beekman Sts, just south of the Brooklyn Bridge • [Map 3]

West Village/Chelsea: St Vincent's • Seventh Ave & 12th St [Map 5]

East Village: Beth Israel Medical Center • 14th St & Broadway/Union Square • [Map 10]

Murray Hill: Bellevue Hospital Center • First Ave & 27th St [Map 10] ; NYU College of Dentistry • First Ave & 24th St [Map 10]

Hell's Kitchen/Upper West Side: St Luke's Roosevelt Hospital • 10th Ave & 58th St [Map 11]

East Side: New York Presbyterian • York Ave & 68th St [Map 15]; Lenox Hill Hospital • Lexington Ave & 77th St [Map 15]; Mt Sinai Medical Center • Madison Ave & 101st St [Map 17]

Columbia/Morningside Heights: St Luke's Hospital Center • Amsterdam Ave & 114th St [Map 18]

El Barrio: North General Hospital • Madison Ave & 125th St [Map 20]

Farther Uptown: Columbia Presbyterian Medical Center • 168th St & Broadway [Map 23]

If you have a condition that isn't immediately threatening, certain hospitals in New York specialize and excel in specific areas of medicine:

Cancer: Memorial Sloan-Kettering

Birthing Center/Labor & Delivery: St Luke's Roosevelt

Digestive Disorders: Mt Sinai

Dentistry: NYU College of Dentistry

Ear, Nose, and Throat: Mt Sinai

Eyes: New York Eye and Ear Infirmary

Geriatrics: Mt Sinai, New York Presbyterian

Heart: New York Presbyterian

Hormonal Disorders: New York Presbyterian

Kidney Disease: New York Presbyterian

Mental Health: Bellevue

Neurology: New York Presbyterian, NYU Medical Center

Orthopedics: Hospital for Special Surgery, New York Presbyterian

Pediatrics: Children's Hospital of New York Presbyterian

Psychiatry: New York Presbyterian, NYU Medical Center

Rheumatology: Hospital for Special Surgery, Hospital for Joint Diseases Orthopedic Institute, NYU Medical Center

Emergency Rooms	*Address*	*Phone*	*Map*
Bellevue Hospital Center	462 First Ave	212-562-1000	10
Beth Israel Medical Center	281 First Ave	212-420-2000	10
Harlem Hospital Center	506 Lenox Ave	212-939-1000	22
Hospital for Joint Diseases	301 E 17th St	212-598-6000	10
Lenox Hill Hospital	110 E 77th St	212-434-2000	15
Manhattan Eye, Ear & Throat	210 E 64th St	212-838-9200	15
Metropolitan Hospital Center	1901 First Ave	212-423-6262	17
Mount Sinai Medical Center	1190 Fifth Ave	212-241-6500	17
New York Downtown Hospital	170 William St	212-312-5000	1
New York Eye & Ear Infirmary	310 E 14th St	212-979-4000	6
New York Presbyterian–Weill Cornell Medical Center	525 E 68th St	212-746-5454	15
New York-Presbyterian Hospital Allen Pavilion	5141 Broadway	212-932-4000	25
New York-Presbyterian Hospital/Columbia University Medical Center	622 W 168th St	212-305-2500	23
North General Hospital	1879 Madison Ave	212-423-4000	20
NYU Langone Medical Center	550 First Ave	212-263-7300	10
St Luke's Hospital	1111 Amsterdam Ave	212-523-4000	18
St Luke's Roosevelt Hospital Center	1000 Tenth Ave	212-523-4000	11
St Vincent's Manhattan	170 W 12th St	212-604-7000	5
VA NY Harbor Healthcare System - Manhattan Campus	423 E 23rd St	212-686-7500	10

Other Hospitals	*Address*	*Phone*	*Map*
Beth Israel – Phillips Ambulatory Care Center	10 Union Sq E	212-844-8000	10
Coler Goldwater–Coler Campus	1 Main St	212-848-6000	p260
Coler Goldwater–Goldwater Campus	1 Main St	212-318-8000	p260
Gouverneur Healthcare Services	227 Madison St	212-238-7000	4
Gracie Square Hospital	420 E 76th St	212-988-4400	15
Hospital for Special Surgery	535 E 70 St	212-606-1000	15
Memorial Sloan-Kettering Cancer Center	1275 York Ave	212-639-2000	15
Renaissance Health Care Network Diagnostic and Treatment Center	215 W 125th St	212-932-6500	18

Beginner's mistake: Walk into the main branch of the New York Public Library at Bryant Park, and ask how to check out books. Trust us; it's happened. Recognizable for its reclining stone lions, Patience and Fortitude, the famous building is a research library with non-circulating materials that you can peruse only in the iconic reading room. If you want to read *War and Peace* or *The Da Vinci Code*, it's best to go to your local branch (there are 80 branch and 5 central libraries). Note: Holds take a very long time to fill, at least a week to a week and a half. If the book you need is only a 20-minute subway ride away, and you need the book now, invest the time and the $4.50. If it's reference material you're after, there are several specialized research libraries to help:

The Schomburg Center for Research in Black Culture (Map 22) is the nation's foremost source on African-American history. **The Science, Industry, and Business Library (Map 9)** is perhaps the newest and swankiest of all of Manhattan's libraries. **The Library for the Performing Arts (Map 14)** contains the Theatre on Film and Tape Archive. If you can give them even a semi-legitimate reason, you can watch taped performances of most Broadway shows from the past 25 years. **The Early Childhood Resource and Information Center (Map 12)** runs workshops for parenting and reading programs for children.

The aforementioned main branch of the **New York Public Library (Map 12)** (one of Manhattan's architectural treasures, designed by Carrère and Hastings in 1897 and renamed for billionaire Stephen A. Schwarzman in 2008) has several special collections and services, such as the Humanities and Social Sciences Library, the Map Division, Exhibition galleries, and divisions dedicated to various ethnic groups. The main branch contains 88 miles of shelves and has more than 10,000 current periodicals from almost 150 countries. Research libraries require an ACCESS card, which you can apply for at the library and which allows you to request materials in any of the reading rooms. Card sign-up can be slow, so be patient. It never hurts to bring along multiple kinds of ID, or a piece of mail if you're a new NYC resident. There's also the **Andrew Heiskell Braille and Talking Book Library (Map 9)**, designed to be barrier-free. The library contains large collections of special format materials and audio equipment for listening to recorded books and magazines. You can check out the full system online at www.nypl.org.

Library	*Address*	*Phone*	*Map*
115th Street	203 W 115th St	212-666-9393	19
125th St	224 E 125th St	212-534-5050	20
58th St	127 E 58th St	212-759-7358	13
67th St	328 E 67th St	212-734-1717	15
96th Street	112 E 96th St	212-289-0908	17
Aguilar	174 E 110th St	212-534-2930	20
Andrew Heiskell Braille & Talking Book Library	40 W 20th St	212-206-5400	9
Bloomingdale	150 W 100th St	212-222-8030	16
Chatham Square	3v East Broadway	212-964-6598	3
Columbus	742 Tenth Ave	212-586-5098	11
Countee Cullen	104 W 136th St	212-491-2070	22
Early Childhood Resource & Information Center	455 5th Ave	917-275-6975	12
Epiphany	228 E 23rd St	212-679-2645	10
Fort Washington	535 W 179th St	212-927-3533	23
Frick Art Reference Library	10 E 71st St	212-547-0641	15
George Bruce	518 W 125th St	212-662-9727	18
Grand Central Branch	135 E 46th St	212-621-0670	13
Hamilton Fish Park	415 E Houston St	212-673-2290	7
Hamilton Grange	503 W 145th St	212-926-2147	21
Harlem	9 W 124th St	212-348-5620	19
Hudson Park	66 Leroy St	212-243-6876	5
Inwood	4790 Broadway	212-942-2445	25
Jefferson Market	425 Sixth Ave	212-243-4334	5
Kips Bay	446 Third Ave	212-683-2520	10
Macomb's Bridge	2650 Adam Clayton Powell Jr Blvd	212-281-4900	22
Mid-Manhattan Library	455 Fifth Ave	917-275-6975	12
Morningside Heights Library	2900 Broadway	212-864-2530	18
Muhlenberg	209 W 23rd St	212-924-1585	9
Mulberry Street	10 Jersey St	212-966-3424	6
New Amsterdam	9 Murray St	212-732-8186	3
New York Academy of Medicine Library	1216 Fifth Ave	212-822-7200	17
New York Public Library for the Performing Arts	40 Lincoln Center Plz	212-870-1630	14
New York Society Library	53 E 79th St	212-288-6900	15
Ottendorfer	135 Second Ave	212-674-0947	6
Riverside	127 Amsterdam Ave	212-870-1810	14
Roosevelt Island	524 Main St	212-308-6243	p260
Schomburg Center for Research	515 Malcolm X Blvd	212-491-2200	22
Science, Industry, and Business Library	188 Madison Ave	212-592-7000	9
Seward Park	192 East Broadway	212-477-6770	4
St Agnes	444 Amsterdam Ave	212-877-4380	14
Stephen A. Schwarzman Building	42nd St & Fifth Ave	212-340-0849	12
Terence Cardinal Cooke-Cathedral	560 Lexington Ave	212-752-3824	13
Tompkins Square	331 E 10th St	212-228-4747	7
Washington Heights	1000 St Nicholas Ave	212-923-6054	23
Webster	1465 York Ave	212-288-5049	15
Yorkville	222 E 79th St	212-744-5824	15

There are few cities in the world that cater to gay men as New York City does; a gay man can find anything and everything he wants, at almost any time of day, in the Big gay Apple. Some bars focus on aesthetics and atmosphere, such as **Therapy**, while others like **Phoenix** and **The Cock** merely provide the space and alcohol—the rest is up to you. Some gay bars play host to particular types of men like **Chi Chiz** (men of color). There are even gay bars that now offer social activities: **Boots & Saddle** provides sports leagues and hi-def TV; **Gym** supplies the city's first gay sports bar; and **Splash** remains one of the hottest dance clubs. Be smart, be safe, and enjoy your status as a "NYC Boy."

There are more lesbian bars and parties than ever in New York City, so all you have to do is decide what night, which neighborhood and how you'll snag a girl! Although you'll find quality drinks, music, and women at **Henrietta Hudson's**, the notorious and intolerable bathroom line might discourage those lesbians who actually have a bladder. **LovergirlNYC@ Club Cache** on Saturday nights boasts 500+ beautiful women, while Thursday nights at **Habibi Lounge** promise a more low-key lesbian gathering. Check out **Snapshot at Delancey** on Tuesday nights for steamy Sapphic scenesters and musicians; and **Nowhere** on any night. For an up-to-the-minute list, visit www.gonycmagazine.com. And if you're not afraid of venturing out of Manhattan, check out **Chueca** in Queens—it's a lesbian bar 7 days a week! In Brooklyn, chill on the patio at **Ginger's**.

Websites

The Lesbian, Gay, Bisexual & Transgender Community Center: www.gaycenter.org — Information about center programs, meetings, publications, and events.

Out & About: www.outandabout.com — Travel website for gays and lesbians including destination information, a gay travel calendar, health information, and listings of gay tour operators.

Gayellow Pages: www.gayellowpages.com — Yellow pages of gay/lesbian-owned and gay/lesbian-friendly businesses in the US and Canada.

Dyke TV: www.myspace.com/dyketv — Whether you're interested in viewing or contributing, this website has all the info you'll need.

Edwina: www.edwina.com — A NY online meeting place for gays and lesbians looking for love, lust, or just friendship.

Shescape: www.shescape.com — Hosts lesbian events at various venues in town year round.

Publications

Free at gay and lesbian venues and shops, and some street corners.

Gay City News (formerly LGNY) — Newspaper for lesbian and gay New Yorkers including current local and national news items. www.gaycitynews.com

Next Magazine – Weekly magazine that includes frisky nightlife listings, film reviews, feature articles, and more. www.nextmagazine.net.

GO NYC — Monthly magazine for the urban lesbian on the go with free arts and entertainment listings, weekly event picks, plus information on community organizations and LGBT-owned and LGBT-friendly businesses. www.gonycmagazine.com

Bookshops

Bluestockings, 172 Allen St, 212-777-6028 — Lesbian/radical bookstore and activist center with regular readings and a fair-trade café. www.bluestockings.com

Health Centers and Support Organizations

Callen-Lorde Community Health Center, 356 W 18th St, 212-271-7200 — Primary Care Center for GLBT New Yorkers. www.callen-lorde.org

Gay Men's Health Crisis, 119 W 24th St, 212-367-1000; Hotline: 212-807-6655 — Non-profit organization dedicated to AIDS awareness and support for those with the disease. www.gmhc.org

The Lesbian, Gay, Bisexual & Transgender Community Center, 208 W 13th, 212-620-7310 — The largest LGBT multi-service organization on the East Coast. www.gaycenter.org

Gay and Lesbian National Hotline, 212-989-0999 — Switchboard for referrals, advice, and counseling. www.glnh.org

Identity House, 208 W 13th St, 212-243-8181 — Offers LGBTQ counseling services, short-term therapy and/or referrals, groups, and workshops. www.identityhouse.org

Lambda Legal Defense and Education Fund, 120 Wall, St Ste 1500, 212 809-8585 — These are the people who fight the good fight in order to secure civil rights for the entire LGBT population. www.lambdalegal.org

National Gay & Lesbian Task Force, 80 Maiden, Ln Ste 1504, 212-604-9830 — This national organization creates change by building LGBT political power and de-marginalizing LGBT issues. www.ngltf.org

New York City Gay & Lesbian Anti-Violence Project, 212-714-1141 — 24-hour crisis support line for violence against LGTBH communities. www.avp.org

PFLAG, 119 W 24th St, 2nd Floor, 212-463-0629 — Parents, Families, and Friends of Lesbians and Gays meet on the second Sunday of every month 3 pm–5 pm for mutual support. www.pflagnyc.org

Lesbian and Gay Immigration Rights Task Force (LGIRTF), 350 W 31st St to 40 Exchange Pl, 17th Floor, 212-714-2904 — Advocates for changing US policy on immigration of permanent partners. www.lgirtf.org

GLAAD (Gay and Lesbian Alliance Against Defamation), W 29th St, 4th Floor, 212-629-3322 — These are the folks who go to bat for you in the media. www.glaad.org

OUTdancing @ Stepping Out Studios, 37 W 26th St, 646-742-9400 — The first LGBT partner dance program in the US. www.steppingoutstudios.com

LGBT Night at Leo Bar, Asia Society, 725 Park Ave, 212-327-9352 — Each third Friday of the month, Asia Society partners with a different LGBT professional organization, mixing people, cocktails, and culture. Free exhibition tours included. www.asiasociety.org

Annual Events

Pride Week — Usually the last full week in June; www.hopinc.org (212-807-7433)

New York Gay and Lesbian Film Festival — Showcase of international gay and lesbian films, May/June; www.newfestival.org (212-571-2170)

Mass Red Ribbon Ride — Replacing the old NYC to Boston AIDS ride, this version is a two-day ride across Massachusetts. The 2006 ride begins in Pittsfield and finishes in Weston, mid-August; www.massredribbonride.org (617-450-1100 or 888-MASSRIDE)

Venues — Lesbian

- **Bamboo 52** (Sun, Ladies Nite) • 344 W 52nd St • 212-315-2777 • www.bamboo52nyc.com • Older, upscale *L Word* gathering. Sushi bar, too!
- **Chueca Bar** • 69-04 Woodside Ave, Queens • 718-424-1171 • www.chuecabar.com • The only Latina lesbian club in NYC.
- **Cubbyhole** • 281 W 12th St • 212-243-9041 • www.cubbyholebar.com • The name says it all, but it's full of fun, flirty women!
- **Escuelita** (Fri) • 301 W 39th St • 212-631-0588 • www.enyclub.com
- **Ginger's** • 363 Fifth Ave, Park Slope • 718-788-0924 • Park Slope's hot lesbian hangout.
- **Habibi Lounge** (Thurs) • 198 Avenue A • 212-982-0932 • www.habibiloungenyc.com • This hookah bar is the place to be, 9 pm–3 am, for a relaxed, lounge-and-flirt-on-cushions evening.
- **Henrietta Hudson** • 438 Hudson St • 212-924-3347 • www.henriettahudson.com
- **Nation** (Sat, girlNation) • 12 West 45th St • 212-391-8053 • Baby dyke gathering in Midtown.
- **Nowhere** • 322 E 14th St • 212-477-4744 • Welcomes both gays and lesbians—imagine that!
- **Slipper Room** • 167 Orchard St • 212-253-7246 • www.slipperroom • Burlesque and drag queens abound at this LGBT-friendly bar.
- **Starbar** • 218 Avenue A • If the now-defunct Starlight and Wonder Bar had a baby, this would be their bar!
- **The Delancey** (Tuesday, Snapshot) • 168 Delancey • 212-254-9920 • www.thedelancey.com • This lesbian party combines art and nightlife on the LES.
- **Club Cache** (Sat, LovergirlNYC) • 221 W 46th St. • 347-385-6745 • www.lovergirlnyc.com •The Big Kahuna of lesbian parties welcomes both members and non-members 10:30 pm–4 am, and includes contests, go-go dancers, and lotsa lesbians!

Venues — Gay

- **Avalon** (Sun. Nights) • 47 W 20th St • 212-807-7780 • www.nycavalonnightclub.com
- **Barracuda** • 275 W 22nd St • 212-645-8613
- **Barrage** • 401 W 47th St • 212-586-9390
- **Billie's Black** • 271 W 119th St • 212-280-2248 • www.billiesblack.com • Bar, lounge, and grill.
- **Boiler Room** • 86 E 4th St • 212-254-7536 • www.boilerroomnyc.com • Internet jukebox with 100,000 selections.
- **Boots & Saddle** • 76 Christopher St • 212-929-9684 • www.bootsnsaddle.com • This place has it all: go-go boys, tarot readers, sports leagues, digital jukebox, and hi-def TV.
- **Candle Bar** • 309 Amsterdam Ave • 212-874-9155 • Small, but not too small to cruise or be cruised!
- **Chi Chiz** • 135 Christopher St • 212-462-0027
- **Cleo's Ninth Avenue Salon** • 656 Ninth Ave •
- **The Dugout** • 185 Christopher St • 212-242-9113 • www.thedugoutny.net
- **The Duplex** • 61 Christopher St • 212-255-5438 • www.theduplex.com
- **Eagle** • 554 W 28th St • 646-473-1866 • www.eaglenyc.com
- **EasternBloc** • 505 E 6th St • 212-777-2555 • www.easternblocnyc.com • Bar for boys who crave strong drinks and stronger DJs.
- **Escuelita** • 301 W 39th St • 212-631-0588 • www.enyclub.com
- **g Lounge** • 225 W 19th St • 212-929-1085 • www.glounge.com
- **Gym** • 167 Eighth Ave • 212-337-2439 • www.gymsportsbar.com • NYC's first gay sports bar.
- **The Hangar Bar** • 115 Christopher St • 212-627-2044
- **Julius'** • 159 W 10th St • 212-929-9672 • Mature men hang at this landmark bar.
- **Marie's Crisis** • 59 Grove St • 212-243-9323 • Cheapest Happy Hour in NYC.
- **Metropolitan** • 559 Lorimer St, Williamsburg • 718-599-4444
- **The Monster** • 80 Grove St • 212-924-3558 .• www.manhattan-monster.com • Part cabaret, part bar, plus comedians.
- **Mr. Black** • 35 E 21st St • 212-253-2560 • www.mrblacknyc.com • Multi-cultural dance mecca with rotating DJs.
- **No Parking** • 4168 Broadway • 212-923-8700 • Washington Heights earns another gay bar!
- **Nowhere** • 322 E 14th St • 212-477-4744 • Boys and girls welcome.
- **Evolve** • 221 E 58th St • 212-355-3395 • Size does matter—check out the longest gay bar in NYC!
- **The Phoenix** • 447 E 13th St • 212-477-9979 • No frills, no cheese, no BS.
- **Pieces Bar** • 8 Christopher St • 212-929-9291• www.piecesbar.com
- **Posh** • 405 W 51st St • 212-957-2222 • www.poshbarnyc.com
- **Pyramid Club** • 101 Avenue A • 212-228-4888 • www.thepyramidclub.com • For '80s dance nights, sans the B&T crowd.
- **Rawhide** • 212 Eighth Ave • 212-242-9332 • Leather crowd.
- **The Ritz** • 369 W 46th St • 212-333-2554 • Another bar/lounge with outdoor patio and guest DJs.
- **Secret** • 525 W 29th St • 212-268-5580 • Shh, another gay lounge.
- **Splash** (SBNY) • 50 W 17th St • 212-691-0073 • www.splashbar.com • Quintessential gay club.
- **Stonewall** • 53 Christopher St • 212-463-0950 • www.stonewall-place.com
- **Suite** • 992 Amsterdam Ave • 212-222-4600 • www.suitenyc.com • Chic bar with drag shows.
- **Xth Avenue Lounge** • 642 Tenth Ave • 212-245-9088
- **Therapy** • 348 W 52nd St • 212-397-1700 • www.therapy-nyc.com
- **Tool Box** • 1742 Second Ave • 212-348-1288
- **Townhouse** • 236 E 58th St • 212-754-4649 • www.townhouseny.com
- **Ty's** • 114 Christopher St • 212-741-9641
- **The Urge** • 33 Second Ave • 212-533-5757 • East Village lounge with 2-tier bar.
- **View Bar** • 232 Eighth Ave • 212-929-2243 • www.viewbarnyc.com
- **Vlada** • 331 West 51st St • 212-974-8030 • www.vladabar.com • Sip one of fifteen infused vodkas at this romantic and sophisticated midtown bar.
- **The Web** • 40 E 58th St • 212-308-1546 • Where the Asian boys are.
- **XES Lounge** • 157 West 24th St • 212-604-0212 • www.xesnyc.com

Restaurants

Restaurants	Address	Phone	Map
Wo Hop	17 Mott St	212-267-2536	3
Sugar Cafe	200 Allen St	212-260-1122	4
Waverly Restaurant	385 Avenue of the Americas	212-675-3181	5
French Roast	78 W 11th St	212-533-2233	5
Around the Clock	8 Stuyvesant St	212-598-0402	6
Ben's Pizza	123 MacDougal St	212-677-0976	6
Cozy Soup & Burger	739 Broadway	212-477-5566	6
Veselka	144 2nd Ave	212-228-9682	6
Lahore	132 Crosby St	212-965-1777	6
Veselka	144 Second Ave	212-228-9682	6
7A	109 Ave A	212-673-6583	7
Bereket Turkish Kebab House	187 E Houston St	212-475-7700	7
Odessa	119 Ave A	212-253-1470	7
Yaffa Café	97 St Marks Pl	212-674-9302	7
Empire Diner	210 Tenth Ave	212-243-2736	8
Skylight Diner	402 W 34th St	212-244-0395	8
Tick Tock Diner	481 Eighth Ave	212-268-8444	8
Kang Suh	1250 Broadway	212-564-6845	9
Kum Gang San	49 W 32nd St	212-967-0909	9
Kunjip	9 W 32nd St	212-216-9487	9
Woo Chon	8 W 36th St	212-695-0676	9
Gemini Diner	641 Second Ave	212-532-2143	10
Gramercy Café	184 Third Ave	212-982-2121	10
L'Express	249 Park Ave S	212-254-5858	10
Lyric Diner & Coffee Shop	283 3rd Ave	212-213-2222	10
Sarge's Deli	548 Third Ave	212-679-0442	10
Hampton's Gourmet	755 9th Ave	212-245-3230	11
H&H Bagels	639 W 46th St	212-765-7200	11
Morningstar	401 W 57th St	212-246-1593	11
Cosmic Diner	888 8th Ave	212-333-5888	12
Maison	1700 Broadway	212-757-2233	12
99 Cents Fresh Pizza	151 E 43rd St	212-922-0257	13
Albert's Mofongo House	4762 Broadway	212-569-3431	14
Big Nick's	2175 Broadway	212-362-9238	14
French Roast	2340 Broadway	212-799-1533	14
Gray's Papaya	2090 Broadway	212-799-0243	14
H&H Bagels	2239 Broadway	212-595-8000	14
Manhattan Diner	2180 Broadway	212-877-7252	14
City Diner	2441 Broadway	212-877-2720	16
Midnight Express	1715 2nd Ave	212-860-2320	17
Viand	300 E 86th St	212-879-9425	17
IHOP	2294 Adam Clayton Powell Jr Blvd	212-234-4747	19
New Caporal Fried Chicken	3772 Broadway	212-862-8986	21
El Malecon	4141 Broadway	212-927-3812	23
Tipico Dominicano	4177 Broadway	212-781-3900	23
White Mana	470 Tonnele Ave	201-963-1441	35

Supermarkets

Supermarkets	Address	Phone	Map
Jubilee Marketplace	99 John St	212-233-0808	1
Jin Market	111 Hudson St	212-226-9310	2
Pathmark	227 Cherry St	212-227-8988	4
Key Food	52 Ave A	212-477-9063	7
Gristedes	460 Third Ave	212-251-9670	10
Gristedes	907 Eighth Ave	212-582-5873	12
Westside Market	2171 Broadway	212-595-2536	14
Gristedes	1446 Second Ave	212-535-4925	15
Gristedes	2704 Broadway	646-352-4676	16
Gristedes Mega Store	262 W 96th St	212-663-5126	16
Gristedes Mega Store	350 E 86th St	212-535-1688	17
Morton Williams	2941 Broadway	212-666-4190	18
Pathmark	300 W 145th St	212-281-3158	22
Pathmark	410 W 207th St	212-569-0600	25
Gourmet Heaven	450 North End Ave	212-233-9333	p234
Gristedes	315 South End Ave	212-233-7797	p234

Plumbers

Plumbers	Address	Phone	Map
Effective Plumbing	Multiple locations	212-545-0100	
New York Plumbing & Heating Service	Multiple locations	212-496-9191	
Roto-Rooter Plumbing	Multiple locations	212-687-1661	
Sanitary Plumbing and Heating	211 E 117th St	212-734-5000	20

Hardware Store

Hardware Store	Address	Phone	Map
Nuthouse Hardware	202 E 29th St	212-545-1447	10

Copy Shops

Copy Shops	Address	Phone	Map
FedEx Kinko's	191 Madison Ave	212-685-3449	9
FedEx Kinko's	239 Seventh Ave	212-929-0623	9
On-Site Sourcing	443 Park Ave S Fl 3	212-252-9700	10
Discovery Copy Services	45 W 45th St	212-827-0039	12
FedEx Kinko's	233 W 54th St	212-977-2679	12
FedEx Kinko's	1211 Sixth Ave	212-391-2679	12
FedEx Kinko's	16 E 52nd St	212-308-2679	12
FedEx Kinko's	240 Central Park S	212-258-3750	12
FedEx Kinko's	60 W 40th St	212-921-1060	12
Skyline Duplication	151 W 46th St	212-302-5153	12
FedEx Kinko's	641 Lexington Ave	212-572-9995	13
FedEx Kinko's	747 Third Ave	212-753-7778	13
FedEx Kinko's	221 W 72nd St	212-362-5288	14
FedEx Kinko's	1122 Lexington Ave	212-628-5500	15
The Village Copier	2872 Broadway	212-666-0600	18

Gym

Gym	Address	Phone	Map
NYSC	125 7th Ave S	212-206-1500	5
24/7 Fitness Club	47 W 14th St	212-206-1504	6
Citi Fitness	244 E 14th St	212-598-9800	6
NYSC	113 E 23rd St	212-982-4400	10
NYSC	2527 Broadway	212-665-0009	16
Big Gym	625 W 181st St	212-568-2444	23
Planet Fitness	177 Dyckman St	212-304-4500	25

Laundromats

Laundromats	Address	Phone	Map
69 Avenue C Laundromat	69 Ave C	212-388-9933	7
Classic Laundry	262 W 145th St	917-507-4865	22
106 Audubon Avenue Laundromat	106 Audubon Ave	212-795-8717	23
Super Laundromats and Dry Cleaners	228 Nagle Ave	na	25

Veterinary

Veterinary	Address	Phone	Map
Animal Emergency Clinic	1 W 15th St	212-924-3311	9
NYC Veterinary Specialists - 24-Hour Emergency Care	410 W 55th St	212-767-0099	11
Animal Medical Center	510 E 62nd St	212-838-8100	15
Center for Veterinary Care	236 E 75th St	212-734-7480	15
Park East Animal Hospital	52 E 64th St	212-832-8417	15

Newsstands

Newsstands	Map
Delancey St & Essex St	4
Sixth Ave & 3rd St	5
Sixth Ave (South of W 8th St)	5
5 Third Ave	6
Second Ave & St Marks Pl	6
23rd St & Third Ave	10
Third Ave (b/w 34th/35th Sts)	10
Seventh Ave & 42nd St	12
Eighth Ave & 49th St	12
Broadway & W 50th St	12
59th St & Third Ave	13
First Ave & 57th St	13
Broadway & W 72nd St	14
Broadway & W 76th St	14
Columbus Ave & 81st St	14
79th St & York (First Ave)	15
First Ave & 63rd St	15
2nd Ave (b/w 60th & 61st Sts)	15
86th St & Lexington Ave	17
Broadway & 116th St	18

Delivery and Messengers

Delivery and Messengers	Phone
Alliance Courier & Freight	212-302-3422
Moonlite Courier	212-473-2246
Need It Now	212-989-1919
Same Day Express	800-982-5910
Urban Express	212-855-5555
Mobile Messenger Service	212-247-7400

Private Investigators

Private Investigators	Phone
Matthew T Cloth, PI	718-449-4100
North American Investigations	800-724-8080
Sherlock Investigations	212-579-4302

Locksmiths

Locksmiths	Phone
A&V Locksmith	212-226-0011
Aaron-Hotz Locksmith	212-675-3358
Abbey Locksmiths	212-535-2289
Advantage Locksmith	212-398-5500
American Locksmiths	212-888-8888
CBS Locksmith	212-410-0090
Certified Locks	917-435-4514
Champion Locksmiths	212-362-7000
East Manhattan Locksmiths	212-369-9063
Emergency Locksmith 24 Hours	212-231-7627
LockDoctors	212-935-6600
Lockmasters Locksmith	212-690-4018
Night and Day Locksmith	212-722-1017
Paragon Security & Locksmith	212-620-9000
Speedway Locksmith	877-917-6500

General Information • **Dog Runs**

Useful websites: www.doglaw.com, www.nycparks.org, www.urbanhound.com

It's good to be a dog in New York. NYC's pooches are among the world's most pampered: they celebrate birthdays, don expensive sweaters, and prance down Fifth Avenue in weather-appropriate gear. But for the rest of us, who would rather step in dog doo than dress our pups in Burberry raincoats, there's still reason to smile. NYC is full of dog runs—both formal and informal—scattered throughout the city's parks and neighborhood community spaces. Good thing too, as the fine for having a dog off-leash can run upward of $100, and park officials are vigilant. While the city takes no active role in the management of the dog runs, it provides space to the community groups who do. These community groups are always eager for help (volunteer time or financial contributions) and many post volunteer information on park bulletin boards. It can take many years and several thousand dollars to build a dog run in New York. NYC boasts more than 40 runs, but that number doesn't seem very big when you consider that the city is home to more than one million pooches. That's not a lot of room for each dog to stretch his four legs. Each dog run is different, but pet lovers can check out www.urbanhounds.com for descriptions. It's good to know, for example, that Riverside Park at 87th Street has a fountain and hose to keep dogs cool in the summer. Formal runs are probably the safest bet for pets, as most are enclosed and maintained. For safety reasons, choke or pronged collars are forbidden, and identification and rabies tags should remain on the flat collar. Most runs prohibit dogs in heat, aggressive dogs, and dogs without up-to-date shots.

There are no dog runs in Central Park, but before 9 am the park is full of people walking their dogs off-leash. While this is a strict no-no the rest of the day (and punishable by hefty fines), park officials unofficially tolerate the practice as long as dogs maintain a low profile, and are leashed immediately at 9 am.

Map Name • Address • Comments

2 **P.S. 234** • 300 Greenwich St at Chambers St • Private run. $50/year membership. www.doglaw.com

3 **Fish Bridge Park** • Dover and Pearl Sts • Concrete-surfaced run. Features water hose, wading pool, and lock box with newspapers. www.nycgovparks.org

4 **Coleman Oval Park** • Pike & Monroe Sts • Under the Manhattan Bridge. www.nycgovparks.org

5 **West Village D.O.G. Run** • Little W 12th St • Features benches, water hose, and drink bowl. Membership costs $40 annually, but there's a waiting list. www.wvdog.org

6 **Washington Square Park** • MacDougal St at W 4th St • Located in the southwest corner of the park, this is a large, gravel-surfaced run with many spectators. This popular run gets very crowded, but is well-maintained nonetheless. www.nycgovparks.org

6 **LaGuardia Place** • Mercer St at Houston St • Private run with a membership (and a waiting list). The benefits include running water and a plastic wading pool for your dog to splash in. www.mhdra.org

6 **Union Square** • Broadway at 15th St • Crushed stone surface. www.nycgovparks.org

7 **Tompkins Square Park** • Avenue B at 10th St • New York City's first dog run (opened in 1990) underwent a $450,000 restoration in 2007. Currently, toys, balls, frisbees, and dogs in heat are all prohibited. This community-centered run offers lots of shade, benches, and running water. www.firstrunfriends.org

8 **Thomas Smith Triangle** • Eleventh Ave at 23rd St • Concrete-surfaced run. www.nycgovparks.org

8 **Chelsea** • 18th St at the West Side Hwy

10 **Madison Square Park** • Madison Ave at 25th St • Medium-sized run with gravel surface and plenty of trees. www.nycgovparks.org

11 **DeWitt Clinton Park** • Eleventh Ave at 52nd & 54th Sts • Two small concrete-surfaced runs. www.nycgovparks.org

11 **Astro's Community Dog Run** • W 39th St at Tenth Ave • A private dog run (membership costs $15 a year) featuring chairs, umbrellas, fenced garden, and woodchip surface. www.hkdogrun.org

13 **E 60th Street Pavilion** • 60th St at the East River • Concrete-surfaced run. www.doglaw.com

13 **Peter Detmold Park** • Beekman Pl at 51st St • Large well-maintained run with cement and dirt surfaces and many trees. www.nycgovparks.org

13 **Robert Moses Park** • First Ave and 42nd St • Concrete surface. www.nycgovparks.org

14 **Theodore Roosevelt Park** • Central Park W at W 81st St • Gravel surface. www.nycgovparks.org

14 **Riverside Park** • Riverside Dr at 72nd St www.nycgovparks.org

14 **Margaret Mead Park** • Columbus Ave at 81st St www.leashline.com

15 **Balto Dog Monument** • Fifth Ave at E 67th St (Central Park)

15,17 **Carl Schurz Park** • East End Ave at 85/86th Sts • Medium-sized enclosed run with pebbled surface and separate space for small dogs. This run has benches and shady trees, and running water is available in the bathrooms. www.nycgovparks.org

16 **Riverside Park** • Riverside Dr at 87th St • Medium-sized run with gravel surface. www.nycgovparks.org

16 **Riverside Park** • Riverside Dr at 105/106th Sts • Medium-sized run with gravel surface. www.nycgovparks.org

18 **Morningside Park** • Morningside Ave b/w 114th & 119th Sts www.nycgovparks.org

20 **Thomas Jefferson Park** • E 112th St at First Ave • Wood chip surface.

23 **J. Hood Wright Park** • Haven Ave at W 173rd St • An enclosed dirt-surfaced run. www.nycgovparks.org

24 **Fort Tryon Park/Sir William's Dog Run** • Margaret Corbin Dr, Washington Heights www.ftdog.org

25 **Inwood Hill Dog Run** • Dyckman St and Payson Ave • Gravel surface. www.nycgovparks.org

p234 Kowsky Plaza Dog Run (**Battery Park City**) • Gateway Plaza • Located near the marina, this area has small hills for your dog to run on, as well as a small fountain and bathing pool. www.bpcdogs.org

p234 **Battery Park City** • Along River Ter between Park Pl W and Murray St • Concrete-surfaced run with a view of the river. www.manhattan.about.com

If you're reading this you're probably not a tourist, and if you're not a tourist you probably don't need a hotel. However, chances are good that at some point your obnoxious friend or relative from out of state will suddenly come a-knockin', bearing news of their long-awaited arrival to the big city. "So I thought I'd stay at your place," they will suggest casually, displaying their complete ignorance of the number of square feet in an average New York apartment—and simultaneously realizing your greatest fear of playing host to someone you greatly dislike. Or there's the possibility that your place is infested with mice, bed bugs, or pigeons and you need to escape, pronto. Or maybe you're just looking for a romantic (or slightly less than romantic) getaway without leaving the city. Whatever the case, be assured that there is a seemingly endless array of possibilities to suit all your overnight desires and needs.

Obviously, your options run from dirt cheap (that's "dirt cheap" by NYC standards) to disgustingly offensive. For those of you with money to spare and/or a respect for high status, there are the elite luxury chains—**The Ritz Carlton** (cheaper to stay at the one in Battery Park **(p 234)** than Central Park **(Map 12)**), **The Four Seasons (Map 12)** at E 57th St, **The W** at Union Square **(Map 10)**, **Times Square (Map 12)**, E 39th St **(Map 10)**, and Lexington Ave at 49th St **(Map 13)**, **Le Parker Meridien (Map 12)**, **The Peninsula (Map 12)**, **The St. Regis (Map 12)**, and **The Mandarin-Oriental (Map 11)**.

Those hotels that are more unique to Manhattan include: **The Lowell (Map 15)**, a fortress of pretentiousness nestled beside Central Park, which successfully captures the feel of a snobby, high-class gentleman's club. For a similar feeling, only with a heavy dose of Renaissance Italy and a design dating back to 1882, check into **The New York Palace (Map 12)**. If you prefer more modern surroundings, the swank-tastic **Bryant Park Hotel (Map 12)** (once the landmark Radiator building before it was transformed) is a favorite amongst entertainment and fashion industry folks. Similarly, The **Regency (Map 15)**, nicknamed "Hollywood East" in the 1960s, is a must for all celeb-stalkers hangers-on alike. Meanwhile, **The Algonquin (Map 12)** offers complimentary delivery of the New Yorker, as if to suggest that they cater to a more literary crowd (maybe in the 1920s, but whether or not that's the case today is up for debate). If you're feeling fabulous, there's **The Muse Hotel (Map 12)**, located in the heart of Times Square, mere steps away from the bright lights of Broadway (Movin' Out, anyone?). If you're more comfortable with the old-money folks (or if you're a nostalgic member of the nouveau-riche), check out the apartment-size rooms at **The Carlyle (Map 15)**. Be a bit easier on your wallet and get a room at **The Excelsior Hotel (Map 14)**—it may be a tad less indulgent, but get over it, you're still right on Central Park. Yet more affordable and not an ounce less attractive is **The Hudson (Map 11)**, a chic boutique hotel from Ian Schrager. Then there's **The Shoreham (Map 12)**, which offers complimentary champagne at the front desk (so it's definitely worth a shot to pose as a guest) in addition to a fantastically retro bar, that looks like it's straight out of A Clockwork Orange. Last but not least, dance on over to the famous **Waldorf Astoria (Map 13)**, where the unrivaled service and $200 million in renovations more than justify the cost of staying.

There are also plenty of places to stay downtown, perfect for those of you who plan on stumbling home after a long night of bar-hopping. The sexier of these hotels include: **The Hotel Gansevoort (Map 5)**, a sleek tower of luxury, located steps away from the Meatpacking District—New York's very own version of Miami Beach! Nearby, you'll find **The Maritime Hotel (Map 10)**, which does a great impression of a cruise ship, replete with porthole-shaped windows and La Bottega, an Italian restaurant with a massive outdoor patio that feels like the deck of a Carnival liner. In trendy SoHo, you'll find **The Mercer Hotel**, 60 Thompson **(Map 6)**, and **The SoHo Grand (Map 2)** (there's also its sister, **The Tribeca Grand (Map 2)**, farther south)—which vary ever-so-slightly in degrees of coolness, depending on your demands. A little ways north, next to Gramercy Park, you'll find **The Inn** at Irving Place **(Map 10)**—things are a tad less modern at this upscale bed and breakfast (it consists of two restored 19th-century townhouses), but the Cibar lounge, the company (it's a favorite of rock and fashion royalty), and the lack of any visible sign outside are all sure to validate your sense of hip. On the newest stretch of NYC hipness, The Bowery, there are a few new boutique hotels to make all your rock star dreams come true. **The Bowery Hotel (Map 6)** was the first to make its mark on this former stretch of skid row. The Lobby Bar is worth checking out even if you can't afford a room. Up the street the semi-sleek **Cooper Square Hotel (Map 6)** is competing for models and I-Bankers expense accounts. Check out how they squeezed the fancy hotel in between two existing tenement buildings. And not too far away is the super fancy **Crosby Street Hotel (Map 6)**, the newest addition to the cool hotels we'll never be able to afford category.

Let's just be honest, shall we? The truth of the matter is that you're poor. All you want is a bargain—and believe it or not, we get it. Thus, behold the most affordable splendors of the New York hotel experience: **The Gershwin Hotel (Map 9)**, **Herald Square Hotel (Map 9)**, **Super 8 Times Square (Map 12)**, **Red Roof Inn (Map 9)**, **Second Home** on Second Avenue **(Map 6)**, and **The Chelsea Savoy (Map 9)**.

More mid-range options include: **Hotel Thirty Thirty (Map 9)**, **The Abington Guest House (Map 5)**, **The Roger Williams Hotel (Map 9)**, **Portland Square Hotel (Map 12)**, **Comfort Inn (Map 9)**, **Clarion Hotel (Map 10)**, and **The New Yorker Hotel (Map 8)**.

Be aware that prices are generally highest during the holiday season and the summer and lowest during the off season. Not all hotels have a star rating, and those that do are sometimes inaccurate. The quoted rates will give you a pretty good idea of the quality of each hotel. Rates are ballpark and subject to change—go to one of the many travel websites (Hotels.com, Priceline, Hotwire, Travelocity, Kayak, Expedia, etc.) or individual company websites (hilton.com, spg.com, holiday-inn.com) to get the best rates. Or call the hotel and ask if they have any specials. The bottom line is that, as is the case with everything in New York, though you have plenty of options, few of them are cheap.

Map 1 • Financial District

		Phone	Rate $
Best Western Seaport Inn	33 Peck Slip	212-766-6600	180
Eurostars Wall Street	129 Front St	212-742-0003	159-329 standard
Gild Hall	15 Gold St	212-232-7700	289-429 standard
Hampton Inn Manhattan - Seaport Financial District	320 Pearl St	212-571-4400	219-319 standard
Millenium Hilton	55 Church St	212-693-2001	279-399 standard
New York Marriott Downtown	85 West St	212-385-4900	149-399 standard
The Wall Street Inn	9 S William St	212-747-1500	379
W New York Downtown	123 Washington St	646-826-8600	489

Map 2 • TriBeCa

Cosmopolitan Hotel	95 W Broadway	212-566-1900	139-199 single
Hilton Garden Inn New York Tribeca	6 York St	212-966-4091	170-280 standard
Smyth Tribeca	85 W Broadway	212-587-7000	295-459 standard
Soho Grand Hotel	310 W Broadway	212-965-3000	474
Tribeca Grand Hotel	2 6th Ave	212-519-6600	464

Map 3 • City Hall / Chinatown

Comfort Inn Manhattan Bridge	61 Chrystie St	212-925-1212	99-189 single
Holiday Inn Soho	138 Lafayette St	212-966-8898	127-280 standard
New World Hotel	101 Bowery	212-226-5522	112 single shared bath
Sun Bright Hotel	140 Hester St	212-226-7070	75
Windsor Hotel	108 Forsyth St	212-226-3009	175

Map 4 • Lower East Side

Hotel on Rivington	107 Rivington St	212-475-2600	260
Thompson Lower East Side	190 Allen St	212-460-5300	269-359

Map 5 • West Village

Abingdon Guest House	21 8th Ave	212-243-5384	229
Chelsea Pines Inn	317 W 14th St	212-929-1023	150
Four Points by Sheraton Manhattan SoHo Village	66 Charlton St	212-229-9988	229-359
Hampton Inn Manhattan - Soho	54 Watts St	212-226-6288	229
Hotel Gansevoort	18 9th Ave	212-206-6700	295-525 standard
Incentra Village House	32 8th Ave	212-206-0007	169
Liberty Inn	51 10th Ave	212-741-2333	159
Rooms to Let	83 Horatio St	212-675-5481	190
The Jane Hotel	113 Jane St	212-924-6700	79
The Standard	848 Washington St	212-645-4646	315-595
Trump Soho	249 Spring St	212-842-5500	389-589
West Eleventh	278 W 11th St	212-675-7897	235-305 single

Map 6 • Washington Square / NYU / NoHo / SoHo

60 Thompson	60 Thompson St	212-431-0400	299 off season, $429 busy season
Bowery's Whitehouse Hotel	340 Bovery	212-477-5623	30
The Bowery Hotel	335 Bowery	212-505-9100	359
Cooper Square Hotel	25 Cooper Sq	212-475-5700	270-425 single
Crosby Street Hotel	79 Crosby St	800-337-4685	505
The Gem Hotel Soho	135 E Houston St	212-358-8844	169
Larchmont Hotel	27 W 11th St	212-989-9333	90
The Mercer	147 Mercer St	212-966-6060	495-595 standard
Off Soho Suites Hotel	11 Rivington St	800-633-7646	119-199 standard
Second Home on Second Avenue	221 2nd Ave	212-677-3161	105 shared / 190 private
Sohotel	341 Broome St	212-226-1482	161, shared bath
St Marks Hotel	2 St Marks Pl	212-674-0100	93-120
Union Square Inn	209 E 14th St	212-614-0500	159
Village House	45 W 9th St	212-473-5500	170
Washington Square Hotel	103 Waverly Pl	212-777-9515	220

Map 7 • East Village

East Village Bed & Coffee	110 Avenue C	917-816-0071	120

Map 8 • Chelsea

Best Western Convention Center Hotel	522 W 38th St	212-405-1700	99
Chelsea Lodge Suites	318 W 20th St	212-243-4499	229
Chelsea Star Hotel	300 W 30th St	212-244-7827	30 dorm, 99 private
Colonial House Inn	318 W 22nd St	212-243-9669	130 shared bath, 180 private bath
Comfort Inn Convention Center	442 W 36th St	212-714-6699	119-299 single
The Gem Hotel Chelsea	300 W 22nd St	212-675-1911	189-289
The Gem Hotel Midtown West	449 W 36th St	212-967-7206	179
Hampton Inn Manhattan - Times Square South	337 W39th St	212-967-2344	129-288
Holiday Inn Express - Times Square	343 W 39th St	212-239-1222	119-315
Manhattan Inn Hostel	303 W 30th St	212-629-4064	40 dorm, 140 private
Maritime Hotel	363 W 16th St	212-242-4300	225-365 standard
New Yorker Hotel	481 8th Ave	212-244-0719	189-349 standard
Vigilant Hotel	370 8th Ave	212-594-5246	140 weekly

Map 9 • Flatiron / Lower Midtown

		Phone	*Rate $*
Ace Hotel	20 W 29th St	212-679-2222	200
Affinia Manhattan	371 7th Ave	212-563-1800	287
Americana Inn	69 W 38th St	212-840-6700	75
The Avalon	16 E 32nd St	212-299-7000	149-319
Broadway Plaza Hotel	1155 Broadway	212-679-7665	159
Carlton Hotel	88 Madison Ave	212-532-4100	295
Chelsea Hotel	222 W 23rd St	212-243-3700	149
Chelsea Inn	46 W 17th St	212-645-8989	89
Chelsea International Hostel	251 W 20th St	212-647-0010	33 dorm, 82 private
Chelsea Savoy Hotel	204 W 23rd St	212-929-9353	99-125 single
Comfort Inn Chelsea	18 W 25th St	212-645-3990	129-249 single
Comfort Inn Manhattan	42 W 35th St	212-947-0200	139-269 single
Doubletree Hotel Chelsea	1287 W 29th St	212-564-0994	119-261 Single
Fashion 26	152 W 26th St	212-858-5888	269-334
Four Points by Sheraton Chelsea	160 W 25th St	212-627-1888	165-389 standard
Gershwin Hotel	7 E 27th St	212-545-8000	45 dorm, 109 private
Hampton Inn Manhattan - 35th St Empire State Building	59 W 35th St	212-564-3688	189-296
Hampton Inn Manhattan/Chelsea	108 W 24th St	212-414-1000	249-349 standard
Hampton Inn Manhattan - Madison Square Garden	116 W 31st St	212-947-9700	199-299 standard
Herald Square Hotel	19 W 31st St	212-279-4017	109-199 standard
Hilton Garden Inn New York Chelsea	121 W 28th St	212-564-2181	159-359 standard
Hilton Garden Inn New York West 35th St	63 W 35th St	212-594-3310	169-399 standard
Holiday Inn Express- Madison Square Garden	232 W 29th St	212-695-7200	119-289 standard
Hotel Chandler	12 E 31st St	212-889-6363	209-369 standard
Hotel Grand Union	34 E 32nd St	212-683-5890	130-175 standard
Hotel Metro	45 W 35th St	212-947-2500	146-365 standard
Hotel Stanford	43 W 32nd St	212-563-1500	139-189 standard
Hotel Thirty Thirty	30 E 30th St	212-689-1900	99-199 standard
Inn on 23rd	131 W 23rd St	212-463-0330	229
Jolly Hotel Madison Towers	22 E 38th St	212-802-0600	148-348 standard
La Quinta Inn–Manhattan	17 W 32nd St	212-736-1600	109-299 standard
La Semana Hotel	25 W 24th St	212-255-5944	98
Latham Hotel	4 E 28th St	212-685-8300	79-139 standard
Madison Hotel	62 Madison Ave	212-532-7373	197
Manhattan Broadway Hotel	273 W 38th St	212-921-9791	179
Morgan's Hotel	237 Madison Ave	212-686-0300	269-509 standard
New York Hotel Pennsylvania	401 7th Ave	212-736-5000	109-209 standard
Radisson Martinique on Broadway	49 W 32nd St	212-736-3800	149-289 standard
Red Roof Inn	6 W 32nd St	212-643-7100	140
Residence Inn Manhattan Times Square	1033 6th Ave	212-768-0007	329
Roger Williams Hotel	131 Madison Ave	212-448-7000	249-349 standard

Senton Hotel	39 W 27th St	212-684-5800	100 shared bath, 120 private bath
The Strand	33 W 37th St	212-448-1024	279
Wolcott Hotel	4 W 31st St	212-268-2900	200

Map 10 • Murray Hill / Gramercy

70 Park Avenue Hotel	70 Park Ave	212-973-2400	265
Affinia Dumont	150 E 34th St	212-481-7600	279
Affinia Shelburne	303 Lexington Ave	212-689-5200	154
American Dream Hostel	168 E 24th St	212-260-9779	75
Clarion Hotel Park Avenue	429 Park Ave S	212-532-4860	99-219
The Hotel Deauville	103 E 29th St	212-683-0990	89-189 single
Eastgate Tower Hotel	222 E 39th St	212-687-8000	130-380 Single
Envoy Club	377 E 33rd St	212-481-4600	129-329 single studio
Gramercy Park Hotel	2 Lexington Ave	212-920-3300	425-665 standard
Hotel 17	225 E 17th St	212-475-2845	79-129 standard
Hotel 31	129 E 31st St	212-685-3060	85-145 standard
Hotel Giraffe	365 Park Ave S	212-685-7700	239-356 standard
Inn at Irving Place	56 Irving Pl	212-533-4600	325
Kitano Hotel New York	66 Park Ave	212-885-7000	174-360 standard
The Marcel Hotel at Gramercy	201 E 24th St	212-696-3800	143-309 standard
Murray Hill East Suites	149 E 39th St	212-661-2100	124-269 standard
Murray Hill Inn	143 E 30th St	212-683-6900	69-109 standard, shared bath
Park South Hotel	122 E 28th St	212-448-0888	259
Ramada Inn Eastside	161 Lexington Ave	212-545-1800	109-299 standard
W New York–The Court	130 E 39th St	212-685-1100	419
W New York–The Tuscany	120 E 39th St	212-686-1600	489
W Union Square	201 Park Ave S	212-253-9119	509
Ye Olde Carlton Arms Hotel	160 E 25th St	212-679-0680	80shared bath, 110 private bath

Map 11 • Hell's Kitchen

		Phone	*Rate $*
414 Inn New York	414 W 46th St	212-399-0006	199
6 Columbus	6 Columbus Cir	212-204-3000	300
Belvedere Hotel	319 W 48th St	212-245-7000	327
The Distrikt Hotel	342 W 40th St	646-831-6780	275
Econo Lodge Times Square	302 W 47th St	212-246-1991	230
Elk Hotel	360 W 42nd St	212-563-2864	50
Four Points by Sheraton Midtown - Times Square	326 W 40th St	212-967-8585	185-245
Holiday Inn	440 W 57th St	212-581-8100	215
Hudson Hotel	356 W 58th St	212-554-6000	299
Ink48	653 11th Ave	212-757-0088	425
Mandarin Oriental New York	80 Columbus Cir	212-805-8800	525
Skyline Hotel	725 10th Ave	212-586-3400	239
Travel Inn	515 W 42nd St	212-695-7171	235
Washington Jefferson Hotel	318 W 51st St	212-246-7550	255

Map 12 • Midtown

Algonquin Hotel	59 W 44th St	212-840-6800	279
Ameritania Hotel	230 W 54th St	212-247-5000	197
Amsterdam Court Hotel	226 W 50th St	212-459-1000	149
Best Western President Hotel	234 W 48th St	212-246-8800	110
Big Apple Hostel	119 W 45th St	212-302-2603	37 dorm, 110 private
Blakely Hotel	136 W 55th St	212-245-1800	210
Bryant Park Hotel	40 W 40th St	212-869-0100	375
Buckingham Hotel	101 W 57th St	212-246-1500	279
Casablanca Hotel	147 W 43rd St	212-869-1212	228
Chambers Hotel	15 W 56th St	212-974-5656	325
The Chatwal	130 W 44th St	212-764-6200	695
City Club Hotel	55 W 44th St	212-921-5500	199-349 single
Comfort Inn Midtown	129 W 46th St	212-221-2600	119-189 single
Courtyard by Marriott Manhattan Fifth Avenue	3 E 40th St	212-447-1500	219-459 single
Courtyard by Marriott Manhattan Times Square South	114 W 40th St	212-391-0088	179-399 single

Crowne Plaza Times Square	1605 Broadway	212-977-4000	199-349 single
Da Vinci Hotel	244 W 56th St	212-489-4100	89-199 single
Doubletree Guest Suites Times Square	1568 Broadway	212-719-1600	141-305 single
Dream	210 W 55th St	212-247-2000	149-399 single
Dylan Hotel	52 E 41st St	212-338-0500	219-339 single
Flatotel International	135 W 52nd St	212-887-9400	229-299 standard
Four Seasons Hotel	57 E 57th St	212-758-5700	655-855 standard
Graze New York	125 W 45th St	212-354-2323	152-239 standard
Hampton Inn Manhattan-Times Square North	851 8th Ave	212-581-4100	129-254 standard
Helmsley Park Lane Hotel	36 Central Park S	212-371-4000	290-545 standard
Hilton Garden Inn Times Square	790 8th Ave	212-581-7000	169-439 standard
Hilton New York	1335 6th Ave	212-586-7000	319
Hilton Times Square	234 W 42nd St	212-840-8222	269-459 standard
Holiday Inn Express Fifth Avenue	15 W 45th St	212-302-9088	128-309 standard
Hotel 41	206 W 41st St	212-703-8600	129-259 standard
The Hotel at Times Square	50 W 46th St	212-719-2300	199-299 standard
Hotel Carter	250 W 43rd St	212-944-6000	99
Hotel Edison	228 W 47th St	212-840-5000	149-189 standard
Hotel Mela	120 W 44th St	212-730-7900	359-619 standard
Hotel St James	109 W 45th St	212-221-3600	99-199 standard
The Iroquois New York	49 W 44th St	212-840-3080	289-409 standard
Jumeirah Essex House	160 Central Park S	212-247-0300	329-529 standard
Le Parker Meridien	119 W 56th St	212-245-5000	358-656 standard
Library Hotel	299 Madison Ave	212-983-4500	259-359 standard
Mansfield Hotel	12 W 44th St	212-277-8700	249-359 standard
Mayfair Hotel	242 W 49th St	212-586-0300	89-190 standard
The Michelangelo Hotel	152 W 51st St	212-765-1900	339-495 standard
Millennium Broadway	145 W 44th St	212-768-4400	169-299 standard
The Moderne Hotel	243 W 55th St	212-397-6767	116-279 standard
The Muse	130 W 46th St	212-485-2400	429
New York Inn	765 8th Ave	212-247-5400	29 dorm style, 159 single private bath
New York Marriott Marquis	1535 Broadway	212-398-1900	259-499 standard
New York Palace Hotel	455 Madison Ave	212-888-7000	299-599 standard deluxe
Novotel New York	226 W 52nd St	212-315-0100	199-299 standard
Omni Berkshire Place	21 E 52nd St	212-753-5800	306-433 standard
Paramount Hotel	235 W 46th St	888-969-0069	266
Park Central Hotel	870 7th Ave	212-247-8000	129-279 standard
Park Savoy Hotel	158 W 58th St	212-245-5755	125
The Peninsula New York	700 5th Ave	212-956-2888	595
Portland Square Hotel	132 W 47th St	212-382-0600	119
The Premier Hotel	133 W 44th St	212-789-7670	399
Radio City Apartments	142 W 49th St	212-730-0728	205
Renaissance New York Times Square	714 7th Ave	212-765-7676	239-499 standard
The Ritz Carlton, Central Park	50 Central Park S	212-308-9100	645-945 standard
Royalton Hotel	44 W 44th St	212-869-4400	299-499 standard
Salisbury Hotel	123 W 57th St	212-246-1300	200
Sheraton Manhattan	790 7th Ave	212-581-3300	215-396 standard
Sheraton New York Hotel and Towers	811 7th Ave	212-581-1000	342
Shoreham Hotel	33 W 55th St	212-247-6700	399
Sofitel	45 W 44th St	212-354-8844	440
St Regis	2 E 55th St	212-753-4500	750-995 standard
Stay	157 W 47th St	212-768-3700	149-389 standard
The Time	224 W 49th St	212-246-5252	149-279
W New York Times Square	1567 Broadway	212-930-7400	479
Warwick New York Hotel	65 W 54th St	212-247-2700	325
Wellington Hotel	871 7th Ave	212-247-3900	319
Westin New York at Times Square	270 W 43rd St	212-201-2700	400

Map 13 • East Midtown

Affinia 50	155 E 50th St	212-751-5710	159
Alex Hotel	205 E 45th St	212-867-5100	305
Bedford Hotel	118 E 40th St	212-697-4800	195
Beekman Tower Hotel	3 Mitchell Pl	212-355-7300	175
The Benjamin	125 E 50th St	212-715-2500	359
Best Western Hospitality House	145 E 49th St	212-753-8781	350

Courtyard by Marriott Midtown East	866 3rd Ave	212-644-1300	219-459 single
Doubletree Metropolitan Hotel	569 Lexington Ave	212-752-7000	139-279
Fitzpatrick Grand Central Hotel	141 E 44th St	212-351-6800	169-395 standard
Fitzpatrick Manhattan Hotel	687 Lexington Ave	212-355-0100	219-435 standard
Grand Hyatt Hotel	109 E 42nd St	212-883-1234	223-373 standard
Helmsley Middletowne Hotel	148 E 48th St	212-755-3000	153-190 standard
Hotel Elysee	60 E 54th St	212-753-1066	189-323 standard
Hotel Lombary	111 E 56th St	212-753-8600	149-294 standard
Intercontinental - The Barclay New York	111 E 48th St	212-755-5900	259-439 standard
Kimberly Hotel	145 E 50th St	212-702-1600	189-309 standard
Marriott New York East Side	525 Lexington Ave	212-755-4000	259-399 standard
Millennium UN Plaza	1 United Nations Plaza	212-758-1234	145-300 standard
The New York Helmsley Hotel	212 E 42nd St	212-490-8900	292
Pod Hotel	230 E 51st St	212-355-0300	109 shared bath, 169 private bath
Radisson Lexington	511 Lexington Ave	212-755-4400	109-249 standard
Renaissance New York Hotel 57	130 E 57th St	212-753-8841	179-359
Roger Smith Hotel	501 Lexington Ave	212-755-1400	149-399 standard
The Roosevelt Hotel	45 E 45th St	212-661-9600	265
San Carlos Hotel	150 E 50th St	212-755-1800	259-395 standard
Seton Hotel	144 E 40th St	212-889-5301	112 (shared bath), 150 (private bath)
Tudor Hotel New York	304 E 42nd St	212-986-8800	279
W New York	541 Lexington Ave	212-755-1200	339
Waldorf Astoria	301 Park Ave	212-355-3000	399
Waldorf Towers	100 E 50th St	212-355-3100	599
YMCA Vanderbilt	224 E 47th St	212-912-2500	89

Map 14 • Upper West Side (Lower)

Amsterdam Inn	340 Amsterdam Ave	212-579-7500	79 shared, 99 private bathroom
Comfort Inn Central Park West	31 W 71st St	212-721-4770	230
Country in the City	270 W 77th St	212-580-4183	204
Excelsior Hotel	45 W 81st St	212-362-9200	299
Hayden Hall Hotel	117 W 79th St	212-787-3300	229
Hotel Beacon	2130 Broadway	212-787-1100	220
Hotel Belleclaire	250 W 77th St	212-362-7700	119 shared bath, 179 private bath
Hotel Lucerne	201 W 79th St	212-875-1000	350
Hotel Riverside Studios	342 W 71st St	212-873-5999	85
Imperial Court Hotel	307 W 79th St	212-787-6600	730 weekly
Inn New York City	266 W 71st St	212-580-1900	475
Milburn Hotel	242 W 76th St	212-362-1006	195
On the Ave Hotel	2178 Broadway	212-362-1100	279
Phillips Club	155 W 66th St	212-835-8800	8000 monthly
Riverside Tower Hotel	80 Riverside Dr	212-877-5200	104
Trump International	1 Central Park West	212-299-1000	595
YMCA West Side	5 W 63rd St	212-875-4100	89 (shared bath)

Map 15 • Upper East Side (Lower)

Affinia Gardens	215 E 64th St	212-355-1230	359
Bentley Hotel	500 E 62nd St	212-644-6000	150
Carlyle Hotel	35 E 76th St	212-744-1600	550
Gracie Inn	502 E 81st St	212-628-1700	129-219 single
Helmsley Carlton House	680 Madison Ave	212-838-3000	250-395 standard
Hotel Plaza Athenee	37 E 64th St	212-734-9100	495-825 standard
Lowell Hotel	28 E 63rd St	212-838-1400	485-625 standard
Regency Hotel	540 Park Ave	212-759-4100	289-589 standard
Surrey Hotel	20 E 76th St	212-288-3700	499
The Pierre	2 E 61st St	212-838-8000	484-750
The Sherry Netherland Hotel	781 5th Ave	212-355-2800	449

Map 16 • Upper West Side (Upper)

Central Park Hostel	19 W 103rd St	212-678-0491	dorm 28, private 89, studio 109
Continental Hostel	330 W 95th St	212-866-1420	15-30 shared, 42-66 private
Days Hotel Broadway	215 W 94th St	212-866-6400	68-169 single
Hostelling International New York	891 Amsterdam Ave	212-932-2300	33 dorm, 150 private

Hotel Newton	2528 Broadway	212-678-6500	85-175 standard
Jazz on the Park	36 W 106th St	212-932-1600	22 shared, 72 private
Marrakech Hotel	2688 Broadway	212-222-2954	99-199 standard
Morningside Inn	235 W 107th St	212-316-0055	85 single, 120 standard
Riverside Terrace	350 W 88th St	212-724-6100	100-200 standard
West End Studios	850 West End Ave	212-662-6000	70
West Side Inn	237 W 107th St	212-866-0061	60

Map 17 • Upper East Side / East Harlem

92nd Street Y de Hirsch Residence	1395 Lexington Ave	212-415-5650	1450 monthly
Courtyard by Marriott Manhattan Upper East Side	410 E 92nd St	212-410-6777	179
Franklin Hotel	164 E 87th St	212-369-1000	309-349 standard
The Marmara-Manhattan	301 E 94th St	212-427-3100	249
Wales Hotel	1295 Madison Ave	212-876-6000	239

Map 19 • Harlem (Lower)

102 Brownstone	102 W 118th St	212-662-4223	250
Efuru Guest House and Suites	106 W 120th St	212-961-9855	95 shared bath, 125 private bath
Fane Dumas Hotel	205 W 135th St	212-281-3400	62 small room, 70 large room
Harlem YMCA	180 W 135th St	212-281-4100	70 (shared bathroom)

Map 21 • Manhattanville / Hamilton Heights

Alga Hotel	828 St Nicholas Ave	212-368-0700	40
Hamilton Heights Casablanca Hotel	511 W 145th St	212-491-0488	70 shared bath, 90 private bath
Hotel Caribe	515 W 145th St	212-368-9915	70 shared bath, 90 private bath
Sugar Hill Harlem Inn	460 W 141st St	212-234-5432	200

Map 22 • Harlem (Upper)

Harlem Vista Hotel	75 Macombs Pl	917-507-4140	77

Battery Park City

Embassy Suites New York City	102 North End Ave	212-945-0100	289-409 single
Ritz-Carlton New York Battery Park	2 West St	212-344-0800	295-375 standard

Eating out in New York...why do we do it? Because our kitchens are small, we're too busy, and hey, cooking is probably only 15% cheaper. Or at least that's what we tell ourselves when we're spending $41 on a hamburger (**Old Homestead Steakhouse (Map 5)**). But even those of us who love to cook can't resist the allure of some of the best and most varied cuisine in the world. For New Yorkers, eating out is simultaneously a science and an art form. Since we have so many options, we don't seem to be able to waste any meal on a haphazard choice of venue. Selecting exactly the right restaurant for an occasion is not just a matter of taste, particularly when you're preparing to splurge; it requires knowledge, logic, strategy, and even risk-assessment (is it beginning to sound like a competitive sport?). We may want a certain type of cuisine, near a subway line convenient for all parties involved, with atmosphere but not romantic, in a specific price range. And with over 25,000 options, we can always find the perfect place. Whether we're looking for a restaurant with a rare 28 from Zagat's (the culinary Bible for many New Yorkers), or we want to roll the dice with an undiscovered hole in the wall where even the Board of Health fears to tread (read: street carts in Chinatown), we will never have to settle. There is, of course, a huge drawback: we are downright spoiled. But I guess we'll just have to live with that.

Eating Old

Since New York City is a culinary hotspot with lots of big names (and wannabe big names) at work in the kitchens, it's easy to get swept up in food trends that often involve dishes that look more like art projects than meals. Many of the more experimental restaurants do merit attention, but when you're not in the mood for Parmesan cheese ice cream with pesto foam in a braised kale emulsion, you can avail yourselves of the Big Apple's time-honored stalwarts. They've recently relaxed the tie and jacket rule, but you can still rub elbows with the who's who at the posh **21 Club (Map 12)** (circa 1929); dine on New American cuisine at the ancient, 213-year-old **Bridge Café (Map 1)**; slurp fresh-shucked oysters under the vaulted, tiled ceiling at **Grand Central Station's Oyster Bar (Map 13)** (circa 1913), and do not miss their desserts; sample more oysters and one of the best burgers in existence at the venerable Midtown watering hole **P.J. Clarke's (Map 13)** (since 1884); since '08 (that's 1908!) people have been ordering the sturgeon scrambled with eggs, onions, and a bialy on the side at **Barney Greengrass (Map 16)**; also going strong since 1938 is the Italian old-school joint **Patsy's Pizzeria (Map 20)**; or expand your culinary horizons with calf's spleen and cheese on a roll at **Ferdinando's Focacceria (Map 32)** (circa 1904).

Eating Cheap

Eating cheap has become more stylish thanks to the recent trend of highbrow chefs and restauranteurs going lowbrow. And oh yeah, that whole economic collapse thing didn't hurt either. At **Shake Shack (Maps 9, 14)**, you can still grab a the famous Shack Burger for $4.75 or one of their legendary Chicago Dogs (a meal in itself) for only $4.25. Ethnic food has always been a great friend to eaters on a budget. For Vietnamese pho and noodle dishes, **Cong Ly (Map 3)** is your best friend. For brilliant Middle Eastern go to **Hummus Place (Map 6, 7)**, **Gazala Place (Map 11)**, or **Taïm (Map 5)** (for some of the best falafel on the planet). For Mexican check out the taqueria at The Corner a.k.a. **La Esquina (Map 6)** or head uptown to **El Paso (Map 17)**. The Indian lunch buffet at **Tiffin Wallah (Map 10)** is only $7.50 and veggie friendly to boot. **Papaya King (Map 17)** has kept hot dog lovers grinning since 1932. For a gut busting plate of Puerto Rican food under ten bucks, sit at the counter of **La Taza De Oro (Map 8)**. For a great cheap breakfast that even celebs appreciate, **La Bonbonniere (Map 5)** can't be beat. And many of us can't survive a day without at least one of the staples of NYC Jewish eats—bagels and knishes. For bagels, go with perennial winners **Ess-a-Bagel (Map 10, 13)** and **H&H Bagels (Map 11, 14)**, or try our favorites: **David's Bagels (Map 10)**, **Kossar's Bialys (Map 4)**, **Absolute Bagels (Map 16)**, or the original **Tal Bagels (Map 13, 15, 16, 17)**. For knishes, nothing beats the **Yonah Schimmel Knish Bakery (Map 6)**. Since the NFT office is in Chinatown and we're always broke (free advice: don't go into independent publishing), we are certified experts on eating cheap in this part of town. At **Nice Green Bo (Map 3)** get the scallion pancakes, at **Joe's Shanghai (Map 3, 12)** get the soup dumplings, at **Food Shing (Map 3)** get the beef noodle soup, at **Fuleen (Map 3)** get the shrimp with chili sauce, and for the best deal in the city head to **Sanur (Map 3)** for a heaping plate of homemade Malayasian food for only $3.50. Try finding that kind of advice in Zagat.

Eating Hip

Eating hip usually involves the food of the moment (small plates, pizza, Asian street food), beautiful people (those who often look like they never eat), and some kind of exclusivity (ridiculously long waits, unpublished phone numbers, impossible-to-come-by reservations, or no reservations at all). Food snobs may warn you that the appetite that's satisfied is the craving to see and be seen, rather than the desire for the city's best culinary experience. Although with this little economic crisis, even the hippest places have had to loosen their policies a little bit. That being said, the ultimate in cool dining is, of course, **Rao's (Map**

20)—or so we hear. But unless you're the Mayor, the Governor, or Woody Allen, you probably won't be getting a reservation anytime soon, so don't hold your breath. People have moved on from the Graydon Carter-owned **The Waverly Inn (Map 5)**, (at least that's what we hear; we never got through the door in the first place) but the West Village is still home to some of the hippest dining experiences in the city. **The Spotted Pig (Map 5)** is still worth the three-hour wait to munch on gourmet gastropub food with Bono and bankers (at least the ones that still have jobs). If you can find the unmarked basement door of **Bobo (Map 5)**, you'll really impress your date. Head east to try the always crowded, no-reservations eatery **Freemans (Map 6)**, which hides itself at the end of an alleyway; do not miss the pork chops. If you just can't wait for the sun to go down for a hip eating experience, head to **202 (Map 8)** for a fantastic breakfast in the middle of a fashionable clothing boutique. For fans of Japanese izakayas, nothing is quite as fun as an evening at **En Japanese Brasserie (Map 5)**. Its gourmet menu brilliantly fuses homemade miso with duck, cod, tofu, and anything else you can think. And the dark lighting will make anyone look good. When you want your pizza in a stark and modern setting, head to **Co (Map 6)** for heavenly crust from the genius behind Sullivan Street Bakery. Meanwhile David Chang's empire continues to grow. Try **Momofuku Ssam Bar (Map 6)** to see what all the hype is about. If the lines are too long at the Momofukus or you don't have friends that can afford to score a table at Spotted Pig, try **Kuma Inn (Map 4)** on the Lower East Side. The small plates like Chinese sausage with Thai chili-lime sauce and pork wasabi dumplings are brilliant, it's BYO sake, and there's no secret phone number.

Eating Late

Luckily New York restaurants rarely sleep (just like New Yorkers), so it's pretty damn easy to find some fine grub late into the night. **Kang Suh's (Map 9)** Korean barbeque runs all night, as well as the Turkish spot **Bereket (Map 7)**, the bar/burger joint **7A (Map 7)**, **Yaffa Café (Map 7)**, and a host of classic diners like **Odessa (Map 7)**, and **Waverly Restaurant (Map 5)**. **Veselka (Map 6)** is the place for late-night Ukrainian soul food. You'll find cabbies chowing down past 3 am at **Lahore (Map 6)**, **Punjabi Deli (Map 7)**, and **Big Arc Chicken (Map 7)**. **French Roast (Map 5, 14)** serves quite good croque-monsieurs 24 hours. If you're near Chinatown at 3 am let the wonton soup and bbq meats at **Great New York Noodletown (Map 3)** soak up all the alcohol you've been imbibing. And, of course, **Blue Ribbon (Map 6)** is still one of the best places to eat after midnight.

Eating Pizza

Pizza constitutes a food group unto itself for New Yorkers. The coal oven spots top most lists: **Grimaldi's (Map 30)**, **Lombardi's (Map 6)**, **Luzzo's (Map 7)**, **John's Pizzeria (Map 5)**, and the original **Patsy's (Map 20)** in East Harlem. The coal oven enjoys extra cachet by virtue of being illegal now, except in the aforementioned eateries where they were already in operation when legislation was passed prohibiting them. The brick oven joints, such as **Franny's (Map 33)**, **Keste (Map 5)**, **Co (Map 8)**, and **Lucali (Map 32)** never seem to slow down either. Trying to find something edible near Wall Street? Check out **Adrienne's (Map 1)** delicious rectangle pies on Stone Street. For a classic Village scene complete with live jazz, check out **Arturo's (Map 6)** on Houston Street. The outer boroughs serious represent here: **Louie & Ernie's** in The Bronx (pp 227), **Nick's Pizza** in Queens (pp 231), **Denino's** in Staten Island (pp 233), and, of course, **DiFara** in Brooklyn (pp 229). Pizza by the slice practically deserves its own category, but the highlights include **Patsy's (Map 20)** (definitely the best slice in the city), **Artichoke Basille's Pizza (Map 6)** (get the grandma slice), **Farinella (Map 3)** (very unique), and **Joe's (Map 5)** (classic NY Style).

Eating Ethnic

Spin a globe, stick your finger onto a spot blindly, and chances are you can find cuisine from that country on offer in New York. And an outstanding offering it will be. To wit: **Sammy's Roumanian (Map 6)**, **Katz's Delicatessen (Map 7)**, and **Carnegie Deli (Map 12)** (Jewish); **Shun Lee (Map 13)**, **Grand Sichuan International (Map 8)**, **Joe's Shanghai (Map 3)**, and **Chef Ho's Peking Duck Grill (Map 17)** (Chinese); **Dawat (Map 13)**, **Banjara (Map 7)**, and **Indian Tandoor Oven (Map 15)** (Indian); **Alma (Map 32)**, **El Paso (Map 17, 20)** and **Rosa Mexicano (Map 14)** (Mexican); **Kang Suh (Map 9)**, **Seoul Garden (Map 9)**, and **Dok Suni's (Map 7)** (Korean); **Nobu (Map 2)**, **Takahachi (Map 7)**, **Ki Sushi (Map 32)**, and about 40 others (Japanese); **Babbo (Map 6)**, **Felidia (Map 13)**, **Il Giglio (Map 2)**, **Sfoglia (Map 17)**, **Al Di La (Map 33)**, **I Trulli (Map 10)**, and countless others (Italian); **Ghenet (Map 33)** and **Zoma (Map 19)** (Ethiopian); **Pakistan Tea House (Map 2)** and **Haandi (Map 10)** (Pakistani); **Café Habana (Map 6)** (Cuban); **Resto (Map 10)** (Belgian); **New Malaysia (Map 3)** (Malayasian); **Kabab Café (Map 26)** (Egyptian); **Eight Mile Creek (Map 6)** and **Bondi Road (Map 4)** (Australian); **Nelson Blue (Map 1)** (New Zealand); **La Fonda Boricua (Map 17)** (Puerto Rican); **El Malecon (Map 23)** and **El Castillo de Jagua (Map 4)** (Dominican); **Balthazar (Map 6)**, **Café D'Alsace (Map 17)**, **La Luncheonette**

(Map 8), **Jules (Map 6)**, and so many more (French); **Socarrat (Map 9)** and **Tia Pol (Map 8)** (Spanish). **Lomzynianka (Map 28)** (Polish). **Aquavit (Map 13)** and **Smörgås Chef (Map 1)** (Scandinavian); **Heidelberg (Map 15)**, **Zum Schneider (Map 7)**, and **Hallo Berlin (Map 11)** (German); **Sylvia's (Map 19)** and **Cheryl's Global Soul (Map 33)** (Southern); **Kefi (Map 14)**, **Periyali (Map 9)**, and **Stamatis (Map 26)** (Greek); **Turkish Kitchen (Map 10)** (Turkish); **Sigiri (Map 7)** (Sri Lankan) **Pongsri Thai (Map 3)** and **Sripraphai** (pp 231) (Thai), etc. etc. etc.

Eating Meat

New York is home to arguably the world's best steakhouse, **Peter Luger's (Map 29)**. But it's competitive at the top, and clawing at Luger's heels are: the newish **Mark Joseph Steakhouse (Map 1)**, and classics like **Sparks (Map 13)**, **Palm (Map 13)**, **Smith & Wollensky (Map 13)**, **Angelo & Maxie's (Map 10)**, and the **Strip House (Map 6)**. For the Brazilian-style "all you can eat meat fest," **Churrascaria Plataforma (Map 11)** does the trick. As for hamburgers, the rankings provide material for eternal debate. Many of the favorites find their way to the top of some list or another: **P.J. Clarke's (Map 13)**, **Corner Bistro (Map 5)**, **Burger Joint** at Le Parker Meridien **(Map 12)**, **J.G. Melon (Map 15)**, **Big Nick's (Map 14)**, and **BLT Burger (Map 5)**, to name a few. New on the scene is **Royale (Map 7)**, where they compliment the perfect patty with stellar fixins, for a song. For a change of pace from your burger tour, look for evidence that we Yankees can indeed produce some damn good BBQ: **Hill Country (Map 9)**, **Dinosaur Bar-B-Que (Map 18)**, and **RUB BBQ (Map 9)** in Manhattan, and **Smoke Joint (Map 31)** and **Fette Sau (Map 29)** in Brooklyn (arrive early at the latter, they run out of the most popular items quickly). And wherever you go, be prepared to wash down your 'cue with some serious bourbon.

Eating Meatless

We're advanced enough here that most restaurants (except perhaps those mentioned directly above) offer at least a few items palatable to vegetarians. But don't worry, every kind of appetite gets special attention here, including non-meat-eaters. Try the quality Indian fare at **Pongal (Map 10)** and **Chennai Garden (Map 10)**, and, for high-end eats, **Candle 79 (Map 15)**, **Dirt Candy (Map 7)**, and **GoBo (Map 5)**. For adventurous veggie heads, nothing beats **HanGawi (Map 9)**, consistently voted one of the best vegetarian and Korean restaurants in the city..

Eating Your Wallet

You don't have to live in this city long before realizing that while we technically use the same currency as the rest of the country, it's actually worth about half as much here as elsewhere. Even the most frugal among us have found ourselves spending 100 New York dollars on a night out and thinking we got off easy. But remember that when it comes to dining out, there is no cap. You can easily spend over $150 (per person) at any number of highly regarded restaurants around town, even if you're feeling abstemious. No doubt you've been just dying to try Batali's this, and Morimoto's that. But handle the decision to dine at the top culinary echelon as you would (or should) handle the prospect of an open bar at your holiday office party: Know your limit (financially, emotionally, morally), and try not to do anything you'll regret in the morning. If you can keep your food down after witnessing triple digits on your share of the tab, start on the slippery slope to gastronomically induced bankruptcy at the following restaurants, which rarely disappoint: **Babbo (Map 6)**, **Per Se (Map 11)**, **Gramercy Tavern (Map 9)**, **Le Bernardin (Map 12)**, **Bouley (Map 2)**, **Union Square Cafe (Map 9)**, **Craft (Map 9)**, **Aquavit (Map 13)**, **Spice Market (Map 5)**, and **Tabla (Map 9)**. And remember to manage your expectations: unless you fall in love with your waiter or waitress, the experience will not change your life. Although **Per Se (Map 11)** comes pretty damn close.

Our Favorite Restaurants

Consensus on such a crucial and personal matter is always elusive, but with a group of New Yorkers opinionated enough to produce the NFT, all we can say is, "Fuhgeddaboutit." We've historically granted the accolade to **Blue Ribbon (Map 6)**—it's open 'til 4 am, it's where the chefs of other restaurants go, it's got fondue, it's got beef marrow, it's got fried chicken, it's got a great vibe, great liquor, and great service. And it will always have that special place in our hearts and stomachs, but we also have to give a shout out to a few other spots: **Sigiri (Map 7)**, a spicy Sri Lankan gem that is BYOB to boot, **Babbo (Map 6)**, well, because it's Babbo (call at least one month ahead), **Arturo's (Map 6)**, a classic, old-school pizza joint with live jazz, Greenwich Village locals, and amazing coal-fired pizza, **Kefi (Map 14)**, gourmet Greek that is the best deal on the Upper West Side, and **Kuma Inn (Map 4)** a hard-to-find Asian tapas restaurant that's cool and hip but also affordable, laid-back, and mind-blowingly delicious.

Overview

If you ever get bored in New York City, you have only yourself to blame. When it comes to nightlife in particular, the only difficulty you'll have is in choosing amongst the seemingly infinite options for entertainment. New York's top weeklies—The Village Voice and Time Out New York—offer their round-ups of goings on about town, as do the e-mail newsletters such as **Flavorpill** (www.flavorpill.com), **My Open Bar** (www.myopenbar.com), **Brooklyn Vegan** (www.brooklynvegan.com), and **Oh My Rockness** (www.ohmyrockness.com) who each week direct you towards various concerts, multimedia events, and new bars. Over time you'll figure out which sources you trust and which venues you favor, and the explorer in you will thrive on checking out the new watering holes that seem to be sprouting like weeds downtown and in Brooklyn. A current favorite for usually cheap and off-beat picks is **The Skint**. For those of you who require more than a perfect drink in the ideal setting: **LVHRD** (www.lvhrd.com) hosts monthly themed parties at secret locations. Below you'll find a few choice destinations for the key genres in evening diversion—dive bars, cocktail lounges, dance spots, music venues, and much more. A word of caution: don't forget to pace yourselves.

Dive Bars

There is no shortage of dumps in this city, so we've done our best to single out the darkest and the dirtiest. A popular choice among our staff is the oh-so derelict **Mars Bar (Map 6)**—clean freaks should use the bathroom wherever they are before they get here. Around Union Square one of the your only (and best) choices is **119 Bar (Map 10)**. Other down-town favorites include **Puffy's Tavern (Map 2)**, **Milano's (Map 6)**, **Blue & Gold (Map 6)**, and **Holiday Lounge (Map 6)**. In Midtown, the classic **Subway Inn (Map 15)** will satisfy all your dive needs, along with Times Square haven **Jimmy's Corner (Map 12)**. Uptown, we like **Reif's Tavern (Map 17)**, **Dublin House (Map 14)**, **1020 Bar (Map 18)**, and **St Nick's Pub (Map 21)**. On the other side of the East River, check out the **Turkey's Nest (Map 29)** in Williamsburg and Red Hook classic **Sunny's (Map 32)**.

Best Beer Selection

When it comes to sheer beer selection, there are a number of worthy contenders. The heavily trodden **Peculier Pub (Map 6)** offers an extensive, though expensive, beer list. Visit this one on a weekday if you want to take advantage of some one-on-one time with the bartender. **The Ginger Man (Map 9)** in lower Midtown stocks over 100 kinds of bottled brew, and has over 60 options on tap. **Vol de Nuit (Map 5)** has a large number of Belgian beers and a warm but reclusive atmosphere. **Zum Schneider (Map 7)** offers a slew of unique German beer choices to wash down its German fare. Hipster-fave **Otherroom (Map 5)** is off the beaten path but has a solid selection too (and it's either beer or wine there, so don't take friends who can't live without the hard stuff). Other places to try: **Blind Tiger Ale House (Map 5)** and **The Waterfront Ale House (Map 10)**. In Brooklyn head to **Beer Table (Map 33)** where the proprietors know more about beer than they probably should (or maybe we're just jealous) or **Draft Barn (Map 33)** to drink ale like a Hungarian king or queen in a medieval fortress minus the moat. In Williamsburg, the cozy **Spuyten Duyvil (Map 29)**, offers many rare finds among its 100-plus beers, while **Barcade (Map 29)** brings joystick junkies and beer-lovers together with its classic '80s arcade games and amazing selection of beers on tap.

Outdoor Spaces

Outdoor space is a precious commodity here, so combine it with cocktails and you've got the perfect destination for city dwellers who just don't want to be cooped up on those all-too-rare temperate evenings. Truth be told, though, you'll find New Yorkers stubbornly holding court at outdoor venues in pretty much any weather short of electrical storms and sub-freezing temperatures, and they'll only retreat in those conditions when chased indoors by the staff. Take note that bars with outdoor patios have circumvented the no-smoking legislation—either a perk or a put-off, depending on your inclination. Unfortunately, you'll never see most of the finest outdoor drinking dens unless you know a supermodel or a European prince—these fashionable places (mostly high up in five-star hotels) have strict door policies. For the rest of us mere mortals, try the **Mé Bar (Map 9)** at the top of La Quinta Inn in Koreatown. They'll let you in no matter who you hang out with or what you wear. For a little fancier night out in the open air but still accessible, try **Bookmarks (Map 12)** the rooftop bar in the Library Hotel. We love the aptly named **Gowanus Yacht Club (Map 32)** in Carroll Gardens. This intimate beer garden serves up cold ones with dogs and burgers in a cookout setting. Other patios to check out include **Sweet & Vicious (Map 6)**, **The Park (Map 8)**, and **The Heights Bar & Grill (Map 18)**. Other Brooklyn highlights include **The Gate (Map 33)** in Park Slope, and Williamsburg's **Iona (Map 29)**, **Union Pool (Map 29)**, and **Huckleberry (Map 29)**. For great views of Manhattan from Long Island City, nothing beats the summer-only **Water Taxi Beach (Map 27)**. In Long Island City, there's an excellent outdoor drinking spot called **Studio Square (Map 26)**, while in Astoria there's a place called **Bohemian Hall & Beer Garden (Map 26)** that you might have heard of, at least once, maybe?

Best Jukebox

Personal taste factors heavily in this category of course, but here is a condensed list of NFT picks. For Manhattan: **Ace Bar (Map 7)** (indie rock/punk), **Hi-Fi (Map 7)** (a huge and diverse selection), **Lakeside Lounge (Map 7)** (a little something for everybody), **7B (Horseshoe Bar) (Map 7)** (rock all the way), **WCOU Radio (Tile Bar) (Map 7)** (eclectic), **Rudy's Bar & Grill (Map 11)** (blues), **Welcome to the Johnsons (Map 4)** (indie rock/punk). For Brooklyn: **Great Lakes (Map 33)** (Park Slope—indie rock), **The Boat (Map 32)** (Carroll Gardens—indie rock), **The Levee (Map 29)** (Williamsburg—good all around), and the **Brooklyn Social Club (Map 32)** (Carroll Gardens—country/soul goodness).

DJs and Dancing

New York's old cabaret laws make it tough to find free dance spots, but they do exist (albeit often with the velvet rope scenario that may deter the impatient). On the weekends, entry into the swankier clubs doesn't come without paying your dues in long lines and pricey cover charges. That's not our style. You'll find us dancing and hanging out at **Santos Party House (Map 3)** as well as **Happy Ending (Map 3)** and **Le Poisson Rouge (Map 6)**. In and around Williamsburg, we suggest checking out the lively dance scenes at **Bembe (Map 29)** or **Glasslands (Map 29)**.

Costly Cocktails

NFT loves dive bars, but sometimes it's nice to grab that blazer or cocktail dress gathering dust in the closet and hit the town for some classy drinking escapades that usually involve fancy hotels. Here are a few places that really are worth the splurge. If you don't want to shell out the $100 cover charge to see Woody Allen play clarinet at the **Café Carlyle (Map 15)**, you can afford the no-cover charge during happy hour at the classy **Bemelmans Bar (Map 15)**, one of the few places worth the money on the Upper East Side. Try to grab one of the ten seats at the famed **King Cole Bar (Map 12)** inside the St Regis Hotel on a weeknight (weekend nights are for tourists remember). For a more downtown cool feel head to **The Lobby Bar (Map 6)** at the Bowery Hotel to mingle with celebrities and models. Other noteworthy settings include **The Campbell Apartment (Map 13)** in Grand Central Station. Phillippe Starck's interior at **The Royalton (Map 12)** is still a damned cool place to have a drink, as well. Or try the **Rose Bar (Map 10)** inside the Grammercy Park Hotel for a taste of opulence you can put on your credit card like everyone else these days.

Music—Overview

New York caters to a wide array of tastes in everything, and music is no exception. From the indie rock clubs of the Lower East Side to the history-steeped jazz clubs in the Village to amateur night at the Apollo, your musical thirst can seemingly be quenched in every possible way.

Jazz, Folk and Country

There are plenty of places to see jazz in the city, starting off with classic joints such as the **Village Vanguard (Map 5)** and **Birdland (Map 11)**. There's also the "Jazz at Lincoln Center" complex in the Time Warner Center on Columbus Circle which has three rooms; the 1,000+ seat, designed-for-jazz Rose Theater, the Allen Room, an amphitheater with a great view of the park, and the nightclub-esque Dizzy's Club Coca Cola.

For a smaller (and cheaper) jazz experience, try the **Lenox Lounge (Map 19)** and **St Nick's Pub (Map 21)** in Harlem, or the **Jazz Gallery** and **Arthur's Tavern (Map 5)** and in the Village. **The Nuyorican Poets Café (Map 7)** has frequent jazz performances. In Brooklyn, one of your best bets is the small back room at Park Slope's **Barbes (Map 33)**.

Easily one of the best weekly jazz experiences is the Mingus Big Band's residency at **The Jazz Standard (Map 10)**. If you've never done it, do it—it's a truly great and unpredicatable band that even surly Mr. Mingus (might) have been proud of.

For folk & country, try **Rodeo Bar (Map 10)**, **Hank's Saloon (Map 33)**, **Lakeside Lounge (Map 7)** or **Parkside Lounge (Map 7)** on Mondays, or **Jalopy's (Map 32)** "Roots & Ruckus" on Wednesdays. BrooklynCountryMusic.com keeps track of who's fiddlin' in Brooklyn.

Rock and Pop

In case you've just moved back to NYC from, say, 7 years in Portland or Mumbai, the rock scene is now firmly entrenched in Brooklyn. Even Bowery Presents, the people behind two of the best clubs in the city—**Mercury Lounge (Map 7)** and **Bowery Ballroom (Map 6)**—have added Brooklyn's **Music Hall of Williamsburg (Map 29)** to their mini-empire. However, larger live shows can be seen at downtown's **Bowery Ballroom (Map 6)**, which remains the top live venue, featuring big acts but with excellent sound and a good layout, as well as **Irving Plaza (Map 10)**, **Terminal 5 (Map 11)**, the **High Line Ballroom (Map 8)**, and, for those of you wishing to check out the Allman Brothers' yearly NYC stand, the **Beacon Theater (Map 14)**. **Roseland**

(Map 12) is billed as an intimate venue for high-profile acts, but good luck getting tickets for the Stones or anyone else of that ilk.

The best remaining small club in Manhattan is **Mercury Lounge (Map 7)**, which gets great bands right before they're ready to move up to Bowery, and features a big stage and audience area (though the bar can be really cramped). As far as the rest of the Lower East Side/East Village area goes, it helps if you like your clubs to be punky basements **(Cake Shop, Map 4)** or former bodegas (**Arlene Grocery, Map 4**).

But it's really the clubs in Brooklyn that generally shine with exciting new talent night after night, including **Union Hall (Map 33)**, **Southpaw (Map 33)**, **Glasslands Gallery (Map 29)**, **Bruar Falls (Map 29)**, **Brooklyn Masonic Temple (Map 31)**, **The Bell House (Map 33)**, or **Trash (Map 29)**. And **Maxwell's (Map 34)** is still your best bet in Hoboken.

Experimental

A number of venues in New York provide a place for experimental music to get exposure. **Experimental Intermedia (Map 3)** and **Roulette (Map 2)** are fully dedicated to showcasing the avant-garde. John Zorn's place, **The Stone (Map 7)**, takes an experimental approach towards the perfor-mance space as well as the music, with a different artist acting as curator for an entire month, no drinks or food, and the artists taking in 100% of door proceeds. **The Kitchen (Map 8)** features experimental music in addition to film, dance, and other art forms. Relative newcomer **Le Poisson Rouge (Map 6)** has brought an exciting mix of different sounds back to the heart of the Village, and is one of our favorite spots. In Brooklyn, the experimental scene is cranking away, especially at **Issue Project Room's (Map 33)** space at the Old American Can Factory, **Glasslands Gallery (Map 29)** in Williamsburg, **Freddy's Back Room (Map 33)** in Prospect Heights and **Jalopy (Map 32)** in Carroll Gardens.

Everything Else

A few places run the gamut of musical genres; folksy artists one night, hot Latin tango the next, and a slew of comedy, spoken word, and other acts. **Joe's Pub (Map 6)** presents an excellent variety of popular styles and often hosts celebrated international musicians. Keep an eye on **BAMcafé (Map 31**) for a variety of great performers.

For cabaret or piano bar, try **Don't Tell Mama (Map 11)**, **Duplex (Map 5)**, or **Brandy's (Map 15)**. For a more plush experience, try the **Café Carlyle (Map 15)** or **Oak Room (Map 12)** at the Algonquin Hotel. But for top cabaret talent at affordable prices, go directly to **The Metropolitan Room (Map 9)**.

If you're seeking some R&B or soul, check out the **Apollo Theater (Map 19)**, though they mostly get "oldies" acts. The Apollo's Amateur Night on Wednesday is your chance to see some up-and-comers. Both the **Bowery Poetry Club (Map 6)** and **The Pyramid Club (Map 7)** have open mic MC'ing nights. Many dance clubs feature hip-hop DJs.

Barbes (Map 33) in Park Slope hosts a wide palette of "world music" (for lack of a better term), including Latin American, European, and traditional US styles, plus more experimental fare. For more sounds of the south, **SOB's (Map 5)** has live South American music and dancing and should definitely be experienced at least once. **Nublu (Map 7)** is always reliable for a fun and sweaty night, especially on Wednesdays when they feature Brazilian bands and DJs.

African music has swelled in NYC in recent years, with fabulous weekly performances at **St. Nick's Pub (Map 21)** on Saturday nights (after midnight is when it really starts to shake), **Barbes (Map 33)** on Wednesday nights with the Mandingo Ambassadors, Afro-fusion masters Asiko at **Zebulon (Map 29)**, as well as occasional performances at **Grand Dakar (Map 31)** in Clinton Hill.

And oh yeah—then there's all that classical music stuff, at places like **Carnegie Hall (Map 12)** and **Lincoln Center (Map 14)**—perhaps you've heard of these venues?

We don't need to hear Liza Minelli or Frank Sinatra sing it to remember the famous line about New York City: "If I can make it there, I'll make it anywhere." A corollary of sorts might be, "If they'll make it anywhere, I can buy it there." From tasteful to tacky, classic to classless, delicious to dangerous, we've got it all: life-size stuffed animals, Ming vases, toys for, shall we say, adventurous adults, live eels, exotic spices, and even illegal fruits (but you didn't hear it here). It requires enormous self-restraint to take a walk, even just to the subway, and not buy something. And while we natives and traditionalists do occasionally lament the "mall-ification" of our fair city, we'll challenge anyone to find another place that combines convenience and quirkiness as well as this town does. You want Prada knock-offs? Chinatown. You want the real thing? Just walk north a few blocks. A real human skeleton? Cross the street. Homemade ricotta? It's practically next door. You can hunt for bargains or blow a year's salary in the blink of an eye. And even if you decide to leave your wallet at home in the interests of self-preservation, you can find endless entertainment in walking the streets and practicing the storied art of window-shopping.

Clothing and Accessories

Shopping for haute couture is no longer strictly an uptown affair, with a few high-end shops appearing in SoHo and the Meatpacking District, but the Upper East Side is still the ultimate destination for designer labels. Madison Avenue is the main artery, in the 50s, 60s, and 70s, rounded out by Fifth Avenue in the 50s and a few blocks east along 57th St. There you will find **Chanel (Map 12)**, **Burberry (Map 12)**, and all other names of that ilk. Take note, these stores still observe the age-old tradition, abandoned in most neighborhoods, of closing on Sundays. For department store shopping, try **Macy's (Map 9)** if you're on a budget and love the crush of tourists and **Saks Fifth Avenue (Map 12)** for the classics, **Henri Bendel (Map 12)** and **Barneys (Map 15)** for trendier lines, and **Bergdorf Goodman (Map 12)** if money is no object. If you have the patience to deal with the crowds and sift through the merchandise to find bargains, **Century 21 (Map 1)** can yield great rewards of name brand clothing, shoes, make-up, accessories, and home wares at significantly discounted prices. For cheap and trendy, **H&M (Map 19)** can't be beat. It's disposable clothing for the fashionistas, but be prepared to change in the aisles on crowded shopping days.

SoHo is one of the neighborhoods that's taken on features of an outdoor mall in recent years, with big chains stores taking the place of the smaller boutiques (and the few art galleries that survived the arrival of said boutiques). That said, if you can handle flocks of tourists, it's still a great place to shop because of the wide range of stores in a concentrated area (and plenty of cafés when you need to refuel). You'll find big names like **Prada (Map 6)**, whose Rem Koolhaas design draws as many visitors as Miuccia's clothes do. In addition to the standards, you'll find many street vendors selling everything from handmade jewelry to floppy-eared children's hats. Some of the quieter streets like Thompson, Sullivan, and Wooster appeal to the shopper who aims to avoid the chain stores. Take advantage of the fact that SoHo is densely packed and great for walking; just cruise the streets to discover hidden gems.

The West Village has its own enclave of hip clothing stores like **Stella McCartney (Map 5)**. Head northwest to the Meatpacking District and you can see the results of an impressive urban magic trick that transformed racks of hanging beef into racks of hanging jeans that cost $800. Check out the punk rock–inspired styles of **Alexander McQueen (Map 5)**, as well as the envelope-pushing and wallet-emptying department store **Jeffrey (Map 5)**, the subject of a reoccurring Saturday Night Live skit that's a send-up of the clerks' reputed snobbery. The other destinations for fashions from up-and-coming designers and great independent boutiques are: NoHo (the area north of Houston and east of Broadway), NoLita (north of Little Italy), and the East Village.

The Upper East Side (particularly along Madison Avenue in the East 80s) has a notable amount of designer consignment stores. **Bis Designer Resale (Map 15)** and others like it sell gently worn items from top tier designers like Chanel and Armani at a fraction of their original cost. You can also meander along "Thrift Row," a string of Upper East Side thrift shops on and near Third Avenue in the East 70s and 80s. Many of these shops, such as the **Housing Works Thrift Shop (Map 15)**, carry a nice selection of designer clothing—not to mention the added bonus that the proceeds from your purchases go toward a good cause, like AIDS-related charities, cancer research, and adoption programs.

Vintage Shopping

The abundance of vintage shops—over 60 at last count—will impress any shopper, whether you're someone who's just looking for a unique piece for a special occasion or a professional stylist purchasing wardrobe for a period film. Check out **What Comes Around Goes Around (Map 2)** in SoHo, for instance, though you can still troll what's left of Broadway's former vintage greatness. In Brooklyn, check out either one of **Beacon's Closet**'s two locations in Williamsburg **(Map 29)** or Park Slope **(Map 33)**, as well as **Amarcord Vintage Fashion (Map 29)**. On the Upper West Side, longtime vintage purveyor **Allan & Suzi (Map 14)** still holds court at the corner of Amsterdam and 80th Street. For you die-hards, be sure to attend the thrice-yearly Manhattan Vintage Clothing Show at the Metropolitan Pavilion, where over 75 dealers sell their vintage finery during two-day stints. And finally, there's always the Triple Pier Antiques Show on the far West Side of Manhattan. It should go without saying that at all of the above-mentioned shops and venues, you must be prepared to pay the usual New York City premium.

Flea Markets, Street Vendors, Street Fairs & Bazaars

New Yorkers who once spent weekends perusing the eclectic finds in the asphalt lot at 26th Street and Sixth Avenue are still mourning the loss of the internationally known Annex Antique Fair & Flea Market. The good news is that many of the same vendors from Annex sell their wares at the **Annex/ Hell's Kitchen Flea Market (Map 11)** on 39th Street between Ninth and Tenth Avenues. There are, of course, many other (albeit smaller) flea markets throughout the city, as well as numerous street fairs in various neighborhoods during warmer months. The best way to find them tends to be to accidentally stumble upon them on an exploratory walk around town. A fantastic indoor market to add to your must-see list is The Market NYC (268 Mulberry St; Sat & Sun; 11 am-7 pm), a refreshingly offbeat collection from young, local designers who aren't afraid to be truly creative. These places provide a cure for chain shopping boredom and the inevitable annoyance at seeing every third person wearing the same H&M shirt as you. Another fun option (particularly during the warmer months) is shopping street side from designers who sell their one-of-a-kind designs al fresco. You can't always identify them by name, but you can't miss their stands along Prince and Spring Streets in SoHo. Look for made-while-you-wait purses and belts, the scrap metal jewelry pieces, handmade leather-bound journals, and other singular and quirky items.

Sports

Paragon Sporting Goods (Map 9) in Union Square is hard to beat as a one-stop shop for all sports gear and accessories. They also take care of your recreational needs, with services like all-inclusive ski packages for Hunter Mountain and permitting for the NYC Parks Department tennis courts. **Sports Authority (Map 13)**, **Foot Locker (Map 21, 24)**, and **Modell's (Map 23)** provide a broad range of affordable sports clothing, shoes, and athletic equipment. For the best cold weather and mountain gear, head to **Tents & Trails (Map 2)** or **Patagonia (Map 14)** (you can expect competitive prices at the former, but definitely not at the latter).

Housewares and Home Design

You can lose hours in **ABC Carpet & Home (Map 9)** just off of Union Square. Design fanatics can appreciate their exotic array of furnishings (much of it antique and imported from Asia and Europe) even if they can't afford the steep prices. For even more amazing and unaffordable housewares, Fifth Avenue's **Takashimaya (Map 12)** will blow your mind with its brilliant Asian aesthetic. For the rest of us, however, much more basic but affordable housewares can be found at the Upper West Side's **Gracious Home (Map 14)**, Chelsea's **The Container Store (Map 9)**, and any one of **Muji's** three Manhattan locations **(Maps 3, 9, 12)**. For paint, window dressings, and other home decorating supplies, try **Janovic (Map 2, 11, 16)**. Prepare for sensory overload if you take on the over 200,000 square feet of commercial and residential furnishings at the **A&D Building (Map 13)**. Showrooms are open to the public, unlike at some of the smaller design shops nearby, which require business cards upon entry.

Kitchenware/Tableware

Fishs Eddy (Map 9) is a "used plateware" alternative to mega-chains like Pottery Barn and Bed, Bath & Beyond, and is easily one of our favorite shops in all of New York. **Zabar's (Map 14)** often-ignored second floor is a favorite among the city's cooks, along with Brooklyn's fabulous **A Cook's Companion (Map 32)**. Downtown, small but sublime **Global Table (Map 6)** has excellent mid-range taste in housewares, and **Lancelotti's (Map 7)** collection of cool kitchenware and tableware is always fun to check out. Our favorite downtown shop, however, is probably coolly unpronouncable **Mxyplyzyk (Map 5)** in the West Village.

Furniture

No cash at all? Easy. Troll the Upper East Side on Sunday nights to see what people are throwing out. Chances are, you'll find something better than what you'd buy new at Brooklyn's **Ikea (Map 32)**, which is indubitably the next step up in the food chain of furniture. Up from there, **West Elm (Map 30)** and **Design Within Reach** (not really within reach) **(Map 30)** will gleefully take your hard-earned dollars if you're ready to graduate from "Aksuldnje" and "Fjosell." Have even more money to spend? Easily done, at places such as **Scott Jordan Furniture (Map 5)**, **Ligne Rosset (Map 10)**, and the Meatpacking's brilliant **Vitra (Map 5)** store. If vintage is your bag, head straight to Williamsburg's **Two Jakes (Map 29)** or check out some of the smaller shops around town such as Fort Greene's **Yu Interiors (Map 31)**. Any way you slice it, you can spend entire paychecks in the blink of an eye. Or not.

Electronics

J&R (Map 1) provides most things electronic, including computers and accessories, iPods, games, cameras, music equipment, CDs, DVDs, and household appliances. **B&H (Map 8)** is the top destination for professionals and amateurs when it comes to photographic, audio, and video equipment. It's worth a visit just to witness the pure spectacle of this well-coordinated operation, as well as the outstanding selection of gear. Note that the megastore is run by Orthodox Jews who strictly observe the Sabbath and holidays, and thus you should always check the hours and days of operation posted on their website before heading over. Audiophiles are wonderfully served by **Stereo Exchange (Map 6)** and the jaw-dropping, price-busting **Sound by Singer (Map 9)**. Other places to shop for electronics include the **Apple Store (Map 12)** and **Tekserve (Map 9)**, the (other) Apple specialists.

Food

With residents from every corner of the globe who collectively speak over 170 languages, New York couldn't help but be an exciting destination for food shopping. The offerings are as diverse as the population, whether you're looking for the best of the basics or exotic spices and other imported specialties. Two revered emporia make the Upper West Side a culinary destination—**Fairway (Maps 14, 18, 32)** and **Zabar's (Map 14)**—and the Zabar's offshoot, **Vinegar Factory (Map 17)**, graces the Upper East. The national chain **Whole Foods (Maps 9, 16)** is multiplying, and now there's even two **Trader Joe's (Map 6)**, though only devotees can brave the crowds there. **The Essex Street Market (Map 4)** on the Lower East Side is a beloved neighborhood institution filled to the brim with amazing cheese (like **Saxleby Cheesemongers (Map 4**), meat, produce, and fish options. Another great public market filled with gourmet goodies can be found in the heart of Grand Central Terminal—the **Grand Central Market (Map 13)**. But the city's real gems come in the form of the increasing number of **Greenmarkets** (the largest is in Union Square **(Map 9)** four days a week), and the ethnic food purveyors stocked with imported goods from around the world. When it comes to Italian, Arthur Ave in the Bronx is famed for its bakeries, butcher shops, grocers, and sundry shops. The more centrally located **Di Palo Fine Foods (Map 3)** offers some of the best imported delicacies as well as their own celebrated fresh ricotta. For Middle Eastern specialties, **Sahadi's (Map 32)** provides the most impressive range of top quality products at prices that cannot be beat (and many of its neighbors on Atlantic Ave deserve a visit while you're in the area). Friendly **Despana (Map 3)** in SoHo will satisfy all your Spanish desires, including three different types of Spanish sparkling water and $100-a-pound Spanish Serrano ham. Chinatown's options will overwhelm and exhaust you before they disappoint even the pickiest of shoppers, and there's even a destination for people in the market for British treats, **Myers of Keswick (Map 5)** in the West Village.

Cheese shops in New York are starting to create their own footprint, neighborhood-by-neighborhood. Your first stop should be brilliant **Murray's (Map 5)** in the West Village, classic **Lamarca Cheese Shop (Map 10)** on the East Side, small but powerful **Stinky (Map 32)** in Carroll Gardens, **Bedford Cheese Shop (Map 29)** in Williamsburg, and, of course, the cheese counter at **Dean & Deluca (Map 15)**. If you're always low on cash (i.e. you work for NFT), **East Village Cheese (Map 6)** is your go-to shop. They don't give out free samples and the line is always long, but it's the cheapest option in Manhattan by far.

You need three other items to go with your cheese, though—bread, meat, and wine. Of course, many neighborhoods have all these things covered as well. For bread, our top favorites are of course the-now-splitsville-duo of **Sullivan Street Bakery (Map 11)** and **Grandaisy Bakery (Maps 2, 5, 14)**. For meats, hit **Faicco's Pork Store (Map 5)**, **Despana (Map 3)**, **G Esposito & Sons (Map 32)**, or **Choice Greene (Map 31)**.

Art Supplies

Running low on Cadmium Red? Use your last stick of charcoal drawing a nude? The best art stores in NYC are scattered loosely around the SoHo area, with **Pearl Paint (Map 3)** being the best known. Located at the corner of Mercer and Canal Streets, the store occupies a full six-story building with every type of art supply you can imagine, including a great separate frame shop out back on Lispenard. Closer to NYU and Cooper Union, you can find the best selection of paper at **New York Central Art Supply (Map 6)** on Third Avenue. **SoHo Art Materials (Map 2)** on Wooster Street is a small, traditional shop that sells super premium paints and brushes for fine artists. Don't forget to check out both **Sam Flax (Map 13)** and **A.I. Friedman (Map 9)** in the Flatiron area for graphic design supplies, portfolios, and gifts. **Lee's Art Shop (Map 12)** is a great store on 57th Street; how it's survived Midtown rents is anyone's guess. Should you find yourself on the Upper East Side needing art supplies in a pinch, the fairly decent selection at **Blacker & Kooby (Map 17)** will do just fine.

As the art scene has made its way to Williamsburg, having a supply store close by is as important as a good supermarket (something folks in the 'burg are still waiting for). **Artist & Craftsman (Map 29)** on North 8th is a good bet for supplies. In Fort Greene, the **Pratt Store (Map 31)** is a combined art supply store/college bookstore.

For photographic equipment, the holy trinity of **B&H Photo (Map 8)**, **Adorama (Map 9)**, and **K & M Camera (Map 3)** will satisfy every possible photographic (digital or darkroom-based) need that you might have. B & H is of course the mothership, Adorama is great if you're nearby, and K & M is in the trinity because it's the only one of the three that's open on f*%&ing Saturdays.

*Remember to flash that student ID card if you've got it, as most art stores offer a decent discount...

Music Equipment & Instruments

New York's large and vibrant music scene supports a thriving instrument trade. To buy a new tuba or get that banjo tuned, head over to 48th Street. You'll find the largest, most well known stores, from generalist shops such as **Manny's (Map 12)** and **Sam Ash (Map 12)**, to more specialized shops like **Roberto's Woodwind Repair (Map 12)**. Just two blocks away, on 46th, drummers can make themselves at home in a store dedicated solely to their craft—**Drummer's World (Map 12)**.

If you can't take the bustle of the Times Square area and are looking for used, vintage, or just plain cool, then you'll want to shop elsewhere. Some of our favorites include: **First Flight (Map 7)**, **30th Street Guitars (Map 9)**, **Rogue Music (Map 9)**, and **Ludlow Guitars (Map 4)**.

For an exquisite purchase where money is no object, find the perfect grand piano at **Steinway Pianos (Map 12)**, where the salespeople pride themselves on matching even beginners with the perfect instrument for their skills and character. Also keep an eye (and an ear) out for special musical evenings at the former, and spontaneous performances at the latter.

Music for Listening

Oops! No record stores left in NYC—or at least that's the way it seems, with Tower, Virgin, and Kim's all now faint memories in our minds (how do you spell "Amoeba" again?). So now it's down to the small "boutique" record shops, and (thank God!) the slightly-larger selection of none other than **J&R Music World (Map 1)** near City Hall. As for the small shops—we still do love hip **Other Music (Map 6)** (look out for occasional in-store performances) and avant-garde **Downtown Music (Map 3)** (now at its postage-stamp-sized new digs in Chinatown). In Brooklyn, **Earwax (Map 29)** in Williamsburg—run by WFMU djs—is our favorite destination. If you're in to trolling through used bins, head to Bleecker Street to check out **Rebel Rebel (Map 5)** and **Bleecker Street Records (Map 5)**. Finally, **Academy Records (Maps 9, 29)** should be able to quench any remaining thirst, especially for the (resurgent) LP.

Weird, Odd, Bizarre, and/or Just Plain Fun

Every once in a while, you walk into a shop in NYC and say, "what is this place?" And while we don't have anything quite as odd as, say, the taxidermy shops that still dot London, for instance, there are a few places that still make us smile. First on the list is the quirky **Brooklyn Superhero Supply (Map 33)**, for all your needs in that department. Next up: SoHo's **Moss (Map 6)**, which sells insanely-priced housewares, watches, furniture, and—our favorite—small sculptures of famous murders/terrorist acts. Our favorite downtown destination (just for the name, even) is City Hall's **Fountain Pen Hospital (Map 3)**. Right underneath the Municipal Building sits the brilliant **New York City Store (Map 3)**, where you can buy old taxi medallions and other NYC ephemera.

Shopping "Districts"

If you're fixated on a specific item, like a sausage maker or a few yards of leopard print fabric, you can shop in specialty districts around Manhattan. Brave the overwhelming selection throughout the Garment District (25th to 40th Sts, Fifth to Ninth Aves) for fabrics, buttons, zippers, ribbons, and anything else you'd need to design your own clothes. Men looking for the perfect romantic gift might want to check out the Diamond and Jewelry District (W 47th between Fifth and Sixth Aves), the world's largest market for diamonds, the Flower District (26th to 29th Sts, along and off Sixth Ave), and the Perfume District (along and off Broadway in the West 20s and 30s). Music Row (48th St between Sixth & Seventh Aves) leaves you with no excuses if you've been meaning to learn to play an instrument. The Bowery around Houston is another well-known strip where you'll find the Kitchenware District for all your culinary endeavors, the Lighting District (past Delancey St) for all your illuminating needs, and the Downtown Jewelry District (turn the corner of Bowery to Canal St) for the more unusual baubles you can't get uptown. High-end home design stores are concentrated on and around Designers Way and Decorators Way (58th and 59th Sts, between Second and Third Aves). The Flatiron District (from 14th to 34th Sts, between Sixth & Park Aves) is another home furnishing mecca. You can also take care of your photography needs where the pros do, with the city's highest concentration of stores and labs (between Fifth and Sixth Aves, from 18th to 22nd Sts). Sadly, Book Row (between 9th and 14th Sts) is no more. What was once an assemblage of over 25 bookstores now houses only the famous Strand Bookstore and Alabaster Bookshop, but avid readers could happily spend days browsing and purchasing in either one of them...

Overview

If you want to see cutting-edge art, go to New York City's galleries. There are more than 500 galleries in the city, with artwork created in every conceivable medium (and of varying quality) on display. SoHo, Chelsea, DUMBO, and Williamsburg are the hot spots for gallery goers, but there are also many famous (and often more traditional) galleries and auction houses uptown, including **Christie's (Map 12)** and **Sotheby's (Map 15)**. With so much to choose from, there's almost always something that's at least *provocative*, if not actually *good*.

The scene at the upscale galleries is sometimes intimidating, especially if you look like you are on a budget. If you aren't interested in buying, they aren't interested in you being there. Some bigger galleries require appointments. Cut your teeth at smaller galleries; they aren't as scary. Also, put your name on the mailing lists. You'll get invites to openings so crowded that no one will try to pressure you into buying (and there's free wine). The Armory Show (www.thearmoryshow.com), an annual show of new art, is also a great way to see what the galleries have to offer without intimidation.

SoHo Area

Five years ago, there were still hundreds of art galleries in SoHo. Now it has practically become an outdoor mall. However, there are still some permanent artworks in gallery spaces, such as Walter De Maria's excellent **The Broken Kilometer (Map 6)** (a Dia-sponsored space at 393 West Broadway), and his sublime **New York Earth Room (Map 6)**. A short jaunt down to TriBeCa will land you in LaMonte Young's awesome aural experience Dream House at the **MELA Foundation (Map 2)**. **Artists Space (Map 2)**, one of the first alternative art galleries in New York, is also in TriBeCa. The **HERE Arts Center (Map 5)** showcases a wide range of work and usually offers an exhibit or performance that warrants a visit

Chelsea

The commercialization of SoHo has helped make Chelsea the center of the city's gallery scene. Our recommendation is to hit at least two streets—W 24th Street between Tenth and Eleventh avenues, and W 22nd Street between Tenth and Eleventh avenues. W 24th Street is anchored by the almost-always-brilliant **Gagosian Gallery (Map 8)** and also includes the **Luhring Augustine (Map 8)**, **Charles Cowles (Map 8)**, **Mary Boone (Map 12)**, **Barbara Gladstone (Map 8)**, and **Matthew Marks (Map 8)** galleries. W 22nd has the architecture-friendly **Max Protech (Map 8)** gallery and the **Julie Saul (Map 8)**, **Leslie Tonkonow (Map 8)**, **Marianne Boesky (Map 8)**, **Pace Wildenstein (Map 8)**, and **Yancey Richardson (Map 8)** galleries. Also, check out the famous "artist's" bookstore **Printed Matter (Map 8)**.

Perhaps the final nail in the coffin of SoHo's art scene was **Exit Art's (Map 8)** move to 475 Tenth Avenue a couple years back. This gallery is well-known for brilliant group shows, exhibiting everything from album covers to multimedia installations, and killer openings. It's highly recommended.

Other recommendations are the **Starrett-Lehigh Building (Map 8)**, not only for the art but also for the great pillars, windows, and converted freight elevators, **Esso (Map 8)** for Pop Art, the **Daniel Reich Gallery (Map 8)**, and the **Jonathan LeVine Gallery (Map 8)**, which consistently features exciting artists. On the Lower East Side check out **Canada (Map 3)** for fun openings and **Envoy Gallery (Map 6)** for cutting edge photography and celebrity sightings.

Map 1 • Financial District

American Indian Community House Gallery	11 Broadway	212-598-0100

Map 2 • TriBeCa

A Taste of Art	147 Duane St	212-964-5493
Adelphi University	75 Varick St, 2nd Fl	212-965-8340
Amazing Art	54 Greene St	
Anthem Gallery	41 Wooster St	347-249-4525
apexart	291 Church St	212-431-5270
Arcadia Fine Arts	51 Greene St	212-965-1387
Art Projects International	429 Greenwich St	212-343-2599
Artists Space	38 Greene St, 3rd Fl	212-226-3970
Atlantic Gallery	40 Wooster St	212-219-3183
Cheryl Hazan Gallery	35 N Moore St	212-343-8964
Cheryl Pelavin Fine Art	13 Jay St	212-925-9424
Dactyl Foundation for the Arts & Humanities	64 Grand St	212-219-2344
Deitch Projects	76 Grand St	212-343-7300
The Drawing Center	35 Wooster St	212-219-2166
Ethan Cohen Fine Arts	18 Jay St	212-625-1250
Gallerie Icosahedron	27 N Moore St	212-966-3897
Jacques Carcanagues Gallery	21 Greene St	212-925-8110
KS Art	73 Leonard St	212-219-9918
Leslie-Lohman Gay Art Foundation	26 Wooster St	212-431-2609
Location One	26 Greene St	212-334-3347
Mela Foundation	275 Church St, 3rd Fl	212-925-8270
National Sculpture Society	75 Varick St	212-764-5645
The Painting Center	52 Greene St	212-343-1060
SoHo Photo Gallery	15 White St	212-266-8571
Spencer Brownstone Gallery	39 Wooster St	212-334-3455
Team Gallery	83 Grand St	212-279-9219

Map 3 • City Hall / Chinatown

Art in General	79 Walker St	212-219-0473
Broadway Gallery	473 Broadway	212-274-8993
Canada	55 Chrystie St	212-925-4631
Christopher Henry Gallery	127 Elizabeth St	212-244-6004
Clic	255 Centre St	212-966-2766
CVZ Contemporary	446 Broadway	917-595-8550
Gallery 456	456 Broadway, 3rd Fl	212-431-9740
The Gallery at Dieu Donne Papermill	433 Broome St	212-226-0573
James Fuentes	35 St James Pl	212-577-1201
Puffin Room	435 Broome St	212-343-2881
Ronald Feldman Fine Arts	31 Mercer St	212-226-3232
Simon Preston Gallery	301 Broome St	212-431-1105
Synagogue for the Arts	49 White St	212-966-7141
White Box	329 Broome St	212-714-2347

Map 4 • Lower East Side

Abrons Art Center	466 Grand St	212-598-0400
Blackston	29 Ludlow St	212-695-8201
Gallery Onetwentyeight	128 Rivington St	212-674-0244
NY Studio Gallery	154 Stanton St	212-627-3276
Ramiken Crucible	221 E Broadway	917-434-4245

Map 5 • West Village

14 Sculptors	332 Bleecker St	212-966-5790
14th Street Painters	110 W 14th St	212-627-9893
Akira Ikeda	17 Cornelia St, #1C	212-366-5449
Art Gotham	192 Ave of the Americas	917-319-2030
Baron/Boisante Editions	421 Hudson St	212-924-9940
Bill Maynes Gallery	55 Bethune St	917-523-7229
Cooper Classics Collection	137 Perry St	212-929-3909

Gavin Brown's Enterprise	620 Greenwich St	212-627-5258
Hal Katzen Gallery	459 Washington St	212-925-9777
Harris Lieberman Gallery	89 Vandam St	212-206-1290
Heller Gallery	420 W 14th St	212-414-4014
HERE	145 Sixth Ave	212-647-0202
hpgrp	32 Little W 12th St	212-727-2491
Kate Werble Gallery	83 Vandam St	212-352-9700
Les Pierre Antiques	369 Bleecker St	212-243-7740
Maccarone	630 Greenwich St	212-431-4977
Parkett Publishers	145 Ave of the Americas	212-673-2660
Pratt Manhattan Gallery	144 W 14th St, 2nd Fl	212-647-7778
Ramscale Gallery	55 Bethune St	212-206-6580
Sperone Westwater	415 W 13th St	212-999-7337
Synchronicity Fine Arts	106 W 13th St	646-230-8199
Tracy Williams Ltd	313 W 4th St	212-229-2757
Westbeth Gallery	57 Bethune St	212-989-4650
White Columns	320 W 13th St	212-924-4212

Map 6 • Washington Square / NYU / NoHo / SoHo

80 Washington Square East Galleries	80 Washington Sq E	212-998-5747
A/D	560 Broadway	212-966-5154
Aicon Gallery	35 Great Jones St	212-725-6092
Art Niche New York	498 Broome St	212-941-0130
Bottom Feeders Studio Gallery	195 Chrystie St, 2nd Fl	917-974-9664
Broadway Windows	80 Washington Square E	212-998-5751
Bronfman Center Gallery at NYU	7 E 10th St	212-998-4123
Brooke Alexander Editions	59 Wooster St	212-925-4338
Campton Gallery	451 West Broadway	212-387-0208
Cecilia De Torres Ltd	140 Greene St	212-431-5869
Clic	424 Broome St	212-219-9308
David Beitzel Gallery	102 Prince St	212-219-2863
DCKT Contemporary	195 Bowery	212-741-9955
Dia Foundation New York Earth Room	141 Wooster St	212-473-8072
Dia Foundation The Broken Kilometer	393 West Broadway	212-989-5566
Dranoff FIne Art	591 Broadway	212-966-0153
Eleanor Ettinger Gallery	119 Sprint St	212-925-7474
El Klein FIne Art	462 West Broadway	212-255-4388
Emily Harvey Gallery	537 Broadway	212-925-7651
Envoy Gallery	131 Chrystie St	212-226-4555
Feature Inc	131 Allen St	212-675-7772
Forbes Galleries	60th Fifth Ave	212-206-5549
Franklin Bowles Galleries	431 West Broadway	212-226-1616
Gallery hanahou	611 Broadway	646-486-6586
Gallery Juno	568 Broadway #604B	212-431-1515
Gracie Mansion Fine Art	101 Second Ave	212-505-9577
Grey Art Gallery	100 Washington Sq E	212-998-6780
Horton Gallery	237 Eldridge St	212-243-2663
ISE Foundation	555 Broadway	212-925-1649
Jamali Fine Art Gallery	413 W Broadway	212-966-3350
Janet Borden	560 Broadway	212-431-0166
Janos Gat Gallery	195 Bowery	212-677-3525
John Szoke Editions	166 Mercer St	212-219-8300
June Kelly Gallery	166 Mercer St	212-226-1660
Kerrigan Cambell Art + Projects	317 E 9th St	212-505-7196
Lehmann Maupin Gallery	201 Chrystie St	212-254-0054
Louis K Meisel Gallery	141 Prince St	212-677-1340
Lumas	77 Wooster St	212-219-9497
Marc Jancou Contemporary	Great Jones Alley	212-473-2100
Margarete Roeder Gallery	545 Broadway, 4th Fl	212-925-6098
Martin Lawrence	457 West Broadway	212-995-8865
Michael Ingbar Gallery	568 Broadway	212-334-1100
Mimi Ferzt Gallery	81 Greene St	212-343-9377
Moss Gallery	150 Greene St	212-204-7100
Nancy Hoffman	429 West Broadway	212-966-6676
National Association of Women Artists Fifth Avenue Gallery	80 Fifth Ave #1405	212-675-1616
New York Open Center Gallery	83 Spring St	212-219-2527
New York Studio School	8 W 8th St	212-673-6466
OK Harris Works of Art	383 West Broadway	212-431-3600
Opera Gallery	115 Spring St	212-966-6675
The Pen & Brush	16 E 10th St	212-475-3669
Peter Blum Gallery SoHo	99 Wooster St	212-343-0441
Peter Freeman	560 Broadway Ste 602	212-966-5154
Pomegranate Gallery	133 Greene St	212-260-4014
Pop International Galleries	473 West Broadway	212-533-4262
Salmagundi Club	47 Fifth Ave	212-255-7740
Salon 94 Freemans	1 Freeman Alley	212-529-7400
Sculptors Guild	110 Greene St Ste 603	212-431-5669
Staley-Wise Gallery	560 Broadway Ste 305	212-966-6223
Stephen Rosenberg Fine Art	115 Wooster St	212-431-4838
Storefront for Art and Architecture	97 Kenmare St	212-431-5795
Susan Teller Gallery	568 Broadway, Ste 103A	212-941-7335
Swiss Institute Contemporary Art	495 Broadway, 3rd Fl	212-925-2035
Tenri Cultural Institute	43A W 13th St	212-645-2800
Terrain Gallery	141 Greene St	212-777-4490
Thierry Goldberg Projects	5 Rivington St	212-967-2260
Vara Global Fine Arts	141 Wooster St	212-475-4404
Walker Fine Art	478 West Broadway	347-563-2100
Ward-Nasse Gallery	178 Prince St	212-925-6951
Washington Square Windows	80 Washington Sq E	212-998-5751
Westwood Gallery	568 Broadway	212-925-5700
William Bennett Gallery	65 Greene St	212- 965-8707
Xanadu	217 Thompson St	646-319-8597

Map 7 • East Village

BlueSky/Eickholt Gallery	93 St Marks Pl	646-613-9610
The Phatory	618 E 9th St	212-777-7922

Map 8 • Chelsea

303 Gallery	547 W 21st St	212-255-1121
ACA Galleries	529 W 20th St, 5th Fl	212-206-8080
Agora Gallery Chelsea	530 W 25th St	212-226-4151
Alexander and Bonin	132 Tenth Ave	212-367-7474
Allen Sheppard Gallery	530 W 25th St	212-989-9919
Ameringer McEnery Yohe	525 W 22nd St	212-445-0051
Amsterdam Whitney	511 W 25th St	212-255-9050
Andrea Meislin Gallery	526 W 26th St	212-627-2552
Andrea Rosen Gallery	525 W 24th St	212-627-6000
Andrew Edlin Gallery	134 10th Ave	212-206-9723
Andrew Kreps	525 W 22nd St	212-741-8849
Anna Kustera	520 W 21st St	212-989-0082
Anton Kern	532 W 20th St	212-367-9663
ATM Gallery	542 W 24th St	212-375-0349
Axelle Fine Arts Ltd	535 W 25th St	212-226-2262
Barry Friedman	515 W 26th St	212-239-8600
Bellwether	134 Tenth Ave	212-929-5959
Betty Cuningham Gallery	541 W 25th St	212-242-2772
Bitforms	529 W 20th St, 2nd Fl	212-366-6939
Blue Mountain Gallery	530 W 25th St, 4th Fl	646-486-4730
Bose Pacia Modern	508 W 26th St, 11th Fl	212-989-7074
Bowery Gallery	530 W 25th St, 4th Fl	646-230-6655
Brenda Taylor	511 W 25th St	212-463-7166
Bruce Silverstein Gallery	535 W 24th St	212-627-3930
Bryce Wolkowitz Gallery	505 W 24th St, Ste 1240	212-243-8830
BUIA Gallery	541 W 23rd St	212-366-9915
Caelum Gallery	526 W 26th St, Ste 315	212-924-4161
Carolina Nitsch	534 W 22nd St	212- 645-2030
Casey Kaplan	525 W 21st St	212-645-7335
Cavin-Morris	210 11th Ave	212-226-3768
Ceres	547 W 27th St, 2nd Fl	212-947-6100
Chambers Fine Art	522 W 19th St	212-414-1169
Chappell Gallery	526 W 26th St, #317	212-414-2673
Charles Cowles Gallery	537 W 24th St	212-741-8999
Cheim & Read	547 W 25th St	212-242-7727
Claire Oliver Gallery	513 W 26th St	212-929-5949
Clementine Gallery	623 W 27th St	212-243-5937
CRG Gallery	535 W 22nd St, 3rd Fl	212-229-2766
Cue Art Foundation	511 W 25th St	212-206-3583
Cynthia Broan Gallery	546 W 29th St	212-760-0809

Gallery	Address	Phone
Cynthia-Reeves	535 W 24th St, 2nd Fl	212-714-0044
D'Amelio Terras	525 W 22nd St	212-352-9460
Danese	535 W 24th St	212-223-2227
Daniel Cooney Fine Art	511 W 25th St	212-255-8158
Daniel Reich Gallery	537 W 23rd St	212-924-4949
David Krut Projects	526 W 26th St	212-255-3094
David Nolan Gallery	527 W 29th St	212-925-6190
David Zwirner	525 W 19th St	212-727-2070
Denise Bibro Fine Art	529 W 20th St, 4th Fl	212-647-7030
Derek Eller Gallery	615 W 27th St	212-206-6411
Dia Foundation 7000 Oaks	535 W 22nd St	212-989-5566
Dieu Donne	315 W 36th St	212-226-0573
Dillon Gallery	555 W 25th St	212-727-8705
Dinter Fine Art	547 W 27th St	212-947-2818
DJT Fine Art	231 Tenth Ave	212-367-0881
Dorfman Projects	529 W 20th St, 7th Fl	212-352-2272
Edward Thorp Gallery	210 Eleventh Ave, 6th Fl	212-691-6565
Elizabeth Dee Gallery	545 W 20th St	212-924-7545
Elizabeth Harris	529 W 20th St	212-463-9666
Esso Gallery	531 W 26th St	212-560-9728
Exit Art	475 Tenth Ave	212-966-7745
Eyebeam	540 W 21st St	212-937-6580
First Street Gallery	526 W 26th St #915	646-336-8053
Fischbach Gallery	210 Eleventh Ave #801	212-759-2345
Flomenhaft Gallery	547 W 27th St	212-268-4952
Florence Lynch Gallery	539 W 25th St	917-327-3580
Flowers	529 W 20th St	212-439-1700
Franklin 54 Gallery	526 W 26th St	917-821-0753
Fredericks & Freiser	536 W 24th St	212-633-6555
Frederieke Taylor Gallery	535 W 22nd St, 6th Fl	646-230-0992
Friedrich Petzel	535 W 22nd St	212-680-9467
Gagosian Gallery	555 W 24th St	212-741-1111
Gagosian Gallery	522 W 21st St	212-741-1717
Galerie Lelong	528 W 26th St	212-315-0470
Gallery Henoch	555 W 25th St	917-305-0003
George Adams Gallery	525 W 26th St	212-564-8480
George Billis Gallery	511 W 25th St	212-645-2621
Gladstone Gallery	515 W 24th St	212-206-9301
Gladstone Gallery	530 W 21st St	212-206-7606
GR N'Namdi Gallery	526 W 26th St	212-929-6645
Greene Naftali	526 W 26th St, 8th Fl	212-463-7770
Heidi Cho Gallery	522 W 23rd St	212-255-6783
Horton Gallery	504 W22nd St	212-243-2663
Hosfelt Gallery	531 W 36th St	212-563-5454
Howard Scott Gallery	529 W 20th St	646-486-7004
HP Garcia Gallery	580 Eight Ave	212-354-7333
I-20 Gallery	557 W 23rd St	212-645-1100
InterArt Gallery	225 Tenth Ave	212-647-1811
International Poster Center	601 W 26th St	212-787-4000
International Print Center New York	526 W 26th St, Rm 824	212-989-5090
J Cacciola Galleries	617 W 27th St	212-462-4646
Jack Shainman Gallery	513 W 20th St	212-645-1701
James Cohan Gallery	533 W 26th St	212-714-9500
Jeff Bailey Gallery	511 W 25th St	212-989-0156
Jenkins Johnson Gallery	521 W 26th St	212-629-0707
Jim Kempner Fine Art	501 W 23rd St	212-206-6872
John Connelly Presents	625 W 27th St	212-337-9563
Jonathan LeVine Gallery	529 W 20th St	212-243-3822
Josee Bienvenu Gallery	529 W 20th St, 2nd Fl	212-206-7990
Julie Saul Gallery	535 W 22nd St, 6th Fl	212-627-2410
Katherine Markel Fine Arts	529 W 20th St	212-366-5368
Kent Gallery	541 W 25th St	212-627-3680
Kim Foster Gallery	529 W 20th St	212-229-0044
Kimcherova	532 W 25th St	212-929-9720
The Kitchen	512 W 19th St	212-255-5793
Klemens Gasser & Tanja Grunert	148 Ninth Ave	212-807-9494
Klotz Sirmon Gallery	511 W 25th St	212-741-4764
Kravets/Wehby Gallery	521 W 21st St	212-352-2238
Larissa Goldston Gallery	530 W 25th St	212-206-7887
Lehmann Maupin	540 W 26th St	212-937-6581
Lennon, Weinberg	514 W 25th St	212-941-0012
Leo Koenig	545 W 23rd St	212-334-9255
Leslie Tonkonow Artworks and Projects	535 W 22nd St, 6th Fl	212-255-8450
Lohin Geduld Gallery	531 W 25th St	212-675-2656
Lombard-Freid Projects	531 W 26th St	212-967-8040
Lost Art	509 W 27th St	212-594-5450
Lucas Schoormans	508 W 26th St #11B	212-243-3159

Gallery	Address	Phone
Luhring Augustine	531 W 24th St	212-206-9100
Luise Ross	511 W 25th St	212-343-2161
Magnan Projects	317 Tenth Ave	212-244-2344
Margaret Thatcher Projects	539 W 23rd St	212-675-0222
Marianne Boesky Gallery	509 W 24th St	212-680-9889
Marlborough Chelsea	545 W 25th St	212-463-8634
Martos Gallery	540 W 29th St	212-560-0670
Marvelli Gallery	526 W 26th St	212-627-3363
Mary Ryan	527 W 26th St	212-397-0669
Massimo Audiello	526 W 26th St #519	212-675-9082
Matthew Marks Gallery	526 W 22nd St	212-243-0200
Matthew Marks Gallery	523 W 24th St	212-243-0200
Max Lang	229 Tenth Ave	212-980-2400
Max Protech	511 W 22nd St	212-633-6999
McKenzie Fine Art	511 W 25th St, 2nd Fl	212-989-5467
Medialia: Rack & Hamper Gallery	335 W 38th St, 4th Fl	212-971-0953
Metro Pictures	519 W 24th St	212-206-7100
Mike Weiss Gallery	520 W 24th St	212-691-6899
Mixed Greens	531 W 26th St	212-331-8888
Miyako Yoshinaga Art Prospects	547 W 27th St	212-268-7132
Montserrat Contemporary Art Gallery	547 W 27th St	212-268-0088
Morgan Lehman Gallery	317 Tenth Ave	212-268-6699
Murray Guy	453 W 17th St	212-463-7372
Nancy Hoffman Gallery	520 W 27th St	212-966-6676
Nancy Margolis Gallery	523 W 25th St	212-242-3013
Neptune Fine Art & Brand X Projects	511 W 25th St	212-989-9080
New Art Center	580 Eighth Ave	212-354-2999
New Century Artists	530 W 25th St Ste 406	212-367-7072
Newman/Popiashvili Gallery	504 W 22nd St	212-274-9166
Nicholas Robinson Gallery	535 W 20th St	212-560-9075
Nicole Klagsbrun Gallery	526 W 26th St #213	212-243-3335
NoHo Gallery in Chelsea	530 W 25th St, 4th Fl	212-367-7063
Nyehaus	538 W 20th St	212-366-4493
Onishi Gallery	521 W 26th St	212-695-8035
Pace Wildenstein	534 W 25th St	212-929-7000
Paul Kasmin Gallery	293 Tenth Ave	212-563-4474
Paul Kasmin Gallery	511 W 27th St	212-563-4474
Paul Rodgers/9W	529 W 20th St, 9th Fl	212-414-9810
Paula Cooper Gallery	534 W 21st St	212-255-1105
Pavel Zoubok Gallery	533 W 23rd St	212-675-7490
Perry Rubenstein Gallery	527 W 23rd St	212-627-8000
Peter Blum Gallery Chelsea	526 W 29th St	212-244-6055
Phoenix	210 Eleventh Ave, 9th Fl	212-226-8711
Pleiades Gallery	530 W 25th St	646-230-0056
Postmasters Gallery	459 W 19th St	212-727-3323
PPOW	511 W 25th St, 2nd Fl	212-647-1044
Prince Street Gallery	530 W 25th St, 4th Fl	646-230-0246
Printed Matter	195 Tenth Ave	212-925-0325
Qui New York/Zwicker Collective USA	601 W 26th St	212-691-2240
Ramis Barquet	532 W 24th St	212-675-3421
Rare	547 W 27th St	
Ricco Maresca Gallery	529 W 20th St, 3rd Fl	212-627-4819
Robert Goff Gallery	537 W 23rd St	212-675-0461
Robert Mann Gallery	210 Eleventh Ave	212-989-7600
Robert Miller	524 W 26th St	212-366-4774
Robert Steele Gallery	511 W 25th St	212-243-0165
Rush Arts Gallery & Resource Center	526 W 26th St #311	212-691-9552
Sara Meltzer Gallery	525 W 26th St	212-727-9330
Sara Tecchia Roma New York	529 W 20th St	212-741-2900
Schellmann Cocken Art Production	210 Eleventh Ave	212-219-1821
Sean Kelly Gallery	528 W 29th St	212-239-1181
Sears-Peyton Gallery	210 Eleventh Ave #802	212-966-7469
Senior & Shopmaker Gallery	210 Eleventh Ave	212-213-6767
Sikkema, Jenkins & Co	530 W 22nd St	212-929-2262
Silas Seandel Studio	551 W 22nd St	212-645-5286
Skoto Gallery	529 W 20th St	212-352-8058
SoHo 20 Chelsea	547 W 27th St	212-367-8994
Sonnabend	536 W 22nd St	212-627-1018
Stefan Stux Gallery	530 W 25th St	212-352-1600
Stellan Holm Gallery	524 W 24th St	212-627-7444
Stendhal Gallery	545 W 20th St	212-366-1549
Stephen Haller Gallery	542 W 26th St	212-741-7777
Steven Kasher Gallery	521 W 23rd St	212-966-3978

Stricoff Fine Art	564 W 25th St	212-219-3977
Studio 601	511 W 25th St	212-367-7300
Sundaram Tagore Gallery	547 W 27th St	212-677-4520
Susan Inglett Gallery	534 W 22nd St	212-647-9111
Susan Sheehan Gallery	535 W 22nd St	212-489-3331
Tamar Hirschi Studio	601 W 26th St	212-255-1440
Tanya Bonakdar Gallery	521 W 21st St	212-414-4144
Thomas Erben Gallery	526 W 26th St	212-645-8701
TIna Kim Gallery	545 W 25th St	212-716-1100
Tony Shafrazi Gallery	544 W 26th St	212-274-9300
Virgil De Voldere Gallery	526 W 26th St	212-343-9694
Viridian Artists	530 W 25th St, #407	212-414-4040
Visual Arts Gallery	601 W 26th St	212-592-2145
Von Lintel Gallery	520 W 23rd St	212-242-0599
Walter Randel Gallery	287 Tenth Ave	212-239-3330
Walter Wickiser Gallery	210 Eleventh Ave	212-941-1817
Wooster Projects	450 W 17th St	212-871-6700
Yancey Richardson Gallery	535 W 22nd St	646-230-9610
Yossi Milo Gallery	525 W 25th St	212-414-0370
Yvon Lambert	550 W 21st St	212-242-3611
Zach Fuer Gallery (LFL)	530 W 24th St	212-989-7700

Map 9 • Flatiron / Lower Midtown

511 Gallery	252 7th Ave	212-255-2885
A-forest Gallery	134 W 29th St	212-673-1168
Alp Galleries	291 Seventh Ave, 5th Fl	212-206-9108
Atlantic Gallery	135 W 29th St	212-219-3183
CFM	237 W 27th St	212-966-3864
Christine Burgin Gallery	239 W 18th St	212-462-2668
Gallery 138	138 W 17th St	212-633-0324
Globe Institute Gallery	500 Seventh Ave	212-349-4330
H Heather Edelman Gallery	141 W 20th St	646-230-1104
Haim Chanin Fine Arts	121 W 19th St	646-230-7200
Illustration House	110 W 25th St	212-966-9444
Lyons Wier Gallery	175 Seventh Ave	212-242-6220
Merton D Simpson Gallery	38 W 28th St, 5th Fl	212-686-6735
Nabi Gallery	1133 Broadway	212-929-6063
NYCoo Gallery	20 W 22nd St	212-380-1149
Sepia International	148 W 24th St	212-645-9444
Space B Gallery	257 W 19th St	917-518-2385
Sragow	153 W 27th St, Rm 505	212-219-1793
The James Gallery at the Graduate Center CUNY	365 Fifth Ave	212-817-7138
Westside Gallery	133 W 21st St	212-592-2145
Wyman Contemporary	227 W 29th St	212-414-0827

Map 10 • Murray Hill / Gramercy

Baruch College/Sidney Mishkin Gallery	135 E 22nd St	212-802-2690
Hayato New York	125 E 23rd St	212-673-7373
The National Arts Club	15 Gramercy Park S	212-475-3424
Swann Galleries	104 E 25th St	212-254-4710
Talwar Gallery	108 E 16th St	212-673-3096
Tepper Galleries	110 E 25th St	212-677-5300

Map 11 • Hell's Kitchen

Art for Healing NYC/Art for Healing Gallery	405 W 50th St	212-946-1160
Fountain Gallery	702 Ninth Ave	212-262-2756
Gallery MC	549 W 52nd St	212-581-1966
Jadite Galleries	413 W 50th St	212-315-2740
TImes Square Gallery - Hunter College	450 W 41st St	212-772-4991
Triton Gallery	630 Ninth Ave	212-765-2472

Map 12 • Midtown

A. Jain Marunouchi Gallery	24 W 57th St	212-969-9660
AFP Galleries	41 E 57th St	212-230-1003
Alexandre Gallery	41 E 57th St, 13th Fl	212-755-2828
Amador Gallery	41 E 57th St	212-759-6740
Austrian Cultural Forum	11 E 52nd St	212-319-5300
Babcock	724 Fifth Ave, 11th Fl	212-767-1852
Bernarducci-Meisel	37 W 57th St, 6th Fl	212-593-3757
Bill Hodges Gallery	24 W 57th St	212-333-2640
Bonni Benrubi	41 E 57th St, 13th Fl	212-888-6007
Christie's	20 Rockefeller Plz	212-636-2000
D Wigmore Fine Art	730 Fifth Ave	212-581-1657
David Findlay Jr Fine Art	41 E 57th St Ste 1120	212-486-7660
DC Moore	724 Fifth Ave, 8th Fl	212-247-2111
Edwynn Houk	745 Fifth Ave, 4th Fl	212-750-7070
Forum Gallery	745 Fifth Ave, 5th Fl	212-355-4545
Francis M Naumann Fine Art	24 W 57th St	212-582-3201
Franklin Parrasch Gallery	20 W 57th St	212-246-5360
Frederico Seve Gallery Latincollector	37 W 57th St	212-334-7813
Galerie St Etienne	24 W 57th St Ste 802	212-245-6734
Gallery: Gertrude Stein	200 W 57th St	212-535-0600
Gering & Lopez Gallery	730 Fifth Ave	646-336-7183
Greenberg Van Doren Gallery	730 Fifth Ave	212-445-0444
Hammer Galleries	33 W 57th St	212-644-4400
Haunch of Venison	1230 Ave of Americas	212-259-0000
Herbert Arnot	250 W 57th St	212-245-8287
Howard Greenberg	41 E 57th St, 14th Fl	212-334-0010
Jain Marunouchi	24 W 57th St, 6th Fl	212-969-9660
James Goodman Gallery	41 E 57th St, 8th Fl	212-593-3737
Jason McCoy	41 E 57th St	212-319-1996
Julian Jadow Ceramics	37 W 57th St #601	212-757-6660
Katharina Rich Perlow	41 E 57th St, 13th Fl	212-644-7171
Laurence Miller	20 W 57th St	212-397-3930
Leonard Hutton	41 E 57th St, 3rd Fl	212-751-7373
Littleton & Hennessey Asian Art	724 Fifth Ave	212-586-4075
Marian Goodman Gallery	24 W 57th St, 4th Fl	212-977-7160
Marlborough Gallery	40 W 57th St, 2nd Fl	212-541-4900
Mary Boone Gallery	745 Fifth Ave, 4th Fl	212-752-2929
Maxwell Davidson Gallery	724 Fifth Ave	212-759-7555
McKee Gallery	745 Fifth Ave, 4th Fl	212-688-5951
Michael Rosenfeld Gallery	24 W 57th St, 7th Fl	212-247-0082
Nippon Gallery	145 W 57th St	212-581-2223
Nohra Haime	41 E 57th St, 6th Fl	212-888-3550
Pace Primitive	32 E 57th St, 7th Fl	212-421-3688
Pace Prints	32 E 57th St, 3rd Fl	212-421-3237
Pace Wildenstein	32 E 57th St	212-421-3292
Pace/MacGill Gallery	32 E 57th St	212-759-7999
Phyllis Harriman Mason	215 W 57th St	212-247-4510
Ramis Barquet	41 E 57th St	212-644-9090
Reece Galleries	24 W 57th St Ste 304	212-333-5830
Scholten Japanese Art	145 W 58th St #2H	212-585-0474
Spanierman Gallery	45 E 58th St	212-832-0208
Tibor de Nagy	724 Fifth Ave, 12th Fl	212-262-5050
Washburn	20 W 57th St	212-397-6780
Zabriskie	41 E 57th St, 4th Fl	212-752-1223
ZONE: Contemporary Art	41 W 57th St	212-255-2177

Map 13 • East Midtown

Dai Ichi Arts	249 E 48th St	212-230-1680
Gallery Korea	460 Park Ave, 6th Fl	212-759-9550
Japan Society	333 E 47th St	212-832-1155
Scott Jacobson Gallery	114 E 57th	212-872-1616
St Peter's Lutheran Church	619 Lexington Ave	212-935-2200
Throckmorton Fine Art	145 E 57th St, 3rd Fl	212-223-1059
Trygve Lie Gallery	319 E 52nd St	212-319-0370
Ubu Gallery	416 E 59th St	212-753-4444
Wally Findlay Galleries	124 E 57th St	212-421-5390

Map 14 • Upper West Side (Lower)

Frederick Schultz Ancient Art	325 W 82nd St	212-721-6007

Map 15 • Upper East Side (Lower)

Achim Moeller Fine Art	36 E 64th St	212-644-2133
Acquavella	18 E 79th St	212-734-6300
Adam Baumgold	60 E 66th St	212-861-7338
Adam Baumgold	40 E 75th St	212-861-7340
Adelson Galleries	19 E 82nd St	212-439-6800
Adler & Conkright Fine Art	24 E 71st St	212-308-0511
American Illustrators Gallery	18 E 77th St Ste 1A	212-744-5190
American Primitive	49 E 78th St	212-628-1530
Americas Society	680 Park Ave	212-249-9850
Andrew Roth	160A E 70th St	212-717-9067
Anita Friedman Fine Arts	980 Madison Ave	212-472-1527
Anita Shapolsky	152 E 65th St	212-452-1094
Barbara Mathes	22 E 80th St	212-570-4190
Bernard Goldberg Fine Arts	667 Madison Ave	212-813-9797
Berry-Hill	11 E 70th St	212-744-2300
Bertha & Karl Leubsdorf Gallery at Hunter College	E 68th & Lexington Ave	212-772-4991
Bruton	40 E 61st St	212-980-1640
CDS Gallery	74 E 79th St	212-772-9555
China 2000 Fine Art Gallery	434 E 75th St	212-472-9800
China Institute	125 E 65th St	212-744-8181
Conner Rosenkranz	19 E 74th St	212-517-3710
Cook Fine Art	1063 Madison Ave	212-737-3550
Craig F Starr Associates	5 E 73rd St	212-570-1739
Daphne Alazraki Fine Art	113 E 64th St	212-734-8658
David Findlay Galleries	1202 Lexington Ave	212-249-2909
Davis & Langdale	231 E 60th St	212-838-0333
Debra Force Fine Art	14 E 73rd St Ste 4B	212-734-3636
Dickinson Roundell	19 E 66th St	212-772-8083
Ekstrom & Ekstrom	417 E 75th St	212-988-8857
Ezair Gallery	905 Madison Ave	212-628-2224
Franklin Riehlman Fine Art	24 E 73rd St	212-879-2545
Friedman & Vallois	27 E 67th St	212-517-3820
Gagosian	980 Madison Ave	212-744-2313
Galerie Rienzo	20 E 69th St #4C	212-288-2226
Gallery 71	974 Lexington Ave	212-744-7779
Gallery Schlesinger	24 E 73rd St, 2nd Fl	212-734-3600
Gemini GEL at Joni Moisant Weyl	980 Madison Ave	212-249-3324
Gerald Peters	24 E 78th St	212-628-9760
Gitterman Gallery	170 E 75th St	212-734-0868
Godel & Co	39 E 72nd St	212-288-7272
Goedhuis Contemporary	42 E 76th St	212-535-6954
Hirschl & Adler Galleries	21 E 70th St	212-535-8810
Hollis Taggart Galleries	958 Madison Ave	212-628-4000
Hubert Gallery	1046 Madison Ave	212-628-2922
Irena Hochman Fine Art	1100 Madison Ave	212-772-2227
Island Weiss Gallery	201 E 69th St	212-861-4608
Jacobson Howard	33 E 68th St	212-570-2362
James Francis Trezza	39 E 78th St Ste 603	212-327-2218
James Graham & Sons	32 E 67th St	212-535-5767
Jan Krugier	980 Madison Ave	212-755-7288
Jane Kahan	922 Madison Ave	212-744-1490
Keith De Lellis	1045 Madison Ave	212-688-2050
Knoedler & Co	19 E 70th St	212-794-0550
Kouros	23 E 73rd St	212-288-5888
Kraushaar	74 E 79th St	212-288-2558
L&M Arts	45 E 78th St	212-861-0020
L'Arc En Seine	15 E 82nd St	212-585-2587
Leila Taghinia-Milani Heller Gallery	39 E 78th St	212-249-7695
Leo Castelli	18 E 77th St	212-249-4470
Leon Tovar Gallery	16 E 71st St	212-585-2400
Littlejohn Contemporary	245 E 72nd St	212-988-4890
M Sutherland Fine Arts	55 E 80th St, 2nd Fl	212-249-0428
M&R Sayer Fine Arts	129 E 71st St	212-517-8811
Mark Murray Fine Paintings	39 E 72nd St	212-585-2380
Martha Parrish & James Reinish	25 E 73rd St, 2nd Fl	212-734-7332
Mary-Anne Martin Fine Art	23 E 73rd St	212-288-2213
Megan Moynihan & Franklin Riehlman	24 E 73rd St	212-879-2545
Menconi & Schoelkopf Fine Art	13 E 69th St	212-879-8815
Meredith Ward Fine Art	44 E 74th	212-744-7306
Michael Werner	4 E 77th St	212-988-1623
Michail-Lombardo Gallery	19 E 69th St Ste 302	212-472-2400
Michelle Rosenfeld	16 E 79th St	212-734-0900
Mitchell-Innes & Nash	1018 Madison Ave, 5th Fl	212-744-7400
MME Fine Art	74 E 79th St	212-439-6600
Otto Naumann	22 E 80th St	212-734-4443
Paul Thiebaud Gallery	42 E 76th St	212-737-9759
Praxis International Art	25 E 73rd St, 4th Fl	212-772-9478
Questroyal Fine Art	903 Park Ave Ste 3A & B	212-744-3586
Richard Gray	1018 Madison Ave, 4th Fl	212-472-8787
Richard L Feigen & Co	34 E 69th St	212-628-0700
Schiller & Bodo	120 E 65th St	212-772-8627
Shepherd & Derom Galleries	58 E 79th St	212-861-4050
Skarstedt Gallery	20 E 79th St	212-737-2060
Soufer	1015 Madison Ave	212-628-3225
Tilton Gallery	8 E 76th St	212-737-2221
Ukrainian Institute of America	2 E 79th St	212-288-8660
Ursus Books and Prints	981 Madison Ave	212-772-8787
Uta Scharf	42 E 76th St	212-744-3840
Van De Weghe Fine Art	1018 Madison Ave	212-744-1900
Vivian Horan Fine Art	35 E 67th St, 2nd Fl	212-517-9410
Wildenstein & Company	19 E 64th St	212-879-0500
William Secord	52 E 76th St	212-249-0075
Winston Wachter Mayer Fine Art	530 W 25th St	212-327-2526
Yoshii	980 Madison Ave	212-744-5550
Zwirner & Wirth	32 E 69th St	212-517-8677

Map 16 • Upper West Side (Upper)

Annina Nosei Gallery	190 Riverside Dr	212-724-0504
Bard Graduate Center for Studies in the Decorative Arts	18 W 86th St	212-501-3000
Broadway Mall Community Center	W 96th St & Broadway	
Catherine Dail Fine Art	40 W 86th St	212-595-3550
Grady Alexis Gallery at the El Taller Latino Americano	2710 Broadway	212-665-9460
Susan Eley Fine Art	46 W 90th St	917-952-7641

Map 17 • Upper East Side / East Harlem

Allan Stone Gallery	113 E 90th St	212-987-4997
Caren Golden Fine Art	170 E 87th St	212-727-8304
Doyle New York	175 E 87th St	212-427-2730
Gallery 221	221 E 88th St	212-426-5646
Jeffrey Myers Primitive & Fine Art	12 E 86th St	212-472-0115
Neue Galerie	1048 Fifth Ave	212-628-6200
Rosa Esman	12 E 86th St	212-737-8944
Salon 94	12 E 94th St	646-672-9212
Taller Boricua Galleries	1680 Lexington Ave	212-831-4333
Uptown Gallery	1194 Madison Ave	212-722-3677

Map 18 • Columbia / Morningside Heights

Galleries at the Interchurch Center	475 Riverside Dr	212-870-2200
Miriam & Ira D Wallach Art Gallery	1190 Amsterdam Ave	212-854-7288

Battery Park City

World Financial Center Courtyard Gallery	200 Vesey St	212-417-7050

The New York City book scene has taken a sharp decline in terms of diversity in recent years, with many excellent bookshops—including Coliseum Books, A Different Light, Academy, A Photographer's Place, Rizzoli SoHo, Tower Books, Brentano's, Spring Street Books, and Shortwave—all going the way of the dodo. The remaining independent stores are now the last outposts before everything interesting or alternative disappears altogether. And some of NYC's richest cultural neighborhoods—such as the East Village and the Lower East Side—don't have enough bookstores to even come close to properly serving their populations of literate hipsters. So we thought we'd take this opportunity to list some of our favorite remaining shops…

General New/Used

The Strand (Map 6) on Broadway, the largest and arguably most popular independent bookstore in town, boasts staggering range and depth in its offerings (and often the best prices around to boot). Whether you're interested in art tomes, rare first editions, foreign language texts, non-fiction works, or the latest bestseller, it's impossible to be disappointed. **St. Mark's Bookshop (Map 6)** anchors the border between the NYU crowd and the East Village hipster contingent. Both Gotham and St. Mark's have excellent literary journal selections. **Argosy Book Store (Map 13)** on 59th Street is still a top destination for antiquarian books. Uptown, **Book Culture (Map 18)** serves the Columbia area well. With four locations around the city, the punchy **Shakespeare & Company (Maps 6, 10, 15)** is a local chain that somehow manages to maintain an aura of independence. In the West Village, **Three Lives and Co. (Map 5)** should be your destination. The **Barnes & Noble (Map 9)** in Union Square is their signature store and has a great feel. The **Housing Works Used Book Café (Map 6)** has a vintage coffeehouse feel and is one of our favorite bookstores—all of the profits go to help homeless New Yorkers living with HIV/AIDS.

Small/Used

Fortunately there are still a lot of used bookstores tucked away all over the city. **Mercer Street Books (Map 6)** serves NYU, **East Village Books (Map 7)** takes care of hipster heaven, and **Skyline (Map 9)** remains a good Chelsea destination. On the Upper East Side both **Corner Bookstore (Map 17)** and **Crawford Doyle (Map 15)** keep it old-school. In Brooklyn, **Park Slope Books (Map 33)**, a.k.a. 7th Avenue Books, is a fun browse. Check out **Unnameable Books (Map 33)** for hyper-local poetry.

Travel

The city's travel book selection is possibly its greatest strength—from the **Hagstrom Map & Travel (Map 12)** near Bryant Park to several independents, such as the elegant **Complete Traveller Bookstore (Map 9)**. But the newest and greatest member of the travel bookstore club is the wonderful **Idlewild Books (Map 9)**. Idlewild curates its collection by country where guidebooks, fiction, and travel writing all happily comingle for a unique way of browsing. So if you can't afford to travel, a trip here is the next best thing.

Art

Printed Matter (Map 8) houses one of the best collections of artists' books in the world and is highly recommended. The **New Museum of Contemporary Art Bookstore (Map 6)** also offers a brilliant selection of both artists' and art books. If you aren't on a budget and have a new coffee table to fill, try **Ursus (Map 15)** in Chelsea. For handsome photography collections, check out **Dashwood Books (Map 6)** on super sleek Bond Street.

NYC/Government

The **City Store (Map 3)** in the Municipal Building is small but carries a solid selection (and is still the only store we've seen that sells old taxicab medallions). The **Civil Service Bookstore (Map 3)** has all the study guides you'll need when you want to change careers and start driving a bus. The **United Nations Bookshop (Map 13)** has a great range of international and governmental titles. The **New York Transit Museum (Map 13)** shop at Grand Central also has an excellent range of books on NYC.

Specialty

Books of Wonder (Map 9) in Chelsea has long been a downtown haven for children's books, and kids love that it adjoins a cupcake bakery. Two mystery shops, **The Mysterious Book Shop (Map 2)** and **Partners & Crime (Map 5)**, slake the need for whodunits. The **Drama Book Shop (Map 12)** is a great source for books on acting and the theater. **Urban Center Books (Map 12)** is well known for its architecture collection. **Bluestockings (Map 4)** is an epicenter for radical and feminist literature. Professional and amateur chefs turn to **Bonnie Slotnick (Map 5)** and **Kitchen Arts and Letters (Map 17)**.

Readings

Anyone can read great authors, but lucky for New Yorkers, we have beaucoup chances to meet the literati, too. The four-story **Barnes & Noble (Map 9)** in Union Square regularly hosts major writers (think: Nick Hornby, Malcolm Gladwell, etc.). **Housing Works Used Book Café (Map 6)** draws some big names; Philip Gourevitch and Jonathan Lethem have discussed their tomes there in the last few years. And **McNally Jackson (Map 6)** in Nolita is another spot known for hosting great author events. Nearly all bookstores present readings, even if irregularly. Check a store's Web page for listings. Literary blogs like www.maudnewton.com list weekly events for bookworms. Even bars have taken a literary turn for the better: KGB Bar features fiction, poetry, and nonfiction readings each week (www.kgbbar.com) and One Story magazine hosts an excellent monthly reading series at Pianos (www.one-story.com). In Brooklyn, Pete's Candy Store and its weekly reading series are a good bet for your weekly dose of literature (www.petescandystore.com).

Map 1 • Financial District

Borders	100 Broadway	212-964-1988	Chain
Chameleon Comics	3 Maiden Ln	212-587-3411	Comics
Metropolitan Museum of Art Bookshop	12 Fulton St	212-248-0954	Specialty - Art books
Pace University Bookstore	41 Park Row	212-346-1605	Academic - General

Map 2 • TriBeCa

Barnes & Noble	97 Warren St	212-587-5389	Chain
Computer Book Works	78 Reade St	212-385-1616	Specialty - Computer
Manhattan Books	150 Chambers St	212-385-7395	New and used textbooks
The Mysterious Book Shop	58 Warren St	212-587-1011	Specialty - Mystery
NY Law School Bookstore	47 Worth St	212-227-7220	Specialty - Law textbooks

Map 3 • City Hall / Chinatown

Civil Service Book Shop	89 Worth St	212-226-9506	Specialty - Civil Services
Computer Book Works	78 Reade St	212-385-1616	Specialty - Computer
Clic	189 Lafayette St	212-966-1161	Art books and an art gallery
Ming Fay Book Store	42 Mott St	212-406-1957	Specialty - Chinese
New York City Store	1 Centre St	212-669-8246	Specialty - NYC books and municipal publications
Oriental Books Stationery & Arts	29 East Broadway	212-962-3634	Specialty - Chinese
Oriental Culture Enterprises	13 Elizabeth St	212-226-8461	Specialty - Chinese

Map 4 • Lower East Side

Bluestockings Bookstore Café and Activist Center	172 Allen St	212-777-6028	Specialty - Political/Left Wing
Eastern Books	15 Pike St	212-964-6869	Specialty - Chinese
World Journal Book Store	379 E Broadway	212-226-5131	Chinese books.

Map 5 • West Village

Barnes & Noble	396 Sixth Ave	212-674-8780	Chain
Bonnie Slotnick Cookbooks	163 W 10th St	212-989-8962	Specialty - Out of print cookbooks
bookbook	266 Bleecker St	212-807-8655	Specialty - Biography
Drougas Books	34 Carmine St	212-229-0079	Used, political, Eastern religious, etc.
Joanne Hendricks Cookbooks	488 Greenwich St	212-226-5731	Specialty - Wine and Cooking
Left Bank Books	304 W 4th St	212-924-5638	Used; Antiquarian
Partners & Crime Mystery Booksellers	44 Greenwich Ave	212-243-0440	Specialty - Mystery
Three Lives and Co	154 W 10th St	212-741-2069	General Interest
Time Machine	207 W 14th St	212-691-0380	Comics

Map 6 • Washington Square / NYU / NoHo / SoHo

12th Street Books & Records	11 E 12th St	212-645-4340	Used
Alabaster Bookshop	122 Fourth Ave	212-982-3550	Used
Barnes & Noble	4 Astor Pl	212-420-1322	Chain
Benjamin Cardozo School of Law Bookstore	55 Fifth Ave	212-790-0339	Academic - Law
Dashwood Books	33 Bond St	212-387-8520	Photography
East West Books	78 Fifth Ave	212-243-5994	Specialty - Spirituality; Self-Help
Forbidden Planet	840 Broadway	212-473-1576	Specialty - Fantasy/Sci-fi
Housing Works Used Book Café	126 Crosby St	212-334-3324	Used
Lomography Gallery Store	41 W 8th St	212-529-4353	Super-cool Lomographic cameras & accessories!
McNally Jackson	52 Prince St	212-274-1160	General Interest
Mercer Street Books and Records	206 Mercer St	212-505-8615	Used
myplasticheart nyc	210 Forsyth St	646-290-6866	Designer toy store and gallery.
New Museum of Contemporary Art Bookstore	235 Bowery	212-343-0460	Art books. And NFT!
New York Open Center Bookstore	83 Spring St	212-219-2527	Specialty - New Age; Spiritual
New York University Book Center-Main Branch	18 Washington Pl	212-998-4667	Academic - General
New York University Book Center-Professional Bookstore	530 LaGuardia Pl	212-998-4680	Academic - Management

NYU Bookstore - Computer Store	242 Greene St	212-998-4672	Academic - Computers
Pageant Book & Print Shop	69 E 4th St	212-674-5296	Just prints, really. But really great prints
Scholastic Store	557 Broadway	212-343-6166	Specialty - Educational
SF Vanni	30 W 12th St	212-675-6336	Specialty - Italian
Shakespeare & Co	716 Broadway	212-529-1330	Good local chain w/ lots of postmodern fiction
Silver Age Comics	47 W 8th St	646-654-7054	Comics
St Mark's Bookshop	31 Third Ave	212-260-7853	General Interest.
St Mark's Comics	11 St Marks Pl	212-598-9439	Comics
Strand	828 Broadway	212-473-1452	Used mecca; world's messiest and best bookstore
Surma Book & Music	11 E 7th St	212-477-0729	Specialty - Ukrainian
Taschen	107 Greene St	212-226-2212	God (and the Devil's) gift to publishing
Zucker Art Books	55 E 9th St	212-679-6332	Art books

Map 7 • East Village

East Village Books and Records	99 St Marks Pl	212-477-8647	Messy pile of used stuff
Rapture Cafe & Books	200 Ave A	212-228-1177	"Indie publishers and eccentric works"

Map 8 • Chelsea

192 Books	192 10th Ave	212-255-4022	Reads like a library—with a premium on art books and literature
Aperture Book Center	547 W 27th St	212-505-5555	Specialty - Photography
Posman Books	75 9th Ave	212-627-0304	Nice location in Chelsea Market
Printed Matter	195 Tenth Ave	212-925-0325	Astounding selection of artist's books; highly recommended

Map 9 • Flatiron / Lower Midtown

Barnes & Noble	33 E 17th St	212-253-0810	Chain
Barnes & Noble	675 Sixth Ave	212-727-1227	Chain
Barnes & Noble College Bookstore	105 Fifth Ave	212-675-5500	Textbook mayhem
Books of Wonder	18 W 18th St	212-989-3270	Top NYC children's bookstore, always has signed copies around too
Borders	2 Penn Plz	212-244-1814	Chain
Center for Book Arts	28 W 27th St, 3rd Fl	212-481-0295	Speciatly - Artist/Handmade
Compleat Strategist	11 E 33rd St	212-685-3880	Specialty - Fantasy/ SciFi
Complete Traveller	199 Madison Ave	212-685-9007	Specialty - Vintage travel books
Cosmic Comics	10 E 23rd St	212-460-5322	Comics
Fashion Design Books	250 W 27th St	212-633-9646	Specialty - Fashion design
Gozlan Sefer Israel	28 W 27th St	212-725-5890	Judaica
Hudson News	Penn Station	212-971-6800	Chain
Idlewild Books	12 W 19th ST	212-414-8888	One of the best travel + literature bookstores on the planet
Jim Hanley's Universe	4 W 33rd St	212-268-7088	Specialty - Comics; SciFi
Koryo Books	35 W 32nd St	212-564-1844	Specialty - Korean
Levine J Co Books & Judaica	5 W 30th St	212-695-6888	Judaica
Metropolis Comics and Collectibles	873 Broadway	212-260-4147	Specialty - Comics
Pathfinder Books	306 W 37th St	212-629-6649	Political books of the working class struggle
Penn Books	1 Penn Plz	212-239-0311	General interest
Revolution Books	9 W 19th St	212-691-3345	Specialty - Political
Rudolf Steiner Bookstore	138 W 15th St	212-242-8945	Specialty - Metaphysics
Russian Bookstore 21	174 Fifth Ave	212-924-5477	Specialty - Russian/Russia
Skyline Books	13 W 18th St	212-759-5463	Used
St Francis Friars	139 W 31st St	212-736-8500	Religious Books

Map 10 • Murray Hill / Gramercy

Baruch College Bookstore	55 Lexington Ave	646-312-4850	Academic - General
Borders	576 Second Ave	212-685-3938	Chain
Butala Emporium	108 E 28th St	212-684-4447	Indian
New York University Book Store– Health Sciences	333 E 29th St	212-998-9990	Academic - Health Sciences
Shakespeare & Co	137 E 23rd St	212-505-2021	Chain

Map 11 • Hell's Kitchen

Hudson News	Port Authority Bldg, North Wing	212-563-1030	Chain
John Jay College - Barnes & Noble	841 W 55th St	212-265-3619	Textbooks

Map 12 • Midtown

AMA Management Bookstore	1601 Broadway	212-903-8286	Specialty - Management
Assouline	768 5th Ave	212-593-7236	Delicious lavishly-produced art, design and fashion books
Barnes & Noble	555 Fifth Ave	212-697-3048	Chain
Bauman Rare Books	535 Madison Ave	212-751-0011	Antiquarian
Bookoff	14 E 41st St	212-685-1410	Used Japanese and English
Chartwell Booksellers	55 E 52nd St	212-308-0643	Specialty - books about Winston Churchill
Collector's Universe	31 W 46th St	212-398-2100	Specialty - Comics
Dahesh Heritage Fine Books	1775 Broadway, Ste 501	212-265-0600	General interest
Drama Book Shop	250 W 40th St	212-944-0595	Alas, poor Yorick…
FAO Schwarz	767 Fifth Ave	212-644-9400	Specialty - Children's
Hagstrom Map and Travel Center	51 W 43rd St	212-398-1222	Specialty - Travel/Maps
J N Bartfield-Fine Books	30 W 57th St	212-245-8890	Rare and antiquarian
Kinokuniya	10 W 49th St	212-765-7766	Specialty - Japanese
Metropolitan Museum of Art Bookshop at Rockefeller Center	15 W 49th St	212-332-1360	Specialty - Art books
Midtown Comics–Times Square	200 W 40th St	212-302-8192	Specialty - Comics
Rakuza	16 E 41st St	212-686-5560	Specialty - Japanese
Rizzoli	31 W 57th St	212-759-2424	Specialty - Art/Design
Urban Center Books	457 Madison Ave	212-935-3595	Sublime architecture & urban planning destination

Map 13 • East Midtown

Argosy Book Store	116 E 59th St	212-753-4455	Rare and antiquarian, great selection of prints, too
Asahiya	360 Madison Ave	212-883-0011	Specialty - Japanese
Barnes & Noble	160 E 54th St	212-750-8033	Chain
Borders	461 Park Ave	212-980-6785	Chain
Come Again	353 E 53rd St	212-308-9394	Specialty - Erotica; Gay/Lesbian
Hudson News	89 E 42nd St	212-687-0833	Chain
Martayan LAN	70 E 55th St	212-308-0018	Specialty - Rare and antiquarian maps, atlases, and books
Midtown Comics–Grand Central	459 Lexington Ave	212-302-8192	Specialty - Comics
New York Transit Museum	Grand Central, Main Concourse	212-878-0106	Specialty - NYC/Transit
Posman Books	9 Grand Central Terminal	212-983-1111	Nice little bookshop. Lots of NFTs
Potterton Books	979 Third Ave	212-644-2292	Specialty - Decorative Arts/Architecture/ Design
Quest Book Shop	240 E 53rd St	212-758-5521	Specialty - New Age
Richard B Arkway Books	59 E 54th St, Ste 62	212-751-8135	Specialty - Rare maps and books
United Nations Bookshop	First Ave & E 46th St	212-963-7680	Good range of everything

Map 14 • Upper West Side (Lower)

Barnes & Noble	1972 Broadway	212-595-6859	Chain
Barnes & Noble	2289 Broadway	212-362-8835	Chain
Borders	10 Columbus Cir	212-823-9775	Chain
Fordham University Bookstore	113 W 60th St	212-636-6080	Academic - General
Juillard School Bookstore	W 66th St b/w Amsterdam Ave & Broadway	212-799-5000	Academic - Music
Music Memorabilia	155 W 72nd St	212-579-0689	Sheet music and books about music.
New York Institute of Technology	1849 Broadway	212-261-1551	Specialty - Technical
Westsider	2246 Broadway	212-362-0706	Used; Antiquarian

Map 15 • Upper East Side (Lower)

Asia Society Bookstore	725 Park Ave	212-327-9217	Specialty - Asian
Bookberries	983 Lexington Ave	212-794-9400	General Interest
Bookstore Of The NY Psychoanalytic Institution	247 E 82nd St	212-772-8282	Specialty - Psychoanalysis
Choices Bookshop- Recovery	220 E 78th St	212-794-3858	Specialty - Self-help and recovery

Cornell University Medical College Bookstore	424 E 70th St	212-988-0400	Academic - Medical
Crawford Doyle Booksellers	1082 Madison Ave	212-288-6300	Lovely place to browse and find a classic
Gotham City Comics Inc	796 Lexington Ave	212-980-0009	Comics
Hunter College Bookstore	695 Park Ave	212-650-3970	Academic - General
Imperial Fine Books	790 Madison Ave, Ste 200	212-861-6620	Antiquarian
James Cummins Book Seller	699 Madison Ave, 7th Fl	212-688-6441	Antiquarian
Locus Solus Rare Books	790 Madison Ave	212-861-9787	Rare and antiquarian
Logos Book Store	1575 York Ave	212-517-7292	Children's books, spiritual lit, and beyond
Metropolitan Museum of Art Bookshop	Fifth Ave & 82nd St	212-570-3894	Specialty - Art books
Shakespeare & Co	939 Lexington Ave	212-570-0201	Chain
Ursus Books	981 Madison Ave	212-772-8787	Specialty - Art
Whitney Museum of American Art Bookstore	945 Madison Ave	212-570-3614	Specialty - Art/ Artists' books

Map 16 • Upper West Side (Upper)

Funny Business Comics	212 W 92nd St	212-799-9477	Specialty - Comics
Westside Judaica	2412 Broadway	212-362-7846	Judaica

Map 17 • Upper East Side / East Harlem

Barnes & Noble	150 E 86th St	212-369-2180	Chain
Corner Bookstore	1313 Madison Ave	212-831-3554	Tiny, old-school shop. Great selection
Islamic Books & Tapes	1711 Third Ave	212-828-4038	Islamic literature
Kitchen Arts & Letters	1435 Lexington Ave	212-876-5550	Fine selection of food and wine books

Map 18 • Columbia / Morningside Heights

Bank Street College Bookstore	610 W 112th St	212-678-1654	Academic - Education/Children
Book Culture	536 W 112th St	212-865-1588	Excellent bookstore servicing Columbia/ Barnard students
Columbia University Bookstore	2922 Broadway	212-854-4132	Academic - General
Morningside Bookshop	2915 Broadway	212-222-3350	General Interest; New and used
Teachers College Bookstore (Columbia University Graduate School of Education)	1224 Amsterdam Ave	212-678-3920	Academic - Education

Map 19 • Harlem (Lower)

Hue-Man	2319 Frederick Douglass Blvd	212-665-7400	African-American
Zoe Christian Bookstore	45 W 116th St	212-828-2776	Christian books

Map 20 • El Barrio / East Harlem

Jehovah jaireh	2028 Third Ave	212-426-9210	Christian

Map 21 • Manhattanville / Hamilton Heights

City College Book Store	W 138th St & Convent Ave	212-368-4000	General - Academic
Sisters Uptown	1942 Amsterdam Ave	212-862-3680	African-American books

Map 23 • Washington Heights

Columbia Medical Books	3954 Broadway	212-923-2149	Academic - Medical
G W Books & Electronics	4211 Broadway	212-927-1104	General Interest
Jumel Terrace Books	426 W 160th St	212-928-9525	African-American and mostly out of print

Map 24 • Fort George / Fort Tryon

Libreria Caliope	170 Dyckman St	212-567-3511	Spanish and English
Metropolitan Museum of Art Bookshop- Cloisters Branch	799 Ft Washington Ave	212-650-2277	Specialty - Art books

Map 25 • Inwood

Libreria Continental	628 W 207th St	212-544-9004	Specialty - Spanish

Map 26 • Astoria

Seaburn Books	33-18 Broadway	718-267-7929	New and used
Silver Age Comics	22-55 31st St	718-721-9691	Comics

Map 27 • Long Island City

PS1 Bookstore	22-25 Jackson Ave	718-784-2084	Fabulous selection of art books

Map 28 • Greenpoint

Ex Libris Polish Book Gallery	140 Nassau Ave	718-349-0468	Polish
Polish American Bookstore	648 Manhattan Ave	718-349-3756	Polish
Polish Bookstore & Publishing	161 Java St	718-349-2738	Polish
Polonia Book Store	882 Manhattan Ave	718-389-1684	Polish
Word	126 Franklin St	718-383-0096	Literary fiction, non-fiction, and kids' books

Map 29 • Williamsburg

The Read Café	158 Bedford Ave	718-599-3032	Used
Spoonbill & Sugartown	218 Bedford Ave	718-387-7322	Art, architecture, design, philosophy, and literature. New and used

Map 30 • Brooklyn Heights / DUMBO / Downtown

A&B Books	146 Lawrence St	718-596-0872	African-American books
A&B Books	223 Duffield St	718-783-7808	General African-American books
Barnes & Noble	106 Court St	718-246-4996	Chain
Heights Books	109 Montague St	718-624-4876	Rare, out of print, used
Long Island University Book Store	1 University Plz	718-858-3888	General
St Mark's Comics	148 Montague St	718-935-0911	Comics
Trazar's Variety Book Store	40 Hoyt St	718-797-2478	African-American books

Map 31 • Fort Greene / Clinton Hill

Dare Books	33 Lafayette Ave	718-625-4651	General
Pratt Bookstore	550 Myrtle Ave	718-789-1105	Art books
Shakespeare & Co. at BAM	30 Lafayette Ave	718-636-4136	General, specializing in film, music, and dance

Map 32 • BoCoCa / Red Hook

Anwaar Bookstore	428 Atlantic Ave	718-875-3791	Arabic books
Book Court	163 Court St	718-875-3677	General
Dar Us Salam	486 Atlantic Ave	718-625-5925	Islamic books
Freebird Books	123 Columbia St	718-643-8484	Used
Pranga Book Store	354 Court St	718-624-2927	General new and used
Rocketship	208 Smith St	718-797-1348	Comic books and graphic novels

Map 33 • Park Slope / Prospect Heights / Windsor Terrace

Adam S Books	456 Bergen St	718-789-1534	General new and used
Babbo's Books	242 Prospect Park W	718-788-3475	Used & new
Barnes & Noble	267 Seventh Ave	718-832-9066	Chain
Community Book Store	143 Seventh Ave	718-783-3075	General
Park Slope Books	200 Seventh Ave	718-499-3064	Mostly used
Seventh Avenue Books	202 Seventh Ave	718-840-0020	Used
Unnameable Books	600 Vanderbilt Ave	718-789-1534	General new and used

Multiplexes abound in NYC, though of course you should brace yourself for far steeper ticket and concession prices than in the rest of the country (with the possible exception of LA). Dinner and a movie turns out to be a rather exorbitant affair, but hey, we don't live in the Big Apple because it's cheap. And whether you're looking for the latest box office hit, or a classic from the French New Wave, there's a theater to meet your needs.

If you're after a first-run Hollywood blockbuster, we highly recommend the **AMC Loews Kips Bay (Map 10)** in Murray Hill. It has spacious theaters with large screens, big sound, comfortable seats, plenty of aisle room, and most importantly, fewer people! The **AMC Loews Village (Map 6)** is gargantuan, too, but movies there sell out hours or days in advance on the weekends. An IMAX theater and a cheesy '30s movie palace decorating theme make **AMC Loews Lincoln Square (Map 14)** a great place to catch a huge film, and its ideal location offers loads of after-movie options. Another great choice is the **Regal Battery Park 16 (p 234)**, but it's starting to get just as crowded as the Union Square location.

For independent or foreign films, the **Landmark Sunshine (Map 6)** has surpassed the **Angelika (Map 6)** as the superior downtown movie house. Don't get us wrong—the Angelika still presents great movies, but the tiny screens and constant subway rumble can sometimes make you wish you'd waited for the DVD. The **IFC Center (Map 5)** always shows great indie flicks, and with a recent expansion it's better than ever. If you're looking for revivals, check the listings at the **Film Forum (Map 5)**, **BAM Rose Cinemas (Map 31)**, and the **MoMA (Map 12)**. Regular attendance at those three venues can provide an excellent education in cinema history. For the truly adventurous, there's **Anthology Film Archives (Map 6)**, which plays a repertory of forgotten classics, obscure international hits, and experimental American shorts. Finally, up in Harlem the tiny but terrific **Maysles Cinema (Map 19)** shows truly brilliant indie movies focusing on New York City. This may be the most unique movie going experience in Manhattan.

The most decadent and enjoyable movie experiences can be found at the theaters that feel the most "New York." Sadly, the Beekman Theatre immortalized in Woody Allen's Annie Hall was demolished in 2005 to make room for a new ward for Sloan-Kettering (it's hard to argue with a cancer hospital, but film buffs can't help but wish they'd found another space for their expansion). Clearview's **Ziegfeld (Map 12)** on 54th Street is a vestige from a time long past when movie theaters were real works of art. This space is so posh with its gilding and red velvet, you'll feel like you're crossing the Atlantic on an expensive ocean liner. The **Paris Theatre (Map 12)** on 58th Street is one of our favorites in the city—it has the best balcony, hands down!

Oh, and don't forget to use Moviefone (777-FILM; www.moviefone.com) or Fandango (www.fandango.com) to purchase tickets in advance for crowded showtimes (opening weekends, holidays, or pretty much any night when you're trying to see a popular film).

Manhattan	*Address*	*Phone*	*Map*	
92nd Street Y	1395 Lexington Ave	212-415-5500	17	Community hub for film, theater, and interesting lectures.
92Y Tribeca	200 Hudson St	212-601-1000	2	Jewish-themed films mixed with popular indies.
AMC Empire 25	234 W 42nd St	212-398-3939	12	Buy tickets ahead. It's Times Square.
AMC Loews 19th Street	890 Broadway	212-260-8173	9	Standard multiplex.
AMC Loews 34th Street 14	312 W 34th St	212-244-4556	8	The biggest and most comfortable of the Midtown multiplexes.
AMC Loews 72nd Street East	1230 Third Ave	212-472-0153	15	Single screen where the movies seem to play forever.
AMC Loews 84th St 6	2310 Broadway	212-721-6023	14	Take the subway to Lincoln Square instead.
AMC Loews Kips Bay 15	570 2nd Ave	212-447-0638	10	This multiplex is starting to show its age.
AMC Loews Lincoln Square 13	1998 Broadway	212-336-5020	14	Classy Upper West Side multiplex with IMAX.
AMC Loews Orpheum 7	1538 Third Ave	212-876-2111	17	The Upper East Side's premier multiplex.
AMC Loews Village VII	66 Third Ave	212-505-6397	6	Good-sized multiplex that keeps Union Square crowds in check.
AMC Magic Johnson Harlem 9	2309 Frederick Douglass Blvd	212-665-6923	19	Owned by Magic. Best choice for Upper Manhattan.
American Museum of Natural History IMAX	200 Central Park West	212-769-5200	14	Rest your tired legs and learn something.
Angelika	18 W Houston St	212-995-2000	6	Higher profile indies play here first.
Anthology Film Archives	32 Second Ave	212-505-5181	6	Quirky retrospectives, revivals, and other rarities.
The Asia Society	725 Park Ave	212-327-9276	15	Special country-themed programs every month.
Beekman Theatre	1271 Second Ave	212-585-4141	15	Another good choice owned by the folks behind the Paris.
Bryant Park Summer Film Festival (outdoors)	Bryant Park, b/w 40th & 42nd Sts	212-512-5700	12	Groovy classics outdoors in sweltering summer heat.
Cinema 123	1001 Third Ave	212-753-6022	15	Ideal cure for Bloomingdale's hangover.
Cinema Village	22 E 12th St	212-924-3363	6	Charming and tiny with exclusive documentaries and foreign films.
City Cinemas: East 86th Street	210 E 86th St	212-744-1999	17	It wouldn't be our first choice.
Clearview Cinemas Chelsea	260 W 23rd St	212-691-5519	9	Manhattan's big, comfy, and gay multiplex.
Clearview Cinemas First & 62nd St	400 E 62nd St	212-752-0694	15	You're better off taking the bus down to Kips Bay.
Coliseum Cinemas	701 W 181st St	212-740-1545	23	We love Washington Heights, but not its movie theater.

Czech Center New York	321 E 73rd St	646-422-3399	15	Czech premieres and special events.
Film Forum	209 W Houston St	212-727-8110	5	Best place to pick up a film geek.
French Institute	22 E 60th St	212-355-6100	15	Frog-centric activities include movies, plays, talks and exhibits.
Guggenheim Museum Movie Theater	1071 Fifth Ave	212-423-3500	17	Special screenings in conjunction with current exhibitions.
IFC Center	323 Sixth Ave	212-924-7771	5	Great midnights, special events, and Manhattan exclusives.
Instituto Cervantes	211 E 49th St	212-308-7720	13	Spanish gems, but call to make sure there's subtitles.
Italian Academy	1161 Amsterdam Ave	212-854-2306	18	Fascinating classic film series at Columbia. Feel smart again.
Jewish Community Center in Manhattan	334 Amsterdam Ave	646-505-4444	14	Jewish premieres, previews, and festivals.
Landmark Sunshine Cinema	143 E Houston St	212-330-8182	6	High luxury indie film multiplex.
Leonard Nimoy Thalia at Symphony Space	2537 Broadway	212-864-5400	16	A different classic movie every week. Good variety.
Lincoln Plaza Cinemas	1886 Broadway	212-757-2280	14	Uptown version of the Angelika.
Maysles Cinema	343 Malcolm X Blvd	212-582-6050	19	Amazing indies and documentaries from local film-makers.
MOMA	11 W 53rd St	212-708-9400	12	Arty programming changes every day.
Museum of TV and Radio	25 W 52nd St	212-621-6800	12	*Gilligan's Island* on the big screen!
New York Public Library Jefferson Market Branch	425 6th Ave	212-243-4334	5	Children's films on Tuesdays.
NYU Cantor Film Center	36 E 8th St	212-998-4100	6	Dirt cheap second-run blockbusters on Monday nights.
The Paley Center for Media	25 W 52nd St	212-621-6800	12	Formerly the Museum of Television & Radio.
Paris Theatre	4 W 58th St	212-688-3800	12	Art house equivalent of the Ziegfeld.
Quad Cinema	34 W 13th St	212-255-8800	6	Gay-themed world premieres and second run Hollywood releases.
Regal 64th and 2nd	1210 Second Ave	212-832-1671	15	Nice big theater with two ugly cousins.
Regal Battery Park City 11	102 North End Ave	212-945-4370	p234	Beautiful downtown multiplex. Getting too crowded.
Regal E Walk Stadium 13	247 W 42nd St	212-505-6397	12	Across the street from the Empire, but not nearly as nice.
Regal East 85th Street 1	1629 1st Ave	212-249-5488	15	Fun single screen.
Regal Union Square Stadium 14	850 Broadway	212-253-6266	6	Extremely crowded but fairly comfortable.
The Scandinavia House	58 Park Ave	212-879-9779	10	Scandinavian movies. Bergman and beyond.
Tribeca Cinemas	54 Varick St	212-941-2001	2	Home base of De Niro's Tribeca Film Festival.
Village East Cinema	181 2nd Ave	212-259-6799	6	Half the theaters are gorgeous, half are dank pits.
Walter Reade Theater	70 Lincoln Plz	212-875-5600	14	Amazing festivals and rare screenings.
Whitney Museum Theater	945 Madison Ave	212-570-3600	15	Artist retrospectives and lectures.
Ziegfeld	141 W 54th St	212-307-1862	12	Beloved NY classic with a gigantic screen. Don't miss.

Brooklyn

BAM Rose Cinemas	30 Lafayette Ave	718-636-4100	31	Great seating and mix of first run + revivals.
Cobble Hill Cinemas	265 Court St	718-596-9113	32	Great indie destination, though theaters are small.
Pavilion Brooklyn Heights	70 Henry St	718-596-7070	30	Intimate, classy, and just about perfect.
Pavilion Movie Theatres	188 Prospect Park W	718-369-0838	33	Nice mix of stuff right across from Propsect Park.
Regal Court Street Stadium 12	108 Court St	718-246-7995	30	Audience-participation-friendly megaplex.
Rooftop Films	various locations	718-417-7362	n/a	Summer rooftop series—check website for locations!

Queens

Museum of the Moving Image	36-01 35th Ave	718-784-4520	26	Excellent alternative to blockbuster crap.
UA Kaufman Studios Cinema 14	35-30 38th St	718-786-2020	26	Astoria

New Jersey

AMC Loews Newport Center 11	30 Mall Dr W [Thomas Gangemi Dr]	201-626-3258	35	Jersey stereotypes at their loudest and ugliest.

Make a resolution: Go to at least one museum in New York City every month. There are over 100 museums in the five boroughs, from the **Metropolitan Museum of Art (Map 15)** to the **Dyckman Farmhouse Museum (Map 25)**, an 18th-century relic in upper Manhattan. Many of these museums have special programs and lectures that are open to the public, as well as children's events and summer festivals. When you've found your favorite museums, look into membership. Benefits include free admission, guest passes, party invites, and a discount at the gift shop.

The famous Museum Mile comprises nine world-class museums along Fifth Avenue between 82nd Street and 105th Street, including the **Met (Map 15)**, and Frank Lloyd Wright's architectural masterpiece, the **Guggenheim (Map 17)**. **El Museo del Barrio (Map 17)**, devoted to early Latin American art, **The Museum of the City of New York (Map 17)**, the **Cooper-Hewitt National Design Museum (Map 17)** (housed in Andrew Carnegie's Mansion), and the **Jewish Museum (Map 17)** are also along the mile. A few blocks off the stretch is the **Whitney Museum of American Art (Map 15)**, which showcases contemporary American artists and features the celebrated Biennial in even-numbered years.

See medieval European art at **The Cloisters (Map 25)** (also a famous picnic spot), exhibitions of up and coming African-American artists at the **Studio Museum in Harlem (Map 19)**, and **PS1 (Map 27)** (MoMA's satellite) for contemporary art. Take the kids to the **Brooklyn Children's Museum** or the **Children's Museum of Manhattan (Map 14)**. The **Lower East Side Tenement Museum (Map 4)** and the **Ellis Island Immigration Museum (Map 1)** stand as reminders of the past, while the **Hayden Planetarium (Map 14)** offers visions of the future. The treasures of the Orient are on display at the **Asia Society (Map 15)**, and coach potatoes can watch the tube all day at **The Paley Center for Media (Map 12)**, formerly known as the Museum of Television and Radio. The **Brooklyn Museum (Map 33)** supplements its wide-ranging permanent collection with edgy exhibitions, performances, and other special events.

Just about every museum in the city is worth a visit. Other favorites include the **New Museum of Contemporary Art (Map 6)** (in its spiffy building on The Bowery), the **New-York Historical Society (Map 14)** (which focuses its exhibits on the birth of the city), the **New York Transit Museum (Map 30)**, **the Morgan Library (Map 9)** (with copies of Gutenberg's Bible on display), the **Museum of the Moving Image (Map 26)**, **The Museum of Sex (Map 9)**, and the **Queens Museum of Art** (check out the panorama of New York City). Finally, the **Museum of Arts and Design (Map 12)**, on the southern edge of Columbus Circle, is a bold redesign of Edward Durrell Stone's quirky masterpiece for Huntington Hartford; the new renovation leaves the curves but replaces the cladding. An excellent permanent collection and diverting exhibitions, plus working artists-in-residence and a small lovely museum store, make the Museum a must-see.

Manhattan	*Address*	*Phone*	*Map*
American Academy of Arts & Letters	633 W 155th St	212-368-5900	21
American Folk Art Museum	45 W 53rd St	212-265-1040	12
American Institute of Graphic Arts	164 Fifth Ave	212-807-1990	9
American Irish Historical Society	991 5th Ave	212-288-2263	15
American Museum of Natural History	Central Park W at 79th St	212-769-5100	15
American Numismatic Society	75 Varick St	212-571-4470	2
Anthology Film Archives	32 Second Ave	212-505-5181	6
Arsenal Gallery	E 64th St & 5th Ave	212-360-8163	15
Asia Society & Museum	725 Park Ave	212-288-6400	15
Asian American Arts Centre	111 Norfolk St	212-233-2154	4
Chelsea Art Museum	556 W 22nd St	212-255-0719	8
Children's Galleries for Jewish Culture	515 W 20th St, Suite 4E	212-924-4500	8
Children's Museum of Manhattan	212 W 83rd St	212-721-1234	14
Children's Museum of the Arts	182 Lafayette St	212-274-0986	3
China Institute	125 E 65th St	212-744-8181	15
The Cloisters	99 Margaret Corbin Dr	212-923-3700	24
Constitution Works	26 Wall St	212-785-1989	1
Cooper-Hewitt National Design Museum	2 E 91st St	212-849-8355	17
Czech Center	321 E 73rd St	646-422-3399	15
Dyckman Farmhouse Museum	4881 Broadway	212-304-9422	25
El Museo del Barrio	1230 Fifth Ave	212-831-7272	17
Ellis Island Immigration Museum	Ellis Island, via ferry at Battery Park	212-561-4588	1
Exit Art	475 Tenth Ave	212-966-7745	8
Fraunces Tavern Museum	54 Pearl St	212-425-1778	1
Frick Collection	1 E 70th St	212-288-0700	15
Gracie Mansion	East End Ave at 88th St	212-570-4773	17

Grant's Tomb	W 122nd St & Riverside Dr	212-666-1640	18
Grey Art Gallery	100 Washington Sq E	212-998-6780	6
Guggenheim Museum	1071 Fifth Ave	212-423-3500	17
Hayden Planetarium	Central Park West & W 79th St	212-769-5100	14
Hispanic Society Museum	613 W 155th St	212-926-2234	21
International Center of Photography (ICP)	1133 Sixth Ave	212-857-0000	12
Intrepid Sea, Air and Space Museum	12th Ave & W 46th St	212-245-0072	11
Japan Society	333 E 47th St	212-832-1155	13
Jewish Museum	1109 Fifth Ave	212-423-3200	17
Lower East Side Tenement Museum	108 Orchard St	212-431-0233	4
Madame Tussauds NY	234 W 42nd St	800-246-8872	12
Merchant's House Museum	29 E 4th St	212-777-1089	6
Metropolitan Museum of Art	1000 Fifth Ave	212-535-7710	15
Morgan Library	225 Madison Ave	212-685-0008	9
Morris-Jumel Mansion	65 Jumel Ter	212-923-8008	23
Mount Vernon Hotel Museum and Garden	421 E 61st St	212-838-6878	15
Municipal Art Society	457 Madison Ave	212-935-3960	12
Museum at Eldridge Street	12 Eldridge St	212-219-0302	3
Museum at the Fashion Institute of Technology	Seventh Ave & 27th St	212-217-4558	9
Museum of American Finance	48 Wall St	212-908-4110	1
Museum of American Illustration	128 E 63rd St	212-838-2560	15
Museum of Arts & Design	2 Columbus Circle	212-299-7777	12
The Museum of Biblical Art	1865 Broadway	212-408-1500	14
Museum of Chinese in America	215 Centre St	212-619-4785	3
Museum of the City of New York	1220 5th Ave	212-534-1672	17
Museum of Comic and Cartoon Art	594 Broadway, Suite 401	212-254-3511	6
Museum of Jewish Heritage	36 Battery Pl	646-437-4200	p 234
Museum of Modern Art (MoMA)	11 W 53rd St	212-708-9400	12
Museum of Sex	233 Fifth Ave	212-689-6337	9
Museum of the City of New York	1220 Fifth Ave	212-534-1672	17
National Academy of Design	1083 Fifth Ave	212-369-4880	17
National Museum of the American Indian	1 Bowling Green	212-514-3700	1
Neue Galerie	1048 Fifth Ave	212-628-6200	17
New Museum of Contemporary Art	235 Bowery	212-219-1222	6
New York City Fire Museum	278 Spring St	212-691-1303	5
New York Police Museum	100 Old Slip	212-480-3100	1
New York Public Library for the Performing Arts	40 Lincoln Center Plaza	212-870-1630	14
The New York Public Library Humanities & Social Sciences Library	Fifth Ave & 42nd St	212-340-0849	12
New-York Historical Society	170 Central Park W	212-873-3400	14
Nicholas Roerich Museum	319 W 107th St	212-864-7752	16
Old Merchant's House	29 E 4th St	212-777-1089	6
The Paley Center for Media	25 W 52nd St	212-621-6800	12
PS1	22-25 Jackson Ave	718-784-2084	27
Rose Museum	154 W 57th St	212-247-7800	12
Rubin Museum of Art	150 W 17th St	212-620-5000	9
Scandinavia House	58 Park Ave	212-879-9779	10
School of Visual Arts Museum	209 E 23rd St	212-592-2000	10
Skyscraper Museum	39 Battery Pl	212-968-1961	p 234
Sony Wonder Technology Lab	550 Madison Ave	212-833-8100	12
South Street Seaport Museum	Fulton St & South St	212-748-8600	1
Statue of Liberty Museum	Liberty Island, via ferry at Battery Park	212-561-4588	1
Studio Museum in Harlem	144 W 125th St	212-864-4500	19
Tibet House	22 W 15th St	212-807-0563	9
Ukrainian Museum	222 E 6th St	212-228-0110	6
US Archives of American Art	1285 Sixth Ave	212-399-5015	12
Whitney Museum of American Art	945 Madison Ave	212-570-3600	15
Yeshiva University Museum	15 W 16th St	212-294-8330	9

Brooklyn

Brooklyn Children's Museum	145 Brooklyn Ave	718-735-4400	n/a
Brooklyn Historical Society	128 Pierrepont St	718-222-4111	30
Brooklyn Museum	200 Eastern Pkwy	718-638-5000	n/a
City Reliquary	370 Metropolitan Ave	718-782-4842	29
Coney Island Museum	1208 Surf Ave	718-372-5159	n/a
Doll & Toy Museum of NYC	157 Montague St	718-243-0820	30
Harbor Defense Museum	230 Sheridan Loop	718-630-4349	n/a
Kurdish Library and Museum	345 Park Pl	718-783-7930	33
Museum of Contemporary African Diasporan Arts	80 Hanson Pl	718-230-0492	31
New York Aquarium	Surf Ave & W 8th St	718-265-3474	n/a
New York Transit Museum	Boerum Pl & Schermerhorn St	718-694-1600	30
The Old Stone House	336 3rd St	718-768-3195	33
Simmons Collection African Arts Museum	1063 Fulton St	718-230-0933	31
Waterfront Museum	290 Conover St	718-624-4719	32
Wyckoff Farmhouse Museum	5816 Clarendon Rd	718-629-5400	n/a

Queens

Bowne House	37-01 Bowne St	718-359 0528	n/a
Fisher Landau Center for Art	38-27 30th St	718-937-0727	27
Godwin-Ternbach Museum	65-30 Kissena Blvd	718-997-4747	n/a
King Manor Museum	Jamaica Ave & 153rd St	718-206-0545	n/a
Kingsland Homestead	Weeping Beech Park, 143-35 37th Ave	718-939-0647	n/a
Louis Armstrong Museum	34-56 107th St,	718-478-8297	n/a
Museum of the Moving Image	36-01 35th Ave	718-784-4520	26
New York Hall of Science	47-01 111th St	718-699-0005	n/a
The Noguchi Museum	9-01 33rd Rd	718-204-7088	27
PS1 Contemporary Art Center	22-25 Jackson Ave	718-784-2084	27
Queens County Farm Museum	73-50 Little Neck Pkwy	718-347-3276	n/a
Queens Museum of Art	Flushing Meadows-Corona Park	718-592-9700	n/a
Socrates Sculpture Park	32-01 Vernon Blvd	718-956-1819	26
Voelker Orth Museum	149-19 38th Ave	718-359-6227	n/a
Weeksville Heritage Center	1698 Bergen St	718-756-5250	n/a

Metropolitan Museum of Art

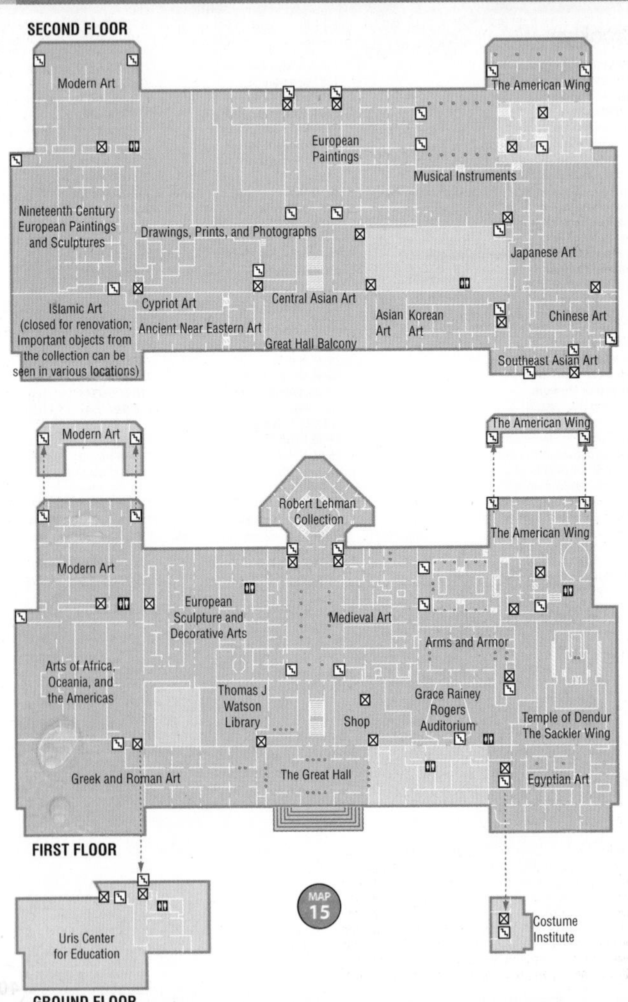

General Information

NFT Map: 15
Address: 1000 Fifth Ave at 82nd St
Phone: 212-535-7710
Website: www.metmuseum.org
Hours: Sun, Tues–Thurs: 9:30 am–5:30 pm; Fri & Sat: 9:30 am–9 pm; Mon, New Year's Day, Christmas & Thanksgiving: closed. The museum is open on select "Holiday Mondays" throughout the year.
Admission: A suggested $20 donation for adults, $10 for students, and $15 for senior citizens. Admission includes the Main Building and The Cloisters on the same day. Free to members and children under twelve with an adult.

Overview

The Metropolitan Museum of Art is touted as the largest and most comprehensive museum in the Western hemisphere. Established by a group of American businessmen, artists, and thinkers back in 1870, the museum was created to preserve and stimulate appreciation for some of the greatest works of art in history.

In the first few years of its existence, the museum moved from its original location at 681 Fifth Avenue to the Douglas Mansion at 128 W 14th Street, and then finally to its current Central Park location in 1880.

Calvert Vaux and Jacob Wrey Mould designed the museum's Gothic Revival red-brick facade, which was later remodeled in 1926 into the grand, white-columned front entrance that you see today. Part of the original facade was left intact and can still be seen from the Robert Lehman Wing looking toward the European Sculpture and Decorative Arts galleries.

The Met's annual attendance reaches over 4 million visitors who flock to see the more than 2 million works of art housed in the museum's permanent collection. You could visit the museum many times and not see more than a small portion of the permanent collection. The vast paintings anthology had a modest beginning in 1870 with a small donation of 174 European paintings and has now swelled to include works spanning 5,000 years of world culture, from the prehistoric to the present and from every corner of the globe.

The Met is broken down into a series of smaller museums within each building. For instance, the American Wing contains the most complete accumulation of American paintings, sculpture, and decorative arts, including period rooms offering a look at domestic life throughout the nation's history. The Egyptian collection is the finest in the world outside of Cairo, and the Islamic art exhibition remains unparalleled, as does the mass of 2,500 European paintings and Impressionist and Post-Impressionist works. The permanent gallery of Islamic art underwent renovations in 2008, following the 10-15 year renovation of the Greek & Roman collection. The redesigned galleries display works that have been in storage for decades, assuring even the most frequent visitor something fresh to check out including the museum's newly restored, world-famous, non-gas-guzzling **Etruscan chariot**.

Other major collections include the arms and armor, Asian art, costumes, European sculpture and decorative arts, medieval and Renaissance art, musical instruments, drawings, prints, ancient antiquities from around the world, photography, and modern art. Add to this the many special exhibits and performances the Met offers throughout the year, and you have a world-class museum with Central Park as its backyard.

This is a massive museum and seating can be difficult to find during busy weekends. When you need a break from all of the culture, sit down for a snack in the American Wing Café or lunch in the cafeteria. If you pal around with a member (or become one yourself), it is a treat to eat in the Trustees Dining Room overlooking the park. In the summer climb up to the Roof Garden Café for a glass of wine and the most beautiful view of Central Park that your lack of money can buy.

The Greatest Hits

You can, of course, spend countless hours at the Met. Pick any style of art and chances are you will find a piece here. But if you're rushed for time, check out the sublime space that houses the **Temple of Dendur** in the Sackler Wing, the elegant **Frank Lloyd Wright Room** in the American Wing, the fabulous **Tiffany Glass** and **Tiffany Mosaics**, also in the American Wing, the **choir screen** in the Medieval Sculpture Hall, the **Caravaggios** and **Goyas** in the Renaissance Rooms, the **Picassos** and **Pollocks** in Modern Art, and that huge **canoe** in Arts of Africa and Oceania. For a moment of tranquility, visit the beautiful Chinese Garden Court in the Asian galleries. When it's open, we highly recommend the **Roof Garden**, which has killer views of Central Park as a side dish to cocktails and conversation. When it's not, check out seasonal specials like the **Christmas "Angel" Tree and Neopolitan Baroque Crèche**, an annual favorite set up in front of the medieval choir screen.

How to Get There—Mass Transit

Subway
Take the 4 5 6 to the 86th Street stop and walk three blocks west to Fifth Avenue and four blocks south to 82nd Street.

Bus
Take the 4 bus along Fifth Avenue (from uptown locations) to 82nd Street or along Madison Avenue (from downtown locations) to 83rd Street.

Museum of Natural History

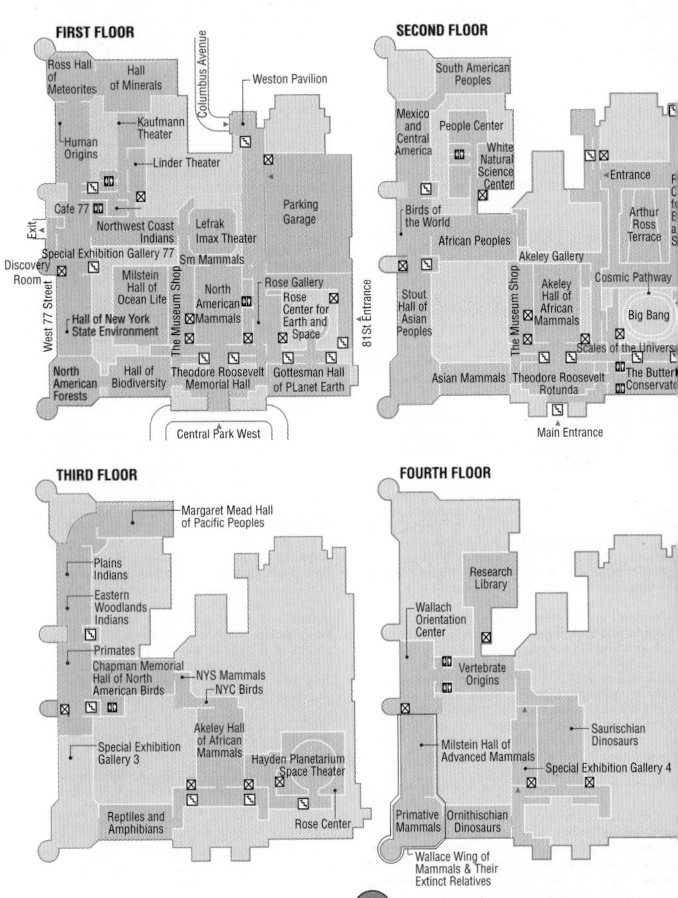

General Information

NFT Map: 14
Address: Central Park West at 79th Street
Phone: 212-769-5100
Website: www.amnh.org
Hours: Daily, 10:00 am–5:45 pm
The Rose Center stays open until 8:45pm the first Friday of every month. Christmas & Thanksgiving: closed.
Admission: Suggested general admission is $14 for adults, $8 for children (2–12), and $10.50 for senior citizens and students. Special exhibitions, IMAX movies, and the space show are extra; packages are available. Free to members.

Overview

Admit it. You secretly TiVo the Discovery Channel and the History Channel. You've even watched one—if not several—episodes of *Star Trek*. Something about African beetles, famous dead guys, and the unknown universe strokes your inner Einstein. Focus your microscope on this one, smarty-pants: the American Museum of Natural History, a paradise for geeks and aspiring geeks alike, not to mention good old nature lovers. And don't worry, your TV-watching secrets are safe with us.

Decades before anyone knew what an atom was, and when relativity was just a twinkle in Einstein's eye, Albert Smith Bickmore established the AMNH. Completed in 1869, the museum held its first exhibition in the Central Park Arsenal a few years later, garnering enough respect to acquire space along classy Central Park West. Architects Calvert Vaux and J. Wrey Mould designed the new, posh building on limited Benjamins and opened it to the public in 1877. Key additions followed: The Hayden Planetarium in 1935, the Theodore Roosevelt Memorial Hall and Rotunda in 1936, and the Rose Center for Earth and Space in 2000.

As Saturday morning museum-going ritual dictates, it's going to be painfully crowded. On those days, you dodge out-of-towners, eyes wide, mouths gaping. It's much the same on weekdays with rowdy school kids on field trips. How to avoid the Excedrin-necessitating atmosphere? Two words: permanent collection. The amazing series of wildlife dioramas even inspired an entire Hollywood movie (albeit not a great one, by adult standards). Don't expect to see any PETA supporters in these halls though.

When you can go at off hours, or if you feel you can brave the crowds, make a point of checking out the fascinating and often provocative special exhibits. Recent highlights have included Darwin and Water: H20=Life.

The Greatest Hits

Five floors of star-lovin', mammal-gazin', bird-watchin', fossil-fuelin' science await. Rain forest fever? Check out the Hall of Biodiversity. Didn't understand why that movie was called *The Squid and The Whale?* Meet the 94-foot long great blue whale and his giant squid companion at the Milstein Hall of Ocean Life. Moby teamed up with MTV2 and the Hayden Planetarium in The Rose Center for Earth and Space to produce SonicVision, an animated alternative music show that poses the question: How do you see your music? Another thought-provoking show with a celebrity element (narration by Harrison Ford) is *The Search for Life: Are We Alone?* For more instant thrills, check out the gigantic meteorites at the Arthur Ross Hall of Meteorites, or the five-story-tall dinosaur display in the Theodore Roosevelt Rotunda. It's the largest freestanding beast in the world. The AMNH also produces spectacular IMAX features, a great alternative to the museum's amazing but creepy taxidermy. The Hall of Gems houses the Star of India, the largest star sapphire in the world. Finally, for recreation of *The Birds* variety with less evil, visit The Butterfly Conservatory. Tropical butterflies flit all around you from, you guessed it, all over the world. It's enough to put TiVo on pause.

How to Get There—Mass Transit

Subway

Take the B C to the 81st Street stop. Or take the 1 to 79th Street and walk two blocks east.

Bus

The 7 10 and 11 all stop within a block of the museum. Take the 79 across Central Park if you are coming from the East Side.

Museum of Modern Art

General Information

NFT Map:	12
Address:	11 W 53rd St
Phone:	212-708-9400
Website:	www.moma.org
Hours:	Sun, Mon, Wed, Thurs, Sat: 10:30 am–5:30 pm; Fri 10:30 am–8 pm; closed Tues, Thanksgiving, and Christmas
Admission:	$20 for adults, $16 for seniors, $12 for students; free to members and children under 16 accompanied by an adult

Overview

The Museum of Modern Art opened in 1929, back when impressionism and surrealism were truly modern art. Originally in the Heckscher Building at 730 Fifth Avenue, MoMA moved to its current address on West 53rd Street in 1932. What started out as a townhouse eventually expanded into an enormous space, with new buildings and additions in 1939 (by Phillip L. Goodwin and Edward Durell Stone), 1953 (including a sculpture garden by Phillip Johnson), 1964 (another Johnson garden), and 1984 (by Cesar Pelli). During the summer of 2002, the museum closed its Manhattan location and moved temporarily to Long Island City (MoMA's affiliate, PS1 Contemporary Art Center, is still there). After a major expansion and renovation by Yoshio Taniguchi, MoMA reopened in September 2004. Opinion varies as to the success of Taniguchi's new design, but the art is the point, right?

Wrong. Museums are one of the last great bastions of inventive, exciting, fun, not-necessarily-practical architecture. Taniguchi's design uses all available space, which, considering the price of midtown real estate, must have been a selling point for his design. Other than that, you'll have to trek up to the Guggenheim, fly off to Bilbao, or head downtown to the New Museum of Contemporary Art's new Bowery digs to see better marriages of art and design.

The re-Manhattanized museum charges $20. If crowds on a typical Saturday afternoon are any indication, the hefty entry fee is not keeping patrons away. Art lovers take note: The yearly $75 membership ($120 for a dual and $150 for a family) is the way to go. Members get a 10% discount at MoMA stores, free tickets to all film screenings, and you're free to pop in whenever you want to see your favorite Picasso (or use the restroom). For the best deal, visit the museum from 4–8 pm on Fridays, when Target sponsors free admission. The crowds aren't as bad as you might think, and you can usually slide right past the main desk and grab one of the free tickets that they scatter there.

What to See

The fourth and fifth floors are where the big names reside—Johns, Pollock, Warhol (fourth floor), Braque, Cezanne, Dali, Duchamp, Ernst, Hopper, Kandinsky, Klee, Matisse, Miro, Monet, Picasso, Rosseau, Seurat, Van Gogh, and Wyeth (fifth floor). More recent works can be found in the contemporary gallery on the second floor. Special exhibitions are featured on the third and sixth floors. The surrealist collection is outstanding, but we suspect that MoMA has only a tiny fraction of its pop art on display. Well, you can't have everything…

Moving downstairs to the third floor, it's clear that the photography collection is, as always, one of the centerpieces of the museum and is highly recommended (although the Gursky pieces are actually dotted throughout the building). The architecture and design gallery showcases a range of cool consumer items, from chairs to cars to the first Mac computers, and is one of the most popular destinations in the museum.

Recent exhibits, such as Doug Aitken's *Sleepwalkers*—which was the first to project film scenes onto MoMA's exterior walls—provide hope that the museum will only continue to be more innovative in the future.

Breakdown of the Space

Floor One: Lobby, Sculpture Garden, Museum Store, Restaurant
Floor Two: Contemporary Galleries, Media Gallery, Prints and Illustrated Books, Café
Floor Three: Architecture and Design, Drawing, Photography, Special Exhibitions
Floor Four: Painting and Sculpture II
Floor Five: Painting and Sculpture I, Café
Floor Six: Special Exhibitions
There are two theater levels below the first floor.

Amenities

Backpacks and large purses are not allowed in gallery spaces, and the free coat check can become messy when the check-in and check-out lines become intertwined. Leave large items (including laptops) at home.

Bathrooms and water fountains are on all floors. We don't think that there are enough of them, and the bathrooms themselves are way too small to handle the crowds.

There are three places to get food in the museum—you'll pay heavily for the convenience and Danny Meyer experience. Café 2, located on the second floor, offers "seasonal Roman fare," also known as "snooty Italian." They also have an espresso bar. Terrace 5, which overlooks the beautiful sculpture garden, has desserts, chocolates, and sandwiches, along with wine, cocktails, coffee, and tea. Both cafes open half an hour after the museum opens its doors and close half an hour before the museum closes.

For the ultimate museum dining experience, The Modern features the cuisine of Gabriel Kreuther. It has two main rooms—the Dining Room overlooks the sculpture garden, and the Bar Room is more casual and overlooks the bar. An outdoor terrace is also made available when the weather permits. The Modern serves French and New American food and features wild game menu items—sounds great if you've got a platinum card.

The Modern is open beyond museum hours, with the Dining Room closing at 10:30 pm Monday–Thursday, and 11:30 pm on Friday and Saturday. The Bar Room closes at 10:30 pm Monday–Thursday, at 11 pm on Friday and Saturday, and 9:30 pm on Sunday. There's a separate street entrance to allow diners access to The Modern after the museum closes.

On warm summer days, a gelato bar in the sculpture garden offers yummy sorbets.

So long as there are adventurous artists putting on plays in abandoned storefronts and opportunistic real estate developers knocking down beautiful old theaters to put up hotels, the New York theater scene will always be adding a few venues here and deleting a few venues there. What remains constant is that on any given night there are at least dozens, and more often hundreds, of live theater performances to be seen. And the best ones are not always the most expensive.

Broadway (theaters in the Times Square vicinity that hold at least 500 people) still has the reputation of being the place to see American theater at its finest, but the peculiar fact of the matter is that there is much more money to be gained by appealing to the infrequent theater goer than there is by trying to please the connoisseur. As a result, shows that are looked down on, if not despised, by many lovers of the theater wind up selling out for years (Mamma Mia, anyone?), while more ambitious, artistically admired plays and musicals struggle to find an audience. Check out theater chat boards like BroadwayWorld.com and TalkinBroadway.com to see what the people who see everything have to say.

Nobody gets famous doing live theater anymore, so if you've never heard of the actor whose name is twinkling in lights (Cherry Jones, Brian Stokes Mitchell, Raul Esparza, Christine Ebersole…) chances are that person has the stage experience and acting chops to keep you enthralled for two and a half hours, unlike the big name celebrities (P. Diddy, Melanie Griffith) who make their stage acting debuts in starring roles they're not prepared for. Of course, there are also actors with extensive stage credits who come back to Broadway regularly after becoming famous. That's why we love John Lithgow, Cynthia Nixon, and Phylicia Rashad.

Many great performers work Off-Broadway (Manhattan theaters seating 100–499 people) where the writing and directing are actually more important than spectacle and scores made up of classic pop songs. Off-Off Broadway (fewer than 100 seats) is a terrific grab bag of both beginners and seasoned pros doing material that is often unlikely to draw in masses. And tickets are pretty cheap, too.

TheaterMania.com keeps an extensive list of just about every show in New York, with direct links to the websites that sell tickets. Many shows offer a limited number of inexpensive standing room and/or same-day rush tickets. A detailed directory of such offers can be found at TalkinBroadway.com.

Thousands of same-day tickets for Broadway and Off-Broadway shows are sold for 20%–50% off at the TKTS booths in Times Square (long lines) and at the South Street Seaport (short lines). They take cash, traveler's checks, and credit cards. Check for hours and to see what's been recently available at www.tdf.org. Don't expect to get a bargain for the top-selling hits, but most shows use this booth at some time or another. You can also download discount coupons at Playbill.com that you can use to get seats in advance.

The dirty little secret of New York theatre is that free tickets for high-quality shows (aka not Billy Elliot, Wicked, or The Lion King etc.) are abundantly available though organizations that specialize in "dressing the house" for productions that depend more on word of mouth than expensive advertising costs. By giving a yearly membership fee of around $100 to AudienceExtras.com or Play-By-Play.com, you can check your computer 24-hours a day to find free tickets (there's a small per-ticket service charge) for a dozen or so Off-, Off-Off-, and sometimes Broadway shows available at the last minute. That dinky little play in some church basement that you went to on a whim might wind up being the next great American classic.

Keep an eye out for shows by these lesser-known companies:

The award-winning Classical Theatre of Harlem (www.classicaltheatreofharlem.org) has earned a reputation for mounting exciting, edgy revivals of classics from Shakespeare and Brecht, as well as solid productions from more recent greats such as August Wilson and Melvin Van Peebles. A multicultural company that frequently casts against racial type, they draw a youthful audience with imaginative interpretations. As of press time the Classical Theater of Harlem has been left nomadic but we're hoping they find a new permanent home soon.

The **Mint Theatre Company (Map 11)** (www.minttheater.org) specializes in reviving Broadway plays from the past they call "worthy, but neglected." In their tiny space you'll see interesting comedies and dramas from the likes of A. A. Milne, Edith Wharton, and Thomas Wolfe played traditionally with sets and costumes that really make you feel like you're watching a production from over 50 years ago.

Musicals Tonight! does the same kind of thing with forgotten musicals, only presenting them in low budgeted, but highly energized, staged readings. Nowadays most musicals revived on Broadway are revised and updated to the point where they lose their authenticity. But if you're in the mood to see what an Irving Berlin ragtime show from 1915 was really like, or if you want to see a Cole Porter tuner from the '30s with all of the dated topical references that confused audiences even back then, Musicals Tonight! serves up the past as it really was written. And check for their special concerts where Broadway understudies sing songs from the roles they are currently covering. Shows take place at **McGinn/Cazale Theatre (Map 14)**.

Broadway insiders know that Monday nights, when most shows are dark, is often the hottest night of the week for entertainment. That's when performers use their night off to partake in benefits and special events. Consistently among the best are shows from Scott Siegel's Broadway By The Year series at **Town Hall (Map 12)** (www.the-townhall-nyc.org). Each one-night concert is packed with theater and cabaret stars singing hits and obscurities introduced on Broadway in one selected year. Siegel also produces Broadway Unplugged at Town Hall, a concert of theater performers singing showtunes without amplification. The atmosphere is like a sports event, with the audience wildly cheering each naturally voiced solo.

Theaters / Performing Arts

Pearl Theatre Company (www.pearltheatre.org) at **City Center (Map 12)** has been mounting kickass productions of classics by Shakespeare, Moliere, Sheridan, Williams and the like since 1984.

Now in its eleventh season, Horse Trade (www.horsetrade.info) has been producing a crazy assortment of readings, workshops and full-out productions. Most events are performed at **The Kraine Theater (Map 6)**, which also houses the **Red Room (Map 6)** on its third floor. The theaters are also available to rent for rehearsals and performances.

HERE (Map 5) (www.here.org) not only houses two small theaters, but it also has an amazing gallery space and a cozy café/bar—perfect for pre- or post-show drinks.

Located in a former school on First Avenue and 9th Street in the East Village, **P.S. 122 (Map 7)** (www.ps122.org) is a not-for-profit arts center serving New York City's dance and performance community. Shows rotate through on a regular basis, so check the website for the latest schedule. The outdoor **Delacorte Theater (Map 15)** in Central Park hosts performances only during the summer months. Tickets to the ridiculously popular and free Shakespeare in the Park performances are given away at 1 pm at the Delacorte and also at the **Public Theater (Map 6)** on the day of each performance. Hopefully, you enjoy camping because people line up for days in their tents and sleeping bags just to secure a ticket!

Just on the other side of the Manhattan Bridge in Brooklyn is the world famous **Brooklyn Academy of Music (Map 31)**. A thriving urban arts center, BAM brings domestic and international performing arts and film to Brooklyn. The center includes two theaters (**Harvey Lichtenstein Theater (Map 31)** and **Howard Gilman Opera House (Map 31)**), the **Bam Rose Cinemas (Map 31)**, and the **BAMcafé (Map 31)**, a restaurant and live music venue. Our favorite season in the Next Wave, an annual three-month celebration of cutting-edge dance, theater, music, and opera. As an alternative to BAM, **St. Ann's Warehouse (Map 30)** in DUMBO also produces cutting-edge work.

Manhattan

Broadway

Al Hirschfeld Theatre	302 W 45th St	212-239-6200	12
Ambassador Theatre	219 W 49th St	212-239-6200	12
American Airlines Theatre	227 W 42nd St	212-719-1300	12
August Wilson Theatre	245 W 52nd St	212-239-6200	12
Belasco Theatre	111 W 44th St	212-239-6200	12
Bernard B Jacobs Theatre	242 W 45th St	212-239-6200	12
Booth Theatre	222 W 45th St	212-239-6200	12
Broadhurst Theatre	235 W 44th St	212-239-6200	12
Broadway Theatre	1681 Broadway	212-239-6200	12
Brooks Atkinson Theatre	256 W 47th St	212-307-4100	12
Circle in the Square Theatre	1633 Broadway	212-307-0388	12
Cort Theatre	138 W 48th St	212-239-6200	12
Ethel Barrymore Theatre	243 W 47th St	212-239-6200	12
Eugene O'Neill Theatre	230 W 49th St	212-239-6200	12
Gershwin Theatre	222 W 51st St	212-307-4100	12
Helen Hayes Theatre	240 W 44th St	212-239-6200	12
Hilton Theater	213 W 42nd St	212-556-4750	12
Imperial Theater	249 W 45th St	212-239-6200	12
John Golden Theatre	252 W 45th St	212-239-6200	12
Longacre Theatre	220 W 48th St	212-239-6200	12
Lunt-Fontanne Theatre	205 W 46th St	212-307-4100	12
Lyceum Theatre	149 W 45th St	212-239-6200	12
Majestic Theater	245 W 44th St	212-239-6200	12
Marquis Theatre	1535 Broadway	212-382-0100	12
Minskoff Theatre	200 W 45th St	212-307-4747	12
Music Box Theatre	239 W 45th St	212-239-6200	12
Nederlander Theatre	208 W 41st St	212-307-4100	12
Neil Simon Theatre	250 W 52nd St	212-307-4100	12
New Amsterdam Theatre	214 W 42nd St	212-307-4100	12
Palace Theatre	1564 Broadway	212-307-4100	12
Richard Rodgers Theatre	226 W 46th St	212-221-1211	12
Roundabout/Laura Pels Theatre	111 W 46th St	212-719-1300	12
Samuel J. Friedman Theatre	261 W 47th St	212-239-6200	12
Schoenfeld Theatre	236 W 45th St	212-239-6200	12
Shubert Theatre	225 W 44th St	212-239-6200	12
St James Theatre	246 W 44th St	212-239-6200	12
Studio 54	254 W 54th St	212-719-1300	12

Vivian Beaumont Theatre	Lincoln Center, W 65th St & Amsterdam Ave	212-362-7600	14
Walter Kerr Theatre	219 W 48th St	212-239-6200	12
Winter Garden Theatre	1634 Broadway	212-239-6200	12
Off-Broadway			
47th Street Theater	304 W 47th St	212-239-6200	12
59E59 Theaters	59 E 59th St	212-753-5959	13
Acorn Theatre	410 W 42nd St	212-714-2442	11
Actor's Playhouse	100 Seventh Ave S	212-239-6200	5
The Actors' Temple	339 W 47th St	212-239-6200	11
American Theatre of Actors	314 W 54th St	212-239-6200	11
Astor Place Theatre	434 Lafayette St	212-254-4370	6
Atlantic Theater Company	336 W 20th St	212-691-5919	8
Barrow Street Theater	27 Barrow St	212-239-6200	5
Beckett Theatre	410 W 42nd St	212-714-2442	11
Cherry Lane Theater	38 Commerce St	212-989-2020	5
Classic Stage Co	136 E 13th St	212-677-4210	6
Connelly Theatre	220 E 4th St	212-982-2287	7
Daryl Roth Theatre	101 E 15th St	212-239-6200	10
Delacorte Theater	Central Park, W 81st St	212-539-8750	15
The Duke on 42nd Street	229 W 42nd St	212-239-6200	12
Ensemble Studio Theatre	549 W 52 St	212-247-3405	11
Harlem School of the Arts Theater	645 St Nicholas Ave	212-868-4444	21
Harold Clurman Theatre	410 W 42nd St	212-714-2442	11
HSA Theater	645 St Nicholas Ave	212-868-4444	21
Irish Repertory Theatre	132 W 22nd St	212-727-2737	9
June Havoc Theatre	312 W 36th St	212-868-4444	8
Kirk Theatre	410 W 42nd St	212-714-2442	11
Lion Theatre	410 W 42nd St	212-714-2442	11
Little Shubert Theatre	422 W 42nd St	212-239-6200	11
Lucille Lortel Theatre	121 Christopher St	212-279-4200	5
Manhattan Ensemble Theatre	55 Mercer St	212-925-1900	3
Manhattan Theatre Club	131 W 55th St	212-581-1212	12
Mazer Theater	197 East Broadway	212-239-6200	4
Minetta Lane Theatre	18 Minetta Ln	212-307-4100	6
Mitzi E Newhouse Theater	Lincoln Center, W 65th & Amsterdam Ave	212-239-6200	14
New World Stages	340 W 50th St	212-239-6200	11
New York Theatre Workshop	79 E 4th St	212-460-5475	6
Orpheum Theater	126 Second Ave	212-477-2477	6
Pearl Theatre Co	80 St Marks Pl	212-598-9802	6
Players Theatre	115 MacDougal St	212-475-1449	6
Playwrights Horizons Theater	416 W 42nd St	212-279-4200	11
The Public Theater	425 Lafayette St	212-260-2400	6
Samuel Beckett Theatre	410 W 42nd St	212-714-2442	11
Second Stage Theatre	307 W 43rd St	212-246-4422	12
Signature Theatre: Peter Norton Space	555 W 42nd St	212-244-7529	11
Snapple Theatre Center	210 W 50th St	212-307-4100	12
St Lukes Church	308 W 46th St	212-239-6200	12
Studio Theatre	410 W 42 St	212-714-2442	11
Theater at St Clement's	423 W 46th St	212-868-4444	11
TriBeCa Performing Arts Center	199 Chambers St	212-220-1460	2
Union Square Theater	100 E 17th St	212-307-4100	10
Upstairs at Studio 54	254 W 54th St	212-719-1300	12
Village Theater	158 Bleecker St	212-307-4100	6
Vineyard Theatre	108 E 15th St	212-353-0303	10
Vinnie Black's Coliseum at the Edison Hotel	221 W 46th St	212-352-3101	12
Westside Theatre	407 W 43rd St	212-239-6200	11
York Theatre at St Peter's Church	619 Lexington Ave	212-935-5820	13

Off-Off Broadway

13th Street Theatre	50 W 13th St	212-675-6677	6
29th Street Repertory Theatre	212 W 29th St	212-465-0575	9
45th St Theater	354 W 45th St	212-279-4200	11
59E59 Theaters	59 E 59th St	212-753-5959	13
78th Street Theatre Lab	236 W 78th St	212-873-9050	14
Abingdon Mainstage Theatre	312 W 36th St	212-868-2055	8
Access Theater	380 Broadway, 4th Fl	212-966-1047	3
Actor's Theater Workshop	145 W 28th St	212-947-1386	9
American Place Theatre	266 W 37th St	212-594-4482	8
American Theatre of Actors	314 W 54th St	212-239-6200	11
ArcLight Theatre	152 W 71st St	212-595-0355	14
Ars Nova Theatre	511 W 54th St	212-868-4444	11
Axis Theater	1 Sheridan Sq	212-807-9300	5
Barrow Group Arts Center	312 W 36th St	212-760-2615	8
Center Stage, NY	48 W 21st St	212-929-2228	9
Collective: Unconscious	279 Church St	212-254-5277	2
DR2 Theatre	103 E 15th St	212-375-1110	10
Duo Theatre	62 E 4th St	212-598-4320	6
Flea Theatre	41 White St	212-226-0051	2
Gene Frankel Theatre	24 Bond St	212-777-1767	6
Gertrude Stein Repertory Theater	15 W 26th St	212-725-7254	9
HERE	145 Sixth Ave	212-647-0202	5
Hudson Guild	441 W 26th St	212-760-9800	8
Irish Arts Center	555 W 51st St	212-757-3318	11
Jewish Community Center	334 Amsterdam Ave	646-505-5700	14
Julia Miles Theater	424 W 55th St	212-765-1706	11
The Kitchen	512 W 19th St	212-255-5793	8
The Kraine Theater	85 E 4th St	212-868-4444	6
La Mama ETC	74A E 4th St	212-475-7710	6
The Looking Glass Theatre	422 W 57th St	212-307-9467	11
Manhattan Theatre Source	177 MacDougal St	212-260-4698	6
McGinn/Cazale Theatre	2162 Broadway	212-579-0528	14
Medicine Show Theatre	549 W 52nd St	212-262-4216	11
Metropolitan Playhouse	220 E 4th St, 2nd Fl	212-995-5302	7
Mint Theatre	311 W 43rd St 5th Fl	212-315-0231	11
National Black Theatre	2031 Fifth Ave	212-722-3800	19
The Ontological Theater at St Mark's Church-in-the-Bowery	131 E 10th St	212-420-1916	6
People's Improv Theater	154 W 29th St, 2nd Fl	212-563-7488	9
Phil Bosakowski Theatre	354 W 45th St	212-352-3101	11
The Producers Club	358 W 44th St	212-315-4743	11
Producers Club II	616 Ninth Ave	212-315-4743	11
PS 122	150 First Ave	212-477-5288	7
Rattlestick Theatre	224 Waverly Pl	212-627-2556	5
The Red Room	85 E 4th St	212-868-4444	6
Repertorio EspaÐol	138 E 27th St	212-889-2850	10
Riverside Church	490 Riverside Dr	212-870-6700	18
Sanford Meisner Theatre	164 Eleventh Ave	212-206-1764	8
Soho Playhouse	15 Vandam St	212-691-1555	5
Soho Repertory Theatre	46 Walker St	212-941-8632	3
St Bart's Playhouse	Park Ave & E 50th St	212-378-0248	13
Storm Theatre	64 E 4th St	212-330-8350	6
T Schreiber Studio	151 W 26th St	212-741-0209	9
TADA! Theater	15 W 28th St	212-252-1619	9
Tenement Theater	97 Orchard St	212-431-0233	4
Theater for the New City	155 First Ave	212-254-1109	7
Theater Ten Ten	1010 Park Ave	212-288-3246	15
Under St Marks	94 St Marks Pl	212-868-4444	7
Urban Stages	259 W 30th St	212-868-4444	9
West End Theatre	263 W 86th St	212-352-3101	16
The Wild Project	195 E 3rd St	212-228-1195	7

Wings Theater	154 Christopher St	212-627-2961	5
WOW Café	59 E 4th St	212-777-4280	6
YMCA	344 E 14th St	212-780-0800	6

Performing Arts

92nd Street Y Theatre	1395 Lexington Ave	212-415-5500	17
Alice Tully Hall	Lincoln Center, 65th & Broadway	212-875-5050	14
Apollo Theater	253 W 125th St	212-531-5300	19
Avery Fisher Hall	Lincoln Center, Columbus Ave at 65th St	212-875-5030	14
Baruch Performing Arts Center	55 Lexington Ave	646-312-4085	10
Beacon Theater	2124 Broadway	212-465-6500	14
Carnegie Hall	881 Seventh Ave	212-247-7800	12
Cedar Lake	547 W 26th St	212-244-0015	8
Chicago City Limits	318 W 53rd St	212-888-5233	12
City Center	131 W 55th St	212-581-7907	12
Dance Theatre Workshop	219 W 19th St	212-691-6500	9
David H. Koch Theater	Columbus Ave & W 63rd St	212-870-5570	14
Dicapo Opera Theatre	184 E 76th St	212-288-9438	15
Dixon Place	161 Chrystie St	212-219-0736	6
French Institute Alliance Francaise	22 E 60th St	212-355-6100	15
The Gerald W Lynch Theater at John Jay College	899 Tenth Ave	212-237-8005	11
Harry DeJur Playhouse	466 Grand St	212-598-0400	4
Joyce Theater	175 Eighth Ave	212-691-9740	8
Manhattan School of Music	120 Claremont Ave	212-749-2802	18
Merkin Concert Hall	129 W 67th St	212-501-3330	14
Metropolitan Opera House	Lincoln Center, Columbus Ave at 64th St	212-362-6000	14
Miller Theater–Columbia University	200 Dodge Hall, 2960 Broadway	212-854-7799	18
New Victory Theatre	209 W 42nd St	212-239-6200	12
New York State Theatre	Lincoln Ctr, Columbus Ave at 63rd St	212-870-5570	14
Radio City Music Hall	1260 Sixth Ave	212-247-4777	12
Sylvia and Danny Kaye Playhouse	695 Park Ave	212-772-5207	15
Symphony Space	2537 Broadway	212-864-5400	16
The Theater at Madison Square Garden	2 Penn Plz	212-307-4111	9
Town Hall	123 W 43rd St	212-840-2824	12
Upright Citizen's Brigade Theatre	307 W 26th St	212-366-9176	8

Brooklyn

651 Arts	651 Fulton St	718-636-4181	31
BAM-Harvey Lichtenstein Theater	651 Fulton St	718-636-4100	31
BAM-Howard Gilman Opera House	30 Lafayette Ave	718-636-4100	31
Bargemusic	Fulton Ferry Landing	718-624-2083	30
BRIC Studio	57 Rockwell Pl	718-855-7882	30
Brick Theatre	575 Metropolitan Ave	718-907-6189	29
Brooklyn Arts Council	55 Washington St	718-625-0080	30
Brooklyn Arts Exchange	421 Fifth Ave	718-832-0018	33
Brooklyn Conservatory of Music	58 Seventh Ave	718-622-3300	33
Brooklyn Family Theatre	1012 Eighth Ave	718-670-7205	33
Brooklyn Lyceum	227 Fourth Ave	718-857-4816	33
Charlie's Pineapple Theater Company	208 N 8th St	718-907-0577	29
Galapagos Art Space	16 Main St	718-222-8500	30
Gallery Players Theater	199 14th St	718-595-0547	33
The Heights Players	26 Willow Pl	718-237-2752	30
Jalopy	315 Columbia St	718-395-3214	32
Paul Robeson Theatre	54 Greene Ave	718-783-9794	31
Public Assembly	70 N 6th St	718-782-5188	29
Puppetworks	338 Sixth Ave	718-965-3391	33
St Ann's Warehouse	38 Water St	718-254-8779	30

Queens

Astoria Performing Arts Center	30-44 Crescent St	718-393-7505	26
The Chocolate Factory	5-49 49th Ave	718-482-7069	27

NOT FOR TOURISTS™ Custom Mapping

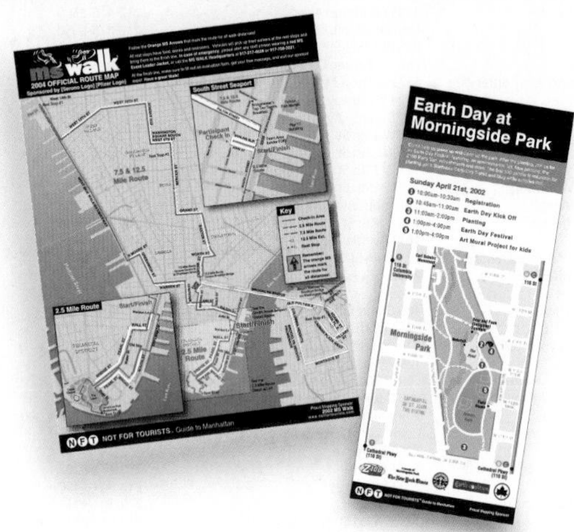

We'll map your world.

Need a custom map?

NFT will work with you to design a custom map that promotes your company or event. NFT's team will come up with something new or put a fresh face on something you already have. We provide custom map-making and information design services to fit your needs—whether simply showing where your organization is located on one of our existing maps, or creating a completely new visual context for the information you wish to convey. NFT will help you—and your audience—make the most of the place you're in, while you're in it.

For more information, call us at 212-965-8650 or visit
www.notfortourists.com/custommapping.aspx

Take the subway to 1904.

You'll feel like you've traveled back in time. The New York Transit Museum is housed in a historic subway station where you can board our vintage collection of subway and elevated trains and check out all the antique treasures from the world's greatest subway system.

If you have children, there are free kids' workshops every weekend. And be sure to visit the Museum Store for all kinds of collectibles and souvenirs.

And get 2-for-1 admission with this ad.

The Museum is located at the corner of Boerum Place and Schermerhorn Street in Brooklyn Heights. Take the 2 3 or 4 train to Borough Hall, then walk 2 blocks south.

For additional information and directions, call 718-694-1600. Or visit us at **www.mta.info**.

It'll be 1904 all over again.

NEW YORK TRANSIT MUSEUM

Metropolitan Transportation Authority *Going your way*

www.mta.info

The Shape of Lies

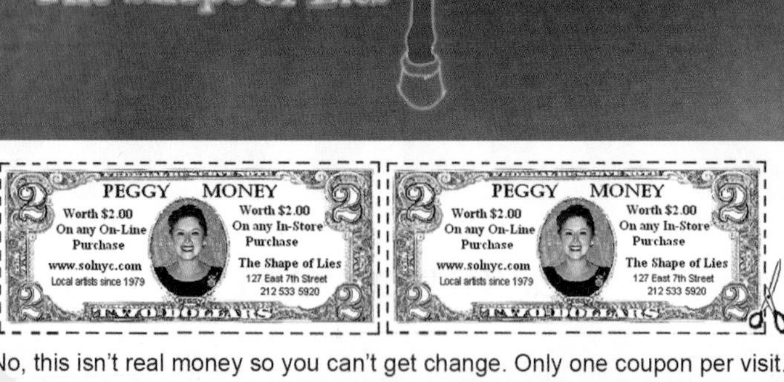

No, this isn't real money so you can't get change. Only one coupon per visit.

Street Index

Street Index

Street Index

WHAT IS THAT?!
HUH? OH, IT'S WWW.NOTFORTOURISTS.COM
BUT WHY?! WHY WOULD YOU USE ANYTHING OTHER THAN ME?
WELL, THE WEBSITE JUST OFFERS A FEW THINGS THAT YOU DON'T: DAILY CONTENT, FUN PHOTOS, SEARCHABLE DATABASE... COOL STUFF LIKE THAT.
DEVASTATED
OH... I SEE...

BUT I FIT IN YOUR POCKET. YOU CAN TAKE ME ANYWHERE.
SWOOP!
OH!
TUCK TUCK
OH PLEASE. THE WEBSITE COULD NEVER REPLACE YOU. I NEED YOU BOTH TO GET THE MOST OUT OF MY CITY!

Address Locator

Streets	Riverside	West End	Broadway	Amsterdam	Columbus	C.P.W.	Central Park
110-116	370-440		2800-2950	995-1120			
102-110	290-370	850-920	2675-2800	856-995	850-1021	419-500	
96-102	240-290	737-850	2554-2675	733-856	740-850	360-419	
90-96	180-240	620-737	2440-2554	620-733	621-740	300-360	
84-90	120-180	500-619	2321-2439	500-619	501-620	241-295	
78-84	60-120	380-499	2201-2320	380-499	381-500	239-241	
72-78	1-60	262-379	2081-2200	261-379	261-380	121-239	
66-72		122-261	1961-2079	140-260	141-260	65-115	
58-66		2-121	1791-1960	1-139	2-140	0-65	

Streets	12th Ave.	11th Ave.	Broadway	10th Ave.	9th Ave.	8th Ave.	7th Ave.	6th Ave.
52-58	710-850	741-854	1674-1791	772-889	782-907	870-992	798-921	1301-1419
46-52	600-710	625-740	1551-1673	654-770	662-781	735-869	701-797	1180-1297
40-46	480-600	503-624	1440-1550	538-653	432-662	620-734	560-701	1061-1178
34-40	360-480	405-502	Macy's-1439	430-537	431-432	480-619	442-559	1060-1061
28-34	240-360	282-404	1178-1282	314-429	314-431	362-479	322-442	815-1060
22-28	0-240	162-281	940-1177	210-313	198-313	236-361	210-321	696-814
14-22		26-161	842-940	58-209	44-197	80-235	64-209	5520-695
8-14			748-842	0-58	0-44	0-80	2-64	420-520
Houston-8			610-748					244-402

The address locator below is formatted north-south, from 116th Street to Houston Street. For east-west addresses, simply remember that Fifth Ave. is the dividing line-2 E 54th would be right off of Fifth, while 200 E 54th would be around Third Ave.

5th Ave.	Madison	Park	Lexington	3rd Ave.	2nd Ave.	1st Ave.	York	Streets
1280-1400	1630-1770	1489-1617	1766-1857	1981-2103	2109-2241	2175-2238		110-116
1209-1280	1500-1630	1350-1489	1612-1766	1820-1981	1880-2109	1975-2175		102-110
1148-1209	1379-1500	1236-1350	1486-1612	1709-1820	1854-1880	1855-1975		96-102
1090-1148	1254-1379	1120-1236	1361-1486	1601-1709	1736-1854	1740-1855	1700-end	90-96
1030-1089	1130-1250	1000-1114	1248-1355	1490-1602	1624-1739	1618-1735	1560-1700	84-90
970-1028	1012-1128	878-993	1120-1248	1374-1489	1498-1623	1495-1617	1477-1560	78-84
910-969	896-1006	760-877	1004-1116	1250-1373	1389-1497	1344-1494	1353-1477	72-78
850-907	772-872	640-755	900-993	1130-1249	1260-1363	1222-1343	1212-1353	66-72
755-849	621-771	476-639	722-886	972-1129	1101-1260	1063-1222	1100-1212	58-66

5th Ave.	Madison	Park	Lexington	3rd Ave.	2nd Ave.	1st Ave.	Avenue A	Streets
656-754	500-611	360-475	596-721	856-968	984-1101	945-1063		52-58
562-655	377-488	240-350	476-593	741-855	862-983	827-944		46-52
460-561	284-375	99-240	354-475	622-735	746-860	701-827		40-46
352-459	188-283	5-99	240-353	508-621	622-747	599-701		34-40
250-351	79-184	4-404	120-239	394-507	500-621	478-598		28-34
172-249	1-78	286-403	9-119	282-393	382-499	390-478		22-28
69-170	University	0-285	1-8	126-281	230-381	240-389		14-22
9-69	0-120			59-126	138-230	134-240	129-210	8-14
0-9				1-59	0-138	0-134	0-129	Houston - 8

NOT FOR TOURISTS™ Custom Books

NFT
Not For Tourists™ Guide to LOS ANGELES
COLLATERAL™
Collateral is a trademark of DreamWorks LLC © 2004

NFT
Not For Tourists™ Guide to CHICAGO
W HOTELS

NFT
Not For Tourists Guide to NEW YORK CITY
NEW YORK UNIVERSITY

Customize your NFT.

We can put **your organization's logo or message** on NFT using custom foil stamps of your (or our) design. Not For Tourists Guidebooks make **great gifts** for employees, clients, and promotional events.

For more information, call us at 212-965-8650, or visit www.notfortourists.com/corporatesales.aspx

Not For Tourists™
www.notfortourists.com
Atlanta • Boston • Chicago • London • Los Angeles • New York City • Philadelphia • San Francisco • Seattle • Washington DC